What Is World Band Radio?

Transmitter tower at Vatican Radio.

I t is no secret why world band radio is now such popular entertainment. Thanks to advanced technology, it allows each of us to enjoy a generous slice of life from every corner of the world. Television and VCRs, for all their virtues, can't begin to equal the wealth of up-to-the-minute newscasts, music, and entertainment available every day on world band radio. There is nothing else quite like it, and it's all free. There are no fees to be paid, and even advertisements are relatively rare.

Special radios are needed, of course, and these are now made by the usual electronics giants, as well as numerous specialty manufacturers. A good set costs about as much as a basic VCR, although simple portables go for much less and monitor models for more. Many are compact, and advanced tuning circuits make listening to the world remarkably straightforward . . . provided you know what's on, and when. There are, after all, **thousands** of stations now on the air.

Passport to World Band Radio provides you with exactly the information you need to enjoy these shows from around the world. Included are schedules for every station on the air, a Buyer's Guide to more than ninety portable radios and tabletop receivers, plus a wide array of articles on how to get started and what you can hear. Share in the thrill of eavesdropping on distant lands and peoples. Tune into world band, and tune in the world.

1989 PASSPORT TO

HOW TO HEAR THE WORLD

WORLD BAND RADIO

WORLDSCAN

GLOSSARIES AND GUIDES

Exclusive Licensee & Distributor of Grundig AG in U.S.A.
Lextronix, INC.
P.O.BOX 2307
Menlo Park, CA 94026
Tel. (415) 361-16 11

800-872-2228

Top Class World Receivers with German Technology
Microcomputer controlled PLL-frequency-synthesizer tuning for AM and FM. Direct frequency key-in for all wave bands with automatic follow-up preselector and three-stage fading control for AM. Short Wave covering 1.6–30.0 MHz. Double superhet for exceptional selectivity and image rejection, switchable SSB/BFO section (adaptable to USB/LSB). AC 110–240 V, 50/60 Hz, DC-operation 9 V with batteries or external power supply.

GRUNDIG

ISSN 0897-0157

International Broadcasting Services, Ltd.

PASSPORT TO WORLD BAND RADIO

1989

Editor-in-Chief	Lawrence Magne
Editor	Tony Jones
Features Editor	Elizabeth Macalaster
Contributing Editors	Tim Akester, Alex Batman, Geoff Cosier, Jock Elliott, Noel Green
Consulting Editors	John Campbell, Don Jensen
Special Contributors	Rogildo Fontenelle Aragão, J.M. Brinker, James A. Conrad, Gordon Darling, Antonio Ribeiro da Motta, DXFL/Isao Ugusa, Ruth M. Hesch, Robert J. Hill, Edward J. Insinger, Konrad Kroszner, Ibrahim Mansour, Larry Miller, Toshimichi Ohtake, Al Quaglieri, RNM/Tetsuya Hirahara, Don Swampo, Craig Tyson, Shelda Tyson, David L. Walcutt
Database Software	Richard Mayell
Laboratory	Sherwood Engineering Inc.
Marketing & Distribution	Mary W. Kroszner
Communications	Consultech Communications, Inc.
Graphic Preparation	The Bookmakers, Incorporated, Wilkes-Barre, Pennsylvania
IBS—Headquarters	Box 300, Penn's Park, Pennsylvania 18943 USA
IBS—Latin America	Casilla 1844, Asunción, Paraguay
IBS—Japan	5-31-6 Tamanawa, Kamakura 247

Take note of the Republic of China on Taiwan

Listen to the Voice of Free China for music, news, culture and insights into Asia's most dynamic economy.

English ● French ● Spanish ● German ● Japanese ● Korean ● Indonesian ● Thai ● Vietnamese ● Arabic ● Mandarin ● Cantonese ● Amoy ● Chaochow ● Hakka ●

5985KHZ   11740KHZ

For a free program guide, please write to:
P.O. Box 24-38, Taipei,
Taiwan, Republic of China

Voice of Free China
自由中國之聲

McKay Dymek, division of:
stoner communications, inc.
9119 Milliken Avenue
Rancho Cucamonga, California 91730 USA
Telephone: (714) 987-4624   Telex: 676-468

DYMEK DA 100D

The World's Most Respected All-Wave Receiving Antenna

- Frequency Coverage: 50 KHz to 30 MHz, continuous
- Output Impedance: Switch selectable 50, 100, 500 Ohms
- Attenuation: Switch selectable 0, 10, 20 dB
- Power Required: Switch selectable 110 or 240VAC, 50–60 Hz, 4 Watts, or 12VDC

DA100DM Marine version also available with fiberglass whip antenna for use on or near salt water.

ICOM RECEIVERS
The World at Your Fingertips

Only ICOM brings the world into your living room...HF, VHF, UHF, and low band receptions. ICOM is the professional's choice to receive international broadcasts, aircraft, marine, business, emergency services, television, and government bands. Tune in with ICOM's IC-R7000 25-2000MHz* and IC-R71A 0.1-30MHz commercial quality scanning receivers for full spectrum coverage.

Incomparable Frequency Control. Both the IC-R71A and IC-R7000 feature **direct frequency access** via their front keypad, main tuning dial, optional infrared remote control and/or computer interface adapter. **Flexibility of this nature can only be accomplished with an ICOM**!

Full Coverage, Maximum Performance. The superb **IC-R71A** is your front row seat to worldwide SSB, CW, RTTY, AM, and FM (optional) communications and foreign broadcasts in the 100kHz to 30MHz range. It features passband, IF Notch, low noise mixer circuits, and 100dB dynamic range. The pacesetting **IC-R7000** receives today's hot areas of

interest, including aircraft, marine, public services, amateur, and satellite transmissions in the 25MHz to 2000MHz* range. It includes **all mode operation** low noise circuits plus outstanding sensitivity and selectivity. The combined IC-R71A/IC-R7000 pair creates a full radio window to the world!

The **IC-R71A** is a shortwave listener's delight. Its **32 tunable memories** store frequency and mode information, and they are single-button reprogrammable **independent of VFO A or VFO B's operations!** This HF reception is further enhanced by a dual width and level adjustable noise blanker, panel selectable RF preamp, selectable AGC, **four scan modes,** and all-mode squelch.

The **IC-R7000** is a high band monitor's masterpiece. Its **99 tunable memories** are complemented by **six scanning modes**. It even scans a band and loads memories 80 to 99 with active frequencies without operator assistance! Additional features include selectable scan speed and pause delays, wide/narrow FM reception, and high frequency stability. Many professional services use IC-R7000's as calibration references.

Options. IC-R7000: RC-12 remote control, EX-310 voice synthesizer, CK-70 DC adapter, MB-12 mobile bracket. IC-R71A: RC-11 remote control, EX-310 voice synthesizer, FM module, CK-70 DC adapter, MB-12 mobile bracket, FL-32A 500Hz, FL-63A 250Hz, and FL-44A filters.

See the IC-R7000 and IC-R71A at your local authorized ICOM dealer.

* Specifications of IC-R7000 guaranteed from 25-100MHz and 1260-1300MHz. No coverage from 1000-1025MHz

First in Communications

ICOM America, Inc., 2380-116th Ave. N.E., Bellevue, WA 98004 **Customer Service Hotline (206) 454-7619**
3150 Premier Drive, Suite 126, Irving, TX 75063 / 1777 Phoenix Parkway, Suite 201, Atlanta, GA 30349
ICOM CANADA, A Division of ICOM America, Inc., 3071 - #5 Road Unit 9, Richmond, B.C. V6X 2T4 Canada
All stated specifications are approximate and subject to change without notice or obligation. All ICOM radios significantly exceed FCC regulations limiting spurious emissions. RCVRS587.

Photo page 11: The Shayad Monument, built to symbolize the "new" Iran, guarded by soldiers in the closing days before the Shah's fall. Photo by Dave Rosenthal

How World Band Radio Saved My Life

Escape from Iran

by Dave Rosenthal

I arrived in Iran during those fateful closing weeks of 1978. An engineer for an American aerospace corporation, I was sent to sell the Shah's military a newly developed shortwave transceiver. Almost incidentally, I had also brought along my own portable world band radio. Little did I know it would save my life.

Dick—the other half of my sales team—and I landed at Tehran's Merhabad Airport just before midnight. Nothing seemed out of the ordinary; things appeared to be moving at a pace typical of any international port-of-call. Upheavals throughout the country had resulted in the Shah's declaring martial law in twelve cities a couple of months back, but there was no sign of any tension here. Armed soldiers were scattered throughout the airport, but they didn't seem to be interested in much except the television sets placed around the lobby.

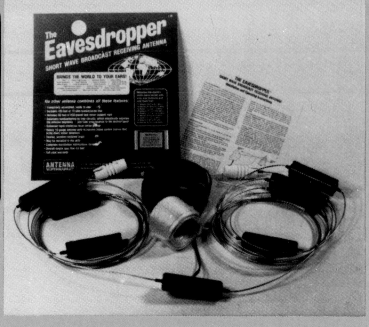

The only things of interest to customs were "instruments of subversion," such as propaganda, weapons—and, unfortunately, shortwave transceivers. It seemed that foreign operatives working against the Shah were receiving their instructions via shortwave transmissions. Once the Iranian customs people saw our declaration forms, all our transceivers wound up in "bonded storage." Dick and I suddenly found ourselves alone, luggage in hand, looking for a ride.

Our taxi took us to the Shah-owned Royal Tehran Hilton. After we passed through the metal detectors to get to the lobby, we were met by a couple of Company employees. They had both been in Iran for almost two years and were very interested in what was happening in the rest of the world. Anticipating something like this, I had bought a *Los Angeles Times* before boarding the plane and presented them with it.

I do not think I had ever seen such genuine gratitude. Once they were over the shock of seeing a newspaper, they literally fought over who got the "World News" section first. I asked them what kind of news coverage they got here, and they related stories about the series of controls the government had put in place over the last year or so.

Iran's official media consisted of the National Iranian Radio and Television (NIRT). The NIRT presented television simulcast in several languages, including English, as well as AM and FM radio. News was carefully prepared, and little or no mention of the developing internal strife was permitted. You heard only about major shifts in policy or "temporary restrictions" on this or that.

I asked about world band radio, and though both were aware of its existence, neither owned a receiver. They did tell me that they were able to monitor an occasional foreign English broadcast on their car's AM radio, but seldom heard any news. The thought of the portable world band radio safely tucked away in my suitcase suddenly became comforting.

After sleeping away the twelve time zones, Dick and I visited the Company's downtown Tehran office. Our in-country Vice President welcomed us, but did not hold much hope for our impounded equipment. "It'll be a couple of weeks before we can negotiate your equipment out of customs," he told us. "Does either of you have an International Driver's License?"

I did. I had gotten it during my post-Vietnam duty in Europe, and Iran was on its list of countries.

The Vice President handed me a set of car keys and told us to check back in a week or two. This would give the Company's Iranian "negotiator" a chance to visit the proper officials and apply the appropriate "lubrication."

Dick and I were somewhat confused, but nonetheless eager to see this place for ourselves.

Dave Rosenthal.

The Company car was a Paykan, an Iranian-built Hillman, and although it was no BMW, it ran.

We set off to see as much of the country as we could in the next couple of weeks. Once out of the city, people and buildings quickly became scarce. We had good maps and planned our trips carefully to make sure we never got in over our heads.

Throughout our travels, everyone seemed friendly and cordial. We would stop for a cold soda at a store, restaurant, or gas station, and the people there would walk up and ask us questions about Los Angeles. Once we rolled up to a mud hut village in the middle of nowhere and were mobbed by children offering us food and asking for any written material we might have in English. I gave one of them the Pan Am inflight magazine I'd stuffed into my camera bag, and he seemed every bit as pleased as the Company fellows who had gotten my *Los Angeles Times*. Dick and I began to wonder what was really happening here.

One night after watching more bland news on television, I pulled out my world band radio and tried some listening for the first time. My room's little balcony faced the broad parkway running by the Hilton, and I strung my forty feet of antenna wire to make the most of what exposure I had.

I was able to monitor the BBC and Radio Nederland news. Both carried headline stories about the big oil worker strike. Television showed nothing about it.

The next day Dick and I decided to go shopping at the Tajrish Bazaar near our hotel in the northern portion of Tehran. It was about a mile up Avenue Pahlave, a broad, tree-lined boulevard named for the Shah's family.

(continued on page 84)

CHECK OUT THE WAVES
OF THE WORLD!

SANGEAN, the world's largest single manufacturer of portable multi-band radio receivers, invites you to enjoy a world of listening with any one of our full feature 4,8,9,10,12 or 15 band receivers.

All SANGEAN receivers are packed with the features and performance you want - at a price just right for your budget. From our flagship model ATS-803A with all the features of many higher priced receivers, to our palm sized MS-101 – just right for those on the go who want to take the world with them.

All models carry the famous SANGEAN guarantee of quality and workmanship; the signature of a company whose only desire is to make the best multi-band portable radios available.

For a FREE full color catalog call 1-800-232-2929 (outside California), or 1-818-288-1661 (in California).

SANGEAN
A World of Listening™

Photo page 17: Cajun musicians give a concert in Louisianna. Photo reprinted from **Southern Living Magazine,** May, 1987

Ten Top Shows for 1989

Passport's "Summary of World Band Broadcasting Activity" shows that world band stations broadcast nearly a quarter *million* hours of programming each week—much of which is in English. Given this vast menu, there is no shortage of delightful programs to fill your available listening time. Indeed, the choice is so generous that a hundred top-notch shows, rather than ten, could easily be selected.

The shows the *Passport* listening panel finally selected are plums worth a portion of any listener's schedule. But there is so much on the air that even entire categories of shows—sports, science and so forth—cannot be included in any one year's choices. For information on these other worthy programs, please see *Passport's* hour-by-hour listening guide, "What's on Tonight?"

News—International

World at Six/As It Happens
Radio Canada International

Brace yourself for a shock. The BBC World Service does not have the best international news broadcast on world band radio.

That is heresy, of course. The British Broadcasting Corporation has been renowned for its complete, accurate, and unbiased news coverage since . . . since . . . well, since as long back as anyone can remember. That reputation dates back to World War II, when the Nazis confiscated millions of radio sets in occupied Europe to prevent captive populations from listening to London. And, since the early Forties, the BBC's *Radio*

Newsreel has been "must" listening for any English-speaking world band listener who wants to be on top of the day's events. It was true then, it's still true now.

But Radio Canada International gets top marks for devoting the time and doing such an outstanding job with its 90-minute weekday combination, the *World at Six* and *As It Happens*. Both emanate from the domestic Canadian Broadcasting Corporation network, but are also heard on RCI's North American and European Services.

The *World at Six* is a thorough half-hour newscast, covering both international and major Canadian stories in a two-reader format, with plenty of on-the-scene reporting.

As It Happens, seemingly patterned after the venerable BBC *Radio Newsreel*, carries in-depth reports on the day's major stories from correspondents abroad. RCI, however, allots a full hour, not just fifteen minutes, to this segment.

The rubs? For one thing, this news feast is aired only on weekdays. For another, it's aimed at merely two of the many parts of the world served by RCI: Europe and North America. Even at that, it's just Americans that get the whole enchilada; Europeans hear only the first 30 minutes of *As It Happens*, after which it vanishes, poof!—sometimes in mid-sentence.

In North America, the *World at Six* is heard weekdays at 0000 Universal Time winters, 2200 summers, on 5960 and 9755 kHz: and also via the CBC at 2300 winters, 2200 summers, on 9625 and 11720 kHz. *As It Happens* is on at 0030 winters, 2330 summers, on 5960 and 9755 kHz: 0200 year-around on 9535, 9755, 11845, and 11940 kHz; and via the CBC at 0200 winters, 0100 summers, on 6195 and 9625 kHz.

In Europe, the *World at Six* and the first half of *As It Happens* are heard back to back weekdays from 2200–2300 Universal Time on 9760 and 11945 kHz winters, 2100–2200 on 11945 and 15325 kHz summers.

National Insight Show

Smith's Weekly
Radio Australia

Besides hard reporting, many world band stations offer glimpses of how the news is played at home in the country's own daily papers. Often this takes the form of a press review of headlines and editorials.

Radio Australia takes a more creative slant with *Smith's Weekly*, "a random look at the (continued on page 86)

A cheese market in Holland. Photo by Tara Van den Hout

"The Best Results throughout the Shortwave Spectrum."

— Larry Magne, Radio Database International White Paper

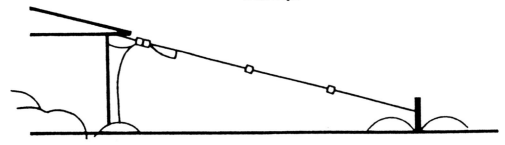

Get world-class, multi-band reception with
ALPHA DELTA DX–SWL SLOPER ANTENNA

Just $69.95 plus shipping from your Alpha Delta dealer!

- Fully assembled, ready to use and built for long life. So strong, it can even be used to transmit — up tp 2 kW!

- Superior multi-band performance on 13, 16, 19, 21, 25, 31, 41, 49, 60, 90, 120 meters plus the AM broadcast band (.5-1.6 MHz). All in a single compact antenna. Alpha Delta first!

- Efficient multi-band frequency selection by means of special RF choke-resonators — instead of lossy, narrow band traps.

- Overall length just 60 feet. Requires only a single elevated support — easier to install than a dipole.

- 50 ohm feedpoint at apex of antenna for maximum DX reception. A UHF connector is provided on the mounting bracket for easy connection to your coax.

- A top overall rating in Radio Database International's hard-hitting White Paper, "RDI Evaluates the Popular Outdoor Antennas."

There's a lot happening on the shortwave broadcast bands. Don't miss a thing by skimping on your antenna. Get world class, multi-band DX reception with the Alpha Delta model DX-SWL Sloper. Just $69.95 plus shipping from your local Alpha Delta dealer.

ALPHA DELTA COMMUNICATIONS, INC.

P.O. Box 571 • Centerville, Ohio 45459

the ICOM experts

√ for years EEB has set high standards for ICOM receiver modifications
√ EEB knows how to release the true potential of these world class receivers
√ you can count on EEB for fast, fair, and friendly service before and after the sale.

ICR71A — .1 to 30 mHz — 32 memories
for the serious HF listener — our best hf seller

EEB IC-R71A HP Options
- FRONT END UPGRADE improves the dynamic range and adds preamp for below 1600 kHz.
- AUDIO OUTPUT MODIFICATION increases your audio output power, lowers distortion, and widens the audio bandwidth for more pleasurable listening.
- AGC MODIFICATION changes the time constant decreasing the slowtime and increasing the fast time.
- 24 HOUR BENCH TEST is a complete checkout and realignment for optimum performance.
- SPIKE PROTECTION - the voltage spike protector is installed where it will do the most good - inside the receiver.
- ICOM options purchased with your new IC-R71A are installed FREE.
- FILTERS replace the stock ceramic SSB filter for improved SSB, ECSS, and Narrow selectivity.
  Filter and Upgrade packages:
      Mechanical 2.4 kHz filter PLUS all upgrades listed above --- order HPMF $200.00
      8 pole crystal filter PLUS all upgrades listed above --- order HPXF $250.00
      Super 2.1 kHz 8 pole crystal filter PLUS all upgrades listed above --- order HPSXF $300.00

IC-R7000 — 25 to 2000 mHz — 99 memories
for the serious V/UHF listener. Our best V/UHF seller

EEB IC-R7000 HP Option $200
- FRONT END UPGRADE improves sensitivity and dynamic range.
- AUDIO OUTPUT MODIFICATION increases your audio output power, lowers distortion, and widens the audio bandwidth for more pleasurable listening.
- 24 HOUR BENCH TEST is a complete checkout and realignment for optimum performance.
- SPIKE PROTECTION - the voltage spike protector is installed where it will do the most good - inside the receiver.

Other Available Options
- R7000 MUX for those listeners desiring to explore the world of hidden subcarriers. $75.00
- R7000 R-SCAN allows scanning to continue after a 5 or 15 second delay regardless of signal condition and allows the scanning to continue after the carrier has dropped. $50.00
- R7000 TURBO SCAN increases the scan speed from 7 to 13 channels per second. $50.00
- R7000 PS is a replacement power supply that reduces line fluctuation receiver degradation. $150.00
- R7000 MEMO EXPAND increases memory to 200 channels. $TBA
- ICOM options purchased with your new IC-R7000 are installed FREE.

 Orders: 800-368-3270   Local & tech info 703-938-3350

Electronic Equipment Bank
516P Mill St. NE, Vienna, VA 22180

An Interview with James A. Michener

World Band Radio

A Real Part of My Life

For those who wait in the backwaters of war, James A. Michener recounts in his classic *Tales of the South Pacific*, there are times when short-wave radio is no less than a lifeline to reality.

"What's the news?" Grant asks in that book's opening pages. The stocky New Zealander elbows his way to the radio set, waiting for the newscast to come crackling through the tropical static. Out there, somewhere, a great naval battle is being fought. What's happening? The bushy-mustachioed flying officer has to know. Once or twice he drowses off, but for 16 hours he stays by the set; no one else dares to touch the dials. *(continued)*

Forty years have passed since the Pulitzer-Prize-winning writer drew that gripping scene from his World War II experiences as a naval officer. More than thirty bestselling titles later, Michener has seen just about everything in his globe-circling travels, observing and recording the ever-changing world and its peoples. But one thing remains unchanged after all the years—Michener's enthusiasm for world band radio, now a prolific medium.

"It's been a real part of my life." the 81-year-old Michener says in a recent interview with *Passport to World Band Radio.*

Tales of his listening experiences come tripping easily in this conversation with the master storyteller, now Distinguished Visiting Professor of English at the University of Miami at Coral Gables, Florida.

He tells of another, and much more recent, naval battle he had followed so closely by radio.

"It was during the Falklands crisis," Michener says, "and I was traveling with a friend who'd been in the British Navy. We were extremely alert to precisely what was happening, particularly after the sinking of that Argentine cruiser, and the probablities of what might happen yet."

With the Englishman, his trusted project editor John Kings, at the wheel, they were motoring west through New Mexico, Arizona, and California as the 1982 war in the South Atlantic unfolded.

> Every night, we used shortwave, from sunset to dawn, as we sailed. We had it on constantly. It was really quite wonderful.

"American radio, commercial radio, the normal band, only gave us some summary information. Fortunately we had a good radio in the car, and with shortwave we tied into the BBC for their 15 minute newscasts, and also for their three minute summaries on the hour," he recalls.

"The reception was really rather good. I followed that with the greatest of care and appreciated more than ever what a service the shortwave does around the world. My friend and I were just two of many people . . . in Canada, the United States, and indeed, in Argentina . . . who were listening to these specially scheduled broadcasts. It was a very dramatic experience."

Michener has long appreciated the real-time drama of world band listening, going back to the earlier war in the South Pacific when he tuned in to Tokyo Rose and the Japanese propaganda machine.

"They were very clever. The Japanese were very able, not at all as burlesqued as they are sometimes depicted. The broadcasts were insidious, but they weren't at all trivial!"

His interest in radio, though, goes back further still. It was in 1933 and 1934, Michener says, when, as a young school teacher in Pennsylvania, he dabbled "way, way ahead of my time" with high fidelity sound, adding filters to a monstrous RCA radio to produce three-channel audio.

> They were very clever. The Japanese were very able, not at all as burlesqued as they are sometimes depicted. The broadcasts were insidious, but they weren't at all trivial!

Years later, he built dozens of electronic kits just for the sheer fun of it. "I'm an old Heathkit man," he says. "I gave them away to schools after I finished them, but I just wanted to see what they were up to. I wanted to know what the technology was."

And as Michener knows well, technology keeps changing. Today, solid state receivers offer signal stability, simple touchpad tuning, and improved sound, replacing the vintage vacuum tube sets with their weak and watery reception. Even the original word, shortwave, is giving way to the more descriptive term world band radio.

It is Michener's unquenchable curiosity about people and places that has repeatedly led him around the world. He has wandered from Afghanistan to Vanuatu, islands near New Caledonia. He has researched his writings from South Africa to Spain. At various times, Michener and his Japanese-American wife, Mari, have called Hawaii, Alaska, Israel, even Texas their home. His travels have taken him to Asia at least twice a year. Michener has been to Burma and back twenty times, and, he estimates, he has flown into Singapore more than fifty times. If you can get from here to there, you can safely wager that Michener has.

"Some years ago, I brought a small boat back across the Pacific from Hawaii," he recalls. "We sailed first to Alaska, then south, down the California coast to Newport Beach. And every night, we used shortwave, from sunset to dawn, as we sailed. We had it on constantly. It was really quite wonderful."

He has a passion for detail—a near flawless ability to observe, remember, and then recreate on the printed page the colorful images of faraway places. His books—all 21 million copies—have been translated into fifty languages, making him America's most popular serious author.

Michener used to carry a portable world band radio on his travels, but now, he says, he's more apt to rely on the hotel where he is staying to provide a suitable radio.

"I'm very much a traveler who uses radio because of the tremendous contribution it makes," says Michener. "I would say that because of the kind of work I do, when I come into an area I try to listen to the radio. I want to find out what's 'biting' the local people. So I probably listen to radio now even more than I used to, as a kind of research tool."

When abroad, he listens frequently to the US Armed Forces Radio and Television Service on world band. "Interestingly, I find that these programs are rather widely listened to not only by those in the American armed services, but by citizens of those countries where American Forces radio can be well heard."

Michener does not criticize the Voice of America's overseas services, but notes that AFRTS may hit "the wider scatter of popular interests" better than does the nation's "official" broadcaster.

A keen observer of political events, Michener has been a participant as well. In 1960, he became chairman of the Bucks County, Pennsylvania,

Citizens for Kennedy Committee—an eye-opening experience he details in his excellent, but little known book, *Report of the County Chairman*. He also ran unsuccessfully for Congress on the Democratic ticket in 1962, and six years later stood as an elector in the presidential campaign.

But it was a Republican president, Richard Nixon, who in 1971 named Michener to the US Advisory Commission on Information, giving him input into the operations of the Voice of America. With fellow author and commission appointee William F. Buckley, Michener accompanied Nixon on his history-making visit to China not long after. "Bill took along to Beijing the shortwave radio which the United States Information Agency had provided. We both listened to it there."

"At the end of the visit, though," Michener recalls with a chuckle, "Bill tried to leave it behind for the people who had cared for us so well. But it was hilarious. Five or six times, very honest Chinese kept running after us to return the radio, thinking he had left it behind. He couldn't get anyone to take it!"

Michener remained on the presidential information commission about eight years.

In 1983, another GOP president, Ronald Reagan, named him to the Board for International *(continued on page 91)*

"Listening is only half the fun. Popular Communications is the other half."

EEB Exclusive Products
NOVEX

CRIS 6000 Computer/Radio Interface System: The ultimate in *Hi-Tech* computer control for your radio. Features auto logging, auto scan, 800 channel memory in RAM, unlimited memory via disk storage, load radio memories, option for remote control, spectral logging, and more. Request the CRIS NEWSLETTER for the lastest information.

SDU 8000 Spectral Display Unit: Allows user to "see" RF activity above and below the operating frequency. Quickly locate activity over 10 mHz bandwidth (with R7000) and easy calibration. A must for the serious listener. Ask for the SDU Newsletter for more details.

RACK MOUNTS: Organize your radio room like the pros, save space, and protect your investment. NOVEX rack mounts are available for most popular receivers and transceivers. Request the *Rack is Back* for details.

FC7100 Frequency Converter: Now your ICOM R7000 can also cover 20 kHz to 30 mHz. The FC7100 has HF and V/UHF antenna connectors and internal switching with manual or remote (TTL) control. Powered from the R7000 and no receiver modifications necessary. Request the FL7100 Bulletin for further info.

FC29 Frequency Converter: Converts DC - 500 kHz up to 29.0 - 29.5 mHz so most HF receivers can tune down to almost DC (depending on filters) to copy OMEGA, Naval ship to shore, WWVB, etc. Use the R7000 with the MUX option to analyze signals for subcarriers using an additional receiver (R71A w/FM) for SCA. Tune in "Reading for the Blind", *elevator* type music, stock reports (digital), and more. Check out these hidden subcarrier transmissions. For more info ask for the FC29 Bulletin.

RC2010 Recorder Controller: Record using your radio's digital clock timer. Just plug into your radio and connect the AC power adapter. When the radio switches on, your recorder will be commanded by the RC2010 to start. LEDs indicate power and recorder status. Typical radios include: SONY 2010, 2003, 7700 - SANGEAN 801, 803 - Panasonic RFB 60.

Orders: 800-368-3270
Local & tech info
703-938-3350

Electronic Equipment Bank
516P Mill St. NE, Vienna, VA 22180

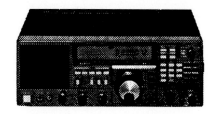

Others May Try to Imitate, But...

Only One Can Be The Best

PAKRATT 232

Advanced Electronic Applications, Inc.

Model PK-2

Morse Code - Baudot - ASCII - AMTOR - Packet - Facsimile - Navtex

Amateur Net Price $319.95

It's a lesson you learn very early in life. Many can be good, some may be better, but only one can be the best. The PK-232 is the best multi-mode data controller you can buy.

1 Versatility

Short-wave listening can be an exciting hobby. But voice broadcasts are just part of the information available to those with short-wave receivers. Digital signals carry everything from foreign news to satellite photos, like the one pictured in this ad. The PK-232 can copy seven different types of digital signals. All you need is a short-wave receiver and an RS-232 compatible computer or data terminal. You will be amazed at how much information you are missing without the PK-232.

The internal decoding program (SIAM^{tm}) feature can even identify different types of signals for you, including some simple types of RTTY encryption. The only software your computer needs is a terminal program.

Facsimile Screen Display

2 Software Support

While you can use most modem or communications programs with the PK-232, AEA has two very special packages available exclusively for the PK-232......PC Pakratt with Fax for IBM PC and compatible computers, and Com Pakratt with Fax for the Commodore 64 and 128.

Each package includes a terminal program with split screen display, QSO buffer, disk storage of received data, and printer operation, and a second program for transmission, reception, and screen display of facsimile signals. The IBM programs are on 5-1/4" disk and the Commodore programs are on plug-in ROM cartridges.

3 Proven Winner

No matter what computer or terminal you plan to use, the PK-232 is the best choice for a multi-mode controller. Over 20,000 amateurs around the world have on-air tested the PK-232 for you. They, along with most major U.S. amateur magazines, have reviewed the PK-232 and found it to be a good value and excellent addition to the radio shack.

No other multi-mode controller offers the features and performance of the PK-232. Don't be fooled by imitations. Ask your friends, or call the local amateur radio store. We're confident the PK-232 reputation will convince you that it's time to order you very own PK-232.

Call an authorized AEA dealer today. You deserve the best you can buy, you deserve the PK-232.

Advanced Electronic Applications, Inc.

P.O. Box C-2160
Lynnwood, WA 98036
206-775-7373

PC Pakratt Packet TX/RX Display

Photo page 31: Puzzle Palace author James Bamford on a research assignment in Europe. Photo by James Bamford

Action between the Bands

by Larry Van Horn

AMERICA'S BIG EAR IN EUROPE

Challenger, you are go at throttle-up, announced the mission controller in Houston. And as usual, the crew replied "Roger, go at throttle-up." And so all appeared normal on that cold day in January, 1986, as the 25th launch of the US Space Shuttle proceeded. Shuttle launches had become so routine that ma-

jor news networks no longer carried them on television or radio. But for those who knew where to listen, the minutes that followed would never be forgotten.

"Flight controllers are looking at the situation. Obviously a major malfunction." For the crew of the Challenger, it was over.

The Challenger disaster is just one example, hopefully a rare one, of the kind of action you can hear on "utility" frequencies. Tuning into utility stations doesn't mean listening to water or sewer repair crews. Instead, utility stations are those within the same shortwave spectrum used by world band radio, but carrying point-to-point traffic instead of broadcasts. They're not meant to be heard by everybody, but with the right equipment—many ordinary world band radios will do—and knowledge, you can eavesdrop on these "hidden" transmissions.

While world band broadcasting stations occupy a major portion of shortwave spectrum, their numbers are dwarfed by the myriad of utility stations. A utility transmission can be from a pilot reporting a hijacking by international terrorists or from a radio operator aboard a cruise ship describing a fire out of control. It can be the strained voices of US Navy personnel cautiously navigating the Persian Gulf.

Utility station monitoring has been likened to a shortwave soup. A utility station may use more than one frequency at once or at different times of the day. There are usually no standard operating schedules. While most stations operate within designated areas of the shortwave spectrum, others, particularly government and military stations, operate just about anywhere they please. Listening to utility frequencies thus is like dipping a spoon into the soup and seeing what comes up. It's pot luck at its best.

> As President Reagan was rushed to the hospital, a communication link was immediately established between the White House and Air Force Two. Listeners monitoring that channel knew exactly the President's condition nearly an hour before the news was broadcast over the networks.

Some of the more common utility stations heard include aeronautical, maritime, military, Coast Guard, and government stations. Aeronautical stations are involved with international and regional flights, with ground controllers helping track the progress of each flight. Within the aeronautical bands, "VOLMET" stations, featured on pages 59–63 of *Passport/88*, broadcast aviation weather for major cities along the world's air routes.

Specialist Fifth Class Kathleen L. Britton is an Air Traffic Control Supervisor assigned to the U.S. Army Communications Command, Ft. Richardson, Alaska. U.S. Army Photograph

The world's most famous utility monitor, Michael Gurdus of Israel, broke the story of the ill-fated Iranian hostage rescue attempt by the American military. He was monitoring aeronautical frequencies and noticed that the aircraft involved in the rescue attempt were overdue in checking in with ground controllers. "Miki," as his friends know him, then notified the Israel Broadcasting Authority and his other media clients of his discovery, and the rest is history.

Maritime frequencies offer the world band listener some interesting material to monitor. Ships communicate with each other and also with shore stations. Listeners can even hear telephone conversations between passengers aboard cruise liners, such as the *QE II*, and folks back home. Discussions about their cruises often are lively and intriguing.

A juicy maritime frequency to tune in is 2182 kHz, an international calling and emergency channel. If you listen long enough, you should hear some exceptional action. One utility listener recently heard the frantic calls for help by the radio operator of the cruise liner *Scandanavian Star* after the ship caught fire off the coast of Mexico. He got the story, blow by blow, exactly as it happened.

The military and the Coast Guard use radio for a variety of communications. Much of the military's communications are in code words, but the Coast Guard's activities are fairly easy to understand. Search and rescue operations, and even the apprehension of drug smugglers, are part of the vast utility menu.

Espionage on the Airwaves: An Interview with James Bamford

James Bamford is author of *The Puzzle Palace*, the bestseller that describes in detail the workings of the National Security Agency—the United States' foremost and most sophisticated organization for gathering signal intelligence.

Bamford spent several years carefully researching the ultra-secret NSA to produce his highly regarded book. Among the fruits of Bamford's labors was that a most displeased NSA twice tried to have him jailed, even though he used only publicly available sources in his research.

For anyone who wonders how governments gather intelligence by snatching signals from the airwaves, *The Puzzle Palace* is "must" reading. Bamford, now a seasoned expert on electronic spookery, continues to write about espionage for a number of publications.

Passport: Can you really hear spies on the radio?

Bamford: Absolutely, but let me set the stage. Starting in the late 1960s and continuing into the early 1980s, a Britisher named Geoffrey Prime made it a habit to listen regularly to world band radio and to record certain "special" transmissions. Prime worked for GCHQ, the British equivalent of the National Security Agency, as a Russian translator. Unfortunately, Prime was not what he seemed. He had been "turned," and was working for the Soviets as a spy. At his trial, it was discovered that his Grundig world band receiver and a tape recorder were key elements in his ability to function as a traitor for more than ten years.

Passport: How's that?

Bamford: At times that were predetermined by his control agent, Prime would tune his radio to an East German station and record a woman reading numbers, in English, in five-digit groups: 03476 74989 30300 and so forth. Prime would then use a one-time pad, also furnished by his control agent, to decode the message.

Passport: A "one-time pad?"

Bamford: Yes. In an ordinary substitution code, such as schoolboys fool around with, 1 always equals "A," 2 always equals "B," 3 always equals "C" . . . well, you get the idea. That kind of code is easy to break, so long as the substitution remains constant.

But in a one-time pad, the first time "A" is used, it might be represented by 1; the second time "A" is used, it may be 16; the next time, 4—and the same random substitution holds true for each letter in the alphabet. It's impossible to break.

The key to this system is that both the sender and the recipient have sheets that show what the substitutions are. After the message is decoded, you throw that sheet away—hence a "one-time pad"—and use a different sheet for decoding the next message. Obviously, the system is very secure, and Prime used the radio, the recorder, and the one-time pads for years to receive his spying instructions.

Passport: What happened to the East German spy station?

Bamford: That's the interesting part. The station was heard operating long after Prime was arrested, the same voice monotonously transmitting five-number groups in English. And this is not an isolated incident. In fact, right now there are a number of stations you can hear on your world band radio that regularly transmit four- or five-digit code groups, either by voice in various languages or in Morse code.

Passport: So the story of espionage on the airwaves continues.

Bamford: Without a doubt, and it raises some interesting questions, such as "Who is transmitting?", "Who is listening?" and, above all, "What are they up to?"

—Interview by Jock Elliot

The United States and other governments use radio for many non-military communications, and their stations are scattered throughout the short-wave spectrum. World band listeners can keep up on the latest happenings in Latin America by listening to Military Assistance Groups. These MAGs, as they are known, can be heard daily passing information among the various embassies throughout Latin America.

Illegal activities also can be heard on utility frequencies. Drug smugglers have taken to the airwaves to coordinate shipments of illicit cargo from Central and South America to the United States. On nearby frequencies, the US Coast Guard and Drug Enforcement Agency can be monitored in hot pursuit. One startled listener reported hearing shouts from a drug runner as machine gun fire punctuated his last transmission.

THE JAPAN RADIO
NRD-525

UNPARALLELED PERFORMANCE AND SOPHISTICATED FEATURES!

Rated a full FIVE STARS by Larry Magne in RADIO DATABASE INTERNATIONAL Whitepaper.

"...it must be said that the NRD-525 is as close to the optimum shortwave listener's receiver as is in existence."

"Japan Radio has taken the features shortwave listeners have always sought...and packaged the lot into what is unquestionably the best overall shortwave listener's receiver on the market today."

"The NRD-525 exemplifies once again that Japan Radio receivers are for the connoisseur."

Larry Magne, International Broadcast Services

The JRC NRD-525 truly stands alone in performance and features! Enjoy exceptional sensitivity and selectivity coupled with rock-solid stability. Continuous coverage from 90.00 to 34000.00 Khz with readout to 10 Hz! Razor-sharp notch filter and passband tuning for digging out that weak DX! All modes are standard including FM and FAX! 24 hour digital clock timer with relay contacts. Incredible 200 channel scanning sweeping memory stores frequency, mode, bandwidth, AGC and ATT settings for each channel. Other standard features include keypad, RIT, MONITOR, AGC, ATT, BFO and dual NB. Available options include VHF/UHF, RS-232, RTTY Demodulator and a wide variety of filters. Operates from 110/220 VAC or 13.8 VDC! Write today for your full color brochure!

Japan Radio Co., Ltd.

Japan Radio Co., Ltd.
USA Branch Office   T. Yamaguchi
405 Park Avenue
New York, New York 10022
(212) 355-1180   Telex 961114

Universal Shortwave Radio
1280 Aida Drive
Reynoldsburg, Ohio 43068
Toll free: 1-800-431-3939
In Ohio: 614-866-4267

Gilfer Associates
52 Park Avenue
Park Ridge, New Jersey 07656
201-391-7887

Passport's "Hot 75" Utility Frequencies

Authoritative references to utility stations run hundreds of pages in length. Here's just a sampling of some of the easiest-to-hear:

Channel	Utility Station	Channel	Utility Station
2182	International Maritime Distress	8778	US Navy Ships
2598	Canadian Coast Guard Marine Warnings	8843	International Aircraft: Pacific
2670	US Coast Guard Marine Warnings	8846	International Aircraft: Caribbean
2869	International Aircraft: Pacific	8879	International Aircraft: Africa/ North Atlantic
2887	International Aircraft: Caribbean		
2899	International Aircraft: North Atlantic	8972	US Navy Aircraft: Atlantic
3123	US Coast Guard Air-to-Ground	8984	US Coast Guard Air-to-Ground
3130	US Navy Ship/Aircraft	9014	US Air Force Air-to-Ground
4495	US Air Force: Strategic Air Command	9027	US Air Force: Strategic Air Command
4627.1	US Air Force: Civil Air Patrol	10493	FEMA-Emergency Net
4670	"Spy Numbers" Broadcast (AM)	10780	NASA Air-to-Ground
4725	US Air Force: Strategic Air Command	11176	US Air Force Air-to-Ground
4746	US Air Force Air-to-Ground	11243	US Air Force: Strategic Air Command
5320	US Coast Guard	11267	US Navy Command
5547	International Aircraft: Pacific	11282	International Aircraft: Pacific
5550	International Aircraft: Caribbean	11300	International Aircraft: Africa
5562	NOAA: Hurricane Hunters	11306	International Aircraft: South America
5598	International Aircraft: North Atlantic	11396	International Aircraft: Caribbean
5658	International Aircraft: Africa/Middle East	13113.2	US Coast Guard
5680	International Search and Rescue	13181	US Navy
5696	US Coast Guard Air-to-Ground	13201	US Air Force Air-to-Ground
5700	US Air Force: Strategic Air Command	13211	US Air Force: Strategic Air Command
5703	US Air Force: Tactical Air Command	13306	International Aircraft: Africa/ North Atlantic
5812	"Spy Numbers" Broadcast (AM)		
6506.4	US Coast Guard Ship-to-Shore	13354	NOAA: Hurricane Hunters
6673	NOAA: Hurricane Hunters	13950	US Air Force South American Embassies
6683	Air Force One/Two/VIP Aircraft (LSB)	15015	US Air Force Air-to-Ground
6697	US Navy Ships/Aircraft	15048	Air Force One/Two/VIP Aircraft (LSB)
6708	NASA Air-to-Ground	15051	US Navy
6715	US Air Force Air-to-Ground	17307.3	US Coast Guard
6723	US Navy Aircraft	17901	NOAA: Hurricane Hunters
6730	Air Force One/Two/VIP Aircraft (LSB)	17946	International Aircraft: North Atlantic
6738	US Air Force Air-to-Ground	17955	International Aircraft: Africa/South America
6761	US Air Force: Strategic Air Command		
6802	"Spy Numbers" Broadcast (AM)	17961	International Aircraft: Africa/Middle East
6840	"Spy Numbers" Broadcast (AM)	17975	US Air Force: Strategic Air Command
6927	Air Force One/Two/VIP Aircraft (LSB)	18002	US Air Force Air-to-Ground
7507	US Navy/US Coast Hurricane Net	19954	USSR Unmanned Satellites (Data)
8418	"Spy Numbers" Broadcast (AM)	20008	USSR Manned Space Stations (CW)

All frequencies in kilohertz/upper sideband unless otherwise noted.

Other tense conversations can be heard by persistent listeners. Air Force One and Two, the planes which carry the President and Vice-President of the United States, are frequent visitors to utility radio. As President Reagan was rushed to the hospital suffering from the gunshot wound from a would-be assassin's bullet, a communication link was immediately established between the White House and Air Force Two. This link kept Vice-President Bush updated on the President's condition. Listeners monitoring that channel knew exactly the President's condition nearly an hour before the news was broadcast over the networks.

Before tuning utility stations, be aware of laws governing this sensitive subject. While listening in the United States to utility stations is usually legal, repeating or divulging the contents of a communication is always against federal law—even though such august publications as *The New York Times* haven't been prosecuted for publishing conversations heard on Air Force One and other utility stations. In a number of countries, simply listening to utility stations is against the law. Even in the normally live-and-let-live

US, listening to radio/TV reporters' "backfeeds" on 26 MHz has recently been made illegal.

Tuning for utility stations can be a mammoth task, but a prospective listener can find help from several sources. *The Shortwave Directory* by Grove Enterprises is one good reference. Many listings in this guide are unusual and include such categories as terrorist networks, freebanders, spy "numbers" communications, hurricane networks, and petroleum platform helicopters. Two other books that no beginner should be without are the *Confidential Frequency List* from Gilfer Associates and the large annual *Guide to Utility Stations* from Klingenfuss Publications.

The utility world band radio scene is constantly changing, and up-to-date information is a must. The monthly publication *Monitoring Times* contains a four-page column called "Utility World." This column will keep you abreast of the newest information on utilities.

The utility frequencies abound with the stuff of life and death, the law and disaster. Do you want to know what's happening right now? Fire up your radio between those world band segments and find out.

Larry Van Horn is an electronics and computer specialist with the US Navy. He has written widely on satellite and utility communications.

U.S. astronaut and ham Tony England airs amateur radio and TV transmissions from his shuttle spacecraft. American Radio Relay League Executive VP David Sumner presents him with an autographed copy of the ARRL Handbook—the "bible" of ham radio operators worldwide. Photo reprinted from May 1988 issue of QST

Yaesu has serious listeners for the serious listener.

Yaesu's serious about giving you better ways to tune in the world around you.

And whether it's for local action or worldwide DX, you'll find our VHF/UHF and HF receivers are the superior match for all your listening needs.

The FRG-9600. A premium VHF/UHF scanning communications receiver. The 9600 is no typical scanner. And it's easy to see why.

You won't miss any local action with continuous coverage from 60 to 905 MHz.

You have more operating modes to listen in on: upper or lower sideband, CW, AM wide or narrow, and FM wide or narrow.

You can even watch television programs by plugging in a video monitor into the optional video output.

Scan in steps of 5, 10, 12½, 25 and 100 KHz. Store any frequency and

related operating mode into any of the 99 memories. Scan the memories. Or in between them. Or simply "dial up" any frequency with the frequency entry pad.

Plus there's more, including a 24-hour clock, multiplexed output, fluorescent readout, signal strength graph, and an AC power adapter.

The FRG-8800 HF communications receiver. A better way to listen to the world. If you want a complete communications package, the FRG-8800 is just right for you.

You get continuous worldwide coverage from 150 KHz to 30 MHz. And local coverage from 118 to 174 MHz with an optional VHF converter.

Listen in on any mode: upper and lower sideband, CW, AM wide or narrow, and FM.

Store frequencies and operating modes into any of the twelve channels for instant recall.

Scan the airwaves with a number of programmable scanning functions.

Plus you get keyboard frequency entry. An LCD display for easy readout. A SINPO signal graph. Computer interface capability for advanced listening functions. Two 24 hour clocks. Recording functions. And much more to make your listening station complete.

Listen in. When you want more from your VHF/UHF or HF receivers, just look to Yaesu. We take your listening seriously.

YAESU

Yaesu USA
17210 Edwards Road, Cerritos, CA 90701
(213) 404-2700

Yaesu Cincinnati Service Center
9070 Gold Park Drive, Hamilton, OH 45011
(513) 874-3100

Dealer inquiries invited.

Prices and specifications subject to change without notice.
FRG-9600 SSB coverage: 60 to 460 MHz.

Photo page 41: The Radio House of Radio France Internationale, Paris. Photo by RFI

Hearing France
Voulez-vous 'coutez avec moi, ce soir?

France. From fabled architecture to notably independent people—it all can be heard on this country's growing world band station, Radio France Internationale.

France. The word brings to the mind's eye images of the Eiffel Tower, lovers along the Seine, sidewalk artists accompanied by soft accordion music. It is the home of legendary wines, sensuous beaches, and mythical scenery—to many, the most romantic country on earth. At the end of *Casa-*

blanca, Bogie and Bergman could live with their anguish because "We will always have Paris."

And the language . . . French ripples with a liquidity and flow unrivaled by any other tongue. It charms the ear. Even heated arguments in French sound like music.

But beyond the stereotypes and quixotic fantasies, there is another France, very much *au courant*—the France of superspeed trains, efficient nuclear power, and coalition governments com-

Make your station really perform

Need to hear the weak ones? No room for an outside long wire? Looking for a great little speaker? Choose the accessories for the

Use this 54 inch active antenna to receive strong signals from all over-the-world MFJ-1024 . . . $129.95

Receive strong clear signals from all-over-the world with this 54 inch active antenna that rivals long wires hundreds of feet long. The authoritative *World Radio TV Handbook* rates the MFJ-1024 as 'a first-rate easy-to-operate active antenna . . . quiet . . . excellent

dynamic range . . . good gain . . . very low noise factor . . . broad frequency coverage . . . excellent choice'.

You'll receive all frequencies 50 KHz to 30 MHz from VLF thru lower VHF - including long wave, medium wave, broadcast and shortwave bands. Mounts anywhere away from electrical noise for maximum signal and minimum noise pickup -- mount on houses, buildings, balconies, mobile homes, apartments, on board ships -- anywhere space is a premium.

High dynamic range eliminates intermodulation so you never hear 'phantom' signals.

A 20 dB attenuator and a gain control prevents overloading your receiver. You can select between 2 receivers and an auxiliary antenna. Has weather-proofed electronics. Use 12 VDC or 110 VAC with MFJ-1312, $9.95.

The MFJ-1024 comes complete with a 50 foot coax cable and connector - ready to use!

WORLD TIME CLOCK

MFJ-109 . . . $18.95

The new MFJ-109 World Time Clock gives you a dual LCD display that shows both the local time and the time in any of 24 world cities.

Easy-slide control lets you instantly select the city.

Or you can instantly check GMT by setting it on our convenient GMT pointer.

It also features an alarm with snooze, night light, Daylight Savings Time adjustment, suede-like carrying case, international date change indicators, and a flip stand. AAA batteries are also included along with an attractive gift box.

It has silver casing, a gray background and black lettering with a red MFJ logo. It measures a shirt-pocket sized 2x4½x½ inches.

MOBILE SHORTWAVE CONVERTER

MFJ-308 . . . $99.95
MFJ-304 . . . $79.95

Enjoy new excitement and variety as you listen to the world while driving with these low cost mobile shortwave converters. Choose the MFJ-304 'World Explorer I' that covers 19, 25, 31 and 49 meter bands or the MFJ-308 'World Explorer II' that adds 13, 16, 41 and 60 meter bands for total shortwave broadcast coverage.

World wide coverage brings in Europe, Africa, Asia, Middle East, South Pacific plus North and South America! Just push a button to select your band and tune in stations with your car radio.

PRESELECTING SW/MW/LW TUNER

MFJ-956 . . . 39.95

This MFJ-956 short, medium, long wave preselector/tuner lets you boost your favorite station while rejecting images, intermod and other phantom signals on your shortwave receiver! It greatly improves reception of 150 KHz thru 30 MHz signals. It has convenient tuner bypass and ground receiver positions. 2x3x4 inches

COMPACT SPEAKER

MFJ-280 . . . $18.95

A rugged, compact communications speaker with a tilt bracket on a magnetic base. Has 3½ mm phone plug on 30 inch cord. Use with all 8 & 4 ohm impedances. Handles up to 3 watts of audio. Mounting plates, screws included. Its dark gray military color matches your rig. 2x2½x3 inches.

12/24 HOUR LCD CLOCKS

MFJ-108B . . . $19.95
MFJ-107B . . . $9.95

Know the exact 24 hour UTC time and your local 12 hour time at a single glance so

you'll tune in your favorite stations on time and keep accurate logs for DXing. Huge 5/8 inch LCD digits makes glare-free reading easy. MFJ-108, dual 24/12 hour clock, 4½x1x2 in. MFJ-107, single 24 hour clock, 2¼x1x2 in. Long lasting lithium battery included.

MFJ . . . making quality affordable

with MFJ shortwave accessories

Troubled by 'phantom' signals? Need convenient access to UTC? kind of performance you need from the many models MFJ offers

ANTENNA MATCHER

MFJ-959B . . . $89.95

Don't lose signal power! The MFJ-959B Antenna Tuner provides proper impedance matching so you transfer maximum power from your antenna to your receiver from 1.8 to 30 MHz. You'll be surprised by significant increases in signal strength.

20 dB preamp with gain control boosts weak stations and 20 dB attenuator prevents overload. Select from 2 antennas and 2 receivers. 9x2x6 inches. 9-18 VDC or 110 VAC with MFJ-1312, $9.95.

RF PRESELECTOR

MFJ-1045B . . . $69.95

Is your receiver "hearing" all it could? Adding an MFJ-1045B RF preselector can make "lost" signals readable while reducing troublesome images and out-of-band signals. It adds 20 dB of low noise gain with a strong, sharp tuning front end and covers all HF amateur and shortwave bands through lower VHF from 1.8 to 54 MHz.

A gain control prevents overload. Select 2 antennas, 2 receivers. 5x2x6 inches. Uses 9-18 VDC or 110 VAC with MFJ-1312, $9.95.

ALL MODE FILTER

MFJ-752C . . . $99.95

Maybe the only filter you'll ever need. Why? Because the all mode dual tunable filters let you zero in AM/SSB/RTTY/CW/AMTOR/Packet signals and notch out interference at the same time.

The primary filter lets you peak, notch, low or high pass filter out interference.

The auxilary filter gives deep notches and sharp peaks.

Both tune 300 to 3000 Hz with variable bandwidth from 40 Hz to virtually flat. Select 2 receivers. Drive speaker. Use 9-18 VDC or 110 VAC with MFJ-1312, $9.95. 10x2x6 in.

RTTY/ASCII/CW COMPUTER INTERFACE

MFJ-1225 . . . $69.95

Open up a whole new and exciting world of shortwave listening with a MFJ-1225 RTTY/ASCII/CW computer interface. Listen to news before it appears on general radio and TV, weather, ship-to-shore communications, hams rag chewing, all kinds of commerical traffic and even the military. You'll be fascinated as traffic scrolls across your home computer screen (some messages may be encrypted).

All you need is a stable shortwave receiver, personal computer and the MFJ-1225 computer interface. Software on disk and cables are supplied for the Commodore 128, 64 and VIC-20 -- everything you need. Most other home computers -- with an RS-232 port, suitable software and cable -- can be used, such as IBM PC and clones, Apple, TRS-80C, Tandy, Atari, TI-99. Uses 12-15 VDC or 110 VAC with MFJ-1312, $9.95.

Rival outside long wires with this INDOOR active antenna

Now you'll rival or exceed the reception of outside long wires with the new and improved MFJ-1020A Indoor Tuned Active Antenna with higher gain. Here's what the 'World Radio TV Handbook' says about the MFJ-1020: 'Fine value...fair price...best offering to date...**performs very well indeed.'**

MFJ-1020A . . . $79.95

You get continuous coverage of low, medium and short wave bands from 300 KHz to 30 MHz so you can listen to all your favorite stations. It even functions as a preselector with an external antenna.

Its unique tuned circuitry minimizes intermodulation, improves selectivity and reduces noise so you're less bothered by images, and other out-of-band signals.

The adjustable telescoping antenna that gives you maximum signal and minimum noise. There's a full set of controls for tuning, band selection, gain, ON/OFF/Bypass and an LED power 'ON' indicator. It measures just 5x2x6 inches. Use a 9 volt battery,9-18 VDC or 110 VAC with MFJ-1312, $19.95.

SUPERPOWER KUSW⊕RADIO WORLDWIDE

FROM THE WEST TO THE WORLD!

Salt Lake City, Utah – United States of America

The World's Newest Commercial World Band Station

* Music * News * Features * Mailbag
* Worldwide Weatherbank Computerized Reports
* Worldwide Listener Contests
* Live Satellite Concerts

Thanks for the positive listener response:

- ⊙ "I have found your station to be a joy to listen to and you can count on me becoming a regular listener." - Toronto, Canada
- ⊙ "Your station was heard with excellent signal strength and nil interference from other radio stations. A very clear signal." - Sweden
- ⊙ "I was impressed to hear advertising sponsorship from the Wall Street Journal. I hope that other major companies will also sponsor your efforts to put a commercial American shortwave station on the air." - Marietta, Georgia
- ⊙ "I am surprised at the good programming you have, especially the music." - West Germany
- ⊙ "I found KUSW's programming to be the best of any domestic shortwave broadcaster." - Lake Villa, Illinois
- ⊙ "This is my first reception of you. I think it's easier to catch your signal than any other short wave from the USA." - Tokyo, Japan
- ⊙ "I've been listening since just after Christmas and you're exactly what the doctor ordered." - S. Deerfield, Mass.

* Send for your Free Superpower KUSW Catalog

KUSW, P.O. Box 7040, Salt Lake City, Utah 84107, USA

prised of strange bedfellows. Today's France is still one of the most romantic spots on the globe, but it is also a modern nation, struggling like every other to play a complex role in a fast-changing world.

Fortunately, for those who want to stay in touch with both the romantic soul and modern reality of France, there is Radio France Internationale. Each week RFI broadcasts 900 hours of programming to a claimed audience of 80 million listeners around the world.

With transmitter sites in France, French Guyana, and Gabon, and with a combined transmitter power of some 7.7 million watts, RFI's primary mission is to broadcast a 24-hour news-and-features service in French. Powerful RFI aims its signals at Europe, the Near and Middle East, Africa, Central and South America, the Caribbean, and most of North America, with a few hours each day to Southeast Asia and Indonesia. RFI also provides programming directly to cable networks in Canada's French-speaking province of Quebec. Short programs for rebroadcast by African national stations are prepared as well.

Beyond the broadcasts aimed primarily at those who speak French, there are also programs in eleven other languages. Some of RFI's foreign language broadcasts use widely spoken languages for listeners in several countries or even several continents, while other broadcasts are tailored to a specific geographic area. For example, Spanish broadcasts to Spain are different from those destined for Latin American countries. Portuguese broadcasts heard in Portugal are also beamed to Portuguese-speaking Africa, but a different news team produces Portuguese programs especially for Brazil. German broadcasts cover both East and West Germany, as well as several other European countries where German is spoken.

Other foreign language programs are created for "target" countries: Russian for the Soviet Union, Polish for Poland, and Serbo-Croatian for Yugoslavia. RFI even produces weekly broadcasts for Caribbean nations where Creole is spoken.

The English Service of RFI produces two hours of live programs each day, prepared by 25 people in Paris and some thirty correspondents around the world. RFI says its English Service is intended to be a "mirror of French life as well as an objective reflection of main world events." Broadcast times are 0315, 1245, and 1600 Universal Time.

What are you likely to hear? RFI's English language programs generally include a comprehensive roundup of world and French news, daily reviews of the French press, sports, and special reports on major events.

In addition, the 0315 and 1600 English broadcasts offer a weekly total of some twenty features on French and African political, cultural, scientific, economic, and social affairs. Other regions of the world, especially the United States, the Third

Some members of the English Service at Radio France Internationale. Photo by F. Duclos, RFI

World, the Middle East, and Latin America, are often the subjects of special features.

For North American listeners, who rarely hear news from Africa—except for reports of drought and famine—the news broadcast at 1600 is particularly refreshing. Formerly called *Paris Calling Africa*, this one-hour program recently featured an in-depth examination of the 25th anniversary of the Organization for African Unity. The report included interviews with African and European observers and gave an original perspective on some of the problems and challenges faced by the African nations. From news to music to culture to press reviews, this broadcast always offers something new and interesting about Africa.

Not only Africa is covered at 1600. Recent broadcasts have also included: a roundup of world news that sounded very similar to the world news summaries produced by other major international broadcasting powers; a French lesson designed to help those planning to visit France; a discussion of a newly emerging French centrist political movement that made American politics sound downright uncomplicated; a review of the French press which, on the eve of a superpower summit, offered a fresh view of the United States and the Soviet Union; and a look at regional elections in France, which showed that no matter where in the world you are, someone is always jockeying for position.

However, for sheer entertainment, the hands-down favorite is the 0345–0400 program called *The Bilingual Show*. Lively and a little racy, this broadcast features a bilingual disc jockey—usually a young *mademoiselle*—who switches rapidly between French and English, and who plays an enchanting variety of music, ranging from modern French rock to French cabaret music of the Twenties and Thirties. When you hear it, you can understand why Paris was so special to Bogart and Bergman.

Recently, RFI added a half hour program at 1245 to its daily English language programming. This change has been heartily applauded by North American listeners interviewed by *Passport*, who were also of the opinion that RFI would be even better if it would increase still further its English programming and produce more programs about those things that make France uniquely itself—its culture, thought, varied geography and environment, and of course, its people.

Then there would be even more reasons to say "Vive La France! Vive La Radio France Internationale!"

Prepared by Jock Elliott.

What's on Radio France in English

	0315 UTC	1245 UTC	1600 UTC
Monday	News Sports Latin American Notes The Bilingual Show	News French Weeklies Sports	News French Weeklies Sports Development Magazine
Tuesday	News French Weeklies Development Magazine The Bilingual Show	News Land of France Science or Guest In France Today	News Land of France and/or Economy Press on Africa In France Today Science or Guest
Wednesday	News Land of France Press on Africa In France Today The Bilingual Show	News Arts in France Latin America Notes	News Arts in France African Panorama Latin America Notes
Thursday	News African Panorama Latin America Notes Sports Arts in France The Bilingual Show	News Made in France Sports	News Made in France Afro-Beat Sports
Friday	News Made in France Afro-Beat The Bilingual Show	News Books or Cinema Medical or Economy	News Books or Cinema Drumbeat or Economy
Saturday	News Books or Cinema Drumbeat or Economy The Bilingual Show	News French Lesson	News Spotlight Focus on France French Lesson

Sunday*	News
	Focus on France
	Spotlight on Africa
	Medical, Science, or
	  Guest.
	The Bilingual Show
		News
		Focus on France
		P.O.B.: Listeners'
		  letters, questions,
		  record requests.
			News
			P.O.B.: Listeners'
			  letters, questions,
			  record requests.
			Latin America Notes

The last Sunday of every month, in all programs: Insight—"the news behind the news."

Photo page 47: The road to Cutervo winds its way through the Peruvian mountains that dominate this townscape. Photo by Don Moore

Small town stations make much
of their money in a unique way—through the sale
of **comunicados** or **servicios sociales**—
everyman's party line in rural Latin America.

Peru
Radio Where Foreigners Never Go

by Don Moore

Visiting a world band radio station in northern Peru turns into an adventure more like a quest for the covenant. Dirt roads, high plateaus plagued by fierce weather, endless bumps and bruises take us only as far as Cochabamba in the Peruvian mountains. And that is only the beginning.

Branching off the main road at Cochabamba is a one-lane dirt track of cutbacks and blind curves clinging to the edge of a mountainside. No cars make this trip—only pickup trucks and rickety old freight trucks, their rotting wooden frames re-bolted and wired together in so many places that they squeak and squeal their way up the mountain like a chorus of haunted staircases. At each curve the driver honks his horn to alert oncoming vehicles. When two trucks meet, a few shouts are exchanged, gestures made, and finally one of the two backs up, its driver praying to the saints that one more time he will avoid the sheer drops. When a wide place is reached, the other may pass. Finally, the mountain is crested and in the valley below, amidst a green plain of fields and meadows, is the town of Cutervo.

I wonder how a town, let alone a world band radio station, can exist in such a rugged, remote corner of the earth. According to the townspeople, a hardy Hungarian adventurer in the 1960s was the only foreign visitor before my wife and I wandered in. How would they react to us? Curious, shy, but with smiles, the townspeople lead us to the Hotel San Juan, the only place in town to stay. Our green, cinderblock room with an unpainted cement floor is complete with a sink, chair, coathook, and a non-too-wide double bed, and goes for the bargain price of 85 American cents double occupancy. That 85 cents doesn't pay for much cleaning or hot water.

We set out to find the local radio station. Along the way, we unearth a simple, secluded town, wakened to the rest of the world mostly through world band radio. Cutervo is a typical Peruvian town of white adobe and cement block row houses roofed with red clay tiles. Life here revolves around the small, shrub-filled central plaza where housewives stop to chat on their way home from the market each morning. After lunch, men gather to pass the bottle and gossip until the midday heat lessens and it is time to return to the fields. After school and through the evening, teenagers take over the plaza to do homework half-heartedly and to flirt.

The town's Catholic church, its interior decorated with colorful local woodworking, dominates the plaza. On the other sides of the plaza are the municipal building, several stores, a pharmacy, a restaurant, and the Hotel San Juan. The hotel's guests are usually government workers or traveling salesmen. Cutervo is far from the tourist route.

Remote as Cutervo is, modern conveniences such as potable water and electricity have arrived. Ice cold water is piped down the mountain and into most homes by a municipal water system. The water's temperature stays ice cold because few can afford gas water heaters. Electricity is more a nightly treat than a convenience. Because bringing kerosene to Cutervo is expensive, the municipal generator is turned on only from six to ten in the evening. For the wealthier families this means a few hours of television from the one station received via a mountaintop repeater. To the poor majority, electricity is a bare light bulb or two hung from the kitchen ceiling.

Paved streets and sidewalks grace the center of town, but a few blocks from the plaza, sidewalks end and the streets become rough cobblestones. Closer to the outskirts of town, the cobblestones give way to dirt or mud streets, depending on the season.

Not only are there many dogs and cats in the streets, but a peek in the front door of many houses reveals a half dozen or more guinea pigs playing on living room floors. *Cuterveños*, however, will be quick to point out that those are not pets, but supper. For centuries the guinea pig, or "cuy" has been a delicacy to Andean peoples. Skinned and

fried it tastes much like rabbit, and is higher in protein than beef or pork. And, as the people of Cutervo know, it is a lot easier to raise a herd of cuy in the living room than a cow or pig.

Unlike many towns in Peru, Cutervo was neither an ancient Inca city nor a Spanish colonial center. For centuries only a few Indian peasants enjoyed the year-round, spring-like climate.

Around the beginning of this century, settlers from the Cajamarca area discovered the fertile valley snuggled among the Andes mountains at 8,000 feet. Realizing its climate was perfect for growing sugarcane, coffee, and vegetables, they established farms, and in 1905 founded Cutervo. With plentiful markets for its produce in coastal desert cities, the town prospered. Today Cuterveños still depend on agriculture to keep their small town's economy going. Everything not consumed locally is sold in nearby Chiclayo. Every day, freight trucks lumber down the mountain, their open-topped backs loaded high with produce.

Besides transporting vegetables, the freight trucks serve another vital function. Few people own cars or trucks, and with only one bus a week to Chiclayo and back, hitching a ride on the flatbed of a freight truck is the easiest way out of town. A person leaves Cutervo sitting atop several tons of potatoes. At least hitching back in the empty trucks is not quite so bumpy.

Like many small farming towns, Cutervo does not boast about its entertainment. The best the town has to offer is a movie theater that shows karate flicks and cheap westerns when they are available. In season, there are *corridas* in a drab cement bullring on the edge of town. At other times, sports fans content themselves with walking to the local high school to watch teenage boys play soccer. But far and away the most colorful pastime in Cutervo is chatting with family or friends while listening to one of the local radio stations.

> A peek in the front door of many houses reveals a half dozen or more guinea pigs playing on living room floors. Cuterveños, however, will be quick to point out that those are not pets, but supper.

Radio has been in Cutervo since the late 1970s and, like the town, it is simple and basic. Located in a long row of adobe brick buildings half a block from the plaza, La Voz de Cutervo looks like the homemade radio station that it is. Under a handpainted wooden sign are a pair of decaying seagreen doors leading into an office. The office has white adobe walls and a high ceiling of rough

The office of La Voz de Cutervo is on the right on this street a half block from the plaza. Photo by Don Moore

plaster held up with huge wooden beams thick with cobwebs in the corners. Inside, to the left, is the secretary's "desk," a green pegboard counter covered with red cloth. Two wooden chairs are the only other furniture.

The wall behind the counter is decorated with beer company calendars and Latin American pop music posters. Sheets of yellow legal paper are taped around the other walls at eye level. Typed onto these are the titles of most of La Voz de Cutervo's record collection, divided into categories by song type: *huaynos; pasillos; vals; ranchera; moderna;* and *infantil.* Listeners use these to pick out songs for record dedications. Above the song lists is a generic black and white clock, a few cheap-looking landscape paintings, and the station's pride, an excellent photograph of Cutervo taken by a local photographer.

Along the back wall, two plain brown doors marked *Locución* and *Audio Master* lead into the car-sized studios. In the middle of the main studio, Locución, is a table with a homemade console, two turntables, a cassette deck, and several microphones. Records, mainly 45s but also some LPs, line shelves on the back wall. Separated from Locución by a fiberboard wall with a large plate glass window, is Audio Master, a special studio with a microphone just for reading the news and doing interviews. Pop music posters decorate both studios.

Station manager Julio César Sánchez is young and enthusiastic about his work. In 1980, he began working for the crosstown competition, Radio Ilucán. Two years later, feeling he had the experience needed to make the big move, he founded La Voz de Cutervo. Undaunted by the many station failures in the region, Julio believes that, with hard work, radio broadcasting in these small towns can be profitable.

And work hard he does to make his the best station in town. He runs the studio feedline through town, and puts his antennas and transmitters on a hilltop outside Cutervo for better coverage. So that his station can broadcast all day, not just when the municipal power is on, there is a generator. Car batteries charged at the transmitter site power the studio during the day.

With an ear for quality, Julio runs his one kilowatt world band transmitters at about 700 watts for better performance and to avoid overmodulation, which causes distorted sound. He is building a 50-watt FM transmitter to give Cutervo true high fidelity. Julio says that, to be the best, he needs FM for listeners in town, AM for the surrounding villages, and world band to reach the more distant towns. His would be the first FM station in the department—province—outside the city of Cajamarca, about 160 miles away.

Julio says that the biggest challenge for La Voz de Cutervo, or for any other small radio station in northern Peru, is getting enough income to survive. Local stores are so small that they cannot afford much advertising, and big national and international companies, such as Tía department stores and Coca-Cola, rarely spend their advertising dollars outside major cities.

Instead, small town stations make much of their money in a unique way—through the sale of

comunicados or *servicios sociales*—everyman's party line in rural Latin America, where telephones are nonexistent and so radio stations have taken their place. Comunicados are simply personal announcements that listeners pay the station to air. In Cutervo the going rate is about 20 American cents for three airings. The main reason that world band is used so extensively in this region is to allow comunicados to reach distant

> **Sometimes expensive parts put a station off the air for months—even years—until the owner can scrape up enough cash for repairs.**

towns. As long as there is no other reliable method of communication, world band will thrive in northern Peru.

All towns are far apart—if not in distance, at least in time. Mail service may take weeks. The only way to keep in touch with family members in places near or distant is by radio.

Maybe Juanita married a man from Chota. Mamá has not seen her daughter since the wedding and decides to visit the newlyweds for a few

Cutervo's Catholic church, its interior decorated with colorful local woodworking, dominates the central plaza.
Photo by Don Moore

days. Having had the good sense to know that Juanita will want a little notice, Mamá sends one of Juanita's younger siblings over to La Voz de Cutervo with a comunicado to warn Juanita and her husband of the upcoming visit. "Juanita Arana de Valencia in Chota, your mother will be coming to visit you next week on Tuesday or Wednesday. She hopes you and your husband are well and looks forward to seeing you."

It does not matter if Juanita does not hear the announcement. One of her neighbors or friends certainly will and they will pass along the news. In fact, within a few hours everyone in Chota will know that Juanita's mother is coming for a visit.

Maybe Don Eduardo wants to send a message to the workers on his coffee plantation, but does not have time to make the four-hour round trip today. He has told them always to listen to La Voz de Cutervo while eating lunch, so he simply drives over to the station to buy a comunicado.

Indeed, the lunch hour is the best time to hear comunicados. People are most likely to listen to the radio during mealtimes, so that is when stations usually air them, in long strings, maybe broken up by an occasional song. The next most popular times are around dinner, the

early evening, and at breakfast. Even people not expecting a message listen. After lunch, mother exchanges gossip with the neighbor who had tuned to a different station. The men at work do not wait any to discuss the day's "news" either.

The record dedication is also an important source of income. For 20 American cents, the station will play the record of one's choice and read an accompanying announcement. It is a great way to wish Happy Birthday to relatives and friends, or for a young man to publically express his affections for a certain young lady. "Jorge sends this romantic message by Julio Iglesias to his one and only love, Luisa."

In a country where the average family lives on 30 to 40 American dollars a month, it is difficult to depend on comunicados and record dedications. Making it tougher in Cutervo are two competitors, Radio Ilucán and Radio Cutervo. With three stations vying for listeners in a town of 6,000, each station tries to play the best music and get the most interesting comunicados to keep people tuned in.

Keeping listeners means staying on the air, and equipment problems can be disastrous. Owners hope breakdowns can be repaired or at

Active Antennas

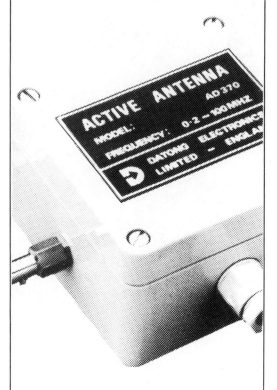

least jury-rigged with local knowhow. If costly imported spare parts are essential, a long overland trip to Lima must be made, putting the station off the air for weeks. Sometimes expensive parts put a station off the air for months—even years—until the owner can scrape up enough cash for repairs. This is why so many poorer Latin stations are listed in *Passport* as "irregular."

> I wonder how a town, let alone a world band radio station, can exist in such a rugged, remote corner of the earth.

La Voz de Cutervo has been fortunate that none of these disasters has snuffed out the station's dreams. In 1986 they changed their world band frequency from 4965 to 5661 kHz, leaving them free of interference. Although their weak signals are rarely heard in North America or Europe, the best time to try is between 0000 and 0400 Universal Time. Maybe you will be lucky enough to hear the voice of Julio Sánchez and his town.

Don Moore has lived in and traveled extensively throughout Latin American with the Peace Corps.

Satisfaction for you and your neighbours! Highly unobtrusive yet ideal for DX reception, Datong actives feature a dipole (not a monopole) for optimum rejection of local interference.

Our full catalogue plus further details of any product are available free on request. Dealers in most countries, please send for list. Credit cards accepted.

Datong Electronics Ltd.,
Clayton Wood Close, West Park, Leeds LS16 6QE, England.

Photo page 53: The Sydney Opera House. Photo by Tara Van den Hout

There's more to Middle East programming
than captivating music—
or even music by captivators.

Twenty of the Easiest-to-Hear Stations

As in *Animal Farm*, some stations are more equal than others. They're stronger, or operate on clearer channels, or are not so far away.

Here is our pick of the tops—twenty of the many world band stations you're likely to hear well. All have shows in English, and a good many broadcast in other languages as well. Unless otherwise noted, reception should be good throughout North America and Europe—and often beyond—especially when it's evening at your location. Complete times and channels are in the "Worldwide Broadcasts" and "Worldscan" sections, and keep in mind that during the summer some stations shift their schedules by an hour.

Europe

Europe is a treasure chest of world band news and entertainment. Nearly every country, including tiny Monaco, has at least one station, and most come in well. Here are just a few of the powerhouses:

France

Radio France Internationale is clearly audible throughout Europe and—thanks to a relay in South America—the United States and Canada, as well. Only a tiny proportion of its considerable menu is in English, but it's expanding and it's good, so tune

in. If you're in eastern North America, listen mornings from 1245–1315 Universal Time on 17720 kHz for English news and features. More news, and music, is on nights from 0315–0400 to North America on 9800 kHz, to Europe on 3965 kHz. Finally, there's also RFI's African-oriented program at 1600, audible in North America and Europe on a variety of frequencies.

Parlez-vous? RFI beams French to eastern North America and Europe morning through evening, and at night it's often heard in western North America, too. Strong channels include 6175, 9790, 17620, 17720 and 21645 kHz.

Germany

Deutsche Welle from West Germany comes to North American and European listeners not only direct from Germany, but also via relay transmitters in Canada, the Caribbean, Rwanda and Malta. Each program in English opens with news and continues with various European topics such as music, opera, life in Germany, and the European economy. For German speakers there's no end of programs to be heard, complete with beer-swilling oompah music. In North America, English is on 9545 kHz at 0100 and 0300 Univer-

sal Time, or two hours later on 6120 and 9635 kHz. German is audible all evening in North America—and all day in Europe—on 6075 kHz.

Holland

Radio Nederland, like Swiss Radio International, specializes in news of European affairs and matters related to European interests. It broadcasts evenings directly to Europe on 6020 kHz, and to North America on 6165 kHz via a relay facility in the Caribbean. Its committment to world band radio was underscored in 1985 by the erection of a large transmitter complex in—where else?—a section of land reclaimed from the sea.

Switzerland

Swiss Radio International, well heard in eastern North America and Europe, is noteworthy for its excellent current events programming, especially on matters in Europe and of concern to Europeans. If all that's a bit heavy for your ears after a long day's work, try the delightful Swiss music that's interspersed throughout many of SRI's programs. In eastern North America, it's on 6135, 9725, and 9885 kHz evenings; in Europe tune in 3985, 6165, 9535, and 12030 kHz day and night.

The Hermitage, Leningrad. Photo by Tara Van den Hout

United Kingdom

The **BBC World Service** is heard loud and clear not only in Europe, but also throughout North America, thanks to relay transmitters in the Caribbean, United States, and Canada. It is on fully 24 hours a day with tens of millions of listeners worldwide. The World Service is renowned for its superb entertainment programs, as well as its profusion of newscasts and commentaries that many consider the highest form of the art. One of the best channels to North America and Europe evenings is 5975 kHz. Other commonly heard channels, night and day, include 6175, 7325, 9410, 9915, 11775, 12095, 15070 and 21710 kHz.

USSR

Radio Moscow, along with kindred Radio Peace and Progress, are on the air in English around the clock. This mammoth operation has at its disposal more transmitters than does any other broadcaster in the world. Some—such as on 11840 kHz to North America daytime—are located in Cuba; yet others, such as on 7115 kHz, emanate from Bulgaria. Most, however, are spread by the hundreds across the vastness of the Soviet Union. It is very, very difficult *not* to hear Radio Moscow!

You can also hear broadcasts in English from Armenia, Lithuania and the Ukraine. These are easily heard evenings—usually on channels beginning with "7" and "9"—in eastern North America and Europe. And if you understand Russian, there are countless domestic channels to be heard.

Africa

Sub-Sahara

Africa is full of world band operations, but most are targeted to Africa proper and are not easily heard in North America or Europe. Some English programs, however, can be heard from afar:

Voice of Nigeria is one of the better sources of English-language news from Africa—two others being the BBC's African Service and Radio France Internationale. But what the BBC and Radio France can't equal are the Voice of Nigeria's lively West African rhythms. Reception is possible in Europe at various times, and in eastern North America the best bet is winter between 0500-0600 Universal Time on 7255 kHz. The only fly in the ointment is that its sound is often distorted.

Radio Cairo's shows cover not only current events but also the history of ancient Egypt. Photo by Tara Van den Hout

Radio RSA in South Africa is the external broadcasting operation of the South African Broadcasting Corporation, the government agency that operates—you guessed it—racially segregated radio and television stations. The quality of reception is variable, but the station tends to be fairly well heard in eastern North America on 9580 and 9615 kHz from 0200 Universal Time during the equinoctal months. In Europe, try 11915, 15405 and 17880 kHz at 1800.

Middle East and North Africa

The Middle East is filled with world band stations best known for music reminiscent of Lawrence of Arabia, or perhaps the Casbah. But there's more to Middle East programming than captivating music—or even music by captivators. Among the biggies:

Radio Cairo sends out a fairly strong signal to eastern North America—to Europe it's much poorer—but the quality of its sound is not ideal. After 0200 Universal Time on 9475 kHz, Americans can enjoy Middle-Eastern news coverage in English, along with shows on Egyptian history and lots of music to belly dance by. Radio Cairo also airs, day and night, all manner of domestic and external service transmissions in Arabic on such channels as 9455 and 12050 kHz.

Kol Israel is well heard in English throughout eastern North America and Europe. Although plagued by occasional strikes and funding problems, it nonetheless manages to produce live newscasts, on-the-scene reports, plus a variety of religious and feature programs. Times and channels change seasonally, but 2000, 2230, 0000, 0100, and 0200 Universal Time on 7465, 9435, and 11605 kHz are excellent possibilities. Almost as well heard is "Reshet Bet," a domestic channel on the air in Hebrew on 9385, 11585, and 15615 kHz.

The Voice of Turkey carries news and features every day in English. But what you'll

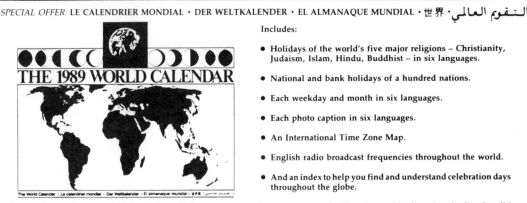

really go for are the generous helpings of exotic Turkish music. In eastern North America it's on at 2200 and 0300 Universal Time on 9445 kHz; in Europe at 2200 on 9685 kHz. You can hear even more of that slithery-zithery music by tuning into the Turkish language services late in the day on 9460 kHz, and evenings from 2300–0300 on 9445 kHz.

South Asia

There are numerous English-language transmissions from South Asia—Pakistan, Bangladesh, and Sri Lanka, for example—but the strongest is All India Radio. The best time to hear other South Asian stations is in the early morning if you're in North America, or evenings if you're in Europe.

All India Radio is a tough catch in North America—the best bet is afternoons, except summers, on 11620 kHz. In Europe, though, it comes in evenings on 9910 and 11620 kHz. AIR is an invaluable source for news of the Subcontinent, and the music will have your pet cobra squirming with joy.

East and Southeast Asia

Eastern Asia is chock-a-block with world band signals—some for foreign audiences, some for the home folks. The strongest, however, are targeted to specific parts of the world via beefy relay transmitters in Europe, Africa, and the Americas. If you wish to listen to non-relayed transmissions from eastern Asia, try early mornings—or even late afternoons—if you're in North America. Evenings are best if you're in Europe.

Radio Beijing in the People's Republic of China broadcasts to North America and Europe both directly and through relay transmitters in West Africa and Europe. Each program opens with news of the world and China and can reveal much about Chinese affairs and politics. There are also features and programs on Chinese folk tales, archeology, and history, along with some Chinese music. Similar programs are also aired in Standard Chinese (Mandarin) and Cantonese.

The best time for Eastern North Americans is at 0000 Universal Time on 9770 and 11715 kHz and at 0500 on 9690 kHz; West Coast Americans can try 9645 and 11980 kHz at 0400. In Europe Beijing is also heard at 0500, and after 1900 between 6800 and 7000 kHz.

The Voice of Free China in Taiwan is only a so-so catch in Europe, but listeners in North America can hear it via powerful relay transmitters in Florida. Its English broadcasts include economic news, feature programs on Chinese culture and history . . . along with doses of traditional gong-banging music worthy of a Confucian celebration. In North America, try 5985 kHz after

Asian children. Photo by Tara Van den Hout

0200 Universal Time. At other times during the evening on that same channel Mandarin and Cantonese programs carry even more of these chopstick-tapping rhythms.

Radio Japan comes to North American and European listeners both directly and through relay transmitters in Canada and West Africa. Its programs include international and Asian news and current affairs, and "DX Corner" for world band radio enthusiasts. In North America the best reception in English is at 0300 Universal Time (0100 summers) on 5960 kHz and at 1100 on 6120 kHz. In Europe, it's 1500 on 21700 kHz. In North America, Japanese is well heard at 1200 (1000 summers) on 6120 kHz and from 0200 on 5960 kHz; in Europe, it's at 1600 on 21700 kHz.

Pacific

Many radio buffs consider the Pacific to be the most tantalizing part of the world to tune in. Almost without exception, the most exotic world band broadcasts from the Pacific are targeted to the home audience, making these signals tough to hear half a world away.

Not every station from the Pacific is low-powered. Radio Australia's woefully underfunded but friendly transmissions are almost never loud and clear outside Asia and the Pacific, but nonetheless can be heard throughout North America and Europe. Its authoritative coverage of Asian and Pacific news is the main course here, but the various feature programs are interesting as well. Best reception in North America is during the early morning hours between about 0800–1400 Universal Time on 9580 kHz. In Europe, try 15395, 15415, and 17715 kHz mornings.

Latin America

Latin America is the least likely part of the world to air strong, clearly heard English programs. Yet, it provides the world's greatest profusion of local world band stations. Most of these are in Spanish or Portuguese, but nearly all burst forth with a variety of Latin rhythms and Indian melodies (for more on Latin music, see "Latin America, Land of Traditional Music" in Passport/88).

Although world band broadcasts in English from Latin America are not yet commonplace, Ecuador is easy to hear both in North America and Europe, thanks to HCJB. Low-keyed evangelism is its *raison d'être*, but interesting programs related to Ecuador and Latin America are also featured. For North America, evening channels include 6205, 6230, 9720, 9870, 11775, and 15155 kHz; for Europe, try 15270 and 17790 kHz evenings.

Radio Japan's English language staff produces programs heard around the world from powerful transmitters in Japan, Canada, South America, and Africa. Photo by NHK

Radio Habana Cuba is often well-heard evenings in North America, and sometimes even in Europe, thanks to relay transmitters in the Soviet Union. Propaganda is the soup du jour here, but some of the news and commentary concerning Central America can be interesting, and there's

plenty of of lively Cuban music. In North America, channels to try include 6090, 6140, 9525, 9550, and 9730 kHz.

North America

Canada

Radio Canada International, with an enormous listenership in the United States, covers a wide variety of Canadian and international issues. "As It Happens" is arguably the finest newscast to be found anywhere, and the popular "SWL Digest" presents the latest in news and features of interest to world band aficionados. In North America, RCI is well heard in English at 0000 Universal Time on 5960 and 9755 kHz, and Sundays at 1400 on 11955 kHz. In Continental Europe—reception is iffy in the United Kingdom—try 2200 on 9760 and 11945 kHz Universal Time. French is also aired on these and other channels at various times. All times are one hour earlier summers.

United States

Although the US is a major user of the international airwaves, in some ways the law treats world band listening as suspect. American world band stations aren't supposed to broadcast to American civilians; and the CIA, which monitors world broadcasts, sometimes classifies programs as "secret" even after they've already been aired for all to hear. Additionally, radio-controlled gadgets in the US soon may soon be permitted by the Government to operate on and disturb world band frequencies.

Fortunately, the laws of nature are less silly than the laws of man, so—wherever you are—enjoy the myriad offerings of America's many stations. Among the strongest:

The Voice of America is the official radio organ of the United States and is generally well heard throughout the world, including North America. To hear it, simply tune around. "Auntie Samantha" airs a surprisingly large number of worthy programs, but if you're looking for sports, weather, or other non-political news, forget it. Try, instead, the Armed Forces Radio and Television Service. The AFRTS relays just about every private US radio network's news, plus live sports. It's the ultimate American news channel—"radio's CNN"—and a so-so catch evenings in single sideband on such frequencies as 9242 and 9334 kHz.

Prepared by Alex Batman and Larry Magne in North America, with John Campbell in Europe.

Pat Gates, popular hostess of The Breakfast Show, is now U.S. Ambassador to Madagascar. Photo by VOA

Photo page 61: The NHK Broadcasting Center, Shibuya, Tokyo. Photo by NHK

News—As You Like It

World band is whatever there is to report, from wherever it may come.

Nothing is more suited to the average news junkie than world band radio. Almost every station that broadcasts in English airs national, regional, and international news ranging from terrorist attacks in Belgium to election frauds in Bangladesh to the overthrow of the Fijian government.

News like this happens fast all over the world, but much of it gets limited or no coverage by major domestic radio and television networks.

Tune around on a world band radio, however, and you'll hear all kinds of news happening—where it's happening. It's all there: short bulletins, news features, propaganda and defensiveness, editorial and press reviews, specialty information. World band is whatever there is to report, from wherever it may come.

Almost every world band broadcast starts off with seven to fifteen minutes of regional, national, and international news. The most respected of these newscasts are those of the BBC, whose lack of bias in reporting has become a world standard. The BBC's scope is both national and international and—unlike Radio Moscow or, sad to say, the Voice of America—it seems to have no "ideological axe" to grind. The BBC's bulletins are comprehensive, accurate, and up to the minute—with plenty of on-the-scene reporting from their vast network of overseas correspondents.

One American voice that appears nearly as fair and unbiased in its reporting is WCSN, the World Service of the *Christian Science Monitor*. Although the station is religiously affiliated, religion and editorial opinion are scrupulously separated from actual news reporting, just as it is at the Pulitzer-Prize winning paper from which the station takes its name. Like its namesake newspaper, the station focuses on analysis of international news rather than reportage of domestic events within the US.

Another news-oriented broadcaster from the Americas is the US Armed Forces Radio and Television Service. Because the AFRTS has almost no news service of its own, it uses those of ABC, CBS, NBC, AP, UPI, NPR, and other American radio networks. This gives the reporting a sufficient cross section to remain unslanted, even if one of those networks has its own bias. It also allows the AFRTS to provide uniquely comprehensive coverage of domestic US events.

Outside Britain and the Americas there are a number of relatively objective news voices on the airwaves. The list includes such venerable names as Swiss Radio International, Radio Austria International, Radio Nederland, Radio Japan, Radio Australia, and Deutsche Welle.

> **Both Radio Baghdad and the Voice of Iran have reported the "glorious victories" of their own armies so often that both sides should have won the war years ago!**

Most stations in the Eastern Bloc, however, do wield the "ideological axe," and editorial opinion distinctly sneaks into what should be strict reporting. For example, references to Afghan "bandits" rather than rebels or Armenian "hooligans" rather than protestors are routine.

Still, the Eastern Bloc has no monopoly on slanted reporting. Both Radio Baghdad and the Voice of the Islamic Republic of Iran have reported the "annihilation" of enemy troops, the "crushing" of enemy offensives, and the "glorious victories" of their own armies so often that both sides should have won the war six or seven years ago!

Radio Japan's news department studios were built in 1987 for exclusive use on the General Service. Photo by NHK

World band radio is also an excellent indicator of regional conflicts. The Voice of Turkey, for example, takes pains to point out instances of repression of the Turkish minority in Bulgaria or "Greek Expansionism" in the Aegean. Radio Sofia, on the other hand, seems to delight in citing instances of Turkish militarism or Turkish repression of its Kurdish and Armenian populations, while the Voice of Greece includes in its brief newscasts a cornucopia of information about the "illegal" Turkish republic of Northern Cyprus.

In addition to regular news bulletins, most world band broadcasters offer news features that focus on a particular story or stories in more detail, much like a "special segment" report on a television network. Arguably the best are the BBC's *Twenty-Four Hours* and *The World Today*, as well as Radio Australia's *International Report*. Other noteworthy news features include Radio Nederland's *Newsline* and Deutsche Welle's *Microphone on Europe*.

For those interested in the Asian region, there is Radio Japan's *Asia Now*. Radio Finland's *Northern Report* and Radio Sweden's *Weekday* discuss Scandanavian concerns, while Radio France International's one-hour broadcast at 1600 UTC and the BBC's special programs for Africa, including *Network Africa*, provide much needed coverage of African issues.

As for the Middle East, there is no truly objective news feature program. Kol Israel's *Spot-light* and Radio Cairo's *Spotlight on the Middle East* suffer from political bias, as does nearly every news feature program from that area of the world.

For a truly international potpourri, tune to the Christian Science Monitor's *News Focus*, which airs at many times during the day. Another program offering an excellent international outlook is Radio Canada International's *As It Happens,* which is aired weekdays (see "Ten Top Shows for 1989").

Propaganda and defensiveness are characteristics of "news" designed to control public opinion. In a world divided into East, West, and Third World, the battle for public opinion is intense—so keen, in fact, that there is a temptation to bend the truth a bit, or even sometimes to stretch it completely out of joint.

> The battle for public opinion is so keen that there is a temptation to bend the truth a bit, or even sometimes to stretch it completely out of joint.

Complete fabrications are relatively rare, but can be heard. Libyan Radio Jamahiriya, for example, supposedly once reported that the streets of New York were littered with the bodies of those who had jumped out of windows because they could no longer stand the insidious pressures of American society.

More common than such complete untruths, however, are the subtle ways certain world band broadcasters have of slanting or exaggerating their reports of international events. Several years ago, for example, when the United States Congress voted $27 million in solely humanitarian aid to the Contras in Central America, Radio Habana Cuba reported that the Congress had approved $30 million in military aid for "mercenaries."

And, not long back, when Secretary Gorbachev was in Washington for a summit meeting, Radio Moscow interviewed a woman with a placard demonstrating outside the White House against the plight of the homeless in the United States. Radio Moscow made no mention of the Ukrainians, Jews, Lithuanians, or Afghans who were protesting during Gorbachev's visit. However, it must be said that while the Voice of America did report on those protestors, it failed to mention the woman with the placard.

There is also the category of countries traditionally more open in news reporting, but which are, fairly or unfairly, under the censure of at least some major elements of world opinion. These countries include South Africa and, more recently, Israel. News from these countries tends to have a defensive quality to it.

Deutsche Welle discusses news events with language service to African and English-speaking countries. Photo © by Deutsche Welle

The South African broadcaster, Radio RSA, commonly reports on the violence of one black group against another, discusses the alleged communist influence in anti-apartheid organizations, and suggests that the western media have blown dissension in South Africa out of all proportion. Kol Israel, during the 1988 demonstrations in the occupied territories, suggested a bias on the part

of the media, and took pains to point out the obvious—that the stones Palestinians were throwing did not necessarily fall harmlessly to the ground, but frequently injured Israeli soldiers and settlers as well.

That a broadcaster's opinion will color the news is unavoidable, if only because of the process of selecting what news will be covered, to what extent, and from what angle. However, aside from these editorial necessities, opinion belongs in editorials—not newscasts. Many world band stations include editorials in their programming; even the venerable BBC has a place for opinion in its thought-provoking *Commentary*.

Some are quick to label editorials from the Eastern Bloc as propaganda, but those who might claim Radio Prague's *Newsview* or Radio Moscow's *As We See It* are merely propaganda pieces misunderstand their purpose. They are avowedly opinionated and, although that opinion may be annoying or even maddening, it is, after all, the official view of the government and should be regarded accordingly.

Similarly, *VOA Editorial* is very much a rehash of the Administration's position on a variety of issues. Indeed, the VOA considers its editorials to be "advertisements for our point of view." Radio Japan's *Current Affairs* more often than not argues on behalf of the Japanese position in its trade disputes, especially those with the United States. *Commentary* on the Voice of Free China does the same type of thing. What's important to remember when listening to editorial comments is that they are usually official opinion.

Perhaps a more reliable assessment of a nation's mood are the "press review" programs, which feature lead stories and editorials from the main newspapers, such as those of Britain, France, Finland, Israel and Belgium. Radio France Internationale each morning reads editorials from the major French newspapers—even those from the political extremes—covering events such as French elections.

Some press reviews, such as those of the Voice of Turkey, Radio Damascus or Radio Baghdad, are suspect because the opinions read are always favorable toward official government policy. Not surprisingly, most Eastern Bloc broadcasters do not bother with a press review, although Radio Budapest's *From the Hungarian Weeklies* is a notable exception.

Aside from politics and the usual newsmaking disasters, there are programs on world band radio devoted to news of special interest. These are the specialty news programs.

Among these, for those who are religiously inclined, HCJB's *What in the World* keeps up with news affecting evangelical Christians, with reporting of such matters as religious persecution in various lands—they have reported on the confiscation of Bibles in China by local governments.

Vatican Radio's *The Church Today* looks at moral and ethical dilemmas presented for the Church and for Christians in general in the week's top news stories. And the BBC's *Report on Religion* each week examines two or three newsworthy stories involving religion—any religion.

Many world band stations offer news programs about their national culture. The BBC's *Meridian* reports on the most important cultural events in Britain, while *Cultural Life in Egypt* and Radio Nederland's *Images* also report on culture in their own respective countries. Other culturally oriented news can be heard on Deutsche Welle's *Arts Magazine*, as part of Spanish Foreign Radio's *Panorama*, on BRT's *Around the Arts*, over Israel Radio's *Studio Three*, in Radio Prague's *Cultural Report* and on Radio Bucharest's *Cultural Survey*.

Science and technology are reported on by many stations. The BBC, for example, airs the excellent *Science in Action*. Radio Moscow offers *Science and Engineering*, which covers such topics as the Soviet space probe for Halley's Comet in 1986. Deutsche Welle and Kol Israel have science-related programs in which advances ranging from agricultural pesticides to research on superconductors are explained.

There are also specialty news reports devoted to sports, agriculture, business, finance and even the rock music industry. Whatever the kind of news you seek, you are likely to find it somewhere, sometime, on world band radio. Keeping up with news around the world may never help most people to have more than a minimal impact on world events, but it can help them understand the world a bit better—which is sufficient reason to listen.

Prepared by Alex Batman.

Picturesque Russian architecture. Photo by Tara Van den Hout

THE ANT FARM

Photo page 67: Ian McFarland is on the air every weekend for Radio Canada International.

Thumbs Up, Thumbs Down!

by Ian McFarland

Do you enjoy a special comedy broadcast on world band radio? Are you dismayed by the cancellation of a gripping drama? Angry at the biased viewpoint of another program?

Feed these feelings back to the stations! Without the same ratings endured by commercial radio, world band broadcasters can only rely on you, the listener, for a measure of their programs' success.

Of course, knowledge of audience preferences can be a mixed blessing. Pity, for example, the poor local radio broadcaster in any major North American city. Life goes on merrily from one ratings period to the next. Those all important ratings are what the station bases its advertising rates on: The better the ratings in the local market, the higher the revenue from commercials. So, in large measure, the broadcaster's job security rides on those all-important numbers. With ratings, there is no doubt who and what is most popular.

As an international broadcaster, I should count my blessings that Nielsen and Arbitron, two top rating services, have not as yet been very active in the world of international broadcasting. While I'm grateful that my job security does not depend on a handful of numbers, I do wish that there were some kind of system for rating the countless programs heard on world band radio.

> **Perhaps they feel that critical letters are tossed into the shredder. This is one myth that most definitely needs exploding.**

I may be dreaming in Technicolor here, because a Nielsen or Arbitron rating system for world band radio might be as difficult to achieve as world peace. There would be an endless number of people to phone to find the four percent who listen to world band radio. The logistics of attempting that feat would boggle the mind of the hardiest demographer.

How do world band broadcasters know what's thought of their programs? For the broadcaster interested in an objective view, there is only feedback from listeners.

I'm well aware that when it comes to rating a program, the views of listeners can differ vastly from those of a station's management. But there is a complicating factor. Some listeners tell a station what they think the station wants to hear, because they believe this will make the station more inclined to send out souvenirs, such as pennants and stickers, or "QSL" cards. Perhaps they feel that international broadcasting stations are only interested in reading good news about their programs, and that critical letters are tossed into the shredder. This is one myth that most definitely needs exploding.

Constructive criticism from listeners is extremely valuable to a world band broadcaster. While the broadcaster and program producer must answer to the station's management, which in most cases is a government agency, it is the *listener* who is the final arbiter of a program's popularity. Having a cross section of listeners' comments on any given program can, therefore, offer a useful balance to other critiques.

When international broadcasters ask for listener feedback, they are not expecting every listener to write in with a weekly critique, or hoping to see another *Rubaiyat of Omar Khayyam*. Any broadcaster would be ecstatic if each regular

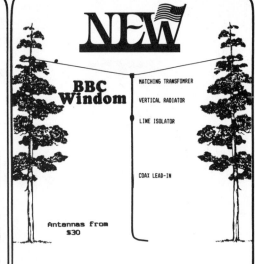

listener wrote only one letter per year, with a few well-written paragraphs of constructive comments about a particular program.

Sometimes a suggestion for improving an aspect of a station's programming or operation is so worthwhile that it may take just one letter from a single listener to get action. For example, a Canadian in Africa used to listen to Radio Canada International on two frequencies. He wrote in to say that the one-minute identification signal did not give enough time to locate the better of the two frequencies. So, Radio Canada International simply added a five-minute frequency identification to one of the frequencies. Just one letter brought satisfaction not only to that listener, but also to many others.

Despite such success stories—and there are many—world band listeners may feel somewhat cynical about the influence their comments can have on a broadcaster. Obviously, that impact will vary from one station to another, especially with letters from listeners in Eastern Bloc countries that are sent to stations in the West. However, the impact can be great.

> ## A Nielsen or Arbitron rating system for world band radio might be as difficult to achieve as world peace.

To take one example, on several occasions during its history the demise of Radio Canada International has been avoided largely as a result of the hundreds of letters sent by loyal listeners abroad. These letters were sent not only to RCI, but also to the Prime Minister of Canada to urge him to lobby against the service's threatened closure. More recently, RCI received considerable numbers of complaints from listeners who were unhappy about being able to hear only the first half of the program *As It Happens*. As a result, more air time was made available for *As It Happens* in order to carry the entire program.

Actually, at times the lack of feedback can be telling, as well. Holding a contest, say, can be a good way to find out how popular a given program is.

Once, I ran a contest in conjunction with a monthly stamp corner show. Since stamp collecting is supposed to be a popular hobby throughout the world, I thought the contest would draw many entries. The contest closed after a couple of months, with a grand total of one entry having been received. That letter was from a fellow international broadcaster who joked, "At least you'll have one entry for your contest."

How right he was. The obvious conclusion was to discontinue the stamp corner feature. If I remember correctly, there was not even a single peep of complaint from listeners.

How to proceed? If you want to write a letter, here are some tested "dos" and "don'ts."

First, write *specific* comments. The vague statement, "I really love the program—keep up the good work," may be great for a broadcaster's ego, but it offers little "food for thought" for producing a better program, or for coming up with material that the broadcaster knows listeners are interested in.

Second, if a comment is about a particular program, then the letter should be addressed to the *host or producer* of that program—not simply to the station in question.

Finally, *don't be shy*. If a favorite program is taken off the air, the worst thing you can do is to resign yourself to being disappointed. Drop a nicely worded note of protest to the station's program director. And send a copy to the program's host as well. Apathy cannot correct anything.

Generally speaking, today's world band radio listeners have many excellent opportunities—an open invitation, in fact—to make their opinions known and to pass their comments directly on to broadcasters and programmers. Not all suggestions from listeners can be acted upon by a station; staff and budget limitations have to be considered, along with technical limitations and station priorities. But, for most international broadcasting stations, the all-important thing is to be in touch with their listeners—their clients, you might say.

So, tickle those ivories and let's hear from you!

Ian McFarland is Announcer-Producer of English Weekend Programming at Radio Canada International. In 1987 he celebrated his 25th year with RCI.

RDI WHITE PAPERS

EVERYTHING YOU NEED TO KNOW BEFORE YOU BUY

World band radios can be a real pleasure to use. But today's best models are also advanced-technology devices with a wide range of perform-ance possibilities . . . and potential pitfalls.

Now, RDI's private library of in-depth test reports—the *RDI White Paper* series—is being made available to you. Within the pages of each report is the full range of measurements and opinions prepared by IBS' award-winning "hands-on" and laboratory experts. Findings are conveniently organized for ready reference and the results—good or ill—are revealed without fear or favor. Nothing is held back, whether for reasons of space or editorial policy.

RDI White Papers are thoroughly up-to-date. Because each report covers only one model, revised editions can be issued from our Database as soon as a manufacturer alters a previously tested model. Only the freshest material appears, and you buy only the reports you need.

The latest editions of these *RDI White Papers* are now available from participating dealers worldwide, or direct from RDI postpaid for US$4 each in North America, $6 each worldwide:

RDI Evaluates the Grundig Satellit 650 Receiver
RDI Evaluates the ICOM IC-R71 Receiver
RDI Evaluates the Japan Radio NRD-93 Receiver
RDI Evaluates the Japan Radio NRD-525U/525E/525J Receiver
RDI Evaluates the Kenwood R-5000 Receiver
RDI Evaluates the Lowe HF-125 Receiver
RDI Evaluates the Sony ICF-2010/ICF-2001D Receiver
RDI Evaluates the Ten-Tec RX325 Receiver
RDI Evaluates the Yaesu FRG-8800 Receiver
RDI Evaluates Popular Outdoor Antennas
How to Interpret Receiver Specifications and Lab Tests
RDI Evaluates Popular Indoor Antennas

Get all the facts before you buy. For a complete, up-to-date list of RDI White Papers and other RDI publications, please write, enclosing a self-addressed envelope, to

RDI Publications Information
Box 300
Penn's Park, PA 18943 USA

Photo page 71: Carp streamers (Koriyama, Fukushima). Photo by NHK

Sports Your Coach Never Taught You

Planet Earth's daily newspaper for the ears. That's what one writer calls world band radio. Listen for a while, and you will find that in addition to news, religion, politics, and entertainment, *this* daily newspaper includes a fat sports section. And your coach probably never even heard of most of the athletic contests found on world band radio.

Would you like a change of pace from the usual weekend sports menu? Try these: cricket from the West Indies, international cross-country ski racing from Switzerland, or full-bore auto rallying from Africa.

If that still seems a bit ordinary, how about a friendly wager with the gang at work on the outcome of a professional endurance race across the outback of Australia. On camels.

Many stations report on sports as part of the regular news broadcast. But for thorough English language coverage, start with the BBC. During the week the BBC puts on *Sports Roundup*, with up-to-the-minute sports news four times a day at 0939, 1245, 1745 and 2245 Universal Time. On Saturdays at 1345 there's *Sportsworld*—a three-hour and 15-minute feast of blow-by-blow commentary, sporting events results and sports commentaries, interrupted occasionally by brief news and current events programs.

The BBC takes a look at the softer side of sports, mixed with issues of the day, on *Sports International*, a magazine program that is broadcast at 2030 Mondays, with repeats Tuesdays at 0230 and 1030.

Finally, BBC's daily *Newsdesk* broadcast at 1800 includes two minutes of sports coverage.

And what are you likely to hear on BBC Sports? As one wag put it, "Stay tuned long enough, and you are liable to hear darn near anything." That may be a bit of an exaggeration, but the variety is truly astounding: British football (soccer); rugby (including Rugby League and Rugby Union); the Grand National, Derby, and Royal Ascot horse races; international cricket test matches (June–September); the European soccer championships (beginning in June); and tennis at Wimbledon.

The elegant but brutal sport of rowing can be heard during the World Rowing Championships, the Henley Regatta on the Thames, and the Cambridge–Oxford Boat Race. For something a bit faster, there's plenty of motor racing: the British Formula One Grand Prix from Silverstone; the Canadian Grand Prix; the Detroit Grand Prix; and the LeMans 24-hour sports car race—as well as Grand Prix Motorcycle racing from Holland and Austria. And for those who crave the rarified air of top-level golf: the US Open; the Belgian Open; the Dunhill British Masters; the Curtis Cup; and the French Open.

The BBC World Service's origins as the "Empire Service" means that its sports coverage is relatively cosmopolitan. However, just as there are sports cities, so there are sports countries, as well. Chief among these is Australia.

Sports is the Australian national religion. Not just sports, but *sports*—the more active, the better. It's no accident that one of swimming's most calorie-gobbling strokes is named after the Land of the 'Roo.

Radio Australia's extensive sports coverage comes complete with a definite "down under" flavor. It was, after all, Australian Rules Football—a form of soccer—that produced "Jacko": the grimacing, outrageous maniac seen in battery commercials and the television series, *The*

Philippe Zickgraf and Gérard Dreyfus of French World Service, sports section, covering the African Nations Football Cup.

Highwayman. Jacko reports that his grandstanding antics—doing handstands, leaping into the bleachers to kiss babies—touched the sentimental side of Aussie spectators. "Some of the fans knew I was thirsty, so they'd toss some bottled drinks at me, and when I was hungry, they'd be nice enough to toss a few tomatoes my way."

Sports bulletins are regularly heard on Radio Australia's main frequencies at 0330, 0830, 1330, 1645, and 1930. On Saturdays, Radio Australia's *Sports World* uses two dedicated sports frequencies, 15240 and 17715 kHz, to provide in-depth sports coverage from 0200 to 0730.

> ## How about the outcome of a professional endurance race across the outback of Australia. On camels.

Radio Australia's *Sports World* covers a wide spectrum of sports: test matches during the Australian cricket season from October through March; Australian Rules football from March through September; the Sydney Rugby League; motor racing; horse racing; and such major international sports events as the Pacific Games and the Asian Games.

Even when the events are the same as those you can hear right at home, world band radio often gives a different perspective. For example, in 1987, Radio Australia's extensive coverage of the

America's Cup offered a fresh slant on the sailing race—that of being the defender.

And what about that camel race? Hardly a Saturday afternoon run for the roses, "The Great Australian Camel Race" is a 2061 mile, or 3297 kilometer, endurance race with dashing dromedaries hoofing it across the outback of Australia.

This select gathering starts off from the monolith of Ayers Rock and lopes across the Simpson Desert to a finish at Surfer's Paradise on the sensous holiday playground of Australia's Gold Coast. The race, which takes 104 camels from fifteen countries twelve weeks to complete, is the brainchild of Arthur Earle, one of Australia's most successful entrepreneurs. He decided to stage the event to highlight outback communities during Australia's 1988 Bicentennial celebrations. And while it may be camels, they aren't playing for cigarettes—there's a guaranteed minimum $100,000 purse.

The land of gourmet chocolates and Oliver North's secret bank accounts also offers world class sports. Swiss Radio International, which produces programs in seven languages, is scheduled to cover a number of major sporting events during 1989. Among these are: World Cup Ski races from Lauberhorn and Adelboden in January; the Swiss Cup Soccer Final in May; the Swiss Tennis Open from Gstaad in July; plus International Cross Country ski races and the "Spengler Cup" International Ice Hockey tournament from Davos in December. Coverage of World Championship Soccer qualifying matches is to include

Switzerland/Czechoslovakia in June, Switzerland/Portugal in September, Switzerland/Belgium in October and Switzerland/Luxembourg in November.

Radio France Internationale also offers a potpourri of sports programming, including coverage of what many commentators consider is the most punishing athletic event in the world—the *Tour de France*. The Tour is a 21-day, 2,500-mile (4,000 kilometer) bicycle race around the perimeter of France, laid out over a new course each year. It involves some 200 riders and *big* prize money. From the flatlands of the south to the high passes of the French alps, the Tour is the physiological equivalent of running a marathon every day for three weeks. You can follow it by tuning in RFI around the beginning of July.

In 1989, Radio France Internationale sports coverage will also include: the 11th Paris–Dakar Automobile Rally in January (if, indeed, it ever takes place; the actual running of this dangerous event is under debate); French Soccer League Games from July 1988 to May/June 1989; the Five Nations Rugby Tournament from February to March; the Rolland Garros Tennis Tournament at the end of May and beginning of June; the French Soccer Cup Finals in June; Track and Field Championships from Paris in June; the Francophone (Olympic-type) Games from Morocco in July; the Lancome Golf Trophy in September; the Bercy Indoor Tennis Tournament in October; African Cup Soccer finals in December; and the Ivory Coast Rally in December.

Even broadcasters who claim no sports programming often produce worthy bits of reportage for the athletically minded. Last year Radio Canada International aired a story on a most unusual expedition. Called "Operation Raleigh," this adventure involved twenty carefully screened and prepared young adults who paddled canoes down 213 miles, or 500 kilometers, of river in the Canadian Arctic. Their purpose: to find signs of ancient human habitation along the riverbanks. While it hardly qualifies as a sports competition, Operation Raleigh certainly offers its participants a good deal of athletic challenge.

On the other hand, if you are interested in typical North American sports, the United States' Armed Forces Radio and Television Service provides excellent coverage of American football, baseball, basketball, and so forth. The only rub is that the AFRTS is a tough catch outside North America and the Carribean. The best bet, if you're in Europe, is to try a special single-sideband transmitter around 9242 or 9334 kHz.

Some private world band stations in Canada broadcast live sports. Fleapowered CFCX on 6005 kHz carries live coverage of Montreal Expos baseball games. Although CFCX isn't meant to be heard for any great distance, it is sometimes audible in parts of the Americas beyond the Canadian border.

But let's just suppose that you crave something utterly exotic in the way of sports, something that will give you the edge in a trivia competition.

Try this. Radio Australia recently covered a sport as part of the Australian Bicentennial celebration. Seventeen teams from around the globe squared off in the categories of accuracy, fast catching, maximum time aloft and distance competitions.

The event? The first World Boomerang Throwing Championship.

All this sports drama—from boomerangs to baseball, from the Davis Cup to dromedaries "down under," from tennis to the Tour de France—is yours on your world band radio. There is one thing world band doesn't cover yet: swimsuit contests. But they're working on it, as you'll find out when you read "World Band Radio in the 21st Century!"

Prepared by Jock Elliott.

World Band News Heard Sundays from Japan

Radio Japan airs *DX Corner* each week especially for active world band radio enthusiasts. Hosted by Illinois-trained broadcasting veteran Kaz Matsuda, it covers news of stations and schedules from an Asian perspective. Also included from time-to-time is *Passport* Editor Larry Magne's "Shortwave Receiver Test," prepared in conjunction with Ian McFarland, with evaluations of newly introduced world band radios and accessories.

Reception in North America is best via the Canada relay, whereas reception in Europe is best via Gabon. In Asia and the Pacific, transmissions direct from the renovated transmission facilities in Japan are usually well heard.

Winter

Sunday

0925–0944 Universal Time to Asia on 11840, 17810 kHz

1525–1544 to North America, Europe, North Africa and the Middle East on 5990, 7210, 11815, 21700 (via Gabon) kHz

Monday (Sunday evening in North America)

0325–0344 to the Americas and Asia on 5960 (via Canada), 15280, 17810, 17835, 17845 kHz

Summer

Sunday

0925–0944 Universal Time to Asia on 11840, 17810 kHz

1525–1544 to North America, Europe, North Africa and the Middle East on 9505, 9695, 11815, 21700 (via Gabon) kHz

Monday (Sunday evening in North America)

0125–0144 to the Americas on 5960 (via Canada), 15195, 17810, 17845 kHz

0325–0344 to Asia on 11840, 15195, 17810 kHz

Kaz Matsuda, taken during the two-hour four-way hook-up, Hands Across the Airwaves.

Photo page 77: A spray of chromospheric material breaks free of magnetic loops that constrain other gases around it, and surges upward away from the sun. The photo was taken by the Solar Telescope of Skylab.

The Sunspots Are Coming!

by Gerry Dexter

Look out, they're coming! What's coming? Sunspots. More and more sunspots. Those flaming furies that whirl and leap on the sun's surface will be growing in numbers over the next few years—the result? World band radio listeners will be better able to tune in far-away, inaccessible stations loud and clear.

Normally, the sun gives off ultraviolet, x-ray, and other types of radiation which ionize, or charge, the earth's atmosphere. Ionization allows radio waves to be reflected back to earth great distances from where the waves were transmitted. This means that world band listeners can hear everything from a military command station in Saudi Arabia, to an explorer's base camp in Antarctica, to the *SWL Digest* program on Radio Canada International.

Anyone acquainted with world band radio is aware of the existence of sunspots and the so-called eleven-year sunspot cycle. At least we

Canada Airs Popular Program for World Band Listeners

Each week Radio Canada International airs "SWL Digest," a program devoted to helping you better understand and enjoy world band radio. Included in this program are tests of new world band radios and accessories by *Passport's* resident equipment expert, Lawrence Magne. *Passport* editors Tony Jones and Don Jensen also highlight worldwide developments, while other features cover a variety of interesting topics, including new world band schedules.

Hosted by award-winning announcer/producer Ian McFarland, "SWL Digest" is heard in many parts of the world—including the Americas, Europe, Africa, and Australia/New Zealand—at various times. Although the 0107/0007, 1330/1230, and 2307 broadcasts are intended for listeners in the Americas, 2208/2108 for Europeans, and 2137 for Africans, in reality these can be heard simultaneously in various parts of the world. Tune around for the best results and handiest times.

1st Saturday/Sunday/Tuesday of the month	Larry Magne's "Test Report" on new world band radios and accessories, and news of stations and schedules.
2nd Saturday/Sunday/Tuesday of the month	Official monthly reports from radio umbrella associations and news of stations and schedules.
3rd Saturday/Sunday/Tuesday of the month	Either Don Jensen's "Journal" or Tony Jones' "Report from South America."
4th Saturday/Sunday/Tuesday of the month	"Potpourri"—special reports and features to aid in listening to world band radio. Also, news of stations and schedules.

A similar program, "Allô DX," is presented weekly in French by Yvan Paquette, animateur.

Universal Time		
Winter Hiver	Summer Été	
1330	1230	Tuesday in English on 9625, 11855, and 17820 kHz (plus C-Span cable network in Washington)
1925	1925	Dimanche en français sur 15260, et 17820 kHz
1955	1855	Dimanche en français sur 5995, 7235 ou 9555, 11945, 15325, et 17875 kHz
2137	2137	Saturday in English on 11880, 15150, and 17820 kHz
2208	2108	Saturday in English on 9760 and 11945 kHz.
2307	2307	Sunday evening in English on 9755 and 11730 kHz (930 kHz AM for the Caribbean)
0107	0007	Saturday night (Sunday UTC date) in English on 5960 and 9755 kHz.
0107	0107	Saturday night (Sunday UTC date) in English on 9535, 11845, and 11940 kHz.
0225	0225	Dimanche soir (lundi UTC) en français sur 6120, 9535, 9755, et 11940 kHz.

should be, since we have been living through the downside of the last cycle for what has seemed a very long period. A cycle begins with little solar activity, including low sunspot numbers. Over the next four or five years, numbers of sunspots increase, peaking after about another five to six years, then the sunspots resume a downward slide, perhaps after plateauing, until they hit the next trough.

> ### Scientists report signs that, like an elevator gone beserk, a great spurt upward to maximum solar activity may be taking place.

Sunspots were first observed several hundred years before the birth of Christ. The first real records of the spots were not made until Galileo invented the telescope back in the early 1600s. It was not until the middle of the 18th century that careful records of cycles and their activity levels were kept. So the data upon which current predictions and educated guesses about a cycle are made rest on some 230 years of recordkeeping.

Throughout that time, scientists have learned that cycles of high and low solar activity run their course over eleven years only as an average. Some have been over and done with in as little as eight years, or have held out for as many as fifteen. We do not know what causes these repeating cycles, but one thing is certain—years of low sunspot activity generally mean poorer radio reception with fewer usable frequency segments, while years of higher sunspot numbers bring about just the opposite. The twenty-first recorded sunspot cycle ended over a year ago, and Cycle 22 is now well underway, already bringing better days for the world band listener.

Sunspots themselves are monstrous whirlwinds in the sun's surface. They contain swirling masses of electrified gasses, very strong magnetic fields, and great emissions of ultraviolet and x-ray radiation. The spots appear dark because their temperature is much lower than that of the sun's surface. Actually, a sunspot is about 100 times brighter than the light reflected by a full moon.

Sunspots tend to be groupies. They appear in clusters which may range from just a few spots spread out over a thousand miles—1600 kilometers—to huge spots grouped together over an area of a quarter million miles—425,000 kilometers—or more. The larger spots in such groups could easily swallow up the Earth, Mars, and Venus, and still have room left over to have several moons for dessert.

The trouble with sunspots is that they often have violent neighbors, called solar flares. These

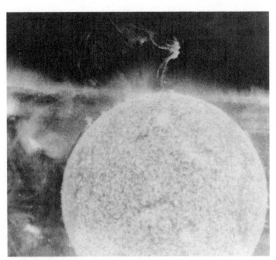

A huge solar eruption can be seen in this enlarged spectroheliogram obtained during the Skylab 3 mission.

are huge and extremely intense bursts of energy. If sunspots are the furies, then these are the fiends. The more sunspots there are, the more solar flare activity can be expected—the sour comes with the sweet. Solar flares usually reach their peak intensity in a minute or less, then take several minutes to a half hour to subside.

The fiendish flares strike the the sun-side of the earth with so much ultraviolet light that the ionosphere—the invisible gaseous layer in the sky that makes world band reception possible—is disrupted. Radio signals may be wiped out or, more typically, reduced in strength. Flares also can create changes in the ability of the ionosphere to reflect signals. To a listener, this means radio stations will fade in and out for a period.

> ### Sunspots tend to be groupies. The larger spots in such groups could easily swallow up the Earth, Mars, and Venus and still have room left over to have several moons for dessert.

Polar blackouts are truly special effects of high solar activity. They are caused by massive levels of radiation from the flares, routed to the polar areas by the earth's magnetic fields. Blackouts can last from a few minutes to a few days and occur mostly at night. World band signals that have the misfortune of passing through the polar areas may be affected by the blackouts, and thus may be only weakly heard. What's special about these are the extraordinary Northern Lights accompanying blackouts. The thrill of seeing this natural light show should not be missed.

Some experts have seen indications that Cycle 22 could prove to be very intense and unusual, perhaps even unprecedented. Scientists report signs that, like an elevator gone beserk, a great spurt upward to maximum solar activity may be taking place. This means that an activity peak, which would not normally occur for another four or five years, could be reached in the coming months. It now appears that during the winter of 1989–1990, there may be an average of over 180 sunspots, with *Passport's* latest estimate for the peak count being 199, occurring in December, 1989.

During this period of solar high activity, listeners may be unlucky on some nights, experiencing occasional poor or erratic reception. But DXers—those who pursue rarely heard signals from afar—will have a heyday: They will be able to tune in stations they've never heard before. Since blackouts mean greatly reduced strengths of signals coming over or near a polar path, exotic stations from southerly directions may be the best to look for.

A very reliable indicator of current propagation conditions is the National Bureau of Standards' station WWV, on the air 24 hours a day on 2500, 5000, 10000 and 15000 kHz. There is a report on propagation conditions aired at 18 minutes past each hour, and during this next cycle WWV should have up-to-date information on what havoc— and blessings—sunspots might create.

> The present cycle may offer a chance of a lifetime for world band radio enthusiasts seeking to hear "impossible" stations.

Keep an ear out for this sort of information. While some signal disruption is bound to happen, the upswing of the present cycle may offer a chance of a lifetime for world band radio enthusiasts seeking to hear "impossible" stations that are normally lost under the "biggies." If the cycle's peak is as unprecedented as expected, then who knows what any of us might hear!

Gerry Dexter, a Contributing Editor at Popular Communications *and Co-Editor at* Numero Uno, *became President of Tiare Publications after leaving a lifetime of broadcasting.*

> World band may be able to broadcast a synthesized "reality" that is all but indistinguishable from the reality around us.

World Band Radio in the Twenty-first Century

Most of the breakthroughs in radio and television—color, stereo, single side-band—have involved new transmission technologies. But world band radio has rarely followed this traditional path, and for good reason: The nearly 160 countries on the air would have to agree on how to proceed. If new technology were not compatible with existing receivers, millions of world band radios would become obsolete. In the first part of the twenty-first century, then, what we are most likely to see are advances that require changes mainly in *receiving* technology.

Nothing is quite so precious as time and information. Forthcoming world band radios will allow you to obtain more information than ever before in a fraction of the time it takes today. Artificial intelligence will analyze the myriad transmissions on the air, edit them for types of content, then store the result to be heard whenever you see fit: immediately on a real-time "hotline" basis, or later upon your command as a custom-packaged "magazine" program.

With the "hotline" option, you'll be notified whenever desired news breaks. For example, you

Also Coming Up: Perestroika in World Band Radio

Many of the most enjoyable stations on the air carry programs intended mainly for domestic consumption, with any foreign audience being incidental. These programs tend to be reasonably good, if only to discourage local complainers from gathering at station doorsteps.

Broadcasts aimed at foreigners lack this sort of proximity to a measurable audience. Consequently, it is possible and sometimes financially necessary to forego systematic audience analysis. In the absence of valid audience data, it is possible to create an illusion of audience interest by using various gimmicks—giveaways, contests, collectable postcards and the like—to stimulate listener mail, which then becomes the yardstick by which audience size is perceived.

The ruse often works—that is, it convinces domestic authorities that a station merits continued funding. But it can become a vicious circle by increasing staff cynicism which, in turn, may help bring about a reduction in program quality. This tends to diminish the real audience, and thus to create an even greater dependence on inflated mail counts and the specialized types of shows and promotions most likely to bring them about.

It is no accident, then, that the best stations tend to be those most concerned with meaningful audience feedback and minimally concerned with gimmickry. The BBC, for example, not only commissions serious audience surveys, but also has panels of listeners to critique programs. It doesn't give away T-shirts, publications, and the like; in fact, it charges handsomely for such things.

There are three reasons the BBC's type of approach should grow more widespread as the twenty-first century draws closer. First, the audience for world band radio is growing in a number of countries. Dubious programming that once attracted little attention increasingly has the potential to cause embarrassment to a station or its country's diplomatic corps.

Second, in most countries government agencies are being forced to justify their existences in a climate of leaner budgets. Gimmickry can succeed for only so long if a station is under close scrutiny.

Finally, national broadcasting monopolies are becoming scarcer, with media administrators increasingly accepting competition as a worthwhile part of the landscape. Audience wishes are thus becoming integrated into the larger broadcasting culture. As a result, "This is what they should hear" carries proportionately less weight in decision-making at the domestic level, with at least some of this thinking rubbing off onto the international sphere—especially when a world band broadcaster is being compared to a new international television operation down the hall.

All this translates into greater professionalism and better programs. It's hard to imagine anything more worthy of welcome by world band listeners.

—L.M.

can request to be made aware of any airplane accidents or whenever a selected financial index varies up or down by more than two percent. The "magazine" format, on the other hand, will allow your radio to monitor the world's stations throughout the day, analyze the contents, then edit out all but those types of material you wish to hear. When you are ready to listen, you can choose—create your own "magazine"—from all that's been been stored during the day.

Video, via facsimile or slow-scan television, is already feasible. Indeed, SSTV is now capable of operating in color, and radio FAX has been used for years for news photos, weather maps, and the like from around the world (see "Action Between the Bands"). All that's missing at present is linking the video to world band broadcasts. Even "real"

television is possible by using a suitable VCR or other storage medium to record incoming pieces of slow-motion video at reduced speed for later playback at normal speed.

One consideration that's held this up has been the lack of available shortwave spectrum space for video signals. But early in the next century world band broadcasters plan to convert to single-sideband transmissions, which take up half the space of conventional transmissions. This, as well as the continued movement away from the shortwave spectrum by "utility" stations, means that there will almost certainly be more space available for world band video. Advances in video processing techniques will eventually allow larger and clearer photos to be created.

For the most part, video is universal in nature.

With dubbed soundtracks or subtitles, a show made in Hollywood can be enjoyed throughout the world, regardless of the diversity of local tongues. The key to this, of course, is the translation.

Since the earliest days of tribes, groups of people have cherished their distinct languages. Nowhere has this been more apparent than on world band radio, where nearly every tongue of humanity is represented, making much of what's on the air incomprehensible to even the most facile multilinguist. Now, computer technology is inching towards a practical remedy: automatic simultaneous translation.

Automatic voice translation has a challenging list of hurdles to overcome before listeners will be able to hear Ayatollah Abdullah inflame distant crowds in pristine English. For example, various differing words sound identical, others have different meanings, and "English" in one country may differ from "English" in another. Speakers' accents don't help matters, either.

But it's coming. Large mainframe computers using sophisticated software already perform a degree of simultaneous translation. Some firms, such as Linguistic Products of Houston, even sell simultaneous-translation software for use with everyday personal computers. While near-perfect translation is probably some decades away, Linguistic predicts acceptable voice translation by as early as the mid-1990s.

The best of today's world band radios feature a variety of noise-reducing characteristics to make listening more pleasurable. Still, even in its finest moments world band audio quality rarely equals that of ordinary AM radio. But there are breathtaking chapters unfolding that will completely change the nature of what you hear.

Significant improvment in fidelity calls for one of two completely new approaches to the medium: either signals transmitted via advanced-fidelity transmission technology, or else standard-fidelity signals converted to high fidelity via advanced technology at the listener's end. The problem with the first option, besides getting numerous countries to agree, is that it takes up too much world band spectrum space. There's simply no place to squeeze in spectrum-hogging hi-fi signals.

Again, computer technology will ride to the rescue. Here's how.

Using a combination of artificial and pseudo-artificial intelligence, database techniques, efficient bulk storage and complex ultra-fast processing, your twenty-first-century world band radio—alone or interfaced with a household computer—will analyze ordinary analog radio signals to discern and break down what is actually being aired. Having done this, it will generate these sounds afresh and with excellent fidelity, synthesizing them from a digital database within your radio. In so doing, it will also have the wherewithal

to reproduce only desired sounds—music, voices and such—and thus to omit unwanted sounds, such as interference, electrical noise, and static.

Now, this seems simple enough. But going from concept to application is a great and extremely complex leap . . . albeit one that is realistic, given the thrust of software and hardware technology. Look for voices to be synthesized first, with music following some time later.

Beyond the twenty-first century? Long-distance reconstruction of matter not only means that instant transportation—"Beam me up, Scotty"—may come to pass, it also means that world band, satellites, and other communications vehicles may be able to broadcast a synthesized "reality" that is all but indistinguishable from the reality around us: not a video screen or loudspeaker, but artificial "real" people in artificial "real" surroundings, with the participant—*viewer* hardly seems appropriate—smack in the middle, interacting with the show as though it were reality. Indeed, this technology, if it ever comes to pass, might allow each of us to be able to create his *own* reality. Thankfully, that and the profound questions it raises will have to be wrestled with in Lord Keynes' famous "long run," by which time we all presumably will have departed for less earthly surroundings.

Prepared by Lawrence Magne, with Aaron Beller, John Campbell, Ralph Dessau and Harry Helms.

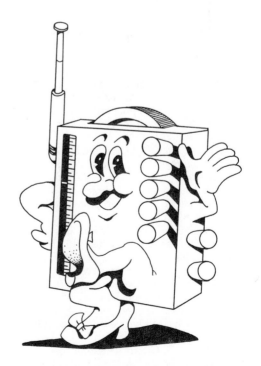

This map illustrates the three day route that took the author's friends to within two miles of the U.S. fleet where they were found floating in life jackets, without money or possessions.

Escape from Iran

(continued from page 13)

As we walked, a man approached us holding a photograph of Khomeini. The man calmly told us, "This is our leader, not the Shah. Soon he will return and drive out those who exploit our country."

At that time, Khomeini was not exactly a household word to me. My natural curiosity, plus my thus-far positive interactions with the average Iranian, made me point to the photograph and ask who it was.

The man calmly explained about the Khomeini Moslem Fundamentalist movement and how they felt the time was ripe for it to replace the present regime. He cautioned us that once the Shah was overthrown, we would probably have to leave the country. I thanked him and we continued.

This encounter apparently had upset Dick quite a bit. He was more familiar with the Khomeini movement than I, as he had been briefed before he left. He told me never to talk with people like that again and that we were lucky the man hadn't killed us. Somehow I doubted Dick was right, but there was no mistaking the fact that something was indeed happening. It was definitely time to turn on the world band radio again.

That night's BBC and Armed Forces Radio and Television Service news contained top stories about oppressive moves being made by the newly appointed military government in response to violence by striking oil workers. The NIRT carried an Olivia Newton-John special.

By then, a 10:00 pm curfew had been imposed. Outside at night, the sound of UH-1 helicopters was almost constant. This meant trouble was brewing. I remember watching the helicopters from my seventh-floor balcony as they circled over distant parts of the city, their gunners raining tracers down onto some trouble spot below. Meanwhile, NIRT's FM service was running a phone-in "Oldies Request" show.

Things were deteriorating fast, according to the foreign broadcast news services which we now monitored religiously. Radio Japan reported that Iranian military reserves were being called up and active forces mobilized. The AFRTS said that US military and Department of Defense personnel here were either restricted to their facilities or residences. Dick and I began thinking about getting out.

At the Company office, there was no news of our equipment and no guidance about our next move. None of the Iranian staff would come to work, and the American employees told us not to go out at night any more. At the same time, the Company's Vice President was telling us not to worry, that this period of tension would pass in a day or two. I quietly arranged a ticket out on Lufthansa via West Germany, while Dick chose to wait.

Radio Nederland that evening reported intermittent closures of Tehran's Merhabad Airport by the military because snipers were shooting at aircraft taking off and landing. Now every night featured a series of firefights between helicopters and "trouble spots" on the ground. Gunfire was getting closer to the hotel, and one morning an Associated Press writer had two rounds come through his window. One of them hit his little refrigerator and shattered the split of California champagne inside. I began listening to my radio more often now, but with the lights out so I wouldn't be seen.

The Voice of America reported massive antigovernment demonstrations taking place in the pro-Khomeini areas of southern Tehran. Indeed, we had seen helicopters orbiting there constantly the previous day and, after nightfall, dropping parachute flares to illuminate the area.

Armored personnel carriers now guarded the entrances to the hotel, while NIRT cheerfully announced that it would carry National Football League games from the US via satellite. In the lobby, you could sign up to be in one of the armed convoys which escorted groups of cars to a release point downtown. Dick and I got on the 7:00 am list, and we finally arrived at the office by about 8:15.

Chaos surrounded the building. There were only three Company employees left now and, when we came in, they were in the Vice President's vacated office. Some time during the previous night, he had departed in the Company jet, taking the contents of the safe and his file cabinet. In the corner was an empty space where the Company's TELEX machine had been. We were now at the mercy of the Iranian telecommunications industry for contact with the outside world.

We got on the phone to call the Company in the United States, and about two hours later we managed to get a line to the 24-hour corporate operations center in Los Angeles. "Don't worry," they said. "We'll let you know what to do soon. Just sit tight." What about the Vice President? "It doesn't concern you. Just sit tight."

This was not comforting at all. We "sat tight" all day. About 3:00 pm, an Iranian knocked on the door. He politely told us that they would be burning this building in thirty minutes and we should get our personal things out. We thanked him and did just that.

The five of us were now squeezed into the company Paykan as we worked our way through the impossible downtown traffic toward the hotel. Looking back, we saw that they were indeed burning the building, with orbiting military helicopters watching.

Once inside our hotel, we went up to my room and made plans. I had an airline ticket for the next day, but none of the others had anything but their passports. Dick's return ticket had been safely tucked away in the Vice President's safe and had departed the country with him.

We turned on my world band radio at the top of the hour and heard the BBC tell that the US Navy was moving its warships in the Persian Gulf closer to the Iranian coastline. The government had shut down all gas stations and imposed a dusk-to-dawn curfew in most cities. Meanwhile, NIRT was running a series of classic Humphrey Bogart films and announcing "temporary interruptions of fuel availability" and a "short curtailment of nighttime activities."

We agreed to stay in the hotel that night and wait for the curfew to lift at dawn. We would then go to the airport, where I could use my ticket to try to get out. With or without me, the others would try to reach the Persian Gulf, about three days' drive to the south.

The next morning we set out at sunup. The airport was mobbed with thousands of people trying to force their way in. The military had sandbag barricades set up at the entrances, and only those with tickets and passports could enter. It looked like I could make it.

It was an emotional moment as I unloaded my gear. My friends seemed pretty confident of being able to make it, though. To help, I gave them all the cash I had . . . and my world band radio. I waded through the crowd and finally got onto the plane after several shakedowns and friskings. Eight hours later I was safe in West Germany and wondering how my friends were doing.

Dick and the other three men had found their way to the Gulf in three days, although they had to give an Iranian all their money and possessions for a boat ride to the US fleet. Unfortunately, the guy took them only to within two miles of one of the ships, then threw them into the water. Thankfully, he did give them life jackets.

Looking back, it seems that the average Iranian is not the wild-eyed radical we see on television. Most of these people were, and are now, caught in the middle of a struggle over which they have no control. The quality of life in Iran has certainly decreased under Khomeini and appears to be continuing downward.

For me, it was a lesson in being aware of a situation around me. Ever since, I have never traveled to any point on this planet without my trusty world band radio and a spool of antenna wire. I guess the only winner was Khomeini, as he wound up with two professional-quality transceivers. He probably has had a hard time finding batteries, though.

Dave Rosenthal is a science correspondent for Radio Nederland and CNN.

Top Ten Shows
(continued from page 19)

week's news and how Australians, young and old, are responding to it."

Keith Smith, a pleasant, whimsical host, guides us through the papers, but his gaze tends to skip past page one and settles on the smaller stories in the back sections—subjects like the transistor's 40th birthday, or Australia's war on cockroaches.

He also plumbs the Australian character as revealed in "letters to the editor" columns. What comes through is the real Aussie spirit—not what you see in beer ads, battery commercials and cute travelogs. Letters have included complaints about such things as celebrating the nation's 200th birthday ("Bicentenary? Obscenity is more like

it.") and joggers ("The beggars run you over with impunity!"). No sacred cows here.

Smith takes his microphone outside for snippets of comment from "Australians on the street." Ordinary folks toss off responses to such questions as, "What's the best age of your life?" (Consensus: Now) and "Do Australians drink too much?" (Yes!)

The quarter-hour show, repeated several times during the week, wraps up with a gimmick—the kiddie interview—lifted from one-time American radio personality Art Linkletter. Thankfully, in Smith's hands, "Romp with Australian Children" is not just cutesy. Youngsters pick out a headline to read and, under Smith's questioning, offer pintsized—often hilarous—opinions.

Witty, insightful, *Smith's Weekly* is smack on target.

They Can't All Be Gems

Unfortunately, not everything in English on world band radio is of sterling quality. Here and there, you'll find real dogs churning out programs that make *I Spit on Your Grave* seem like high culture.

Does that mean you should steer clear? No way! There's a mine lode of unintended humor—remember *Reefer Madness*?—to be found among these humorless haranguers of the airwaves. Here are five yawners to test your endurance on a slow night:

Radio Pyongyang, North Korea. News on Radio Pyongyang zeroes in on the tireless doings of the "great leader," Kim Il-Sung, or the "dear leader," Kim Il-Chung—"great" and "dear" being nearly indispensible adjectives. Songs have such inspiring titles as "We Will Always Follow Our Leader," and political commentary uses the phrase "US imperialists" so often that one wonders if it is a hyphenated word.

Radio Tirana, Albania. Radio Tirana may be impartial in directing its verbal abuse against both the United States and the Soviet Union, but it also has what are probably the longest titles for the shortest programs. Common are five-minute groaners with such titles as, "The Future of the Marxist-Leninist Movement Is Growing in Scope and Strength."

Voice of the Islamic Republic of Iran. News from this station usually centers on the tireless "annihilation" of Iraqi troops, with the juiciest political invective being directed against the "Great Satans" of Zionism—"Israel" doesn't exist in Ayatolese—and the United States. The station also offers such spellbinding features as, "Analysis of the True Character of Western Radio Stations." Fortunately for North Americans, the English language broadcasts air from 1930-2030 Universal Time, when few people in the Western Hemisphere are home to hear them. Europeans, however, are deserving of sympathy.

Radio Cultural, Guatemala. Generally, this evangelical station in Guatemala broadcasts in Spanish or plays Easy Listening music. But once a day it airs such English-language everbores as "Back to the Bible." It is much like television evangelism without the visual effects—perhaps, actually, a plus.

RAI, Italy. Although RAI's Italian language programs are quite good, its English language coverage to North America is limited to only twenty minutes. The real problem isn't the twenty minutes; it's the woman who reads the news. She pauses, stumbles, hesitates, mispronounces, corrects herself, coughs, sniffles, and, in general, gives the most incompetent performance on world band radio. She is so boring that from time to time she yawns, presumably in concert with her hapless listeners.

—Alex Batman

In North America, the best time is 1313 Universal Time Sunday mornings on 6080, 7205, and 9580 kHz. Other possibilities are 2330 Tuesday evenings on 15320, 15395, and 17795 kHz; or, if you keep vampire's hours, at 0930 Friday mornings on 9580 kHz.

In Europe, try 0930 Universal Time Friday mornings on 9655 and 15415 kHz or 1713 Thursday evenings on 6035 and 7205 kHz.

Listener Response Show

Anything Goes
British Broadcasting Corporation

The BBC's audio archives are said to be unrivaled anywhere in the world. And each Sunday night *Anything Goes* is the listener's entree to it all. It is a listener request program, but unlike any other. The program's premise is that if it has been recorded, somewhere, sometime, regular host Bob Holness will find it in the files and play it.

Anything Goes responds to letter writers from around the globe, Oregon to Oman, Andorra to Australia, playing whatever—or nearly so—they ask to hear, drawn from the BBC's vast audio collection.

Music? How about a 1927 version of *My Blue Heaven*, Mel Torme's slickly hip *Mountain Greenery* or a 50-year-old recording of Ethel Waters' *Frankie and Johnny*? Or you might hear Jimmy Rodgers' folksy *Kisses Sweeter than Wine*, something by Rudy Vallee or the Beatles, or another listener's favorite: the classical theme from the 1975 BBC-TV series, *Anna Karenina*.

A spot of comedy? A healthy sense of humor is as much a part of the English makeup as the Ploughman's Lunch. You'll hear such classics as Peter Sellers from the hilarious BBC *Goon Show*, or the hoary "Who's on First" routine by Abbott and Costello.

Historic speech is sometimes a writer's choice, and the wellspring of British history runs deep. Recent excerpts include Churchill's so-called "Blood, Sweat, and Tears" speech (you discover why it's "so-called" when you hear it), the "I-do's" of a royal wedding, and the recollections of an aging, 1930s-era champion cricketer.

Anything Goes is a novelty, but a delightful one. For North America, it's on Sunday nights (Monday UTC) at 0330 Universal Time on 5975 and 6175 kHz. For Europe, it's on Mondays at 0830 and 1330 on 5975, 9410, and 12095 kHz.

Drama

Play of the Week
British Broadcasting Corporation

The true art of radio is its drama, commented broadcasting historian Jim Harmon some years

The faces behind the Royal Canadian Air Farce (L to R): Don Ferguson, Luba Goy, Roger Abbott, and John Morgan. Photo by Fred Phipps, CBC

ago, back when pop music deejays first shoved radio theatre off the airwaves in North America.

With radio drama and the fertility of the imagination, you can have entertainment and excitement your own way. The special effects the mind produces can run rings around any movie stuntman's act or computer-generated graphics. After all, what can equal the terror of a youngster alone in a dark room during a thunderstorm, when there's little to fear except roof leaks and what's sprung forth from his imagination?

"The greatest impresario of radio," said Harmon, "was not Cecil B. DeMille or Orson Welles. The one who really ushered you into the world of strange and commonplace delight that was radio—the guide through the mind's inner rooms—was always yourself!" Fortunately, Harmon noted, "in Great Britain . . . radio drama still retains an important share of the general audience." That remains true today.

World band listeners can share in those radio experiences, thanks to the BBC's hourlong *Play of the Week* aired each Sunday night. The playbill is varied, from contemporary drama to Shakespeare. Production values and the actors themselves are first rate. Longer plays, such as a recent *Romeo and Juliet*, are presented in parts over several consecutive weekly shows.

In North America, the best bet is 0101 Universal Time Sunday evenings (technically, Monday UTC) on 5975, 6175, and 7325 kHz. In Europe, best is 1901 Saturday evenings on 6195, 7325, 9410, and 12095 kHz. It's also repeated daytime Sundays at 1201 for eastern North America on 6195, 9510, and 11775 kHz, and for Europe on 7325, 9410, and 12095 kHz.

Comedy

Royal Canadian Air Farce
Canadian Broadcasting Corporation

Comedy generally doesn't travel well, which may be why it is not heard all that often on world band radio. What's funny to one culture tends to sail over the heads of another half a world away.

But there are exceptions. The BBC presents comedy on its English-language World Service, but they usually are not long-running shows. There's a BBC panel show called *Just a Minute*. Problem is, it's only on the air for a few months, then disappears from the schedule for a while. When on, though, it is a good listen, with a witty panel which is given a far-out topic—such as "roast hippopotamus"—and must speak for a full minute on the subject without pause, verbal "padding," or repetition. It's a lot harder—and funnier—than you might imagine. If you stumble across this one, stick with it.

But it is the Canadian home service CBC network that keeps us laughing day in and day out with a topical humor program called the *Royal Canadian Air Farce*, now in its 16th year. This program is not carried on Radio Canada International's foreign service, probably because the humor is too Canadian to be fully appreciated abroad. And it is true that to "get" all the jokes, a useful primer for non-Canadians is the previously mentioned RCI-relayed news duo, if only to keep straight the public figures and foibles that get neatly skewered.

If not on RCI, then where, and when? Why, on the CBC's Northern Quebec Service, the world band transmission intended for Canadians living in the far frozen north, beyond the normal ranges of AM and FM stations.

For a laugh and a half, take off weekly with the *Royal Canadian Air Farce* at 1808 Universal Time (1708 UTC summers) Sunday on 9625 and 11720 kHz. In North America—it's hard to hear this gem in Europe—that means 1:08 PM Eastern Time, not necessarily the best hour for a comedy show, so you might want to tape the program for playback at a more appropriate time.

Family Entertainment

The Happy Station
Radio Nederland

Some will disagree with this selection as one of the best. Radio Nederland's Sunday night fare is occasionally viewed as old fashioned, unchanging, predictable.

Yes, it is old fashioned radio. After all, it is the oldest continuous program—not only on world band, but on any sort of radio, anywhere. *The Happy Station* originated sixty years ago, hosted by the late Eddie Startz over Holland's pioneer world band station, PCJ. The high point of each program was when a barnyard full of Startz's imaginary animals would trot out, bleating and whinnying, to share "a nice cupper" tea with him. Even then, it was different.

Willis Conover, host of the immensely popular VOA Jazz Hour.

When Startz retired in 1970, the show got its second host, Tom Meyer, who remains firmly at the helm of this legendary program. Meyer serves up a blend of music—everything from Shorty Rogers' '50ish cool jazz to Northern Ireland's No. 2 country and western artist, Billy McFarland—and talk (light banter and features, listeners' letters, giveaways, children's coloring contests and more).

It bills itself as the Sunday family show of "smiles across the miles," something of everything for everyone. The one taboo is controversy; the 50-year-old Meyer, like his predecessor, is not looking to makes waves. It is an easygoing, gentle show, as easy to slip on as an old shoe. Maybe *The Happy Station* is not for you, or maybe it is. But they must be doing something right to have endured all these years.

Heard often, but in North America the best bet is Sunday evenings (Monday UTC) at 0235 Universal Time on 6165 and 9590 kHz, or later at 0535 on 6165 and 9715 kHz. In Europe, try Sundays at 1835 on 6020 kHz.

Music—Popular/Rock/Jazz

Jazz Hour/Music USA
Voice of America

In Poland, during a visit, they cheered and strew flowers in his path. In Moscow, they kissed his hand in adoration. In America, though, relatively few even know the name Willis Conover.

Since 1955, the host of the VOA's *Jazz Hour* on *Music USA* has been the world's most famous disc jockey. But the curse the 67-year-old Conover has lived with for nearly 12,000 programs is to be unrecognized and unappreciated in his native land.

He has been called America's most effective ambassador. Countless jazz buffs abroad grew up listening to and taping his voice and music. On the occasion of his ten-thousandth broadcast in 1982, he visited the Soviet Union, where throngs welcomed him as a musical deity.

Six days a week Conover's show goes out to listeners in Europe, North Africa and the Middle East from VOA transmitters, including those at Greenville, North Carolina. But not long ago, the program was eliminated from the "Americas" beam which, while not officially directed to US audiences, is widely listened to there.

"There's not that much interest in jazz on this side of the Atlantic," a VOA official notes ruefully. That, seemingly, has been a disappointment to the serious Conover. But there's nothing downbeat about his program, beginning each day with the evergreen theme, Ellington's *Take the "A" Train*, and Conover's mellifluous opening words, "Time for jazz!"

For specialized musical tastes, perhaps, but the VOA's *Jazz Hour* is truly one of the class acts on world band radio.

Europeans and even some North Americans can tune in at 2010 Universal Time Monday through Saturday on 6040, 9760, 11760, and 15205 kHz. It's distinctive, so you'll know it when you hear it.

Music—Regional

Nuevo Día
Faro del Caribe

No list of superior world band radio programs would be complete without Latin American music. But there are so many musical types and tempos that it's no easy job settling on just one. For example, there's *Música del Ecuador*, a fifteen-minute offering frequently tucked into the English programming of pioneer religious broadcaster, HCJB, in Quito, Ecuador.

There's also the mellow *Best in Brazilian Popular Music* on Radiobras. Or Peruvian huaynos—the haunting, flute-filled sound which can sometimes be heard faintly on any number of Spanish-language world band outlets, such as Radio Andina in Huancayo, Peru. Radio Habana Cuba airs *From the Land of Music*—short segments of super Cuban rhythms which serve as fillers around the more ideological fare during the nightly English broadcasts.

Instead, the *Passport* listening panel opted for an obscure but delightful wake-up program, *Nuevo Día*—"New Day"—on TIFC from San José, Costa Rica. TIFC, like most Latin stations, more commonly identifies by its slogan *Faro del Caribe* which, translated from the Spanish, means "Caribbean Lighthouse." It is a world band station with a religious orientation and purpose, although the inspirational messages, in Spanish, are very brief.

The program's big attraction to non-Spanish-speaking listeners is its music—a rousing mix of Central American rhythms, including mariachis, ranchera, norteñas, Mexican-style polkas and marimba selections. It's the perfect elixir to arouse slumbering bones.

"Adiós a las estrellas," begins the *Nuevo Día* announcer each morning. "Buenos días a la luz de un día nuevo."

"Goodbye to the stars; hello to the light of a new day!" It's a great way for early risers—we're talking *early* here . . . 5:15 in New York, 4:15 in Winnipeg—to kick off your morning.

The signal isn't strong, but in North America *Nuevo Día* can be heard, with the right equipment and reasonable odds, winters at 1015 Universal Time daily on 5056 kHz. In Europe it's inaudible, which isn't entirely inappropriate, considering it's almost lunchtime in Berlin at that hour.

Pete Bergeron prepares a weekly menu of lively Cajun music over WRNO Worldwide. Photo by WRNO

Music—Specialty

Voix de la Louisiane
WRNO Worldwide

A "sleeper" on the list is this half-hour non-English program aired Tuesday nights and repeated at other times—scheduled and unscheduled—during the week on this United States commercial world band station.

Nearly two hundred weekly programs ago, the French consul in New Orleans contacted Pete Bergeron, program director for an FM public radio station, about producing a world band program that would showcase the French culture and traditions of the Cajun country of southern Louisiana.

The Cajun dialect—Bergeron explains that it is French as spoken two centuries ago when Acadian exiles from Canada's Atlantic coast settled in Louisiana—is easily understood by Francophone listeners from Quebec to Paris. And the 48-year-old, Cajun-speaking host has the fan mail to prove it.

Why should English-speaking listeners tune to a program in a French dialect?

The music, that's why. Bergeron, along with his interviews and features on different aspects of his region's culture, each week plays a nifty sampling of Cajun and Creole music, records seldom played outside the "bayou belt."

Cajun music is a footstompin' melange of Anglo country and western, French-Canadian folk themes, and Spanish and African rhythms played on fiddle, guitar, drum, bass, and the diatonic or German "push-button" accordion.

Creole originally described the "Born-in-America" first-generation offspring of early white French and Spanish settlers. But as television viewers of the critically acclaimed *Frank's Place* are aware, today Creole means black New Orleans. Creole music, explains Bergeron, borders on rhythm and blues, with a large dollop of piano accordion.

Voix de la Louisiane is good listening, even if you don't parlez-vous.

For Europeans, WRNO Worldwide is a tough catch and the show's timing is far from ideal. But North Americans will have little difficulty tuning in on Tuesday nights (Wednesday UTC) at 0430 Universal Time on 6185 kHz.

Creative Programming

The Bilingual Show
Radio France Internationale

The Bilingual Show is an innovative free-form musical presentation tucked into a tiny empty corner between RFI's regular English and French newscasts.

...a Paris au jourd hui...

This is most definitely not your average show. For starters, it has a changing cast, with such *noms-de-micro* as "Claudele Louvre" and "Michele Apollo." Voice timbre and inflection vary a bit from night to night, depending on the nominal hostess, who may be French or Anglo-Saxon; but the persona is the same—Gallic in spirit, flip, and just a touch sexy, with the ability to switch between French and English with the speed of summer lightning.

"A shot of French, a jigger of English . . . just shake and pour for a fantastique cocktail," purrs Claudele. "I do weekends, but I don't do windows."

It's *fou*, but it works!

The music is an easygoing and enjoyable grabbag of pops and romantic ballads, mostly French, presented *vite, vite*. Sometimes, though, there's a thread through it all, as with a St. Valentine's Day show built upon the eternal emotion, love, with vocalists from Baez to Piaf singing *toujours l'amour*. At other times, you may race through a time warp into the raucous cabaret music of Paris *entre les Guerres*.

The Bilingual Show is a bit like a sailor's bouillabaise—a casual mixture of ingredients, but very tasty. It's on, ever so briefly, at 0345 Universal Time to the Americas on 9800 and 11670 kHz, and to Europe on 3965 kHz. It's sometimes introduced as "the second broadcast of the day." We're still trying to find the first, but suspect these are airings of vintage tapes from back when the show was presented twice, instead of once, each morning.

Prepared by Passport/89 *Program Panel Chairman Don Jensen. Panel Members are Alex Batman, Don Moore, Sheryl Paszkiewicz, John Tuchscherer and George Zeller.*

The Taj Mahal, the world's most famous monument to a man's love for a woman. Photo by Tara Van den Hout

Michener

(continued from page 26)

Broadcasting. He remains a member, and, on the day following the *Passport/89* interview, he left for Washington and a scheduled BIB meeting.

The Board for International Broadcasting was established in the 1970s, in the wake of disclosures that the nominally private shortwave voices of Radio Liberty and Radio Free Europe were being covertly funded by the Central Intelligence Agency.

Michener and his fellow BIB members oversee the operations of Radio Liberty, which broadcasts from European-based world band stations to listeners in the Soviet Union, and of Radio Free Europe, which has a similar mission for eastern European audiences. Not the least of the BIB's duties is lobbying Congress to fund these two stations, a role which finds the Board in a kind of competition with the Voice of America.

"Considerable money is being pumped into the VOA," Michener says, carefully measuring his words. "I'd really better not comment on that. A great deal of the increased funds are [the result] of the personal factor relating to [VOA director] Charles Wick's remarkable and continued friendship with the President.

"I don't think that was money wasted, but I think it might not have been so allocated under a different situation. That's interfamily politics," he wryly observes.

Despite Gorbachev's *glasnost*, Michener says Radio Liberty remains "on the front line" of broadcasting into the Soviet Union. "What glasnost really means is for somebody else to say. But just look within the Soviet Union today. You have four, maybe five dissident groups . . . in Armenia, out beyond Lake Baikal in the Balkan states, for example. Those people still look to Radio Liberty as their principal source of information."

For service to his country, Michener has been awarded the Presidential Medal of Freedom, the highest civilian honor the nation can bestow.

Michener, it is said, specializes in long books with short titles — *Caravans*, *Centennial*, *Poland*, *Texas* and the rest. It is a demanding regimen — the herculean research, the odysseyan travel, and, only then, long hours of two-fingered typing, creating yet another bestseller. And the octogenarian author still has five or six books yet to write, he laughs, before he retires and is free to "travel and meet interesting people."

Spellbinding narration makes his non-fiction read like an adventure novel. But a reporter's feel for the facts gives his fiction the clear ring of authenticity. As much a journalist as a novelist, Michener flashes his press credentials easily and is comfortable among other newsmen like his good friend Walter Cronkite.

"When I lived at the Press Club, the famous Press Club in Tokyo, a number of the fellows had shortwave receivers. We used to listen to the BBC and Deutsche Welle, sort of to compare notes," says Michener. "And now, when I'm in Europe, I try to monitor Radio Moscow or Albania's Radio Tirana."

Recently back from yet another Pacific junket, Michener talks about broadcasting developments there. In Micronesia, world band is coming of age. A new station, WSZO, is on the air as the voice of the newly independent Republic of the Marshall Islands. On Palau, there is talk of a possible religious station which may be established by an American Gospel preacher-broadcaster. Elsewhere in the region, there is potential trouble in Paradise, particularly on the Francophone islands with their restive local populations.

"I've just been to Vanuatu," Michener says, "and, well, everybody there tries to hear what is going on in Noumea, New Caledonia. And I'm sure that's very important to them."

Meanwhile, he notes, the French do seem to be trying to bolster their broadcasting presence in that area.

He speaks also of the "very painful" situation in Fiji, where unrest between the native Fijians and the sizeable Hindi population led, not long ago, to a bloodless coup that overthrew the elected government.

"I believe that India is broadcasting into Fiji by shortwave . . . just to give them courage," Michener says. "I don't think it is at all venal, but it is disruptive."

Michener says radio is a first-rate tool in projecting a country's culture to others in this world, and to him music makes the biggest impact.

"I know world music intimately! I am a scholar in kabuki. Oh yes, and I have had the warmest experience with Chinese opera, which I love. I know Indonesian music. World music . . . the impact is very strong. I really think that on radio musical programs will be around for a long, long time," he says. "You know, the broadcasting of music is terribly seductive to listeners."

It is a happy tune—or maybe one of his favorite operatic arias—he hums each day. Unjaded, even after all those years and all those miles, he can still say of the world around him, "I can hardly wait to get up in the morning and see it all. I've never been bored."

And world band radio broadcasting, happily, lets the rest of us share at least a part of James A. Michener's never-boring, ever-interesting world.

Interview by Don Jensen.

Photo page 93: Lab tests provide valuable information for the Buyer's Guide. Here, technician Kathleen Nace of Sherwood Engineering checks for dynamic range, an important measurement of world band performance.

1989 Buyer's Guide
to World Band Radios

HOW TO BUY
A WORLD BAND RADIO

World band radios have to receive signals from afar, so it's not surprising that some better models are on the leading edge of technology. That's the good news. Less encouraging is that there is no shortage of low-technology clunkers on the market.

Specialized Tests for Evaluating Radios

That's why, starting eleven years ago, International Broadcasting Services conceived of and carried out the concept of specialized systematic testing of world band radios. These tests have grown over the years to involve a number of individuals, including "hands on" test panelists and specialized laboratory personnel. The reports, which have nothing to do with advertising, form the basis of our "Buyer's Guide," and even more detailed data on sophisticated world band receivers is available via *RDI White Papers*.

Taken together, these findings indicate that while really cheap world band radios serve little good purpose except for occasional use on trips, it's not necessary to spend hefty sums to obtain a really pleasant radio. Quality advanced-technology portables list from $199, and sometimes sell for less.

Best-Value Performers Start at $199

The best values are usually found among portables in the $199-280 range that are given a two-star rating in the "Buyer's Guide." These perform surprisingly well and are more than adequate for most listeners' needs. Too, they can be used both in the home and on trips, and they don't require a special antenna.

Higher-priced portables can have advantages, especially if you are a seasoned listener or inclined to go for the best. Even costlier tabletop models are available, but these are primarily for ferreting out the weakest and most obstinate stations. Tabletop models usually require a separate antenna, too.

What Do You Want to Hear?

In the final analysis, it's what you're trying to hear that should determine what you purchase. If you're interested only in the strong, clear stations, then there's no need to spend a king's ransom on equipment designed to hear a fly scratch its back on a Pacific Island. Look for a reasonably performing portable with high-quality audio.

Ratings of Overall Performance

★★★★★ Superb
★★★★ Excellent
★★★ Very Good
★★ Good
★ Fairly Good
☐ Fair
◫ Fair to Poor
◪ Poor to Fair
■ Poor

Classement General

★★★★★ Superbe
★★★★ Excellent
★★★ Très Bon
★★ Bon
★ Assez Bon
☐ Moyen
◫ Moyen à Médiocre
◪ Médiocre à Moyen
■ Médiocre

Clasificacion General

★★★★★ Magnífico
★★★★ Sobresaliente
★★★ Muy Bueno
★★ Bueno
★ Bastante Bueno
☐ Regular
◫ Regular hasta Mediocre
◪ Mediocre hasta Regular
■ Mediocre

Einteilung in Klassen

★★★★★ Ausgezeichnet
★★★★ Vorzüglich
★★★ Sehr Gut
★★ Gut
★ Ziemlich Gut
☐ Nicht Sehr Gut
◫ Nicht Sehr Gut zu Schlecht
◪ Schlecht zu Nicht Sehr Gut
■ Schlecht

Editor's Choice
The Bottom Line

In a recent analysis of television sets, *Consumer Reports* found that all but one of the models tested produced an acceptably good picture. "That's not surprising," the magazine explains, "because TV sets are a mature product, composed largely of goof-proof solid-state electronic circuitry, and the secrets of their manufacture are well understood all over the world."

World band radios aren't like TVs. Although, like television, world band radio is a mature product, it is only in the last decade or so that advances in technology have allowed them to perform well. Before that, affordable radios were hard to tune and programs were often disrupted by a cacophony of howls and squeals. There were a few good models, mostly for specialized use, but they were large and cost the equivalent of thousands of today's dollars.

Old-technology world band radios may be doomed to eventual extinction, but they're not there yet. Indeed, because they're so cheap they are sometimes among the best sellers to the uninitiated—who, understandably, tend to be turned off by the world band medium after having been jolted by their new radio's dubious performance. Some canny manufacturers, such as Sony, have realized the harm such poor first impressions can do to their longer-term market, and so have culled the really poor performers from their lines. Others, however, have not.

The best values in world band radios are list-priced between $150 and $250 and incorporate a number of technological advances. The Magnavox D2935, sold in Europe as the Philips D2935, is particularly interesting, inasmuch as it performs unusually well and is often available for under $200. The Sangean ATS-803, which appears under various names, also tends to sell for under $200. Although these Best Value designs have a number of important differences, either should please all but the most fastidious listener.

Although lower-priced sets suffer from significantly reduced performance, there are some reasonable offerings for as little as $69.99, before discounts.

At the other end of the price scale, costly tabletop models typically excel at flushing out the hardest-to-hear stations. However, they usually don't perform better at receiving the stronger stations most people are interested in hearing. On the other hand, some costly portables, such as the Sony ICF-2010 (sold outside North America as the ICF-2001D) and the Grundig Satellit 650, contain exceptional performance plusses to make everyday listening particularly enjoyable.

Here, then, are your editor's choices as the best sets in their price and function categories.

Under $100

Magnavox D1835/Philips D1835
Sangean MS 101

None of these diminutive models, which sell for $70 or less, will knock your socks off. Not only are their speakers small, they also let in quite a few unwanted sounds from competing stations. Their lists of features are tinier than the radios themselves, and they don't even receive some portions of the world band spectrum containing stations you may want to hear. Because there are so many stations on the air, their relatively modest ability to separate one signal from another is a real drawback.

Still, if you want a really inexpensive travel portable, certain of these—especially the Magnavox and Philips offerings—are good values.

$100 to $150

Sony ICF-4920/Sony ICF-4900 Mark II/
Sony ICF-5100
Sony ICF-7601
Toshiba RP-F11

Portables in this price category usually don't provide the "bang-per-buck" that the better low-cost portables do. Best Bet: Look for special deals. The Toshiba, for example, sometimes sells for only $20 or so more than models in the "low-cost" category.

$150 to $250

Magnavox D2935/Philips D2935
Sangean ATS-803A/Realistic DX440/
Eskab RX33

Here are the values! For less than the cost of a Korean TV, you can have a world band radio that provides very pleasant performance, indeed.

For most listeners, the Magnavox and Philips D2935 have an edge because of their superior audio quality and relative simplicity of operation.

They have, arguably, the best intersection of performance and price of any world band radio, and are often steeply discounted too. However, the Sangean series has advantages for certain specialized uses—listening to "utility" stations, for example (see "Action between the Bands"), and the Sangean has two bandwidths to the 'D2935's one.

The Magnavox/Philips D2935 is an exceptional performer within its price class

$250 to $400

Sony ICF-2010/Sony ICF-2001D
Magnavox D2999/Philips D2999
Panasonic RF-B60
Sony ICF-SW1S
Sony ICF-2003/Sony ICF-7600DS

This is the price range of most interest to listeners looking for premium portables.

Leading the pack in raw performance is Sony's high-tech ICF-2010 and ICF-2001D. Indeed, such is Sony's engineering superiority that even though these twin models have been out for some time, now, they are still the most advanced portables to be found at any price, anywhere.

That's the good news. The bad news is that these Sonys are not easy to operate—although they're no harder to handle than a VCR. Their audio quality is also not equal to the price tag. So, if simplicity of operation is of overriding importance to you, consider the Panasonic RF-B60. The 'B60 won't begin to do the handstands of Sony's high-tech model, but its performance is still quite good and its operation is all but foolproof.

The Sony SW-1S is easily the top performer in the tiny-for-traveling category. Indeed, it's the only pocket portable that provides worthy reception quality. Although its speaker is tiny, when stereo earpieces are used the audio quality is among the best of any set around.

At the other end of the size scale is the Magnavox and Philips D2999. Its audio quality is very good, and it's one of the few models laid out for horizontal operation. This allows it to serve not

only as a portable, but also as a de facto tabletop set. Still, audio quality, layout, and features aside, it doesn't differ appreciably from from its lower-cost 'D2935 sibling.

$400 to $900

Yaesu FRG-8800
Lowe HF-125
Grundig Satellit 400

This price range tends to disappoint. Yes, the Yaesu is a pleasant, well-made set, and is clearly the best in its price class. But like the Lowe it lacks the value of certain less costly models without having the pizzazz of monitor receivers.

The Yaesu and Lowe are tabletop models, whereas the Grundig is a conventional midsized portable.

$900 and Up

Japan Radio NRD-93
Kenwood R-5000
Japan Radio NRD-525
ICOM IC-R71
Grundig Satellit 650

Although none of these models has the advanced-technology synchronous detection feature found on the much cheaper Sony ICF-2010 and ICF-2001D, all have certain virtues over less costly sets.

The Japan Radio NRD-93's standout characteristic, although hardly a virtue, is its price. The '93 costs several *times* more than any other model tested, and for that you get exceptional ruggedness, quality of construction, high-caliber audio, and ease of repair. Its slightly less costly sibling, the NRD-92, looks similar but has certain drawbacks.

Those with less stratospheric budgets will find that although there are differences among the R-5000, NRD-525 and IC-R71 models, the similarities—including price—are far greater. All are superb for reception of hard-to-hear stations and are reasonably well-constructed. However, the R-5000 has the clear edge among the three in audio quality except for taping.

The maverick in the pack is the Grundig Satellit 650. Unlike other monitor receivers, which are designed mainly for the radio aficionado tuning faint signals, the '650 is designed for those listening to stronger, more conventional world band broadcasts. The '650's tone quality is unsurpassed—or even equalled—by any other model on the market, and it tapes well, too.

Comparative Ratings of Portable World Band Radios

World band portables are handy, affordable, and increasingly widely distributed. Many are even versatile enough to use not only for travel, but also for high-quality listening around the house.

Still, buying a world band portable isn't like buying, say, a VCR. All VCRs are made by three giant producers, regardless of the brand name on the cabinet, and they all perform similarly. World band portables, on the other hand, are made by ten separate producers. Not only do models vary greatly in performance from producer to producer, they often also vary markedly in performance from model to model within a given producer's line.

Performance vs. Price and Size

While price is often an indication of quality, it can be a fickle barometer. For example, the Sangean ATS-803A performs, overall, comparably to Sony's ICF-PRO80. But for the price of one 'PRO80, you can buy *two* '803As.

Size can also be misleading. That larger doesn't necessarily mean better is shown by the Magnavox/Philips D1835, a $69.99 compact that outperforms the full-sized $79.85 Rhapsody. Partly this is because the D1835 concentrates on world band performance, whereas the Rhapsody is characterized by glitzy appearance and features unrelated to world band performance.

The best performers are the two top-rated, but very different, three-star models: Sony's high-tech ICF-2010 and ICF-2001D (both are essentially identical; Sony model designations for the same radio often differ from country to country) and Grundig's quality-audio Satellit 650. However, very pleasant results can also be had, at lower cost, from some of the two-star models, notably the BEST VALUE Magnavox D2935 and Philips D2935.

Several Good Travel Portables Available

Most models tested, aside from those that are full-sized, are compact enough to be taken on flights. But if you travel with only a carry-on bag, you'll probably want to concentrate on the mini and compact portables. Sony recently introduced the first mini-portable—the ICF-SW1S—that is also a serious high-tech performer. Indeed, when earpieces are used, the 'SW1 provides audio fidelity that in some ways is superior to that of any other world band radio on the market . . . regardless of size or price.

Less costly small travel radios worth considering include the Sony ICF-4920 and identical siblings, along with the slightly larger Sony ICF-7601, Panasonic RF-B20 and Toshiba RP-F11. If price is the overriding consideration, there's the Magnavox D1835 and Philips D1835.

Models are listed in order of suitability for listening to world band radio broadcasts. Those models found to provide exceptional performance for the price are listed as "A BEST VALUE." For the US, list—suggested retail—prices are quoted. In the US discounts of 10 to 15 percent are not uncommon, whereas in Canada prices tend to run higher than US list. As list prices are largely an American phenomenon, the observed *selling* price ranges, expressed in dollars to permit comparison, are cited for the European Economic Community.

Certain models' ratings have been downgraded slightly from those in *Passport/88* to reflect advances in receiving technology and the emergence of the new 13 MHz world band segment. This new segment, along with expansion of the 11, 15, 17, and 21 MHz bands, comes into official use on July 1, 1989.

Mini-Portables

Welcome news for 1989 is Sony's ICF-SW1S, easily the best mini-portable available

---

★ ★ Sony ICF-SW1S

Price: $339.95 in US; $370–470 in Europe
Advantages: Superb high-quality, low distortion audio when earpieces used. Various helpful tuning features. Unusually straightforward to operate for a high-tech model. Universal Time clock. Alarm/sleep facilities. Quality-audio FM stereo when earpieces, which come standard with set, used. Comes standard with active (amplified) outboard antenna, in addition to the usual built-in antenna, to enhance reception of weak signals. Comes standard with ac power adaptor that adjusts automatically to local current level anywhere in the world. Night light for LCD.

Disadvantages: Tiny speaker provides mediocre audio quality. Lacks tuning knob. Tunes only in coarse 5 kHz increments, making for substandard reception of some "off-channel" broadcasts. Universal Time clock can be read only when radio is switched off. Volume control located at rear, making it easy to change accidentally. Mediocre image (spurious signal) rejection for price class. Earpieces, which rest loosely in the ears, fall out easily.

Overall: Although relatively costly, the new Sony ICF-SW1—the closest thing to a world band "Walkman" available—is, hands down, the best mini-portable on the market.

Sangean's latest small portable, new for 1989, includes coverage of the important 13 MHz segment

A   B E S T   V A L U E

☐ **Sony ICF-4920**

☐ **Sony ICF-4900 Mark II** Outside North America

☐ **Sony ICF-5100** Outside North America

Sony's mini ICF-4920 is also sold under other model designations

Price: $99.95 in US; $120–160 in Europe

Advantages: Superior adjacent-channel rejection, comparable to that of pricier sibling ICF-SW1S, for size class.

Disadvantages: Mediocre audio quality. Limited coverage of world band spectrum includes omission of important 13 MHz segment. Lacks digital channel display.

Overall: The best of the lower-cost minis, the '4920 is nonetheless of interest almost exclusively to the weight-conscious traveler.

◪ Sangean MS 101

Price: $89.95 in US; $65–125 in Europe

Advantages: Inexpensive.

Disadvantages: Mediocre overall performance. Limited coverage of world band spectrum. Lacks digital channel display. Inferior audio quality. Less likely than most models to be steeply discounted.

Overall: A low-priced, modest mini portable of interest almost exclusively to the weight- and price-conscious traveler. Also sold under a wide and ever-changing variety of brand names, including Emerson, Goodmans and Siemens.

◪ Panasonic RF-B10
◪ National B10 Asia

Panasonic's RF-B10 is tiny, but not much else

Price: $94.95 in US; $95–135 in Europe

Advantages: Relatively inexpensive. Two-year warranty.

Disadvantages: Substandard overall performance. Limited coverage of world band spectrum includes omission of important 13 MHz segment. Mediocre audio quality. Lacks digital channel display.

Overall: Better, more advanced choices available at same or lower prices.

Compact Portables

★ ★ Panasonic RF-B60
★ ★ Panasonic RF-B60L
★ ★ National B60 Asia

Price: (RF-B60): $279.95 in US; (RF-B60L): $280–400 in Europe

Advantages: Very easy-to-operate advanced-technology radio. Pleasant audio quality. Various helpful tuning features. Universal Time clock. Alarm/sleep facilities. Two-year warranty.

Disadvantages: Tuning knob cumbersome to turn rapidly.

Overall: A very nice, easy-to-use portable for listening to noncritical favorite programs.

Panasonic's RF-B60 is pleasant sounding and unusually straightforward to operate

★ ★ Sony ICF-2003 North America
★ ★ Sony ICF-7600DS Outside North America

Sony's ICF-2003/ICF-7600DS, a time-tested compact portable

Price: $289.95 in US; $260–400 in Europe
Advantages: Various helpful tuning features. Separately displayed Universal Time clock. Alarm/sleep facilities. One of the few lightweight portables suitable for reception of "utility" signals (see "Action between the Bands").
Disadvantages: Sensitivity slightly below par with built-in antenna. Pedestrian audio quality. Lacks tuning knob.
Overall: Similar to the new Sony ICF-SW1, but a bit larger and lacking accessories and high-quality ear-piece audio, the Sony ICF-2003/ICF-7600DS is a worthy portable for air travel.

★ ★ Sony ICF-PRO80 North America and certain other markets
★ ★ Sony ICF-PRO70 Elsewhere

Price: $439.95 in US; $550–700 in Europe; (ICF-PRO70): $600–650 in Europe
Advantages: Comes equipped with versatile VHF scanner (reduced coverage in 'PRO70 version). Above average at bringing in weak world band stations. One of the few lightweight portables suitable for reception of "utility" signals (see "Action between the Bands").
Disadvantages: Awkward to operate. Operation of outboard scanner module especially cumbersome, as it

requires removal and replacement of battery pack and antenna. Mediocre audio quality. Lacks tuning knob and most travel features.
Overall: Of interest mainly to "DXers" in need of a small world band portable with a VHF scanner.

Sony's handheld scanner doubles as a world band portable

★ Panasonic RF-B40
★ Panasonic RF-B40L
★ National B40 Asia

Panasonic's RF-B40 is very easy to use

Price: $219.95 in US; (Panasonic RF-B40L): $220–320 in Europe
Advantages: Very easy to use. Two-year warranty.
Disadvantages: Tunes only in coarse 5 kHz increments, which leads to suboptimal adjacent-channel rejection. Lacks tuning knob.
Overall: Although lacking in any strong pluses or minuses, the 'B40 is a pleasant, easy-to-operate portable for noncritical listening.

★ Sony ICF-7700 North America
★ Sony ICF-7600DA Outside North America

Price: $259.95 in US; $230–300 in Europe
Advantages: Very easy to use. Universal Time clock. Alarm/sleep functions.

Disadvantages: Coarse 5 kHz tuning increments create performance shortcomings, including substandard adjacent-channel rejection. Slightly limited coverage of world band spectrum.

Overall: A better bet for the technically timid is the comparably priced Panasonic RF-B60.

Sony's ICF-7700/ICF-7600DA is unusually easy to operate

A   B   E   S   T   V   A   L   U   E
☐ Sony ICF-7601

The Sony ICF-7601, new for 1989, is the latest version of one of Sony's best-selling world band models

Price: $139.95 in US; $125–170 in Europe

Advantages: High sensitivity aids in reception of weak stations.

Disadvantages: Lacks digital channel display. Slightly limited coverage of world band spectrum. Adjacent-channel rejection, although reasonable, not equal to that of many other Sony models.

Overall: This latest entrant in the popular ICF-7600 series—well over a million have been sold—represents a slight, but noticeable, improvement over earlier versions.

A   B   E   S   T   V   A   L   U   E
☐ Toshiba RP-F11

Price: $129.95 in US; $170–200 in Europe, therefore a best value only in some countries

Advantages: More likely than most models to be steeply discounted.

Disadvantages: Limited coverage of world band spectrum. Lacks digital channel display. Modest overall performance. Not widely available.

Overall: A reasonable performer that, when steeply discounted, can be an above-average value.

Toshiba's RP-F11 is one of the few compact portables with an analog signal-strength meter

A   B   E   S   T   V   A   L   U   E
▨ Panasonic RF-B20 Most countries
▨ Panasonic RF-B20L Europe
▨ National B20 Asia

Panasonic RF-B20 has good audio for a compact, but lacks coverage of 13 MHz

Price: $134.95 in US; (RF-B20L): $120–195 in Europe

Advantages: Unusually good audio for such a small radio. Two-year warranty.

Disadvantages: Limited coverage of world band spectrum includes omission of important 13 MHz segment. Mediocre adjacent-channel rejection. Lacks digital channel display.

Overall: A reasonable performer that would be much better were it able to sort stations out more successfully.

☑ Magnavox D1835   North America
☑ Philips D1835   Outside North America
☑ Philips D7476   Outside North America

Price: (D1835): $69.99 in US; $85–120 in Europe;
(D7476): $150–220 in Europe
Advantages: Inexpensive. Built-in cassette recorder
(D7476 only).
Disadvantages: Modest overall performance. Limited
coverage of world band spectrum. Lacks digital chan-
nel display.
Overall: A so-so performer, the D1835 is nonetheless the
best of the truly inexpensive portables.

"King of The Cheaps" is the Magnavox/Philips D1835, a
reasonable performer for very little money

☑ Grundig Yacht Boy 215

Grundig's Yacht Boy 215 lacks coverage of 13 MHz segment

Price: $119.95; $105–155 in Europe
Advantages: Universal Time clock/timer.
Disadvantages: Modest overall performance. Limited
coverage of world band spectrum includes omission of
important 13 MHz segment. Lacks digital channel
display.
Overall: Of interest primarily to travelers seeking a
low-cost portable with clock/timer facilities.

☑ Grundig Yacht Boy 210

Price: $99.95 in US; $90–140 in Europe.
Identical to preceding Grundig Yacht Boy 215, except
that clock/timer facilities are omitted.

☑ Opal OP-35   Various countries
☑ Siemens RK 702   Europe

The new Opal OP-35, a great clock with a mediocre radio, is
also sold as the Siemens RK 702

Price: $99.95 in US; (RK 702): $75–160 in Europe
Advantages: Relatively inexpensive. Includes Universal
Time and worldwide multicountry clock/timer.
Disadvantages: Very limited coverage of world band
spectrum. Mediocre overall performance. Drifts off
channel when held. Lacks digital channel display. Not
widely available.
Overall: A clock that comes with a radio, rather than *vice
versa*.

■ Sangean ATS-801

Sangean's ATS-801 is one of the worst sets tested

Price: $109.95 in US; $85–140 in Europe
Advantages: Digital channel display, an unusual feature
in this price class.
Disadvantages: Dreadful overall performance. Tortoise-
slow tuning. Limited coverage of world band spectrum.
Overall: Although with improved battery operation for
1989, the ATS-801 remains a model with little to
commend it.

Midsized Portables

★ ★ ★ **Sony ICF-2010** North America

★ ★ ★ **Sony ICF-2001D** Outside North America

High-tech Sony ICF-2010 is the most advanced portable tested

Price: $419.95 in US; $500–690 in Europe

Advantages: Innovative synchronous detector circuit results in unsurpassed adjacent-channel rejection within world, longwave, and mediumwave AM bands. Two bandwidths allow for superior tradeoff between audio fidelity and adjacent-channel rejection. Numerous helpful tuning features. Separately displayed Universal Time clock. Alarm/sleep/timer facilities. Pushbuttons for 36 memory channels unusually useful and handy to operate. Some reception of air band signals. The best portable for reception of "utility" signals (see "Action between the Bands").

Disadvantages: Audio quality below par for price class. Proliferation of controls and high-tech features may intimidate or confuse some. Memories and time setting sometimes erase when set is jostled.

Overall: Except for audio quality and ease of operation, the best performer among midsized-and-smaller portables.

A   B   E   S   T   V   A   L   U   E

★ ★ **Grundig Satellit 400**

Grundig's Satellit 400 is easier to carry around than its '650 sibling

Price: $449.00 in US; $300-380 in Europe, therefore a best value only in some countries

Advantages: Fairly pleasant world band audio quality, superior FM audio quality. Numerous helpful tuning features. Good overall world band performance. Universal Time clock. Alarm facility. Superior FM reception. Unusually handy carrying handle.

Disadvantages: Unstable synthesizer produces "whooshing" oscillating sound in lower world radio bands and degrades reception of "utility" signals. Less likely than most models to be steeply discounted.

Overall: A pleasant, all-around receiver.

A   B   E   S   T   V   A   L   U   E

★ ★ **Magnavox D2935** North America

★ ★ **Philips D2935** Outside North America

Magnavox/Philips D2935 is an excellent set for the price

Price: $249.99 in US; $280–370 in Europe

Advantages: Pleasant audio quality. Numerous helpful tuning features. Performance good in most bands. More likely than most models to be steeply discounted.

Disadvantages: Membrane keypad lacks "feel." A bit larger and heavier for travel than most midsized portables.

Overall: A simplified and more compact version of the Magnavox and Philips D2999, the D2935 is an exceptional performer within its price class.

A   B   E   S   T   V   A   L   U   E

★ ★ **Sangean ATS-803A**

★ ★ **Realistic DX-440**

★ ★ **Eska RX 33** Europe

★ ★ **Matsui MR 4099** Europe

Price: (ATS-803A): $239.95 in US; $170–330 in Europe; (DX-440): $199.95 in US; $225–260 in Europe; (RX-33): $250–300 in Europe; (MR 4099): £99.99 in UK

Advantages: Numerous helpful tuning features. Performance slightly above average. Two bandwidths allow for superior tradeoff between audio fidelity and adjacent-channel rejection. Superior reception of "utility" stations for price class (see "Action between the Bands").

Disadvantages: Rarely steeply discounted.

Overall: With balanced, all-around performance, the various designations of the ATS-803A, an improved version of the earlier ATS-803, are runner-up Best Buys in their price class. Also reportedly sold recently in Canada as the Emerson ATS-803A and in Europe as the Siemens RK 641 (on new version, "mono stereo" switch also reads "wide narrow"; otherwise, it is the original version; see "Discontinued Models").

Sangean's top-of-the-line ATS-803A is also sold under various other designations, such as Radio Shack's new Realistic DX-440

▣ Realistic DX-360

Price: $99.95 in US

Advantages: Fairly pleasant audio quality.

Disadvantages: Lacks any form of even remotely accurate channel display, making it an arduous, hit-and-miss procedure to locate a desired station. Mediocre overall performance. Slightly limited coverage of world band spectrum.

Overall: The archetypal "shortwave radio" of twenty years ago. One can but wonder how many people have obtained a DX-360 from Radio Shack stores "to see what world band radio is like," only to be turned off for good by the DX-360's disappointing performance.

Radio Shack's disappointing Realistic DX-360 performs much more poorly than its DX-440 sibling

Full-Sized Portables

★ ★ ★ Grundig Satellit 650

Grundig's beefy Satellit 650 has outstanding audio quality

Price: $1,149.00 in US; $650–950 in Europe

Advantages: Excellent audio quality. Above-average performance in all bands. Two full bandwidths and a third pseudo-bandwidth allow for superior tradeoff between audio fidelity and adjacent-channel rejection. Numerous helpful tuning features. Universal Time clock. Alarm/timer facilities. Superior FM reception. Large size and heft make it relatively well-suited for use as a home receiver.

Disadvantages: Too large and heavy for portable use except around the home and on automobile trips. Less likely than most models to be steeply discounted. Motorized preselector tuning results in above-average mechanical complexity.

Overall: A favorite for hour-after-hour listening, the massive '650 is arguably the best-sounding world band radio available new.

★ ★ Magnavox D2999 North America
★ ★ Philips D2999 Outside North America

The D-2999, sold by Philips and Magnavox alike, is larger and heavier than the D-2935

Price: $399.00 in US; $420–650 in Europe

Advantages: Unusually pleasant audio quality—even better than that of its D2935 sibling. Numerous helpful tuning features. Performance above average in most bands. Two bandwidths allow for superior tradeoff between audio fidelity and adjacent-channel rejection. Lays down horizontally, with speakers on both the top and front, and thus is one of the few portables tested that also serves as a true tabletop receiver for use at home. Universal Time clock. Alarm facility.

Disadvantages: Mediocre reception of "utility" stations for a full-sized portable.

Overall: A fine-sounding world band receiver, the D2999 combines many of the virtues of a portable with those of a tabletop model, but in many other respects is remarkably similar to its less-costly D2935 sibling.

☑ Marc II
☑ Pan Crusader

Price: $400–600 Worldwide; (Pan): $350–500 in Europe
Advantages: Unusually broad coverage of radio frequency spectrum. Universal Time clock. Sleep/timer facilities.
Disadvantages: Marginal overall performance within certain portions of the world band spectrum. Poor adjacent-channel rejection. Preselector tuning control adds greatly to complexity to operation. Not widely available.
Overall: A dreary performer at any price.

■ Venturer Multiband
■ Rhapsody Multiband

The Venturer Multiband, sold under various names, is long on glitz and short on guts

Price: $99.95 in US ($129.95 with Cassette Recorder); (Rhapsody): $79.85 in US
Advantages: Inexpensive. Covers VHF-TV and air/weather bands. Audio quality at least average. Genuine signal-strength meter, a rarity at this price. Built-in cassette recorder (one version only).
Disadvantages: World band coverage omits the 2, 3, 13, 15, 17, 21, and 26 MHz segments. Lacks any form of even remotely accurate channel display, making it an

arduous, hit-and-miss procedure to locate a desired station. Mediocre overall performance.

Overall: For those who don't know any better. Sold widely under various names, but with identical appearance, by mail order stores, such as Haverhills ("Venturer") and Blair Shoppe ("Rhapsody"), as well as by credit-card companies.

Discontinued Models

The following models have reportedly been discontinued, but may still be available new at some retail outlets. Prices are in the range of actual or estimated sale prices as of the time *Passport/89* went to press. Because these are discontinued models, prices vary widely and interesting bargains can sometimes be struck with retailers seeking to unload outdated inventory. In one very recent case, a *Passport* reader in Houston, Texas, purchased a brand-new Sony CRF-1—originally an $1,800 receiver—from a local radio dealer for $100!

★ ★ ★ ★ Sony CRF-1

A moderately large semi-professional communications receiver suited to field portable applications. Nearly every aspect of performance, including reception of "utility" signals, is top-drawer. Only the "wide" bandwidth and audio quality disappoint, and tuning features are limited. Very few sets were ever made, so this is a tough find. Under $1,000.

★ ★ ★ Panasonic RF-9000
★ ★ ★ National DR-90

Excellent audio quality and overall performance, but much too large and heavy for portable use. Grossly overpriced when in Panasonic's line, but if you can find it for under $1,000 it could be worth considering. Very few sets were ever made, so this is a tough find. Under $2,000.

★ ★ ★ Grundig Satellit 600

All but identical to Grundig Satellit 650. Under $700.

★ ★ Panasonic RF-B600
★ ★ National B600

Fairly good performance. Lays down horizontally, with speaker on front panel, and thus is one of the few portables tested that also serves as a true tabletop receiver for use at home. However, synthesizer's "laggy" operation slows down bandscanning on all bands. Reasonably good reception of "utility" signals. Only very recently discontinued. Under $600.

★ ★ Sony ICF-2002
★ ★ Sony ICF-7600D

Essentially identical, except for cosmetics, to Sony ICF-2003. Still sold new in many parts of the world. Under $250.

★ ★ Panasonic RF-3100
★ ★ National DR-31

Serves as either a large portable or a home-based set with pleasant, but not distinguished, overall performance. Suffers from high battery consumption. Under $400.

★ Panasonic RF-B300
★ National B300

Very similar in performance to the Panasonic RF-2900 and GE World Monitor (see following). A pleasant, if slightly old fashioned, model that was only very recently discontinued. Under $250.

★ Panasonic RF-2900
★ National DR-29

Similar to the General Electric World Monitor. Very scarce on the new market anywhere, but still found new as the similar and more recent Panasonic RF-B300 (see preceding). Under $175.

★ General Electric World Monitor

Pleasant overall performance, but with modest frequency stability. Originally sold new in US and PXs only. Under $200.

★ Sony ICF-2001

Modest adjacent-channel rejection, excessive battery consumption and its keypad is prone to failure. Otherwise, in most respects it's similar to the smaller and lighter ICF-2003/ICF-7600DS. In principle, this should have vanished long ago from the new-radio market, but from time to time new samples emerge on dealer shelves and catalogs. Around $170.

★ Sangean ATS-803

Also available (not tested) as:

Goodmans ATS-803
Matsui 4099
Saisho SW5000
Siemens RK641
Supertech SR-16H

The earlier version of the Sangean ATS-803A. Lacks the second and much tighter selectivity position that can be chosen on the current version, as well as various other operating and performance improvements. This version still available new in many parts of the world, but not desirable unless sold at a substantial discount over current price of newer and better "A" version. Inferior to "A" version for reception of "utility" signals. Under $200.

☐ Panasonic RF-2200
☐ National DR-22

Similar to the General Electric World Monitor, above, except that the '2200 utilizes a tiresome Rube Goldberg arrangement to tune in stations. Very, very hard to find new. Under $150.

☐ Sharp FV-610

Notable mainly for its high sensitivity and concomitant propensity to "overload." Limited coverage of world band spectrum includes omission of important 13 MHz segment. Selectivity only fair. Under $150.

☐ Panasonic RF-6300
☐ National DR-63

Pleasant audio, but overall performance not appropriate to a set in this price class. Under $350.

☐ Panasonic RF-B50
☐ National B50

Above-average audio for such a small set and covers much, but not all, of the world radio spectrum; for example, the new 13 MHz segment is omitted. Not sensitive to weak signals. Analog frequency readout. Under $150.

☐ Sony ICF-4910
☐ Sony ICF-4900

Identical in all but styling to Sony ICF-4920/ICF-4900 Mark II. Still found for sale new in various parts of the world. Under $100.

☐ Kenwood R-11
☐ Trio R-11

Virtually identical to the Toshiba RP-F11. Rarely found, inasmuch as few were ever produced. Under $100.

☐ Sony ICF-7600A
☐ Sony ICF-7600AW

Similar to the Sony ICF-7601 (see), but with reduced coverage of world band spectrum; notably, the 13 MHz segment is omitted. Still available new in many parts of the world. Under $120.

☐ Grundig Yacht Boy 700

Mediocre overall performance. Still available new in some European stores. About $200.

☑ Grundig Satellit 300

Uninspiring performance, notably insensitivity to weak signals. Rarely found and even more rarely missed. Under $250.

☑ Sharp FV-310

Identical to the Sharp FV-610, but lacks digital frequency readout, clock/timer and stereo FM. Under $130.

☑ Grundig Yacht Boy 650

Limited coverage of world band spectrum includes omission of important 13 MHz segment. Audio quality is above average in quality and strength, but world band radio performance is only so-so, overall. Under $200.

☑ Panasonic RF-799

Limited coverage of world band spectrum includes omission of important 13 MHz segment. Mediocre overall performance. Under $300.

☑ Silver XF1900 Europe only

Pleasant audio and digital frequency readout, but otherwise mediocre performance from an outdated design. Recently introduced world band radios from Silver have been even worse than the discontinued XF1900. About $150.

◪ Sangean SG-789

Mediocre overall performance and audio quality, and limited coverage of world band spectrum. Sold under a wide variety of brand names, some of which may still be available. According to Sangean America, superseded by the Sangean MS-101, although the SG-789, which omits 13 MHz, continues to be advertised. Under $70.

◼ Panasonic RF-9
◼ Panasonic RF-9L
◼ National Micro 00

More a toy than a serious radio. Replaced by the very similar model RF-B10. Under $100.

The Passport *equipment review team is led by* Lawrence Magne. Laboratory tests are performed by J. Robert Sherwood.

Comparative Ratings of Tabletop World Band Receivers

I n almost any field, there is a version that may be considered a class apart. In world band radio, as in television, this is the monitor set. All world band monitor sets are tabletop models, but not all tabletop models are monitor sets.

In world band, the receiver carries most of the burden of converting often faint signals from a congested radio spectrum into intelligible programming you can enjoy. True, a good outboard antenna can help significantly, but it's not as in satellite reception in which the television set itself is far less important than are the antenna dish and intermediate outboard electronic hardware.

This difference shows in the price. A TV set typically constitutes less than 25 percent of the total cost of a satellite receiving system, whereas a world band radio usually equals more than 90 percent of the total system cost. It's almost the whole ballgame, so it's important to choose your world band radio prudently.

In principle, a monitor-class world band receiver should process difficult signals as far as the cutting edge of technology allows and with the best fidelity possible. Professional-class equipment has the added task of doing this day-in and day-out with a high "MTBF" (mean time between failures, a measure of reliability). Fortunately, as professional receivers can set you back thousands of dollars, a super-high MTBF is of little relevance for ordinary world band listening. Nevertheless, we included one particularly attractive model of professional receiver in our tests.

In practice, models rated with four or more stars qualify as monitor receivers. They excel at reception of weak, difficult-to-hear signals, and they're well-constructed. Unfortunately, they all fall short in fidelity. The Japan Radio NRD-525 and ICOM IC-R71 are particularly disappointing in this regard, and even the Kenwood R-5000 and the professional Japan Radio NRD-93 are far from exceptional.

Among other things, none of these monitor-grade receivers possesses synchronous detection, a high-tech feature that enhances fidelity by eliminating unwanted intrusion from adjacent-channel signals, and also by reducing certain types of distortion. Fortunately, as we go to press there are encouraging signs that at least one enhanced-fidelity monitor receiver may be reaching the market by the time you read this (see page 113).

The bottom line is that we have found only four tabletop models—all costly—that significantly outperform the best of the available portables. If you're a dedicated world band listener, one of these high-quality tabletops may be close to ideal. But if you're a relative newcomer to the medium, or are looking for your first set, stick to the three- and two-star portables—some of which have better audio fidelity than most monitor receivers. If you decide later on to get a tabletop receiver, you can always use the portable for trips and listening on the balcony or in the backyard.

Among the four highest-rated tabletops—from Kenwood, Japan Radio, and ICOM—differences in overall performance, other than audio quality, are relatively minor, although the specific differences may very well be enough to make you prefer one model over the rest. However, variations in actual selling prices, especially in Europe, can be considerable. Any of these four top sets should be a delight to own, with the only disappointment being the collective absence of fidelity-enhancing synchronous detection.

If these models are too pricey for you, the Yaesu FRG-8800 or Lowe HF-125 may be appealing. Although neither is a stellar performer, both provide reception quality that is quite pleasing. Too, you may wish to consider the full-sized Magnavox D2999 or Philips D2999 portables reviewed in the "Comparative Ratings of Portable World Band Radios" section of this *Passport*. Although these are, strictly speaking, portables, they also possess a number of characteristics of tabletop models, but at a much lower cost.

If you're interested in hearing "utility" signals, nearly any tabletop model will suffice. This is hardly surprising as—unlike nearly all portables—most tabletops have been specifically designed for this purpose. For more on this subject, please refer to the article, "Action between the Bands." If you're interested in computer control of your monitor receiver, contact Electronic Equipment Bank (C.R.I.S. Department) or Universal Shortwave, both of which are in the US.

Our unabridged laboratory and hands-on test results are far too exhaustive to reproduce here, as they run quite a number of pages for each model of receiver. If you are interested in these detailed reports, they are now available as *RDI White Papers*, details of which may be found elsewhere in this *Passport*.

Receivers are listed in order of suitability for listening to world band radio broadcasts. Keep in mind that if you listen mainly to weaker stations—or to speech, such as newscasts—audio quality will be of less importance than if you listen mainly to musical programs over strong, clear stations. Most tabletop models are available only from electronics and world band specialty outlets.

For the US, list prices are quoted. In the US,

discounts of 10 to 15 percent are not unusual, whereas in Canada prices tend to run slightly higher than US list. As list prices are largely an American phenomenon, the observed *selling* price ranges, expressed in dollars to permit comparison, are cited for Europe (Common Market).

Professional Monitor Receiver

★ ★ ★ ★ ★ Japan Radio NRD-93

Japan Radio NRD-93—built tough for professional applications

Price: $7,995.00 in US; around $10,000 in Europe
Advantages: Superb reception of all types of world band signals. Professional-quality construction with exceptional durability to survive around-the-clock use in such difficult environments as the tropical high seas. Unusually easy to repair. Excellent ergonomics. Above-average audio for a tabletop model. Sophisticated optional scanner allows for a certain degree of automated listening. Superb reception of "utility" signals.
Disadvantages: Dreadfully expensive. Lacks certain advanced-technology features.
Overall: A sterling professional-quality receiver when money is no object. Nevertheless, even though it is a pleasure to operate and as tough as a tank, its performance is not appreciably different from that of less-costly monitor models. Sold through Japan Radio marine outlets, as well as a few world band specialty firms.

Tabletop Monitor Receivers

★ ★ ★ ★ ★ Kenwood R-5000

Price: $999.00 in US; $1,100–1,600 in Europe
Advantages: Superb reception of all types of world band signals. Unusually good audio for a tabletop, provided a suitable outboard speaker is used. Exceptionally flexible operating controls. Excellent reception of "utility" signals.

Disadvantages: Ergonomics only fair. Replacement of standard, but mediocre, wide bandwidth filter with high-quality YK-88A-1 substitute adds $80 to cost. Audio badly distorted at tape-recording output.
Overall: Superb performance at a non-stratospheric price. In UK, some samples may appear under "Trio" brand name.

Kenwood R-5000 is excellent performer with audio quality to match

★ ★ ★ ★ ★ Japan Radio NRD-525

Japan Radio NRD-525 features top-notch performance with slide-in circuit boards for ease of repair

Price: $1,295.00 in US; $1,350–2,000 in Europe
Advantages: Superb reception of all types of world band signals. Highly flexible operating controls. Very good ergonomics. Quality of construction slightly above average. Modular plug-in circuit boards enhance ease of repair. Sophisticated scanner allows for a certain degree of automated listening. Excellent-to-superb reception of "utility" signals.
Disadvantages: Audio quality only fair. Surface-mounted devices make replacement of discrete components very difficult. Relatively limited dealer network.
Overall: A superb performer that's well put together, but is somewhat lacking in fidelity.

★ ★ ★ ★ ICOM IC-R71

Price: $999.00 in US; $1,100–1,600 in Europe
Advantages: Superb reception of weak, hard-to-hear signals. Highly flexible operating controls. Excellent reception of "utility" signals.

Disadvantages: Mediocre audio quality. Substandard ergonomics. Operating system software erases, requiring reprogramming by ICOM service center, should backup battery die.

Overall: A favorite among serious DXers, but not equal to other tabletop models for quality-audio program listening.

ICOM IC-R71A—a favorite among radio aficionados

Regular Tabletop Receivers

★ ★ ★ Yaesu FRG-8800

FRG-8800 is Yaesu's latest offering

Price: $699.95 in US; $800–1,000 in Europe

Advantages: Flexible operating controls. Audio quality slightly above average for tabletop model. Fairly good ergonomics. Universal Time clock.

Disadvantages: Bandwidths too broad. Reportedly above-average rate of microprocessor failure, usually user-correctable. Reception of "utility" stations, although acceptable, is below average for tabletop model.

Overall: A well-balanced performer.

★ ★ ★ Lowe HF-125

Price: £375.00 in UK; around $700 on Continent

Advantages: Unusually straightforward to operate for tabletop model. Generous bandwidth flexibility. Unusually rugged. Very good audio for tabletop model. Optional battery pack allows for field portable use. Optional synchronous detection (see "Disadvantages," below). Attractively priced within the UK.

Disadvantages: Some operating controls provide limited flexibility. Slight insensitivity to weak signals. Trace of digital-circuit "whine." Excessively slow automatic-gain control recovery. Optional synchronous detector circuit, not recommended, cannot select one sideband over another, thus defeating its main purpose. Extremely limited dealer network; no longer distributed within the US. Not particularly appropriate for reception of "utility" stations.

Overall: A plain vanilla, but tough and easy-to-operate little unit that appears to have sold poorly more because it lacks "bells and whistles" than because of its performance, which is quite respectable, and its audio quality, which is superior.

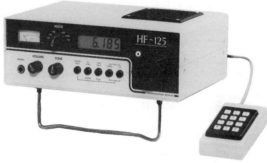

Lowe's rugged HF-125 receiver is easy to operate

★ ★ Kenwood R-2000

R-2000 is Kenwood's lowest priced model

Price: $749.95 in US; $750–1,250 in Europe

Advantages: Straightforward to operate, with good ergonomics. Audio quality slightly above average for tabletop model. Universal Time clock. Reception of "utility" stations, although not outstanding, is the best among portables or tabletops in the under-$900 price bracket.

Disadvantages: Performance materially compromised by "overloading." Bandwidths too broad.

Overall: Generally pleasurable for listening to most world band programs, but not much more. Occasionally sold under "Trio" brand name.

☐ Heathkit/Zenith SW-7800

Heath's SW-7800 is the only world band radio available as a kit

Price: $349.95 in US

Advantages: Lowest-priced tabletop model tested. Relatively visible availability in North America through Heath's vast catalog mailings.

Disadvantages: Poorest performance of any tabletop tested. Barely functional for reception of "utility" stations. Available only in kit form, requiring dozens of hours to construct.

Overall: Unless kits are your special passion, you'd be better off with one of the higher-rated portables.

Discontinued Models

A number of recently discontinued models are still occasionally found new on dealer shelves or, more frequently, nearly new on the used receiver market. However, unlike discontinued portables, discontinued tabletop models are not always heavily discounted.

Prices, except where otherwise indicated, are selling prices for new units in the US. Used sets usually sell for very roughly half price or a bit more. Availability of most discontinued models on the new receiver market is extremely limited.

★ ★ ★ ★ ★ Japan Radio NRD-515

Price: $650-700 (used)
The near-professional Japan Radio NRD-515 is built like a fortress and provides intelligible signal reception under all but the most excruciating situations. It's also the only set in our list of discontinued tabletops that provides top-drawer reception of "utility" signals.

How rugged is the '515? In 1988, lightning all but destroyed our South American monitoring post, blowing furniture into splinters, fusing wire into blobs, and partially melting the aluminum cabinet of the main '515 monitoring receiver and its memory accessory. The set was pulled from the debris, plugged in, and it worked—and continues to work—perfectly.

Operation of this hairy-chested receiver is straightforward and pleasant, but the '515's woolly audio is not well-suited to the reproduction of music. However, Sherwood Engineering in the US offers modifications and an SE-3 outboard synchronous detector that turn the '515 into an enhanced-fidelity device.

Because it's so tough, the '515 is actively sought out on the used market, where samples in excellent condition fetch around $700—add to that amount if it has accessories or is is Sherwood-modified. A classic that was scooped up quickly, so only used samples—highly prized—appear to be available for 1989.

Sherwood SE-3 synchronous detector helps make Japan Radio NRD-515 into an excellent enhanced-fidelity receiver

★ ★ ★ Sony ICF-6800W

Price: Under $600
Lacking the "bells and whistles" found on most other tabletop models, the Sony ICF-6800W provides unusually well-rounded and pleasant results, along with uncomplicated operation. In particular, its audio quality is well above average. Another unusual plus with the '6800 is that it operates off either ac power or batteries. Its chief shortcoming lies in its modest dynamic range, which can result in "overloading," with stations sounding as though they're piled atop each other when they really aren't. New samples still surface every now and then.

★ ★ ★ McKay Dymek DR 101-6

Price: Under $1,000
The best of the McKay Dymek line, the DR 101-6 manages to incorporate McKay's innovative ideas, such as a variable-rate slewing knob, without some of the drawbacks evidenced on earlier versions of the DR 22 and DR 33 series. As with other models in the McKay line, the DR 101-6 comes equipped with a substandard speaker and mediocre front-end selectivity. But with a worthy external speaker the end result can be quite pleasant. Few sets made, so very hard to find—new or used.

★ ★ ★ Yaesu FRG-7700

Price: Under $550

Similar in performance to the newer FRG-8800, but lacking many of the '8800's "bells and whistles," the '7700—which has three bandwidths, instead of the '8800's two—can be an attractive alternative when it is priced to move.

★ ★ Kenwood R-1000
★ ★ Trio R-1000

Price: Under $500

Although the current Kenwood R-2000 is in many ways a more modern receiver than the older R-1000, the '1000 is less prone to "overloading," and thus continues to be preferred where long antennas are used. All but impossible to find new.

★ ★ McKay Dymek DR 33-C

Price: Under $1,000

McKay's earliest models, the DR 22 and DR 33 series, were not entirely successful performers—the McKay Dymek DR 101 series (see) is better. New samples may still be available from the manufacturer and others.

★ ★ Ten-Tec RX325

Price: Under $700

Discontinued because of lack of parts availability. Simple, rugged, with overall performance somewhat below par. Few were made, but it may still found new here and there in North America and Western Europe.

★ Bearcat DX1000

Price: Under $600

A serviceable, but uninspiring, radio seemingly designed to be produced at rock-bottom cost. Given the several better alternatives, there is precious little reason to select this model. Sometimes still surfaces new in various parts of the world.

★ Kenwood R-600
★ Trio R-600

Price: Under $400

Decent, uncomplicated reception with a minimum of operating controls and features. All but impossible to find new.

★ Panasonic RF-4900
★ National DR-49

Price: Under $500

A modest performer with surprisingly pleasant audio quality. Operates off both ac power and batteries. All but impossible to find new.

Passport's equipment review team led by Lawrence Magne. Laboratory tests performed by J. Robert Sherwood.

WHY YOU SHOULD—OR SHOULD NOT—BUY A TABLETOP RECEIVER

Most of us who have discovered world band radio are delighted with what we hear on our portables. But if you want to have a greater chance of tuning in the small local stations that proliferate in the lower "tropical" ranges below 5.73 MHz, you may wish to consider a tabletop receiver. These elite models don't come cheap, and they require a good outboard antenna and electrically quiet location to strut their stuff. But when all the pieces fall into place, most of these supersets can really perform.

Eavesdropping on the Home Folks

For most listeners, the point of spending a lot of money on a world band radio is to eavesdrop on what the home folks are hearing. In the exotic countries to the south, world band is often used instead of FM or mediumwave AM for local radio broadcasts. These domestic broadcasts aren't intended to be heard outside the home turf, but at night in the winter you can often hear them anyway, thanks to world band radio's exceptional ability to circumnavigate the globe.

Local Signals Often Heard Far Away

The problem is that these stations are intended for local audiences. This means that they're usually far less powerful than the international giants that come in so nicely on $250 portables. You need a highly effective set to flush out these sorts of faint signals. And, because there are so many stations crammed on the air at the same time, you need a set that is unusually able to lasso any given one of these little radio heifers from a vast thundering herd. This is where high-quality tabletop receivers—at least those with good audio quality—and outboard antennas come into the picture.

Local Broadcasts Often Beamed Abroad

Fortunately, it's not necessary to purchase a costly tabletop receiver to hear some of these exotic domestic stations. In selected cases, local broadcasts are targeted abroad, rather than to the home audience, via powerful transmitters. Usually these are intended for expatriates, mariners and diplomats abroad. But, with a good radio, anybody can listen.

The Liniplex enhanced fidelity configuration can now be tuned to 22 MHz

COMING UP: A MONITOR RECEIVER WITH FIDELITY POTENTIAL

The quest for a world band receiver that really sounds good—or at least as good as the state of technology will allow—seems to be like the mythical quest for an honest man. Some world band receivers come closer than others, but to date there's always been some missing element in each of the available models.

A few years ago, Phase Track, a small firm in Reading in the United Kingdom, came up with an unusual little world band receiver called the Liniplex F1. Its aim was to provide enhanced fidelity reception by the use of a particularly effective synchronous-detector design, coupled with a "clean" signal path offering low distortion.

The new Liniplex F2 is an upgrade of the earlier F1 model we tested in 1985. A number of small improvements and changes have been made—gone, for example, are the soft, nipplelike controls—but the real news concerns the options.

Set Now Tunable

The main problem with the F1 was that it was not tunable—you could only select among eight predetermined channels that could be changed only by ordering special parts from the factory. This made it about as popular as fleas with the public.

The new F2 is also not tunable, but by early 1989 it will be possible to pair it with the forthcoming Liniplex OSC-1 tuning synthesizer. This will allow the F2 to tune the world band spectrum up to about 22 MHz—which is to say, everything but the rarely used 11 meter segment. The F2 can also be equipped with a factory outboard speaker, another plus over the F1, which used an inferior inboard speaker.

Unsurpassed Synchronous Detection

Assuming the F2 performs at least as well as did the F1 we tested, it should be a success as an enhanced-fidelity device. Its synchronous detector design is exceptionally effective—much more so than those found on various Sony, Eska, and Escom receivers. One can but wonder why only a small firm in the hinterland of England can come up with such an effective solution, while the sleeping electronic giants of Asia and Europe continue to be oblivious to what today's technology can accomplish.

All this having been said, the Liniplex receiver is not without its shortcomings. It's a typically "English" design, all but devoid of features and user-selectable choices. There's only one bandwidth, no circuitry to cope with heterodyne ("whistle") interference, no passband-tuning—not even a set of tone controls. And the new synthesizer continues in this vein: no memories, no keypad, no slewing controls—not even so much as a tuning knob. Instead, tuning is only by thumbwheel switches reminiscent of classic professional receivers from bygone years.

It's too early to comment on the F2's performance. However, the earlier F1 performed very well, overall, although it did suffer from substandard sensitivity. Too, mediocre "blocking" allowed powerful nearby signals to desensitize the set yet further. For these reasons, the F1, more than most monitor receivers, was in need of an effective external antenna. A small such antenna comes with the receiver, or a larger outdoor design—trap dipole, sloper, inverted-L, or whathaveyou—may be used instead.

For Now, None of This Comes Cheap

The whole kit and kaboodle—receiver, synthesizer and outboard speaker—is to sell via the factory in the UK for £1,399. It can also be ordered from California's Radio West, which prices the complete assembly at $2,400. However, the equipment is drop-shipped directly from the factory in England to the purchaser in North America. There's a $75 or so customs fee, payable to the postal carrier upon receipt, and if the set is damaged en route it may be forwarded to Radio West for warranty repair or replacement.

What seems most likely to expect from the Liniplex system is not a DX or so-called "hobby" receiver—for this, there are already ample choices from Japanese manufacturers. What you are likely to find, instead, is an enhanced-fidelity device, pure and simple. It may or may not be for you, but it could be just what some perfectionistic listeners have been waiting for.   —*L.M.*

A Speaker That Improves Audio Quality

While we take it for granted that today's AM/FM radios and even television sets will have at least reasonably good audio quality, we can't make the same assumption when it comes to world band radios. Many have sound that is tinny and distorted, with narrow-range audio reproduction and a paucity of tone controls.

In part, this is the inheritance of old technology "shortwave radios." These reproduced so many squeals and squawks from the congested airwaves that it hardly seemed worth the candle to provide low distortion, wideband audio. In fact, good audio on mediocre sets could actually make matters worse.

Now, with such advances as sharp bandwidth filtering, multiple bandwidths, passband tuning, heterodyne rejection, and—most recently—synchronous detection, woolly audio is often the most disappointing aspect of a receiver's performance.

Take, for example, Sony's high-tech ICF-2010 and ICF-2001D. Nearly everything about these models is first class . . . until you get to the audio stage, which is underpowered and lacking in any real tone controls, and the speaker, which is strictly el cheapo. However, if you feed the radio's tape-recorder output into a good amplifier and speaker, it is transformed from blah into something quite pleasant.

Grove Enterprises has attempted to go after at least a portion of this problem by introducing a special outboard speaker for world band radios. Called the Grove SP-100 Sound Enhancer, it comes in a compact black metal box with a single 3 1/2", or 9 cm, speaker with a big, beefy magnet. Controls consist of an on-off switch and a pair of tone (bass and treble) controls, as well as a headphone jack.

The prototype we tested did, in fact, sound better than do most outboard accessory speakers that come standard—or even as options—with world band tabletops.

Placing tone controls between a speaker and its amplifier, as opposed to within the amplifier itself, is not the high water point of good elec-

Grove SP-100 Sound Enhancer

tronic design. However, on the SP-100, which has no amplifier, it is a necessity. Fortunately, the tone controls do work and can be a real plus. The only problem—one which Grove indicates is due to the lack of availability of alternative parts—is that the controls do virtually nothing until they are turned nearly fully clockwise. Thankfully, this is only an ergonomics question, inasmuch as with careful manipulation the controls can be set exactly where you wish.

The SP-100 is passive; that is, it has no amplication of its own. When the SP-100 is used with most tabletop models, this is not much of a drawback, as these quality sets usually have adequate audio power to drive the SP-100. However, most portables don't. For example, when we used the SP-100 with the popular Sony '2010/2001D, there was intolerable distortion unless the volume was kept very, very low. Grove indicates they plan to offer an optional amplifier to remedy this.

The SP-100, which lists at $99.50, fills an important niche. It is well worth considering if you are looking for improved audio quality.—*L.M.*

Antennas to Hear the World By

High-tech radios usually come equipped with foolproof little telescopic antennas that make an outdoor antenna unnecessary. But then so do TVs. Yet most of us hook up our televisions to an outdoor antenna or cable system for better reception.

Portables Rarely Need Extra Antenna

The same isn't always true of world band radios, though. Nearly all portables—even the better ones—are designed to be operated off the telescopic antenna that comes with the set . . . or perhaps a bit of wire, at best. If you try to be too fancy and hook a portable up to a powerful antenna, you may overload the radio's circuits. This won't damage the radio, but you could end up with a mishmash of signals—Radio Canada International on the wrong frequency, for example. Remove the fancy antenna and, *voilà!* The radio works as it should.

But if you're using a truly excellent receiver, you need to feed it with something other than a meager diet of signals grasped from the air by a short telescopic antenna. That's why most table-top world band receivers don't come with a built-in antenna: You don't feed table scraps to a thoroughbred.

The main reason for using an outboard antenna is that it can be mounted away from local electrical noises and walls that might absorb radio signals before they reach your antenna. As a result, more radio signals and fewer noises work their way into your set. More signal and less noise—those are the prime objectives. A so-so antenna that's mounted where signals are strong and noises are weak will do better than a fancy antenna mounted next to a microwave oven or hidden behind thick walls.

So get your antenna out into the fresh air, and especially keep it away from the radio, which itself emits electrical noises. The best place to mount it is outdoors, well away from buildings and utility lines. However, if you're in an apartment, at least try to place your antenna near a window or out on the balcony.

Outdoor Antennas for Tabletop Models

In our tests of various popular outdoor wire antennas, we found two clear winners: Alpha Delta's "Sloper" and Antenna Supermarket's "Eavesdropper." Since these tests were completed, Antenna Supermarket has come out with its own "sloper" design to compete with that of Alpha Delta, and new antenna designs are also emerging from The Ant Farm as well. These sorts of antennas

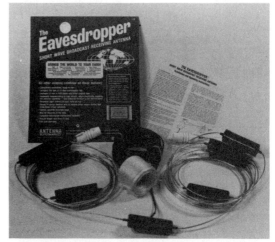

Antenna Supermarket's popular "Eavesdropper" antenna is designed to be mounted outdoors

are ideal for tabletop receivers, and they aren't terribly big or difficult to erect, either.

Unless you live in a totally lightning-free area, such as the moon, you should use your outdoor antenna in conjunction with a high-quality surge protector, such as the Alpha Delta "Transi-Trap" or a comparable device produced by the R.L. Drake Company. Static from nearby lightning strikes, along with similar charges from windy snow and sand storms, are more than enough to damage your receiver's sensitive solid-state innards.

Antennas Available for Apartment Dwellers

Not everyone has the room or desire to erect an outside antenna. One solution is what's called an "active" antenna. What distinguishes an active antenna from something like the Eavesdropper—or even a simple hank of wire—is amplification. An active antenna contains electronic circuitry that actually amplifies the strength of signals it receives.

Active antennas, however, are mixed blessings. True, their smaller size allows them to be affixed to windowsills and the like, and they're inconspicuous. The drawback is that their electrical circuitry is prone to the same foibles as any other electrical circuitry. If the antenna has a so-so circuit and you're connecting it to a superset, you're almost certain to be disappointed. Too much antenna amplification can strain—"overload"—many receivers . . . especially portables.

The most balanced overall performers, as found in our extensive *RDI White Paper* tests, are

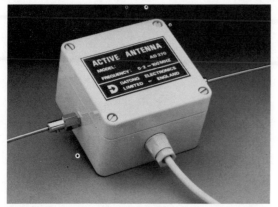

Datong AD 370 antenna works indoors or out

the Datong AD370, for outdoors or indoors, and the Datong AD270 for indoors only. However, depending on your individual situation—the presence of powerful AM stations in your area, for example—you may find the Dymek DA100D or the MFJ-1024 to be more appropriate.

The Bottom Line

If you are using a portable, you probably won't need an outboard antenna of any sort. However, if you have a tabletop receiver, you will almost certainly need one. The best choice, if it's feasible, is an outdoor wire antenna. Otherwise, choose the most suitable active antenna based on the conditions at your location. —L.M.

Dymek DA100D can also be obtained in a marine version

Photo page 117: Rotative Antenna for 500 kW transmitter near Sottens, Switzerland.

Worldscan

What's on Tonight?

Passport's Hour-by-Hour Guide to World Band Shows

The Menorah outside the Knesset, Israel. Photo by Tara Van den Hout

With nearly a quarter-*million* hours of world band programming on the air in all languages each week, an unabridged hour-by-hour directory of shows might qualify as the World's Heftiest Book. What follows is somewhat more practical: what's on in English that's also likely to be audible and worth hearing. Keep in mind that some operations, such as the World and regional services of the BBC and Radio Moscow, are on 24 hours a day on numerous channels, and thus may be heard almost any time simply by dialing about until a clear channel is found.

All shows are listed in Universal Time (UTC), which is easy to figure out, as it's announced by nearly all stations at the top of the hour. "Repeat" programs usually start with fresh news, but include the same features aired earlier. Key channels for North America and Europe are given, but rigorously complete information on all available channels worldwide may be found elsewhere in the "Worldscan" section.

Evening Prime Time—North America

0000

Kol Israel. A variety of feature programs, depending on the day of the week and time of year. Begins with news, then in summer features *Israel Sound* (pop songs), *Calling All Listeners*, *Studio Thirty-three* (arts in Israel), or *Shabbat Shalom*. On Sunday, the news is shortened and the current events show *Spotlight* is aired. Half-hour on 9435 kHz. *Tov!*

Radio Beijing. News, then a series of feature programs, including *Economic Horizons*, *Profiles*, *Travel Talk*, *Sports Beat*, *Chinese Folk Tales*, and *Letterbox*. One hour on 9770 and 11715 kHz. Yangtze for the Yankee.

Spanish Foreign Radio. News, then *Panorama* which features current events, literature, science, the arts, and so forth. Followed by a feature on a different region of Spain for each day and *Learn Spanish*, a language course. On weekends, different features, usually on a serial basis, followed by sports news. One hour on 9630 kHz. *Olé!*

Radio Baghdad, Iraq. Heard at this time summer only. See 2100 winter transmission for details, except 0000 beamed to North America on 11775 kHz.

0030

Radio Canada International. (2330 summer) Weekdays, there is a relay of the eminent CBC home service program called *As It Happens*, which features international news stories, Canadian news and weather, and general human interest features. On Saturday evenings (Sunday UTC) after the news, sports and weather, it's *Coast to Coast*, followed by *SWL Digest*, *Canada Rocks*, and *Spotlight on Science*. Sunday's main feature is *Listeners' Corner*. A pleasant hour—a full ninety minutes weekends—for North America on 5960 and 9755 kHz. Do right, Dudley, and tune in!

Radio Kiev, Ukrainian SSR. (summer 2330) Similar to 1900 transmission, but directed to North America on 6020, 6200, 7165, 11790, 11860, and 13645 kHz.

Radio Austria International. Heard at this time

summer only. See 0130 winter transmission for details.

0050

Vatican Radio. Different feature programs each day of the week, including *A Many Splendored Thing* (biographies of Christian martyrs), *The Pope, The Church and the World, Talking Point,* and *The Church Today* (a look at the moral and ethical issues in the week's top news stories). The last five minutes of each broadcast, except for Saturdays, is *Newsdesk*, a brief rundown of main news headlines. Twenty minutes of fair reception on 6150 and 9605 kHz. For the Curias listener.

0100

Deutsche Welle, West Germany. News, followed on Tuesdays through Saturdays by *Microphone on Europe*, a current events feature, then *Germany Today*, a lighter look at news stories. The rest of the transmission is devoted to feature programs, including *Science Magazine*, *Spotlight on Modern Life*, *People and Places* and *Arts Magazine*. Sunday's program features *Mailbag* on the first and third weekends of the month, and *To the Top*, German pop/rock music, on the fourth. Monday's program airs a variety of musical shows, different for each day of the month, but usually concentrating on classical or folk music. Fifty minutes on 6085 kHz. An earfest for cheermans.

Kol Israel. News at the top of the hour, then feature programs including *With Me in the Studio*, *Living Here* and *Spectrum* (advances in Israeli science). On Sundays, this half hour features *Spotlight*, plus the same current events show aired in the previous hour. On 9435 kHz for a half hour, so it doesn't pita out.

Radio Japan. Heard at this time summers only. See 0300 winter transmission for details.

Spanish Foreign Radio. Repeat of the 0000 transmission.

Radio Baghdad, Iraq. (starts 0000 summer) Same as 2100 program, but to North America for two hours on 6110, 9770, or 9875 kHz. Heard better summer than winter.

0130

Radio Austria International. (0030 summer) News, followed by a series of current events and human interest stories, including interviews with news makers and such features as a cooking show on Viennese pastries. Monday's program features *Postfach 700*, a listener contact or mailbag show. Half-hour on 9875 kHz. Yummy.

Voice of Greece. Mostly in Greek, but with a five minute English newscast nominally at 0130 heard at least most days except Saturday nights (Sunday UTC date). The bulk of air time is devoted to delightful Greek popular music, with very little commentary in between. One hour on 7430, 9395, and 9420 kHz.

0200

BBC World Service. News, then a cornucopia of features, such as *Network UK, People and Politics, Album Time*, a dramatized novel, *Science in Action, Sports International, Citizens* (a radio comedy/drama), and *Assignment*, just to name a few. One hour on 5975 kHz. Top drawer—Britannia definitely still rules the airwaves.

Radiobras, Brazil. Starts with Brazilian news, followed by *The Best in Brazilian Popular Music*, which features some of the most melodious sounds on world band radio, accompanied by occasional critical commentary on the music or biographies of the composers. This program takes an intermission for short features on Brazilian folklore, cultural events, contemporary Brazil, tourist attractions, and so forth. The musical feature is then resumed for the rest of the broadcast. Fifty minutes on 11745 kHz. A carnival for the ears.

Radio Cairo. Begins with Egyptian music, followed by a feature program, more sultry music, then news and commentary. The news is succeeded by more feature programs, including *Quiz of the Month, Cultural Life in Egypt, Focus, Reader's Corner,* and *Mailbag*. All programs are interlaced with tummy-rubbing Egyptian songs. One-and-a-half hours of fair reception on 9475 kHz. Nile polish.

Voice of Free China, Taiwan. Chinese news and commentary, then three different features. The last is *Let's Learn Chinese*, which has a series of segments for beginners, intermediate and advanced learners. Other features include *Republic of China Today, Chinese Old Songs, Journey into Chinese Culture,* and *Stories from*

St. Stephen's monastery, Greece. Photo by Tara Van den Hout

Ancient China. One hour on 5985 kHz. Formosa our listeners.

R.A.E., Argentina. Reception varies, but is rarely good. Begins with news and includes a number of "microprograms," such as *Argentine Personalities, Our Fauna, Mailbag,* and *Sports in Argentina.* Microprograms are separated by interludes of Argentine music, primarily tangos, but with an occasional folk song thrown in. One hour on 9690 and 11710 kHz. *Bailemos!*

Radio Kiev, Ukrainian SSR. (summer only) Repeat of 2330 transmission.

0230

Radio Nederland. World news followed by *Newsline,* a current affairs program. Then a different feature each night including *Rembrandt Express, Images* (arts in Holland), or *Shortwave Feedback,* a listener response program. Sunday nights (Monday UTC date) are devoted to *The Happy Station,* a program of chat, letters and light music. This program has the distinction of being the oldest program on radio, having begun in the 1920s. One hour on 6165 kHz. Even though they've been on the air with such frequency, it never hertz to listen.

0300

Radio Japan. (0100 summer) News, followed by *Current Affairs, Commentary* and *Tokyo Pop-Inn* which plays a different Japanese pop song each day. The last half hour offers different features, including *Japan Travelogue, Crosscurrents, Asia Now,* and *Japan Music Scene.* One hour on 5960 kHz. Pop in.

Radio Five, South Africa. Designed for (white) South African listeners. Programs include (white) pop songs, (white) traffic reports, (white) contest announcements and (white) advertisements, as well as racially neutral weather reports. Two hours of fair-to-poor reception—summer is worst—on 4880 kHz. Like listening in on a next door neighbor's private conversations without the guilt of eavesdropping.

Radio RSA, South Africa. This is the second half of Radio RSA's transmission to North America, which actually begins at 0200 with world news, followed by *Africa Today.* This second half of the broadcast features *Black Choirs, Historical Almanac, Personality of the Week, Talk Point,* and so forth. Two hours of iffy reception on 9580 and 9615 kHz. Racy programming.

United Arab Emirates Radio, Dubai. Similar to transmission at 1330, but on 11940 and 15435 kHz. Heard best in warm-weather months. See 1330 transmission for program description.

Voice of Free China, Taiwan. Repeat of the 0200 transmission.

Radio Beijing. Repeat of the 0000 transmission.

Voice of Greece. Repeat of the 0130 transmission.

Radio Kiev, Ukrainian SSR. Repeat of 0030 transmission.

0315

Radio France Internationale. Begins with news, then a review of the French press, followed by such feature programs as *Land of France, Drum Beat, Science Notes,* and *Afro Beat.* The last ten minutes are bilingual in French and English, and consist of all kinds of music interspersed with lively commentary between songs. Forty-five minutes on 3965, 9800, or 11670 kHz. Play it again, Sam!

0400

BBC World Service. First is *Newsdesk,* which airs world news, British news and press reviews, then a different feature program each day. This is followed by *Reflections* (an erudite sermonette) and *Financial News* at 0450. One hour on 5975 kHz. Dry as a martini.

Radio Habana Cuba. Biased news and propaganda, along with some interesting Latin American news, followed by fine Cuban, Caribbean, and Latin American music, as well as popular and traditional music, salsa, and jazz. A short sports program follows. Heard for some hours throughout the evening—on 5965, 6035, and 6140 kHz, at last check—but Habana changes frequencies often, so you may have to dial around to find them.

Swiss Radio International. News bulletins, followed by human interest features. On Sundays, the last fifteen minutes airs *Swiss Shortwave Merry-go-Round,* which answers technical questions sent in by listeners; Mondays are devoted alternately to *Supplement,* a feature on life in Switzerland, and *The Grapevine,* a listeners' contact program with a unique sense of humor. One-half-hour on 6135, 9725, and 9885 kHz. Best thing from Switzerland since chocolate.

Zebras grazing in South Africa. Photo by Tara Van den Hout

Voice of America. Directed to Africa, but widely heard elsewhere. Begins with news, then *VOA Morning*, a conglomeration of popular music, interviews, human interest stories, science digest, sports news, and so on, with news summaries at half past the hour. Two hours on 5995 and 9575 kHz. World class performance from where you might least expect it—a US government agency.

R.A.E., Argentina. Repeat of the 0200 transmission.

0500

Deutsche Welle, West Germany. Repeat of the 0100 transmission, but on 6010 kHz.

HCJB, Ecuador. Part of a continuous transmission starting at 0030. Programs include *Unshackled, Música del Ecuador, Here and Now, Psychology for Living*, and *The Christian Brotherhood Hour*. At 0530, the station begins its broadcast with *Passport*, an hourlong program containing news, music and special features from both an Ecuadorian and international perspective. One hour on various frequencies. No snake oil, just honest evangelism.

Spanish Foreign Radio. Repeat of the 0000 and 0100 transmissions, but on 6125 or 9630 kHz.

Voice of Nigeria. Usually clearer in winter than in summer, but never a barnburner. First, *Jamboree* (African popular music and mailbag), followed by news, editorials, and commentary until 0600, when the station begins its broadcast in other languages. One hour on 7255 kHz. Hi-life as you like it.

0530

HCJB, Ecuador. *Passport*, followed at 0630 by a variety of programs including *DX Party Line, Saludos Amigos* (listener contact), *Musical Mailbag,* and *Discovery*. Friendly.

Radio Nederland. Repeat of the 0230 transmission.

Outside Prime Time

0600

BBC World Service. First, *Newsdesk*, then features such as *Meridian* (an arts show), *Jazz for the Asking*, dramatized novels, *Rock Salad, Time for Verse*, and *The Farming World*. One hour on 5975 kHz, with diverse programming.

Radio Korea, South Korea. Starts with news and commentary, then *Seoul Calling*, a magazine program of interviews, pop music, and human interest segments, followed by *Let's Learn Korean*. The remainder of the broadcast offers a variety of one-day-a-week features, including *KBS Salon* (interviews with visitors to South

Three Asian children out for a mid-morning stroll.
Photo by Tara Van den Hout

Korea), *Sports Report* and *Inside North Korea.* Heard in Europe, but reception iffy in North America. One hour on 6060 and 9570 kHz. At least a bronze medal for Seoulful programming.

Radio Finland International. Heard at this time summer only. See 0730 winter transmission for details.

0645

Ghana Broadcasting Corporation. Designed for Ghanaian listeners rather than foreigners, so reception is marginal—especially during the warm months. African music begins the program, followed by a news bulletin. At 0730, more traditional African music is played. Half-hour on 6130 kHz. Ghana with the wind.

0700

Radio Australia. News, then a variety of feature programs, including *You Asked for It* (answers to listeners' questions), *Window on Australia, Health Report* and *Communicator*, as well as interludes of popular music. Continuous on 9655 (and 11720 from 0730) kHz, but see 0800 transmission for even better reception. Underfunded operation—with a weak signal, to boot—but still great 'roodio.

RFO, New Caledonia. Much of this feeble transmission is in French, and even though there is an English news bulletin scheduled for 0700, a French bulletin usually appears instead. Even for those who do not speak French, however, the remainder of the transmission can be entertaining, since the station largely airs French, British, and American popular music as well as some South Pacific Island music. Continuous on 7170 kHz. *Écoutez, si vous pouvez!*

Voice of Free China, Taiwan. Repeat of the 0200 transmission.

Old Country Church, Norway. Photo by Tara Van den Hout

0730

Radio Finland International. (0630 summer) Heard in Europe, but inaudible in North America, the entire transmission is called the "Northern Report." First is Finnish and Nordic news, followed by press review. Then different feature programs are aired each day of the week, some of which include *Arts Review, Enterprise Finland,* and *Starting Finnish*. There are various program changes on weekends. Half-hour on 9560 and 11755 kHz.

0800

KYOI, Saipan, Northern Marianas. Sometimes audible in North America and Europe. Part of the World Service network of Christian Science Monitor. Two hours on 17780 kHz. Good current and oldies light rock and pop . . . including, presumably, "Marianne."

Radio Australia. Begins with news summary, followed by *International Report*, a current affairs program that looks at two or three major stories in more detail. The second part focuses on sports results and popular music. Heard continuously on 9580 kHz to shortly after local sunrise in

North America. Inaudible in Europe, but reasonably good in North America most months. Great sports review.

Radio Korea, South Korea. Repeat of the 0600 transmission. Audible in Europe but rarely in North America. One hour on 7550 and 13670 kHz.

Voice of Nigeria. In addition to news, there is a variety of feature programs including *Weekend Magazine, Ecology, Nigerian Music, Literature, Nigerian Geography*, as well as *Spotlight*, a focus on topical issues. Two hours on 7255 kHz. Heard occasionally in mid-winter.

0900

NBC, Papua New Guinea. Entire broadcast is in Pidgin, except for an English newscast at the top of the hour. Present reception usually poor, but there are tentative plans to add a higher-power transmitter on 9520 kHz. Currently continuous on 4890 kHz at low power. One of the heads of the pack in unusual island music.

1000

ABC, Perth, Western Australia. Service of the Australian Broadcasting Corporation intended for listeners in Australia, but also heard intelligibly for a few hours many days in North America. Continuous from 0950 on 9610 kHz. Best way to get the flavor of the Australian outback.

1100

Radio Canada International. Heard this time summer only. See 1200 winter transmission for details.

1130

Radio Austria International. Heard at this time summer only. See 1230 winter transmission for details.

Radio Berlin International, East Germany. Heard at this time summer only. See 1230 winter transmission for details.

1200

Radio Tashkent, Uzbek SSR. Begins with national news and commentary, followed by features such as *Life in the Village, Youth Program, On the Asian Continent,* and *Muslims of the Soviet East*. Better heard in Europe. Half-hour on 9540, 9600, 9715, 11785, or 15460 kHz.

Radio Canada International. Heard at this time summer only. See 1300 transmission for details.

1230

Radio Austria International. (1130 summer) Repeat of broadcast at 0130, but on Sundays transmission begins at 1200 with *Austrian Coffee Table*, which each week features light chat and different kinds of music including classical, popular, jazz, or German and Austrian popular songs from the Twenties and—yes—those unforgettable Thirties. One-half-hour Monday through Saturday, one hour on Sunday, on 6155 and 15320 kHz.

Radio Berlin International, East Germany. (1130 summer) Directed toward Southeast Asia, though increased sunspot activity has allowed for occasional good reception in North America. Starts with news and commentary, then specific untitled features, followed by the titled feature programs, *Round About the GDR, GDR Report, Sports Round-Up,* and *RBI DX Club*. Forty-five minutes long on 17880, 21465, and 21540 kHz. Like a good shotgun, RBI operates at full bore.

1245

Radio France Internationale. New for North and Central America, as well as parts of Europe, RFI's news gives in-depth coverage to French politics and international events, usually followed by short features. Half-hour on 9805, 11670 and 17720 kHz. *Bonjour!*

Radio Berlin International, East Germany. Heard this time summer only; see 1345 winter transmission for details. Repeat of the 1130 transmission.

1300

Radio Canada International. (1200 summer) *North Country* begins with news, then interviews, human interest stories, current events and, on Tuesday, *SWL Digest*. One hour Monday through Friday on 9625, 11855, and 17820 kHz. A tough catch in Europe.

Radio Moscow. Part of an earlier segment of the World Service beginning at 1200 and extending to 2200; for example, on 11840 kHz. World news, followed by *Inside Report*, then a series of interviews and features designed to give a picture of life in the Soviet Union. Focus is on the effects of restructuring and increased openess now underway in the USSR. One hour on a vast number of channels—simply tune around the 11, 15, or 17 MHz band segments for best reception. *Glasnost* has greatly improved this station.

Radio Finland International. Heard at this time summer only. See 1400 winter transmission for details.

1330

United Arab Emirates Radio. Arguably the most unusual station on the air. Starts with news, of course, but then goes into a documentary feature which runs in a series from beginning to

"Little Mermaid" stands watch over Copenhagen Harbor. Photo by Tara Van den Hout

end. Often centering around traditional Arab fables, some titles have included *Follow the Wind* (a history of music), *Arab Women and the Koran,* and *Arabic Music*. Half hour on 17865 and 21605 kHz. Well researched, thorough—an unexpected treat.

Belgische Radio en Televisie, Belgium. For North America, Monday through Saturday only. Called *Brussels Calling*; begins with news, followed by press reviews and *Belgium Today*, a feature on an item of particular national interest. More features follow on economics, Third World development efforts, arts, and a mailbag. Half-hour on 15590 kHz.

Radio Tashkent, Uzbek SSR. Repeat of the 1200 transmission.

1345

Radio Berlin International, East Germany. Heard at this time winter only. Repeat of the 1230 transmission.

1400

Radio Finland International. (1300 summer) Repeat of the 0700 transmission, but on 11945 and 15400 kHz.

Radio Korea, South Korea. Repeat of the 0600 transmission, but modestly audible on 9750 and 15575 kHz.

Radio Sweden. For North America. Broadcast is called *Weekday, Saturday, or Sunday*, and begins with world and Nordic news, followed by human interest features and interviews. Occasionally documentaries are offered—Scandanavian émigrés to New Zealand in the late 19th and early 20th centuries, for example. Half-hour of variable reception on 15345 kHz.

1500

Afrique Numero Un, Gabon, West Africa. Commercially, rather than nationally, sponsored world band broadcaster. Although almost entirely in French, much air time is devoted to hi-life and jeje music, two enjoyable African popular rhythms. For those who know French, and can afford it, the station frequently accepts telephone requests. To 1700 on 15200 kHz, then to 2130 on 15475 kHz. Get down!

BBC World Service. Begins with *Radio Newsreel*, followed by several different features, including *Sportsworld, International Recital*, or *Concert Hall, A Jolly Good Show*, radio dramas and *The Pleasure's Yours*. One hour to Europe on 12095 and 15070, and to North America weekends on 11775 and 15260 kHz. Jolly good!

Deutsche Welle, West Germany. DW's African Service, similar programming to that on at 0100, but with some changes for the African audience. One hour on 15135, 17765, 17810, or 21600 kHz.

Radio Moscow. World news, followed by *Focus on Asia and the Pacific*, a current events show about those regions' concerns. The last part airs Soviet pop music and special features. Continuous on a wealth of frequencies—just dial around the 15, 17, or 21 MHz band segments.

1600

Radio France Internationale. Formerly called *Paris Calling Africa*, RFI is heard quite well in North America for most of the year. Begins with world and African news, followed by feature programs, including *Land of France, Turntable, Mailbag, Drumbeat* (African arts), *Spotlight on Africa* and, perhaps surprisingly, *Latin American Magazine*. One hour on 6175, 15360, 17620, and 17795 kHz.

United Arab Emirates Radio. Comparable to the 1330 transmission, but on 15320 and 17865 kHz.

WCSN, USA. World Service of the *Christian Science Monitor*. News, editorials, then *Monitor Forum*, which features human interest stories; and *Music Program*, which each day of the week offers a different singer, group, or style of music. Weekend broadcasts follow a different format,

with Sundays devoted to church services and religious programming. Two hours on 21640 kHz. Don't miss it!

1630

Belgische Radio en Televisie, Belgium. Repeat of the 1330 transmission, but on 17595 and 21810 kHz.

1645

Radio Pakistan. News, followed by a series of *ad hoc* interviews and current events, as well as a good bit of delightful Pakistani music. Heard better in Europe, to which it is targeted, than in North America. Weak for one hour on 11570 kHz.

1700

Radio Moscow. News, then feature programs, including *Mailbag, Culture and the Arts, Science and Engineering, Round About the USSR,* and *Jazz Show*, as well as interesting music. 24 hours a day on countless frequencies—dial around to find the best channel.

Radio-Télévision Marocaine, Morocco. One of the newest additions to world band radio, but in English Monday through Saturday only. Most of the transmission is devoted to uninterrupted western popular music, both current and classic. One hour on 17815 kHz.

Voice of America. Produced for Africa. Starts with world news, then *African Panorama*, interviews, current affairs, music, and human interest features. One hour on 15410, 15445, 15580, 15600, 17785, 17800, and 17870 kHz.

WCSN, USA. World news, followed by *Mailbag, Kaleidescope*, a current events magazine, and either *Conversations* (interviews), or *Young Ideas* (a program designed for young people, complete with games and puzzles). One hour, the second half of a two-hour broadcast beginning at 1600 on 21640 kHz.

Evening Prime Time—Europe

1800

Radio Canada International. Targeted to Africa, but quite well heard in Europe and North America. Includes news, weather, and sports, as well as *Spectrum*. Expands to an hour on weekends, and includes *Canada Rocks* and *Spotlight on Science*. Half-hour weekdays, one hour weekends on 15260 and 17820 kHz. Sparkly.

Radio Kiev, Ukrainian SSR. Heard summers only at this time, but on 7330, 9560, 9710, and 11780 kHz. See 1900 winter transmission for details.

Radio Kuwait. Mostly popular and rock music, with such occasional features as *The Study of the Mosque* and *Kuwait, Our Beloved Homeland.* Three hours on 11665 kHz. Too much everyday AM/FM musical fare to have world band appeal.

AFRTS, USA. Nonstop North American and international news from all US radio networks, plus live American sports. Audible in Europe on the *single-sideband* frequencies of 9239.5 USB, 9242 LSB, 9244 LSB and 9334 LSB. If your radio can pick this up, it's the next best thing to being in the US. 24 hours a day, but not all days.

1830

Radio Habana Cuba. Similar to 0400, but an hour-and-a-half targeted to Europe on 9670 and 11795 kHz. Variable reception.

1900

Radio Algiers, Algeria. Starts with news, then rock and popular music and also some occasional brief features, such as *Algiers in a Week*, which runs down the main events in Algeria during the past week. One hour of so-so reception on 9509, 9640, 9685, 15215, and 17745. Pretty run down.

Radio Kiev, Ukrainian SSR. (winter only) Regional and international news, followed by commentary. Monday through Friday, features *The Ukraine Today*, a show about Ukrainian life. On Saturday, the feature after commentary is *The Dialogue*, a listener contact program, and on Sundays it's *Music from the Ukraine* and *The Stamp Collector*. High point is the beautiful Ukrainian choral music. Best heard in Europe, to which it is targeted. Half-hour on 6010, 6090, 6165, and 7170 kHz. Typical but for exceptional choral music.

1920

Voice of Greece. Comparable to 0130 transmission, but to Europe on 7430 and 9425 kHz.

1930

Voice of the Islamic Republic of Iran. One full hour of radio Tehrantula. Barely audible in North America—winter is best—but fairly strong in Europe on 9022 kHz.

2000

All India Radio. Starts on some channels at 1845, and includes Indian music up to 2000, when it is followed by regional and international news, then interviews on current events and more Indian music. Continuous, with fairly good reception in Europe, but mediocre in North America. To 2230 on 7412, 9910, and 11620 kHz. Heaps of exotic music.

Radio Damascus, Syria. Actually starts at 2005. Directed to European listeners, but often audible in North America. Starts with news, followed by Syrian music, a daily press review, and a different feature for each day of the week, including *Portrait from Our Country, Around the World in a Week,* and *Syria in a Week.* Most of the transmission, however, airs Syrian and some western music. One hour on 12085 and 15095 kHz. In parts, there's more music than talk.

Radio Baghdad, Iraq. Heard at this time summer only. See 2100 winter transmission for details.

WCSN, USA. Repeat of the 1600 transmission, but on 15390 kHz.

2100

Radio Baghdad, Iraq. (2000 summer) Directed to Europe, but often heard in North America. News, mostly about the war with Iran, then a generous helping of Iraqi music and a press review just prior to the second hour of transmission. A few brief features, including *Guests in Baghdad* and *The Song of Today*, with some *ad hoc* interviews and current events. Two hours on 7295, 9770, 9875, or 15230 kHz. Tough slogging.

Radio Sweden International. Repeat of the 1400 transmission, but directed to Europe on 6065 kHz.

Belgische Radio en Televisie, Belgium. (summer only) Similar to 1330 transmission, but daily to Europe on 5910 and 9925 kHz.

2130

Radio Canada International. See 1800, but includes *SWL Digest* on Saturday. Directed for one-half hour to Africa on 1880, 15150, and 17820 kHz. Often heard well in North America and in Europe.

2200

BBC. World news, then feature programs, such as *From Our Own Correspondent*, dramatized novels, and so on. On Mondays through Fridays, these also include *The World Today, Financial News* and *Reflections*, and every day brings *Sports Roundup* at 2245. Continuous on 5975 kHz.

Radio Australia. Best heard on the West Coast of North America. Starts with world news summary, followed by *International Report, Window on Australia* and popular music. Weekends feature *You Asked for It* and *What Do You Do for a Crust?*. Roughly continuous on 15160, 15240, 15320, 15395, and 17795 kHz. Go for it, especially in the warmer months, at this hour or later.

Voice of Free China, Taiwan. See 0200. For Western Europe, but on 7355 or 9955 kHz.

Voice of Turkey. Heard this time summer only. See 2300 winter transmission for details.

Radio Vilnius, Lithuanian SSR. Heard this time summer only. See 2300 winter transmission for details.

Belgische Radio en Televisie, Belgium. (winter only) Similar to 1330 transmission, but daily to Europe on 5910 and 9925 kHz.

2300

BBC. News, then *Commentary* and a variety of feature programs including: *Multitrack* (rock music) on Mondays, Wednesdays, and Fridays, special segments, *Write On, The Farming World*, and *From the Weeklies*. One hour on 5975 kHz. Right on!

Voice of Turkey. (2200 summer) Begins with news and press reviews, followed by such cliffhangers as *The Kemalist Reforms and Religion, Turkish Panorama* and *The Western Thrace Question*. Then Turkish popular music and more features, more music, until signoff at 2350. One hour on 9445 and 9685 kHz. A real turkey, all right, except for the exotic Turkish music.

Radio Vilnius, Lithuanian SSR. (2200 summer)

News, followed by such features as *The Way We Live, Musical Panorama, Youth Club, Letterbox* and *Lithuanian by Radio*. Half-hour on 6100, 11790, and 13645 kHz. Standard Soviet fare except for some very pleasant Lithuanian music.

Radio Polonia, Poland. Starts at 2305 with news, followed by features, including folk music and *Learn Polish*, a language course. *Castles, Palaces, and Legends*, aired at 0345 Saturdays, details the history, anecdotes, and legends that surround some of Poland's best known historical monuments. Fifty minutes on 5995, 6135, 7125, 7145, and 7270 kHz. Friendly, charming, but hard to hear in North America.

2330

Radio Canada International. Heard at this time summer only. See 0030 winter transmission for details.

Radio Kiev, Ukrainian SSR. Heard at this time summer only. Similar to 1900 transmission, but to North America on 9640, 9800, 11790, 13645, 15180, and 15455 kHz.

Prepared by Alex Batman.

Worldwide Broadcasts in English
Country-by-Country Guide to World Band Radio

More than one hundred countries air broadcasts on world band radio. This "Worldwide Broadcasts" section gives the times and channels you are most likely to hear.

Times and days given are in UTC, which is explained in the "Terms and Abbreviations" section at the back of the book. During summer, some broadcasts are heard one hour earlier to compensate for savings, or summer, time. Programs that are heard summers only are preceded by "J" for June, whereas those heard winter only are preceded by "D" for December. Transmissions not preceded by a "J" or "D" are heard year-round. Channels in **bold** type often come in best, as these are from relay transmission facilities located near the intended listening audience.

More World Band Channels for 1989

On July 1, 1989, the official world band segments are to be expanded considerably above 10 MHz. Not only will the existing 11, 15, 17, and 21 MHz segments be increased, but also an entirely new 13 MHz segment—from 13600 to 13800 kHz—is to be created.

The exact parameters of these reconfigured bands are outlined in the "Terms and Abbreviations" section in the back of this book. Also given is the new upper parameter—9900 kHz, replacing 9775 kHz—for the 9 MHz band. Even though this expansion is not scheduled to go into effect until July 1, 1994, such large numbers of broadcasters have already moved into the new range that the revised 9 MHz upper parameter has become a *fait accompli*.

This means that the world band spectrum, currently overcrowded with stations trying to girdle the globe, will become somewhat less congested. This couldn't have come at a better time. Because of the rising sunspot cycle (see "The Sunspots Are Coming!"), the spectrum above 10 MHz is needed now more than ever before.

The forthcoming presence of so many new channels means that by the autumn of 1989 there will have been a major "shuffling" of channel usage by many of the world's broadcasters. At *Passport*, we are keeping keenly abreast of this activity, and will detail our findings in the forthcoming *Passport/90*, due out in the fall.

ALBANIA
RADIO TIRANA
6200	2330–2400 (NA)
7065	0230–0300 (NA), 0330–0400 (NA), 2330–2400 (NA)
7120	1830–1900 (EU)
7205	0630–0700 (EU)
9480	0430–0500 (CAF/SAF), 1130–1200 (CAF/SAF), 1530–1600 (CAF/SAF), 1830–1900 (EU), 2030–2100 (SAF), 2230–2300 (EU)
9500	0630–0700 (EU), 0800–0830 (SEA/ANZ), 1400–1430 (SEA/ANZ)
9760	0230–0300 (NA), 0330–0400 (NA), 2330–2400 (NA)

ARGENTINA
RADIO ARGENTINA—RAE
9690	0200–0300 (AM), 0400–0500 (AM), 2200–2300 (AM)
11710	0200–0300 (AM), 0400–0500 (AM), 2200–2300 (AM)
15345	1730–1830 (EU/NAF)

AUSTRALIA
ABC—PERTH (Domestic Programs)
9610	24h (PAC)
15245	2100–0945 (PAC)

RADIO AUSTRALIA
5995	0700–0800 (PAC), 1100–1900 (PAC)
6035	1530–2040 (EU/SAS/SEA)
6060	1130–1400 (PAC/NA), 1430–2030 (PAC/NA)
6080	1100–2000 (PAC/NA)
7205	1200–1330 (SEA), 1430–2040 (SAS/SEA), J 1330–1430 (SEA)
9580	0800–2130 (PAC/NA)
9655	0700–1030 (PAC/EU)

11910	0400–0630 (EU/PAC)
15320	0300–0500 (PAC/NA/CA), 2200–0200 (PAC/NA/CA)
15395	0100–0200 (PAC/AS), 2100–0100 (PAC/NA), 0300–0500 (EAS/SEA), 0500–0900 (EAS/SEA)
15415	0900–1100 (SAS/SEA)
17715	Sa 0100–0400 (EAS), 0100–0900 (SAS/SEA), Sa 0500–0630 (EAS), 0400–0900 (EAS)
17795	2200–0640 (PAC/NA)

AUSTRIA
RADIO AUSTRIA INTERNATIONAL
5945	1830–1900 (EU), 2200–2300 (EU)
6155	Su/M 0500–0530 (EU), 0530–0600 (EU), Su 0800–0830 (EU), 0830–0900 (EU), 1230–1300 (EU), Su 1300–1330 (EU), 1730–1900 (EU), Su 2200–2230 (EU), 2230–2300 (EU)
9870	Su 2200–2230 (EU), 2230–2300 (EU)
9875	0130–0200 (NA), Su 0200–0300 (NA), Su/M 0500–0530 (NA), 0530–0600 (NA)
12010	1830–1900 (WEU)

BANGLADESH
RADIO BANGLADESH
6240	D 1815–1900 (EU)
7505	1815–1900 (EU)
15525	D 0800–0830 (EU), D 1230–1300 (EU)
17870	J 0800–0830 (EU), J 1230–1300 (EU)

BELGIUM
BELGISCHE RADIO & TV
5910	1830–1855 (EU), 2200–2225 (EU), D Tu–Su 0030–0055 (ENA), D M–F 0800–0825 (ANZ)
9925	D Tu–Su 0030–0055 (SA), J 2100–2125

	(AM), J M–Sa 2330–2355 (AM)
11695	D 1830–1855 (EU), J M–F 0800–0825 (ANZ), J Su 1730–1755 (EU)
15510	D M–F 1000–1025 (AF), D M–Sa 1630–1655 (AF), J M–F 0800–0825 (SEA), J M–Sa 1330–1355 (SEA)
15590	M–Sa 1330–1355 (ENA)

BRAZIL
RADIO NACIONAL
11745	0200–0250 (CA/NA)
15265	1800–1850 (EU)

BULGARIA
RADIO SOFIA
7115	0400–0500 (ENA/EU), D 2130–2200 (EU)
11750	J 2030–2100 (EU)

CANADA
CBC (Domestic Programs to NA)
6065	1200–1300, Sa–Su 1300–1400
6195	Su 0000–0300, Tu–Sa 0200–0300, M 0300–0310, M 0330–0400, Su/M 0400–0500, 0500–0610
9625	Su 0000–0200, 0200–0300, M 0300–0310, M 0330–0400, Su 0400–0500, 0500–0610, 1200–1255, Sa/Su 1255–1505, Su 1505–1700, Sa 1700–1805, Su 1800–2200, Su–F 2200–2225, Su 2225–2240, Su–F 2240–2330, Su 2330–2400
11720	Sa/Su 1400–1505, Su 1505–1700, Sa 1700–1800, Su 1800–2200, Su–F 2200–2225, Su 2225–2240, Su–F 2240–2330, Su 2330–2400

RADIO CANADA INTERNATIONAL
5960	M–F 0930–0940 (CA), D 0000–0130 (ENA/CA), J Su/M 0030–0100, J Su/M 0130–0200, M–F 0930–0940, J 2330–0030 (ENA/CA)
5995	D 1715–1730 (EU), D M–F 1930–2000 (EU)
6050	M–F 0615–0630 (EU), M–F 0645–0700 (EU)
6140	M–F 0615–0630 (EU), M–F 0645–0700 (EU)
7155	D M–F 0615–0630 (EU), D M–F 0645–0700 (EU)
7235	1715–1730 (EU), M–F 1930–2000 (EU)
7295	J M–F 0515–0530 (EU), J M–F 0545–0600 (EU)
9535	Su/M 0100–0200 (CA/SA), Tu–Sa 0200–0300 (CA/SA)
9555	D 1545–1600 (EU), J M–F 1830–1900 (EU)
9625	M–F 1300–1400 (ENA)
9740	D M–F 0615–0630 (AF), D M–F 0645–0700 (AF)
9750	J M–F 0515–0530 (EU), J M–F 0545–0600 (EU)
9755	D 0000–0130 (ENA/CA), J Su/M 0030–0100 (SA), J Su/M 0100–0130 (SA), Su/M 0130–0200 (SA), Tu–Sa 0200–0300 (SA), M–F 0930–0940 (CA/SA), 2300–2330 (ENA/CA)
9760	D M–F 0615–0630 (EU), D M–F 0645–0700 (EU), D 2200–2300 (EU)
11705	2200–2230 (SEA)
11775	J M–F 0515–0530 (AF), J M–F 0545–0600 (AF)
11840	M–F 0615–0630 (ME), M–F 0645–0700 (ME)
11845	Su/M 0100–0200 (CA/SA), Tu–Sa 0200–0300 (SA)
11855	M–F 1300–1400 (ENA)

11915	1545–1600 (EEU)
11935	D 1545–1600 (EU), J 1445–1500 (EU)
11940	Su/M 0100–0300 (SA)
11945	D M–F 1930–2000 (EU), D 2200–2300 (EU), J M–F 1830–1900 (EU), J 2100–2200 (EU)
11955	Su 1400–1700 (ENA/CA)
15150	2130–2200 (WAF/SAF)
15160	J 1445–1500 (EEU)
15235	D M–F 0615–0630 (ME), D M–F 0645–0700 (ME)
15245	J M–F 0515–0530 (ME), J M–F 0545–0600 (ME)
15260	1800–1900 (WAF/SAF), M–F 1900–1930 (WAF/SAF)
15325	1545–1600 (EU), 1715–1730 (EU), M–F 1930–2000 (EU)
15385	1200–1230 (SEA)
17710	1200–1230 (SEA)
17820	1800–1900 (WAF/SAF), M–F 1900–1930 (WAF/SAF), 2130–2200 (WAF/SAF), D M–F 1300–1700 (CA/SA), D M–Sa 1545–1600 (EU), D 1715–1730 (EU), J M–F 1200–1600 (CA/SA), J M–Sa 1445–1500 (EU), J 1615–1630 (EU)
17875	D M–F 1930–2000 (EU), J M–F 1830–1900 (EU)

CHINA (PR)
RADIO BEIJING
3985	2230–2300 (EU)
7335	D 1200–1400 (WNA)
9645	D 0300–0500 (WNA/CA)
9665	D Su 0000–0100 (ENA/CA/SA), D Su 1100–1300 (ENA/CA/SA)
9690	0500–0600 (ENA), 0500–0600 (ENA/CA)
9744	2030–2130 (EU/NAF)
9770	0000–0100 (NA), 0300–0400 (NA), 0500–0600 (NA)
9820	J 2000–2200 (EU)
11715	0000–0100 (NA), 0300–0400 (NA)
11790	1600–1700 (CAF/EAF), 2030–2130 (EU/NAF)
11980	D 0300–0500 (WNA)
15130	1600–1700 (CAF/EAF)
15290	J 0300–0500 (WNA/CA)
15455	0300–0400 (WNA), J 0000–0100 (ENA/CA/SA), J 1100–1300 (ENA/CA/SA)

CHINA (TAIWAN)
VOICE OF FREE CHINA
5945	D 0200–0400 (NA)
5985	0200–0300 (ENA), 0300–0400 (ENA/CA), 0700–0800 (CA)
7355	D 2200–2300 (EU)
9680	J 0200–0400 (WNA)
9955	2200–2300 (EU/NAF/SA)
11740	0200–0300 (CA)
11805	D 2200–2300 (EU)
15440	J 2200–2300 (EU)
17845	J 2200–2300 (EU)

VOICE OF ASIA
7445	1100–1200 (SEA/EAS), 1530–1630 (SEA/EAS)

COSTA RICA
ADVENTIST WORLD RADIO
15460	1500–1700 (CA)

RADIO FOR PEACE INTERNATIONAL
7375	0015-0400 (CA/ENA)
13660	0415-0600, 2100-2400 (CA/WNA)

CUBA
RADIO HABANA
6090	D 0000-0600 (NA)
6115	D 0200-0600 (SA)
6140	D 0200-0450 (NA)
9525	0600-0800 (WNA)
9655	J 0000-0600 (NA)
9670	D 1830-2000 (EU)
11795	J 1830-2000 (EU)

CZECHOSLOVAKIA
RADIO PRAGUE
5930	0100-0200 (EU/AM), 0300-0400 (EU/AM), 1800-1830 (EU), 1900-2000 (EU)
6055	0100-0200 (WEU/ENA/CA), 0300-0400 (WEU/ENA/CA), 1530-1630 (EU), 2200-2230 (WEU/ENA/CA)
7345	0100-0200 (AM), 0300-0400 (AM), 1530-1630 (EU), 1800-1830 (EU), 1900-2000 (EU)
9540	0100-0200 (ENA/CA), 0300-0400 (ENA/CA)
9740	0100-0200 (AM), 0300-0400 (AM)
11990	0100-0200 (AM), 0300-0400 (AM), 1530-1630 (AF), 1730-1830 (AF)
13715	1430-1500 (ME/EAF), 1530-1630 (SAS), 1730-1830 (ME/EAF)
15340	2040-2140 (AM)

ECUADOR
HCJB – VOICE OF THE ANDES
6205	D 0645-0830 (EU)
6230	0200-0700 (NA/CA)
9610	0645-0830 (EU)
9720	0030-0700 (NA/CA)
11740	1130-1600 (CA/ENA)
11775	0030-0700 (CA/NA)
11790	D 1900-2000 (EU), D 2130-2200 (EU)
11835	0700-0830 (EU)
11910	0030-0130 (AM)
15115	1200-1600 (AM)
15155	0030-0200 (NA/CA)
15270	1900-2000 (EU), 2130-2200 (EU)
17790	1900-2000 (EU), 2130-2200 (EU)
17890	1200-1600 (NA/CA)

EGYPT
RADIO CAIRO
9475	0200-0330 (NA/CA)
9675	0200-0330 (NA)
9900	2115-2245 (EU)
17595	1215-1330 (SAS/SEA)

FINLAND
RADIO FINLAND
9530	D M-F 1930-1955 (EU/WAF)
9550	J Su 1830-1855 (EU/WAF)
9560	0730-0755 (EU/WAF)
9635	0330-0355 (NA)
11755	D 0530-0555 (ME), D 0730-0755 (EU/WAF), D 1930-1955 (EU/WAF), J 0230-0255 (NA), J 0630-0655 (EU/WAF), J 1405-1430 (EEU), J 1830-1855 (EU/WAF), J 2100-2125 (SA)

11945	M-F 1200-1225 (ENA/CA), M-Sa 1300-1325 (ENA/CA), 1400-1500 (ENA/CA), D 0330-0355 (NA), J 2100-2125 (EAS)
15270	J 0630-0655 (WEU/WAF)
15400	M-F 1200-1225 (ENA/CA), M-Sa 1300-1325 (ENA/CA), 1400-1500 (ENA/CA), J 2100-2125 (SA)

FRANCE
RADIO FRANCE INTERNATIONAL
6055	D 0315-0345 (CA)
6175	1600-1700 (EU/NAF), D 0315-0345 (EEU/ME/EAF)
9790	0315-0345 (AF)
9800	0315-0345 (CA)
9805	1245-1315 (EEU/WUSSR)
9860	D 1600-1700 (ME)
11670	1245-1315 (EEU)
11670	J 0315-0345 (CA)
11995	0315-0345 (SA)
15155	1245-1315 (EEU)
15195	1245-1315 (EEU/WUSSR)
15315	D 1600-1700 (WAF)
15360	J 1600-1700 (ME)
15365	1245-1315 (CA/ENA)
17620	J 1600-1700 (AF)
17720	1245-1315 (ENA/CA)
17795	J 1600-1700 (EAF)
21645	1245-1315 (NA/CA)

GABON
ADVENTIST WORLD RADIO
17890	Su 1200-1300 (WAF)

GERMANY (DR)
RADIO BERLIN INTERNATIONAL
6010	D 0245-0330 (NA/CA), D 0400-0530 (NA/CA)
6080	0045-0130 (ENA), 0200-0330 (ENA)
7185	Sa/Su 0845-0930 (EU)
7260	1815-1900 (EU)
7295	1645-1730 (WEU), 1815-1900 (WEU)
9560	D 0400-0530 (WNA)
9620	J 0145-0230 (NA), J 0300-0430 (NA)
9730	0045-0130 (ENA/CA), 0200-0330 (ENA/CA), Sa/Su 0845-0930 (WEU)
11785	D 1200-1245 (WAF), D 1645-1730 (WAF), J 0145-0230 (WNA), J 0300-0430 (WNA)
13610	J 0500-0545 (ME/EAF), J 1730-1815 (ME/EAF), J 1915-2000 (AF)
21465	Sa/Su 0845-0930 (EAS), 1230-1315 (SAS/SEA), 1345-1430 (SAS/SEA)
21540	0845-0930 (EAS/ANZ), 1000-1045 (EAS/ANZ), 1230-1315 (SAS/SEA), 1345-1430 (SAS/SEA)

GERMANY (FR)
DEUTSCHE WELLE
5960	0500-0550 (NA/CA)
6040	0100-0150 (NA)
6085	0100-0150 (NA/CA)
6120	0500-0550 (NA)
6130	0500-0550 (NA)
9565	0430-0515 (CAF/SAF), D 0100-0150 (CA)
9605	D 2100-2150 (SEA), J 0300-0350 (NA/CA)
9700	J 0500-0550 (NA)
9735	J 0100-0150 (NA)

11785	J 0300–0350 (CA), J 1000–1030 (CAF/SAF)
11795	D 0100–0150 (CA)
11865	J 0100–0150 (NA/CA)
13790	1800–1850 (AF)

GHANA
RADIO GHANA

6130	0645–0800 (WAF), 1845–2000 (WAF)

GREECE
I FONI TIS HELLADAS

7430	0135–0145 (NA), 0335–0345 (NA), 1920–1930 (EU)
9395	0335–0345 (NA/PAC), 1920–1930 (EU), 2335–2345 (SA), D 0135–0145 (NA/PAC)
9420	0135–0145 (NA), 0335–0345 (NA)
9425	1920–1930 (EU)
9855	D 1235–1245 (NA/EU)
9905	J 1235–1245 (NA/EU)
11645	1035–1045 (EAS), 1235–1245 (NA/EU), 1535–1545 (NA/EU), 2335–2345 (SA), J 0135–0145 (NA/PAC), J 1835–1845 (AF)
15630	0835–0845 (ANZ), 1035–1050 (EAS), 1235–1245 (NA/EU), 1535–1545 (NA/EU), 1835–1845 (AF)

GUAM
ADVENTIST WORLD RADIO

9465	2100–2200 (SEA)
11810	1500–1600 (SAS)

15125	0000–0100 (SEA)
17865	0200–0300 (EAS)

KTWR – TRANS WORLD RADIO

9840	J 1500–1630 (SAS), J Th-Sa 1630–1640 (SAS)
9870	D 1500–1630 (SAS), D Th-Sa 1630–1640 (SAS)
11805	0805–0930 (EAS), 0930–1100 (ANZ)

HOLLAND
RADIO NEDERLAND

5955	1130–1225 (EU), 1430–1525 (EU)
6020	0230–0325 (ENA)
6020	1030–1125 (CA/SA), 1630–1725 (SAF), 1830–1925 (SAF)
6020	1830–1925 (EU)
6165	0230–0325 (ENA/CA), 0530–0625 (WNA/CA)
9590	0230–0325 (ENA)
9715	0530–0625 (WNA), 0730–0825 (ANZ)
9715	1130–1225 (EU)
9895	0230–0325 (ENA), 0400–0425 (ME), 0630–0655 (WEU/WAF), 2030–2125 (WEU/WAF)
15180	D 1830–1925 (EAF)
15560	1130–1225 (SAS), 1430–1525 (SAS)
15570	D 1630–1725 (EAF)
17575	0830–0925 (SAS), 1130–1225 (EAS), 1430–1525 (SAS)
17605	1830–1925 (WAF)
21685	1830–1925 (WAF/CAF)

HUNGARY
RADIO BUDAPEST
9520   Tu–Su 0030–0100 (ENA), 0130–0230
        (ENA), W/Sa 0200–0230, Tu/W/F/Sa 0230–
        0245 (ENA), Tu/F 2230–2300 (SA)
9585   Tu–Su 0030–0100 (ENA), 0130–0200
        (ENA), W/Sa 0200–0230, Tu/W/F/Sa 0230–
        0245 (ENA), Su 1045–1100 (EU), Sa 1130–
        1145 (EU), M/Th 1615–1630 (EU), 1930–
        2000 (EU), 2100–2130 (EU), Tu/F 2230–
        2300 (SA)
9835   Tu–Su 0030–0100 (NA), 0130–0200 (NA),
        W/Sa 0200–0230 (NA), Tu/W/F/Sa 0230–
        0245 (NA), Su 1045–1100 (EU), Sa 1130–
        1145 (EU), M/Th 1615–1630 (EU), 1930–
        2000 (EU), 2100–2130 (EU)

INDIA
ALL INDIA RADIO
7412   1845–2230 (EU)
9910   2000–2230, 2245–0115 (EU)
11620   1845–2230 (EU)

INDONESIA
VOICE OF INDONESIA
11788   0100–0200 (SEA/EAS), 0800–0900 (SEA/
        EAS), 1500–1600 (SEA/EAS)
15150   0100–0200 (AS/PAC), 0800–0900 (AS/
        PAC), 1500–1600 (AS/PAC)

IRAN
VOICE OF THE ISLAMIC REPUBLIC
9022   1930–2030 (EU/NAF/CA)

IRAQ
RADIO BAGHDAD
6110   D 0100–0300 (ENA), D
        0100–0250 (ENA/CA)
7295   D 2100–2250 (EU)
9770   J 2000–2150 (EU)
11775   J 0000–0150 (ENA/CA)
11810   0100–0250 (SAS)
15230   J Su 2000–2150 (EU)

ISRAEL
KOL ISRAEL
7462   D 0000–0030 (EU/ENA), D 0100–0125
        (EU/ENA), D 0200–0225 (EU/ENA), D
        0500–0515 (EU/ENA), D 2000–2030 (EU/
        ENA), D 2230–2300 (EU/ENA)
9010   D 2000–2030 (AF/SA), D 2230–2300 (AF/
        SA), J 1900–1930 (AF/SA)
9435   0000–0030 (WEU/ENA), 0100–0125
        (WEU/ENA), D 0200–0225 (WEU/ENA), D
        0500–0515 (EU/NAF/CA), D 2000–2030
        (WEU/ENA), D 2230–2300 (WEU/ENA), J
        0400–0415 (EU), J 2300–2330 (WEU/ENA)
9855   D 0000–0030 (EU/NAF/CA), D 0100–0125
        (EU/NAF/CA), D 0200–0225 (EU/NAF/
        CA), D 2000–2030 (EU), D 2230–2300
        (EU/NAF/CA)
11605   J 0000–0025 (EU/ENA), J 0100–0125 (EU/
        ENA), J 1900–1930 (EU/ENA), J 2130–2200
        (EU/ENA), J 2300–2330 (EU/ENA)
12080   J 0000–0025 (EU/NAF/CA), J 0100–0125
        (EU/NAF/CA), J 0400–0415 (EU/NAF/
        CA), J 2130–2200 (EU/ENA), J 2300–2330

(EU/NAF/CA)
15485   J 1900–1930 (WEU/ENA)
15585   J 1900–1930 (WUSSR/EEU), J 2130–2200
        (WUSSR/EEU)
17635   D 1100–1130 (EU/WUSSR)

ITALY
RAI-RTV ITALIANA
6165   J 0425–0440 (EU/NAF/ME)
7235   2025–2045 (EEU/ME)
7275   0425–0440 (EU/NAF/ME), 1935–1955 (EU)
7290   D 1930–1955 (EU)
9575   0100–0120 (ENA), 2025–2045 (ME)
9710   0350–0410 (SAS/SEA), 1935–1955 (EU),
        2200–2225 (EAS)
11800   0100–0120 (ENA/CA), 2025–2045 (ME/
        EAF), 2200–2225 (EAS), J 1935–1955 (EU)

JAPAN
RADIO JAPAN/NHK
5960   D 0300–0400 (ENA/CA), J 0100–0300
        (ENA/CA)
5990   D 0500–0600 (WNA), D 0700–0800 (WNA),
        D 1100–1200 (WNA), D 1400–1600 (WNA),
        D 1700–1800 (WNA)
6120   1100–1200 (NA)
9505   1900–1930 (PAC/WNA), 2000–2030
        (PAC/WNA), J 0500–0600 (PAC/WNA), J
        1500–1600 (PAC/WNA), J 1700–1800
        (PAC/WNA)
11800   2300–2400 (EU/NAF)
15195   0700–0800 (EU/NAF)
15300   D 2300–2400 (NA)
17825   0300–0330 (WNA/CA/SA)
21695   0700–0800 (EU/NAF)
21700   1500–1600 (EU)

KOREA (DPR)
RADIO PYONGYANG
6576   1100–1150 (CA), 2000–2050 (EU)
9325   1300–1350 (EU), 1500–1550 (EU), 1700–
        1750 (EU)
9345   1300–1350 (EU/ME), 2000–2050 (EU/ME)
9600   1200–1250 (EU)
11735   1100–1150 (CA), 2300–2350 (CA)
11740   1500–1550 (EU), 1700–1750 (EU)
13650   2300–2350 (CA)

KOREA (REPUBLIC)
RADIO KOREA
6060   0600–0700 (ENA)
6480   2030–2130 (EU)
7550   0800–0900 (EU), 2030–2130 (ME/AF)
9570   0600–0700 (WNA/CA), 0915–0930 (SA),
        1400–1500 (SEA)
9750   1400–1500 (NA/CA)
13670   0800–0900 (EU), 0915–0930 (EU)
15575   0045–0100 (ENA), 0245–0300 (ENA), 1100–
        1200 (AF), 1400–1500 (ENA), 1800–1900
        (EU), 2030–2130 (EU), 2330–0030 (ENA)

KUWAIT
RADIO KUWAIT
11665   1800–2100 (EU/ENA)
15345   0500–0800 (SAS)

LUXEMBOURG
RADIO LUXEMBOURG
  6090   0000–0300 (EU)

MALTA
RADIO MEDITERRANEAN
  6110   2230–2330 (EU)

MONACO
TRANS WORLD RADIO
  7105   0725–1010 (EU), Sa 1010–1100 (EU)
  7205   1800–1830 (EU)

NEW ZEALAND
RADIO NEW ZEALAND
  9540   0930–1115 (ANZ/SEA)
  11780   D Sa/Su 0930–1115 (PAC), D Sa/Su 1730–
          2015 (PAC)
  15150   0045–0630 (PAC), 1730–2015 (PAC),
          2245–0045 (PAC)
  17705   D 0045–0630 (PAC), D 2245–0045 (PAC)

NICARAGUA
LA VOZ DE NICARAGUA
  6100   Tu–Su 0300–0400 (CA/NA), Tu–Su 0600–
          0700 (CA/NA)

NIGERIA
VOICE OF NIGERIA
  7255   0500–0600 (WAF)
  15120   0500–0600 (EU/PAC), 0700–0800 (EU/
          PAC), 0830–1700 (EU/PAC), 1800–1900
          (EU/PAC), 2100–2200 (EU/PAC)

NORWAY
RADIO NORWAY INTERNATIONAL
  6015   D M 0500–0530 (WNA)
  6040   D Su 1300–1330 (EU)
  7125   D Su 2000–2030 (EU)
  9590   Su 1300–1330 (EU), Su 1900–1930 (NA/
          EU/AF), D Su 1000–1030 (EAS/ANZ), J Su
          2000–2030 (EU)
  9605   D M 0000–0030 (ENA/CA/SA)
  9650   J M 0400–0430 (WNA)
  9655   Su 1700–1730 (EU/AF)
  11840   J M 0000–0030 (ENA/CA)
  11850   D Su 1600–1630 (WNA), D Su 1700–1730
          (WNA)
  11870   J Su 1000–1030 (EU/WAF)
  15180   D Su 1000–1030 (ANZ), J Su 2200–2230
          (WEU/WAF/SA)
  15220   J Su 1600–1630 (ME/EAF), J Su 1700–1730
          (EU/ME/AF), J Su 1900–1930 (ANZ)
  15230   D Su 1000–1030 (EU/ME/AF)
  15300   J Su 1400–1430 (EU/EAF)
  15310   Su 1300–1330 (NA), Su 1400–1430 (ENA/
          CA), Su 1600–1630 (NA/CA), J M 0500–
          0530 (AF), J Su 1700–1730 (WNA), J Su
          1900–1930 (ENA/CA), J Su 2000–2030 (NA)
  21730   J Su 1000–1030 (EU/WAF)

PAKISTAN
RADIO PAKISTAN
  6210   D 1600–1630 (ME)

  9795   D 1600–1630 (ME)
  11570   D 0230–0245 (SEA)
  11615   J 1600–1630 (ME)
  15115   0230–0245 (SAS/SEA)
  15605   J 1600–1630 (ME)
  17660   1100–1120 (EU), J 0230–0245 (SEA)

PHILIPPINES
FAR EAST BROADCASTING CO
  9670   D 1500–1600 (SAS)
  11850   0400–0600 (ANZ/EAS), 0830–0930 (ANZ/
          EAS), 1300–1500 (SEA/SAS), J 1500–1600
          (SAS)
  15445   0000–0200 (SAS/SEA)

POLAND
RADIO POLONIA
  6095   1200–1225 (EU), 1400–1430 (EU)
  6135   0630–0700 (EU), 1600–1630 (EU), 1830–
          1855 (EU), 2230–2355 (EU)
  7125   1630–1700 (NAF/WAF), 1830–1855 (NAF/
          WAF), 2000–2030 (NAF/WAF), 2230–
          2355 (EU)
  7145   2000–2030 (WEU/WAF), 2305–2355
          (WEU/WAF)
  7270   0630–0700 (EU), 2230–2355 (EU)
  7285   1200–1225 (EU), 1400–1430 (EU), 1830–
          1855 (EU)
  9525   1230–1300 (EU/WAF), 1630–1700 (EU/
          WAF), 1830–1855 (EU/WAF), 2000–2030
          (EU/WAF)
  9540   1600–1630 (EU)
  11840   1230–1300 (WEU/WAF), 1630–1700
          (WEU/WAF), 1830–1855 (WEU/WAF)
  15120   0630–0700 (WAF), 1230–1300 (WAF)

PORTUGAL
RDP INTERNATIONAL
  6060   Tu–Sa 0230–0300 (ENA)
  7155   D M–F 2030–2100 (EU)
  9605   J M–F 1930–2000 (EU)
  9680   Tu–Sa 0230–0300 (ENA)
  9705   Tu–Sa 0230–0300 (NA)
  9740   D M–F 2030–2100 (EU)
  11800   J M–F 1930–2000 (EU)
  11840   Tu–Sa 0230–0300 (SA)

ROMANIA
RADIO BUCHAREST
  5990   0200–0300 (AM), 0400–0430 (AM), D 1930–
          2030 (EU), D 2100–2130 (EU)
  6055   D 1930–2030 (EU), D 2100–2130 (EU)
  6155   0200–0300 (AM), 0400–0430 (AM)
  7105   D 1730–1800 (EU)
  7135   D 1730–1800 (EU)
  7145   1930–2030 (EU), 2100–2130 (EU), D 1500–
          1530 (SAS/SEA)
  7195   D 1500–1530 (EU), D 1930–2030 (EU), D
          2100–2130 (EU)
  9510   0200–0300 (AM), 0400–0430 (AM), D 1500–
          1530 (SAS)
  9570   0200–0300 (AM), 0400–0430 (AM), 1730–
          1800 (AF)
  9690   M–Sa 1045–1100 (EU), 1300–1330 (EU),
          1500–1530 (ME/SAS), J 1930–2030 (EU), J
          2100–2130 (EU)
  9750   J 1930–2030 (EU), J 2100–2130 (EU)

11810	0200-0300 (AM), 0400-0430 (AM)
11940	0200-0300 (AM), 0400-0430 (AM), 0530-0600 (EAF/SAF), 0645-0715 (ANZ), M-Sa 1045-1100 (EU/WUSSR), 1300-1330 (EU), 1500-1530 (ME/SAS), 1730-1800 (AF), J 1930-2030 (EU), J 2100-2130 (EU)
15250	0645-0715 (SEA/ANZ), M-Sa 1045-1100 (EU), 1300-1330 (EU), J 1500-1530 (SAS/SEA), J M-F 1500-1530 (ME)

SOUTH AFRICA
RADIO RSA

6010	J 0200-0400 (NA)
7245	J 1800-1900 (EU/AF)
9580	0200-0400 (NA), 0400-0430 (AF), 1900-2100 (AF/EU), D 1100-1200 (SAF)
9615	0200-0400 (NA)
11730	D 0200-0400 (NA)
11900	D 0400-0430 (EAF), D 2100-2200 (AF/EU)
11915	J 1800-1900 (EU/AF)
15125	D 1400-1600 (AF/EU)
17755	J 1400-1600 (AF/WEU)
17810	D 1400-1600 (AF/WEU)
21535	J 1400-1600 (AF/WEU)
21590	1100-1200 (AF/WEU), 1400-1600 (AF/WEU)

SPAIN
RADIO EXTERIOR DE ESPANA

6125	D 0000-0200 (ENA/CA), D 0500-0600 (NA/CA)
7275	D 1830-1930 (EU), D 2030-2130 (EU)
9630	0000-0200 (ENA/CA), J 0500-0600 (NA/CA)
9765	D 1830-1930 (EU), D 2030-2130 (EU), J 1900-2000 (EU), J 2100-2200 (EU)
11840	D 1830-1930 (ME)
11880	J 0000-0200 (ENA/CA)
15125	J 1800-1900 (ME)
15375	D 1830-1930 (NAF/WAF), J 1900-2000 (NAF/WAF)
15395	J 1900-2000 (ME)

SURINAME
RADIO SURINAME INTERNATIONAL
English/Dutch

17875	M-F 1730-1745 (EU)

SWEDEN
RADIO SWEDEN

6065	M-F 1100-1130 (EU), 2100-2130 (EU/WAF), D 1600-1630 (EU/WAF), D 2300-2330 (ENA/CA), J 1700-1730 (EU/WAF)
9630	1100-1130 (EU/WAF), D 0930-1000 (EU/WAF)
9695	0230-0300 (NA), 2300-2330 (ENA/CA), D 1400-1430 (NA)
11705	0330-0400 (ME), J 2300-2330 (ENA/CA)
15345	1400-1430 (ENA/CA)
15390	0930-1000 (ANZ), J 1400-1430 (NA)

SWITZERLAND
SWISS RADIO INTERNATIONAL

3985	0730-0800 (EU), 1800-1830 (EU)
6135	0200-0230 (NA/CA), 0400-0430 (NA/CA)
6165	0730-0800 (EU/NAF), 1300-1330 (EU/

	NAF), 1800-1830 (EU/NAF)
6190	2230-2300 (WEU)
9535	0730-0800 (EU/NAF), 1300-1330 (EU/NAF), 1800-1830 (EU/NAF)
9725	0200-0230 (CA), 0400-0430 (NA/CA)
9885	0200-0230 (ENA/CA), 0400-0430 (NA), 1830-1900 (AF), 2100-2130 (AF), D 0830-0900 (ANZ), D 1000-1030 (ANZ), D 1100-1130 (EAS), D 1530-1600 (ME/EAF)
11695	1330-1400 (SEA)
12030	0630-0700 (WAF), 1300-1330 (EU/NAF)
12035	0200-0230 (ENA/CA), 0400-0430 (NA), 2100-2130 (ME/EAF)
13685	J 0830-0900 (ANZ), J 1000-1030 (ANZ), J 1100-1130 (ANZ), J 1330-1400 (SAS/SEA), J 1530-1600 (ME/EAF)
15135	1330-1400 (SEA)
15570	1100-1130 (EAS/ANZ), 1330-1400 (SAS/SEA), 2100-2130 (WAF)
17730	0200-0230 (CA/WNA)

SYRIA
SYRIAN BROADCASTING SERVICE

9950	2110-2210 (ENA), D 2005-2105 (EU)
11625	2005-2105 (EU)
12085	2005-2105 (EU), 2110-2210 (ANZ)
15095	J 2005-2105 (EU), J 2110-2210 (ANZ)

TURKEY
TURKISH RADIO TV CORP

7135	D 2300-2350 (EU/ENA)
7215	D 2100-2150 (EU)
9445	0400-0450 (ENA), 2300-2350 (ENA)
9685	J Su 2200-2250 (EU)
9825	J 2000-2050 (EU)
17760	0400-0450 (NA), 2300-2350 (NA)

UNITED ARAB EMIRATES
UAE RADIO (Domestic/Intl Programs)

11940	0330-0400 (CA)
15320	1600-1645 (EU/ENA)
15435	0330-0400 (CA), 0530-0600 (ANZ), 1030-1100 (EU), 1330-1400 (EU)
17865	1030-1100 (EU), 1330-1400 (EU), 1600-1645 (EU)
17890	0330-0400 (ENA/CA)
21605	1030-1100 (EU), 1330-1400 (EU)
21700	0530-0600 (ANZ), J 0330-0400 (NA)

UNITED KINGDOM
BBC World Service

3955	0500-0730 (EU/NAF)
3975	0645-0730 (EU), 0730-0745 (EU), 1715-1745 (EU)
5975	0430-0730 (NA)
5975	0730-1515 (EU), 2200-0430 (AM)
5995	0900-0945 (EAS), 1300-1400 (EAS), 1500-1615 (EAS)
6010	0545-0730 (EU)
6045	0900-1330 (EU)
6050	0300-0730 (EU)
6065	1200-1215 (SAS/SEA)
6080	2330-2345 (SEA/EAS)
6125	1215-1300 (WEU)
6140	0530-0545 (EEU/ME)
6150	0645-0700 (EEU)

6175	2300-0430 (NA)
6195	0500-0530 (EU), 0545-0630 (EU), 0630-0745 (EU)
6195	0900-0915 (AM), 1100-1330 ((M)
6195	1400-0030 (EU), 1645-1700 (EU), 1945-2115 (EU), D 2115-2315 (EU)
7105	0400-0430 (WAF/CAF), 0445-0500 (WAF/CAF), 0600-0630 (WAF/CAF)
7120	0500-0730 (EU)
7120	2200-2245 (SEA/EAS)
7135	0000-0230 (ME/SAS)
7150	0545-0700 (ANZ), 0700-0730 (EU/ANZ), Sa/Su 0730-0915 (EU), D 0700-0915 (EU/ANZ)
7160	0300-0330 (EAF), 0300-0400 (EAF/SAF), 0330-0400 (EAF), 0400-0500 (SAF), 0500-0545 (SAF)
7165	1715-1745 (WEU)
7170	0200-0230 (WUSSR)
7180	0815-0945 (EAS), 1300-1400 (EAS), 1645-1700 (SAS), 2330-2345 (SEA/EAS)
7185	0300-0730 (EU/NAF)
7210	0300-0330 (EEU)
7230	0730-0745 (WEU/NAF)
7260	0400-0430 (WUSSR)
7260	0645-0700 (EEU)
7320	1300-2315 (EU)
9410	0300-0915 (EU/AF), 0915-1500 (EU), 1500-2315 (EU/AF)
9510	0430-0545 (NA), 1100-1330 (NA)
9515	0230-0330 (ENA/CA/SA), 1500-1745 (NA), 2300-0330 (SA)
9535	0900-1330 (ME)
9590	0030-0230 (ENA/CA/SA), 2200-0030 (NA)
9600	0400-0430 (WAF), 0445-0515 (WAF), 0545-0730 (WAF), 0730-0815 (WAF), J 0300-0400 (CAF/EAF)
9600	J 1130-1200 (EU)
9610	J 1130-1200 (EU)
9640	0545-0915 (CA/ANZ)
9660	D Su 1230-1300 (EU)
9715	J 1800-2030 (SAF)
9750	0900-1515 (EU), J 0430-0445 (EEU)
9760	0730-1615 (EU)
9915	0330-0430 (NAF/WAF), 2200-0330 (AM), 0445-0530 (NAF/WAF), 0600-0630 (NAF/WAF), 0700-0745 (NAF/WAF), Tu/F 2130-2200 (ATL/SA)
11750	0600-0730 (EEU), 1615-1745 (EAF)
11775	1500-1745 (NA)
11780	1230-1300 (WEU), 1230-1300 (EU/WUSSR)
11820	D 2215-2230 (SA)
11860	J 0600-0730 (WAF/CAF), J 0730-0815 (WAF/CAF), J 0815-0915 (WAF/CAF)
11945	2245-0030 (EAS)
11955	0600-0915 (WAF), 2300-2330 (SEA), 2330-0330 (SAS/SEA)
12040	1230-1300 (EEU)
12095	0600-1830 (EU/AF), J 0300-0600 (EU/AF), J 1830-2245 (EU/AF)
15070	0900-1830 (EU), J 0300-0900 (EU), J 1830-2115 (EU)
15105	0730-0800 (WAF), 1300-1330 (WAF)
15260	2000-2315 (SA)
15270	1230-1300 (WUSSR)
15360	0600-0915 (ANZ), 0930-1000 (EAS)
15390	1230-1300 (EEU/ME)

15390	D 2315-2330 (SA)
15420	0400-0900 (ME/EAF/SAF), 0900-1615 (ME/EAF/SAF), J 1615-1745 (ME/EAF/SAF)
15440	1500-1530 (EAF)
17695	1230-1300 (WUSSR)
17705	0900-1515 (WAF)
17710	0000-0045 (EAS)
17740	1500-1530 (EAF)
17790	1030-1515 (SAF)
17810	1130-1200 (EAF/WAF)
17880	0900-0945 (EAS), 1600-1700 (SAF), 1700-1745 (SAF)
17885	0500-0900 (SAF), 0900-1600 (SAF)
18080	0900-1330 (ME), 1500-1530 (EAF), J 1700-1745 (EAF)
21470	0900-1330 (EAF), J 1330-1615 (EAF)
21710	1100-1515 (AF), J 1515-1615 (AF)

USA

AFRTS (Domestic Programs)

6155	24h (EAS)
9293.3	USB 24h/Irr (ATL/EU)
9242.3	LSB 24h/Irr (ATL/EU)
9244.3	LSB 24h/Irr (ATL/EU)
9334.3	LSB 24h/Irr (ATL/EU)
15260	24h (EAS)

KNLS—NEW LIFE STATION

6150	D 0800-1100 (EAS)
7355	D 1730-2030 (EAS)
9750	J 1500-1700 (EAS)
11700	J 1800-1900 (EAS)
11860	J 0800-0900 (EAS)
11930	J 1000-1100 (EAS)

KUSW

6130	D Su 1100-1400 (ENA)
6135	Su 0700-1100 (ENA)
6155	J Su 0500-0700 (ENA)
6175	D Su 0500-0700 (ENA)
9815	Tu-Su 0300-0500 (ENA)
9850	Su 1400-1600 (ENA), J Su 1100-1400 (ENA)
11680	D Tu-Su 0000-0300 (ENA)
11695	J Tu-Su 0100-0300 (ENA)
15225	1600-1900 (ENA)
15580	M-Sa 2200-2400 (ENA), J Tu-Su 0000-0100 (ENA)
15690	J M-Sa 1900-2200 (ENA)
17715	D M-Sa 1900-2200 (ENA)

KVOH—VOICE OF HOPE

13695	D M-Sa 0100-0335 (CA), D Tu-Sa 0235-0300 (CA)
17775	2100-0100 (CA), J M-Sa 0100-0235 (CA), J Tu-Sa 0235-0300 (CA), Su 2000-2030 (CA) Sa/Su 2030-2100 (CA)

VOICE OF AMERICA

5975	1000-1200 (CA)
5985	1000-1200 (PAC/ANZ)
5995	0000-0300 (CA/SA), J 0400-0700 (EU)
6035	0300-0700 (WAF)
6040	0300-0700 (EU), J 1700-2200 ¼EU/NAF
6045	D 1900-2200 (WAF/SAF)
6060	0530-0700 (EEU), D 0500-0530 (EEU)
6080	0600-0700 (WAF)
6125	0600-0700 (NAF)
6130	0000-0200 (CA/SA)

6160	1000–1200 (CA)
7170	0400–0700 (NAF), J 0300–0400 (NAF)
7200	0300–0700 (EU/ME)
7280	0300–0700 (WAF/CAF)
7325	D 0600–0700 (EU), J 0600–0700 (EU)
9455	0000–0200 (CA/SA)
9525	0300–0500 (WAF/CAF)
9530	0600–0700 (WAF)
9540	0500–0700 (WAF/CAF)
9550	0600–0700 (NAF/WAF)
9575	0300–0600 (NAF), Th 0845–0915 (WAF)
9575	1600–1900 (EAF)
9590	1000–1200 (CA)
9640	M–F 2200–2215 (CA)
9650	D 0000–0300 (CA/SA)
9760	1100–1700 (AS), J 1700–2200 (EU/ME)
9775	0000–0300 (CA/SA)
9815	0000–0300 (CA/SA)
11580	0000–0300 (CA/SA)
11695	0000–0100 (CA/SA)
11715	D 1100–1330 (EAS)
11740	0000–0200 (CA/SA), M–F 2200–2215 (CA/SA)
11760	1700–2200 (EU/ME), 2200–0100 (SEA)
11805	0600–0700 (NAF/WAF)
11915	Th 0845–0915 (WAF)
15120	M–F 2200–2215 (CA/SA)
15160	J 0100–0400 (SAS), J 1100–1500 (EAS)
15205	0000–0300 (CA/SA)
15205	0500–0600 (ME/SAS), 1400–1500 (ME/SAS), 1500–1700 (EU/WUSSR), J 0400–0500 (ME/SAS)
15260	J 1500–1800 (ME)
15410	1600–2200 (WAF)
15445	1600–2200 (WAF/CAF)
15580	1600–2200 (WAF/SAF)
15600	D 1600–1830 (WAF), J 1830–2200 (WAF)
17740	2200–0100 (EAS/ANZ)
17785	1600–2200 (WAF/SAF)
17800	1600–2200 (WAF/SAF)
17870	1600–2200 (WAF/SAF)

WCSN—CHRISTIAN SCIENCE MONITOR

5980	1200–1315 (ENA)
7365	D 0600–0755 (EU)
9465	D 1800–2200 (EAS)
9495	D 2000–2155 (EU), D 2200–2355 (AF), J 0600–0755 (EU)
9495	J 1800–2200 (EAS)
9852.5	0000–0155 (AF), 0200–0355 (AF)
9870	0400–0555 (AF)
11900	0800–1600 (EAS)
13760	1400–1515 (EU)
15300	J 2200–2355 (WAF)
15390	J 1800–1955 (NAF/EAF), J 2000–2155 (EU)
15405	2200–0200 (EAS)
17780	0200–0800 (EAS)
21640	1600–1755 (WAF/SAF), D 1800–1955 (NAF/EAF)

WINB—WORLD INTERNATIONAL BC

15185	2000–2245 (EU/NAF)
15295	1600–1700 (EU/NAF), 1800–2000 (EU/NAF)

WMLK—ASSEMBLIES OF YAWEH

9465	0400–0700 (EU/ME), 1700–2000 (EU/ME)

WORLD HARVEST RADIO

5995	1100–1300 (ENA)
6100	D 0600–0800 (ENA/WEU)

The Great Wall of China.

7355	0800–1100 (ENA/CA), J 0300–0400 (CA/SA)
7365	D 0000–0200 (ENA), J 0400–0800 (CA/SA)
7400	0200–0600 (ENA), D 0600–0800 (CA/SA), J 0000–0200 (ENA)
9455	1300–1500 (ENA), D 1500–1600 (ENA)
9495	J 0000–0300 (ENA)
9510	J 0800–1100 (CA/SA)
9580	1300–1500 (ENA)
9620	J 0600–0800 (ENA/WEU)
9770	2100–2400 (ENA/EU)
9852.5	D 0400–0600 (CA/SA)
9870	D 0000–0400 (CA/SA)
11790	1100–1500 (CA)
13760	1800–2100 (ENA/WEU), D 1600–1800 (ENA/WEU)
15105	1500–1800 (CA), J 1700–1800 (ENA/WEU)
17830	1800–2400 (CA/SA)
21655	J 1500–1700 (ENA/WEU)

WRNO WORLDWIDE

6185	0400–0500 (ENA), 0500–0600 (ENA), J 0300–0400 (ENA)
7355	0000–0300 (ENA), 2300–2400 (ENA), D 0300–0400 (ENA)
13760	2100–2400 (ENA)
15420	1700–2100 (ENA), D 1600–1700 (ENA)

WYFR—FAMILY RADIO

5950	D 0100–0800 (NA), D 1200–1545 (NA), J 2300–0145 (NA)
6065	0600–0800 (NA)
6175	D 1300–1545 (NA)
6185	D 1200–1245 (NA)
7355	0600–0745 (EU/NAF)
9455	D 2000–2045 (EU)
9535	J 1400–2245 (ENA)
9555	D 0100–0145 (ENA)
9660	D 2300–0045 (NA)
9680	2300–0245 (ENA)
9852.5	0600–0745 (EU), D 2100–2145 (EU)
11550	1500–1520 (SAS)
11580	0700–0900 (WAF), 1700–1900 (EU)
11830	1300–1545 (NA), D 1545–2245 (NA)
11905	D 2100–2145 (EU)
13695	1300–2300 (ENA)
15055	1300–1500 (SAS)

15170	D 1300–2245 (NA)
15440	1600–1700 (EU), J 1900–2045 (EU)
15566	1900–2045 (EU), J 0300–0345 (SA), J 2045–2145 (EU)
17612.5	D 1600–0045 (NA), J 1500–1600 (SA)
17750	D 1600–1700 (EU), J 2000–2200 (U)
17845	D 1900–1945 (EU), D 2000–2145 (WAF), J 1600–1700 (EU)
21525	1600–1700 (WAF/SAF), J 2000–2245 (WAF/SAF)
21615	J 1600–1700 (EU), J 1900–1945 (EU)

USSR

RADIO KIEV

6010	D 1900–1930 (EU)
6020	D 0030–0100 (ENA), D 0300–0330 (ENA)
6090	D 1900–1930 (EU)
6165	D 1900–1930 (EU)
6200	D 0030–0100 (ENA), D 0300–0330 (ENA)
7165	D 0030–0100 (ENA), D 0300–0330 (ENA)
7170	D 1900–1930 (EU)
7195	D 1900–1930 (EU)
7330	J 1800–1900 (EU)
9560	J 1800–1900 (EU)
9640	J 0200–0230 (ENA/CA), J M–F 2330–2400 (ENA/CA)
9710	J 1800–1830 (EU)
9800	J 0200–0230 (ENA/CA), J 2330–2400 (ENA/CA)
11780	J 1800–1830 (EU)
11790	0030–0100 (WNA), 0300–0330 (WNA)
11860	D 0030–0100 (WNA), D 0300–0330 (WNA)
13645	0030–0100 (WNA), 0300–0330 (WNA)
15180	J 0200–0230 (WNA), J 2330–2400 (WNA)
15455	J 0200–0230 (WNA), J 2330–2400 (WNA)

RADIO MOSCOW/RADIO PEACE & PROGRESS

6000	0000–0500 (NA), D 1000–1300 (NA)
6045	D 2200–0400 (NA)
7100	D 0400–0900 (EU), D 2300–0400 (ENA)
7115	D 2300–0400 (ENA)
7150	D 0400–0600 (EU), D 1800–2200 (EU), D 2300–0400 (ENA)
7165	D 0400–0800 (EU/ENA)
7215	D 2300–0300 (ENA)
7320	D 2300–0400 (ENA)
7335	D 0500–0700 (NA/CA), D 1730–2300 (EU), D 2300–0100 (NA/CA)
7440	J 2030–2200 (EU/ATL)
9520	D 0500–0700 (CA/EU)
9530	J 2300–0700 (ENA/WEU)
9600	J 0000–0500 (NA), J 1000–1300 (NA)
9610	D 0400–0500 (EU)
9640	J 0300–0700 (WEU/ENA/CA)
9765	J 2200–0800 (ENA/CA/WEU)
11710	J 2200–0400 (NA)
11750	J 2100–0300 (NA)
11770	2200–0400 (ENA)
11840	1330–2200 (NA)
12045	2000–2200 (EU)
12060	J 2200–0300 (ENA/CA)
12070	J 0300–0700 (EU/WAF/ATL)
12075	2100–2400 (SEA/ANZ)
13705	1200–1600 (WEU)
15125	0500–0900 (EU), 1000–1600 (EU)

15135	1000–1400 (ENA)
15150	1000–1530 (EAF/EU/ATL)
15175	J Su 2100–2200 (WEU)
15370	1530–1600 (ME)

RADIO TASHKENT

7325	J 1200–1230 (SAS), J 1330–1400 (SAS)
9540	D 1200–1230 (SAS), D 1330–1400 (SAS)
9600	D 1200–1230 (SAS), D 1330–1400 (SAS)
9715	J 1200–1230 (SAS), J 1330–1400 (SAS)
11785	1200–1230 (SAS), 1330–1400 (SAS)
15460	J 1200–1230 (SAS), J 1330–1400 (SAS)

RADIO VILNIUS

6020	D 2300–2330 (ENA)
6200	D 2300–2330 (ENA)
7165	D 2300–2330 (ENA)
9640	J 2200–2230 (ENA/CA)
11720	J 2200–2230 (ENA/CA)
11790	2300–2330 (WNA)
11860	D 2300–2330 (WNA)
13645	2300–2330 (WNA)
15180	J 2200–2230 (WNA)
15455	J 2200–2230 (WNA)

RADIO YEREVAN

11790	0350–0400 (WNA)
11860	D 0350–0400 (WNA)
13645	0350–0400 (WNA)
15180	J 0250–0300 (WNA)
15455	J 0250–0300 (WNA)

VATICAN STATE

VATICAN RADIO

6150	0050–0115, 0310–0330 (NA/CA)
6190	1950–2010 (EU)
6248	1445–1500 (EU)
7250	1950–2010 (EU)
9605	0050–0115 (NA/CA)
9645	1950–2010 (EU)
11780	0050–0115 (NA/CA)

English/Multilingual

6248	M–Sa 0700–0800 (EU), M–Sa 1130–1200 (EU), M–Sa 1600–1630 (EU)

VIETNAM

VOICE OF VIETNAM

9840	1000–1030 (SEA), 1330–1400 (EAS/AM), 1600–1630 (EAS/AM), 1800–1830 (EAS/AM), 1900–1930 (EAS/AM), 2030–2100 (EAS/AM), 2230–2300 (SEA), 2330–2400 (SEA)
15010	J 1000–1030 (SEA), J 1330–1400 (EAS/AM), J 1600–1630 (EAS/AM), J 1800–1830 (EAS/AM), J 1900–1930 (EAS/AM), J 2030–2100 (EAS/AM), J 2230–2300 (SEA), J 2330–2400 (SEA)

YUGOSLAVIA

RADIO YUGOSLAVIA

5980	1830–1900 (WEU), 2000–2030 (WEU)
6100	1830–1900 (EU/NAF/ME), 2000–2030 (EU/NAF/ME), 2215–2230 (EU/NAF/ME)
7240	1530–1600 (EU/NAF/ME), 1830–1900 (EU/NAF/ME), 2000–2030 (EU/NAF/ME), 2215–2230 (EU/NAF/ME)
9620	2000–2030 (ME/EAF), 2215–2230 (EU/ME/NAF)

Worldscan: The Blue Pages

Quick-Access Guide to World Band Schedules

There are hundreds upon hundreds of channels of news and entertainment available on world band radio. As if this were not enough, each channel is often shared by several stations. With such an abundance from which to choose, it can take some doing to figure out what is actually on the air.

Ordinary listings of what's on world band radio are unwieldy because there is such a vast quantity of data. This is why *Passport to World Band Radio* includes the quick-access Blue Pages. With these comprehensive charts, all you need—stations, times, languages, targets, and more—are available at a glance. If something is not clear, the "Terms and Abbreviations" section at the back of the book explains it. There is even a handy key to languages and symbols at the bottom of each Blue Page.

For example, if you're in North America listening to the channel of 6175 kHz at 2300 Universal Time, a glance at the appropriate page shows that the BBC World Service is broadcast in English to this area at that time.

Universal Time Simplifies Listening

Universal Time (UTC)—a handy concept also known as World Time or GMT—is used to eliminate the potential complication of so many time zones throughout the world. It treats the entire world as a single zone and is announced regularly on the hour by many world band stations.

For example, if you're in New York and it's 6:00 AM EST, you will hear the time announced as "11 hours UTC." A glance at your clock shows that this is five hours ahead of your local time. You can either keep this "add five hours" figure in your head or use a separate clock for Universal Time. A growing number of world band radios come with Universal Time clocks built in, and 24-hour UTC clocks are also widely available as accessories.

World Band Stations Heard Outside Intended Target

With several hundred stations on the air at the same time, many piled atop each other like so much cordwood, you can't begin to hear all—or even most—of them. Nevertheless, even stations not targeted to your part of the world may be heard loud and clear. Tune around with the Blue Pages alongside your radio and you'll discover a wealth of stations that can be enjoyed even though they're beamed to a completely different part of our planet.

GUIDE TO WORLDSCAN FORMAT

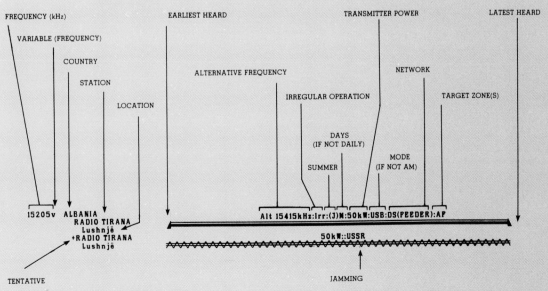

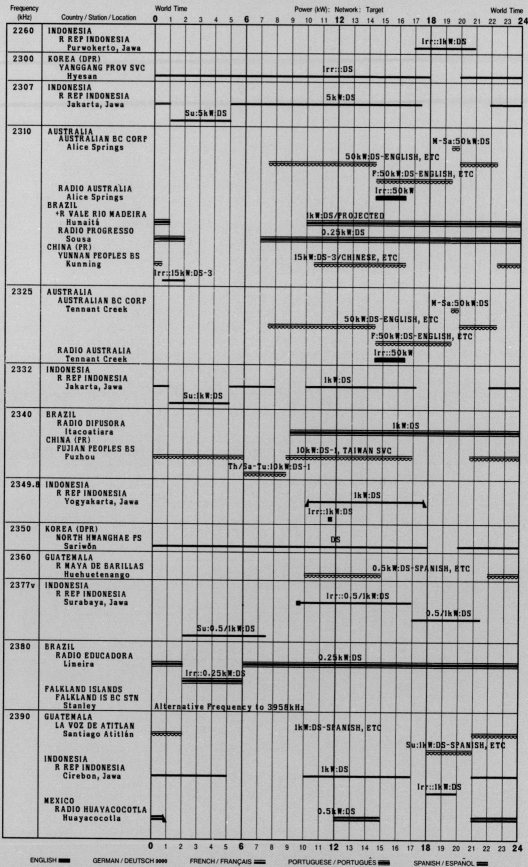

Frequency (kHz)	Country / Station / Location	Details
2260	INDONESIA — R REP INDONESIA — Purwokerto, Jawa	Irr::1kW:DS
2300	KOREA (DPR) — YANGGANG PROV SVC — Hyesan	Irr::DS
2307	INDONESIA — R REP INDONESIA — Jakarta, Jawa	5kW:DS / Su:5kW:DS
2310	AUSTRALIA — AUSTRALIAN BC CORP — Alice Springs	M-Sa:50kW:DS / 50kW:DS-ENGLISH, ETC / F:50kW:DS-ENGLISH, ETC
	RADIO AUSTRALIA — Alice Springs	Irr::50kW
	BRAZIL — +R VALE RIO MADEIRA — Humaitá	1kW:DS/PROJECTED
	RADIO PROGRESSO — Sousa	0.25kW:DS
	CHINA (PR) — YUNNAN PEOPLES BS — Kunming	15kW:DS-3/CHINESE, ETC / Irr::15kW:DS-3
2325	AUSTRALIA — AUSTRALIAN BC CORP — Tennant Creek	M-Sa:50kW:DS / 50kW:DS-ENGLISH, ETC / F:50kW:DS-ENGLISH, ETC
	RADIO AUSTRALIA — Tennant Creek	Irr::50kW
2332	INDONESIA — R REP INDONESIA — Jakarta, Jawa	1kW:DS / Su:1kW:DS
2340	BRAZIL — RADIO DIFUSORA — Itacoatiara	1kW:DS
	CHINA (PR) — FUJIAN PEOPLES BS — Fuzhou	10kW:DS-1, TAIWAN SVC / Th/Sa-Tu:10kW:DS-1
2349.8	INDONESIA — R REP INDONESIA — Yogyakarta, Jawa	1kW:DS / Irr::1kW:DS
2350	KOREA (DPR) — NORTH HWANGHAE PS — Sariwŏn	DS
2360	GUATEMALA — R MAYA DE BARILLAS — Huehuetenango	0.5kW:DS-SPANISH, ETC
2377v	INDONESIA — R REP INDONESIA — Surabaya, Jawa	Irr::0.5/1kW:DS / 0.5/1kW:DS / Su:0.5/1kW:DS
2380	BRAZIL — RADIO EDUCADORA — Limeira	0.25kW:DS / Irr::0.25kW:DS
	FALKLAND ISLANDS — FALKLAND IS BC STN — Stanley	Alternative Frequency to 3958kHz
2390	GUATEMALA — LA VOZ DE ATITLAN — Santiago Atitlán	1kW:DS-SPANISH, ETC / Su:1kW:DS-SPANISH, ETC
	INDONESIA — R REP INDONESIA — Cirebon, Jawa	1kW:DS / Irr::1kW:DS
	MEXICO — RADIO HUAYACOCOTLA — Huayacocotla	0.5kW:DS

ENGLISH ■■■   GERMAN / DEUTSCH ◊◊◊◊   FRENCH / FRANÇAIS ═══   PORTUGUESE / PORTUGUÊS ▬▬▬   SPANISH / ESPAÑOL ▬▬▬

ARABIC / عربي ═══   RUSSIAN / РУССКИЙ ═══   CHINESE / 中文 ◊◊◊◊   JAPANESE / 日本語 ■■■   MULTILINGUAL ∞∞∞   OTHER ▬▬

SUMMER ONLY (J)   WINTER ONLY (D)   JAMMING ∧∧∧ or / or \   EARLIEST HEARD ◢   LATEST HEARD ◣   + TENTATIVE

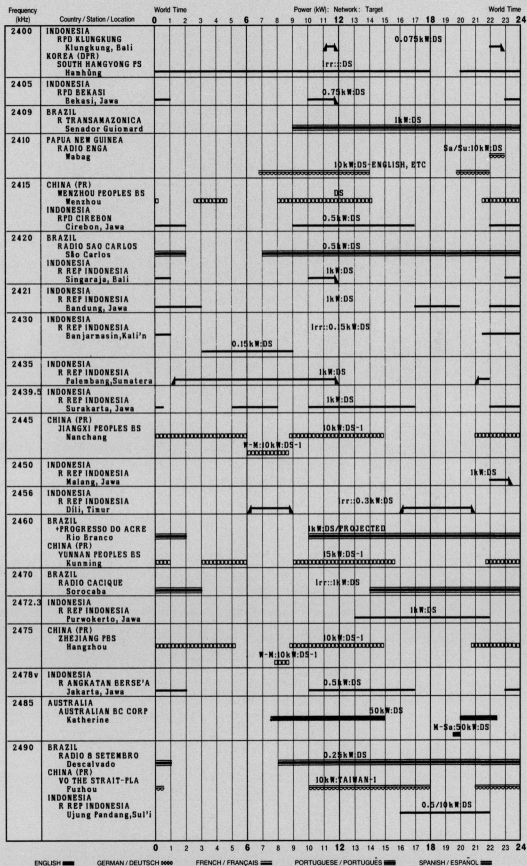

Frequency (kHz)	Country / Station / Location	Power (kW): Network: Target
2400	INDONESIA — RPD KLUNGKUNG — Klungkung, Bali	0.075kW:DS
	KOREA (DPR) — SOUTH HAMGYONG PS — Hamhŭng	Irr::DS
2405	INDONESIA — RPD BEKASI — Bekasi, Jawa	0.75kW:DS
2409	BRAZIL — R TRANSAMAZONICA — Senador Guiomard	1kW:DS
2410	PAPUA NEW GUINEA — RADIO ENGA — Wabag	Sa/Su:10kW:DS — 10kW:DS-ENGLISH, ETC
2415	CHINA (PR) — WENZHOU PEOPLES BS — Wenzhou	DS
	INDONESIA — RPD CIREBON — Cirebon, Jawa	0.5kW:DS
2420	BRAZIL — RADIO SAO CARLOS — São Carlos	0.5kW:DS
	INDONESIA — R REP INDONESIA — Singaraja, Bali	1kW:DS
2421	INDONESIA — R REP INDONESIA — Bandung, Jawa	1kW:DS
2430	INDONESIA — R REP INDONESIA — Banjarmasin,Kali'n	Irr::0.15kW:DS — 0.15kW:DS
2435	INDONESIA — R REP INDONESIA — Palembang,Sumatera	1kW:DS
2439.5	INDONESIA — R REP INDONESIA — Surakarta, Jawa	1kW:DS
2445	CHINA (PR) — JIANGXI PEOPLES BS — Nanchang	10kW:DS-1 — W-M:10kW:DS-1
2450	INDONESIA — R REP INDONESIA — Malang, Jawa	1kW:DS
2456	INDONESIA — R REP INDONESIA — Díli, Timur	Irr::0.3kW:DS
2460	BRAZIL — +PROGRESSO DO ACRE — Rio Branco	1kW:DS/PROJECTED
	CHINA (PR) — YUNNAN PEOPLES BS — Kunming	15kW:DS-1
2470	BRAZIL — RADIO CACIQUE — Sorocaba	Irr::1kW:DS
2472.3	INDONESIA — R REP INDONESIA — Purwokerto, Jawa	1kW:DS
2475	CHINA (PR) — ZHEJIANG PBS — Hangzhou	10kW:DS-1 — W-M:10kW:DS-1
2478v	INDONESIA — R ANGKATAN BERSE'A — Jakarta, Jawa	0.5kW:DS
2485	AUSTRALIA — AUSTRALIAN BC CORP — Katherine	50kW:DS — M-Sa:50kW:DS
2490	BRAZIL — RADIO 8 SETEMBRO — Descalvado	0.25kW:DS
	CHINA (PR) — VO THE STRAIT-PLA — Fuzhou	10kW:TAIWAN-1
	INDONESIA — R REP INDONESIA — Ujung Pandang,Sul'i	0.5/10kW:DS

ENGLISH ▬   GERMAN / DEUTSCH ◊◊◊◊   FRENCH / FRANÇAIS ▬   PORTUGUESE / PORTUGUÊS ▬   SPANISH / ESPAÑOL ▬

ARABIC /ﻉﺏﺭ ▬   RUSSIAN / РУССКИИ ▬   CHINESE / ✦✕ ◊◊◊◊   JAPANESE / 日本語 ▬   MULTILINGUAL ▬   OTHER ▬

SUMMER ONLY (J)   WINTER ONLY (D)   JAMMING ∧∧ or / or \   EARLIEST HEARD ◢   LATEST HEARD ◣   +TENTATIVE

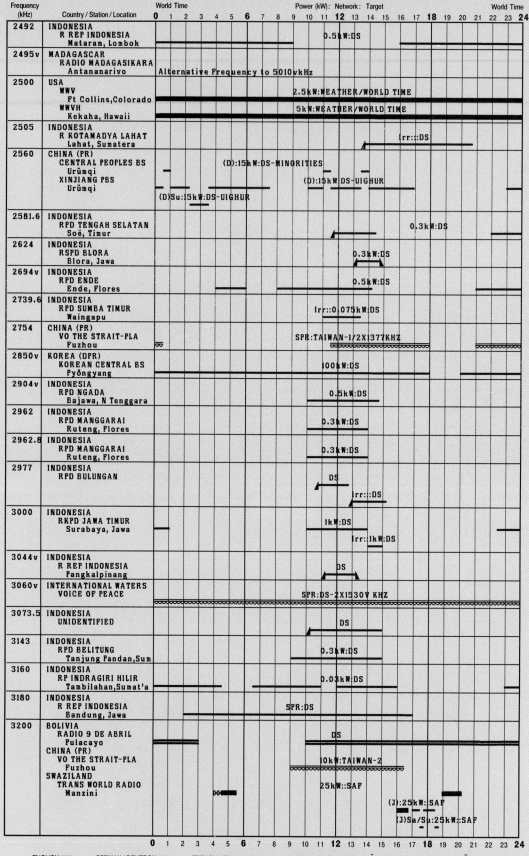

Frequency (kHz)	Country / Station / Location	Transmission details
2492	INDONESIA — R REP INDONESIA, Mataram, Lombok	0.5kW:DS
2495v	MADAGASCAR — RADIO MADAGASIKARA, Antananarivo	Alternative Frequency to 5010vkHz
2500	USA — WWV, Ft Collins, Colorado	2.5kW:WEATHER/WORLD TIME
	WWVH, Kekaha, Hawaii	5kW:WEATHER/WORLD TIME
2505	INDONESIA — R KOTAMADYA LAHAT, Lahat, Sumatera	Irr:::DS
2560	CHINA (PR) — CENTRAL PEOPLES BS, Urümqi	(D):15kW:DS-MINORITIES
	XINJIANG PBS, Urümqi	(D):15kW:DS-UIGHUR / (D)Su:15kW:DS-UIGHUR
2581.6	INDONESIA — RPD TENGAH SELATAN, Soë, Timur	0.3kW:DS
2624	INDONESIA — RSPD BLORA, Blora, Jawa	0.3kW:DS
2694v	INDONESIA — RPD ENDE, Ende, Flores	0.5kW:DS
2739.6	INDONESIA — RPD SUMBA TIMUR, Waingapu	Irr::0.075kW:DS
2754	CHINA (PR) — VO THE STRAIT-PLA, Fuzhou	SPR:TAIWAN-1/2X1377KHZ
2850v	KOREA (DPR) — KOREAN CENTRAL BS, Pyŏngyang	100kW:DS
2904v	INDONESIA — RPD NGADA, Bajawa, N Tenggara	0.5kW:DS
2962	INDONESIA — RPD MANGGARAI, Ruteng, Flores	0.3kW:DS
2962.8	INDONESIA — RPD MANGGARAI, Ruteng, Flores	0.3kW:DS
2977	INDONESIA — RPD BULUNGAN	DS / Irr:::DS
3000	INDONESIA — RKPD JAWA TIMUR, Surabaya, Jawa	1kW:DS / Irr:1kW:DS
3044v	INDONESIA — R REP INDONESIA, Pangkalpinang	DS
3060v	INTERNATIONAL WATERS — VOICE OF PEACE	SPR:DS-2X1530V KHZ
3073.5	INDONESIA — UNIDENTIFIED	DS
3143	INDONESIA — RPD BELITUNG, Tanjung Pandan, Sum	0.3kW:DS
3160	INDONESIA — RP INDRAGIRI HILIR, Tambilahan, Sumat'a	0.03kW:DS
3180	INDONESIA — R REP INDONESIA, Bandung, Jawa	SPR:DS
3200	BOLIVIA — RADIO 9 DE ABRIL, Pulacayo	DS
	CHINA (PR) — VO THE STRAIT-PLA, Fuzhou	10kW:TAIWAN-2
	SWAZILAND — TRANS WORLD RADIO, Manzini	25kW::SAF / (J):25kW::SAF / (J)Sa/Su:25kW::SAF

World Time: 0 1 2 3 4 5 6 7 8 9 10 11 12 13 14 15 16 17 18 19 20 21 22 23 24

Power (kW): Network: Target

ENGLISH ▬   GERMAN / DEUTSCH ▨▨   FRENCH / FRANÇAIS ▬   PORTUGUESE / PORTUGUÊS ▬   SPANISH / ESPAÑOL ▬

ARABIC / عربي ▬   RUSSIAN / РУССКИЙ ▬   CHINESE / 中文 ▨▨   JAPANESE / 日本語 ▨▨   MULTILINGUAL ▨▨   OTHER ▬

SUMMER ONLY (J)   WINTER ONLY (D)   JAMMING ∧∧ or / or \   EARLIEST HEARD ◢   LATEST HEARD ◣   + TENTATIVE

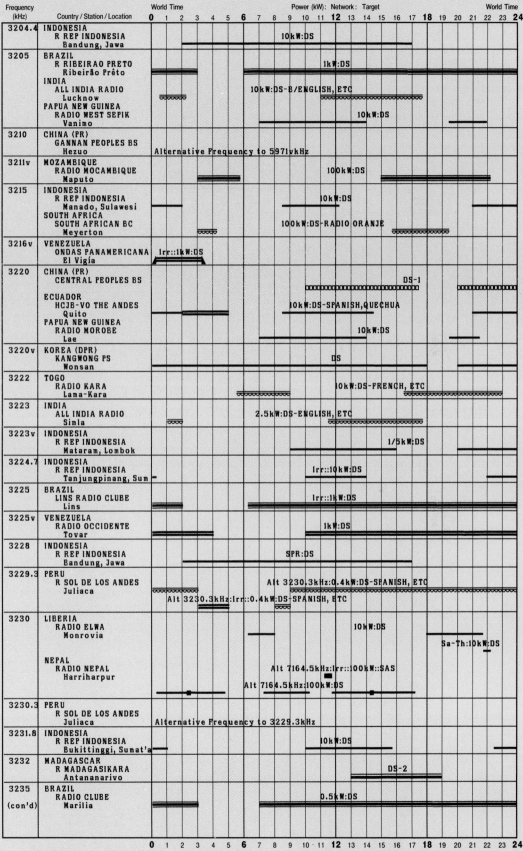

Frequency (kHz)	Country / Station / Location	Schedule / Power (kW): Network : Target
3204.4	**INDONESIA** R REP INDONESIA Bandung, Jawa	10kW:DS
3205	**BRAZIL** R RIBEIRAO PRETO Ribeirão Prêto	1kW:DS
	INDIA ALL INDIA RADIO Lucknow	10kW:DS-B/ENGLISH, ETC
	PAPUA NEW GUINEA RADIO WEST SEPIK Vanimo	10kW:DS
3210	**CHINA (PR)** GANNAN PEOPLES BS Hezuo	Alternative Frequency to 5971vkHz
3211v	**MOZAMBIQUE** RADIO MOCAMBIQUE Maputo	100kW:DS
3215	**INDONESIA** R REP INDONESIA Manado, Sulawesi	10kW:DS
	SOUTH AFRICA SOUTH AFRICAN BC Meyerton	100kW:DS-RADIO ORANJE
3216v	**VENEZUELA** ONDAS PANAMERICANA El Vigía	Irr::1kW:DS
3220	**CHINA (PR)** CENTRAL PEOPLES BS	DS-1
	ECUADOR HCJB-VO THE ANDES Quito	10kW:DS-SPANISH,QUECHUA
	PAPUA NEW GUINEA RADIO MOROBE Lae	10kW:DS
3220v	**KOREA (DPR)** KANGWONG PS Wonsan	DS
3222	**TOGO** RADIO KARA Lama-Kara	10kW:DS-FRENCH, ETC
3223	**INDIA** ALL INDIA RADIO Simla	2.5kW:DS-ENGLISH, ETC
3223v	**INDONESIA** R REP INDONESIA Mataram, Lombok	1/5kW:DS
3224.7	**INDONESIA** R REP INDONESIA Tanjungpinang, Sum	Irr::10kW:DS
3225	**BRAZIL** LINS RADIO CLUBE Lins	Irr::1kW:DS
3225v	**VENEZUELA** RADIO OCCIDENTE Tovar	1kW:DS
3228	**INDONESIA** R REP INDONESIA Bandung, Jawa	SPR:DS
3229.3	**PERU** R SOL DE LOS ANDES Juliaca	Alt 3230.3kHz:0.4kW:DS-SPANISH, ETC Alt 3230.3kHz:Irr::0.4kW:DS-SPANISH, ETC
3230	**LIBERIA** RADIO ELWA Monrovia	10kW:DS Sa-Th:10kW:DS
	NEPAL RADIO NEPAL Harriharpur	Alt 7164.5kHz:Irr::100kW::SAS Alt 7164.5kHz:100kW:DS
3230.3	**PERU** R SOL DE LOS ANDES Juliaca	Alternative Frequency to 3229.3kHz
3231.8	**INDONESIA** R REP INDONESIA Bukittinggi, Sumat'a	10kW:DS
3232	**MADAGASCAR** R MADAGASIKARA Antananarivo	DS-2
3235 (con'd)	**BRAZIL** RADIO CLUBE Marília	0.5kW:DS

ENGLISH ▆▆ GERMAN / DEUTSCH ▨▨▨ FRENCH / FRANÇAIS ▬▬ PORTUGUESE / PORTUGUÊS ▬▬ SPANISH / ESPAÑOL ▬▬

ARABIC / ﻉﺏﺭ ▤ RUSSIAN / PУССКИИ ▬ CHINESE / ✶✶ ▭▭ JAPANESE / 日本語 ▬▬ MULTILINGUAL ▭▭ OTHER ▬

SUMMER ONLY (J) WINTER ONLY (D) JAMMING ∧∧ or / or \ EARLIEST HEARD ◢ LATEST HEARD ◣ + TENTATIVE

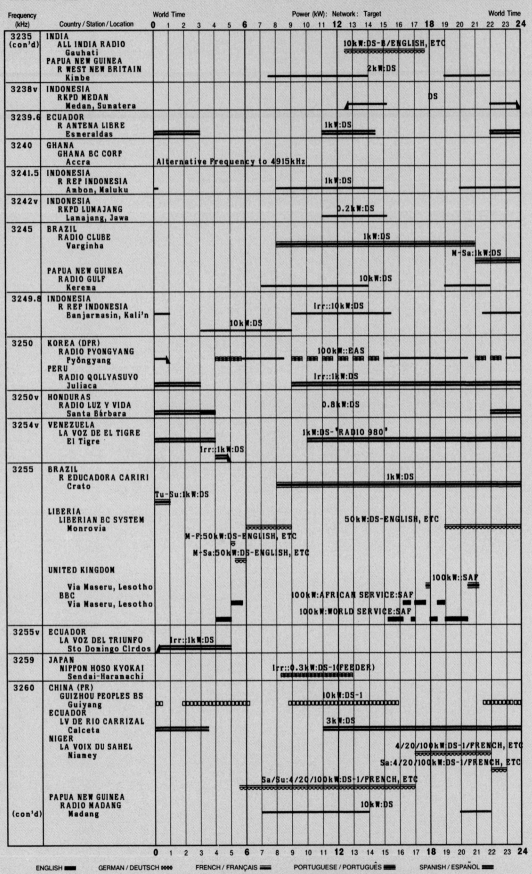

Frequency (kHz)	Country / Station / Location	World Time / Power (kW): Network : Target
3235 (con'd)	INDIA — ALL INDIA RADIO — Gauhati	10kW:DS-B/ENGLISH, ETC
	PAPUA NEW GUINEA — R WEST NEW BRITAIN — Kimbe	2kW:DS
3238v	INDONESIA — RKPD MEDAN — Medan, Sumatera	DS
3239.6	ECUADOR — R ANTENA LIBRE — Esmeraldas	1kW:DS
3240	GHANA — GHANA BC CORP — Accra	Alternative Frequency to 4915kHz
3241.5	INDONESIA — R REP INDONESIA — Ambon, Maluku	1kW:DS
3242v	INDONESIA — RKPD LUMAJANG — Lamajang, Jawa	0.2kW:DS
3245	BRAZIL — RADIO CLUBE — Varginha	1kW:DS / M-Sa:1kW:DS
	PAPUA NEW GUINEA — RADIO GULF — Kerema	10kW:DS
3249.8	INDONESIA — R REP INDONESIA — Banjarmasin, Kali'n	Irr::10kW:DS / 10kW:DS
3250	KOREA (DPR) — RADIO PYONGYANG — Pyŏngyang	100kW::EAS
	PERU — RADIO QOLLYASUYO — Juliaca	Irr::1kW:DS
3250v	HONDURAS — RADIO LUZ Y VIDA — Santa Bárbara	0.8kW:DS
3254v	VENEZUELA — LA VOZ DE EL TIGRE — El Tigre	1kW:DS-"RADIO 980" / Irr::1kW:DS
3255	BRAZIL — R EDUCADORA CARIRI — Crato	1kW:DS / Tu-Su:1kW:DS
	LIBERIA — LIBERIAN BC SYSTEM — Monrovia	50kW:DS-ENGLISH, ETC / M-F:50kW:DS-ENGLISH, ETC / M-Sa:50kW:DS-ENGLISH, ETC
	UNITED KINGDOM — Via Maseru, Lesotho BBC — Via Maseru, Lesotho	100kW::SAF / 100kW:AFRICAN SERVICE:SAF / 100kW:WORLD SERVICE:SAF
3255v	ECUADOR — LA VOZ DEL TRIUNFO — Sto Domingo Clrdos	Irr::1kW:DS
3259	JAPAN — NIPPON HOSO KYOKAI — Sendai-Haramachi	Irr::0.3kW:DS-1(FEEDER)
3260	CHINA (PR) — GUIZHOU PEOPLES BS — Guiyang	10kW:DS-1
	ECUADOR — LV DE RIO CARRIZAL — Calceta	3kW:DS
	NIGER — LA VOIX DU SAHEL — Niamey	4/20/100kW:DS-1/FRENCH, ETC / Sa:4/20/100kW:DS-1/FRENCH, ETC / Sa/Su:4/20/100kW:DS-1/FRENCH, ETC
(con'd)	PAPUA NEW GUINEA — RADIO MADANG — Madang	10kW:DS

ENGLISH ▬ GERMAN / DEUTSCH ∞ FRENCH / FRANÇAIS ═ PORTUGUESE / PORTUGUÊS ▬ SPANISH / ESPAÑOL ▬
ARABIC /لال ≡ RUSSIAN / РУССКИИ ═ CHINESE / ✦✗ ∞ JAPANESE / 日本語 ▬ MULTILINGUAL ∞ OTHER ▬
SUMMER ONLY (J) WINTER ONLY (D) JAMMING ∧∧ or \ or \ EARLIEST HEARD ◢ LATEST HEARD ◣ ✦ TENTATIVE

Frequency (kHz)	Country / Station / Location	World Time / Power (kW): Network: Target

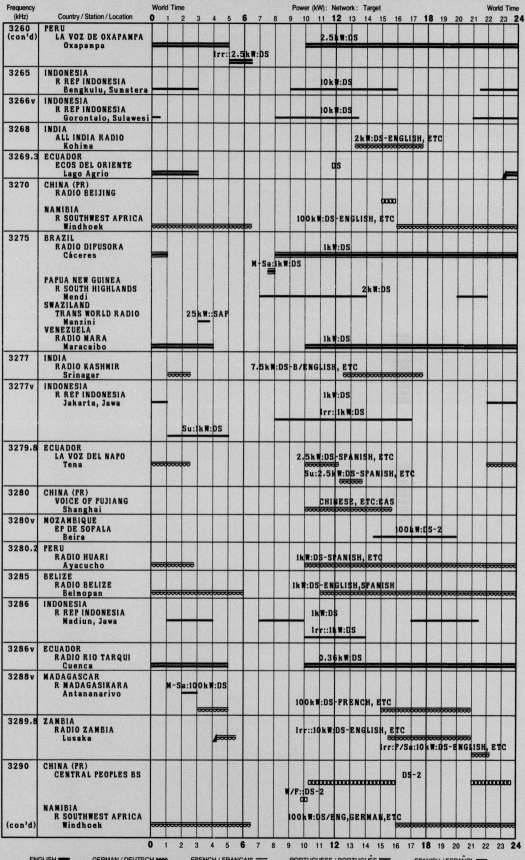

3260 (con'd) — PERU — LA VOZ DE OXAPAMPA — Oxapampa — 2.5kW:DS / Irr:2.5kW:DS

3265 — INDONESIA — R REP INDONESIA — Bengkulu, Sumatera — 10kW:DS

3266v — INDONESIA — R REP INDONESIA — Gorontalo, Sulawesi — 10kW:DS

3268 — INDIA — ALL INDIA RADIO — Kohima — 2kW:DS-ENGLISH, ETC

3269.3 — ECUADOR — ECOS DEL ORIENTE — Lago Agrio — DS

3270 — CHINA (PR) — RADIO BEIJING
NAMIBIA — R SOUTHWEST AFRICA — Windhoek — 100kW:DS-ENGLISH, ETC

3275 — BRAZIL — RADIO DIFUSORA — Cáceres — 1kW:DS / M-Sa:1kW:DS
PAPUA NEW GUINEA — R SOUTH HIGHLANDS — Mendi — 2kW:DS
SWAZILAND — TRANS WORLD RADIO — Manzini — 25kW::SAF
VENEZUELA — RADIO MARA — Maracaibo — 1kW:DS

3277 — INDIA — RADIO KASHMIR — Srinagar — 7.5kW:DS-B/ENGLISH, ETC

3277v — INDONESIA — R REP INDONESIA — Jakarta, Jawa — 1kW:DS / Irr:1kW:DS / Su:1kW:DS

3279.8 — ECUADOR — LA VOZ DEL NAPO — Tena — 2.5kW:DS-SPANISH, ETC / Su:2.5kW:DS-SPANISH, ETC

3280 — CHINA (PR) — VOICE OF PUJIANG — Shanghai — CHINESE, ETC:EAS

3280v — MOZAMBIQUE — EP DE SOFALA — Beira — 100kW:DS-2

3280.2 — PERU — RADIO HUARI — Ayacucho — 1kW:DS-SPANISH, ETC

3285 — BELIZE — RADIO BELIZE — Belmopan — 1kW:DS-ENGLISH, SPANISH

3286 — INDONESIA — R REP INDONESIA — Madiun, Jawa — 1kW:DS / Irr::1kW:DS

3286v — ECUADOR — RADIO RIO TARQUI — Cuenca — 0.36kW:DS

3288v — MADAGASCAR — R MADAGASIKARA — Antananarivo — M-Sa:100kW:DS / 100kW:DS-FRENCH, ETC

3289.8 — ZAMBIA — RADIO ZAMBIA — Lusaka — Irr::10kW:DS-ENGLISH, ETC / Irr:F/Sa:10kW:DS-ENGLISH, ETC

3290 — CHINA (PR) — CENTRAL PEOPLES BS — DS-2 / W/F:DS-2
NAMIBIA — R SOUTHWEST AFRICA — Windhoek **(con'd)** — 100kW:DS/ENG,GERMAN,ETC

ENGLISH ▬ GERMAN / DEUTSCH ◊◊◊◊ FRENCH / FRANÇAIS ▬ PORTUGUESE / PORTUGUÊS ▬ SPANISH / ESPAÑOL ▬
ARABIC / ﻉﺮﺑ ▬ RUSSIAN / РУССКИИ ▬ CHINESE / 中文 ◊◊◊◊ JAPANESE / 日本語 ▬ MULTILINGUAL ◊◊◊◊ OTHER ▬
SUMMER ONLY (J) WINTER ONLY (D) JAMMING /\/\ or / or \ EARLIEST HEARD ◢ LATEST HEARD ◣ + TENTATIVE

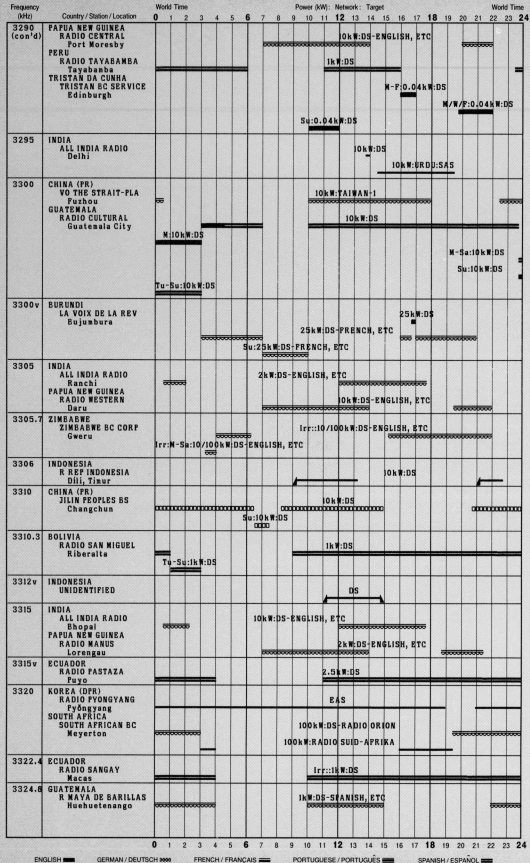

Frequency (kHz)	Country / Station / Location
3290 (con'd)	PAPUA NEW GUINEA — RADIO CENTRAL — Port Moresby — 10kW:DS-ENGLISH, ETC
	PERU — RADIO TAYABAMBA — Tayabamba — 1kW:DS
	TRISTAN DA CUNHA — TRISTAN BC SERVICE — Edinburgh — M-F:0.04kW:DS / M/W/F:0.04kW:DS / Su:0.04kW:DS
3295	INDIA — ALL INDIA RADIO — Delhi — 10kW:DS / 10kW:URDU:SAS
3300	CHINA (PR) — VO THE STRAIT-PLA — Fuzhou — 10kW:TAIWAN-1
	GUATEMALA — RADIO CULTURAL — Guatemala City — 10kW:DS / M:10kW:DS / M-Sa:10kW:DS / Su:10kW:DS / Tu-Su:10kW:DS
3300v	BURUNDI — LA VOIX DE LA REV — Bujumbura — 25kW:DS / 25kW:DS-FRENCH, ETC / Su:25kW:DS-FRENCH, ETC
3305	INDIA — ALL INDIA RADIO — Ranchi — 2kW:DS-ENGLISH, ETC
	PAPUA NEW GUINEA — RADIO WESTERN — Daru — 10kW:DS-ENGLISH, ETC
3305.7	ZIMBABWE — ZIMBABWE BC CORP — Gweru — Irr::10/100kW:DS-ENGLISH, ETC / Irr:M-Sa:10/100kW:DS-ENGLISH, ETC
3306	INDONESIA — R REP INDONESIA — Díli, Timur — 10kW:DS
3310	CHINA (PR) — JILIN PEOPLES BS — Changchun — 10kW:DS / Su:10kW:DS
3310.3	BOLIVIA — RADIO SAN MIGUEL — Riberalta — 1kW:DS / Tu-Su:1kW:DS
3312v	INDONESIA — UNIDENTIFIED — DS
3315	INDIA — ALL INDIA RADIO — Bhopal — 10kW:DS-ENGLISH, ETC
	PAPUA NEW GUINEA — RADIO MANUS — Lorengau — 2kW:DS-ENGLISH, ETC
3315v	ECUADOR — RADIO PASTAZA — Puyo — 2.5kW:DS
3320	KOREA (DPR) — RADIO PYONGYANG — Pyŏngyang — EAS
	SOUTH AFRICA — SOUTH AFRICAN BC — Meyerton — 100kW:DS-RADIO ORION / 100kW:RADIO SUID-AFRIKA
3322.4	ECUADOR — RADIO SANGAY — Macas — Irr::1kW:DS
3324.8	GUATEMALA — R MAYA DE BARILLAS — Huehuetenango — 1kW:DS-SPANISH, ETC

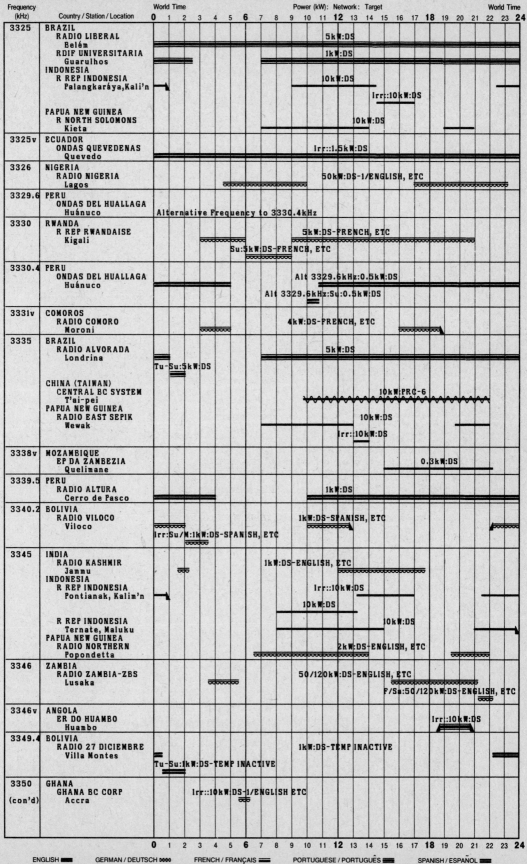

Frequency (kHz)	Country / Station / Location	Schedule / Notes
3325	**BRAZIL** — RADIO LIBERAL, Belém	5kW:DS
	RDIF UNIVERSITARIA, Guarulhos	1kW:DS
	INDONESIA — R REP INDONESIA, Palangkaráya, Kali'n	10kW:DS / Irr::10kW:DS
	PAPUA NEW GUINEA — R NORTH SOLOMONS, Kieta	10kW:DS
3325v	**ECUADOR** — ONDAS QUEVEDENAS, Quevedo	Irr::1.5kW:DS
3326	**NIGERIA** — RADIO NIGERIA, Lagos	50kW:DS-1/ENGLISH, ETC
3329.6	**PERU** — ONDAS DEL HUALLAGA, Huánuco	Alternative Frequency to 3330.4kHz
3330	**RWANDA** — R REP RWANDAISE, Kigali	5kW:DS-FRENCH, ETC / Su:5kW:DS-FRENCH, ETC
3330.4	**PERU** — ONDAS DEL HUALLAGA, Huánuco	Alt 3329.6kHz:0.5kW:DS / Alt 3329.6kHz:Su:0.5kW:DS
3331v	**COMOROS** — RADIO COMORO, Moroni	4kW:DS-FRENCH, ETC
3335	**BRAZIL** — RADIO ALVORADA, Londrina	5kW:DS / Tu-Su:5kW:DS
	CHINA (TAIWAN) — CENTRAL BC SYSTEM, T'ai-pei	10kW:PRC-6
	PAPUA NEW GUINEA — RADIO EAST SEPIK, Wewak	10kW:DS / Irr::10kW:DS
3338v	**MOZAMBIQUE** — EP DA ZAMBEZIA, Quelimane	0.3kW:DS
3339.5	**PERU** — RADIO ALTURA, Cerro de Pasco	1kW:DS
3340.2	**BOLIVIA** — RADIO VILOCO, Viloco	1kW:DS-SPANISH, ETC / Irr:Su/M:1kW:DS-SPANISH, ETC
3345	**INDIA** — RADIO KASHMIR, Jammu	1kW:DS-ENGLISH, ETC
	INDONESIA — R REP INDONESIA, Pontianak, Kalim'n	Irr::10kW:DS / 10kW:DS
	R REP INDONESIA, Ternate, Maluku	10kW:DS
	PAPUA NEW GUINEA — RADIO NORTHERN, Popondetta	2kW:DS-ENGLISH, ETC
3346	**ZAMBIA** — RADIO ZAMBIA-ZBS, Lusaka	50/120kW:DS-ENGLISH, ETC / F/Sa:50/120kW:DS-ENGLISH, ETC
3346v	**ANGOLA** — ER DO HUAMBO, Huambo	Irr::10kW:DS
3349.4	**BOLIVIA** — RADIO 27 DICIEMBRE, Villa Montes	1kW:DS-TEMP INACTIVE / Tu-Su:1kW:DS-TEMP INACTIVE
3350 (con'd)	**GHANA** — GHANA BC CORP, Accra	Irr::10kW:DS-1/ENGLISH ETC

ENGLISH ▬   GERMAN / DEUTSCH ◗◖◗◖   FRENCH / FRANÇAIS ▰▰   PORTUGUESE / PORTUGUÊS ▰▰   SPANISH / ESPAÑOL ▰▰

ARABIC /ﻉﺭﺏ ▰▰   RUSSIAN / PУССКИИ ══   CHINESE /中文 ▢▢▢▢   JAPANESE / 日本語 ▰▰   MULTILINGUAL ▱▱▱   OTHER ▬

SUMMER ONLY (J)   WINTER ONLY (D)   JAMMING ∧∧ or / or \   EARLIEST HEARD ◢   LATEST HEARD ◣   + TENTATIVE

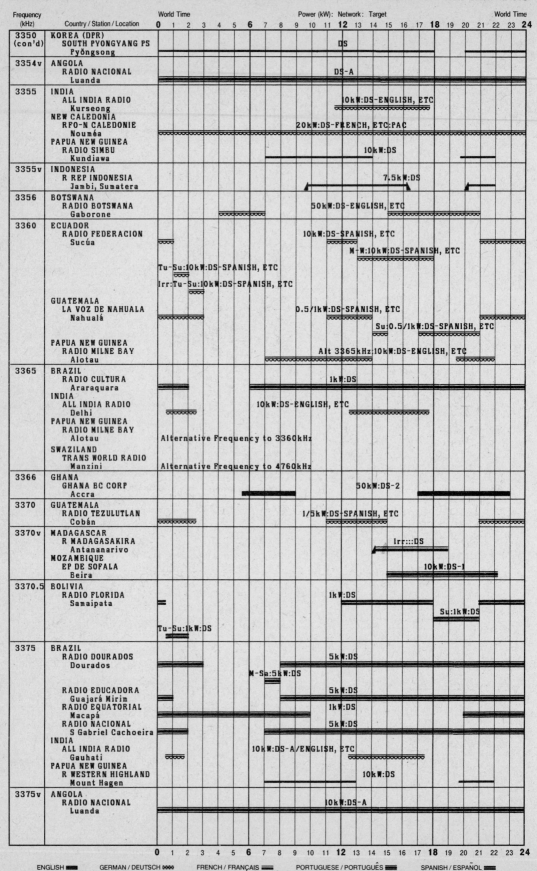

Frequency (kHz)	Country / Station / Location	Power (kW): Network: Target
3350 (con'd)	KOREA (DPR) SOUTH PYONGYANG PS Pyŏngsong	DS
3354v	ANGOLA RADIO NACIONAL Luanda	DS-A
3355	INDIA ALL INDIA RADIO Kurseong	10kW:DS-ENGLISH, ETC
	NEW CALEDONIA RFO-N CALEDONIE Nouméa	20kW:DS-FRENCH, ETC:PAC
	PAPUA NEW GUINEA RADIO SIMBU Kundiawa	10kW:DS
3355v	INDONESIA R REP INDONESIA Jambi, Sumatera	7.5kW:DS
3356	BOTSWANA RADIO BOTSWANA Gaborone	50kW:DS-ENGLISH, ETC
3360	ECUADOR RADIO FEDERACION Sucúa	10kW:DS-SPANISH, ETC / M-W:10kW:DS-SPANISH, ETC / Tu-Su:10kW:DS-SPANISH, ETC / Irr:Tu-Su:10kW:DS-SPANISH, ETC
	GUATEMALA LA VOZ DE NAHUALA Nahualá	0.5/1kW:DS-SPANISH, ETC / Su:0.5/1kW:DS-SPANISH, ETC
	PAPUA NEW GUINEA RADIO MILNE BAY Alotau	Alt 3365kHz:10kW:DS-ENGLISH, ETC
3365	BRAZIL RADIO CULTURA Araraquara	1kW:DS
	INDIA ALL INDIA RADIO Delhi	10kW:DS-ENGLISH, ETC
	PAPUA NEW GUINEA RADIO MILNE BAY Alotau	Alternative Frequency to 3360kHz
	SWAZILAND TRANS WORLD RADIO Manzini	Alternative Frequency to 4760kHz
3366	GHANA GHANA BC CORP Accra	50kW:DS-2
3370	GUATEMALA RADIO TEZULUTLAN Cobán	1/5kW:DS-SPANISH, ETC
3370v	MADAGASCAR R MADAGASAKIRA Antananarivo	Irr:::DS
	MOZAMBIQUE EP DE SOFALA Beira	10kW:DS-1
3370.5	BOLIVIA RADIO FLORIDA Samaipata	1kW:DS / Su:1kW:DS / Tu-Su:1kW:DS
3375	BRAZIL RADIO DOURADOS Dourados	5kW:DS / M-Sa:5kW:DS
	RADIO EDUCADORA Guajará Mirim	5kW:DS
	RADIO EQUATORIAL Macapá	1kW:DS
	RADIO NACIONAL S Gabriel Cachoeira	5kW:DS
	INDIA ALL INDIA RADIO Gauhati	10kW:DS-A/ENGLISH, ETC
	PAPUA NEW GUINEA R WESTERN HIGHLAND Mount Hagen	10kW:DS
3375v	ANGOLA RADIO NACIONAL Luanda	10kW:DS-A

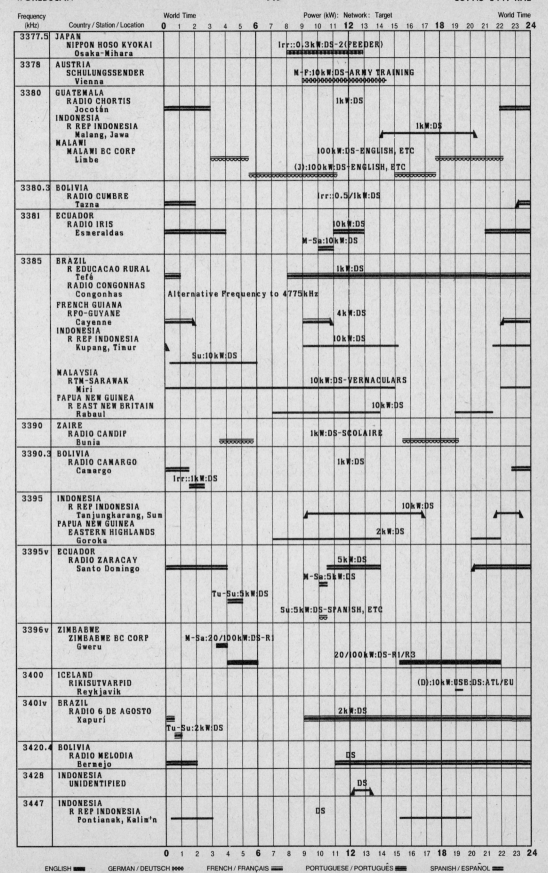

Frequency (kHz)	Country / Station / Location	Details
3377.5	JAPAN — NIPPON HOSO KYOKAI — Osaka-Mihara	Irr::0.3kW:DS-2(FEEDER)
3378	AUSTRIA — SCHULUNGSSENDER — Vienna	M-F:10kW:DS-ARMY TRAINING
3380	GUATEMALA — RADIO CHORTIS — Jocotán	1kW:DS
	INDONESIA — R REP INDONESIA — Malang, Jawa	1kW:DS
	MALAWI — MALAWI BC CORP — Limbe	100kW:DS-ENGLISH, ETC / (J):100kW:DS-ENGLISH, ETC
3380.3	BOLIVIA — RADIO CUMBRE — Tazna	Irr::0.5/1kW:DS
3381	ECUADOR — RADIO IRIS — Esmeraldas	10kW:DS / M-Sa:10kW:DS
3385	BRAZIL — R EDUCACAO RURAL — Tefé	1kW:DS
	RADIO CONGONHAS — Congonhas	Alternative Frequency to 4775kHz
	FRENCH GUIANA — RFO-GUYANE — Cayenne	4kW:DS
	INDONESIA — R REP INDONESIA — Kupang, Timur	10kW:DS / Su:10kW:DS
	MALAYSIA — RTM-SARAWAK — Miri	10kW:DS-VERNACULARS
	PAPUA NEW GUINEA — R EAST NEW BRITAIN — Rabaul	10kW:DS
3390	ZAIRE — RADIO CANDIP — Bunia	1kW:DS-SCOLAIRE
3390.3	BOLIVIA — RADIO CAMARGO — Camargo	1kW:DS / Irr::1kW:DS
3395	INDONESIA — R REP INDONESIA — Tanjungkarang, Sum	10kW:DS
	PAPUA NEW GUINEA — EASTERN HIGHLANDS — Goroka	2kW:DS
3395v	ECUADOR — RADIO ZARACAY — Santo Domingo	5kW:DS / M-Sa:5kW:DS / Tu-Su:5kW:DS / Su:5kW:DS-SPANISH, ETC
3396v	ZIMBABWE — ZIMBABWE BC CORP — Gweru	M-Sa:20/100kW:DS-R1 / 20/100kW:DS-R1/R3
3400	ICELAND — RIKISUTVARPID — Reykjavik	(D):10kW:USB:DS:ATL/EU
3401v	BRAZIL — RADIO 6 DE AGOSTO — Xapurí	2kW:DS / Tu-Su:2kW:DS
3420.4	BOLIVIA — RADIO MELODIA — Bermejo	DS
3428	INDONESIA — UNIDENTIFIED	DS
3447	INDONESIA — R REP INDONESIA — Pontianak, Kalim'n	DS

ENGLISH ▬▬   GERMAN / DEUTSCH ××××   FRENCH / FRANÇAIS ═══   PORTUGUESE / PORTUGUÊS ▬▬   SPANISH / ESPAÑOL ▬▬

ARABIC / عربى ═══   RUSSIAN / РУССКИИ ═══   CHINESE / 中文 ××××   JAPANESE / 日本語 ▬▬   MULTILINGUAL ▒▒▒   OTHER ▬▬

SUMMER ONLY (J)   WINTER ONLY (D)   JAMMING ∧∧ or / or \   EARLIEST HEARD ◢   LATEST HEARD ◣   + TENTATIVE

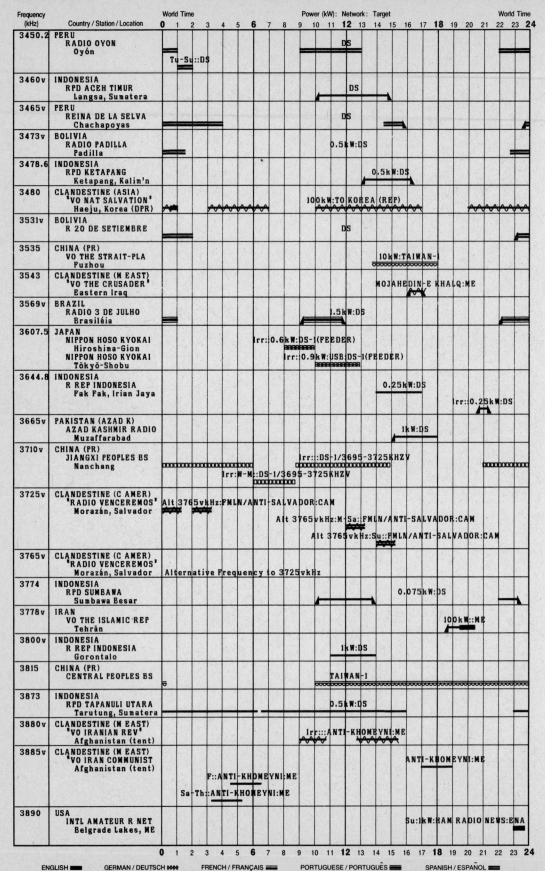

Frequency (kHz)	Country / Station / Location	World Time 0-24 / Power (kW): Network: Target
3450.2	PERU RADIO OYON Oyón	DS / Tu-Su::DS
3460v	INDONESIA RPD ACEH TIMUR Langsa, Sumatera	DS
3465v	PERU REINA DE LA SELVA Chachapoyas	DS
3473v	BOLIVIA RADIO PADILLA Padilla	0.5kW:DS
3478.6	INDONESIA RPD KETAPANG Ketapang, Kalim'n	0.5kW:DS
3480	CLANDESTINE (ASIA) 'VO NAT SALVATION' Haeju, Korea (DPR)	100kW:TO KOREA (REP)
3531v	BOLIVIA R 20 DE SETIEMBRE	DS
3535	CHINA (PR) VO THE STRAIT-PLA Fuzhou	10kW:TAIWAN-1
3543	CLANDESTINE (M EAST) 'VO THE CRUSADER' Eastern Iraq	MOJAHEDIN-E KHALQ:ME
3569v	BRAZIL RADIO 3 DE JULHO Brasiléia	1.5kW:DS
3607.5	JAPAN NIPPON HOSO KYOKAI Hiroshima-Gion NIPPON HOSO KYOKAI Tōkyō-Shobu	Irr:0.6kW:DS-1(FEEDER) / Irr:0.9kW:USB:DS-1(FEEDER)
3644.8	INDONESIA R REP INDONESIA Fak Fak, Irian Jaya	0.25kW:DS / Irr::0.25kW:DS
3665v	PAKISTAN (AZAD K) AZAD KASHMIR RADIO Muzaffarabad	1kW:DS
3710v	CHINA (PR) JIANGXI PEOPLES BS Nanchang	Irr::DS-1/3695-3725KHZV / Irr:W-M::DS-1/3695-3725KHZV
3725v	CLANDESTINE (C AMER) 'RADIO VENCEREMOS' Morazán, Salvador	Alt 3765vkHz:FMLN/ANTI-SALVADOR:CAM / Alt 3765vkHz:M-Sa::FMLN/ANTI-SALVADOR:CAM / Alt 3765vkHz:Su::FMLN/ANTI-SALVADOR:CAM
3765v	CLANDESTINE (C AMER) 'RADIO VENCEREMOS' Morazán, Salvador	Alternative Frequency to 3725vkHz
3774	INDONESIA RPD SUMBAWA Sumbawa Besar	0.075kW:DS
3778v	IRAN VO THE ISLAMIC REP Tehrān	100kW::ME
3800v	INDONESIA R REP INDONESIA Gorontalo	1kW:DS
3815	CHINA (PR) CENTRAL PEOPLES BS	TAIWAN-1
3873	INDONESIA RPD TAPANULI UTARA Tarutung, Sumatera	0.5kW:DS
3880v	CLANDESTINE (M EAST) 'VO IRANIAN REV' Afghanistan (tent)	Irr::::ANTI-KHOMEYNI:ME
3885v	CLANDESTINE (M EAST) 'VO IRAN COMMUNIST' Afghanistan (tent)	ANTI-KHOMEYNI:ME / F::ANTI-KHOMEYNI:ME / Sa-Th::ANTI-KHOMEYNI:ME
3890	USA INTL AMATEUR R NET Belgrade Lakes, ME	Su:1kW:HAM RADIO NEWS:ENA

ENGLISH ▬▬ GERMAN / DEUTSCH ⋄⋄⋄⋄ FRENCH / FRANÇAIS ▬▬ PORTUGUESE / PORTUGUÊS ▬▬ SPANISH / ESPAÑOL ▬▬

ARABIC / عربي ▬▬ RUSSIAN / РУССКИИ ▬▬ CHINESE / 中文 ⋄⋄⋄⋄ JAPANESE / 日本語 ▬▬ MULTILINGUAL ⋄⋄⋄⋄ OTHER ▬▬

SUMMER ONLY (J) WINTER ONLY (D) JAMMING ∧∧ or / or \ EARLIEST HEARD ⌐ LATEST HEARD ⌐ ✝ TENTATIVE

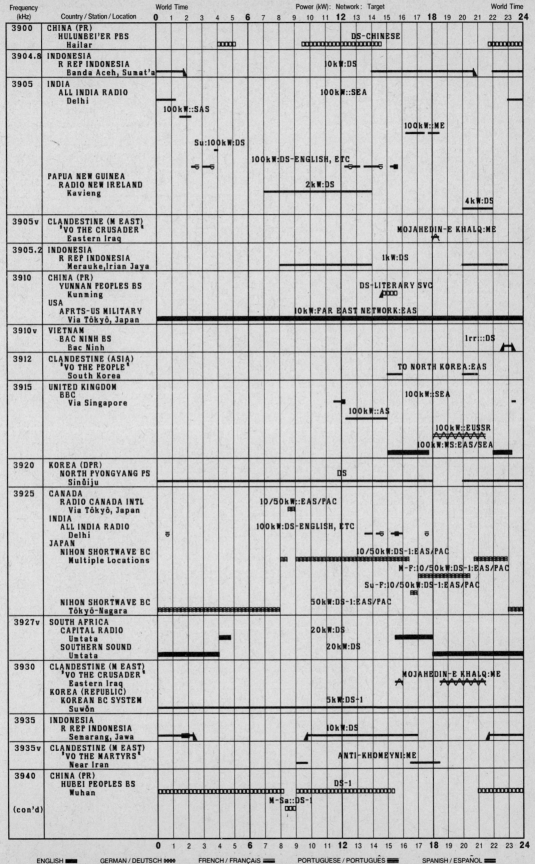

Frequency (kHz)	Country / Station / Location	Details
3900	CHINA (PR) HULUNBEI'ER PBS Hailar	DS-CHINESE
3904.8	INDONESIA R REP INDONESIA Banda Aceh, Sumat'a	10kW:DS
3905	INDIA ALL INDIA RADIO Delhi	100kW::SEA 100kW::SAS 100kW::ME Su:100kW:DS 100kW:DS-ENGLISH, ETC
	PAPUA NEW GUINEA RADIO NEW IRELAND Kavieng	2kW:DS 4kW:DS
3905v	CLANDESTINE (M EAST) VO THE CRUSADER Eastern Iraq	MOJAHEDIN-E KHALQ:ME
3905.2	INDONESIA R REP INDONESIA Merauke,Irian Jaya	1kW:DS
3910	CHINA (PR) YUNNAN PEOPLES BS Kunming	DS-LITERARY SVC
	USA AFRTS-US MILITARY Via Tōkyō, Japan	10kW:FAR EAST NETWORK:EAS
3910v	VIETNAM BAC NINH BS Bac Ninh	1rr:::DS
3912	CLANDESTINE (ASIA) VO THE PEOPLE South Korea	TO NORTH KOREA:EAS
3915	UNITED KINGDOM BBC Via Singapore	100kW::SEA 100kW::AS 100kW::EUSSR 100kW:WS:EAS/SEA
3920	KOREA (DPR) NORTH PYONGYANG PS Sinŭiju	DS
3925	CANADA RADIO CANADA INTL Via Tōkyō, Japan	10/50kW::EAS/PAC
	INDIA ALL INDIA RADIO Delhi	100kW:DS-ENGLISH, ETC
	JAPAN NIHON SHORTWAVE BC Multiple Locations	10/50kW:DS-1:EAS/PAC M-F:10/50kW:DS-1:EAS/PAC Su-F:10/50kW:DS-1:EAS/PAC
	NIHON SHORTWAVE BC Tōkyō-Nagara	50kW:DS-1:EAS/PAC
3927v	SOUTH AFRICA CAPITAL RADIO Umtata	20kW:DS
	SOUTHERN SOUND Umtata	20kW:DS
3930	CLANDESTINE (M EAST) VO THE CRUSADER Eastern Iraq	MOJAHEDIN-E KHALQ:ME
	KOREA (REPUBLIC) KOREAN BC SYSTEM Suwŏn	5kW:DS-1
3935	INDONESIA R REP INDONESIA Semarang, Jawa	10kW:DS
3935v	CLANDESTINE (M EAST) VO THE MARTYRS Near Iran	ANTI-KHOMEYNI:ME
3940	CHINA (PR) HUBEI PEOPLES BS Wuhan	DS-1
(con'd)		M-Sa::DS-1

Frequency (kHz) — Country / Station / Location — World Time — Power (kW): Network: Target — World Time

0 1 2 3 4 5 6 7 8 9 10 11 12 13 14 15 16 17 18 19 20 21 22 23 24

ENGLISH ▬▬ GERMAN / DEUTSCH ◊◊◊◊ FRENCH / FRANÇAIS ▬▬ PORTUGUESE / PORTUGUÊS ▬▬ SPANISH / ESPAÑOL ▬▬

ARABIC / ﻉﺮﻉ ▬ RUSSIAN / РУССКИИ ▬ CHINESE / ╈✕ ◊◊◊◊ JAPANESE / 日本語 ▬ MULTILINGUAL ▭▭▭ OTHER ▬

SUMMER ONLY (J) WINTER ONLY (D) JAMMING ∧∧ or / or \ EARLIEST HEARD ◢ LATEST HEARD ◣ + TENTATIVE

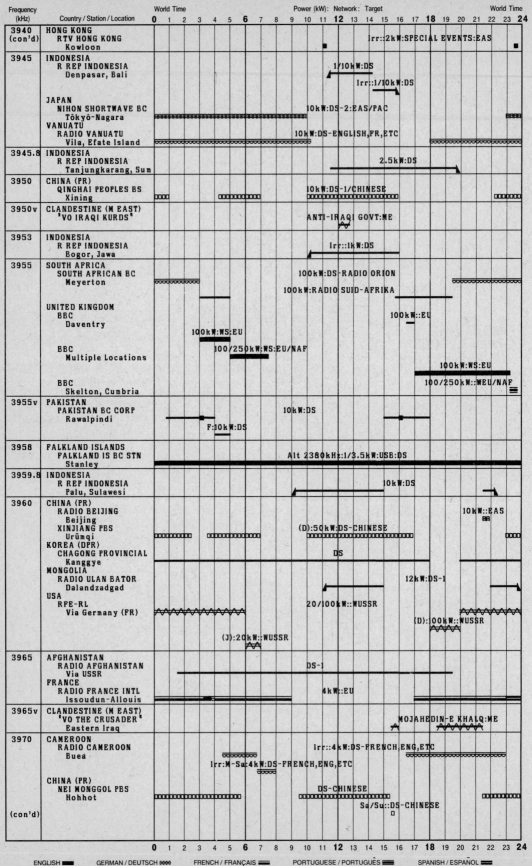

Frequency (kHz)	Country / Station / Location	World Time 0 1 2 3 4 5 6 7 8 9 10 11 12 13 14 15 16 17 18 19 20 21 22 23 24
3940 (con'd)	HONG KONG / RTV HONG KONG / Kowloon	Irr::2kW:SPECIAL EVENTS:EAS
3945	INDONESIA / R REP INDONESIA / Denpasar, Bali	1/10kW:DS — Irr::1/10kW:DS
	JAPAN / NIHON SHORTWAVE BC / Tōkyō-Nagara	10kW:DS-2:EAS/PAC
	VANUATU / RADIO VANUATU / Vila, Efate Island	10kW:DS-ENGLISH,FR,ETC
3945.8	INDONESIA / R REP INDONESIA / Tanjungkarang, Sum	2.5kW:DS
3950	CHINA (PR) / QINGHAI PEOPLES BS / Xining	10kW:DS-1/CHINESE
3950v	CLANDESTINE (M EAST) / 'VO IRAQI KURDS'	ANTI-IRAQI GOVT:ME
3953	INDONESIA / R REP INDONESIA / Bogor, Jawa	Irr::1kW:DS
3955	SOUTH AFRICA / SOUTH AFRICAN BC / Meyerton	100kW:DS-RADIO ORION — 100kW:RADIO SUID-AFRIKA
	UNITED KINGDOM / BBC / Daventry	100kW::EU
	BBC / Multiple Locations	100kW:WS:EU — 100/250kW:WS:EU/NAF — 100kW:WS:EU
	BBC / Skelton, Cumbria	100/250kW::WEU/NAF
3955v	PAKISTAN / PAKISTAN BC CORP / Rawalpindi	10kW:DS — F:10kW:DS
3958	FALKLAND ISLANDS / FALKLAND IS BC STN / Stanley	Alt 2380kHz:1/3.5kW:USB:DS
3959.8	INDONESIA / R REP INDONESIA / Palu, Sulawesi	10kW:DS
3960	CHINA (PR) / RADIO BEIJING / Beijing	10kW::EAS
	XINJIANG PBS / Urümqi	(D):50kW:DS-CHINESE
	KOREA (DPR) / CHAGONG PROVINCIAL / Kanggye	DS
	MONGOLIA / RADIO ULAN BATOR / Dalandzadgad	12kW:DS-1
	USA / RFE-RL / Via Germany (FR)	20/100kW::WUSSR — (D):100kW::WUSSR — (J):20kW::WUSSR
3965	AFGHANISTAN / RADIO AFGHANISTAN / Via USSR	DS-1
	FRANCE / RADIO FRANCE INTL / Issoudun-Allouis	4kW::EU
3965v	CLANDESTINE (M EAST) / 'VO THE CRUSADER' / Eastern Iraq	MOJAHEDIN-E KHALQ:ME
3970	CAMEROON / RADIO CAMEROON / Buea	Irr::4kW:DS-FRENCH,ENG,ETC — Irr:M-Sa:4kW:DS-FRENCH,ENG,ETC
	CHINA (PR) / NEI MONGGOL PBS / Hohhot	DS-CHINESE — Sa/Su::DS-CHINESE
(con'd)		

ENGLISH ▬▬ GERMAN / DEUTSCH 0000 FRENCH / FRANÇAIS ═══ PORTUGUESE / PORTUGUÊS ▬▬ SPANISH / ESPAÑOL ▬▬

ARABIC /ﻉﻑ ≡≡ RUSSIAN / PУССКИИ ▬▬ CHINESE /中文 0000 JAPANESE / 日本語 ▬▬ MULTILINGUAL 0000 OTHER ▬▬

SUMMER ONLY (J) WINTER ONLY (D) JAMMING /\/\ or / or \ EARLIEST HEARD ◢ LATEST HEARD ◣ ✦ TENTATIVE

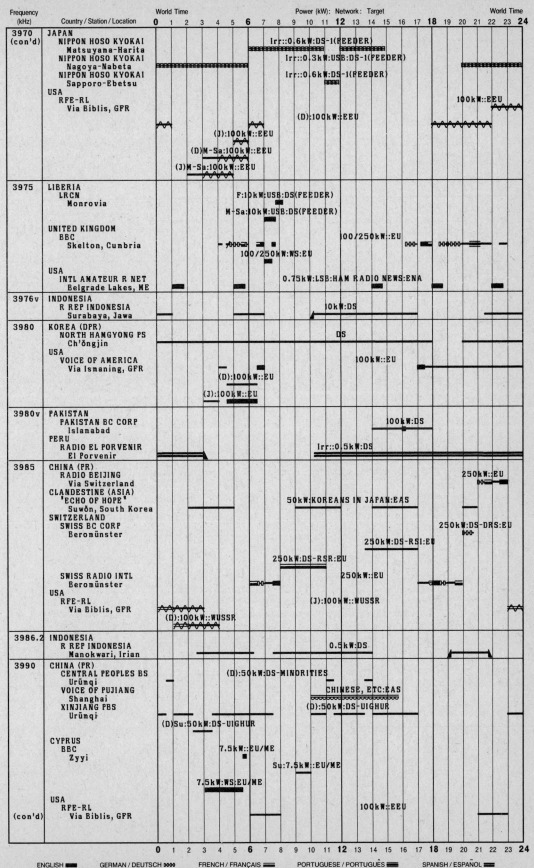

The chart lists broadcast schedules by frequency:

3970 (con'd) — JAPAN
- NIPPON HOSO KYOKAI, Matsuyama-Harita — Irr::0.6kW:DS-1(FEEDER)
- NIPPON HOSO KYOKAI, Nagoya-Nabeta — Irr::0.3kW:USB:DS-1(FEEDER)
- NIPPON HOSO KYOKAI, Sapporo-Ebetsu — Irr::0.6kW:DS-1(FEEDER)
- USA, RFE-RL, Via Biblis, GFR — 100kW::EEU; (D):100kW::EEU; (J):100kW::EEU; (D)M-Sa:100kW::EEU; (J)M-Sa:100kW::EEU

3975 — LIBERIA
- LRCN, Monrovia — F:10kW:USB:DS(FEEDER); M-Sa:10kW:USB:DS(FEEDER)
- UNITED KINGDOM, BBC, Skelton, Cumbria — 100/250kW::EU; 100/250kW:WS:EU
- USA, INTL AMATEUR R NET, Belgrade Lakes, ME — 0.75kW:LSB:HAM RADIO NEWS:ENA

3976v — INDONESIA
- R REP INDONESIA, Surabaya, Jawa — 10kW:DS

3980 — KOREA (DPR)
- NORTH HAMGYONG PS, Ch'ŏngjin — DS
- USA, VOICE OF AMERICA, Via Ismaning, GFR — 100kW::EU; (D):100kW::EU; (J):100kW::EU

3980v — PAKISTAN
- PAKISTAN BC CORP, Islamabad — 100kW:DS
- PERU, RADIO EL PORVENIR, El Porvenir — Irr::0.5kW:DS

3985 — CHINA (PR)
- RADIO BEIJING, Via Switzerland — 250kW::EU
- CLANDESTINE (ASIA), "ECHO OF HOPE", Suwŏn, South Korea — 50kW:KOREANS IN JAPAN:EAS
- SWITZERLAND, SWISS BC CORP, Beromünster — 250kW:DS-DRS:EU; 250kW:DS-RSI:EU; 250kW:DS-RSR:EU
- SWISS RADIO INTL, Beromünster — 250kW::EU
- USA, RFE-RL, Via Biblis, GFR — (J):100kW::WUSSR; (D):100kW::WUSSR

3986.2 — INDONESIA
- R REP INDONESIA, Manokwari, Irian — 0.5kW:DS

3990 — CHINA (PR)
- CENTRAL PEOPLES BS, Urŭmqi — (D):50kW:DS-MINORITIES
- VOICE OF PUJIANG, Shanghai — CHINESE, ETC:EAS
- XINJIANG PBS, Urŭmqi — (D):50kW:DS-UIGHUR; (D)Su:50kW:DS-UIGHUR
- CYPRUS, BBC, Zyyi — 7.5kW::EU/ME; Su:7.5kW::EU/ME; 7.5kW:WS:EU/ME
- USA, RFE-RL, Via Biblis, GFR (con'd) — 100kW::EEU

ENGLISH ▰▰   GERMAN / DEUTSCH ∞∞   FRENCH / FRANÇAIS ▰▰   PORTUGUESE / PORTUGUÊS ▰▰   SPANISH / ESPAÑOL ▰▰

ARABIC / ﻉﺮﺑ ▰   RUSSIAN / РУССКИЙ ▰   CHINESE / ✶✶ ∞∞   JAPANESE / 日本語 ▰▰   MULTILINGUAL ∞∞   OTHER ▬

SUMMER ONLY (J)   WINTER ONLY (D)   JAMMING ∧∧ or / or \   EARLIEST HEARD ◢   LATEST HEARD ◣   ✝ TENTATIVE

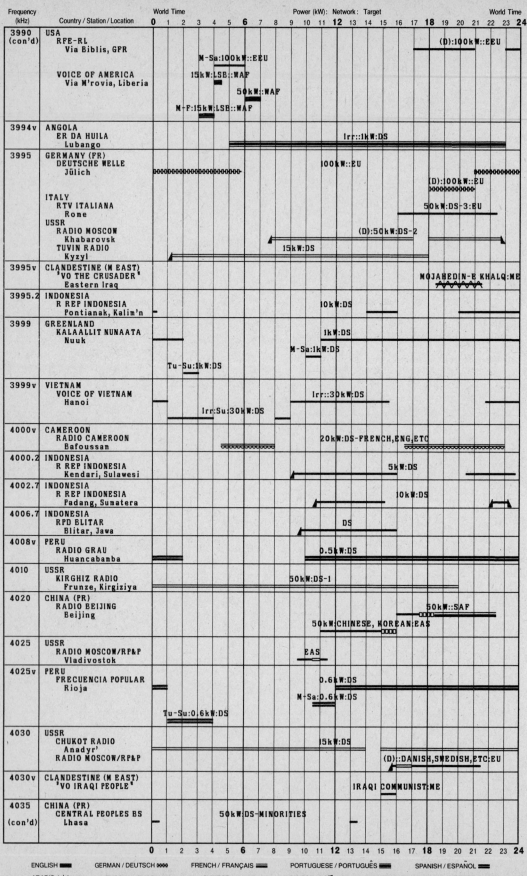

Frequency (kHz)	Country / Station / Location	Power (kW) : Network : Target
3990 (con'd)	USA — RFE-RL, Via Biblis, GFR	(D):100kW::EEU; M-Sa:100kW::EEU
	VOICE OF AMERICA, Via M'rovia, Liberia	15kW:LSB::WAF; 50kW::WAF; M-F:15kW:LSB::WAF
3994v	ANGOLA — ER DA HUILA, Lubango	Irr::1kW:DS
3995	GERMANY (FR) — DEUTSCHE WELLE, Jülich	100kW::EU; (D):100kW::EU
	ITALY — RTV ITALIANA, Rome	50kW:DS-3:EU
	USSR — RADIO MOSCOW, Khabarovsk	(D):50kW:DS-2
	TUVIN RADIO, Kyzyl	15kW:DS
3995v	CLANDESTINE (M EAST) — "VO THE CRUSADER", Eastern Iraq	MOJAHEDIN-E KHALQ:ME
3995.2	INDONESIA — R REP INDONESIA, Pontianak, Kalim'n	10kW:DS
3999	GREENLAND — KALAALLIT NUNAATA, Nuuk	1kW:DS; M-Sa:1kW:DS; Tu-Su:1kW:DS
3999v	VIETNAM — VOICE OF VIETNAM, Hanoi	Irr::30kW:DS; Irr:Su:30kW:DS
4000v	CAMEROON — RADIO CAMEROON, Bafoussam	20kW:DS-FRENCH,ENG,ETC
4000.2	INDONESIA — R REP INDONESIA, Kendari, Sulawesi	5kW:DS
4002.7	INDONESIA — R REP INDONESIA, Padang, Sumatera	10kW:DS
4006.7	INDONESIA — RPD BLITAR, Blitar, Jawa	DS
4008v	PERU — RADIO GRAU, Huancabamba	0.5kW:DS
4010	USSR — KIRGHIZ RADIO, Frunze, Kirgiziya	50kW:DS-1
4020	CHINA (PR) — RADIO BEIJING, Beijing	50kW::SAF; 50kW:CHINESE, KOREAN:EAS
4025	USSR — RADIO MOSCOW/RP&P, Vladivostok	EAS
4025v	PERU — FRECUENCIA POPULAR, Rioja	0.6kW:DS; M-Sa:0.6kW:DS; Tu-Su:0.6kW:DS
4030	USSR — CHUKOT RADIO, Anadyr'	15kW:DS
	RADIO MOSCOW/RP&P	(D)::DANISH,SWEDISH,ETC:EU
4030v	CLANDESTINE (M EAST) — "VO IRAQI PEOPLE"	IRAQI COMMUNIST:ME
4035 (con'd)	CHINA (PR) — CENTRAL PEOPLES BS, Lhasa	50kW:DS-MINORITIES

ENGLISH ▰▰▰   GERMAN / DEUTSCH ∞∞∞   FRENCH / FRANÇAIS ▰▰▰   PORTUGUESE / PORTUGUÊS ▰▰▰   SPANISH / ESPAÑOL ▰▰▰

ARABIC / عربي ▰▰▰   RUSSIAN / РУССКИИ ▰▰▰   CHINESE / ●★ ∞∞∞   JAPANESE / 日本語 ▰▰▰   MULTILINGUAL ∞∞∞   OTHER ▬▬

SUMMER ONLY (J)   WINTER ONLY (D)   JAMMING ∧∧ or / or \   EARLIEST HEARD ◢   LATEST HEARD ◣   ✦ TENTATIVE

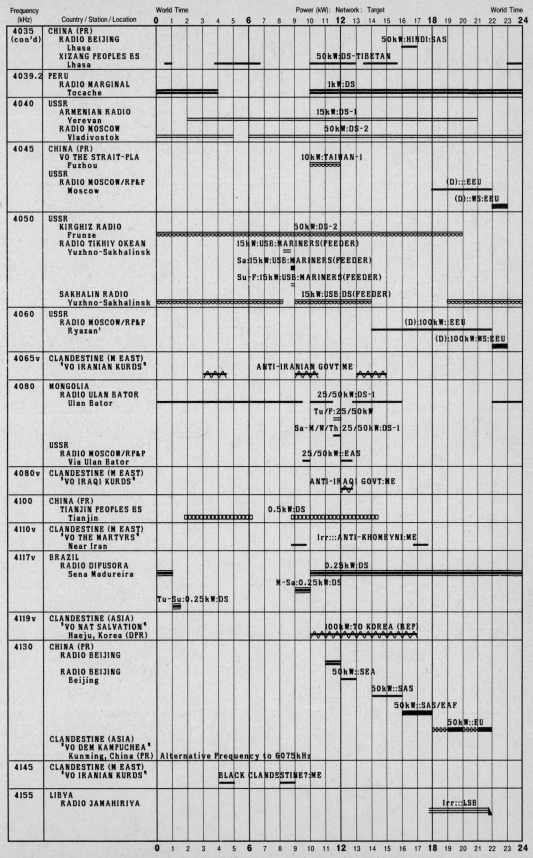

Frequency (kHz)	Country / Station / Location	Power (kW): Network: Target
4035 (con'd)	CHINA (PR) RADIO BEIJING Lhasa	50kW:HINDI:SAS
	XIZANG PEOPLES BS Lhasa	50kW:DS-TIBETAN
4039.2	PERU RADIO MARGINAL Tocache	1kW:DS
4040	USSR ARMENIAN RADIO Yerevan	15kW:DS-1
	RADIO MOSCOW Vladivostok	50kW:DS-2
4045	CHINA (PR) VO THE STRAIT-PLA Fuzhou	10kW:TAIWAN-1
	USSR RADIO MOSCOW/RP&P Moscow	(D):::EEU
		(D)::WS:EEU
4050	USSR KIRGHIZ RADIO Frunze	50kW:DS-2
	RADIO TIKHIY OKEAN Yuzhno-Sakhalinsk	15kW:USB:MARINERS(FEEDER)
		Sa:15kW:USB:MARINERS(FEEDER)
		Su-F:15kW:USB:MARINERS(FEEDER)
	SAKHALIN RADIO Yuzhno-Sakhalinsk	15kW:USB:DS(FEEDER)
4060	USSR RADIO MOSCOW/RP&P Ryazan'	(D):100kW::EEU
		(D):100kW:WS:EEU
4065v	CLANDESTINE (M EAST) "VO IRANIAN KURDS"	ANTI-IRANIAN GOVT:ME
4080	MONGOLIA RADIO ULAN BATOR Ulan Bator	25/50kW:DS-1
		Tu/F:25/50kW
		Sa-M/W/Th:25/50kW:DS-1
	USSR RADIO MOSCOW/RP&P Via Ulan Bator	25/50kW::EAS
4080v	CLANDESTINE (M EAST) "VO IRAQI KURDS"	ANTI-IRAQI GOVT:ME
4100	CHINA (PR) TIANJIN PEOPLES BS Tianjin	0.5kW:DS
4110v	CLANDESTINE (M EAST) "VO THE MARTYRS" Near Iran	Irr:::ANTI-KHOMEYNI:ME
4117v	BRAZIL RADIO DIFUSORA Sena Madureira	0.25kW:DS
		M-Sa:0.25kW:DS
		Tu-Su:0.25kW:DS
4119v	CLANDESTINE (ASIA) "VO NAT SALVATION" Haeju, Korea (DPR)	100kW:TO KOREA (REP)
4130	CHINA (PR) RADIO BEIJING	
	RADIO BEIJING Beijing	50kW::SEA
		50kW::SAS
		50kW::SAS/EAF
		50kW::EU
	CLANDESTINE (ASIA) "VO DEM KAMPUCHEA" Kunming, China (PR)	Alternative Frequency to 6075kHz
4145	CLANDESTINE (M EAST) "VO IRANIAN KURDS"	BLACK CLANDESTINE?:ME
4155	LIBYA RADIO JAMAHIRIYA	Irr:::LSB

ENGLISH ▬ GERMAN / DEUTSCH ◊◊◊◊ FRENCH / FRANÇAIS ▬ PORTUGUESE / PORTUGUÊS ▬ SPANISH / ESPAÑOL ▬

ARABIC / عربية ▬ RUSSIAN / РУССКИЙ ▬ CHINESE / 中文 ◻◻◻◻ JAPANESE / 日本語 ▬▬ MULTILINGUAL ▬▬ OTHER ▬

SUMMER ONLY (J) WINTER ONLY (D) JAMMING /\/\ or / or \ EARLIEST HEARD ◢ LATEST HEARD ◣ + TENTATIVE

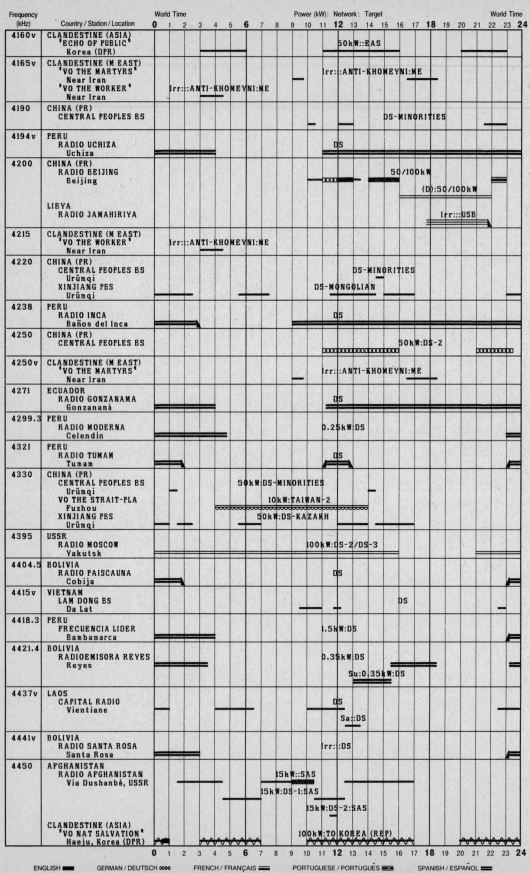

Frequency (kHz)	Country / Station / Location	Power (kW) : Network : Target
4160v	CLANDESTINE (ASIA) "ECHO OF PUBLIC" Korea (DPR)	50kW::EAS
4165v	CLANDESTINE (M EAST) "VO THE MARTYRS" Near Iran "VO THE WORKER" Near Iran	Irr:::ANTI-KHOMEYNI:ME / Irr:::ANTI-KHOMEYNI:ME
4190	CHINA (PR) CENTRAL PEOPLES BS	DS-MINORITIES
4194v	PERU RADIO UCHIZA Uchiza	DS
4200	CHINA (PR) RADIO BEIJING Beijing	50/100kW (D):50/100kW
	LIBYA RADIO JAMAHIRIYA	Irr:::USB
4215	CLANDESTINE (M EAST) "VO THE WORKER" Near Iran	Irr:::ANTI-KHOMEYNI:ME
4220	CHINA (PR) CENTRAL PEOPLES BS Urümqi XINJIANG PBS Urümqi	DS-MINORITIES / DS-MONGOLIAN
4238	PERU RADIO INCA Baños del Inca	DS
4250	CHINA (PR) CENTRAL PEOPLES BS	50kW:DS-2
4250v	CLANDESTINE (M EAST) "VO THE MARTYRS" Near Iran	Irr:::ANTI-KHOMEYNI:ME
4271	ECUADOR RADIO GONZANAMA Gonzanamá	DS
4299.3	PERU RADIO MODERNA Celendín	0.25kW:DS
4321	PERU RADIO TUMAM Tumam	DS
4330	CHINA (PR) CENTRAL PEOPLES BS Urümqi VO THE STRAIT-PLA Fuzhou XINJIANG PBS Urümqi	50kW:DS-MINORITIES / 10kW:TAIWAN-2 / 50kW:DS-KAZAKH
4395	USSR RADIO MOSCOW Yakutsk	100kW:DS-2/DS-3
4404.5	BOLIVIA RADIO PAISCAUNA Cobija	DS
4415v	VIETNAM LAM DONG BS Da Lat	DS
4418.3	PERU FRECUENCIA LIDER Bambamarca	1.5kW:DS
4421.4	BOLIVIA RADIOEMISORA REYES Reyes	0.35kW:DS / Su:0.35kW:DS
4437v	LAOS CAPITAL RADIO Vientiane	DS / Sa::DS
4441v	BOLIVIA RADIO SANTA ROSA Santa Rosa	Irr:::DS
4450	AFGHANISTAN RADIO AFGHANISTAN Via Dushanbé, USSR	15kW::SAS / 15kW:DS-1:SAS / 15kW:DS-2:SAS
	CLANDESTINE (ASIA) "VO NAT SALVATION" Haeju, Korea (DPR)	100kW:TO KOREA (REP)

World Time: 0 1 2 3 4 5 6 7 8 9 10 11 12 13 14 15 16 17 18 19 20 21 22 23 24

ENGLISH ▬   GERMAN / DEUTSCH ◻◻◻◻   FRENCH / FRANÇAIS ▬   PORTUGUESE / PORTUGUÊS ▬   SPANISH / ESPAÑOL ▬

ARABIC / ﻋﺮﺑﻲ ▬   RUSSIAN / РУССКИИ ▬   CHINESE / ✦✗ ◻◻◻◻   JAPANESE / 日本語 ▬   MULTILINGUAL ◻◻◻◻   OTHER ▬

SUMMER ONLY (J)   WINTER ONLY (D)   JAMMING ∧∧ or / or \   EARLIEST HEARD ◢   LATEST HEARD ◣   ✦ TENTATIVE

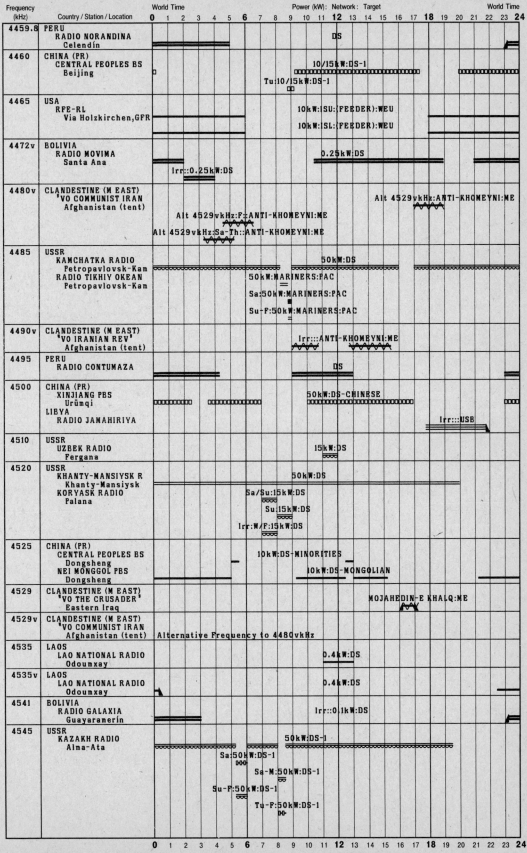

Frequency (kHz)	Country / Station / Location	World Time / Power (kW): Network: Target
4459.8	PERU RADIO NORANDINA Celendín	DS
4460	CHINA (PR) CENTRAL PEOPLES BS Beijing	10/15kW:DS-1 / Tu:10/15kW:DS-1
4465	USA RFE-RL Via Holzkirchen,GFR	10kW:ISU:(FEEDER):WEU / 10kW:ISL:(FEEDER):WEU
4472v	BOLIVIA RADIO MOVIMA Santa Ana	0.25kW:DS / Irr::0.25kW:DS
4480v	CLANDESTINE (M EAST) 'VO COMMUNIST IRAN' Afghanistan (tent)	Alt 4529vkHz:ANTI-KHOMEYNI:ME / Alt 4529vkHz:F::ANTI-KHOMEYNI:ME / Alt 4529vkHz:Sa-Th::ANTI-KHOMEYNI:ME
4485	USSR KAMCHATKA RADIO Petropavlovsk-Kam RADIO TIKHIY OKEAN Petropavlovsk-Kam	50kW:DS / 50kW:MARINERS:PAC / Sa:50kW:MARINERS:PAC / Su-F:50kW:MARINERS:PAC
4490v	CLANDESTINE (M EAST) 'VO IRANIAN REV' Afghanistan (tent)	Irr:::ANTI-KHOMEYNI:ME
4495	PERU RADIO CONTUMAZA	DS
4500	CHINA (PR) XINJIANG PBS Urümqi LIBYA RADIO JAMAHIRIYA	50kW:DS-CHINESE / Irr:::USB
4510	USSR UZBEK RADIO Fergana	15kW:DS
4520	USSR KHANTY-MANSIYSK R Khanty-Mansiysk KORYASK RADIO Palana	50kW:DS / Sa/Su:15kW:DS / Su:15kW:DS / Irr:W/F:15kW:DS
4525	CHINA (PR) CENTRAL PEOPLES BS Dongsheng NEI MONGGOL PBS Dongsheng	10kW:DS-MINORITIES / 10kW:DS-MONGOLIAN
4529	CLANDESTINE (M EAST) 'VO THE CRUSADER' Eastern Iraq	MOJAHEDIN-E KHALQ:ME
4529v	CLANDESTINE (M EAST) 'VO COMMUNIST IRAN' Afghanistan (tent)	Alternative Frequency to 4480vkHz
4535	LAOS LAO NATIONAL RADIO Odoumxay	0.4kW:DS
4535v	LAOS LAO NATIONAL RADIO Odoumxay	0.4kW:DS
4541	BOLIVIA RADIO GALAXIA Guayaramerín	Irr::0.1kW:DS
4545	USSR KAZAKH RADIO Alma-Ata	50kW:DS-1 / Sa:50kW:DS-1 / Sa-M:50kW:DS-1 / Su-F:50kW:DS-1 / Tu-F:50kW:DS-1

World Time: 0 1 2 3 4 5 6 7 8 9 10 11 12 13 14 15 16 17 18 19 20 21 22 23 24

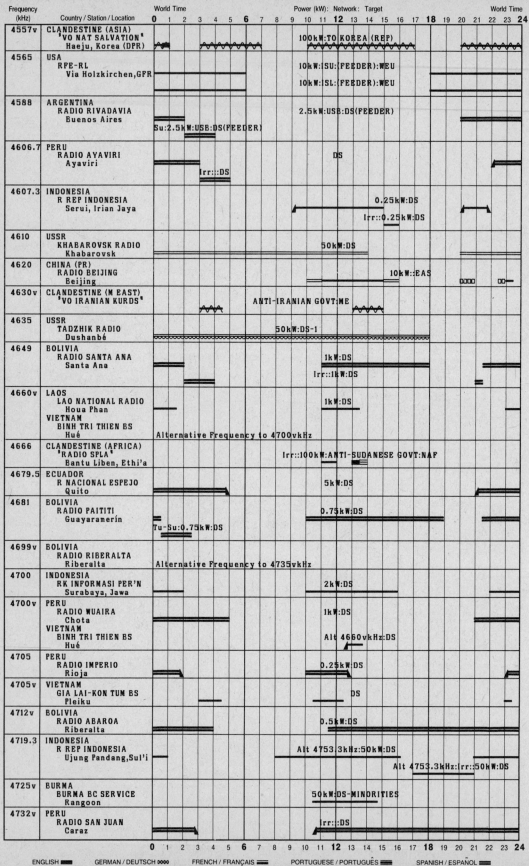

Frequency (kHz)	Country / Station / Location	World Time 0 1 2 3 4 5 6 7 8 9 10 11 12 13 14 15 16 17 18 19 20 21 22 23 24	Power (kW): Network: Target
4557v	CLANDESTINE (ASIA) "VO NAT SALVATION" Haeju, Korea (DPR)		100kW:TO KOREA (REP)
4565	USA RFE-RL Via Holzkirchen,GFR		10kW:|SU:(FEEDER):WEU / 10kW:|SL:(FEEDER):WEU
4588	ARGENTINA RADIO RIVADAVIA Buenos Aires	Su:2.5kW:USB:DS(FEEDER)	2.5kW:USB:DS(FEEDER)
4606.7	PERU RADIO AYAVIRI Ayaviri	Irr::DS	DS
4607.3	INDONESIA R REP INDONESIA Serui, Irian Jaya		0.25kW:DS / Irr::0.25kW:DS
4610	USSR KHABAROVSK RADIO Khabarovsk		50kW:DS
4620	CHINA (PR) RADIO BEIJING Beijing		10kW::EAS
4630v	CLANDESTINE (M EAST) "VO IRANIAN KURDS"		ANTI-IRANIAN GOVT:ME
4635	USSR TADZHIK RADIO Dushanbé		50kW:DS-1
4649	BOLIVIA RADIO SANTA ANA Santa Ana		1kW:DS / Irr::1kW:DS
4660v	LAOS LAO NATIONAL RADIO Houa Phan VIETNAM BINH TRI THIEN BS Hué	Alternative Frequency to 4700vkHz	1kW:DS
4666	CLANDESTINE (AFRICA) "RADIO SPLA" Bantu Liben, Ethi'a		Irr::100kW:ANTI-SUDANESE GOVT:NAF
4679.5	ECUADOR R NACIONAL ESPEJO Quito		5kW:DS
4681	BOLIVIA RADIO PAITITI Guayaramerín	Tu-Su:0.75kW:DS	0.75kW:DS
4699v	BOLIVIA RADIO RIBERALTA Riberalta	Alternative Frequency to 4735vkHz	
4700	INDONESIA RK INFORMASI PER'N Surabaya, Jawa		2kW:DS
4700v	PERU RADIO WUAIRA Chota VIETNAM BINH TRI THIEN BS Hué		1kW:DS / Alt 4660vkHz:DS
4705	PERU RADIO IMPERIO Rioja		0.25kW:DS
4705v	VIETNAM GIA LAI-KON TUM BS Pleiku		DS
4712v	BOLIVIA RADIO ABAROA Riberalta		0.5kW:DS
4719.3	INDONESIA R REP INDONESIA Ujung Pandang,Sul'i		Alt 4753.3kHz:50kW:DS / Alt 4753.3kHz:Irr::50kW:DS
4725v	BURMA BURMA BC SERVICE Rangoon		50kW:DS-MINORITIES
4732v	PERU RADIO SAN JUAN Caraz		Irr::DS

World Time 0 1 2 3 4 5 6 7 8 9 10 11 12 13 14 15 16 17 18 19 20 21 22 23 24

ENGLISH ▬ GERMAN / DEUTSCH ▭▭▭ FRENCH / FRANÇAIS ▬ PORTUGUESE / PORTUGUÊS ▬ SPANISH / ESPAÑOL ▬

ARABIC /ﻉﺏﺝ ▬ RUSSIAN / РУССКИЙ ▬ CHINESE / ✳✕ ▭▭ JAPANESE / 日本語 ▬ MULTILINGUAL ▭▭ OTHER ▬

SUMMER ONLY (J) WINTER ONLY (D) JAMMING /\/\ or / or \ EARLIEST HEARD ◢ LATEST HEARD ◣ + TENTATIVE

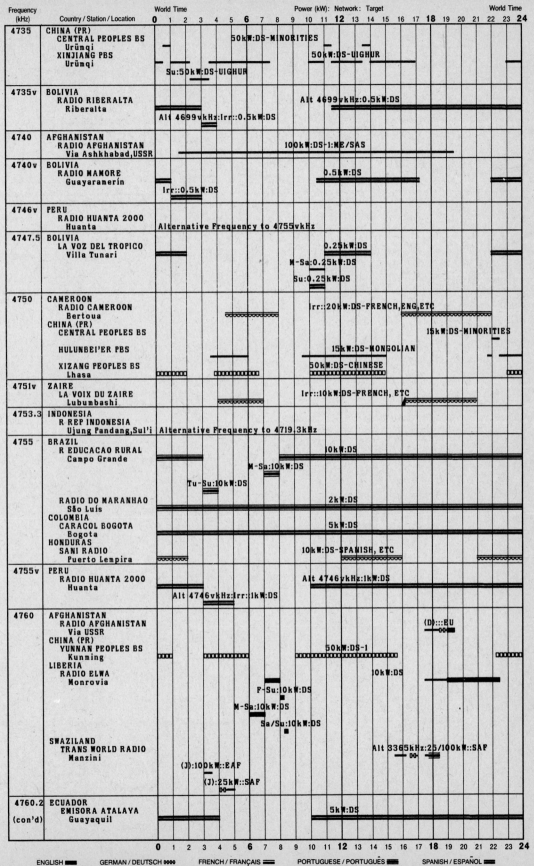

Frequency (kHz)	Country / Station / Location	Transmission details
4735	CHINA (PR) CENTRAL PEOPLES BS Urümqi	50kW:DS-MINORITIES
	XINJIANG PBS Urümqi	50kW:DS-UIGHUR
		Su:50kW:DS-UIGHUR
4735v	BOLIVIA RADIO RIBERALTA Riberalta	Alt 4699vkHz:0.5kW:DS
		Alt 4699vkHz:Irr::0.5kW:DS
4740	AFGHANISTAN RADIO AFGHANISTAN Via Ashkhabad,USSR	100kW:DS-1:ME/SAS
4740v	BOLIVIA RADIO MAMORE Guayaramerín	0.5kW:DS
		Irr::0.5kW:DS
4746v	PERU RADIO HUANTA 2000 Huanta	Alternative Frequency to 4755vkHz
4747.5	BOLIVIA LA VOZ DEL TROPICO Villa Tunari	0.25kW:DS
		M-Sa:0.25kW:DS
		Su:0.25kW:DS
4750	CAMEROON RADIO CAMEROON Bertoua	Irr::20kW:DS-FRENCH,ENG,ETC
	CHINA (PR) CENTRAL PEOPLES BS	15kW:DS-MINORITIES
	HULUNBEI'ER PBS	15kW:DS-MONGOLIAN
	XIZANG PEOPLES BS Lhasa	50kW:DS-CHINESE
4751v	ZAIRE LA VOIX DU ZAIRE Lubumbashi	Irr::10kW:DS-FRENCH, ETC
4753.3	INDONESIA R REP INDONESIA Ujung Pandang,Sul'i	Alternative Frequency to 4719.3kHz
4755	BRAZIL R EDUCACAO RURAL Campo Grande	10kW:DS
		M-Sa:10kW:DS
		Tu-Su:10kW:DS
	RADIO DO MARANHAO São Luís	2kW:DS
	COLOMBIA CARACOL BOGOTA Bogota	5kW:DS
	HONDURAS SANI RADIO Puerto Lempira	10kW:DS-SPANISH, ETC
4755v	PERU RADIO HUANTA 2000 Huanta	Alt 4746vkHz:1kW:DS
		Alt 4746vkHz:Irr::1kW:DS
4760	AFGHANISTAN RADIO AFGHANISTAN Via USSR	(D):::EU
	CHINA (PR) YUNNAN PEOPLES BS Kunming	50kW:DS-1
	LIBERIA RADIO ELWA Monrovia	10kW:DS
		F-Su:10kW:DS
		M-Sa:10kW:DS
		Sa/Su:10kW:DS
	SWAZILAND TRANS WORLD RADIO Manzini	Alt 3365kHz:25/100kW::SAF
		(J):100kW::EAF
		(J):25kW::SAF
4760.2 (con'd)	ECUADOR EMISORA ATALAYA Guayaquil	5kW:DS

World Time: 0 1 2 3 4 5 6 7 8 9 10 11 12 13 14 15 16 17 18 19 20 21 22 23 24

Power (kW): Network: Target

ENGLISH ▬ GERMAN / DEUTSCH ∞∞ FRENCH / FRANÇAIS ⟩⟩ PORTUGUESE / PORTUGUÊS ▬ SPANISH / ESPAÑOL ▬

ARABIC / بي ≡ RUSSIAN / РУССКИЙ ▬ CHINESE / 中文 ∞∞ JAPANESE / 日本語 ▬ MULTILINGUAL ∞∞ OTHER ▬

SUMMER ONLY (J)   WINTER ONLY (D)   JAMMING /\/\ or / or \   EARLIEST HEARD ◢   LATEST HEARD ◣   ＊ TENTATIVE

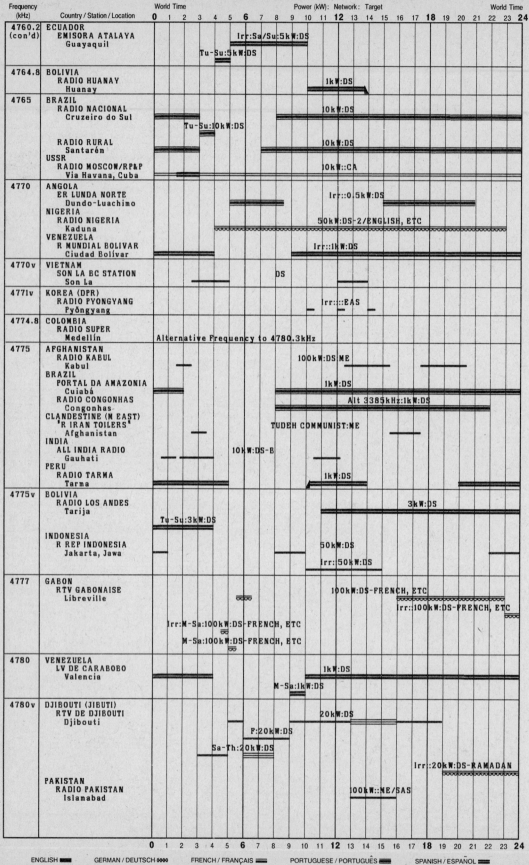

Frequency (kHz)	Country / Station / Location		World Time / Power (kW): Network: Target
4760.2 (con'd)	**ECUADOR** EMISORA ATALAYA Guayaquil		Irr:Sa/Su:5kW:DS / Tu-Su:5kW:DS
4764.8	**BOLIVIA** RADIO HUANAY Huanay		1kW:DS
4765	**BRAZIL** RADIO NACIONAL Cruzeiro do Sul		10kW:DS / Tu-Su:10kW:DS
	RADIO RURAL Santarém		10kW:DS
	USSR RADIO MOSCOW/RP&P Via Havana, Cuba		10kW::CA
4770	**ANGOLA** ER LUNDA NORTE Dundo-Luachimo		Irr::0.5kW:DS
	NIGERIA RADIO NIGERIA Kaduna		50kW:DS-2/ENGLISH, ETC
	VENEZUELA R MUNDIAL BOLIVAR Ciudad Bolívar		Irr::1kW:DS
4770v	**VIETNAM** SON LA BC STATION Son La		DS
4771v	**KOREA (DPR)** RADIO PYONGYANG Pyŏngyang		Irr::::EAS
4774.8	**COLOMBIA** RADIO SUPER Medellín		Alternative Frequency to 4780.3kHz
4775	**AFGHANISTAN** RADIO KABUL Kabul		100kW:DS:ME
	BRAZIL PORTAL DA AMAZONIA Cuiabá		1kW:DS
	RADIO CONGONHAS Congonhas		Alt 3385kHz:1kW:DS
	CLANDESTINE (M EAST) "R IRAN TOILERS" Afghanistan		TUDEH COMMUNIST:ME
	INDIA ALL INDIA RADIO Gauhati		10kW:DS-B
	PERU RADIO TARMA Tarma		1kW:DS
4775v	**BOLIVIA** RADIO LOS ANDES Tarija		3kW:DS / Tu-Su:3kW:DS
	INDONESIA R REP INDONESIA Jakarta, Jawa		50kW:DS / Irr:50kW:DS
4777	**GABON** RTV GABONAISE Libreville		100kW:DS-FRENCH, ETC / Irr::100kW:DS-FRENCH, ETC / Irr:M-Sa:100kW:DS-FRENCH, ETC / M-Sa:100kW:DS-FRENCH, ETC
4780	**VENEZUELA** LV DE CARABOBO Valencia		1kW:DS / M-Sa:1kW:DS
4780v	**DJIBOUTI (JIBUTI)** RTV DE DJIBOUTI Djibouti		20kW:DS / F:20kW:DS / Sa-Th:20kW:DS / Irr::20kW:DS-RAMADAN
	PAKISTAN RADIO PAKISTAN Islamabad		100kW::ME/SAS

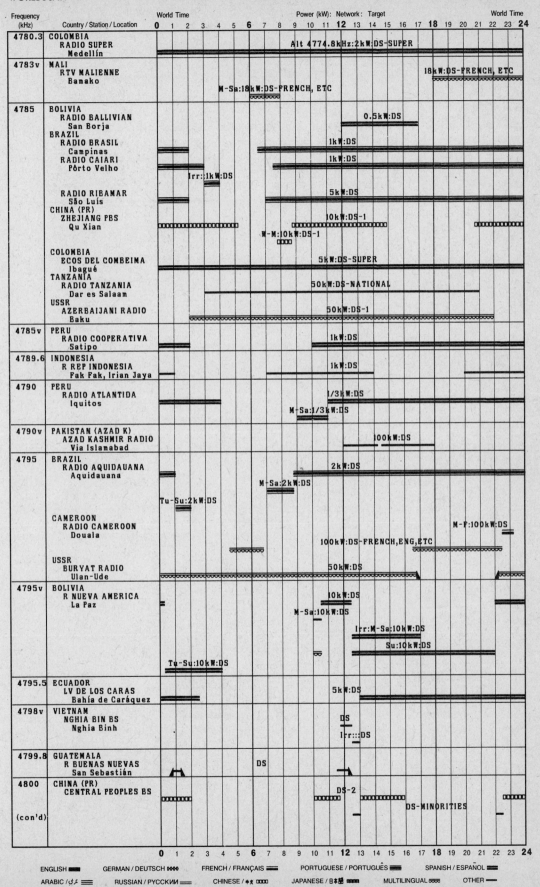

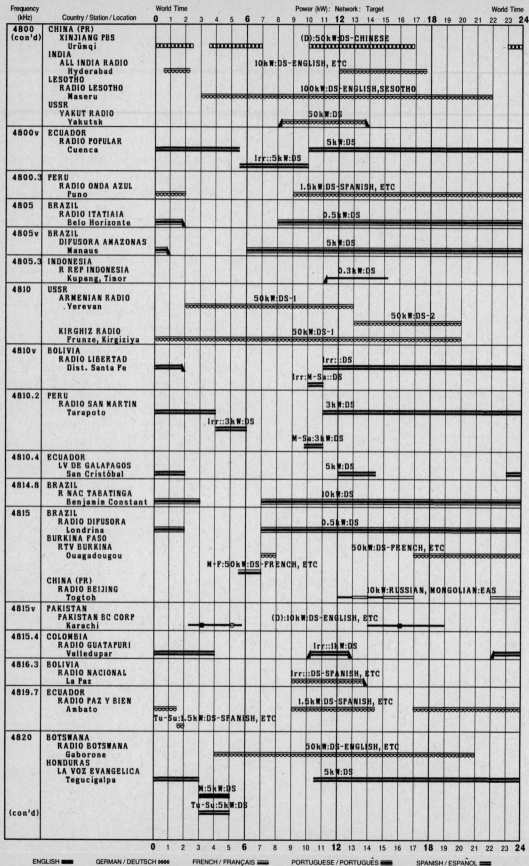

ENGLISH ▄▄▄   GERMAN / DEUTSCH ००००   FRENCH / FRANÇAIS ▭▭▭   PORTUGUESE / PORTUGUÊS ▭▭▭   SPANISH / ESPAÑOL ▭▭▭

ARABIC / عربية ≡   RUSSIAN / РУССКИИ ▭▭   CHINESE / ●★ ००००   JAPANESE / 日本語 ▭▭▭   MULTILINGUAL ००००   OTHER ▬

SUMMER ONLY (J)   WINTER ONLY (D)   JAMMING /\/\ or / or \   EARLIEST HEARD ◢   LATEST HEARD ◣   + TENTATIVE

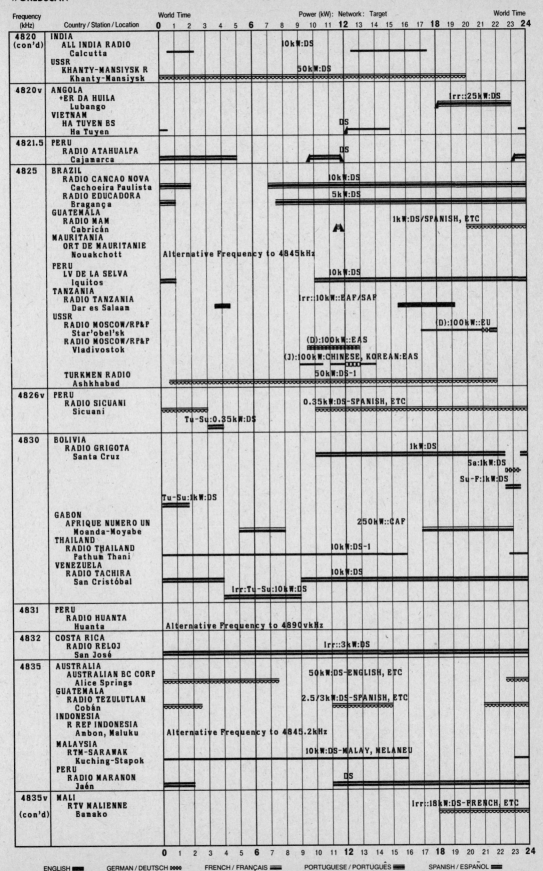

Frequency (kHz)	Country / Station / Location	World Time — Power (kW): Network: Target
4820 (con'd)	**INDIA** ALL INDIA RADIO Calcutta	10kW:DS
	USSR KHANTY-MANSIYSK R Khanty-Mansiysk	50kW:DS
4820v	**ANGOLA** +ER DA HUILA Lubango	Irr::25kW:DS
	VIETNAM HA TUYEN BS Ha Tuyen	DS
4821.5	**PERU** RADIO ATAHUALPA Cajamarca	DS
4825	**BRAZIL** RADIO CANCAO NOVA Cachoeira Paulista	10kW:DS
	RADIO EDUCADORA Bragança	5kW:DS
	GUATEMALA RADIO MAM Cabricán	1kW:DS/SPANISH, ETC
	MAURITANIA ORT DE MAURITANIE Nouakchott	Alternative Frequency to 4845kHz
	PERU LV DE LA SELVA Iquitos	10kW:DS
	TANZANIA RADIO TANZANIA Dar es Salaam	Irr::10kW::EAF/SAF
	USSR RADIO MOSCOW/RP&P Star'obel'sk	(D):100kW::EU
	RADIO MOSCOW/RP&P Vladivostok	(D):100kW::EAS (J):100kW:CHINESE, KOREAN:EAS
	TURKMEN RADIO Ashkhabad	50kW:DS-1
4826v	**PERU** RADIO SICUANI Sicuani	0.35kW:DS-SPANISH, ETC Tu-Su:0.35kW:DS
4830	**BOLIVIA** RADIO GRIGOTA Santa Cruz	1kW:DS Sa:1kW:DS Su-F:1kW:DS Tu-Su:1kW:DS
	GABON AFRIQUE NUMERO UN Moanda-Moyabe	250kW::CAF
	THAILAND RADIO THAILAND Pathum Thani	10kW:DS-1
	VENEZUELA RADIO TACHIRA San Cristóbal	10kW:DS Irr:Tu-Su:10kW:DS
4831	**PERU** RADIO HUANTA Huanta	Alternative Frequency to 4890vkHz
4832	**COSTA RICA** RADIO RELOJ San José	Irr::3kW:DS
4835	**AUSTRALIA** AUSTRALIAN BC CORP Alice Springs	50kW:DS-ENGLISH, ETC
	GUATEMALA RADIO TEZULUTLAN Cobán	2.5/3kW:DS-SPANISH, ETC
	INDONESIA R REP INDONESIA Ambon, Maluku	Alternative Frequency to 4845.2kHz
	MALAYSIA RTM-SARAWAK Kuching-Stapok	10kW:DS-MALAY, MELANEU
	PERU RADIO MARANON Jaén	DS
4835v (con'd)	**MALI** RTV MALIENNE Bamako	Irr::18kW:DS-FRENCH, ETC

World Time: 0 1 2 3 4 5 6 7 8 9 10 11 12 13 14 15 16 17 18 19 20 21 22 23 24

ENGLISH ▬ GERMAN / DEUTSCH ◊◊◊◊ FRENCH / FRANÇAIS ▬ PORTUGUESE / PORTUGUÊS ▬ SPANISH / ESPAÑOL ▬
ARABIC / العربية ▬ RUSSIAN / РУССКИИ ▬ CHINESE / 中文 ◊◊◊◊ JAPANESE / 日本語 ▬ MULTILINGUAL ▬ OTHER ▬
SUMMER ONLY (J) WINTER ONLY (D) JAMMING ∧∧ or / or \ EARLIEST HEARD ◢ LATEST HEARD ◣ + TENTATIVE

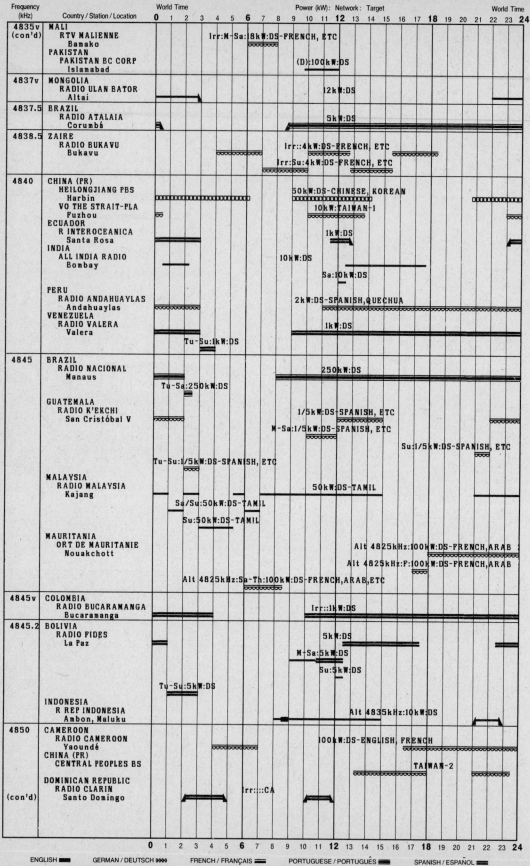

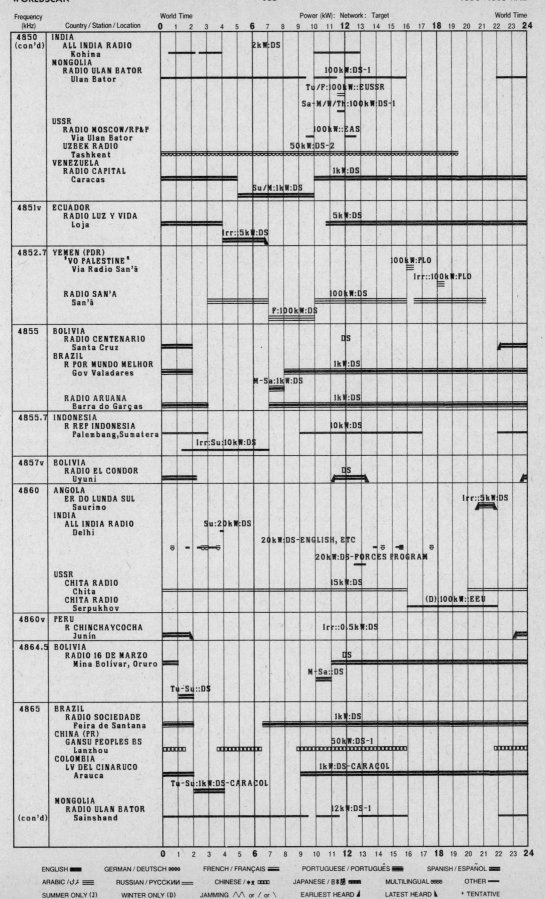

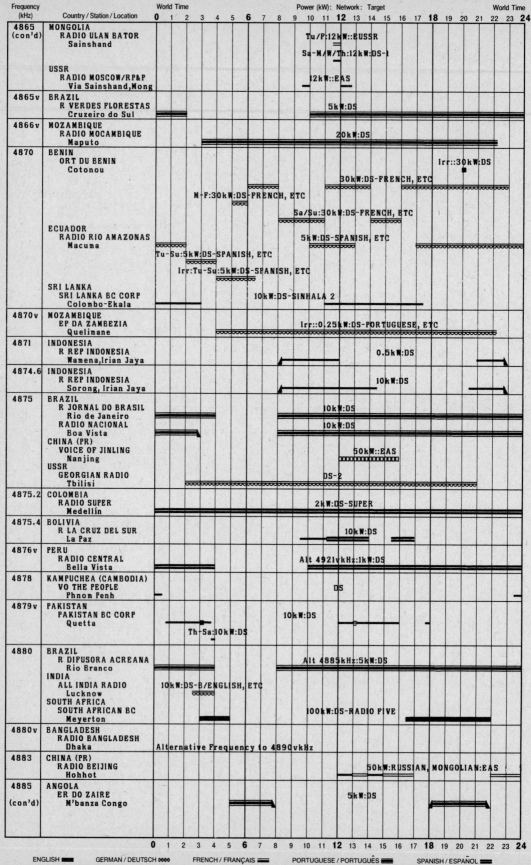

Frequency (kHz)	Country / Station / Location	World Time 0–24 / Power (kW): Network: Target
4865 (con'd)	MONGOLIA RADIO ULAN BATOR Sainshand	Tu/F:12kW::EUSSR / Sa-M/W/Th:12kW:DS-1
	USSR RADIO MOSCOW/RP&P Via Sainshand, Mong	12kW::EAS
4865v	BRAZIL R VERDES FLORESTAS Cruzeiro do Sul	5kW:DS
4866v	MOZAMBIQUE RADIO MOCAMBIQUE Maputo	20kW:DS
4870	BENIN ORT DU BENIN Cotonou	Irr::30kW:DS / 30kW:DS-FRENCH, ETC / M-F:30kW:DS-FRENCH, ETC / Sa/Su:30kW:DS-FRENCH, ETC
	ECUADOR RADIO RIO AMAZONAS Macuma	5kW:DS-SPANISH, ETC / Tu-Su:5kW:DS-SPANISH, ETC / Irr:Tu-Su:5kW:DS-SPANISH, ETC
	SRI LANKA SRI LANKA BC CORP Colombo-Ekala	10kW:DS-SINHALA 2
4870v	MOZAMBIQUE EP DA ZAMBEZIA Quelimane	Irr::0.25kW:DS-PORTUGUESE, ETC
4871	INDONESIA R REP INDONESIA Wamena, Irian Jaya	0.5kW:DS
4874.6	INDONESIA R REP INDONESIA Sorong, Irian Jaya	10kW:DS
4875	BRAZIL R JORNAL DO BRASIL Rio de Janeiro	10kW:DS
	RADIO NACIONAL Boa Vista	10kW:DS
	CHINA (PR) VOICE OF JINLING Nanjing	50kW::EAS
	USSR GEORGIAN RADIO Tbilisi	DS-2
4875.2	COLOMBIA RADIO SUPER Medellín	2kW:DS-SUPER
4875.4	BOLIVIA R LA CRUZ DEL SUR La Paz	10kW:DS
4876v	PERU RADIO CENTRAL Bella Vista	Alt 4921vkHz:1kW:DS
4878	KAMPUCHEA (CAMBODIA) VO THE PEOPLE Phnom Penh	DS
4879v	PAKISTAN PAKISTAN BC CORP Quetta	10kW:DS / Th-Sa:10kW:DS
4880	BRAZIL R DIFUSORA ACREANA Rio Branco	Alt 4885kHz:5kW:DS
	INDIA ALL INDIA RADIO Lucknow	10kW:DS-B/ENGLISH, ETC
	SOUTH AFRICA SOUTH AFRICAN BC Meyerton	100kW:DS-RADIO FIVE
4880v	BANGLADESH RADIO BANGLADESH Dhaka	Alternative Frequency to 4890vkHz
4883	CHINA (PR) RADIO BEIJING Hohhot	50kW:RUSSIAN, MONGOLIAN:EAS
4885 (con'd)	ANGOLA ER DO ZAIRE M'banza Congo	5kW:DS

World Time: 0 1 2 3 4 5 6 7 8 9 10 11 12 13 14 15 16 17 18 19 20 21 22 23 24

ENGLISH ▪▪▪   GERMAN / DEUTSCH ০০০০   FRENCH / FRANÇAIS ▭▭▭   PORTUGUESE / PORTUGUÊS ▰▰▰   SPANISH / ESPAÑOL ◣◣◣

ARABIC / ﻉﺭﺐ ▬▬   RUSSIAN / РУССКИЙ ══   CHINESE / ★☆ ০০০০   JAPANESE / 日本語 ▦▦▦   MULTILINGUAL ০০০০   OTHER ▬▬

SUMMER ONLY (J)   WINTER ONLY (D)   JAMMING ∧∧ or / or \   EARLIEST HEARD ◢   LATEST HEARD ◣   ✦ TENTATIVE

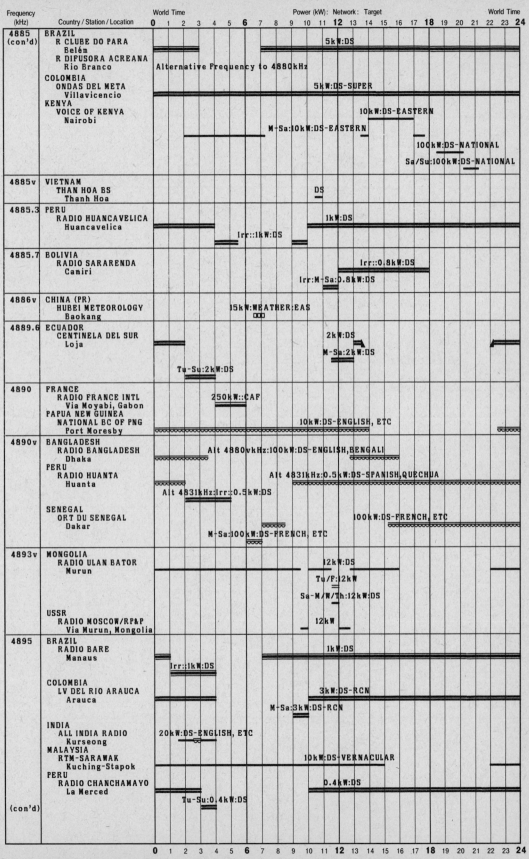

Frequency (kHz)	Country / Station / Location	Power (kW): Network: Target

4885 (con'd) — BRAZIL, R CLUBE DO PARA, Belém — 5kW:DS

R DIFUSORA ACREANA, Rio Branco — Alternative Frequency to 4880kHz

COLOMBIA, ONDAS DEL META, Villavicencio — 5kW:DS-SUPER

KENYA, VOICE OF KENYA, Nairobi — 10kW:DS-EASTERN / M-Sa:10kW:DS-EASTERN / 100kW:DS-NATIONAL / Sa/Su:100kW:DS-NATIONAL

4885v — VIETNAM, THAN HOA BS, Thanh Hoa — DS

4885.3 — PERU, RADIO HUANCAVELICA, Huancavelica — 1kW:DS / Irr::1kW:DS

4885.7 — BOLIVIA, RADIO SARARENDA, Camiri — Irr::0.8kW:DS / Irr:M-Sa:0.8kW:DS

4886v — CHINA (PR), HUBEI METEOROLOGY, Baokang — 15kW:WEATHER:EAS

4889.6 — ECUADOR, CENTINELA DEL SUR, Loja — 2kW:DS / M-Sa:2kW:DS / Tu-Su:2kW:DS

4890 — FRANCE, RADIO FRANCE INTL, Via Moyabi, Gabon — 250kW::CAF

PAPUA NEW GUINEA, NATIONAL BC OF PNG, Port Moresby — 10kW:DS-ENGLISH, ETC

4890v — BANGLADESH, RADIO BANGLADESH, Dhaka — Alt 4880vkHz:100kW:DS-ENGLISH,BENGALI

PERU, RADIO HUANTA, Huanta — Alt 4831kHz:0.5kW:DS-SPANISH,QUECHUA / Alt 4831kHz:Irr::0.5kW:DS

SENEGAL, ORT DU SENEGAL, Dakar — 100kW:DS-FRENCH, ETC / M-Sa:100kW:DS-FRENCH, ETC

4893v — MONGOLIA, RADIO ULAN BATOR, Murun — 12kW:DS / Tu/F:12kW / Sa-M/W/Th:12kW:DS

USSR, RADIO MOSCOW/RP&P, Via Murun, Mongolia — 12kW

4895 — BRAZIL, RADIO BARE, Manaus — 1kW:DS / Irr::1kW:DS

COLOMBIA, LV DEL RIO ARAUCA, Arauca — 3kW:DS-RCN / M-Sa:3kW:DS-RCN

INDIA, ALL INDIA RADIO, Kurseong — 20kW:DS-ENGLISH, ETC

MALAYSIA, RTM-SARAWAK, Kuching-Stapok — 10kW:DS-VERNACULAR

PERU, RADIO CHANCHAMAYO, La Merced — 0.4kW:DS / Tu-Su:0.4kW:DS

(con'd)

ENGLISH ▰▰▰   GERMAN / DEUTSCH ◊◊◊◊   FRENCH / FRANÇAIS ▭▭   PORTUGUESE / PORTUGUÊS ▰▰▰   SPANISH / ESPAÑOL ▰▰▰

ARABIC /ﻉﻉ ▰▰   RUSSIAN / РУССКИИ ▰▰   CHINESE / ✦✦ ◻◻◻◻   JAPANESE / 日本語 ▰▰▰   MULTILINGUAL ◊◊◊◊   OTHER ▬▬

SUMMER ONLY (J)   WINTER ONLY (D)   JAMMING ∧∧ or / or \   EARLIEST HEARD ◢   LATEST HEARD ◣   ✦ TENTATIVE

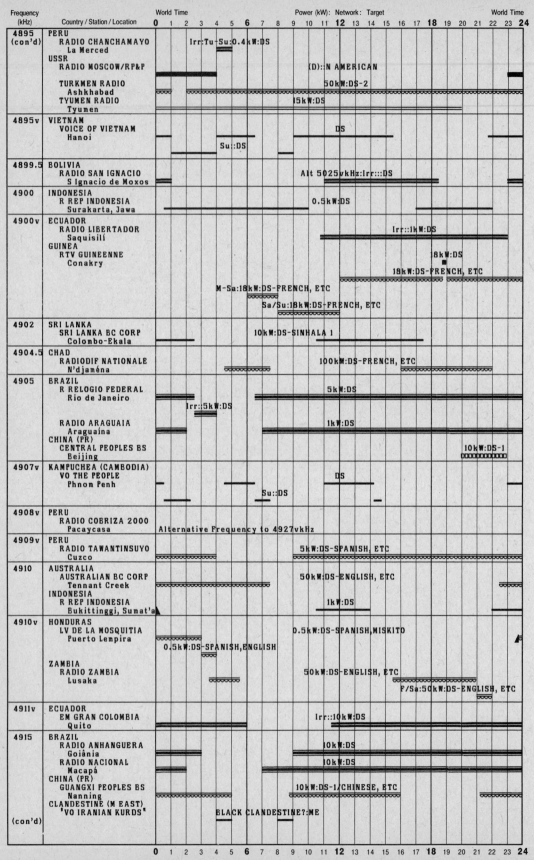

Frequency (kHz)	Country / Station / Location	World Time / Power (kW) : Network : Target
4895 (con'd)	**PERU** **RADIO CHANCHAMAYO** La Merced	Irr:Tu-Su:0.4kW:DS
	USSR **RADIO MOSCOW/RP&P**	(D)::N AMERICAN
	TURKMEN RADIO Ashkhabad	50kW:DS-2
	TYUMEN RADIO Tyumen	15kW:DS
4895v	**VIETNAM** **VOICE OF VIETNAM** Hanoi	DS Su:|:DS
4899.5	**BOLIVIA** **RADIO SAN IGNACIO** S Ignacio de Moxos	Alt 5025vkHz:Irr:::DS
4900	**INDONESIA** **R REP INDONESIA** Surakarta, Jawa	0.5kW:DS
4900v	**ECUADOR** **RADIO LIBERTADOR** Saquisilí	Irr::1kW:DS
	GUINEA **RTV GUINEENNE** Conakry	18kW:DS 18kW:DS-FRENCH, ETC M-Sa:18kW:DS-FRENCH, ETC Sa/Su:18kW:DS-FRENCH, ETC
4902	**SRI LANKA** **SRI LANKA BC CORP** Colombo-Ekala	10kW:DS-SINHALA 1
4904.5	**CHAD** **RADIODIF NATIONALE** N'djaména	100kW:DS-FRENCH, ETC
4905	**BRAZIL** **R RELOGIO FEDERAL** Rio de Janeiro	5kW:DS Irr::5kW:DS
	RADIO ARAGUAIA Araguaína	1kW:DS
	CHINA (PR) **CENTRAL PEOPLES BS** Beijing	10kW:DS-1
4907v	**KAMPUCHEA (CAMBODIA)** **VO THE PEOPLE** Phnom Penh	DS Su::DS
4908v	**PERU** **RADIO COBRIZA 2000** Pacaycasa	Alternative Frequency to 4927vkHz
4909v	**PERU** **RADIO TAWANTINSUYO** Cuzco	5kW:DS-SPANISH, ETC
4910	**AUSTRALIA** **AUSTRALIAN BC CORP** Tennant Creek	50kW:DS-ENGLISH, ETC
	INDONESIA **R REP INDONESIA** Bukittinggi, Sumat'a	1kW:DS
4910v	**HONDURAS** **LV DE LA MOSQUITIA** Puerto Lempira	0.5kW:DS-SPANISH,MISKITO 0.5kW:DS-SPANISH,ENGLISH
	ZAMBIA **RADIO ZAMBIA** Lusaka	50kW:DS-ENGLISH, ETC F/Sa:50kW:DS-ENGLISH, ETC
4911v	**ECUADOR** **EM GRAN COLOMBIA** Quito	Irr::10kW:DS
4915	**BRAZIL** **RADIO ANHANGUERA** Goiânia	10kW:DS
	RADIO NACIONAL Macapá	10kW:DS
	CHINA (PR) **GUANGXI PEOPLES BS** Nanning	10kW:DS-1/CHINESE, ETC
(con'd)	**CLANDESTINE (M EAST)** "VO IRANIAN KURDS"	BLACK CLANDESTINE?:ME

ENGLISH ▰▰▰   GERMAN / DEUTSCH ◊◊◊◊   FRENCH / FRANÇAIS ▰▰▰   PORTUGUESE / PORTUGUÊS ▰▰▰   SPANISH / ESPAÑOL ▰▰▰

ARABIC /ﻉﻑﻉ ▰▰▰   RUSSIAN / РУССКИИ ▰▰▰   CHINESE / ✶★ ◻◻◻◻   JAPANESE / 日本語 ▰▰▰   MULTILINGUAL ⸿⸿⸿⸿   OTHER ▬▬

SUMMER ONLY (J)   WINTER ONLY (D)   JAMMING /\/\/\ or / or \   EARLIEST HEARD ◢   LATEST HEARD ◣   + TENTATIVE

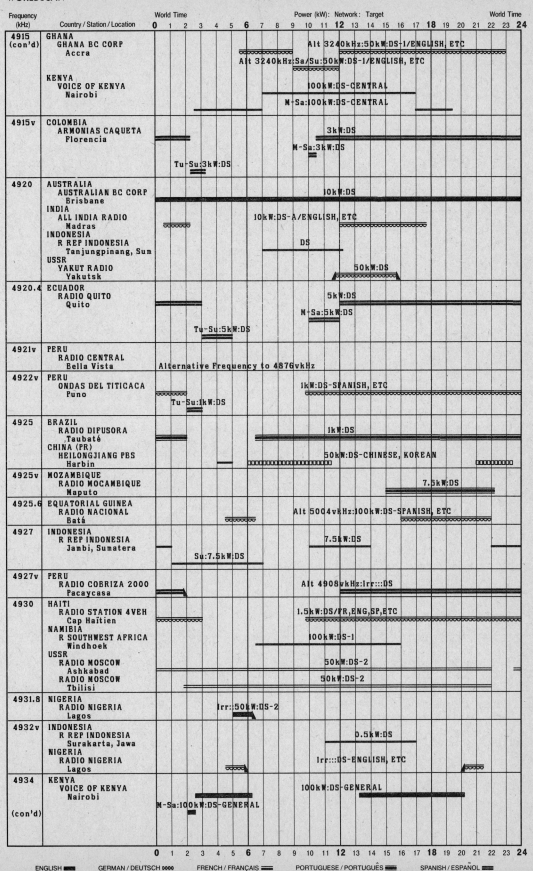

Frequency (kHz)	Country / Station / Location	Power (kW): Network: Target
4915 (con'd)	GHANA / GHANA BC CORP / Accra	Alt 3240kHz:50kW:DS-1/ENGLISH, ETC / Alt 3240kHz:Sa/Su:50kW:DS-1/ENGLISH, ETC
	KENYA / VOICE OF KENYA / Nairobi	100kW:DS-CENTRAL / M-Sa:100kW:DS-CENTRAL
4915v	COLOMBIA / ARMONIAS CAQUETA / Florencia	3kW:DS / M-Sa:3kW:DS / Tu-Su:3kW:DS
4920	AUSTRALIA / AUSTRALIAN BC CORP / Brisbane	10kW:DS
	INDIA / ALL INDIA RADIO / Madras	10kW:DS-A/ENGLISH, ETC
	INDONESIA / R REP INDONESIA / Tanjungpinang, Sum	DS
	USSR / YAKUT RADIO / Yakutsk	50kW:DS
4920.4	ECUADOR / RADIO QUITO / Quito	5kW:DS / M-Sa:5kW:DS / Tu-Su:5kW:DS
4921v	PERU / RADIO CENTRAL / Bella Vista	Alternative Frequency to 4876vkHz
4922v	PERU / ONDAS DEL TITICACA / Puno	1kW:DS-SPANISH, ETC / Tu-Su:1kW:DS
4925	BRAZIL / RADIO DIFUSORA / ,Taubaté	1kW:DS
	CHINA (PR) / HEILONGJIANG PBS / Harbin	50kW:DS-CHINESE, KOREAN
4925v	MOZAMBIQUE / RADIO MOCAMBIQUE / Maputo	7.5kW:DS
4925.6	EQUATORIAL GUINEA / RADIO NACIONAL / Batá	Alt 5004vkHz:100kW:DS-SPANISH, ETC
4927	INDONESIA / R REP INDONESIA / Jambi, Sumatera	7.5kW:DS / Su:7.5kW:DS
4927v	PERU / RADIO COBRIZA 2000 / Pacaycasa	Alt 4908vkHz:Irr:::DS
4930	HAITI / RADIO STATION 4VEH / Cap Haïtien	1.5kW:DS/FR,ENG,SP,ETC
	NAMIBIA / R SOUTHWEST AFRICA / Windhoek	100kW:DS-1
	USSR / RADIO MOSCOW / Ashkabad	50kW:DS-2
	RADIO MOSCOW / Tbilisi	50kW:DS-2
4931.8	NIGERIA / RADIO NIGERIA / Lagos	Irr::50kW:DS-2
4932v	INDONESIA / R REP INDONESIA / Surakarta, Jawa	0.5kW:DS
	NIGERIA / RADIO NIGERIA / Lagos	Irr:::DS-ENGLISH, ETC
4934 (con'd)	KENYA / VOICE OF KENYA / Nairobi	100kW:DS-GENERAL / M-Sa:100kW:DS-GENERAL

ENGLISH ▬▬   GERMAN / DEUTSCH ০০০০   FRENCH / FRANÇAIS ▬▬   PORTUGUESE / PORTUGUÊS ▬▬   SPANISH / ESPAÑOL ▬▬

ARABIC /ﻉﺏﺭ ▬▬   RUSSIAN / РУССКИИ ▬▬   CHINESE / 中文 ০০০০   JAPANESE / 日本語 ▬▬   MULTILINGUAL ০০০০   OTHER ▬

SUMMER ONLY (J)   WINTER ONLY (D)   JAMMING ∧∧ or / or \   EARLIEST HEARD ◢   LATEST HEARD ◣   + TENTATIVE

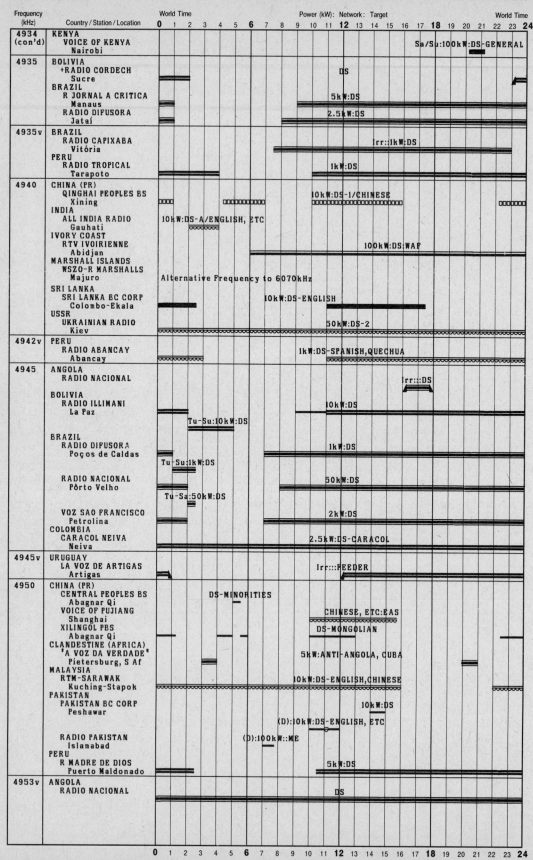

ENGLISH ▬▬   GERMAN / DEUTSCH ◊◊◊◊   FRENCH / FRANÇAIS ▬▬   PORTUGUESE / PORTUGUÊS ▬▬   SPANISH / ESPAÑOL ▬▬

ARABIC / العربية ▬▬   RUSSIAN / РУССКИЙ ▬▬   CHINESE / 中文 ◌◌◌◌   JAPANESE / 日本語 ▬▬   MULTILINGUAL ◌◌◌◌   OTHER ▬▬

SUMMER ONLY (J)   WINTER ONLY (D)   JAMMING /\/\ or / or \   EARLIEST HEARD ◢   LATEST HEARD ◣   + TENTATIVE

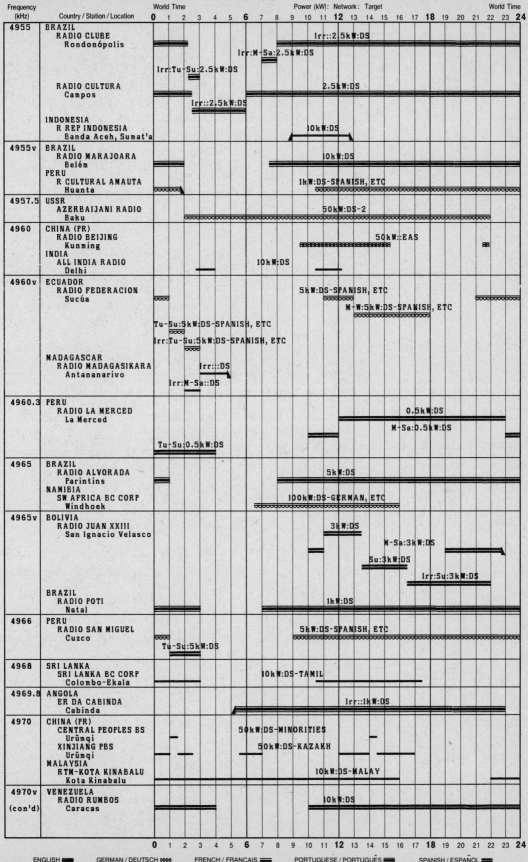

Frequency (kHz)	Country / Station / Location	
4955	BRAZIL	
	RADIO CLUBE	Irr::2.5kW:DS
	Rondonópolis	Irr:M-Sa:2.5kW:DS
		Irr:Tu-Su:2.5kW:DS
	RADIO CULTURA	2.5kW:DS
	Campos	Irr::2.5kW:DS
	INDONESIA	
	R REP INDONESIA	10kW:DS
	Banda Aceh, Sumat'a	
4955v	BRAZIL	
	RADIO MARAJOARA	10kW:DS
	Belém	
	PERU	
	R CULTURAL AMAUTA	1kW:DS-SPANISH, ETC
	Huanta	
4957.5	USSR	
	AZERBAIJANI RADIO	50kW:DS-2
	Baku	
4960	CHINA (PR)	
	RADIO BEIJING	50kW::EAS
	Kunming	
	INDIA	
	ALL INDIA RADIO	10kW:DS
	Delhi	
4960v	ECUADOR	
	RADIO FEDERACION	5kW:DS-SPANISH, ETC
	Sucúa	M-W:5kW:DS-SPANISH, ETC
		Tu-Su:5kW:DS-SPANISH, ETC
		Irr:Tu-Su:5kW:DS-SPANISH, ETC
	MADAGASCAR	
	RADIO MADAGASIKARA	Irr:::DS
	Antananarivo	Irr:M-Sa::DS
4960.3	PERU	
	RADIO LA MERCED	0.5kW:DS
	La Merced	M-Sa:0.5kW:DS
		Tu-Su:0.5kW:DS
4965	BRAZIL	
	RADIO ALVORADA	5kW:DS
	Parintins	
	NAMIBIA	
	SW AFRICA BC CORP	100kW:DS-GERMAN, ETC
	Windhoek	
4965v	BOLIVIA	
	RADIO JUAN XXIII	3kW:DS
	San Ignacio Velasco	M-Sa:3kW:DS
		Su:3kW:DS
		Irr:Su:3kW:DS
	BRAZIL	
	RADIO POTI	1kW:DS
	Natal	
4966	PERU	
	RADIO SAN MIGUEL	5kW:DS-SPANISH, ETC
	Cuzco	Tu-Su:5kW:DS
4968	SRI LANKA	
	SRI LANKA BC CORP	10kW:DS-TAMIL
	Colombo-Ekala	
4969.8	ANGOLA	
	ER DA CABINDA	Irr::1kW:DS
	Cabinda	
4970	CHINA (PR)	
	CENTRAL PEOPLES BS	50kW:DS-MINORITIES
	Urümqi	
	XINJIANG PBS	50kW:DS-KAZAKH
	Urümqi	
	MALAYSIA	
	RTM-KOTA KINABALU	10kW:DS-MALAY
	Kota Kinabalu	
4970v	VENEZUELA	
(con'd)	RADIO RUMBOS	10kW:DS
	Caracas	

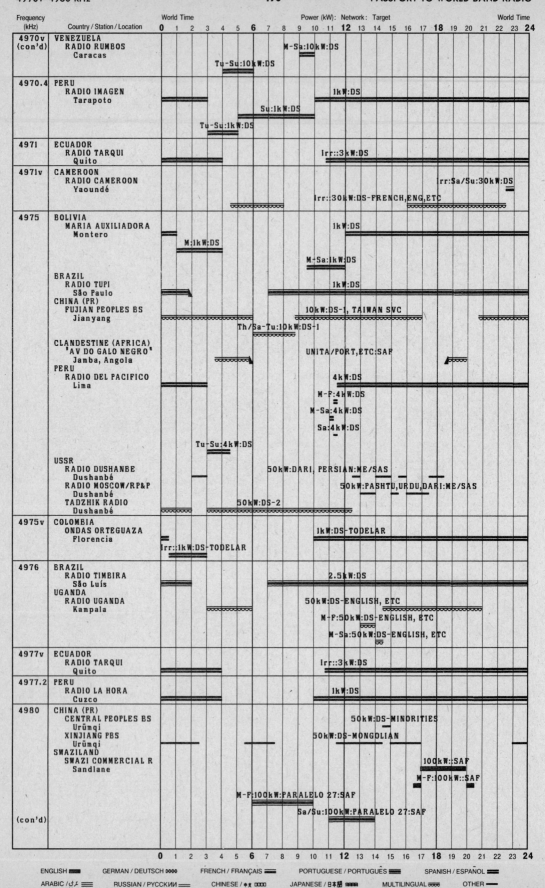

Frequency (kHz)	Country / Station / Location	Schedule / Power / Target
4970v (con'd)	VENEZUELA — RADIO RUMBOS — Caracas	M-Sa:10kW:DS / Tu-Su:10kW:DS
4970.4	PERU — RADIO IMAGEN — Tarapoto	1kW:DS / Su:1kW:DS / Tu-Su:1kW:DS
4971	ECUADOR — RADIO TARQUI — Quito	Irr::3kW:DS
4971v	CAMEROON — RADIO CAMEROON — Yaoundé	Irr:Sa/Su:30kW:DS / Irr:30kW:DS-FRENCH,ENG,ETC
4975	BOLIVIA — MARIA AUXILIADORA — Montero	1kW:DS / M:1kW:DS / M-Sa:1kW:DS
	BRAZIL — RADIO TUPI — São Paulo	1kW:DS
	CHINA (PR) — FUJIAN PEOPLES BS — Jianyang	10kW:DS-1, TAIWAN SVC / Th/Sa-Tu:10kW:DS-1
	CLANDESTINE (AFRICA) — "AV DO GALO NEGRO" — Jamba, Angola	UNITA/PORT,ETC:SAF
	PERU — RADIO DEL PACIFICO — Lima	4kW:DS / M-F:4kW:DS / M-Sa:4kW:DS / Sa:4kW:DS / Tu-Su:4kW:DS
	USSR — RADIO DUSHANBE — Dushanbé	50kW:DARI, PERSIAN:ME/SAS
	RADIO MOSCOW/RP&P — Dushanbé	50kW:PASHTU,URDU,DARI:ME/SAS
	TADZHIK RADIO — Dushanbé	50kW:DS-2
4975v	COLOMBIA — ONDAS ORTEGUAZA — Florencia	1kW:DS-TODELAR / Irr::1kW:DS-TODELAR
4976	BRAZIL — RADIO TIMBIRA — São Luís	2.5kW:DS
	UGANDA — RADIO UGANDA — Kampala	50kW:DS-ENGLISH, ETC / M-F:50kW:DS-ENGLISH, ETC / M-Sa:50kW:DS-ENGLISH, ETC
4977v	ECUADOR — RADIO TARQUI — Quito	Irr::3kW:DS
4977.2	PERU — RADIO LA HORA — Cuzco	1kW:DS
4980	CHINA (PR) — CENTRAL PEOPLES BS — Urümqi	50kW:DS-MINORITIES
	XINJIANG PBS — Urümqi	50kW:DS-MONGOLIAN
	SWAZILAND — SWAZI COMMERCIAL R — Sandlane	100kW::SAF / M-F:100kW::SAF / M-F:100kW:PARALELO 27:SAF / Sa/Su:100kW:PARALELO 27:SAF
(con'd)		

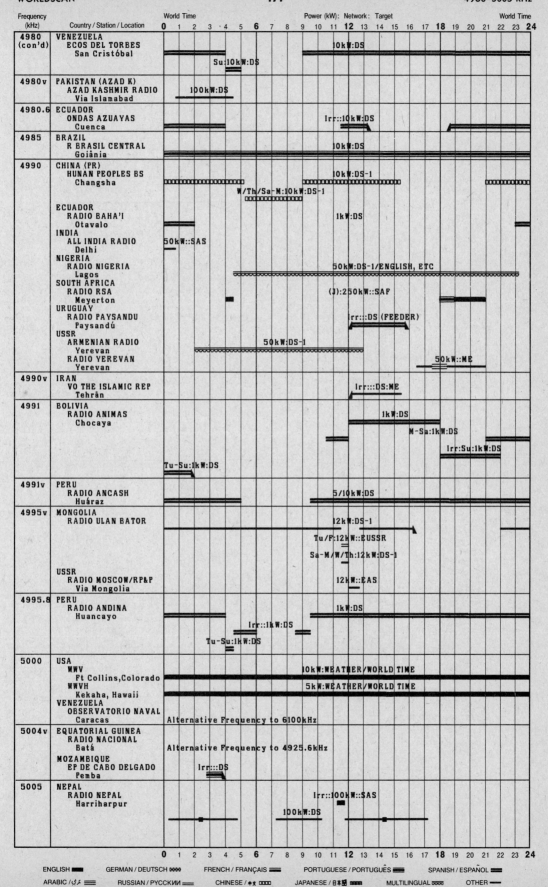

Frequency (kHz)	Country / Station / Location	Power (kW): Network: Target
4980 (con'd)	VENEZUELA ECOS DEL TORBES San Cristóbal	10kW:DS · Su:10kW:DS
4980v	PAKISTAN (AZAD K) AZAD KASHMIR RADIO Via Islamabad	100kW:DS
4980.6	ECUADOR ONDAS AZUAYAS Cuenca	Irr::10kW:DS
4985	BRAZIL R BRASIL CENTRAL Goiânia	10kW:DS
4990	CHINA (PR) HUNAN PEOPLES BS Changsha	10kW:DS-1 · W/Th/Sa-M:10kW:DS-1
	ECUADOR RADIO BAHA'I Otavalo	1kW:DS
	INDIA ALL INDIA RADIO Delhi	50kW::SAS
	NIGERIA RADIO NIGERIA Lagos	50kW:DS-1/ENGLISH, ETC
	SOUTH AFRICA RADIO RSA Meyerton	(J):250kW::SAF
	URUGUAY RADIO PAYSANDU Paysandú	Irr:::DS (FEEDER)
	USSR ARMENIAN RADIO Yerevan	50kW:DS-1
	RADIO YEREVAN Yerevan	50kW::ME
4990v	IRAN VO THE ISLAMIC REP Tehrān	Irr:::DS:ME
4991	BOLIVIA RADIO ANIMAS Chocaya	1kW:DS · M-Sa:1kW:DS · Irr:Su:1kW:DS · Tu-Su:1kW:DS
4991v	PERU RADIO ANCASH Huáraz	5/10kW:DS
4995v	MONGOLIA RADIO ULAN BATOR	12kW:DS-1 · Tu/F:12kW::EUSSR · Sa-M/W/Th:12kW:DS-1
	USSR RADIO MOSCOW/RP&P Via Mongolia	12kW::EAS
4995.8	PERU RADIO ANDINA Huancayo	1kW:DS · Irr::1kW:DS · Tu-Su:1kW:DS
5000	USA WWV Ft Collins, Colorado	10kW:WEATHER/WORLD TIME
	WWVH Kekaha, Hawaii	5kW:WEATHER/WORLD TIME
	VENEZUELA OBSERVATORIO NAVAL Caracas	Alternative Frequency to 6100kHz
5004v	EQUATORIAL GUINEA RADIO NACIONAL Batá	Alternative Frequency to 4925.6kHz
	MOZAMBIQUE EP DE CABO DELGADO Pemba	Irr::::DS
5005	NEPAL RADIO NEPAL Harriharpur	Irr::100kW::SAS · 100kW:DS

ENGLISH ▬▬ GERMAN / DEUTSCH ◊◊◊◊ FRENCH / FRANÇAIS ▬▬ PORTUGUESE / PORTUGUÊS ▬▬ SPANISH / ESPAÑOL ▬▬

ARABIC / ﻋ ﺮ ﺑ ﻲ ▬ RUSSIAN / РУССКИЙ ▬ CHINESE / 中文 ◊◊◊◊ JAPANESE / 日本語 ▬▬ MULTILINGUAL ▬▬ OTHER ▬

SUMMER ONLY (J) WINTER ONLY (D) JAMMING /\/\ or / or \ EARLIEST HEARD ◢ LATEST HEARD ◣ + TENTATIVE

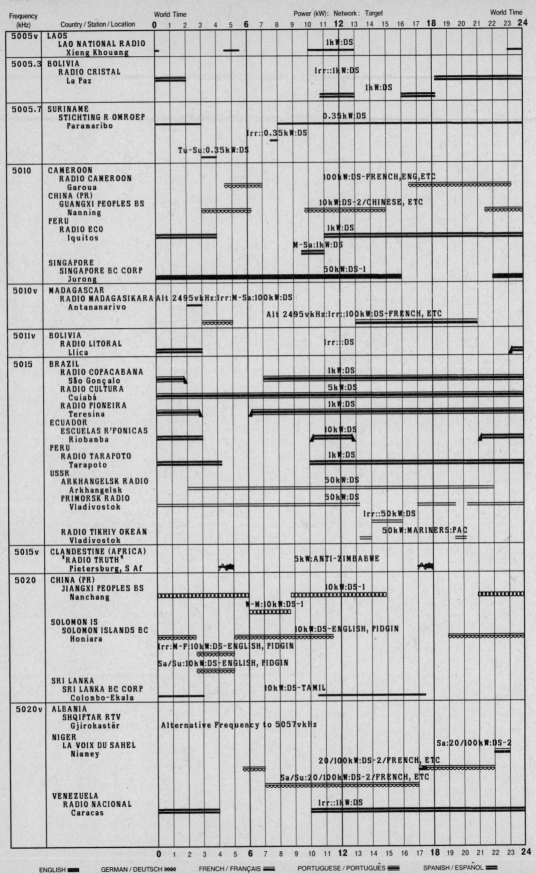

Frequency (kHz)	Country / Station / Location	Transmission details
5005v	LAOS — LAO NATIONAL RADIO — Xieng Khouang	1kW:DS
5005.3	BOLIVIA — RADIO CRISTAL — La Paz	Irr::1kW:DS / 1kW:DS
5005.7	SURINAME — STICHTING R OMROEP — Paramaribo	0.35kW:DS / Irr::0.35kW:DS / Tu-Su:0.35kW:DS
5010	CAMEROON — RADIO CAMEROON — Garoua	100kW:DS-FRENCH,ENG,ETC
	CHINA (PR) — GUANGXI PEOPLES BS — Nanning	10kW:DS-2/CHINESE, ETC
	PERU — RADIO ECO — Iquitos	1kW:DS / M-Sa:1kW:DS
	SINGAPORE — SINGAPORE BC CORP — Jurong	50kW:DS-1
5010v	MADAGASCAR — RADIO MADAGASIKARA — Antananarivo	Alt 2495vkHz:Irr:M-Sa:100kW:DS / Alt 2495vkHz:Irr::100kW:DS-FRENCH, ETC
5011v	BOLIVIA — RADIO LITORAL — Llica	Irr::DS
5015	BRAZIL — RADIO COPACABANA — São Gonçalo	1kW:DS
	RADIO CULTURA — Cuiabá	5kW:DS
	RADIO PIONEIRA — Teresina	1kW:DS
	ECUADOR — ESCUELAS R'FONICAS — Riobamba	10kW:DS
	PERU — RADIO TARAPOTO — Tarapoto	1kW:DS
	USSR — ARKHANGELSK RADIO — Arkhangelsk	50kW:DS
	PRIMORSK RADIO — Vladivostok	50kW:DS / Irr::50kW:DS
	RADIO TIKHIY OKEAN — Vladivostok	50kW:MARINERS:PAC
5015v	CLANDESTINE (AFRICA) — "RADIO TRUTH" — Pietersburg, S Af	5kW:ANTI-ZIMBABWE
5020	CHINA (PR) — JIANGXI PEOPLES BS — Nanchang	10kW:DS-1 / W-M:10kW:DS-1
	SOLOMON IS — SOLOMON ISLANDS BC — Honiara	10kW:DS-ENGLISH, PIDGIN / Irr:M-F:10kW:DS-ENGLISH, PIDGIN / Sa/Su:10kW:DS-ENGLISH, PIDGIN
	SRI LANKA — SRI LANKA BC CORP — Colombo-Ekala	10kW:DS-TAMIL
5020v	ALBANIA — SHQIPTAR RTV — Gjirokastër	Alternative Frequency to 5057vkHz
	NIGER — LA VOIX DU SAHEL — Niamey	Sa:20/100kW:DS-2 / 20/100kW:DS-2/FRENCH, ETC / Sa/Su:20/100kW:DS-2/FRENCH, ETC
	VENEZUELA — RADIO NACIONAL — Caracas	Irr::1kW:DS

ENGLISH ▰▰▰   GERMAN / DEUTSCH ⋈⋈⋈   FRENCH / FRANÇAIS ▰▰▰   PORTUGUESE / PORTUGUÊS ▰▰▰   SPANISH / ESPAÑOL ▰▰▰

ARABIC /ﻉﺏ ▰   RUSSIAN / РУССКИИ ▰▰   CHINESE /✶✶ ⊡⊡⊡   JAPANESE / 日本語 ▰▰   MULTILINGUAL ⌇⌇⌇   OTHER ▬

SUMMER ONLY (J)   WINTER ONLY (D)   JAMMING /\/\ or / or \   EARLIEST HEARD ◢   LATEST HEARD ◣   ✝ TENTATIVE

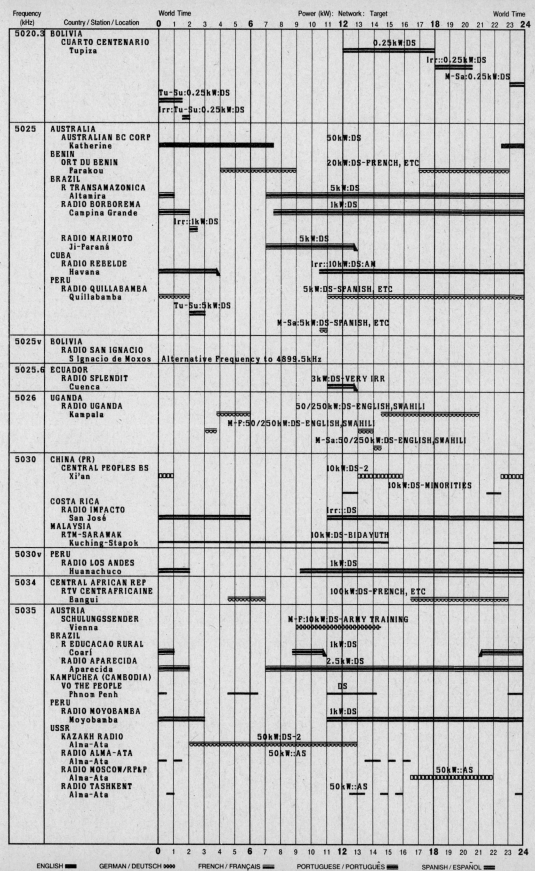

Frequency (kHz)	Country / Station / Location	Power (kW): Network: Target
5020.3	BOLIVIA CUARTO CENTENARIO Tupiza	0.25kW:DS / Irr::0.25kW:DS / M-Sa:0.25kW:DS / Tu-Su:0.25kW:DS / Irr:Tu-Su:0.25kW:DS
5025	AUSTRALIA AUSTRALIAN BC CORP Katherine	50kW:DS
	BENIN ORT DU BENIN Parakou	20kW:DS-FRENCH, ETC
	BRAZIL R TRANSAMAZONICA Altamira	5kW:DS
	RADIO BORBOREMA Campina Grande	1kW:DS / Irr:1kW:DS
	RADIO MARIMOTO Ji-Paraná	5kW:DS
	CUBA RADIO REBELDE Havana	Irr::10kW:DS:AM
	PERU RADIO QUILLABAMBA Quillabamba	5kW:DS-SPANISH, ETC / Tu-Su:5kW:DS / M-Sa:5kW:DS-SPANISH, ETC
5025v	BOLIVIA RADIO SAN IGNACIO S Ignacio de Moxos	Alternative Frequency to 4899.5kHz
5025.6	ECUADOR RADIO SPLENDIT Cuenca	3kW:DS-VERY IRR
5026	UGANDA RADIO UGANDA Kampala	50/250kW:DS-ENGLISH,SWAHILI / M-F:50/250kW:DS-ENGLISH,SWAHILI / M-Sa:50/250kW:DS-ENGLISH,SWAHILI
5030	CHINA (PR) CENTRAL PEOPLES BS Xi'an	10kW:DS-2 / 10kW:DS-MINORITIES
	COSTA RICA RADIO IMPACTO San José	Irr::DS
	MALAYSIA RTM-SARAWAK Kuching-Stapok	10kW:DS-BIDAYUTH
5030v	PERU RADIO LOS ANDES Huamachuco	1kW:DS
5034	CENTRAL AFRICAN REP RTV CENTRAFRICAINE Bangui	100kW:DS-FRENCH, ETC
5035	AUSTRIA SCHULUNGSSENDER Vienna	M-F:10kW:DS-ARMY TRAINING
	BRAZIL R EDUCACAO RURAL Coarí	1kW:DS
	RADIO APARECIDA Aparecida	2.5kW:DS
	KAMPUCHEA (CAMBODIA) VO THE PEOPLE Phnom Penh	DS
	PERU RADIO MOYOBAMBA Moyobamba	1kW:DS
	USSR KAZAKH RADIO Alma-Ata	50kW:DS-2
	RADIO ALMA-ATA Alma-Ata	50kW::AS
	RADIO MOSCOW/RP&P Alma-Ata	50kW::AS
	RADIO TASHKENT Alma-Ata	50kW::AS

ENGLISH ▬▬   GERMAN / DEUTSCH ᴰᴰᴰᴰ   FRENCH / FRANÇAIS ▬▬   PORTUGUESE / PORTUGUÊS ▬▬   SPANISH / ESPAÑOL ▬▬

ARABIC / عربى ▬▬   RUSSIAN / РУССКИИ ▬▬   CHINESE / 中文 ᴰᴰᴰᴰ   JAPANESE / 日本語 ▬▬   MULTILINGUAL ᴰᴰᴰᴰ   OTHER ▬▬

SUMMER ONLY (J)   WINTER ONLY (D)   JAMMING ∧∧ or / or \   EARLIEST HEARD ◢   LATEST HEARD ◣   + TENTATIVE

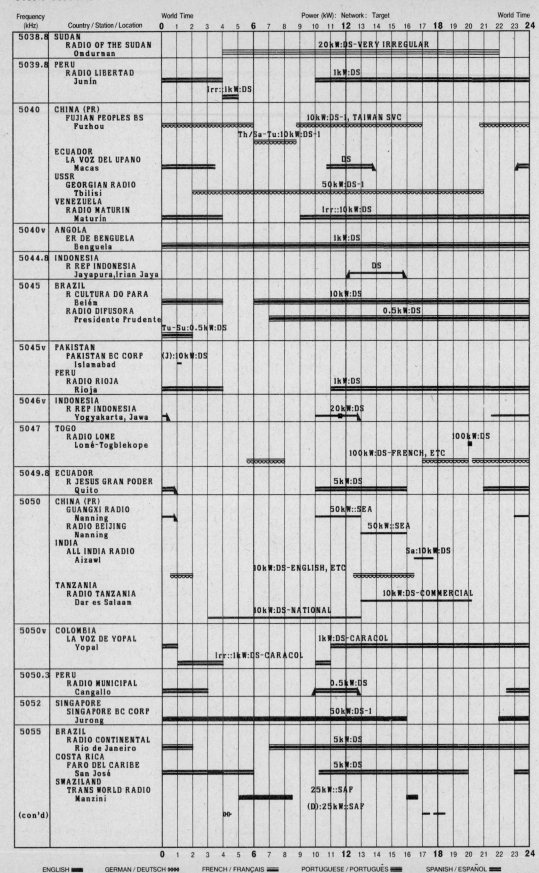

Frequency (kHz)	Country / Station / Location	Power (kW): Network: Target / World Time
5038.8	**SUDAN** — RADIO OF THE SUDAN — Omdurman	20kW:DS-VERY IRREGULAR
5039.8	**PERU** — RADIO LIBERTAD — Junín	1kW:DS / Irr::1kW:DS
5040	**CHINA (PR)** — FUJIAN PEOPLES BS — Fuzhou	10kW:DS-1, TAIWAN SVC / Th/Sa-Tu:10kW:DS-1
	ECUADOR — LA VOZ DEL UPANO — Macas	DS
	USSR — GEORGIAN RADIO — Tbilisi	50kW:DS-1
	VENEZUELA — RADIO MATURIN — Maturín	Irr::10kW:DS
5040v	**ANGOLA** — ER DE BENGUELA — Benguela	1kW:DS
5044.8	**INDONESIA** — R REP INDONESIA — Jayapura,Irian Jaya	DS
5045	**BRAZIL** — R CULTURA DO PARA — Belém	10kW:DS
	RADIO DIFUSORA — Presidente Prudente	0.5kW:DS / Tu-Su:0.5kW:DS
5045v	**PAKISTAN** — PAKISTAN BC CORP — Islamabad	(J):10kW:DS
	PERU — RADIO RIOJA — Rioja	1kW:DS
5046v	**INDONESIA** — R REP INDONESIA — Yogyakarta, Jawa	20kW:DS
5047	**TOGO** — RADIO LOME — Lomé-Togblekope	100kW:DS / 100kW:DS-FRENCH, ETC
5049.8	**ECUADOR** — R JESUS GRAN PODER — Quito	5kW:DS
5050	**CHINA (PR)** — GUANGXI RADIO — Nanning	50kW::SEA
	RADIO BEIJING — Nanning	50kW::SEA
	INDIA — ALL INDIA RADIO — Aizawl	Sa:10kW:DS / 10kW:DS-ENGLISH, ETC
	TANZANIA — RADIO TANZANIA — Dar es Salaam	10kW:DS-COMMERCIAL / 10kW:DS-NATIONAL
5050v	**COLOMBIA** — LA VOZ DE YOPAL — Yopal	1kW:DS-CARACOL / Irr::1kW:DS-CARACOL
5050.3	**PERU** — RADIO MUNICIPAL — Cangallo	0.5kW:DS
5052	**SINGAPORE** — SINGAPORE BC CORP — Jurong	50kW:DS-1
5055	**BRAZIL** — RADIO CONTINENTAL — Rio de Janeiro	5kW:DS
	COSTA RICA — FARO DEL CARIBE — San José	5kW:DS
	SWAZILAND — TRANS WORLD RADIO — Manzini	25kW::SAF
(con'd)		(D):25kW::SAF

ENGLISH ▬▬   GERMAN / DEUTSCH ◊◊◊◊   FRENCH / FRANÇAIS ▬▬   PORTUGUESE / PORTUGUÊS ▬▬   SPANISH / ESPAÑOL ▬▬

ARABIC / عربى ▬▬   RUSSIAN / РУССКИИ ▬▬   CHINESE / 中文 ◻◻◻◻   JAPANESE / 日本語 ▬▬   MULTILINGUAL ▭▭▭▭   OTHER ▬

SUMMER ONLY (J)   WINTER ONLY (D)   JAMMING ∧∧ or / or \   EARLIEST HEARD ◢   LATEST HEARD ◣   ◆ TENTATIVE

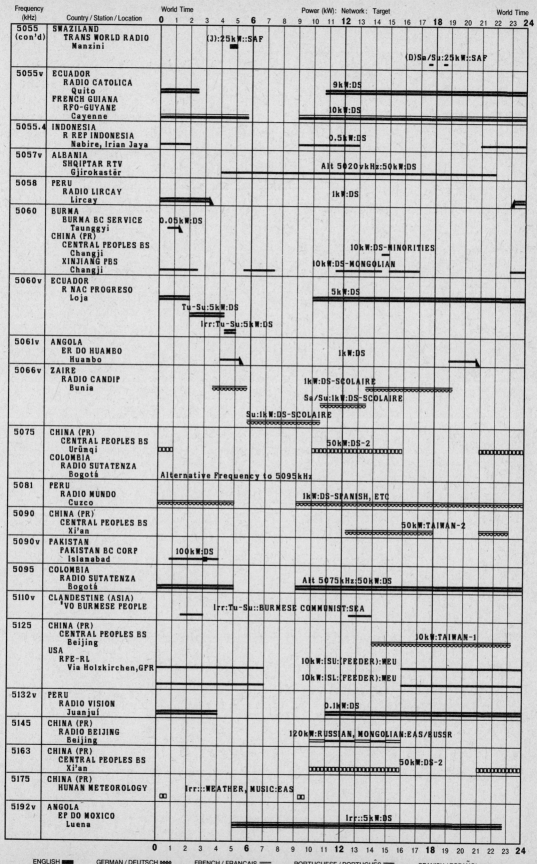

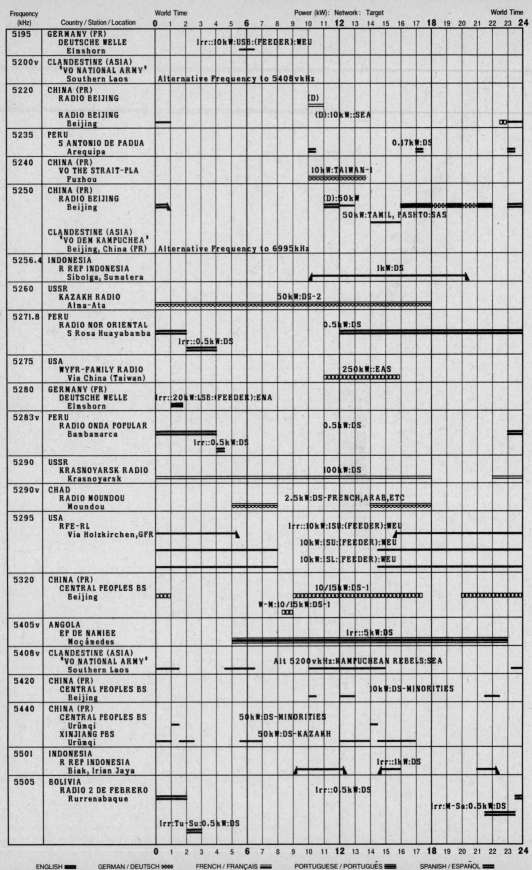

Frequency (kHz)	Country / Station / Location	Schedule notes
5195	GERMANY (FR) DEUTSCHE WELLE Elmshorn	Irr::10kW:USB:(FEEDER):WEU
5200v	CLANDESTINE (ASIA) 'VO NATIONAL ARMY' Southern Laos	Alternative Frequency to 5408vkHz
5220	CHINA (PR) RADIO BEIJING	(D)
	RADIO BEIJING Beijing	(D):10kW::SEA
5235	PERU S ANTONIO DE PADUA Arequipa	0.17kW:DS
5240	CHINA (PR) VO THE STRAIT-PLA Fuzhou	10kW:TAIWAN-1
5250	CHINA (PR) RADIO BEIJING Beijing	(D):50kW
		50kW:TAMIL, PASHTO:SAS
	CLANDESTINE (ASIA) 'VO DEM KAMPUCHEA' Beijing, China (PR)	Alternative Frequency to 6995kHz
5256.4	INDONESIA R REP INDONESIA Sibolga, Sumatera	1kW:DS
5260	USSR KAZAKH RADIO Alma-Ata	50kW:DS-2
5271.8	PERU RADIO NOR ORIENTAL S Rosa Huayabamba	0.5kW:DS
		Irr::0.5kW:DS
5275	USA WYFR-FAMILY RADIO Via China (Taiwan)	250kW::EAS
5280	GERMANY (PR) DEUTSCHE WELLE Elmshorn	Irr::20kW:LSB:(FEEDER):ENA
5283v	PERU RADIO ONDA POPULAR Bambamarca	0.5kW:DS
		Irr::0.5kW:DS
5290	USSR KRASNOYARSK RADIO Krasnoyarsk	100kW:DS
5290v	CHAD RADIO MOUNDOU Moundou	2.5kW:DS-FRENCH,ARAB,ETC
5295	USA RFE-RL Via Holzkirchen,GFR	Irr::10kW:ISU:(FEEDER):WEU
		10kW:ISU:(FEEDER):WEU
		10kW:ISL:(FEEDER):WEU
5320	CHINA (PR) CENTRAL PEOPLES BS Beijing	10/15kW:DS-1
		W-M:10/15kW:DS-1
5405v	ANGOLA EP DE NAMIBE Moçâmedes	Irr::5kW:DS
5408v	CLANDESTINE (ASIA) 'VO NATIONAL ARMY' Southern Laos	Alt 5200vkHz:KAMPUCHEAN REBELS:SEA
5420	CHINA (PR) CENTRAL PEOPLES BS Beijing	10kW:DS-MINORITIES
5440	CHINA (PR) CENTRAL PEOPLES BS Urümqi	50kW:DS-MINORITIES
	XINJIANG PBS Urümqi	50kW:DS-KAZAKH
5501	INDONESIA R REP INDONESIA Biak, Irian Jaya	Irr::1kW:DS
5505	BOLIVIA RADIO 2 DE FEBRERO Rurrenabaque	Irr::0.5kW:DS
		Irr::M-Sa:0.5kW:DS
		Irr:Tu-Su:0.5kW:DS

World Time: 0 1 2 3 4 5 6 7 8 9 10 11 12 13 14 15 16 17 18 19 20 21 22 23 24

Power (kW): Network: Target

ENGLISH ▰▰▰   GERMAN / DEUTSCH ∞∞∞   FRENCH / FRANÇAIS ═══   PORTUGUESE / PORTUGUÊS ▰▰▰   SPANISH / ESPAÑOL ▰▰▰

ARABIC / عربى ═══   RUSSIAN / РУССКИИ ═══   CHINESE / ◆文 ∞∞∞   JAPANESE / 日本語 ▰▰▰   MULTILINGUAL ∞∞∞   OTHER ▬▬▬

SUMMER ONLY (J)   WINTER ONLY (D)   JAMMING ∧∧ or / or \   EARLIEST HEARD ◢   LATEST HEARD ◣   ✦ TENTATIVE

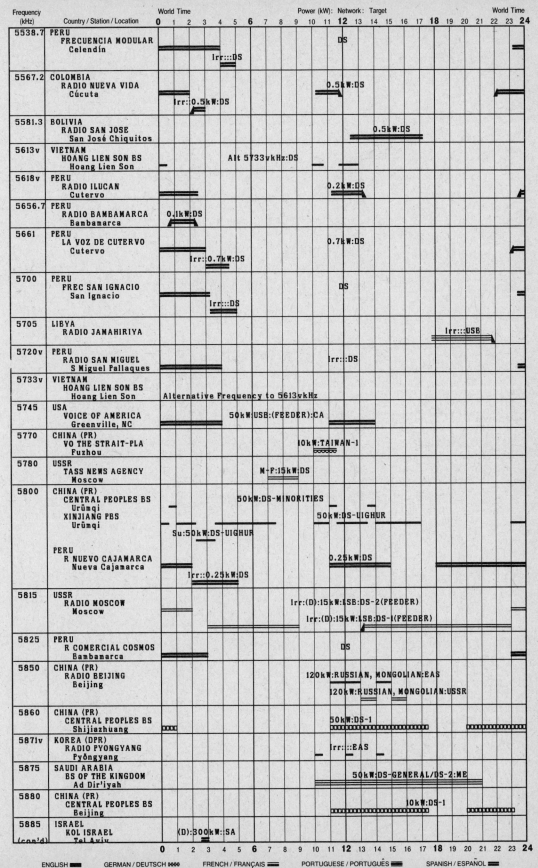

Frequency (kHz)	Country / Station / Location	Details
5538.7	PERU FRECUENCIA MODULAR Celendín	DS / Irr:::DS
5567.2	COLOMBIA RADIO NUEVA VIDA Cúcuta	0.5kW:DS / Irr::0.5kW:DS
5581.3	BOLIVIA RADIO SAN JOSE San José Chiquitos	0.5kW:DS
5613v	VIETNAM HOANG LIEN SON BS Hoang Lien Son	Alt 5733vkHz:DS
5618v	PERU RADIO ILUCAN Cutervo	0.2kW:DS
5656.7	PERU RADIO BAMBAMARCA Bambamarca	0.1kW:DS
5661	PERU LA VOZ DE CUTERVO Cutervo	0.7kW:DS / Irr::0.7kW:DS
5700	PERU FREC SAN IGNACIO San Ignacio	DS / Irr:::DS
5705	LIBYA RADIO JAMAHIRIYA	Irr:::USB
5720v	PERU RADIO SAN MIGUEL S Miguel Pallaques	Irr::DS
5733v	VIETNAM HOANG LIEN SON BS Hoang Lien Son	Alternative Frequency to 5613vkHz
5745	USA VOICE OF AMERICA Greenville, NC	50kW:USB:(FEEDER):CA
5770	CHINA (PR) VO THE STRAIT-PLA Fuzhou	10kW:TAIWAN-1
5780	USSR TASS NEWS AGENCY Moscow	M-F:15kW:DS
5800	CHINA (PR) CENTRAL PEOPLES BS Urümqi XINJIANG PBS Urümqi	50kW:DS-MINORITIES / 50kW:DS-UIGHUR / Su:50kW:DS-UIGHUR
	PERU R NUEVO CAJAMARCA Nueva Cajamarca	0.25kW:DS / Irr::0.25kW:DS
5815	USSR RADIO MOSCOW Moscow	Irr:(D):15kW:LSB:DS-2(FEEDER) / Irr:(D):15kW:LSB:DS-1(FEEDER)
5825	PERU R COMERCIAL COSMOS Bambamarca	DS
5850	CHINA (PR) RADIO BEIJING Beijing	120kW:RUSSIAN, MONGOLIAN:EAS / 120kW:RUSSIAN, MONGOLIAN:USSR
5860	CHINA (PR) CENTRAL PEOPLES BS Shijiazhuang	50kW:DS-1
5871v	KOREA (DPR) RADIO PYONGYANG Pyöngyang	Irr::::EAS
5875	SAUDI ARABIA BS OF THE KINGDOM Ad Dir'iyah	50kW:DS-GENERAL/DS-2:ME
5880	CHINA (PR) CENTRAL PEOPLES BS Beijing	10kW:DS-1
5885 (con'd)	ISRAEL KOL ISRAEL Tel Aviv	(D):300kW:SA

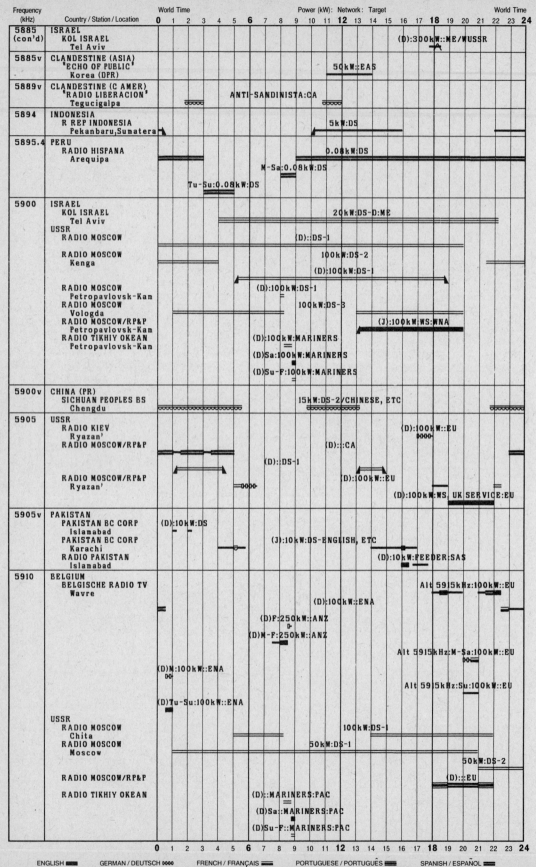

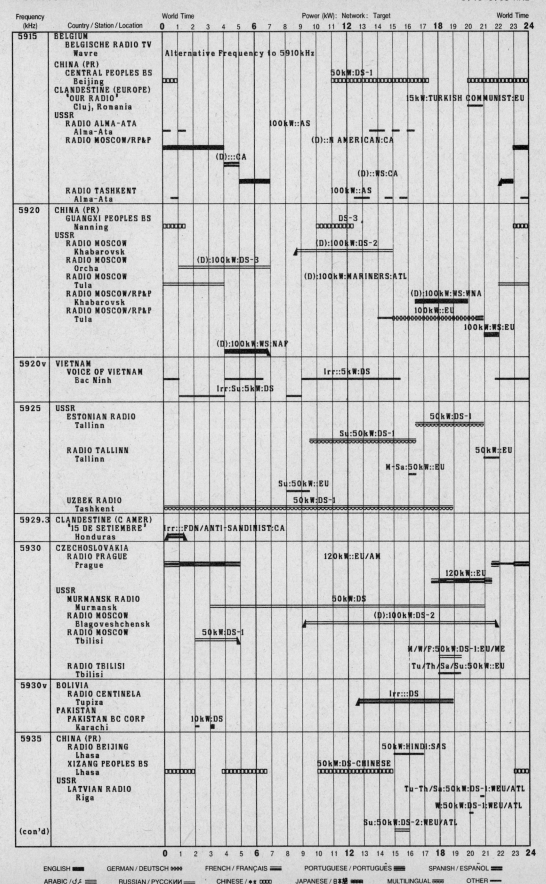

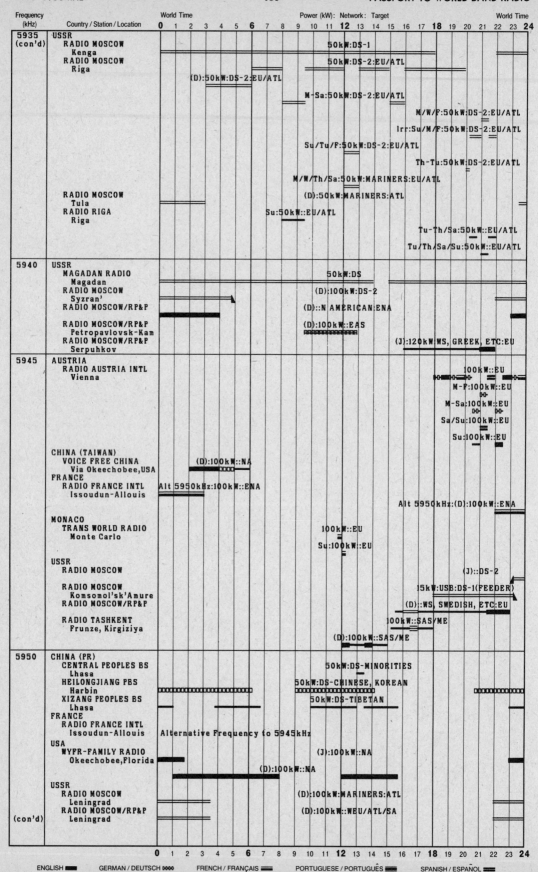

Frequency (kHz)	Country / Station / Location	World Time 0 1 2 3 4 5 6 7 8 9 10 11 12 13 14 15 16 17 18 19 20 21 22 23 24
5935 (con'd)	USSR	
	RADIO MOSCOW Kenga	50kW:DS-1
	RADIO MOSCOW Riga	50kW:DS-2:EU/ATL
		(D):50kW:DS-2:EU/ATL
		M-Sa:50kW:DS-2:EU/ATL
		M/W/F:50kW:DS-2:EU/ATL
		Irr:Su/M/F:50kW:DS-2:EU/ATL
		Su/Tu/F:50kW:DS-2:EU/ATL
		Th-Tu:50kW:DS-2:EU/ATL
		M/W/Th/Sa:50kW:MARINERS:EU/ATL
	RADIO MOSCOW Tula	(D):50kW:MARINERS:ATL
	RADIO RIGA Riga	Su:50kW::EU/ATL
		Tu-Th/Sa:50kW::EU/ATL
		Tu/Th/Sa/Su:50kW::EU/ATL
5940	USSR	
	MAGADAN RADIO Magadan	50kW:DS
	RADIO MOSCOW Syzran'	(D):100kW:DS-2
	RADIO MOSCOW/RP&P	(D)::N AMERICAN:ENA
	RADIO MOSCOW/RP&P Petropavlovsk-Kam	(D):100kW::EAS
	RADIO MOSCOW/RP&P Serpuhkov	(J):120kW:WS, GREEK, ETC:EU
5945	AUSTRIA	
	RADIO AUSTRIA INTL Vienna	100kW::EU
		M-F:100kW::EU
		M-Sa:100kW::EU
		Sa/Su:100kW::EU
		Su:100kW::EU
	CHINA (TAIWAN)	
	VOICE FREE CHINA Via Okeechobee,USA	(D):100kW::NA
	FRANCE	
	RADIO FRANCE INTL Issoudun-Allouis	Alt 5950kHz:100kW::ENA
		Alt 5950kHz:(D):100kW::ENA
	MONACO	
	TRANS WORLD RADIO Monte Carlo	100kW::EU
		Su:100kW::EU
	USSR	
	RADIO MOSCOW	(J)::DS-2
	RADIO MOSCOW Komsomol'sk'Amure	15kW:USB:DS-1(FEEDER)
	RADIO MOSCOW/RP&P	(D)::WS, SWEDISH, ETC:EU
	RADIO TASHKENT Frunze, Kirgiziya	100kW::SAS/ME
		(D):100kW::SAS/ME
5950	CHINA (PR)	
	CENTRAL PEOPLES BS Lhasa	50kW:DS-MINORITIES
	HEILONGJIANG PBS Harbin	50kW:DS-CHINESE, KOREAN
	XIZANG PEOPLES BS Lhasa	50kW:DS-TIBETAN
	FRANCE	
	RADIO FRANCE INTL Issoudun-Allouis	Alternative Frequency to 5945kHz
	USA	
	WYFR-FAMILY RADIO Okeechobee,Florida	(J):100kW::NA
		(D):100kW::NA
	USSR	
	RADIO MOSCOW Leningrad	(D):100kW:MARINERS:ATL
	RADIO MOSCOW/RP&P	(D):100kW::WEU/ATL/SA
(con'd)	Leningrad	

0 1 2 3 4 5 6 7 8 9 10 11 12 13 14 15 16 17 18 19 20 21 22 23 24

ENGLISH ▬▬　GERMAN / DEUTSCH ▭▭▭▭　FRENCH / FRANÇAIS ▬▬　PORTUGUESE / PORTUGUÊS ▬▬　SPANISH / ESPAÑOL ▬▬

ARABIC / عربي ▬▬　RUSSIAN / РУССКИИ ▬▬　CHINESE / 中文 ▭▭▭▭　JAPANESE / 日本語 ▬▬　MULTILINGUAL ▭▭▭▭　OTHER ▬▬

SUMMER ONLY (J)　WINTER ONLY (D)　JAMMING ∧∧ or / or \　EARLIEST HEARD ◢　LATEST HEARD ◣　⁺ TENTATIVE

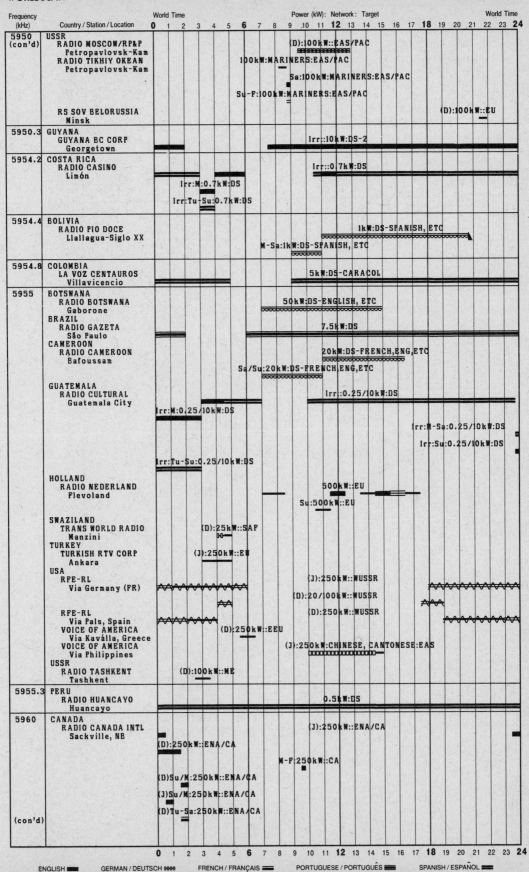

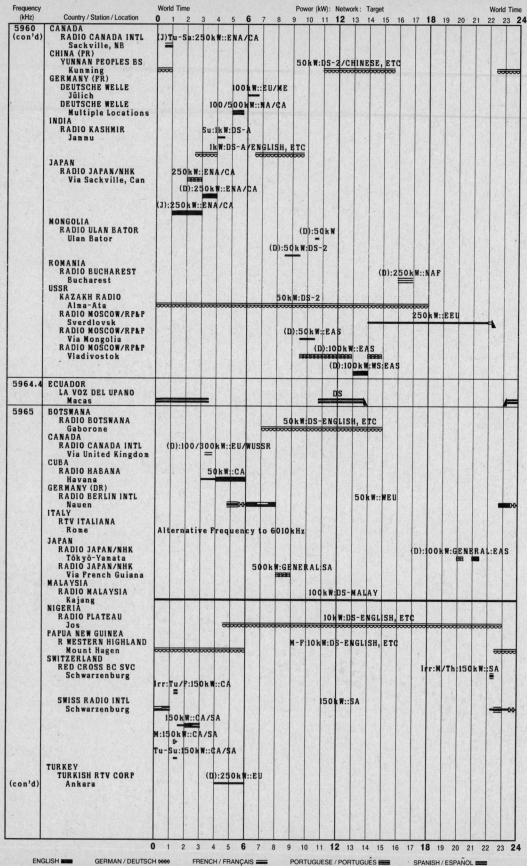

Frequency (kHz)	Country / Station / Location	World Time 0 – 24
5960 (con'd)	**CANADA**	
	RADIO CANADA INTL — Sackville, NB	(J)Tu-Sa:250kW::ENA/CA
	CHINA (PR)	
	YUNNAN PEOPLES BS — Kunming	50kW:DS-2/CHINESE, ETC
	GERMANY (FR)	
	DEUTSCHE WELLE — Jülich	100kW::EU/ME
	DEUTSCHE WELLE — Multiple Locations	100/500kW::NA/CA
	INDIA	
	RADIO KASHMIR — Jammu	Su:1kW:DS-A / 1kW:DS-A/ENGLISH, ETC
	JAPAN	
	RADIO JAPAN/NHK — Via Sackville, Can	250kW::ENA/CA / (D):250kW::ENA/CA / (J):250kW::ENA/CA
	MONGOLIA	
	RADIO ULAN BATOR — Ulan Bator	(D):50kW / (D):50kW:DS-2
	ROMANIA	
	RADIO BUCHAREST — Bucharest	(D):250kW::NAF
	USSR	
	KAZAKH RADIO — Alma-Ata	50kW:DS-2
	RADIO MOSCOW/RP&P — Sverdlovsk	250kW::EEU
	RADIO MOSCOW/RP&P — Via Mongolia	(D):50kW::EAS
	RADIO MOSCOW/RP&P — Vladivostok	(D):100kW::EAS / (D):100kW:WS:EAS
5964.4	**ECUADOR**	
	LA VOZ DEL UPANO — Macas	DS
5965	**BOTSWANA**	
	RADIO BOTSWANA — Gaborone	50kW:DS-ENGLISH, ETC
	CANADA	
	RADIO CANADA INTL — Via United Kingdom	(D):100/300kW::EU/WUSSR
	CUBA	
	RADIO HABANA — Havana	50kW::CA
	GERMANY (DR)	
	RADIO BERLIN INTL — Nauen	50kW::WEU
	ITALY	
	RTV ITALIANA — Rome	Alternative Frequency to 6010kHz
	JAPAN	
	RADIO JAPAN/NHK — Tōkyō-Yamata	(D):100kW:GENERAL:EAS
	RADIO JAPAN/NHK — Via French Guiana	500kW:GENERAL:SA
	MALAYSIA	
	RADIO MALAYSIA — Kajang	100kW:DS-MALAY
	NIGERIA	
	RADIO PLATEAU — Jos	10kW:DS-ENGLISH, ETC
	PAPUA NEW GUINEA	
	R WESTERN HIGHLAND — Mount Hagen	M-F:10kW:DS-ENGLISH, ETC
	SWITZERLAND	
	RED CROSS BC SVC — Schwarzenburg	Irr:M/Th:150kW::SA / Irr:Tu/F:150kW::CA
	SWISS RADIO INTL — Schwarzenburg	150kW::SA / 150kW::CA/SA / M:150kW::CA/SA / Tu-Su:150kW::CA/SA
	TURKEY	
(con'd)	TURKISH RTV CORP — Ankara	(D):250kW::EU

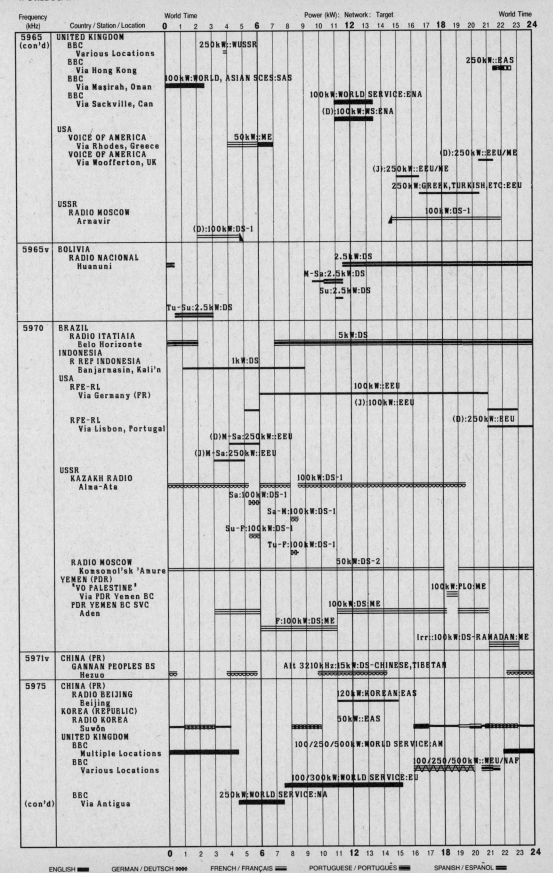

Frequency (kHz)	Country / Station / Location	World Time
5965 (con'd)	UNITED KINGDOM	
	BBC	
	Various Locations	250kW::WUSSR
	BBC	
	Via Hong Kong	250kW::EAS
	BBC	
	Via Maṣirah, Oman	100kW:WORLD, ASIAN SCES:SAS
	BBC	
	Via Sackville, Can	100kW:WORLD SERVICE:ENA
		(D):100kW:WS:ENA
	USA	
	VOICE OF AMERICA	
	Via Rhodes, Greece	50kW::ME
	VOICE OF AMERICA	
	Via Woofferton, UK	(D):250kW::EEU/ME
		(J):250kW::EEU/ME
		250kW:GREEK,TURKISH,ETC:EEU
	USSR	
	RADIO MOSCOW	
	Armavir	100kW:DS-1
		(D):100kW:DS-1
5965v	BOLIVIA	
	RADIO NACIONAL	2.5kW:DS
	Huanuni	M-Sa:2.5kW:DS
		Su:2.5kW:DS
		Tu-Su:2.5kW:DS
5970	BRAZIL	
	RADIO ITATIAIA	5kW:DS
	Belo Horizonte	
	INDONESIA	
	R REP INDONESIA	1kW:DS
	Banjarmasin, Kali'n	
	USA	
	RFE-RL	100kW::EEU
	Via Germany (FR)	(J):100kW::EEU
	RFE-RL	(D):250kW::EEU
	Via Lisbon, Portugal	(D)M-Sa:250kW::EEU
		(J)M-Sa:250kW::EEU
	USSR	
	KAZAKH RADIO	100kW:DS-1
	Alma-Ata	Sa:100kW:DS-1
		Sa-M:100kW:DS-1
		Su-F:100kW:DS-1
		Tu-F:100kW:DS-1
	RADIO MOSCOW	50kW:DS-2
	Komsomol'sk 'Amure	
	YEMEN (PDR)	
	"VO PALESTINE"	100kW:PLO:ME
	Via PDR Yemen BC	
	PDR YEMEN BC SVC	100kW:DS:ME
	Aden	F:100kW:DS:ME
		Irr::100kW:DS-RAMADAN:ME
5971v	CHINA (PR)	
	GANNAN PEOPLES BS	Alt 3210kHz:15kW:DS-CHINESE,TIBETAN
	Hezuo	
5975	CHINA (PR)	
	RADIO BEIJING	120kW:KOREAN:EAS
	Beijing	
	KOREA (REPUBLIC)	
	RADIO KOREA	50kW::EAS
	Suwŏn	
	UNITED KINGDOM	
	BBC	100/250/500kW:WORLD SERVICE:AM
	Multiple Locations	
	BBC	100/250/500kW::WEU/NAF
	Various Locations	
		100/300kW:WORLD SERVICE:EU
	BBC	250kW:WORLD SERVICE:NA
(con'd)	Via Antigua	

World Time scale: 0 1 2 3 4 5 6 7 8 9 10 11 12 13 14 15 16 17 18 19 20 21 22 23 24

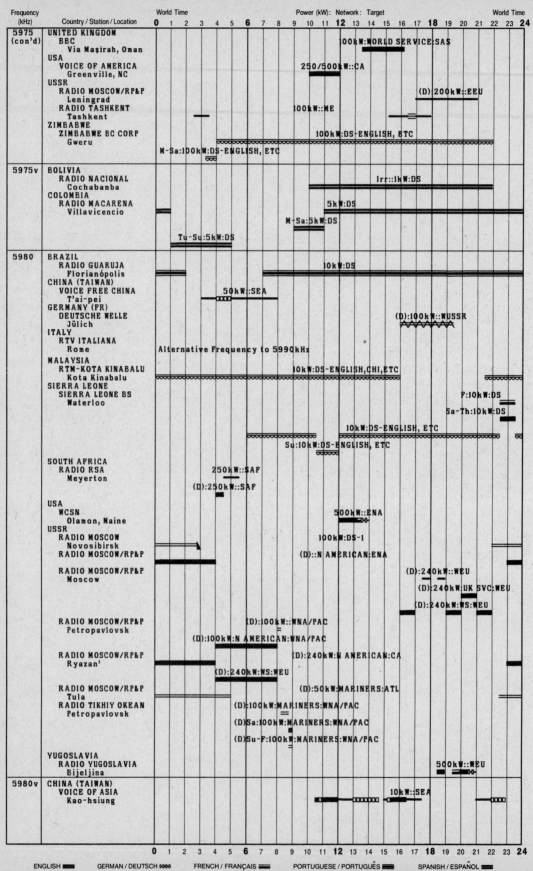

Frequency (kHz)	Country / Station / Location	World Time / Power (kW): Network: Target
5975 (con'd)	**UNITED KINGDOM** BBC, Via Maşirah, Oman	100kW:WORLD SERVICE:SAS
	USA VOICE OF AMERICA, Greenville, NC	250/500kW::CA
	USSR RADIO MOSCOW/RP&P, Leningrad	(D) 200kW::EEU
	RADIO TASHKENT, Tashkent	100kW::ME
	ZIMBABWE ZIMBABWE BC CORP, Gweru	100kW:DS-ENGLISH, ETC / M-Sa:100kW:DS-ENGLISH, ETC
5975v	**BOLIVIA** RADIO NACIONAL, Cochabamba	Irr::1kW:DS
	COLOMBIA RADIO MACARENA, Villavicencio	5kW:DS / M-Sa:5kW:DS / Tu-Su:5kW:DS
5980	**BRAZIL** RADIO GUARUJA, Florianópolis	10kW:DS
	CHINA (TAIWAN) VOICE FREE CHINA, T'ai-pei	50kW::SEA
	GERMANY (FR) DEUTSCHE WELLE, Jülich	(D):100kW::WUSSR
	ITALY RTV ITALIANA, Rome	Alternative Frequency to 5990kHz
	MALAYSIA RTM-KOTA KINABALU, Kota Kinabalu	10kW:DS-ENGLISH,CHI,ETC
	SIERRA LEONE SIERRA LEONE BS, Waterloo	F:10kW:DS / Sa-Th:10kW:DS / 10kW:DS-ENGLISH, ETC / Su:10kW:DS-ENGLISH, ETC
	SOUTH AFRICA RADIO RSA, Meyerton	250kW::SAF / (D):250kW::SAF
	USA WCSN, Olamon, Maine	500kW::ENA
	USSR RADIO MOSCOW, Novosibirsk	100kW:DS-1
	RADIO MOSCOW/RP&P	(D)::N AMERICAN:ENA
	RADIO MOSCOW/RP&P, Moscow	(D):240kW::WEU / (D):240kW:UK SVC:WEU / (D):240kW:WS:WEU
	RADIO MOSCOW/RP&P, Petropavlovsk	(D):100kW::WNA/PAC / (D):100kW:N AMERICAN:WNA/PAC
	RADIO MOSCOW/RP&P, Ryazan'	(D):240kW:N AMERICAN:CA / (D):240kW:WS:WEU
	RADIO MOSCOW/RP&P, Tula	(D):50kW:MARINERS:ATL
	RADIO TIKHIY OKEAN, Petropavlovsk	(D):100kW:MARINERS:WNA/PAC / (D)Sa:100kW:MARINERS:WNA/PAC / (D)Su-F:100kW:MARINERS:WNA/PAC
	YUGOSLAVIA RADIO YUGOSLAVIA, Bijeljina	500kW::WEU
5980v	**CHINA (TAIWAN)** VOICE OF ASIA, Kao-hsiung	10kW::SEA

ENGLISH ▬▬   GERMAN / DEUTSCH booo   FRENCH / FRANÇAIS ▬▬   PORTUGUESE / PORTUGUÊS ▬▬   SPANISH / ESPAÑOL ▬▬

ARABIC / ﻉﺏﺭ ▬   RUSSIAN / РУССКИИ ▬   CHINESE / ✦✖ ooooo   JAPANESE / 日本語 ▬   MULTILINGUAL ▬   OTHER ▬

SUMMER ONLY (J)   WINTER ONLY (D)   JAMMING ∧∧ or / or \   EARLIEST HEARD ◢   LATEST HEARD ◣   ✦ TENTATIVE

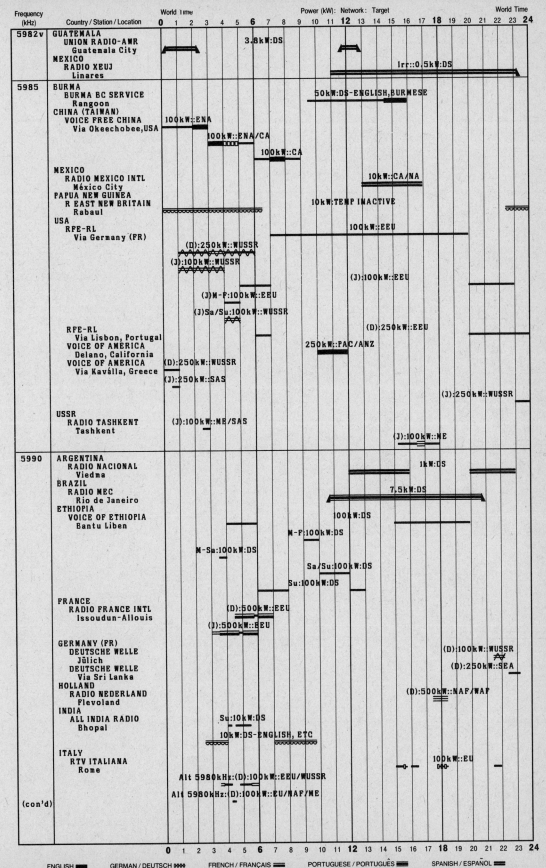

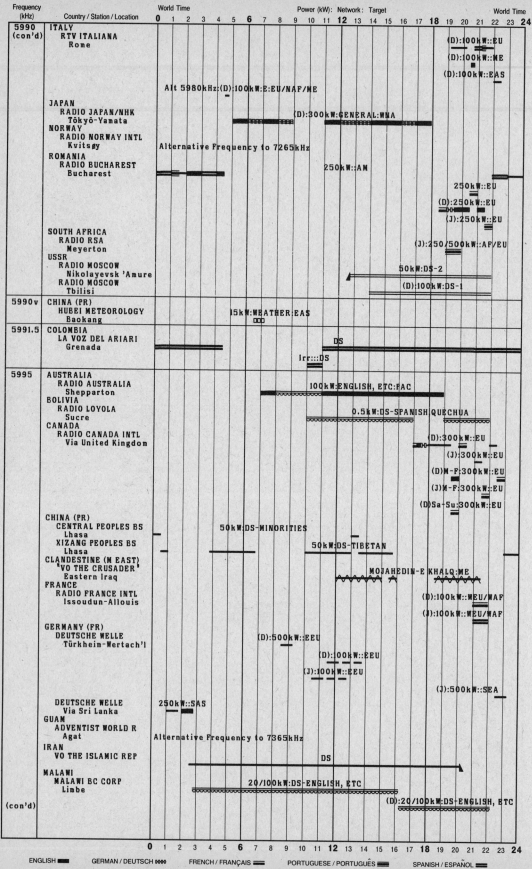

Frequency (kHz)	Country / Station / Location	Transmission details
5990 (con'd)	ITALY RTV ITALIANA Rome	(D):100kW::EU
		(D):100kW::ME
		(D):100kW::EAS
		Alt 5980kHz:(D):100kW:E:EU/NAF/ME
	JAPAN RADIO JAPAN/NHK Tôkyô-Yamata	(D):300kW:GENERAL:WNA
	NORWAY RADIO NORWAY INTL Kvitsøy	Alternative Frequency to 7265kHz
	ROMANIA RADIO BUCHAREST Bucharest	250kW::AM
		250kW::EU
		(D):250kW::EU
		(J):250kW::EU
	SOUTH AFRICA RADIO RSA Meyerton	(J):250/500kW:AF/EU
	USSR RADIO MOSCOW Nikolayevsk 'Amure	50kW:DS-2
	RADIO MOSCOW Tbilisi	(D):100kW:DS-1
5990v	CHINA (PR) HUBEI METEOROLOGY Baokang	15kW:WEATHER:EAS
5991.5	COLOMBIA LA VOZ DEL ARIARI Grenada	DS
		Irr:::DS
5995	AUSTRALIA RADIO AUSTRALIA Shepparton	100kW:ENGLISH, ETC:PAC
	BOLIVIA RADIO LOYOLA Sucre	0.5kW:DS-SPANISH QUECHUA
	CANADA RADIO CANADA INTL Via United Kingdom	(D):300kW::EU
		(J):300kW::EU
		(D)M-F:300kW::EU
		(J)M-F:300kW::EU
		(D)Sa-Su:300kW::EU
	CHINA (PR) CENTRAL PEOPLES BS Lhasa	50kW:DS-MINORITIES
	XIZANG PEOPLES BS Lhasa	50kW:DS-TIBETAN
	CLANDESTINE (M EAST) "VO THE CRUSADER" Eastern Iraq	MOJAHEDIN-E KHALQ:ME
	FRANCE RADIO FRANCE INTL Issoudun-Allouis	(D):100kW::WEU/WAF
		(J):100kW::WEU/WAF
	GERMANY (FR) DEUTSCHE WELLE Türkheim-Wertach'l	(D):500kW::EEU
		(D):100kW::EEU
		(J):100kW::EEU
		(J):500kW::SEA
	DEUTSCHE WELLE Via Sri Lanka	250kW::SAS
	GUAM ADVENTIST WORLD R Agat	Alternative Frequency to 7365kHz
	IRAN VO THE ISLAMIC REP	DS
	MALAWI MALAWI BC CORP Limbe	20/100kW:DS-ENGLISH, ETC
(con'd)		(D):20/100kW:DS-ENGLISH, ETC

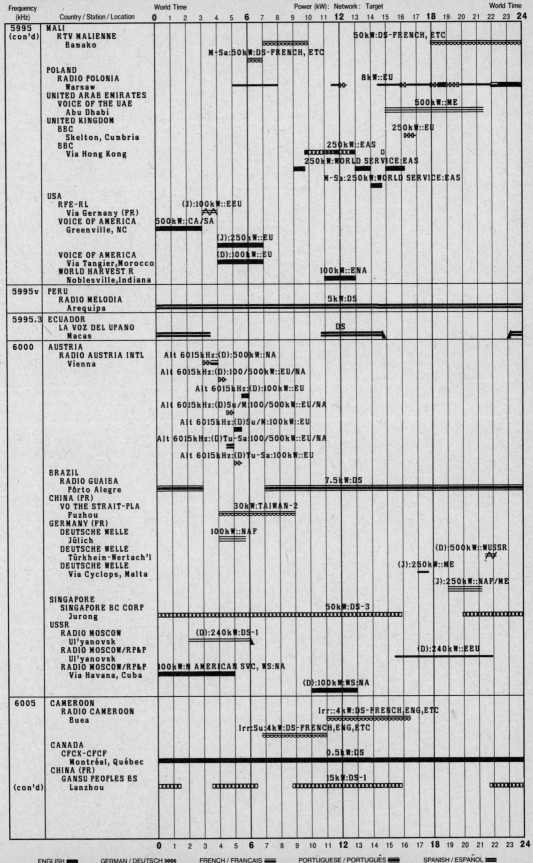

Frequency (kHz)	Country / Station / Location	Schedule
5995 (con'd)	MALI — RTV MALIENNE — Bamako	50kW:DS-FRENCH, ETC / M-Sa:50kW:DS-FRENCH, ETC
	POLAND — RADIO POLONIA — Warsaw	8kW::EU
	UNITED ARAB EMIRATES — VOICE OF THE UAE — Abu Dhabi	500kW::ME
	UNITED KINGDOM — BBC — Skelton, Cumbria	250kW::EU
	BBC — Via Hong Kong	250kW::EAS / 250kW:WORLD SERVICE:EAS / M-Sa:250kW:WORLD SERVICE:EAS
	USA — RFE-RL — Via Germany (FR)	(J):100kW::EEU
	VOICE OF AMERICA — Greenville, NC	500kW::CA/SA / (J):250kW::EU
	VOICE OF AMERICA — Via Tangier, Morocco	(D):100kW::EU
	WORLD HARVEST R — Noblesville, Indiana	100kW::ENA
5995v	PERU — RADIO MELODIA — Arequipa	5kW:DS
5995.3	ECUADOR — LA VOZ DEL UPANO — Macas	DS
6000	AUSTRIA — RADIO AUSTRIA INTL — Vienna	Alt 6015kHz:(D):500kW::NA / Alt 6015kHz:(D):100/500kW::EU/NA / Alt 6015kHz:(D):100kW::EU / Alt 6015kHz:(D)Su/M:100/500kW::EU/NA / Alt 6015kHz:(D)Su/M:100kW::EU / Alt 6015kHz:(D)Tu-Sa:100/500kW::EU/NA / Alt 6015kHz:(D)Tu-Sa:100kW::EU
	BRAZIL — RADIO GUAIBA — Pôrto Alegre	7.5kW:DS
	CHINA (PR) — VO THE STRAIT-PLA — Fuzhou	30kW:TAIWAN-2
	GERMANY (FR) — DEUTSCHE WELLE — Jülich	100kW::NAF
	DEUTSCHE WELLE — Türkheim-Wertach'l	(D):500kW::WUSSR
	DEUTSCHE WELLE — Via Cyclops, Malta	(J):250kW::ME / (J):250kW::NAF/ME
	SINGAPORE — SINGAPORE BC CORP — Jurong	50kW:DS-3
	USSR — RADIO MOSCOW — Ul'yanovsk	(D):240kW:DS-1
	RADIO MOSCOW/RP&P — Ul'yanovsk	(D):240kW::EEU
	RADIO MOSCOW/RP&P — Via Havana, Cuba	100kW:N AMERICAN SVC, WS:NA / (D):100kW:WS:NA
6005	CAMEROON — RADIO CAMEROON — Buea	Irr::4kW:DS-FRENCH,ENG,ETC / Irr:Su:4kW:DS-FRENCH,ENG,ETC
	CANADA — CFCX-CFCF — Montréal, Québec	0.5kW:DS
(con'd)	CHINA (PR) — GANSU PEOPLES BS — Lanzhou	15kW:DS-1

ENGLISH ▬▬   GERMAN / DEUTSCH ◊◊◊◊   FRENCH / FRANÇAIS ═══   PORTUGUESE / PORTUGUÊS ▬▬▬   SPANISH / ESPAÑOL ▬▬

ARABIC /ىبرع ══   RUSSIAN / РУССКИИ ══   CHINESE / ✶✸ ◊◊◊◊   JAPANESE / 日本語 ▬▬   MULTILINGUAL ◊◊◊◊   OTHER ▬

SUMMER ONLY (J)   WINTER ONLY (D)   JAMMING /\/\ or / or \   EARLIEST HEARD ◢   LATEST HEARD ◣   ✝ TENTATIVE

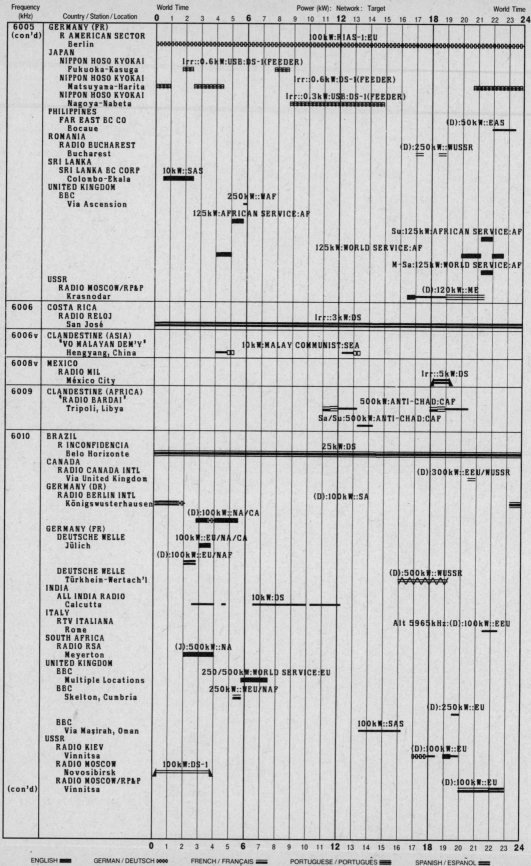

Frequency (kHz)	Country / Station / Location	World Time 0–24 / Power (kW): Network: Target
6005 (con'd)	GERMANY (FR) R AMERICAN SECTOR / Berlin	100kW:RIAS-1:EU
	JAPAN NIPPON HOSO KYOKAI / Fukuoka-Kasuga	Irr::0.6kW:USB:DS-1(FEEDER)
	NIPPON HOSO KYOKAI / Matsuyama-Harita	Irr::0.6kW:DS-1(FEEDER)
	NIPPON HOSO KYOKAI / Nagoya-Nabeta	Irr::0.3kW:USB:DS-1(FEEDER)
	PHILIPPINES FAR EAST BC CO / Bocaue	(D):50kW::EAS
	ROMANIA RADIO BUCHAREST / Bucharest	(D):250kW::WUSSR
	SRI LANKA SRI LANKA BC CORP / Colombo-Ekala	10kW::SAS
	UNITED KINGDOM BBC / Via Ascension	250kW::WAF / 125kW:AFRICAN SERVICE:AF / Su:125kW:AFRICAN SERVICE:AF / 125kW:WORLD SERVICE:AF / M-Sa:125kW:WORLD SERVICE:AF
	USSR RADIO MOSCOW/RP&P / Krasnodar	(D):120kW::ME
6006	COSTA RICA RADIO RELOJ / San José	Irr::3kW:DS
6006v	CLANDESTINE (ASIA) "VO MALAYAN DEM'Y" / Hengyang, China	10kW:MALAY COMMUNIST:SEA
6008v	MEXICO RADIO MIL / México City	Irr::5kW:DS
6009	CLANDESTINE (AFRICA) "RADIO BARDAI" / Tripoli, Libya	500kW:ANTI-CHAD:CAF / Sa/Su:500kW:ANTI-CHAD:CAF
6010	BRAZIL R INCONFIDENCIA / Belo Horizonte	25kW:DS
	CANADA RADIO CANADA INTL / Via United Kingdom	(D):300kW::EEU/WUSSR
	GERMANY (DR) RADIO BERLIN INTL / Königswusterhausen	(D):100kW::SA / (D):100kW::NA/CA
	GERMANY (FR) DEUTSCHE WELLE / Jülich	100kW::EU/NA/CA / (D):100kW::EU/NAF
	DEUTSCHE WELLE / Türkheim-Wertach'l	(D):500kW::WUSSR
	INDIA ALL INDIA RADIO / Calcutta	10kW:DS
	ITALY RTV ITALIANA / Rome	Alt 5965kHz:(D):100kW::EEU
	SOUTH AFRICA RADIO RSA / Meyerton	(J):500kW::NA
	UNITED KINGDOM BBC / Multiple Locations	250/500kW:WORLD SERVICE:EU
	BBC / Skelton, Cumbria	250kW::WEU/NAF
	BBC / Via Maşirah, Oman	100kW::SAS / (D):250kW::EU
	USSR RADIO KIEV / Vinnitsa	(D):100kW::EU
	RADIO MOSCOW / Novosibirsk	100kW:DS-1
(con'd)	RADIO MOSCOW/RP&P / Vinnitsa	(D):100kW::EU

ENGLISH ▰▰ GERMAN / DEUTSCH ⋈⋈⋈ FRENCH / FRANÇAIS ═══ PORTUGUESE / PORTUGUÊS ▰▰▰ SPANISH / ESPAÑOL ▰▰

ARABIC / ﻋﺮﺑﻰ ═══ RUSSIAN / РУССКИИ ═══ CHINESE / ✷✷ ⋈⋈⋈⋈ JAPANESE / 日本語 ▰▰▰ MULTILINGUAL ⋈⋈⋈⋈ OTHER ━━

SUMMER ONLY (J)   WINTER ONLY (D)   JAMMING /\/\ or / or \   EARLIEST HEARD ◢   LATEST HEARD ◣   ✦ TENTATIVE

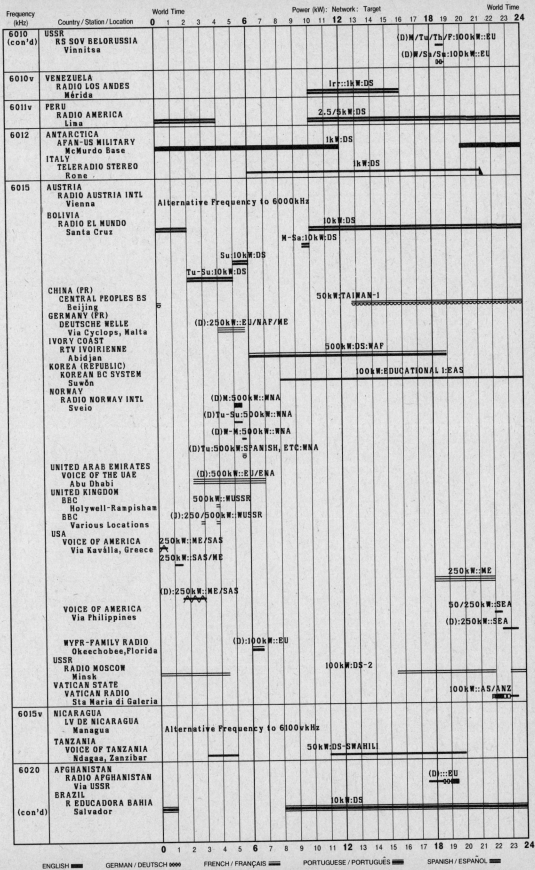

Frequency (kHz)	Country / Station / Location	Schedule
6010 (con'd)	USSR — RS SOV BELORUSSIA, Vinnitsa	(D)M/Tu/Th/F:100kW::EU; (D)W/Sa/Su:100kW::EU
6010v	VENEZUELA — RADIO LOS ANDES, Mérida	Irr::1kW:DS
6011v	PERU — RADIO AMERICA, Lima	2.5/5kW:DS
6012	ANTARCTICA — AFAN-US MILITARY, McMurdo Base	1kW:DS
	ITALY — TELERADIO STEREO, Rome	1kW:DS
6015	AUSTRIA — RADIO AUSTRIA INTL, Vienna	Alternative Frequency to 6000kHz
	BOLIVIA — RADIO EL MUNDO, Santa Cruz	10kW:DS; M-Sa:10kW:DS; Su:10kW:DS; Tu-Su:10kW:DS
	CHINA (PR) — CENTRAL PEOPLES BS, Beijing	50kW:TAIWAN-1
	GERMANY (FR) — DEUTSCHE WELLE, Via Cyclops, Malta	(D):250kW::EU/NAF/ME
	IVORY COAST — RTV IVOIRIENNE, Abidjan	500kW:DS:WAF
	KOREA (REPUBLIC) — KOREAN BC SYSTEM, Suwŏn	100kW:EDUCATIONAL 1:EAS
	NORWAY — RADIO NORWAY INTL, Sveio	(D)M:500kW::WNA; (D)Tu-Su:500kW::WNA; (D)W-M:500kW::WNA; (D)Tu:500kW:SPANISH, ETC:WNA
	UNITED ARAB EMIRATES — VOICE OF THE UAE, Abu Dhabi	(D):500kW::EU/ENA
	UNITED KINGDOM — BBC, Holywell-Rampisham	500kW::WUSSR
	UNITED KINGDOM — BBC, Various Locations	(J):250/500kW::WUSSR
	USA — VOICE OF AMERICA, Via Kaválla, Greece	250kW::ME/SAS; 250kW::SAS/ME; 250kW::ME; (D):250kW::ME/SAS
	VOICE OF AMERICA, Via Philippines	50/250kW::SEA; (D):250kW::SEA
	WYFR-FAMILY RADIO, Okeechobee, Florida	(D):100kW::EU
	USSR — RADIO MOSCOW, Minsk	100kW:DS-2
	VATICAN STATE — VATICAN RADIO, Sta Maria di Galeria	100kW::AS/ANZ
6015v	NICARAGUA — LV DE NICARAGUA, Managua	Alternative Frequency to 6100vkHz
	TANZANIA — VOICE OF TANZANIA, Ndagaa, Zanzibar	50kW:DS-SWAHILI
6020	AFGHANISTAN — RADIO AFGHANISTAN, Via USSR	(D):::EU
	BRAZIL — R EDUCADORA BAHIA, Salvador	10kW:DS
(con'd)		

World Time: 0 1 2 3 4 5 6 7 8 9 10 11 12 13 14 15 16 17 18 19 20 21 22 23 24

Power (kW) : Network : Target

ENGLISH ▬▬   GERMAN / DEUTSCH ∞∞   FRENCH / FRANÇAIS ▬▬   PORTUGUESE / PORTUGUÊS ▬▬   SPANISH / ESPAÑOL ▬▬

ARABIC / عربي ▬▬   RUSSIAN / РУССКИЙ ▬▬   CHINESE / 中文 ∞∞   JAPANESE / 日本語 ∞∞   MULTILINGUAL ∞∞   OTHER ▬▬

SUMMER ONLY (J)   WINTER ONLY (D)   JAMMING ∧∧ or / or \   EARLIEST HEARD ◢   LATEST HEARD ◣   + TENTATIVE

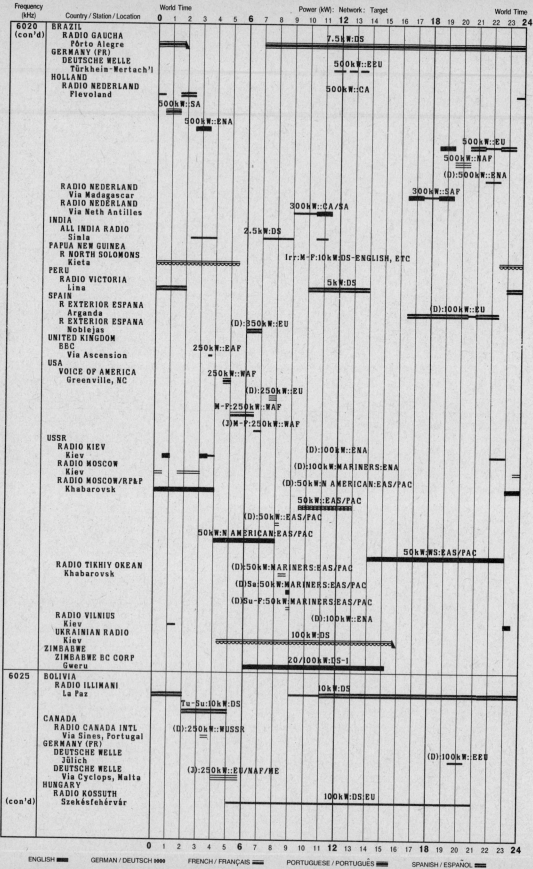

6020 (con'd)

BRAZIL
RADIO GAUCHA
Pôrto Alegre — 7.5kW:DS

GERMANY (FR)
DEUTSCHE WELLE
Türkheim-Wertach'l — 500kW::EEU

HOLLAND
RADIO NEDERLAND
Flevoland — 500kW::CA
500kW:SA
500kW::ENA
500kW::EU
500kW::NAF
(D):500kW::ENA

RADIO NEDERLAND
Via Madagascar — 300kW::SAF

RADIO NEDERLAND
Via Neth Antilles — 300kW::CA/SA

INDIA
ALL INDIA RADIO
Simla — 2.5kW:DS

PAPUA NEW GUINEA
R NORTH SOLOMONS
Kieta — Irr:M-F:10kW:DS-ENGLISH, ETC

PERU
RADIO VICTORIA
Lima — 5kW:DS

SPAIN
R EXTERIOR ESPANA
Arganda — (D):100kW::EU

R EXTERIOR ESPANA
Noblejas — (D):350kW::EU

UNITED KINGDOM
BBC
Via Ascension — 250kW::EAF

USA
VOICE OF AMERICA
Greenville, NC — 250kW::WAF
(D):250kW::EU
M-F:250kW::WAF
(J)M-F:250kW::WAF

USSR
RADIO KIEV
Kiev — (D):100kW::ENA

RADIO MOSCOW
Kiev — (D):100kW:MARINERS:ENA

RADIO MOSCOW/RP&P
Khabarovsk — (D):50kW:N AMERICAN:EAS/PAC
50kW::EAS/PAC
(D):50kW::EAS/PAC
50kW:N AMERICAN:EAS/PAC
50kW:WS:EAS/PAC

RADIO TIKHIY OKEAN
Khabarovsk — (D):50kW:MARINERS:EAS/PAC
(D)Sa:50kW:MARINERS:EAS/PAC
(D)Su-F:50kW:MARINERS:EAS/PAC

RADIO VILNIUS
Kiev — (D):100kW::ENA

UKRAINIAN RADIO
Kiev — 100kW:DS

ZIMBABWE
ZIMBABWE BC CORP
Gweru — 20/100kW:DS-1

6025

BOLIVIA
RADIO ILLIMANI
La Paz — 10kW:DS
Tu-Su:10kW:DS

CANADA
RADIO CANADA INTL
Via Sines, Portugal — (D):250kW::WUSSR

GERMANY (FR)
DEUTSCHE WELLE
Jülich — (D):100kW::EEU

DEUTSCHE WELLE
Via Cyclops, Malta — (J):250kW::EU/NAF/ME

HUNGARY
RADIO KOSSUTH
Szekésfehérvár **(con'd)** — 100kW:DS:EU

ENGLISH ■■■ GERMAN / DEUTSCH 0000 FRENCH / FRANÇAIS ≡≡ PORTUGUESE / PORTUGUÊS ≡≡ SPANISH / ESPAÑOL ≡≡
ARABIC / عربي ≡≡ RUSSIAN / РУССКИИ ≡≡ CHINESE / 中文 □□□□ JAPANESE / 日本語 ■■■ MULTILINGUAL ∞∞∞ OTHER ▬▬
SUMMER ONLY (J) WINTER ONLY (D) JAMMING /\/\ or / or \ EARLIEST HEARD ◢ LATEST HEARD ◣ + TENTATIVE

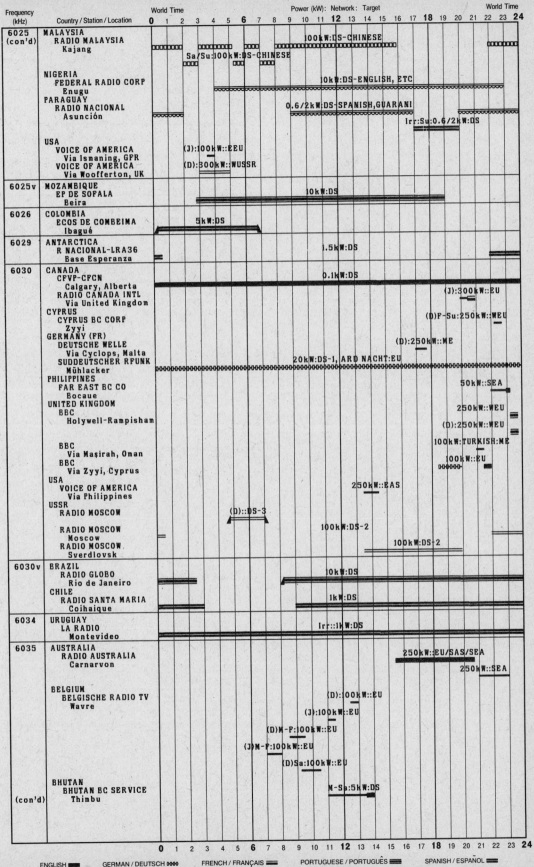

Frequency (kHz)	Country / Station / Location	Details
6025 (con'd)	MALAYSIA / RADIO MALAYSIA / Kajang	100kW:DS-CHINESE / Sa/Su:100kW:DS-CHINESE
	NIGERIA / FEDERAL RADIO CORP / Enugu	10kW:DS-ENGLISH, ETC
	PARAGUAY / RADIO NACIONAL / Asunción	0.6/2kW:DS-SPANISH,GUARANI / Irr:Su:0.6/2kW:DS
	USA / VOICE OF AMERICA / Via Ismaning, GFR	(J):100kW::EEU
	VOICE OF AMERICA / Via Woofferton, UK	(D):300kW::WUSSR
6025v	MOZAMBIQUE / EP DE SOFALA / Beira	10kW:DS
6026	COLOMBIA / ECOS DE COMBEIMA / Ibagué	5kW:DS
6029	ANTARCTICA / R NACIONAL-LRA36 / Base Esperanza	1.5kW:DS
6030	CANADA / CFVP-CFCN / Calgary, Alberta	0.1kW:DS
	RADIO CANADA INTL / Via United Kingdom	(J):300kW::EU
	CYPRUS / CYPRUS BC CORP / Zyyi	(D)F-Su:250kW::WEU
	GERMANY (FR) / DEUTSCHE WELLE / Via Cyclops, Malta	(D):250kW::ME
	SUDDEUTSCHER RFUNK / Mühlacker	20kW:DS-1, ARD NACHT:EU
	PHILIPPINES / FAR EAST BC CO / Bocaue	50kW::SEA
	UNITED KINGDOM / BBC / Holywell-Rampisham	250kW::WEU / (D):250kW::WEU
	BBC / Via Maşirah, Oman	100kW:TURKISH:ME
	BBC / Via Zyyi, Cyprus	100kW::EU
	USA / VOICE OF AMERICA / Via Philippines	250kW::EAS
	USSR / RADIO MOSCOW	(D)::DS-3
	RADIO MOSCOW / Moscow	100kW:DS-2
	RADIO MOSCOW / Sverdlovsk	100kW:DS-2
6030v	BRAZIL / RADIO GLOBO / Rio de Janeiro	10kW:DS
	CHILE / RADIO SANTA MARIA / Coihaique	1kW:DS
6034	URUGUAY / LA RADIO / Montevideo	Irr::1kW:DS
6035	AUSTRALIA / RADIO AUSTRALIA / Carnarvon	250kW::EU/SAS/SEA / 250kW::SEA
	BELGIUM / BELGISCHE RADIO TV / Wavre	(D):100kW::EU / (J):100kW::EU / (D)M-F:100kW::EU / (J)M-F:100kW::EU / (D)Sa:100kW::EU
	BHUTAN / BHUTAN BC SERVICE / Thimbu	M-Sa:5kW:DS
(con'd)		

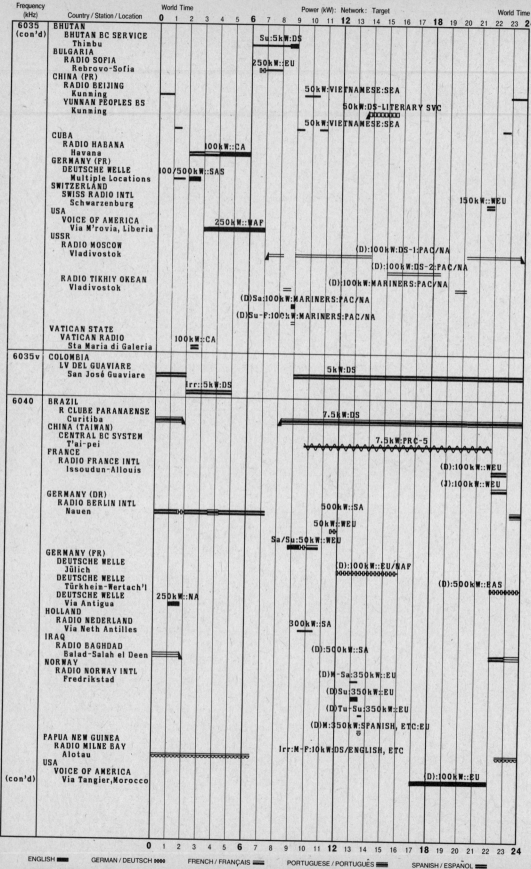

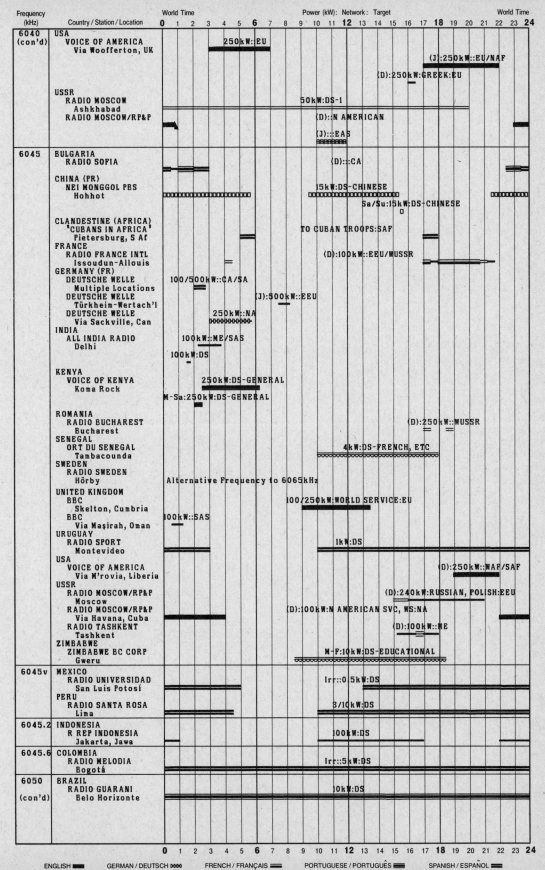

Frequency (kHz)	Country / Station / Location	Power (kW): Network: Target	

6040 (con'd)

USA
VOICE OF AMERICA Via Woofferton, UK — 250kW::EU
(J):250kW::EU/NAF
(D):250kW:GREEK:EU

USSR
RADIO MOSCOW Ashkhabad — 50kW:DS-1
RADIO MOSCOW/RP&P — (D)::N AMERICAN
(J):::EAS

6045

BULGARIA
RADIO SOFIA — (D):::CA

CHINA (PR)
NEI MONGGOL PBS Hohhot — 15kW:DS-CHINESE
Sa/Su:15kW:DS-CHINESE

CLANDESTINE (AFRICA)
'CUBANS IN AFRICA' Pietersburg, S Af — TO CUBAN TROOPS:SAF
FRANCE
RADIO FRANCE INTL Issoudun-Allouis — (D):100kW::EEU/WUSSR
GERMANY (FR)
DEUTSCHE WELLE Multiple Locations — 100/500kW::CA/SA
DEUTSCHE WELLE Türkheim-Wertach'l — (J):500kW::EEU
DEUTSCHE WELLE Via Sackville, Can — 250kW::NA
INDIA
ALL INDIA RADIO Delhi — 100kW::ME/SAS
100kW:DS

KENYA
VOICE OF KENYA Koma Rock — 250kW:DS-GENERAL
M-Sa:250kW:DS-GENERAL

ROMANIA
RADIO BUCHAREST Bucharest — (D):250kW::WUSSR
SENEGAL
ORT DU SENEGAL Tambacounda — 4kW:DS-FRENCH, ETC
SWEDEN
RADIO SWEDEN Hörby — Alternative Frequency to 6065kHz
UNITED KINGDOM
BBC Skelton, Cumbria — 100/250kW:WORLD SERVICE:EU
BBC Via Maşirah, Oman — 100kW::SAS
URUGUAY
RADIO SPORT Montevideo — 1kW:DS
USA
VOICE OF AMERICA Via M'rovia, Liberia — (D):250kW::WAF/SAF
USSR
RADIO MOSCOW/RP&P Moscow — (D):240kW:RUSSIAN, POLISH:EEU
RADIO MOSCOW/RP&P Via Havana, Cuba — (D):100kW:N AMERICAN SVC, WS:NA
RADIO TASHKENT Tashkent — (D):100kW::ME
ZIMBABWE
ZIMBABWE BC CORP Gweru — M-F:10kW:DS-EDUCATIONAL

6045v

MEXICO
RADIO UNIVERSIDAD San Luis Potosí — Irr::0.5kW:DS
PERU
RADIO SANTA ROSA Lima — 3/10kW:DS

6045.2

INDONESIA
R REP INDONESIA Jakarta, Jawa — 100kW:DS

6045.6

COLOMBIA
RADIO MELODIA Bogotá — Irr::5kW:DS

6050 (con'd)

BRAZIL
RADIO GUARANI Belo Horizonte — 10kW:DS

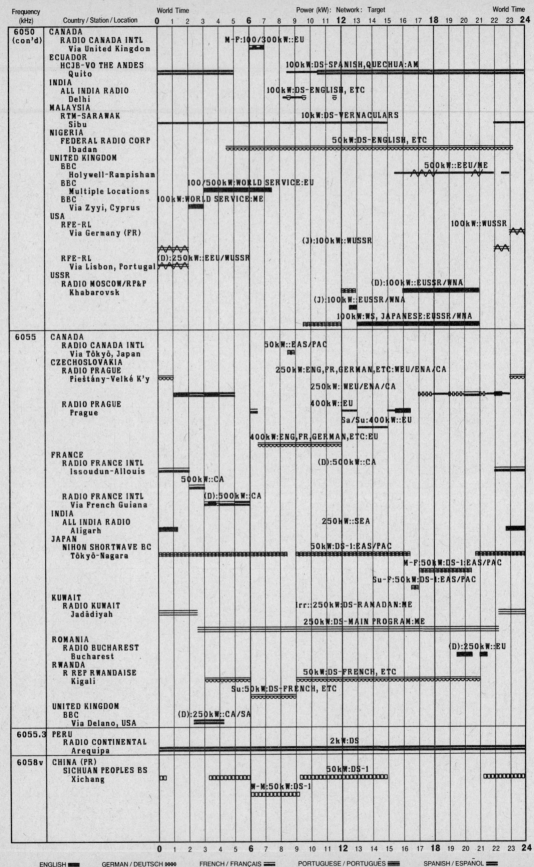

Frequency (kHz)	Country / Station / Location	World Time / Power (kW) : Network : Target
6050 (con'd)	CANADA	
	RADIO CANADA INTL — Via United Kingdom	M-F:100/300kW::EU
	ECUADOR	
	HCJB-VO THE ANDES — Quito	100kW:DS-SPANISH,QUECHUA:AM
	INDIA	
	ALL INDIA RADIO — Delhi	100kW:DS-ENGLISH, ETC
	MALAYSIA	
	RTM-SARAWAK — Sibu	10kW:DS-VERNACULARS
	NIGERIA	
	FEDERAL RADIO CORP — Ibadan	50kW:DS-ENGLISH, ETC
	UNITED KINGDOM	
	BBC — Holywell-Rampisham	500kW::EEU/ME
	BBC — Multiple Locations	100/500kW:WORLD SERVICE:EU
	BBC — Via Zyyi, Cyprus	100kW:WORLD SERVICE:ME
	USA	
	RFE-RL — Via Germany (FR)	100kW::WUSSR / (J):100kW::WUSSR
	RFE-RL — Via Lisbon, Portugal	(D):250kW::EEU/WUSSR
	USSR	
	RADIO MOSCOW/RP&P — Khabarovsk	(D):100kW::EUSSR/WNA / (J):100kW::EUSSR/WNA / 100kW:WS, JAPANESE:EUSSR/WNA
6055	CANADA	
	RADIO CANADA INTL — Via Tōkyō, Japan	50kW::EAS/PAC
	CZECHOSLOVAKIA	
	RADIO PRAGUE — Pieštány-Velké K'y	250kW:ENG,FR,GERMAN,ETC:WEU/ENA/CA
		250kW: WEU/ENA/CA
	RADIO PRAGUE — Prague	400kW:EU / Sa/Su:400kW::EU
		400kW:ENG,FR,GERMAN,ETC:EU
	FRANCE	
	RADIO FRANCE INTL — Issoudun-Allouis	(D):500kW::CA
		500kW::CA
	RADIO FRANCE INTL — Via French Guiana	(D):500kW::CA
	INDIA	
	ALL INDIA RADIO — Aligarh	250kW::SEA
	JAPAN	
	NIHON SHORTWAVE BC — Tōkyō-Nagara	50kW:DS-1:EAS/PAC / M-F:50kW:DS-1:EAS/PAC / Su-F:50kW:DS-1:EAS/PAC
	KUWAIT	
	RADIO KUWAIT — Jadādiyah	Irr::250kW:DS-RAMADAN:ME / 250kW:DS-MAIN PROGRAM:ME
	ROMANIA	
	RADIO BUCHAREST — Bucharest	(D):250kW::EU
	RWANDA	
	R REP RWANDAISE — Kigali	50kW:DS-FRENCH, ETC / Su:50kW:DS-FRENCH, ETC
	UNITED KINGDOM	
	BBC — Via Delano, USA	(D):250kW::CA/SA
6055.3	PERU	
	RADIO CONTINENTAL — Arequipa	2kW:DS
6058v	CHINA (PR)	
	SICHUAN PEOPLES BS — Xichang	50kW:DS-1 / M-M:50kW:DS-1

ENGLISH ▬   GERMAN / DEUTSCH ▭▭▭   FRENCH / FRANÇAIS ▬   PORTUGUESE / PORTUGUÊS ▬   SPANISH / ESPAÑOL ▬

ARABIC / العربية   RUSSIAN / РУССКИЙ ▬   CHINESE / 中文 ▭▭▭   JAPANESE / 日本語 ▬   MULTILINGUAL ▭▭▭   OTHER ▬

SUMMER ONLY (J)   WINTER ONLY (D)   JAMMING ∧∧ or / or \   EARLIEST HEARD ◢   LATEST HEARD ◣   ✦ TENTATIVE

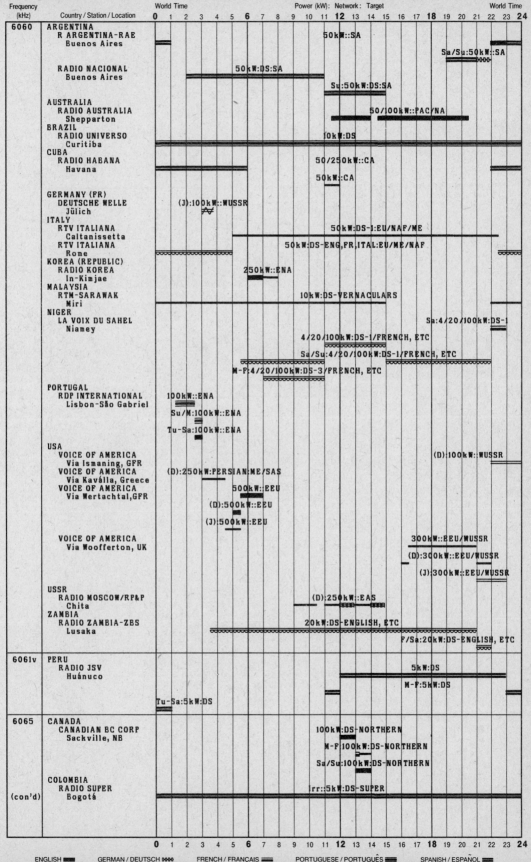

Frequency (kHz)	Country / Station / Location		
6060	**ARGENTINA**		
	R ARGENTINA-RAE	50kW::SA	
	Buenos Aires	Sa/Su:50kW::SA	
	RADIO NACIONAL	50kW:DS:SA	
	Buenos Aires	Su:50kW:DS:SA	
	AUSTRALIA		
	RADIO AUSTRALIA	50/100kW::PAC/NA	
	Shepparton		
	BRAZIL		
	RADIO UNIVERSO	10kW:DS	
	Curitiba		
	CUBA		
	RADIO HABANA	50/250kW::CA	
	Havana	50kW::CA	
	GERMANY (FR)		
	DEUTSCHE WELLE	(J):100kW::WUSSR	
	Jülich		
	ITALY		
	RTV ITALIANA	50kW:DS-1:EU/NAF/ME	
	Caltanissetta		
	RTV ITALIANA	50kW:DS-ENG,FR,ITAL:EU/ME/NAF	
	Rome		
	KOREA (REPUBLIC)		
	RADIO KOREA	250kW::ENA	
	In-Kimjae		
	MALAYSIA		
	RTM-SARAWAK	10kW:DS-VERNACULARS	
	Miri		
	NIGER		
	LA VOIX DU SAHEL	Sa:4/20/100kW:DS-1	
	Niamey	4/20/100kW:DS-1/FRENCH, ETC	
		Sa/Su:4/20/100kW:DS-1/FRENCH, ETC	
		M-F:4/20/100kW:DS-3/FRENCH, ETC	
	PORTUGAL		
	RDP INTERNATIONAL	100kW::ENA	
	Lisbon-São Gabriel	Su/M:100kW::ENA	
		Tu-Sa:100kW::ENA	
	USA		
	VOICE OF AMERICA	(D):100kW::WUSSR	
	Via Ismaning, GFR		
	VOICE OF AMERICA	(D):250kW:PERSIAN:ME/SAS	
	Via Kaválla, Greece		
	VOICE OF AMERICA	500kW::EEU	
	Via Wertachtal,GFR	(D):500kW::EEU	
		(J):500kW::EEU	
	VOICE OF AMERICA	300kW::EEU/WUSSR	
	Via Woofferton, UK	(D):300kW::EEU/WUSSR	
		(J):300kW::EEU/WUSSR	
	USSR		
	RADIO MOSCOW/RP&P	(D):250kW::EAS	
	Chita		
	ZAMBIA		
	RADIO ZAMBIA-ZBS	20kW:DS-ENGLISH, ETC	
	Lusaka	F/Sa:20kW:DS-ENGLISH, ETC	
6061v	**PERU**		
	RADIO JSV	5kW:DS	
	Huánuco	M-F:5kW:DS	
		Tu-Sa:5kW:DS	
6065	**CANADA**		
	CANADIAN BC CORP	100kW:DS-NORTHERN	
	Sackville, NB	M-F:100kW:DS-NORTHERN	
		Sa/Su:100kW:DS-NORTHERN	
	COLOMBIA		
(con'd)	RADIO SUPER	Irr::5kW:DS-SUPER	
	Bogotá		

ENGLISH ▬▬ GERMAN / DEUTSCH ◊◊◊◊ FRENCH / FRANÇAIS ═══ PORTUGUESE / PORTUGUÊS ▬▬ SPANISH / ESPAÑOL ▬▬

ARABIC /ﻉﻑ ═══ RUSSIAN / РУССКИИ ═══ CHINESE / ★★ ▭▭▭ JAPANESE / 日本語 ▬▬ MULTILINGUAL ▭▭▭ OTHER ▬▬

SUMMER ONLY (J) WINTER ONLY (D) JAMMING ∧∧ or / or \ EARLIEST HEARD ◢ LATEST HEARD ◣ + TENTATIVE

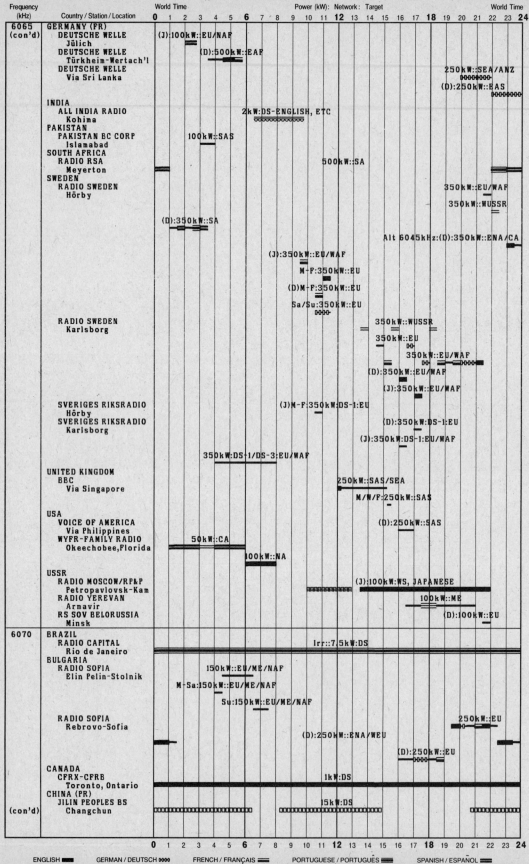

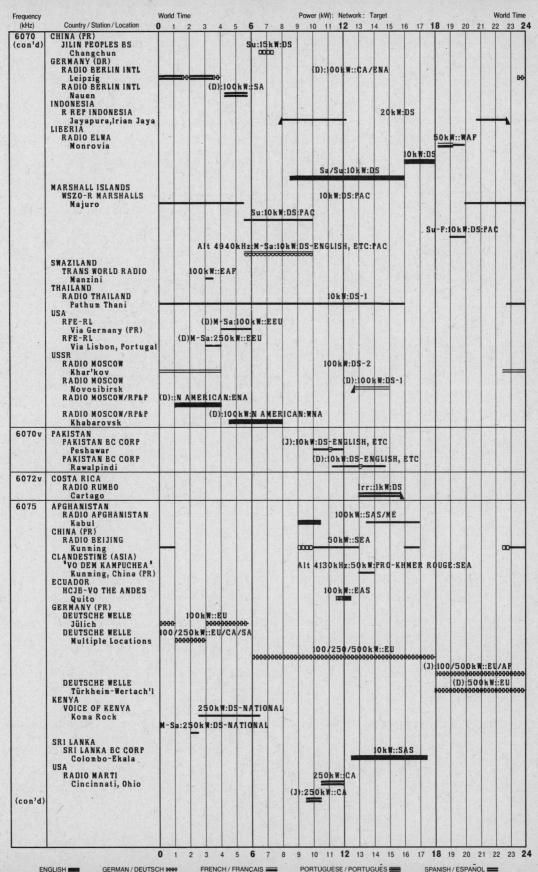

Frequency (kHz)	Country / Station / Location		Power (kW): Network: Target

6070 (con'd)

CHINA (PR)
- JILIN PEOPLES BS — Changchun — Su:15kW:DS

GERMANY (DR)
- RADIO BERLIN INTL — Leipzig — (D):100kW::CA/ENA
- RADIO BERLIN INTL — Nauen — (D):100kW::SA

INDONESIA
- R REP INDONESIA — Jayapura,Irian Jaya — 20kW:DS

LIBERIA
- RADIO ELWA — Monrovia — 50kW::WAF — 10kW:DS — Sa/Su:10kW:DS

MARSHALL ISLANDS
- WSZO-R MARSHALLS — Majuro — 10kW:DS:PAC — Su:10kW:DS:PAC — Su-F:10kW:DS:PAC — Alt 4940kHz:M-Sa:10kW:DS-ENGLISH, ETC:PAC

SWAZILAND
- TRANS WORLD RADIO — Manzini — 100kW::EAF

THAILAND
- RADIO THAILAND — Pathum Thani — 10kW:DS-1

USA
- RFE-RL — Via Germany (FR) — (D)M-Sa:100kW::EEU
- RFE-RL — Via Lisbon, Portugal — (D)M-Sa:250kW::EEU

USSR
- RADIO MOSCOW — Khar'kov — 100kW:DS-2
- RADIO MOSCOW — Novosibirsk — (D):100kW:DS-1
- RADIO MOSCOW/RP&P — (D)::N AMERICAN:ENA
- RADIO MOSCOW/RP&P — Khabarovsk — (D):100kW:N AMERICAN:WNA

6070v

PAKISTAN
- PAKISTAN BC CORP — Peshawar — (J):10kW:DS-ENGLISH, ETC
- PAKISTAN BC CORP — Rawalpindi — (D):10kW:DS-ENGLISH, ETC

6072v

COSTA RICA
- RADIO RUMBO — Cartago — Irr::1kW:DS

6075

AFGHANISTAN
- RADIO AFGHANISTAN — Kabul — 100kW::SAS/ME

CHINA (PR)
- RADIO BEIJING — Kunming — 50kW::SEA

CLANDESTINE (ASIA)
- "VO DEM KAMPUCHEA" — Kunming, China (PR) — Alt 4130kHz:50kW:PRO-KHMER ROUGE:SEA

ECUADOR
- HCJB-VO THE ANDES — Quito — 100kW::EAS

GERMANY (FR)
- DEUTSCHE WELLE — Jülich — 100kW::EU
- DEUTSCHE WELLE — Multiple Locations — 100/250kW::EU/CA/SA — 100/250/500kW::EU — (J):100/500kW::EU/AF
- DEUTSCHE WELLE — Türkheim-Wertach'l — (D):500kW::EU

KENYA
- VOICE OF KENYA — Koma Rock — 250kW:DS-NATIONAL — M-Sa:250kW:DS-NATIONAL

SRI LANKA
- SRI LANKA BC CORP — Colombo-Ekala — 10kW::SAS

USA
- RADIO MARTI — Cincinnati, Ohio — 250kW::CA — (J):250kW::CA

(con'd)

ENGLISH ▬ GERMAN / DEUTSCH ◊◊◊◊ FRENCH / FRANÇAIS ▬ PORTUGUESE / PORTUGUÊS ▬ SPANISH / ESPAÑOL ▬

ARABIC / عربي ▬ RUSSIAN / РУССКИЙ ▬ CHINESE / 中文 ◊◊◊◊ JAPANESE / 日本語 ▬ MULTILINGUAL ▭▭▭ OTHER ▬

SUMMER ONLY (J) WINTER ONLY (D) JAMMING /\/\ or / or \ EARLIEST HEARD ◢ LATEST HEARD ◣ + TENTATIVE

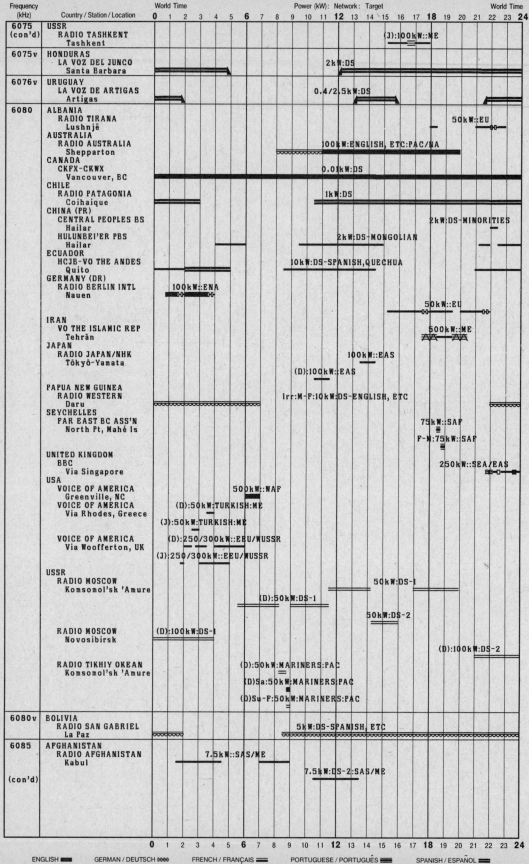

Frequency (kHz)	Country / Station / Location	World Time	Power (kW): Network: Target	World Time

Frequency (kHz)	Country / Station / Location	Details
6075 (con'd)	**USSR** RADIO TASHKENT Tashkent	(J):100kW::ME
6075v	**HONDURAS** LA VOZ DEL JUNCO Santa Barbara	2kW:DS
6076v	**URUGUAY** LA VOZ DE ARTIGAS Artigas	0.4/2.5kW:DS
6080	**ALBANIA** RADIO TIRANA Lushnjë	50kW::EU
	AUSTRALIA RADIO AUSTRALIA Shepparton	100kW:ENGLISH, ETC:PAC/NA
	CANADA CKFX-CKWX Vancouver, BC	0.01kW:DS
	CHILE RADIO PATAGONIA Coihaique	1kW:DS
	CHINA (PR) CENTRAL PEOPLES BS Hailar	2kW:DS-MINORITIES
	HULUNBEI'ER PBS Hailar	2kW:DS-MONGOLIAN
	ECUADOR HCJB-VO THE ANDES Quito	10kW:DS-SPANISH,QUECHUA
	GERMANY (DR) RADIO BERLIN INTL Nauen	100kW:ENA / 50kW::EU
	IRAN VO THE ISLAMIC REP Tehrān	500kW::ME
	JAPAN RADIO JAPAN/NHK Tōkyō-Yamata	100kW::EAS / (D):100kW::EAS
	PAPUA NEW GUINEA RADIO WESTERN Daru	Irr:M-F:10kW:DS-ENGLISH, ETC
	SEYCHELLES FAR EAST BC ASS'N North Pt, Mahé Is	75kW::SAF / F-M:75kW:SAF
	UNITED KINGDOM BBC Via Singapore	250kW::SEA/EAS
	USA VOICE OF AMERICA Greenville, NC	500kW::WAF
	VOICE OF AMERICA Via Rhodes, Greece	(D):50kW:TURKISH:ME / (J):50kW:TURKISH:ME
	VOICE OF AMERICA Via Woofferton, UK	(D):250/300kW::EEU/WUSSR / (J):250/300kW::EEU/WUSSR
	USSR RADIO MOSCOW Komsomol'sk 'Amure	50kW:DS-1 / (D):50kW:DS-1 / 50kW:DS-2
	RADIO MOSCOW Novosibirsk	(D):100kW:DS-1 / (D):100kW:DS-2
	RADIO TIKHIY OKEAN Komsomol'sk 'Amure	(D):50kW:MARINERS:PAC / (D)Sa:50kW:MARINERS:PAC / (D)Su-F:50kW:MARINERS:PAC
6080v	**BOLIVIA** RADIO SAN GABRIEL La Paz	5kW:DS-SPANISH, ETC
6085 (con'd)	**AFGHANISTAN** RADIO AFGHANISTAN Kabul	7.5kW::SAS/ME / 7.5kW:DS-2:SAS/ME

ENGLISH ▬▬   GERMAN / DEUTSCH ∞∞∞   FRENCH / FRANÇAIS ══   PORTUGUESE / PORTUGUÊS ▬   SPANISH / ESPAÑOL ▬

ARABIC / العربية ═══   RUSSIAN / РУССКИИ ═══   CHINESE / 中文 □□□□   JAPANESE / 日本語 ▬▬   MULTILINGUAL ∞∞∞   OTHER ──

SUMMER ONLY (J)   WINTER ONLY (D)   JAMMING /\/\ or / or \   EARLIEST HEARD ◢   LATEST HEARD ◣   * TENTATIVE

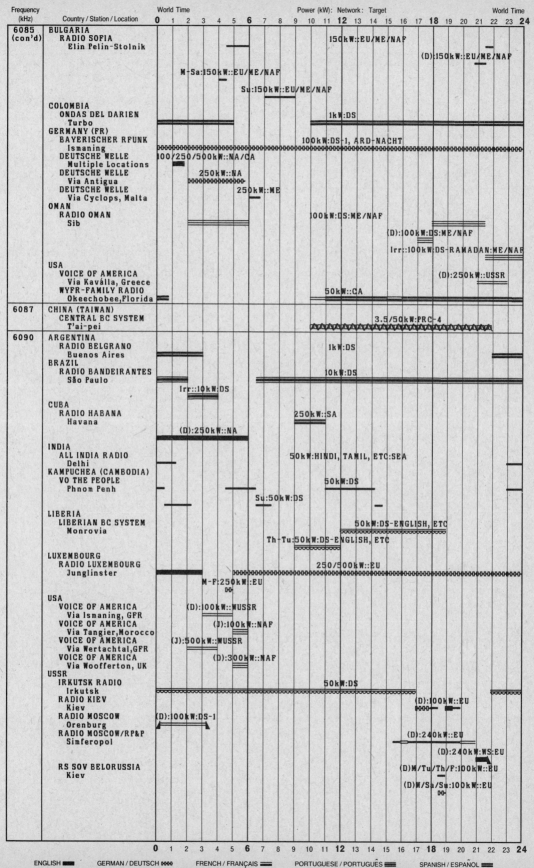

Frequency (kHz)	Country / Station / Location	Schedule details
6085 (con'd)	**BULGARIA**	
	RADIO SOFIA	150kW::EU/ME/NAF
	Elin Pelin-Stolnik	(D):150kW::EU/ME/NAF
		M-Sa:150kW::EU/ME/NAF
		Su:150kW::EU/ME/NAF
	COLOMBIA	
	ONDAS DEL DARIEN	1kW:DS
	Turbo	
	GERMANY (FR)	
	BAYERISCHER RFUNK	100kW:DS-1, ARD-NACHT
	Ismaning	
	DEUTSCHE WELLE	100/250/500kW::NA/CA
	Multiple Locations	
	DEUTSCHE WELLE	250kW::NA
	Via Antigua	
	DEUTSCHE WELLE	250kW::ME
	Via Cyclops, Malta	
	OMAN	
	RADIO OMAN	100kW:DS:ME/NAF
	Sib	(D):100kW:DS:ME/NAF
		Irr::100kW:DS-RAMADAN:ME/NAF
	USA	
	VOICE OF AMERICA	(D):250kW::USSR
	Via Kaválla, Greece	
	WYFR-FAMILY RADIO	50kW::CA
	Okeechobee,Florida	
6087	**CHINA (TAIWAN)**	
	CENTRAL BC SYSTEM	3.5/50kW:PRC-4
	T'ai-pei	
6090	**ARGENTINA**	
	RADIO BELGRANO	1kW:DS
	Buenos Aires	
	BRAZIL	
	RADIO BANDEIRANTES	10kW:DS
	São Paulo	Irr::10kW:DS
	CUBA	
	RADIO HABANA	250kW::SA
	Havana	(D):250kW::NA
	INDIA	
	ALL INDIA RADIO	50kW:HINDI, TAMIL, ETC:SEA
	Delhi	
	KAMPUCHEA (CAMBODIA)	
	VO THE PEOPLE	50kW:DS
	Phnom Penh	Su:50kW:DS
	LIBERIA	
	LIBERIAN BC SYSTEM	50kW:DS-ENGLISH, ETC
	Monrovia	Th-Tu:50kW:DS-ENGLISH, ETC
	LUXEMBOURG	
	RADIO LUXEMBOURG	250/500kW::EU
	Junglinster	M-F:250kW:EU
	USA	
	VOICE OF AMERICA	(D):100kW::WUSSR
	Via Ismaning, GFR	
	VOICE OF AMERICA	(J):100kW::NAF
	Via Tangier,Morocco	
	VOICE OF AMERICA	(J):500kW::WUSSR
	Via Wertachtal,GFR	
	VOICE OF AMERICA	(D):300kW::NAF
	Via Woofferton, UK	
	USSR	
	IRKUTSK RADIO	50kW:DS
	Irkutsk	
	RADIO KIEV	(D):100kW::EU
	Kiev	
	RADIO MOSCOW	(D):100kW:DS-1
	Orenburg	
	RADIO MOSCOW/RP&P	(D):240kW::EU
	Simferopol	
		(D):240kW:WS:EU
	RS SOV BELORUSSIA	(D)M/Tu/Th/F:100kW::EU
	Kiev	(D)W/Sa/Su:100kW::EU

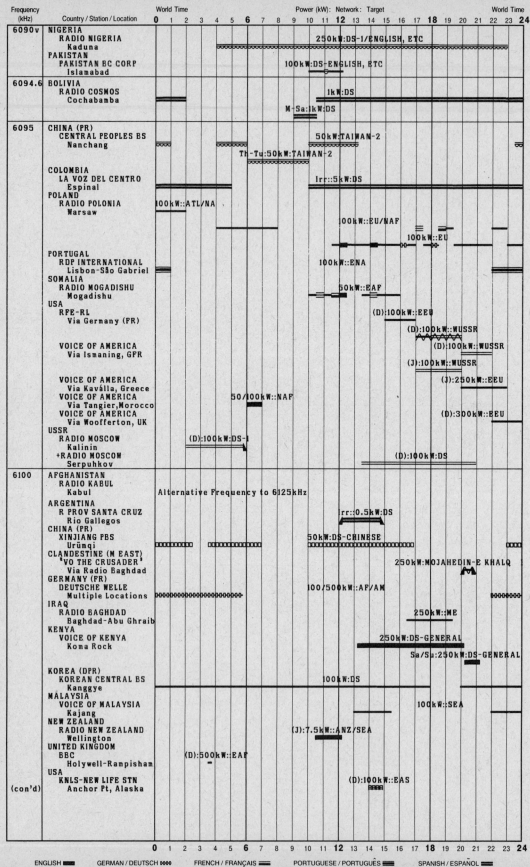

Frequency (kHz)	Country / Station / Location	World Time / Power (kW): Network: Target
6090v	**NIGERIA**	
	RADIO NIGERIA	250kW:DS-1/ENGLISH, ETC
	Kaduna	
	PAKISTAN	
	PAKISTAN BC CORP	100kW:DS-ENGLISH, ETC
	Islamabad	
6094.6	**BOLIVIA**	
	RADIO COSMOS	1kW:DS
	Cochabamba	M-Sa:1kW:DS
6095	**CHINA (PR)**	
	CENTRAL PEOPLES BS	50kW:TAIWAN-2
	Nanchang	Th-Tu:50kW:TAIWAN-2
	COLOMBIA	
	LA VOZ DEL CENTRO	Irr::5kW:DS
	Espinal	
	POLAND	
	RADIO POLONIA	100kW::ATL/NA
	Warsaw	100kW::EU/NAF
		100kW::EU
	PORTUGAL	
	RDP INTERNATIONAL	100kW::ENA
	Lisbon-São Gabriel	
	SOMALIA	
	RADIO MOGADISHU	50kW::EAF
	Mogadishu	
	USA	
	RFE-RL	(D):100kW::EEU
	Via Germany (FR)	
	VOICE OF AMERICA	(D):100kW::WUSSR
	Via Ismaning, GFR	(D):100kW::WUSSR
		(J):100kW::WUSSR
	VOICE OF AMERICA	(J):250kW::EEU
	Via Kaválla, Greece	
	VOICE OF AMERICA	50/100kW::NAF
	Via Tangier, Morocco	
	VOICE OF AMERICA	(D):300kW::EEU
	Via Woofferton, UK	
	USSR	
	RADIO MOSCOW	(D):100kW:DS-1
	Kalinin	
	+RADIO MOSCOW	(D):100kW:DS
	Serpuhkov	
6100	**AFGHANISTAN**	
	RADIO KABUL	Alternative Frequency to 6125kHz
	Kabul	
	ARGENTINA	
	R PROV SANTA CRUZ	Irr::0.5kW:DS
	Rio Gallegos	
	CHINA (PR)	
	XINJIANG PBS	50kW:DS-CHINESE
	Urümqi	
	CLANDESTINE (M EAST)	
	"VO THE CRUSADER"	250kW:MOJAHEDIN-E KHALQ
	Via Radio Baghdad	
	GERMANY (FR)	
	DEUTSCHE WELLE	100/500kW::AF/AM
	Multiple Locations	
	IRAQ	
	RADIO BAGHDAD	250kW::ME
	Baghdad-Abu Ghraib	
	KENYA	
	VOICE OF KENYA	250kW:DS-GENERAL
	Koma Rock	Sa/Su:250kW:DS-GENERAL
	KOREA (DPR)	
	KOREAN CENTRAL BS	100kW:DS
	Kanggye	
	MALAYSIA	
	VOICE OF MALAYSIA	100kW::SEA
	Kajang	
	NEW ZEALAND	
	RADIO NEW ZEALAND	(J):7.5kW::ANZ/SEA
	Wellington	
	UNITED KINGDOM	
	BBC	(D):500kW::EAF
	Holywell-Rampisham	
	USA	
	KNLS-NEW LIFE STN	(D):100kW::EAS
(con'd)	Anchor Pt, Alaska	

World Time scale: 0 1 2 3 4 5 6 7 8 9 10 11 12 13 14 15 16 17 18 19 20 21 22 23 24

ENGLISH ▬▬▬ GERMAN / DEUTSCH ◊◊◊◊ FRENCH / FRANÇAIS ═══ PORTUGUESE / PORTUGUÊS ▬▬ SPANISH / ESPAÑOL ▬▬

ARABIC / ‫ګ ﻋ‬ ═══ RUSSIAN / РУССКИИ ▬▬ CHINESE / 中文 ◊◊◊◊ JAPANESE / 日本語 ▬▬▬ MULTILINGUAL ▬▬▬ OTHER ▬▬

SUMMER ONLY (J)   WINTER ONLY (D)   JAMMING ∧∧ or / or \   EARLIEST HEARD ◢   LATEST HEARD ◣   + TENTATIVE

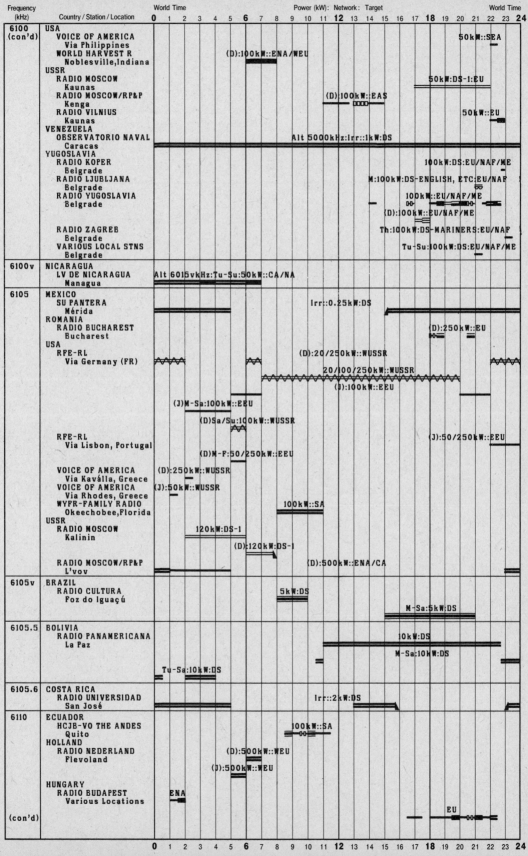

Frequency (kHz)	Country / Station / Location	Details
6100 (con'd)	USA	
	VOICE OF AMERICA Via Philippines	50kW::SEA
	WORLD HARVEST R Noblesville,Indiana	(D):100kW::ENA/WEU
	USSR	
	RADIO MOSCOW Kaunas	50kW:DS-1:EU
	RADIO MOSCOW/RP&P Kenga	(D):100kW::EAS
	RADIO VILNIUS Kaunas	50kW::EU
	VENEZUELA	
	OBSERVATORIO NAVAL Caracas	Alt 5000kHz:Irr::1kW:DS
	YUGOSLAVIA	
	RADIO KOPER Belgrade	100kW:DS:EU/NAF/ME
	RADIO LJUBLJANA Belgrade	M:100kW:DS-ENGLISH, ETC:EU/NAF
	RADIO YUGOSLAVIA Belgrade	100kW::EU/NAF/ME (D):100kW::EU/NAF/ME
	RADIO ZAGREB Belgrade	Th:100kW:DS-MARINERS:EU/NAF
	VARIOUS LOCAL STNS Belgrade	Tu-Su:100kW:DS:EU/NAF/ME
6100v	NICARAGUA	
	LV DE NICARAGUA Managua	Alt 6015vkHz:Tu-Su:50kW::CA/NA
6105	MEXICO	
	SU PANTERA Mérida	Irr::0.25kW:DS
	ROMANIA	
	RADIO BUCHAREST Bucharest	(D):250kW::EU
	USA	
	RFE-RL Via Germany (FR)	(D):20/250kW::WUSSR 20/100/250kW::WUSSR (J):100kW::EEU (J)M-Sa:100kW::EEU (D)Sa/Su:100kW::WUSSR
	RFE-RL Via Lisbon, Portugal	(D)M-F:50/250kW::EEU (J):50/250kW::EEU
	VOICE OF AMERICA Via Kaválla, Greece	(D):250kW::WUSSR
	VOICE OF AMERICA Via Rhodes, Greece	(J):50kW::WUSSR
	WYFR-FAMILY RADIO Okeechobee,Florida	100kW::SA
	USSR	
	RADIO MOSCOW Kalinin	120kW:DS-1 (D):120kW:DS-1
	RADIO MOSCOW/RP&P L'vov	(D):500kW::ENA/CA
6105v	BRAZIL	
	RADIO CULTURA Foz do Iguaçú	5kW:DS M-Sa:5kW:DS
6105.5	BOLIVIA	
	RADIO PANAMERICANA La Paz	10kW:DS M-Sa:10kW:DS Tu-Sa:10kW:DS
6105.6	COSTA RICA	
	RADIO UNIVERSIDAD San José	Irr::2kW:DS
6110	ECUADOR	
	HCJB-VO THE ANDES Quito	100kW::SA
	HOLLAND	
	RADIO NEDERLAND Flevoland	(D):500kW::WEU (J):500kW::WEU
	HUNGARY	
	RADIO BUDAPEST Various Locations	ENA EU
(con'd)		

ENGLISH ▬▬   GERMAN / DEUTSCH ◊◊◊◊   FRENCH / FRANÇAIS ▬▬   PORTUGUESE / PORTUGUÊS ▬▬   SPANISH / ESPAÑOL ▬▬

ARABIC / ﻋﺮﺑﻲ ▬▬   RUSSIAN / РУССКИИ ▬▬   CHINESE / ●▼ ◻◻◻◻   JAPANESE / 日本語 ▬▬▬   MULTILINGUAL ▭▭▭   OTHER ▬▬

SUMMER ONLY (J)   WINTER ONLY (D)   JAMMING /\/\ or / or \   EARLIEST HEARD ◢   LATEST HEARD ◣   + TENTATIVE

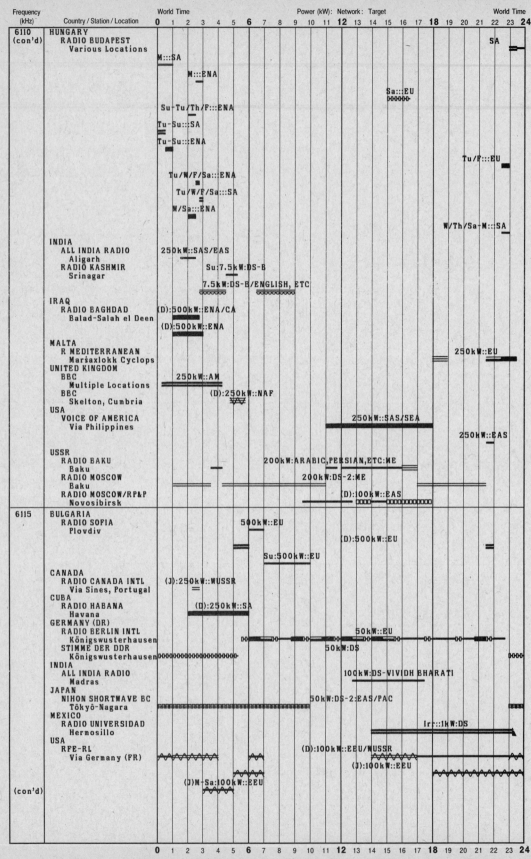

Frequency (kHz)	Country / Station / Location	World Time / Power (kW): Network : Target
6110 (con'd)	**HUNGARY**	
	RADIO BUDAPEST	
	Various Locations	SA / M:::SA / M:::ENA / Sa:::EU / Su-Tu/Th/F:::ENA / Tu-Su:::SA / Tu-Su:::ENA / Tu/F:::EU / Tu/W/F/Sa:::ENA / Tu/W/F/Sa:::SA / W/Sa:::ENA / W/Th/Sa-M:::SA
	INDIA	
	ALL INDIA RADIO	250kW::SAS/EAS
	Aligarh	
	RADIO KASHMIR	Su:7.5kW:DS-B
	Srinagar	7.5kW:DS-B/ENGLISH, ETC
	IRAQ	
	RADIO BAGHDAD	(D):500kW::ENA/CA
	Balad-Salah el Deen	(D):500kW::ENA
	MALTA	
	R MEDITERRANEAN	250kW::EU
	Marśaxlokk Cyclops	
	UNITED KINGDOM	
	BBC	250kW::AM
	Multiple Locations	
	BBC	(D):250kW::NAF
	Skelton, Cumbria	
	USA	
	VOICE OF AMERICA	250kW::SAS/SEA
	Via Philippines	250kW::EAS
	USSR	
	RADIO BAKU	200kW:ARABIC,PERSIAN,ETC:ME
	Baku	
	RADIO MOSCOW	200kW:DS-2:ME
	Baku	
	RADIO MOSCOW/RP&P	(D):100kW::EAS
	Novosibirsk	
6115	**BULGARIA**	
	RADIO SOFIA	500kW::EU
	Plovdiv	(D):500kW::EU / Su:500kW::EU
	CANADA	
	RADIO CANADA INTL	(J):250kW::WUSSR
	Via Sines, Portugal	
	CUBA	
	RADIO HABANA	(D):250kW::SA
	Havana	
	GERMANY (DR)	
	RADIO BERLIN INTL	50kW::EU
	Königswusterhausen	
	STIMME DER DDR	50kW:DS
	Königswusterhausen	
	INDIA	
	ALL INDIA RADIO	100kW:DS-VIVIDH BHARATI
	Madras	
	JAPAN	
	NIHON SHORTWAVE BC	50kW:DS-2:EAS/PAC
	Tōkyō-Nagara	
	MEXICO	
	RADIO UNIVERSIDAD	Irr::1kW:DS
	Hermosillo	
	USA	
	RFE-RL	(D):100kW::EEU/WUSSR
	Via Germany (FR)	(J):100kW::EEU / (J)M-Sa:100kW::EEU
(con'd)		

World Time: 0 1 2 3 4 5 6 7 8 9 10 11 12 13 14 15 16 17 18 19 20 21 22 23 24

ENGLISH ▬▬ GERMAN / DEUTSCH ◊◊◊◊ FRENCH / FRANÇAIS ══ PORTUGUESE / PORTUGUÊS ▬▬ SPANISH / ESPAÑOL ══

ARABIC / ﻉﺭﺏ ≡≡ RUSSIAN / РУССКИИ ══ CHINESE / ✦✦ ◊◊◊◊ JAPANESE / 日本語 ▬▬ MULTILINGUAL ▭▭▭ OTHER ▬▬

SUMMER ONLY (J)   WINTER ONLY (D)   JAMMING ∧∧ or / or \   EARLIEST HEARD ◢   LATEST HEARD ◣   + TENTATIVE

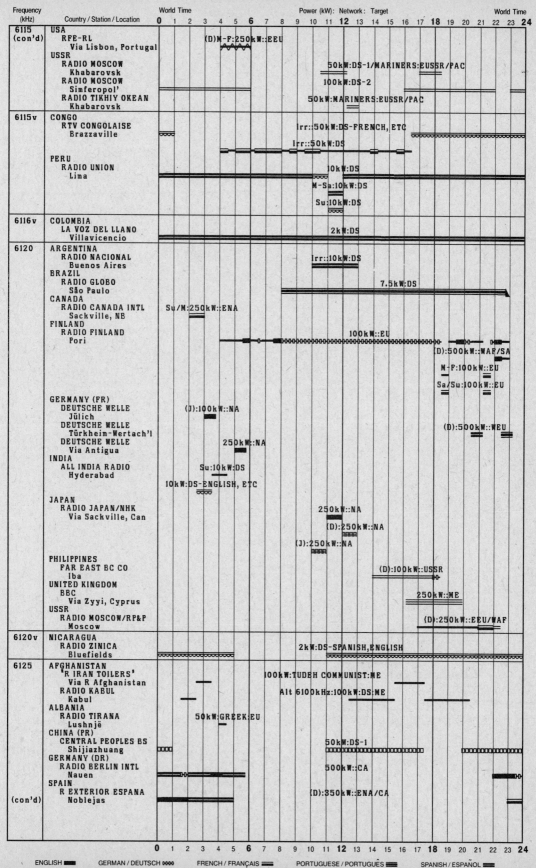

Frequency (kHz)	Country / Station / Location	Power (kW) : Network : Target
6115 (con'd)	USA	
	RFE-RL / Via Lisbon, Portugal	(D)M-F:250kW::EEU
	USSR	
	RADIO MOSCOW / Khabarovsk	50kW:DS-1/MARINERS:EUSSR/PAC
	RADIO MOSCOW / Simferopol'	100kW:DS-2
	RADIO TIKHIY OKEAN / Khabarovsk	50kW:MARINERS:EUSSR/PAC
6115v	CONGO	
	RTV CONGOLAISE / Brazzaville	Irr::50kW:DS-FRENCH, ETC ; Irr::50kW:DS
	PERU	
	RADIO UNION / Lima	10kW:DS ; M-Sa:10kW:DS ; Su:10kW:DS
6116v	COLOMBIA	
	LA VOZ DEL LLANO / Villavicencio	2kW:DS
6120	ARGENTINA	
	RADIO NACIONAL / Buenos Aires	Irr::10kW:DS
	BRAZIL	
	RADIO GLOBO / São Paulo	7.5kW:DS
	CANADA	
	RADIO CANADA INTL / Sackville, NB	Su/M:250kW::ENA
	FINLAND	
	RADIO FINLAND / Pori	100kW::EU ; (D):500kW::WAF/SA ; M-F:100kW::EU ; Sa/Su:100kW::EU
	GERMANY (FR)	
	DEUTSCHE WELLE / Jülich	(J):100kW::NA
	DEUTSCHE WELLE / Türkheim-Wertach'l	(D):500kW::WEU
	DEUTSCHE WELLE / Via Antigua	250kW::NA
	INDIA	
	ALL INDIA RADIO / Hyderabad	Su:10kW:DS ; 10kW:DS-ENGLISH, ETC
	JAPAN	
	RADIO JAPAN/NHK / Via Sackville, Can	250kW::NA ; (D):250kW::NA ; (J):250kW::NA
	PHILIPPINES	
	FAR EAST BC CO / Iba	(D):100kW::USSR
	UNITED KINGDOM	
	BBC / Via Zyyi, Cyprus	250kW::ME
	USSR	
	RADIO MOSCOW/RP&P / Moscow	(D):250kW::EEU/WAF
6120v	NICARAGUA	
	RADIO ZINICA / Bluefields	2kW:DS-SPANISH,ENGLISH
6125	AFGHANISTAN	
	'R IRAN TOILERS' / Via R Afghanistan	100kW:TUDEH COMMUNIST:ME
	RADIO KABUL / Kabul	Alt 6100kHz:100kW:DS:ME
	ALBANIA	
	RADIO TIRANA / Lushnjë	50kW:GREEK:EU
	CHINA (PR)	
	CENTRAL PEOPLES BS / Shijiazhuang	50kW:DS-1
	GERMANY (DR)	
	RADIO BERLIN INTL / Nauen	500kW::CA
	SPAIN	
(con'd)	R EXTERIOR ESPANA / Noblejas	(D):350kW::ENA/CA

World Time scale: 0 1 2 3 4 5 6 7 8 9 10 11 12 13 14 15 16 17 18 19 20 21 22 23 24

ENGLISH ▬▬   GERMAN / DEUTSCH ◊◊◊◊   FRENCH / FRANÇAIS ▬▬   PORTUGUESE / PORTUGUÊS ▬▬   SPANISH / ESPAÑOL ▬▬

ARABIC / عربي ▬   RUSSIAN / РУССКИИ ▬   CHINESE / ★★ ◊◊◊◊   JAPANESE / 日本語 ▬▬   MULTILINGUAL ◊◊◊   OTHER ▬

SUMMER ONLY (J)   WINTER ONLY (D)   JAMMING /\/\ or / or \   EARLIEST HEARD ◢   LATEST HEARD ◣   ⁺ TENTATIVE

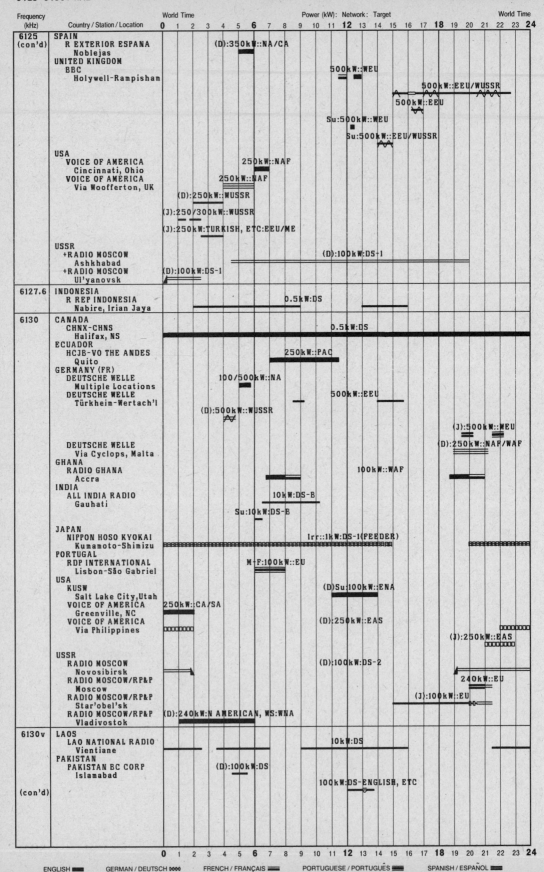

Frequency (kHz) — Country / Station / Location — World Time — Power (kW): Network: Target

6125 (con'd)

SPAIN
R EXTERIOR ESPANA
Noblejas — (D):350kW::NA/CA

UNITED KINGDOM
BBC
Holywell-Rampisham — 500kW::WEU — 500kW::EEU/WUSSR — 500kW::EEU — Su:500kW::WEU — Su:500kW::EEU/WUSSR

USA
VOICE OF AMERICA
Cincinnati, Ohio — 250kW::NAF
VOICE OF AMERICA
Via Woofferton, UK — 250kW::NAF
— (D):250kW::WUSSR
— (J):250/300kW::WUSSR
— (J):250kW:TURKISH, ETC:EEU/ME

USSR
+RADIO MOSCOW
Ashkhabad — (D):100kW:DS-1
+RADIO MOSCOW
Ul'yanovsk — (D):100kW:DS-1

6127.6

INDONESIA
R REP INDONESIA
Nabire, Irian Jaya — 0.5kW:DS

6130

CANADA
CHNX-CHNS
Halifax, NS — 0.5kW:DS

ECUADOR
HCJB-VO THE ANDES
Quito — 250kW::PAC

GERMANY (FR)
DEUTSCHE WELLE
Multiple Locations — 100/500kW::NA
DEUTSCHE WELLE
Türkheim-Wertach'l — 500kW::EEU — (D):500kW::WUSSR

DEUTSCHE WELLE
Via Cyclops, Malta — (J):500kW::WEU — (D):250kW::NAF/WAF

GHANA
RADIO GHANA
Accra — 100kW::WAF

INDIA
ALL INDIA RADIO
Gauhati — 10kW:DS-B — Su:10kW:DS-B

JAPAN
NIPPON HOSO KYOKAI
Kumamoto-Shimizu — Irr::1kW:DS-1(FEEDER)

PORTUGAL
RDP INTERNATIONAL
Lisbon-São Gabriel — M-F:100kW::EU

USA
KUSW
Salt Lake City,Utah — (D)Su:100kW::ENA
VOICE OF AMERICA
Greenville, NC — 250kW::CA/SA
VOICE OF AMERICA
Via Philippines — (D):250kW::EAS — (J):250kW::EAS

USSR
RADIO MOSCOW
Novosibirsk — (D):100kW:DS-2
RADIO MOSCOW/RP&P
Moscow — 240kW::EU
RADIO MOSCOW/RP&P
Star'obel'sk — (J):100kW::EU
RADIO MOSCOW/RP&P
Vladivostok — (D):240kW:N AMERICAN, WS:WNA

6130v

LAOS
LAO NATIONAL RADIO
Vientiane — 10kW:DS

PAKISTAN
PAKISTAN BC CORP
Islamabad — (D):100kW:DS

(con'd) — 100kW:DS-ENGLISH, ETC

ENGLISH ▬   GERMAN / DEUTSCH ▯▯▯▯   FRENCH / FRANÇAIS ▬▬   PORTUGUESE / PORTUGUÊS ▬▬   SPANISH / ESPAÑOL ▬▬

ARABIC / ‫ةيبرعلا‬ ▬   RUSSIAN / PУССКИЙ ▬   CHINESE / ✦✗ ▯▯▯▯   JAPANESE / 日本語 ▬▬   MULTILINGUAL ▯▯▯▯   OTHER ▬

SUMMER ONLY (J)   WINTER ONLY (D)   JAMMING /\/\ or / or \   EARLIEST HEARD ◢   LATEST HEARD ◣   ✦ TENTATIVE

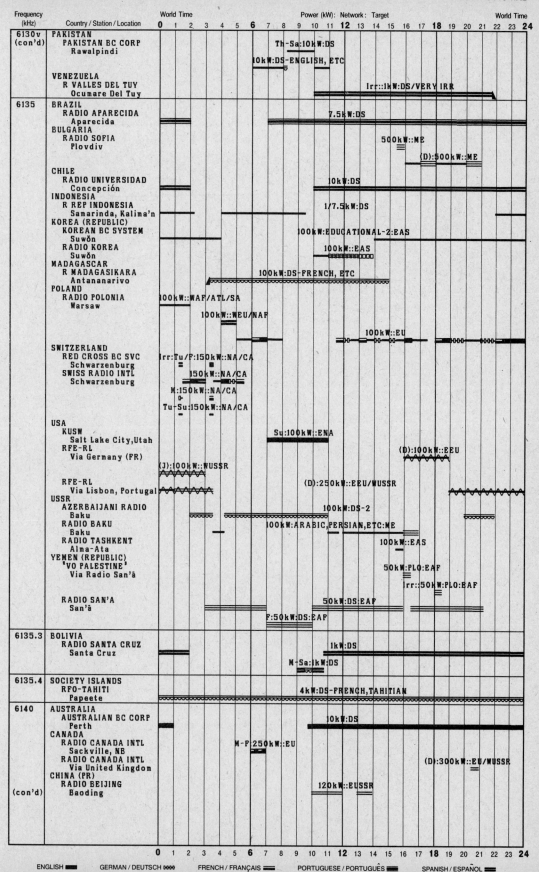

6130v PAKISTAN
(con'd)   PAKISTAN BC CORP — Th–Sa:10kW:DS
          Rawalpindi
              10kW:DS–ENGLISH, ETC

          VENEZUELA
              R VALLES DEL TUY — Irr::1kW:DS/VERY IRR
              Ocumare Del Tuy

6135 BRAZIL
          RADIO APARECIDA — 7.5kW:DS
              Aparecida
          BULGARIA
              RADIO SOFIA — 500kW::ME
              Plovdiv
                              (D):500kW::ME

          CHILE
              RADIO UNIVERSIDAD — 10kW:DS
              Concepción
          INDONESIA
              R REP INDONESIA — 1/7.5kW:DS
              Samarinda, Kalima'n
          KOREA (REPUBLIC)
              KOREAN BC SYSTEM — 100kW:EDUCATIONAL-2:EAS
              Suwŏn
              RADIO KOREA — 100kW::EAS
              Suwŏn
          MADAGASCAR
              R MADAGASIKARA — 100kW:DS-FRENCH, ETC
              Antananarivo
          POLAND
              RADIO POLONIA — 100kW::WAF/ATL/SA
              Warsaw
                              100kW::WEU/NAF

                              100kW::EU

          SWITZERLAND
              RED CROSS BC SVC — Irr:Tu/F:150kW::NA/CA
              Schwarzenburg
              SWISS RADIO INTL — 150kW::NA/CA
              Schwarzenburg
                              M:150kW::NA/CA
                              Tu-Su:150kW::NA/CA

          USA
              KUSW — Su:100kW::ENA
              Salt Lake City,Utah
              RFE-RL — (D):100kW::EEU
              Via Germany (FR)
                              (J):100kW::WUSSR

              RFE-RL — (D):250kW::EEU/WUSSR
              Via Lisbon, Portugal
          USSR
              AZERBAIJANI RADIO — 100kW:DS-2
              Baku
              RADIO BAKU — 100kW:ARABIC,PERSIAN,ETC:ME
              Baku
              RADIO TASHKENT — 100kW::EAS
              Alma-Ata
          YEMEN (REPUBLIC)
              "VO PALESTINE" — 50kW:PLO:EAF
              Via Radio San'ā
                              Irr::50kW:PLO:EAF

              RADIO SAN'A — 50kW:DS:EAF
              San'ā
                              F:50kW:DS:EAF

6135.3 BOLIVIA
              RADIO SANTA CRUZ — 1kW:DS
              Santa Cruz
                              M-Sa:1kW:DS

6135.4 SOCIETY ISLANDS
          RFO-TAHITI — 4kW:DS-FRENCH,TAHITIAN
              Papeete

6140 AUSTRALIA
              AUSTRALIAN BC CORP — 10kW:DS
              Perth
          CANADA
              RADIO CANADA INTL — M-F:250kW::EU
              Sackville, NB
              RADIO CANADA INTL — (D):300kW::EU/WUSSR
              Via United Kingdom
          CHINA (PR)
              RADIO BEIJING — 120kW::EUSSR
(con'd)   Baoding

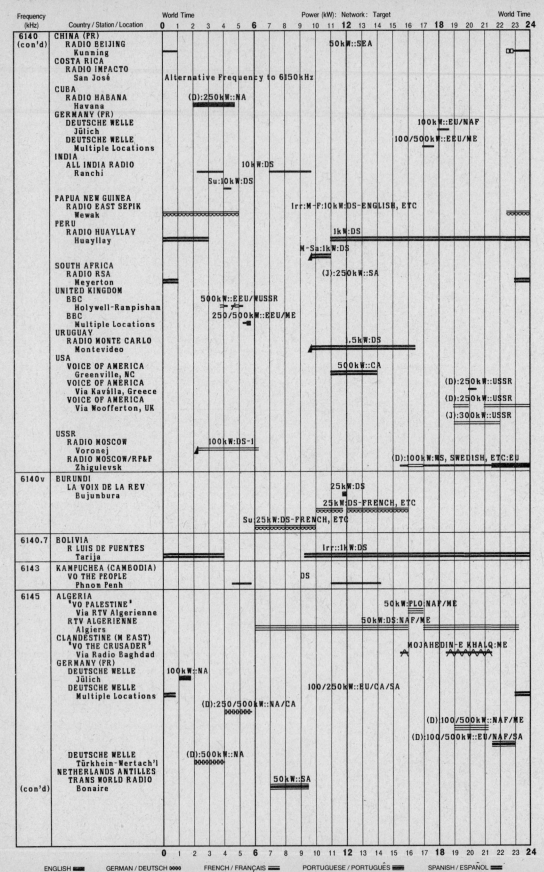

Frequency (kHz) / Country / Station / Location — World Time 0–24, Power (kW) / Network: Target

Frequency (kHz)	Country / Station / Location	Schedule details
6140 (con'd)	CHINA (PR) RADIO BEIJING — Kunming	50kW::SEA
	COSTA RICA RADIO IMPACTO — San José	Alternative Frequency to 6150kHz
	CUBA RADIO HABANA — Havana	(D):250kW::NA
	GERMANY (FR) DEUTSCHE WELLE — Jülich	100kW::EU/NAF
	DEUTSCHE WELLE — Multiple Locations	100/500kW::EEU/ME
	INDIA ALL INDIA RADIO — Ranchi	10kW:DS / Su:10kW:DS
	PAPUA NEW GUINEA RADIO EAST SEPIK — Wewak	Irr:M-F:10kW:DS-ENGLISH, ETC
	PERU RADIO HUAYLLAY — Huayllay	1kW:DS / M-Sa:1kW:DS
	SOUTH AFRICA RADIO RSA — Meyerton	(J):250kW::SA
	UNITED KINGDOM BBC — Holywell-Rampisham	500kW::EEU/WUSSR
	BBC — Multiple Locations	250/500kW::EEU/ME
	URUGUAY RADIO MONTE CARLO — Montevideo	.5kW:DS
	USA VOICE OF AMERICA — Greenville, NC	500kW::CA
	VOICE OF AMERICA — Via Kaválla, Greece	(D):250kW::USSR
	VOICE OF AMERICA — Via Woofferton, UK	(D):250kW::USSR
		(J):300kW::USSR
	USSR RADIO MOSCOW — Voronej	100kW:DS-1
	RADIO MOSCOW/RP&P — Zhigulevsk	(D):100kW:WS, SWEDISH, ETC:EU
6140v	BURUNDI LA VOIX DE LA REV — Bujumbura	25kW:DS / 25kW:DS-FRENCH, ETC / Su:25kW:DS-FRENCH, ETC
6140.7	BOLIVIA R LUIS DE FUENTES — Tarija	Irr::1kW:DS
6143	KAMPUCHEA (CAMBODIA) VO THE PEOPLE — Phnom Penh	DS
6145	ALGERIA "VO PALESTINE" — Via RTV Algerienne	50kW:PLO:NAF/ME
	RTV ALGERIENNE — Algiers	50kW:DS:NAF/ME
	CLANDESTINE (M EAST) "VO THE CRUSADER" — Via Radio Baghdad	MOJAHEDIN-E KHALQ:ME
	GERMANY (FR) DEUTSCHE WELLE — Jülich	100kW::NA
	DEUTSCHE WELLE — Multiple Locations	100/250kW::EU/CA/SA / (D):250/500kW::NA/CA / (D):100/500kW::NAF/ME / (D):100/500kW::EU/NAF/SA
	DEUTSCHE WELLE — Türkheim-Wertach'l	(D):500kW::NA
(con'd)	NETHERLANDS ANTILLES TRANS WORLD RADIO — Bonaire	50kW::SA

ENGLISH ▬▬   GERMAN / DEUTSCH ◊◊◊◊   FRENCH / FRANÇAIS ══   PORTUGUESE / PORTUGUÊS ▬▬   SPANISH / ESPAÑOL ▬▬

ARABIC / بيبرع ══   RUSSIAN / РУССКИИ ═══   CHINESE / 中文 ◊◊◊◊   JAPANESE / 日本語 ▬▬   MULTILINGUAL ◊◊◊◊   OTHER ▬▬

SUMMER ONLY (J)   WINTER ONLY (D)   JAMMING /\/\ or / or \   EARLIEST HEARD ◢   LATEST HEARD ◣   + TENTATIVE

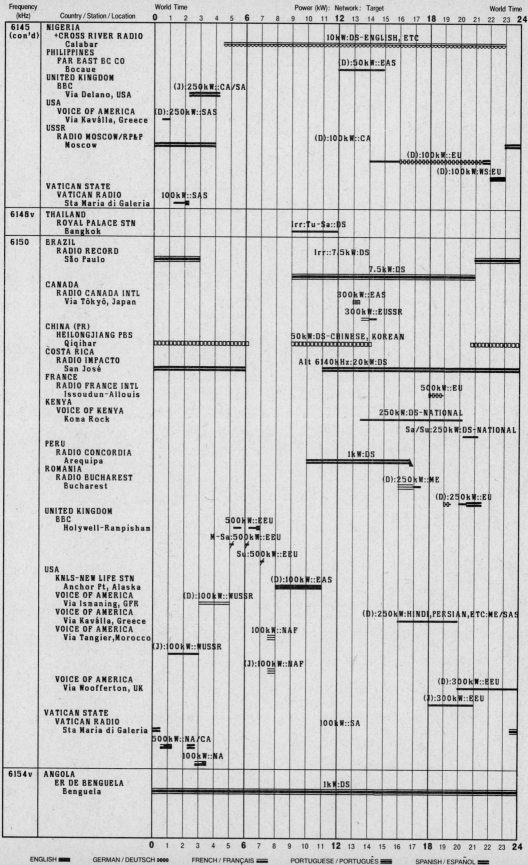

Frequency (kHz)	Country / Station / Location	Details
6145 (con'd)	NIGERIA +CROSS RIVER RADIO Calabar	10kW:DS-ENGLISH, ETC
	PHILIPPINES FAR EAST BC CO Bocaue	(D):50kW::EAS
	UNITED KINGDOM BBC Via Delano, USA	(J):250kW::CA/SA
	USA VOICE OF AMERICA Via Kaválla, Greece	(D):250kW::SAS
	USSR RADIO MOSCOW/RP&P Moscow	(D):100kW::CA / (D):100kW::EU / (D):100kW:WS:EU
	VATICAN STATE VATICAN RADIO Sta Maria di Galeria	100kW::SAS
6148v	THAILAND ROYAL PALACE STN Bangkok	Irr:Tu-Sa::DS
6150	BRAZIL RADIO RECORD São Paulo	Irr::7.5kW:DS / 7.5kW:DS
	CANADA RADIO CANADA INTL Via Tōkyō, Japan	300kW::EAS / 300kW::EUSSR
	CHINA (PR) HEILONGJIANG PBS Qiqihar	50kW:DS-CHINESE, KOREAN
	COSTA RICA RADIO IMPACTO San José	Alt 6140kHz:20kW:DS
	FRANCE RADIO FRANCE INTL Issoudun-Allouis	500kW::EU
	KENYA VOICE OF KENYA Koma Rock	250kW:DS-NATIONAL / Sa/Su:250kW:DS-NATIONAL
	PERU RADIO CONCORDIA Arequipa	1kW:DS
	ROMANIA RADIO BUCHAREST Bucharest	(D):250kW::ME / (D):250kW::EU
	UNITED KINGDOM BBC Holywell-Rampisham	500kW::EEU / M-Sa:500kW::EEU / Su:500kW::EEU
	USA KNLS-NEW LIFE STN Anchor Pt, Alaska	(D):100kW::EAS
	VOICE OF AMERICA Via Ismaning, GFR	(D):100kW::WUSSR
	VOICE OF AMERICA Via Kaválla, Greece	(D):250kW:HINDI,PERSIAN,ETC:ME/SAS
	VOICE OF AMERICA Via Tangier,Morocco	100kW::NAF / (J):100kW::WUSSR / (J):100kW::NAF
	VOICE OF AMERICA Via Woofferton, UK	(D):300kW::EEU / (J):300kW::EEU
	VATICAN STATE VATICAN RADIO Sta Maria di Galeria	100kW::SA / 500kW::NA/CA / 100kW::NA
6154v	ANGOLA ER DE BENGUELA Benguela	1kW:DS

ENGLISH ▬▬ GERMAN / DEUTSCH ୦୦୦୦ FRENCH / FRANÇAIS ▭▭ PORTUGUESE / PORTUGUÊS ▦▦▦ SPANISH / ESPAÑOL ▬▬

ARABIC / عربي ▤▤ RUSSIAN / РУССКИЙ ══ CHINESE / 中文 ୦୦୦୦ JAPANESE / 日本語 ▨▨▨ MULTILINGUAL ▩▩▩ OTHER ▬▬

SUMMER ONLY (J)   WINTER ONLY (D)   JAMMING /\/\ or / or \   EARLIEST HEARD ◢   LATEST HEARD ◣   + TENTATIVE

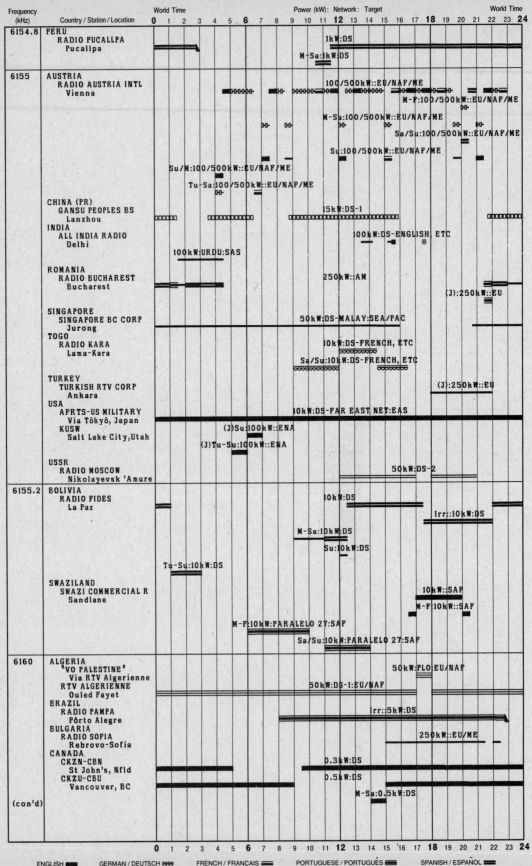

Frequency (kHz) — Country / Station / Location — Power (kW): Network: Target

6154.8	PERU
	RADIO PUCALLPA
	Pucallpa

1kW:DS
M-Sa:1kW:DS

6155	AUSTRIA
	RADIO AUSTRIA INTL
	Vienna

100/500kW::EU/NAF/ME
M-F:100/500kW::EU/NAF/ME
M-Sa:100/500kW::EU/NAF/ME
Sa/Su:100/500kW::EU/NAF/ME
Su:100/500kW::EU/NAF/ME
Su/M:100/500kW::EU/NAF/ME
Tu-Sa:100/500kW::EU/NAF/ME

CHINA (PR)
GANSU PEOPLES BS
Lanzhou — 15kW:DS-1

INDIA
ALL INDIA RADIO
Delhi — 100kW:DS-ENGLISH, ETC
100kW:URDU:SAS

ROMANIA
RADIO BUCHAREST
Bucharest — 250kW:AM
(J):250kW::EU

SINGAPORE
SINGAPORE BC CORP
Jurong — 50kW:DS-MALAY:SEA/PAC

TOGO
RADIO KARA
Lama-Kara — 10kW:DS-FRENCH, ETC
Sa/Su:10kW:DS-FRENCH, ETC

TURKEY
TURKISH RTV CORP
Ankara — (J):250kW::EU

USA
AFRTS-US MILITARY
Via Tōkyō, Japan — 10kW:DS-FAR EAST NET:EAS
KUSW
Salt Lake City,Utah — (J)Su:100kW::ENA
(J)Tu-Su:100kW::ENA

USSR
RADIO MOSCOW
Nikolayevsk 'Amure — 50kW:DS-2

6155.2	BOLIVIA
	RADIO FIDES
	La Paz

10kW:DS
Irr::10kW:DS
M-Sa:10kW:DS
Su:10kW:DS
Tu-Su:10kW:DS

SWAZILAND
SWAZI COMMERCIAL R
Sandlane — 10kW::SAF
M-F:10kW::SAF
M-F:10kW:PARALELO 27:SAF
Sa/Su:10kW:PARALELO 27:SAF

6160	ALGERIA
	'VO PALESTINE'
	Via RTV Algerienne — 50kW:PLO:EU/NAF
	RTV ALGERIENNE
	Ouled Fayet — 50kW:DS-1:EU/NAF
	BRAZIL
	RADIO PAMPA
	Pôrto Alegre — Irr::5kW:DS
	BULGARIA
	RADIO SOFIA
	Rebrovo-Sofia — 250kW::EU/ME
	CANADA
	CKZN-CBN
	St John's, Nfld — 0.3kW:DS
	CKZU-CBU
	Vancouver, BC — 0.5kW:DS
	M-Sa:0.5kW:DS

(con'd)

ENGLISH ▬▬ GERMAN / DEUTSCH ∞∞∞ FRENCH / FRANÇAIS ▭▭ PORTUGUESE / PORTUGUÊS ▬▬ SPANISH / ESPAÑOL ▬▬

ARABIC / ﻉﺭﺑﻲ ≡≡ RUSSIAN / РУССКИИ ▬▬ CHINESE / 中文 ▭▭▭ JAPANESE / 日本語 ▬▬▬ MULTILINGUAL ∞∞∞ OTHER ▬

SUMMER ONLY (J)   WINTER ONLY (D)   JAMMING ∧∧ or / or \   EARLIEST HEARD ◢   LATEST HEARD ◣   + TENTATIVE

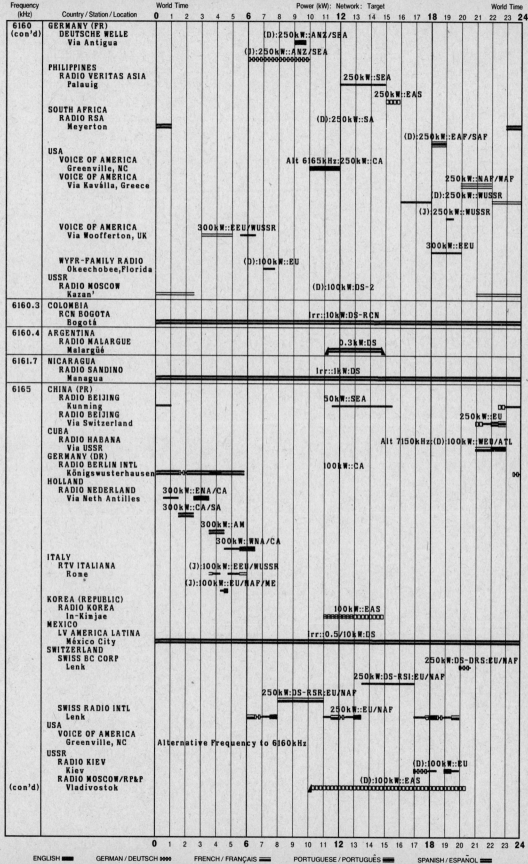

Frequency (kHz)	Country / Station / Location	Details
6160 (con'd)	GERMANY (FR) — DEUTSCHE WELLE, Via Antigua	(D):250kW::ANZ/SEA; (J):250kW::ANZ/SEA
	PHILIPPINES — RADIO VERITAS ASIA, Palauig	250kW::SEA; 250kW::EAS
	SOUTH AFRICA — RADIO RSA, Meyerton	(D):250kW::SA; (D):250kW::EAF/SAF
	USA — VOICE OF AMERICA, Greenville, NC	Alt 6165kHz:250kW::CA
	VOICE OF AMERICA, Via Kaválla, Greece	250kW::NAF/WAF; (D):250kW::WUSSR; (J):250kW::WUSSR
	VOICE OF AMERICA, Via Woofferton, UK	300kW::EEU/WUSSR; 300kW::EEU
	WYFR-FAMILY RADIO, Okeechobee, Florida	(D):100kW::EU
	USSR — RADIO MOSCOW, Kazan'	(D):100kW:DS-2
6160.3	COLOMBIA — RCN BOGOTA, Bogotá	Irr::10kW:DS-RCN
6160.4	ARGENTINA — RADIO MALARGUE, Malargüe	0.3kW:DS
6161.7	NICARAGUA — RADIO SANDINO, Managua	Irr::1kW:DS
6165	CHINA (PR) — RADIO BEIJING, Kunming	50kW::SEA
	RADIO BEIJING, Via Switzerland	250kW::EU
	CUBA — RADIO HABANA, Via USSR	Alt 7150kHz:(D):100kW::WEU/ATL
	GERMANY (DR) — RADIO BERLIN INTL, Königswusterhausen	100kW::CA
	HOLLAND — RADIO NEDERLAND, Via Neth Antilles	300kW::ENA/CA; 300kW::CA/SA; 300kW::AM; 300kW::WNA/CA
	ITALY — RTV ITALIANA, Rome	(J):100kW::EEU/WUSSR; (J):100kW::EU/NAF/ME
	KOREA (REPUBLIC) — RADIO KOREA, In-Kimjae	100kW::EAS
	MEXICO — LV AMERICA LATINA, México City	Irr::0.5/10kW:DS
	SWITZERLAND — SWISS BC CORP, Lenk	250kW:DS-DRS:EU/NAF; 250kW:DS-RSI:EU/NAF; 250kW:DS-RSR:EU/NAF
	SWISS RADIO INTL, Lenk	250kW::EU/NAF
	USA — VOICE OF AMERICA, Greenville, NC	Alternative Frequency to 6160kHz
	USSR — RADIO KIEV, Kiev	(D):100kW::EU
(con'd)	RADIO MOSCOW/RP&P, Vladivostok	(D):100kW::EAS

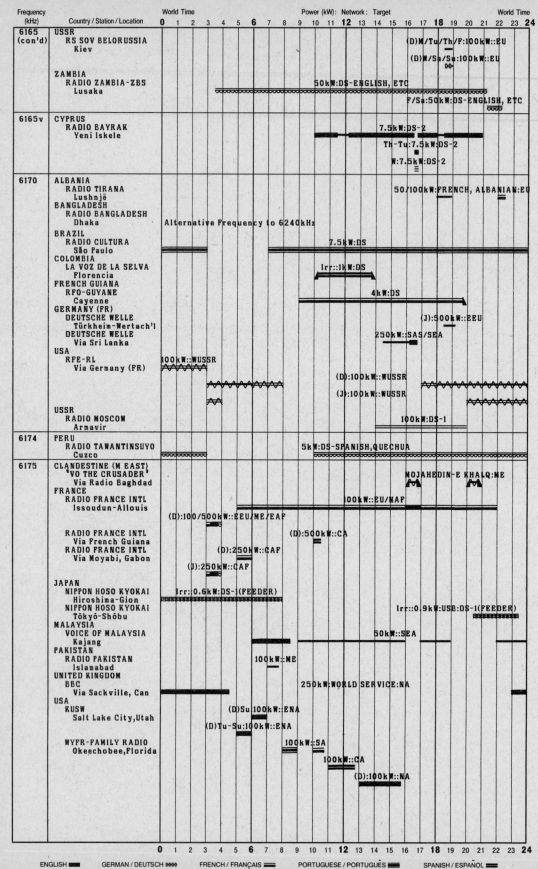

Frequency (kHz)	Country / Station / Location	World Time 0–24
6165 (con'd)	USSR RS SOV BELORUSSIA Kiev	(D)M/Tu/Th/F:100kW::EU (D)W/Sa/Su:100kW::EU
	ZAMBIA RADIO ZAMBIA-ZBS Lusaka	50kW:DS-ENGLISH, ETC F/Sa:50kW:DS-ENGLISH, ETC
6165v	CYPRUS RADIO BAYRAK Yeni Iskele	7.5kW:DS-2 Th-Tu:7.5kW:DS-2 W:7.5kW:DS-2
6170	ALBANIA RADIO TIRANA Lushnjë	50/100kW:FRENCH, ALBANIAN:EU
	BANGLADESH RADIO BANGLADESH Dhaka	Alternative Frequency to 6240kHz
	BRAZIL RADIO CULTURA São Paulo	7.5kW:DS
	COLOMBIA LA VOZ DE LA SELVA Florencia	Irr::1kW:DS
	FRENCH GUIANA RFO-GUYANE Cayenne	4kW:DS
	GERMANY (FR) DEUTSCHE WELLE Türkheim-Wertach'l	(J):500kW::EEU
	DEUTSCHE WELLE Via Sri Lanka	250kW:SAS/SEA
	USA RFE-RL Via Germany (FR)	100kW::WUSSR (D):100kW::WUSSR (J):100kW::WUSSR
	USSR RADIO MOSCOW Armavir	100kW:DS-1
6174	PERU RADIO TAWANTINSUYO Cuzco	5kW:DS-SPANISH,QUECHUA
6175	CLANDESTINE (M EAST) 'VO THE CRUSADER' Via Radio Baghdad	MOJAHEDIN-E KHALQ:ME
	FRANCE RADIO FRANCE INTL Issoudun-Allouis	100kW::EU/NAF (D):100/500kW::EEU/ME/EAF
	RADIO FRANCE INTL Via French Guiana	(D):500kW::CA
	RADIO FRANCE INTL Via Moyabi, Gabon	(D):250kW::CAF (J):250kW::CAF
	JAPAN NIPPON HOSO KYOKAI Hiroshima-Gion	Irr::0.6kW:DS-1(FEEDER)
	NIPPON HOSO KYOKAI Tōkyō-Shōbu	Irr::0.9kW:USB:DS-1(FEEDER)
	MALAYSIA VOICE OF MALAYSIA Kajang	50kW::SEA
	PAKISTAN RADIO PAKISTAN Islamabad	100kW::ME
	UNITED KINGDOM BBC Via Sackville, Can	250kW:WORLD SERVICE:NA
	USA KUSW Salt Lake City,Utah	(D)Su:100kW::ENA (D)Tu-Su:100kW::ENA
	WYFR-FAMILY RADIO Okeechobee,Florida	100kW::SA 100kW::CA (D):100kW::NA

ENGLISH ▬▬   GERMAN / DEUTSCH ০০০০   FRENCH / FRANÇAIS ▬▬   PORTUGUESE / PORTUGUÊS ▬▬   SPANISH / ESPAÑOL ▬▬

ARABIC / ﻉﺏ ▬   RUSSIAN / РУССКИИ ▬   CHINESE / ✦✗ ০০০০   JAPANESE / 日本❖ ▬▬   MULTILINGUAL ০০০০   OTHER ▬

SUMMER ONLY (J)   WINTER ONLY (D)   JAMMING ∧∧ or / or \   EARLIEST HEARD ◢   LATEST HEARD ◣   ✦ TENTATIVE

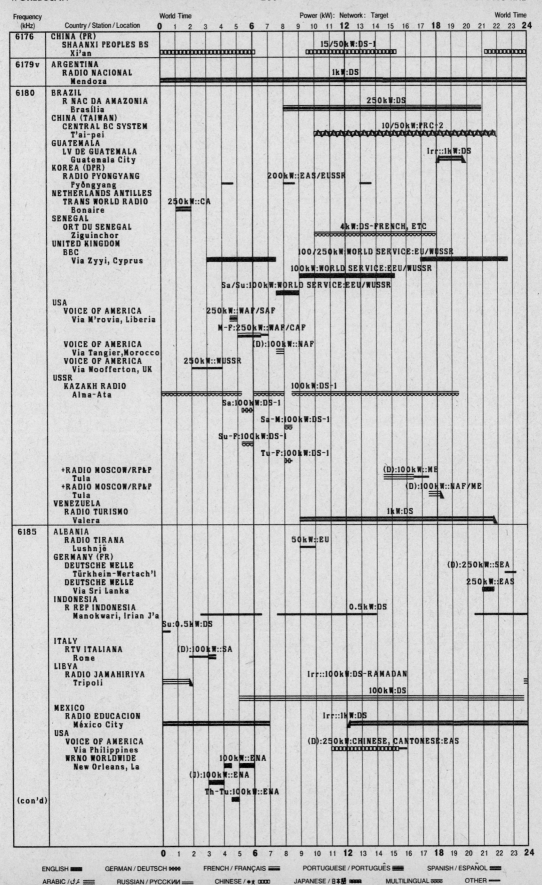

Frequency (kHz)	Country / Station / Location	Power (kW): Network: Target
6176	CHINA (PR) SHAANXI PEOPLES BS Xi'an	15/50kW:DS-1
6179 v	ARGENTINA RADIO NACIONAL Mendoza	1kW:DS
6180	BRAZIL R NAC DA AMAZONIA Brasília	250kW:DS
	CHINA (TAIWAN) CENTRAL BC SYSTEM T'ai-pei	10/50kW:PRC-2
	GUATEMALA LV DE GUATEMALA Guatemala City	Irr::1kW:DS
	KOREA (DPR) RADIO PYONGYANG Pyǒngyang	200kW::EAS/EUSSR
	NETHERLANDS ANTILLES TRANS WORLD RADIO Bonaire	250kW::CA
	SENEGAL ORT DU SENEGAL Ziguinchor	4kW:DS-FRENCH, ETC
	UNITED KINGDOM BBC Via Zyyi, Cyprus	100/250kW:WORLD SERVICE:EU/WUSSR 100kW:WORLD SERVICE:EEU/WUSSR Sa/Su:100kW:WORLD SERVICE:EEU/WUSSR
	USA VOICE OF AMERICA Via M'rovia, Liberia	250kW::WAF/SAF M-F:250kW::WAF/CAF (D):100kW::NAF
	VOICE OF AMERICA Via Tangier,Morocco VOICE OF AMERICA Via Woofferton, UK	250kW::WUSSR
	USSR KAZAKH RADIO Alma-Ata	100kW:DS-1 Sa:100kW:DS-1 Sa-M:100kW:DS-1 Su-F:100kW:DS-1 Tu-F:100kW:DS-1
	+RADIO MOSCOW/RP&P Tula	(D):100kW::ME
	+RADIO MOSCOW/RP&P Tula	(D):100kW::NAF/ME
	VENEZUELA RADIO TURISMO Valera	1kW:DS
6185	ALBANIA RADIO TIRANA Lushnjë	50kW::EU
	GERMANY (FR) DEUTSCHE WELLE Türkheim-Wertach'l DEUTSCHE WELLE Via Sri Lanka	(D):250kW::SEA 250kW::EAS
	INDONESIA R REP INDONESIA Manokwari, Irian J'a	0.5kW:DS Su:0.5kW:DS
	ITALY RTV ITALIANA Rome	(D):100kW::SA
	LIBYA RADIO JAMAHIRIYA Tripoli	Irr::100kW:DS-RAMADAN 100kW:DS
	MEXICO RADIO EDUCACION México City	Irr::1kW:DS
	USA VOICE OF AMERICA Via Philippines WRNO WORLDWIDE New Orleans, La	(D):250kW:CHINESE, CANTONESE:EAS 100kW::ENA (J):100kW::ENA Th-Tu:100kW::ENA
(con'd)		

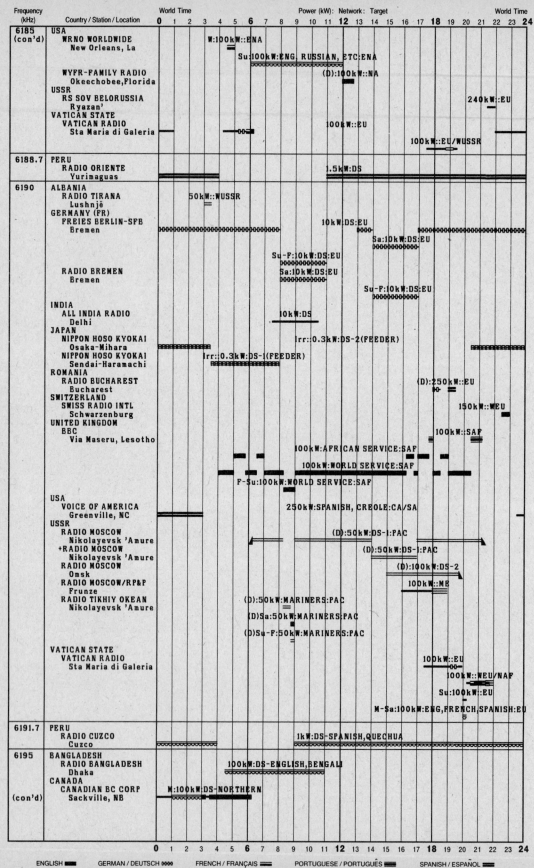

Frequency (kHz)	Country / Station / Location	Details
6185 (con'd)	USA — WRNO WORLDWIDE, New Orleans, La	W:100kW::ENA / Su:100kW:ENG, RUSSIAN, ETC:ENA
	WYFR-FAMILY RADIO, Okeechobee, Florida	(D):100kW::NA
	USSR — RS SOV BELORUSSIA, Ryazan'	240kW::EU
	VATICAN STATE — VATICAN RADIO, Sta Maria di Galeria	100kW::EU / 100kW::EU/WUSSR
6188.7	PERU — RADIO ORIENTE, Yurimaguas	1.5kW:DS
6190	ALBANIA — RADIO TIRANA, Lushnjë	50kW::WUSSR
	GERMANY (FR) — FREIES BERLIN-SFB, Bremen	10kW:DS:EU / Sa:10kW:DS:EU / Su-F:10kW:DS:EU
	RADIO BREMEN, Bremen	Sa:10kW:DS:EU / Su-F:10kW:DS:EU
	INDIA — ALL INDIA RADIO, Delhi	10kW:DS
	JAPAN — NIPPON HOSO KYOKAI, Osaka-Mihara	Irr::0.3kW:DS-2(FEEDER)
	NIPPON HOSO KYOKAI, Sendai-Haramachi	Irr::0.3kW:DS-1(FEEDER)
	ROMANIA — RADIO BUCHAREST, Bucharest	(D):250kW::EU
	SWITZERLAND — SWISS RADIO INTL, Schwarzenburg	150kW::WEU
	UNITED KINGDOM — BBC, Via Maseru, Lesotho	100kW::SAF / 100kW:AFRICAN SERVICE:SAF / 100kW:WORLD SERVICE:SAF / F-Su:100kW:WORLD SERVICE:SAF
	USA — VOICE OF AMERICA, Greenville, NC	250kW:SPANISH, CREOLE:CA/SA
	USSR — RADIO MOSCOW, Nikolayevsk 'Amure	(D):50kW:DS-1:PAC
	+RADIO MOSCOW, Nikolayevsk 'Amure	(D):50kW:DS-1:PAC
	RADIO MOSCOW, Omsk	(D):100kW:DS-2
	RADIO MOSCOW/RP&P, Frunze	100kW::MB
	RADIO TIKHIY OKEAN, Nikolayevsk 'Amure	(D):50kW:MARINERS:PAC / (D)Sa:50kW:MARINERS:PAC / (D)Su-F:50kW:MARINERS:PAC
	VATICAN STATE — VATICAN RADIO, Sta Maria di Galeria	100kW::EU / 100kW::WEU/NAF / Su:100kW::EU / M-Sa:100kW:ENG,FRENCH,SPANISH:EU
6191.7	PERU — RADIO CUZCO, Cuzco	1kW:DS-SPANISH,QUECHUA
6195	BANGLADESH — RADIO BANGLADESH, Dhaka	100kW:DS-ENGLISH,BENGALI
(con'd)	CANADA — CANADIAN BC CORP, Sackville, NB	M:100kW:DS-NORTHERN

ENGLISH ▬ GERMAN / DEUTSCH ◊◊◊◊ FRENCH / FRANÇAIS ▬ PORTUGUESE / PORTUGUÊS ▬ SPANISH / ESPAÑOL ▬

ARABIC /ﻉﻑ ▬ RUSSIAN / РУССКИИ ▬ CHINESE / ✳✗ ◻◻◻◻ JAPANESE / 日本語 ▬ MULTILINGUAL ◗◗◗◗ OTHER ▬

SUMMER ONLY (J)   WINTER ONLY (D)   JAMMING ∧∧ or / or \   EARLIEST HEARD ◢   LATEST HEARD ◣   + TENTATIVE

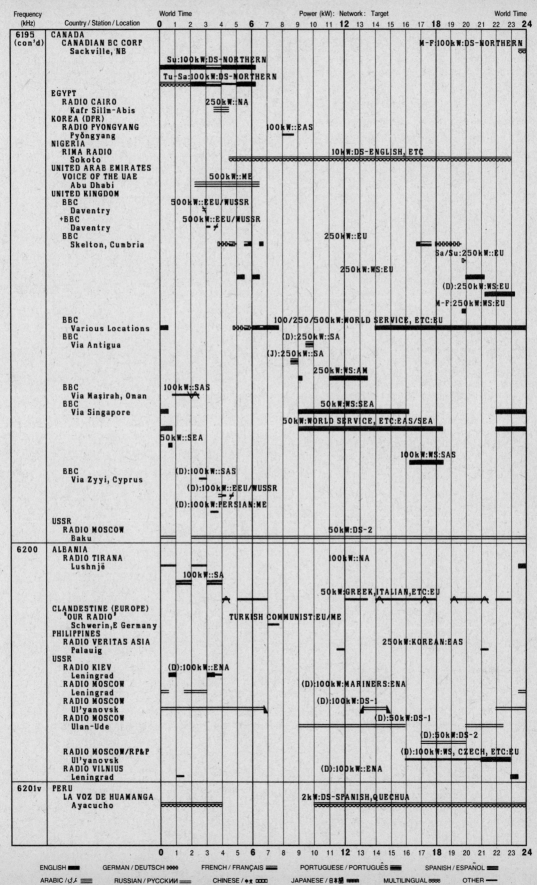

Frequency (kHz)	Country / Station / Location	Power (kW): Network: Target
6195 (con'd)	**CANADA**	
	CANADIAN BC CORP Sackville, NB	M-F:100kW:DS-NORTHERN
		Su:100kW:DS-NORTHERN
		Tu-Sa:100kW:DS-NORTHERN
	EGYPT	
	RADIO CAIRO Kafr Silim-Abis	250kW::NA
	KOREA (DPR)	
	RADIO PYONGYANG Pyŏngyang	100kW::EAS
	NIGERIA	
	RIMA RADIO Sokoto	10kW:DS-ENGLISH, ETC
	UNITED ARAB EMIRATES	
	VOICE OF THE UAE Abu Dhabi	500kW::ME
	UNITED KINGDOM	
	BBC Daventry	500kW::EEU/WUSSR
	+BBC Daventry	500kW::EEU/WUSSR
	BBC Skelton, Cumbria	250kW::EU
		Sa/Su:250kW::EU
		250kW:WS:EU
		(D):250kW:WS:EU
		M-F:250kW:WS:EU
	BBC Various Locations	100/250/500kW:WORLD SERVICE, ETC:EU
	BBC Via Antigua	(D):250kW::SA
		(J):250kW::SA
		250kW:WS:AM
	BBC Via Maşirah, Oman	100kW::SAS
	BBC Via Singapore	50kW:WS:SEA
		50kW:WORLD SERVICE, ETC:EAS/SEA
		50kW::SEA
		100kW:WS:SAS
	BBC Via Zyyi, Cyprus	(D):100kW::SAS
		(D):100kW::EEU/WUSSR
		(D):100kW:PERSIAN:ME
	USSR	
	RADIO MOSCOW Baku	50kW:DS-2
6200	**ALBANIA**	
	RADIO TIRANA Lushnjë	100kW::NA
		100kW::SA
		50kW:GREEK,ITALIAN,ETC:EU
	CLANDESTINE (EUROPE)	
	'OUR RADIO' Schwerin,E Germany	TURKISH COMMUNIST:EU/ME
	PHILIPPINES	
	RADIO VERITAS ASIA Palauig	250kW:KOREAN:EAS
	USSR	
	RADIO KIEV Leningrad	(D):100kW::ENA
	RADIO MOSCOW Leningrad	(D):100kW:MARINERS:ENA
	RADIO MOSCOW Ul'yanovsk	(D):100kW:DS-1
	RADIO MOSCOW Ulan-Ude	(D):50kW:DS-1
		(D):50kW:DS-2
	RADIO MOSCOW/RP&P Ul'yanovsk	(D):100kW:WS, CZECH, ETC:EU
	RADIO VILNIUS Leningrad	(D):100kW::ENA
6201v	**PERU**	
	LA VOZ DE HUAMANGA Ayacucho	2kW:DS-SPANISH,QUECHUA

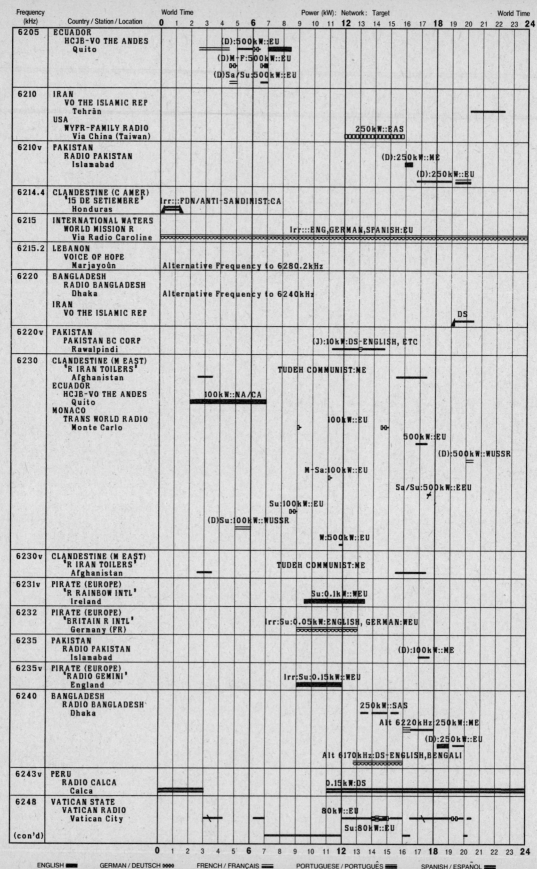

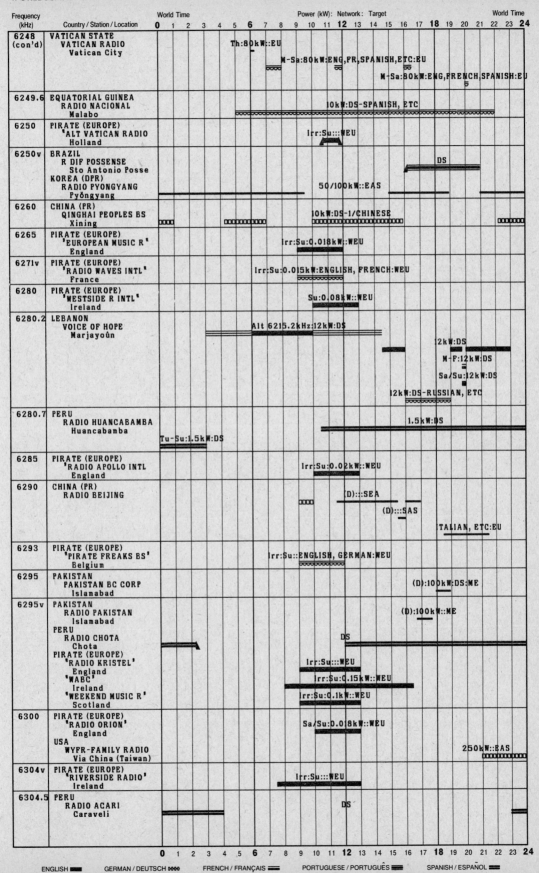

Frequency (kHz)	Country / Station / Location	Schedule (World Time 0–24)
6248 (con'd)	VATICAN STATE — VATICAN RADIO — Vatican City	Th:80kW::EU; M-Sa:80kW:ENG,FR,SPANISH,ETC:EU; M-Sa:80kW:ENG,FRENCH,SPANISH:EU
6249.6	EQUATORIAL GUINEA — RADIO NACIONAL — Malabo	10kW:DS-SPANISH, ETC
6250	PIRATE (EUROPE) — "ALT VATICAN RADIO" — Holland	Irr:Su:::WEU
6250v	BRAZIL — R DIF POSSENSE — Sto Antonio Posse	DS
	KOREA (DPR) — RADIO PYONGYANG — Pyŏngyang	50/100kW:EAS
6260	CHINA (PR) — QINGHAI PEOPLES BS — Xining	10kW:DS-1/CHINESE
6265	PIRATE (EUROPE) — "EUROPEAN MUSIC R" — England	Irr:Su:0.018kW::WEU
6271v	PIRATE (EUROPE) — "RADIO WAVES INTL" — France	Irr:Su:0.015kW:ENGLISH, FRENCH:WEU
6280	PIRATE (EUROPE) — "WESTSIDE R INTL" — Ireland	Su:0.08kW::WEU
6280.2	LEBANON — VOICE OF HOPE — Marjayoûn	Alt 6215.2kHz:12kW:DS; 12kW:DS; M-F:12kW:DS; Sa/Su:12kW:DS; 12kW:DS-RUSSIAN, ETC
6280.7	PERU — RADIO HUANCABAMBA — Huancabamba	1.5kW:DS; Tu-Su:1.5kW:DS
6285	PIRATE (EUROPE) — "RADIO APOLLO INTL" — England	Irr:Su:0.02kW::WEU
6290	CHINA (PR) — RADIO BEIJING	(D):::SEA; (D):::SAS; ITALIAN, ETC:EU
6293	PIRATE (EUROPE) — "PIRATE FREAKS BS" — Belgium	Irr:Su::ENGLISH, GERMAN:WEU
6295	PAKISTAN — PAKISTAN BC CORP — Islamabad	(D):100kW:DS:ME
6295v	PAKISTAN — RADIO PAKISTAN — Islamabad	(D):100kW::ME
	PERU — RADIO CHOTA — Chota	DS
	PIRATE (EUROPE) — "RADIO KRISTEL" — England	Irr:Su:::WEU
	"WABC" — Ireland	Irr:Su:0.15kW::WEU
	"WEEKEND MUSIC R" — Scotland	Irr:Su:0.1kW::WEU
6300	PIRATE (EUROPE) — "RADIO ORION" — England	Sa/Su:0.018kW::WEU
	USA — WYFR-FAMILY RADIO — Via China (Taiwan)	250kW::EAS
6304v	PIRATE (EUROPE) — "RIVERSIDE RADIO" — Ireland	Irr:Su:::WEU
6304.5	PERU — RADIO ACARI — Caraveli	DS

ENGLISH ▬▬ GERMAN / DEUTSCH ∞∞∞ FRENCH / FRANÇAIS ▬▬ PORTUGUESE / PORTUGUÊS ▬▬ SPANISH / ESPAÑOL ▬▬

ARABIC / عربي ▬▬ RUSSIAN / РУССКИИ ▬▬ CHINESE / 中文 ▭▭ JAPANESE / 日本語 ▬▬ MULTILINGUAL ∞∞∞ OTHER ▬

SUMMER ONLY (J) WINTER ONLY (D) JAMMING /\/\ or / or \ EARLIEST HEARD ◢ LATEST HEARD ◣ * TENTATIVE

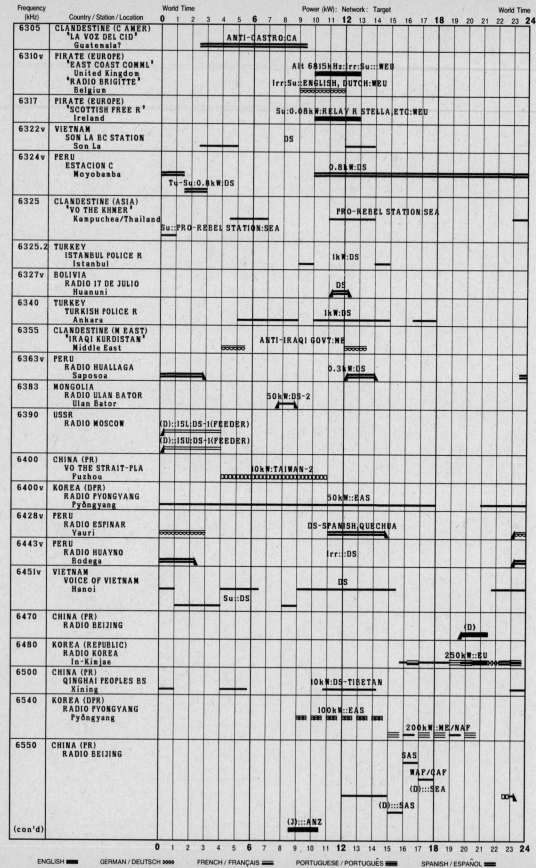

Frequency (kHz)	Country / Station / Location	World Time 0 ... 24
6305	CLANDESTINE (C AMER) "LA VOZ DEL CID" Guatemala?	ANTI-CASTRO:CA
6310v	PIRATE (EUROPE) "EAST COAST COMML" United Kingdom "RADIO BRIGITTE" Belgium	Alt 6815kHz:Irr:Su:::WEU / Irr:Su:ENGLISH, DUTCH:WEU
6317	PIRATE (EUROPE) "SCOTTISH FREE R" Ireland	Su:0.08kW:RELAY R STELLA,ETC:WEU
6322v	VIETNAM SON LA BC STATION Son La	DS
6324v	PERU ESTACION C Moyobamba	0.8kW:DS / Tu-Su:0.8kW:DS
6325	CLANDESTINE (ASIA) "VO THE KHMER" Kampuchea/Thailand	PRO-REBEL STATION:SEA / Su::PRO-REBEL STATION:SEA
6325.2	TURKEY ISTANBUL POLICE R Istanbul	1kW:DS
6327v	BOLIVIA RADIO 17 DE JULIO Huanuni	DS
6340	TURKEY TURKISH POLICE R Ankara	1kW:DS
6355	CLANDESTINE (M EAST) "IRAQI KURDISTAN" Middle East	ANTI-IRAQI GOVT:ME
6363v	PERU RADIO HUALLAGA Saposoa	0.3kW:DS
6383	MONGOLIA RADIO ULAN BATOR Ulan Bator	50kW:DS-2
6390	USSR RADIO MOSCOW	(D)::ISL:DS-1(FEEDER) / (D)::ISU:DS-1(FEEDER)
6400	CHINA (PR) VO THE STRAIT-PLA Fuzhou	10kW:TAIWAN-2
6400v	KOREA (DPR) RADIO PYONGYANG Pyŏngyang	50kW::EAS
6428v	PERU RADIO ESPINAR Yauri	DS-SPANISH,QUECHUA
6443v	PERU RADIO HUAYNO Bodega	Irr::DS
6451v	VIETNAM VOICE OF VIETNAM Hanoi	DS / Su::DS
6470	CHINA (PR) RADIO BEIJING	(D)
6480	KOREA (REPUBLIC) RADIO KOREA In-Kimjae	250kW::EU
6500	CHINA (PR) QINGHAI PEOPLES BS Xining	10kW:DS-TIBETAN
6540	KOREA (DPR) RADIO PYONGYANG Pyŏngyang	100kW::EAS / 200kW:ME/NAF
6550	CHINA (PR) RADIO BEIJING	SAS / WAF/CAF / (D):::SEA / (D):::SAS / (J):::ANZ
(con'd)		

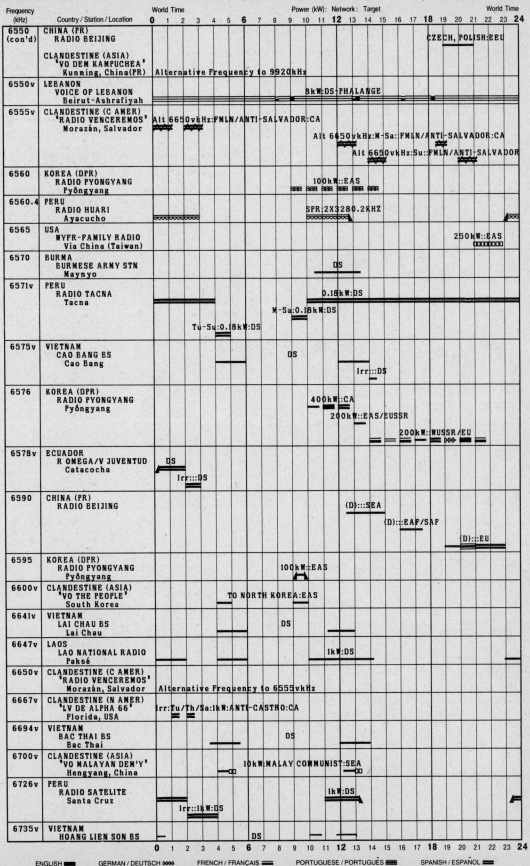

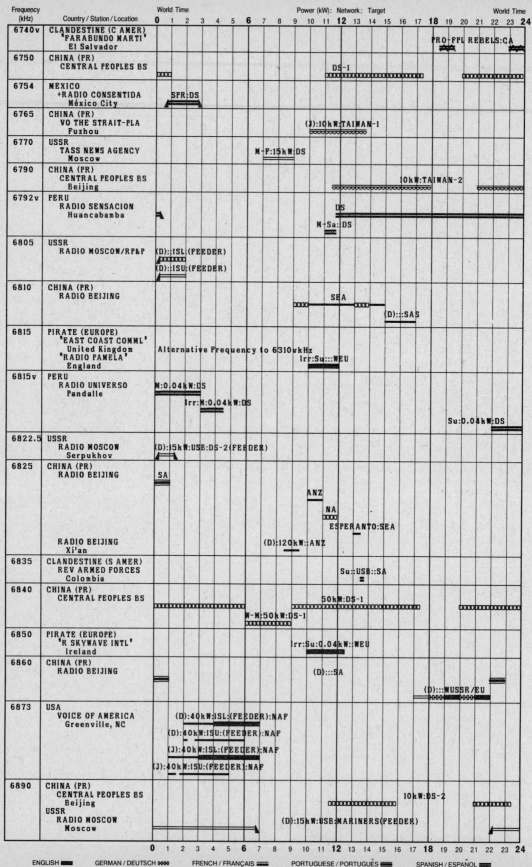

Frequency (kHz)	Country / Station / Location	Notes
6740v	CLANDESTINE (C AMER) "FARABUNDO MARTI" El Salvador	PRO-FPL REBELS:CA
6750	CHINA (PR) CENTRAL PEOPLES BS	DS-1
6754	MEXICO +RADIO CONSENTIDA México City	SPR:DS
6765	CHINA (PR) VO THE STRAIT-PLA Fuzhou	(J):10kW:TAIWAN-1
6770	USSR TASS NEWS AGENCY Moscow	M-F:15kW:DS
6790	CHINA (PR) CENTRAL PEOPLES BS Beijing	10kW:TAIWAN-2
6792v	PERU RADIO SENSACION Huancabamba	DS / M-Sa:DS
6805	USSR RADIO MOSCOW/RP&P	(D)::ISL:(FEEDER) / (D)::ISU:(FEEDER)
6810	CHINA (PR) RADIO BEIJING	SEA / (D):::SAS
6815	PIRATE (EUROPE) "EAST COAST COMML" United Kingdom "RADIO PAMELA" England	Alternative Frequency to 6310vkHz / Irr:Su:::WEU
6815v	PERU RADIO UNIVERSO Pandalle	M:0.04kW:DS / Irr:M:0.04kW:DS / Su:0.04kW:DS
6822.5	USSR RADIO MOSCOW Serpukhov	(D):15kW:USB:DS-2(FEEDER)
6825	CHINA (PR) RADIO BEIJING	SA / ANZ / NA / ESPERANTO:SEA
	RADIO BEIJING Xi'an	(D):120kW::ANZ
6835	CLANDESTINE (S AMER) REV ARMED FORCES Colombia	Su::USB::SA
6840	CHINA (PR) CENTRAL PEOPLES BS	50kW:DS-1 / W-M:50kW:DS-1
6850	PIRATE (EUROPE) "R SKYWAVE INTL" Ireland	Irr:Su:0.04kW::WEU
6860	CHINA (PR) RADIO BEIJING	(D):::SA / (D):::WUSSR/EU
6873	USA VOICE OF AMERICA Greenville, NC	(D):40kW:ISL:(FEEDER):NAF / (D):40kW:ISU:(FEEDER):NAF / (J):40kW:ISL:(FEEDER):NAF / (J):40kW:ISU:(FEEDER):NAF
6890	CHINA (PR) CENTRAL PEOPLES BS Beijing	10kW:DS-2
	USSR RADIO MOSCOW Moscow	(D):15kW:USB:MARINERS(FEEDER)

ENGLISH ▪▪▪ GERMAN / DEUTSCH ◊◊◊◊ FRENCH / FRANÇAIS ▬▬ PORTUGUESE / PORTUGUÊS ▬▬ SPANISH / ESPAÑOL ▬▬

ARABIC / عربية ▬▬ RUSSIAN / РУССКИИ ▬▬ CHINESE / 中文 ▯▯▯▯ JAPANESE / 日本語 ▬▬▬ MULTILINGUAL ▭▭▭▭ OTHER ▬

SUMMER ONLY (J) WINTER ONLY (D) JAMMING ∧∧ or / or \ EARLIEST HEARD ◢ LATEST HEARD ◣ + TENTATIVE

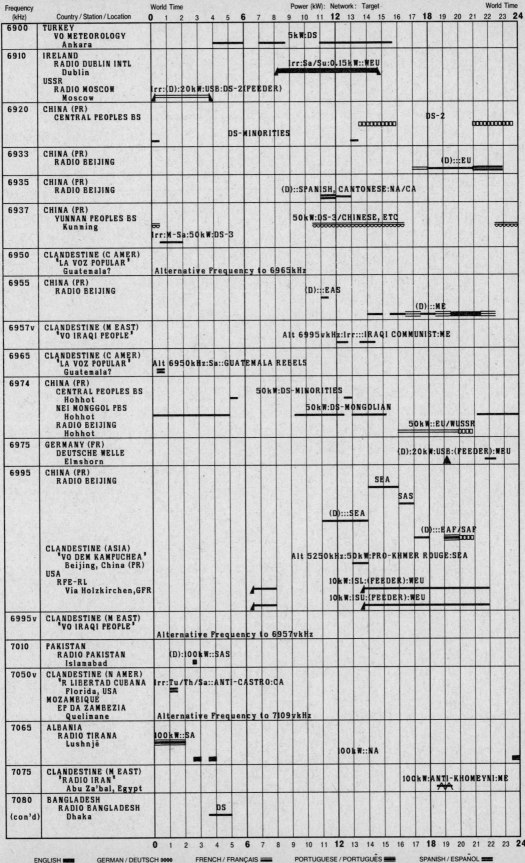

Frequency (kHz)	Country / Station / Location	World Time / Power (kW): Network: Target
6900	TURKEY VO METEOROLOGY Ankara	5kW:DS
6910	IRELAND RADIO DUBLIN INTL Dublin	Irr:Sa/Su:0.15kW::WEU
	USSR RADIO MOSCOW Moscow	Irr:(D):20kW:USB:DS-2(FEEDER)
6920	CHINA (PR) CENTRAL PEOPLES BS	DS-2 / DS-MINORITIES
6933	CHINA (PR) RADIO BEIJING	(D):::EU
6935	CHINA (PR) RADIO BEIJING	(D)::SPANISH, CANTONESE:NA/CA
6937	CHINA (PR) YUNNAN PEOPLES BS Kunming	50kW:DS-3/CHINESE, ETC / Irr:M-Sa:50kW:DS-3
6950	CLANDESTINE (C AMER) 'LA VOZ POPULAR' Guatemala?	Alternative Frequency to 6965kHz
6955	CHINA (PR) RADIO BEIJING	(D):::EAS / (D)::ME
6957v	CLANDESTINE (M EAST) 'VO IRAQI PEOPLE'	Alt 6995vkHz:Irr:::IRAQI COMMUNIST:ME
6965	CLANDESTINE (C AMER) 'LA VOZ POPULAR' Guatemala?	Alt 6950kHz:Sa::GUATEMALA REBELS
6974	CHINA (PR) CENTRAL PEOPLES BS Hohhot	50kW:DS-MINORITIES
	NEI MONGGOL PBS Hohhot	50kW:DS-MONGOLIAN
	RADIO BEIJING Hohhot	50kW::EU/WUSSR
6975	GERMANY (FR) DEUTSCHE WELLE Elmshorn	(D):20kW:USB:(FEEDER):WEU
6995	CHINA (PR) RADIO BEIJING	SEA / SAS / (D):::SEA / (D):::EAF/SAF
	CLANDESTINE (ASIA) 'VO DEM KAMPUCHEA' Beijing, China (PR)	Alt 5250kHz:50kW:PRO-KHMER ROUGE:SEA
	USA RFE-RL Via Holzkirchen,GFR	10kW:ISL:(FEEDER):WEU / 10kW:ISU:(FEEDER):WEU
6995v	CLANDESTINE (M EAST) 'VO IRAQI PEOPLE'	Alternative Frequency to 6957vkHz
7010	PAKISTAN RADIO PAKISTAN Islamabad	(D):100kW::SAS
7050v	CLANDESTINE (N AMER) 'R LIBERTAD CUBANA' Florida, USA	Irr:Tu/Th/Sa::ANTI-CASTRO:CA
	MOZAMBIQUE EP DA ZAMBEZIA Quelimane	Alternative Frequency to 7109vkHz
7065	ALBANIA RADIO TIRANA Lushnjë	100kW::SA / 100kW::NA
7075	CLANDESTINE (M EAST) 'RADIO IRAN' Abu Za'bal, Egypt	100kW:ANTI-KHOMEYNI:ME
7080 (con'd)	BANGLADESH RADIO BANGLADESH Dhaka	DS

ENGLISH ▬▬ GERMAN / DEUTSCH ◊◊◊◊ FRENCH / FRANÇAIS ▬▬ PORTUGUESE / PORTUGUÊS ▬▬ SPANISH / ESPAÑOL ▬▬

ARABIC / ﺏﺮﻋ ▬▬ RUSSIAN / РУССКИИ ▬▬ CHINESE / ✳ ☆ ◻◻◻◻ JAPANESE / 日本語 ▬▬ MULTILINGUAL ◊◊◊◊ OTHER ▬▬

SUMMER ONLY (J) WINTER ONLY (D) JAMMING ∧∧ or / or \ EARLIEST HEARD ◢ LATEST HEARD ◣ ✦ TENTATIVE

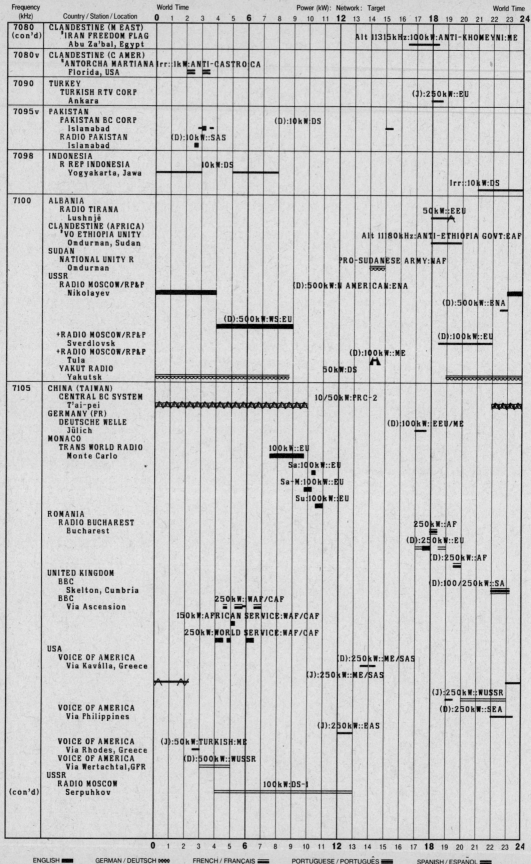

Frequency (kHz)	Country / Station / Location	World Time / Power (kW): Network: Target
7080 (con'd)	CLANDESTINE (M EAST) 'IRAN FREEDOM FLAG Abu Za'bal, Egypt	Alt 11315kHz:100kW:ANTI-KHOMEYNI:ME
7080v	CLANDESTINE (C AMER) 'ANTORCHA MARTIANA Florida, USA	Irr:1kW:ANTI-CASTRO:CA
7090	TURKEY TURKISH RTV CORP Ankara	(J):250kW::EU
7095v	PAKISTAN PAKISTAN BC CORP Islamabad RADIO PAKISTAN Islamabad	(D):10kW:DS (D):10kW::SAS
7098	INDONESIA R REP INDONESIA Yogyakarta, Jawa	10kW:DS Irr::10kW:DS
7100	ALBANIA RADIO TIRANA Lushnjë CLANDESTINE (AFRICA) 'VO ETHIOPIA UNITY Omdurman, Sudan SUDAN NATIONAL UNITY R Omdurman USSR RADIO MOSCOW/RP&P Nikolayev +RADIO MOSCOW/RP&P Sverdlovsk +RADIO MOSCOW/RP&P Tula YAKUT RADIO Yakutsk	50kW::EEU Alt 11180kHz:ANTI-ETHIOPIA GOVT:EAF PRO-SUDANESE ARMY:NAF (D):500kW:N AMERICAN:ENA (D):500kW::ENA (D):500kW:WS:EU (D):100kW::EU (D):100kW::ME 50kW:DS
7105	CHINA (TAIWAN) CENTRAL BC SYSTEM T'ai-pei GERMANY (FR) DEUTSCHE WELLE Jülich MONACO TRANS WORLD RADIO Monte Carlo ROMANIA RADIO BUCHAREST Bucharest UNITED KINGDOM BBC Skelton, Cumbria BBC Via Ascension USA VOICE OF AMERICA Via Kaválla, Greece VOICE OF AMERICA Via Philippines VOICE OF AMERICA Via Rhodes, Greece VOICE OF AMERICA Via Wertachtal, GFR USSR RADIO MOSCOW Serpuhkov	10/50kW:PRC-2 (D):100kW: EEU/ME 100kW::EU Sa:100kW::EU Sa-M:100kW::EU Su:100kW::EU 250kW::AF (D):250kW::EU (D):250kW::AF (D):100/250kW::SA 250kW::WAF/CAF 150kW:AFRICAN SERVICE:WAF/CAF 250kW:WORLD SERVICE:WAF/CAF (D):250kW::ME/SAS (J):250kW::ME/SAS (J):250kW::WUSSR (D):250kW::SEA (J):250kW::EAS (J):50kW:TURKISH:ME (D):500kW::WUSSR 100kW:DS-1
(con'd)		

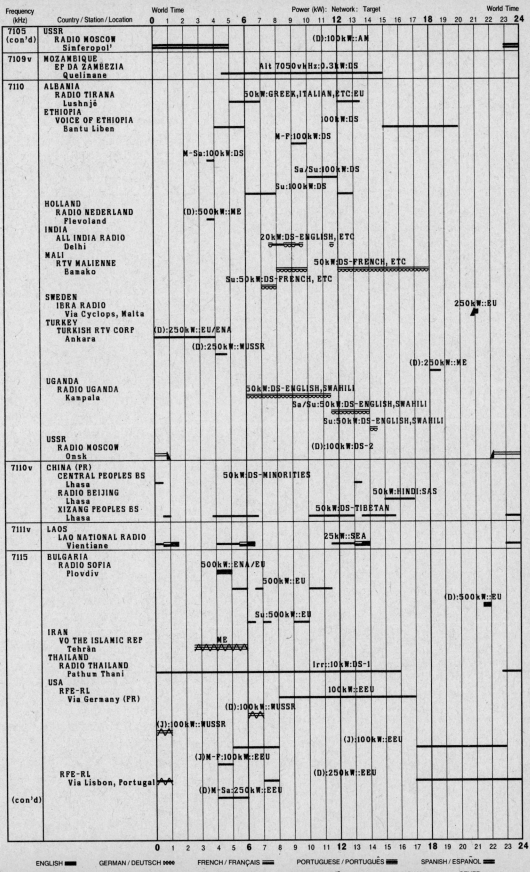

Frequency (kHz) — Country / Station / Location — World Time 0–24 — Power (kW): Network: Target

7105 (con'd) — USSR — RADIO MOSCOW — Simferopol'
(D):100kW::AM

7109v — MOZAMBIQUE — EP DA ZAMBEZIA — Quelimane
Alt 7050vkHz:0.3kW:DS

7110 — ALBANIA — RADIO TIRANA — Lushnjë
50kW:GREEK,ITALIAN,ETC:EU

ETHIOPIA — VOICE OF ETHIOPIA — Bantu Liben
100kW:DS
M-F:100kW:DS
M-Sa:100kW:DS
Sa/Su:100kW:DS
Su:100kW:DS

HOLLAND — RADIO NEDERLAND — Flevoland
(D):500kW::ME

INDIA — ALL INDIA RADIO — Delhi
20kW:DS-ENGLISH, ETC

MALI — RTV MALIENNE — Bamako
50kW:DS-FRENCH, ETC
Su:50kW:DS-FRENCH, ETC

SWEDEN — IBRA RADIO — Via Cyclops, Malta
250kW::EU

TURKEY — TURKISH RTV CORP — Ankara
(D):250kW::EU/ENA
(D):250kW::WUSSR
(D):250kW::ME

UGANDA — RADIO UGANDA — Kampala
50kW:DS-ENGLISH,SWAHILI
Sa/Su:50kW:DS-ENGLISH,SWAHILI
Su:50kW:DS-ENGLISH,SWAHILI

USSR — RADIO MOSCOW — Omsk
(D):100kW:DS-2

7110v — CHINA (PR) — CENTRAL PEOPLES BS — Lhasa
50kW:DS-MINORITIES

RADIO BEIJING — Lhasa
50kW:HINDI:SAS

XIZANG PEOPLES BS — Lhasa
50kW:DS-TIBETAN

7111v — LAOS — LAO NATIONAL RADIO — Vientiane
25kW::SEA

7115 — BULGARIA — RADIO SOFIA — Plovdiv
500kW:ENA/EU
500kW::EU
(D):500kW::EU
Su:500kW::EU

IRAN — VO THE ISLAMIC REP — Tehrān
ME

THAILAND — RADIO THAILAND — Pathum Thani
Irr::10kW:DS-1

USA — RFE-RL — Via Germany (FR)
100kW::EEU
(D):100kW::WUSSR
(J):100kW::WUSSR
(J):100kW::EEU
(J)M-F:100kW::EEU

RFE-RL — Via Lisbon, Portugal
(D):250kW::EEU
(D)M-Sa:250kW::EEU

(con'd)

ENGLISH ▬ GERMAN / DEUTSCH ∞∞ FRENCH / FRANÇAIS ═ PORTUGUESE / PORTUGUÊS ▬ SPANISH / ESPAÑOL ▬
ARABIC / ﺏﺮﻋ ═ RUSSIAN / PYCCKИЙ ═ CHINESE / ♦✗ ∞∞ JAPANESE / 日本語 ▬ MULTILINGUAL ∞∞ OTHER ▬
SUMMER ONLY (J) WINTER ONLY (D) JAMMING /\/\ or / or \ EARLIEST HEARD ◢ LATEST HEARD ◣ ♦ TENTATIVE

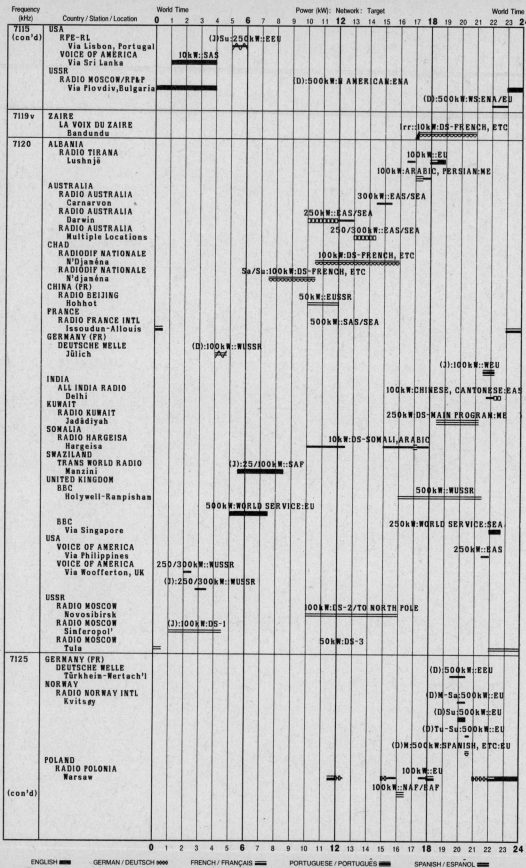

Frequency (kHz)	Country / Station / Location	World Time / Power (kW): Network: Target
7115 (con'd)	USA RFE-RL Via Lisbon, Portugal	(J)Su:250kW::EEU
	VOICE OF AMERICA Via Sri Lanka	10kW:SAS
	USSR RADIO MOSCOW/RP&P Via Plovdiv,Bulgaria	(D):500kW:N AMERICAN:ENA
		(D):500kW:WS:ENA/EU
7119 v	ZAIRE LA VOIX DU ZAIRE Bandundu	Irr:10kW:DS-FRENCH, ETC
7120	ALBANIA RADIO TIRANA Lushnjë	100kW::EU
		100kW:ARABIC, PERSIAN:ME
	AUSTRALIA RADIO AUSTRALIA Carnarvon	300kW::EAS/SEA
	RADIO AUSTRALIA Darwin	250kW::EAS/SEA
	RADIO AUSTRALIA Multiple Locations	250/300kW::EAS/SEA
	CHAD RADIODIF NATIONALE N'Djaména	100kW:DS-FRENCH, ETC
	RADIODIF NATIONALE N'djaména	Sa/Su:100kW:DS-FRENCH, ETC
	CHINA (PR) RADIO BEIJING Hohhot	50kW:EUSSR
	FRANCE RADIO FRANCE INTL Issoudun-Allouis	500kW::SAS/SEA
	GERMANY (FR) DEUTSCHE WELLE Jülich	(D):100kW::WUSSR
		(J):100kW::WEU
	INDIA ALL INDIA RADIO Delhi	100kW:CHINESE, CANTONESE:EAS
	KUWAIT RADIO KUWAIT Jadādiyah	250kW:DS-MAIN PROGRAM:ME
	SOMALIA RADIO HARGEISA Hargeisa	10kW:DS-SOMALI,ARABIC
	SWAZILAND TRANS WORLD RADIO Manzini	(J):25/100kW::SAF
	UNITED KINGDOM BBC Holywell-Rampisham	500kW::WUSSR
		500kW:WORLD SERVICE:EU
	BBC Via Singapore	250kW:WORLD SERVICE:SEA
	USA VOICE OF AMERICA Via Philippines	250kW::EAS
	VOICE OF AMERICA Via Woofferton, UK	250/300kW::WUSSR
		(J):250/300kW::WUSSR
	USSR RADIO MOSCOW Novosibirsk	100kW:DS-2/TO NORTH POLE
	RADIO MOSCOW Simferopol'	(J):100kW:DS-1
	RADIO MOSCOW Tula	50kW:DS-3
7125	GERMANY (FR) DEUTSCHE WELLE Türkheim-Wertach'l	(D):500kW::EEU
	NORWAY RADIO NORWAY INTL Kvitsøy	(D)M-Sa:500kW::EU
		(D)Su:500kW::EU
		(D)Tu-Su:500kW::EU
		(D)M:500kW:SPANISH, ETC:EU
	POLAND RADIO POLONIA Warsaw	100kW::EU
(con'd)		100kW::NAF/EAF

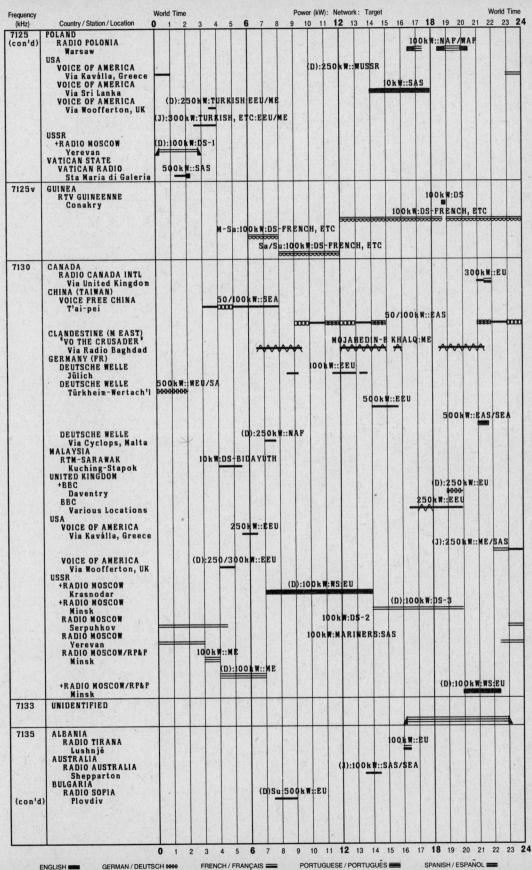

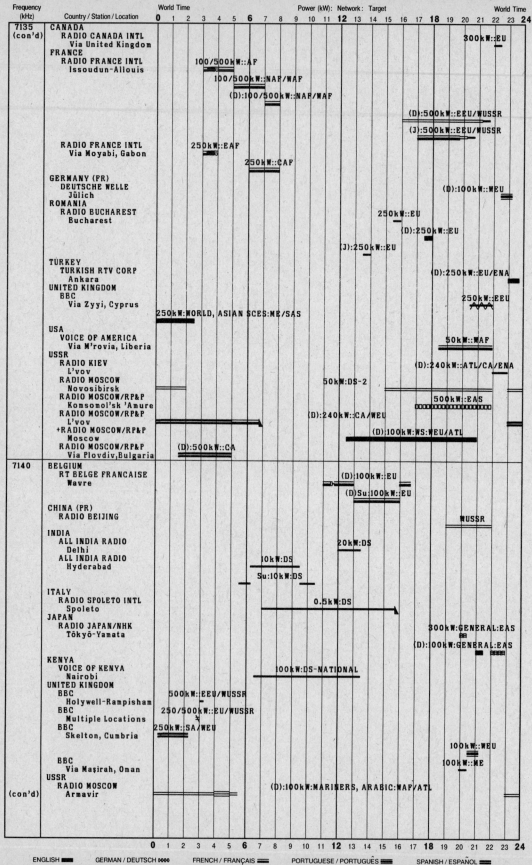

Frequency (kHz)	Country / Station / Location		
7135 (con'd)	**CANADA**		
	RADIO CANADA INTL Via United Kingdom		300kW::EU
	FRANCE		
	RADIO FRANCE INTL Issoudun-Allouis	100/500kW::AF	
		100/500kW::NAF/WAF	
		(D):100/500kW::NAF/WAF	
			(D):500kW::EEU/WUSSR
			(J):500kW::EEU/WUSSR
	RADIO FRANCE INTL Via Moyabi, Gabon	250kW::EAF	
		250kW::CAF	
	GERMANY (FR)		
	DEUTSCHE WELLE Jülich		(D):100kW::WEU
	ROMANIA		
	RADIO BUCHAREST Bucharest	250kW::EU	
		(D):250kW::EU	
		(J):250kW::EU	
	TURKEY		
	TURKISH RTV CORP Ankara		(D):250kW::EU/ENA
	UNITED KINGDOM		
	BBC Via Zyyi, Cyprus		250kW::EEU
		250kW:WORLD, ASIAN SCES:ME/SAS	
	USA		
	VOICE OF AMERICA Via M'rovia, Liberia		50kW::WAF
	USSR		
	RADIO KIEV L'vov		(D):240kW::ATL/CA/ENA
	RADIO MOSCOW Novosibirsk	50kW:DS-2	
	RADIO MOSCOW/RP&P Komsomol'sk 'Amure		500kW::EAS
	RADIO MOSCOW/RP&P L'vov	(D):240kW::CA/WEU	
	+RADIO MOSCOW/RP&P Moscow	(D):100kW:WS:WEU/ATL	
	RADIO MOSCOW/RP&P Via Plovdiv,Bulgaria	(D):500kW::CA	
7140	**BELGIUM**		
	RT BELGE FRANCAISE Wavre	(D):100kW::EU	
		(D):Su:100kW::EU	
	CHINA (PR)		
	RADIO BEIJING		WUSSR
	INDIA		
	ALL INDIA RADIO Delhi	20kW:DS	
	ALL INDIA RADIO Hyderabad	10kW:DS	
		Su:10kW:DS	
	ITALY		
	RADIO SPOLETO INTL Spoleto	0.5kW:DS	
	JAPAN		
	RADIO JAPAN/NHK Tōkyō-Yamata		300kW:GENERAL:EAS
			(D):100kW:GENERAL:EAS
	KENYA		
	VOICE OF KENYA Nairobi	100kW:DS-NATIONAL	
	UNITED KINGDOM		
	BBC Holywell-Rampisham	500kW::EEU/WUSSR	
	BBC Multiple Locations	250/500kW::EU/WUSSR	
	BBC Skelton, Cumbria	250kW::SA/WEU	
	BBC Via Maşirah, Oman		100kW::WEU
			100kW::ME
	USSR		
(con'd)	RADIO MOSCOW Armavir	(D):100kW:MARINERS, ARABIC:WAF/ATL	

ENGLISH ▬ GERMAN / DEUTSCH ०००० QUOTE FRENCH / FRANÇAIS ▭▭ PORTUGUESE / PORTUGUÊS ▬ SPANISH / ESPAÑOL ▬

ARABIC /ﻋﺮﺑﻲ ≣ RUSSIAN / РУССКИИ ▭ CHINESE / 中文 ०००० JAPANESE / 日本語 ▭▭ MULTILINGUAL ०००० OTHER ▬

SUMMER ONLY (J)   WINTER ONLY (D)   JAMMING ∧∧ or / or \   EARLIEST HEARD ◢   LATEST HEARD ◣   ♦ TENTATIVE

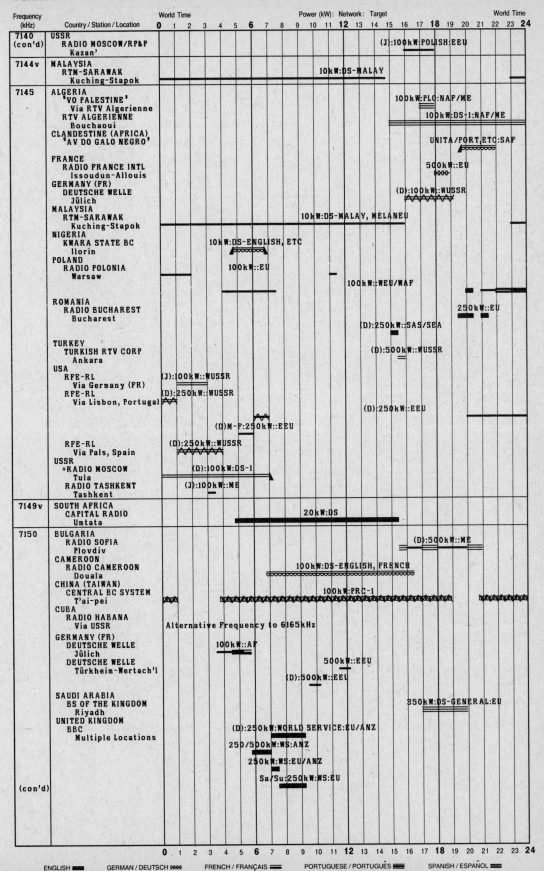

Frequency (kHz)	Country / Station / Location	World Time — Power (kW): Network: Target

7140 (con'd) — USSR / RADIO MOSCOW/RP&P / Kazan' — (J):100kW:POLISH:EEU

7144v — MALAYSIA / RTM-SARAWAK / Kuching-Stapok — 10kW:DS-MALAY

7145 — ALGERIA
- 'VO PALESTINE' Via RTV Algerienne — 100kW:PLO:NAF/ME
- RTV ALGERIENNE Bouchaoui — 100kW:DS-1:NAF/ME
- CLANDESTINE (AFRICA) 'AV DO GALO NEGRO' — UNITA/PORT,ETC:SAF

FRANCE / RADIO FRANCE INTL / Issoudun-Allouis — 500kW::EU

GERMANY (FR) / DEUTSCHE WELLE / Jülich — (D):100kW::WUSSR

MALAYSIA / RTM-SARAWAK / Kuching-Stapok — 10kW:DS-MALAY, MELANEU

NIGERIA / KWARA STATE BC / Ilorin — 10kW:DS-ENGLISH, ETC

POLAND / RADIO POLONIA / Warsaw — 100kW::EU — 100kW::WEU/WAF

ROMANIA / RADIO BUCHAREST / Bucharest — 250kW::EU — (D):250kW::SAS/SEA

TURKEY / TURKISH RTV CORP / Ankara — (D):500kW::WUSSR

USA
- RFE-RL Via Germany (FR) — (J):100kW::WUSSR
- RFE-RL Via Lisbon, Portugal — (D):250kW:WUSSR — (D):250kW::EEU — (D)M-F:250kW::EEU
- RFE-RL Via Pals, Spain — (D):250kW::WUSSR

USSR
- +RADIO MOSCOW Tula — (D):100kW:DS-1
- RADIO TASHKENT Tashkent — (J):100kW::ME

7149v — SOUTH AFRICA / CAPITAL RADIO / Umtata — 20kW:DS

7150 — BULGARIA / RADIO SOFIA / Plovdiv — (D):500kW::ME

CAMEROON / RADIO CAMEROON / Douala — 100kW:DS-ENGLISH, FRENCH

CHINA (TAIWAN) / CENTRAL BC SYSTEM / T'ai-pei — 100kW:PRC-1

CUBA / RADIO HABANA / Via USSR — Alternative Frequency to 6165 kHz

GERMANY (FR)
- DEUTSCHE WELLE Jülich — 100kW::AF
- DEUTSCHE WELLE Türkheim-Wertach'l — 500kW::EEU — (D):500kW::EEU

SAUDI ARABIA / BS OF THE KINGDOM / Riyadh — 350kW:DS-GENERAL:EU

UNITED KINGDOM / BBC / Multiple Locations
- (D):250kW:WORLD SERVICE:EU/ANZ
- 250/500kW:WS:ANZ
- 250kW:WS:EU/ANZ
- Sa/Su:250kW:WS:EU

(con'd)

ENGLISH ▬ GERMAN / DEUTSCH ००० FRENCH / FRANÇAIS ◀ PORTUGUESE / PORTUGUÊS ▬ SPANISH / ESPAÑOL ▬

ARABIC / عربى ▬ RUSSIAN / РУССКИИ ▬ CHINESE / 中文 ००० JAPANESE / 日本語 ▬ MULTILINGUAL ०००० OTHER ▬

SUMMER ONLY (J)   WINTER ONLY (D)   JAMMING ∧∧∧ or / or \   EARLIEST HEARD ◀   LATEST HEARD ▶   + TENTATIVE

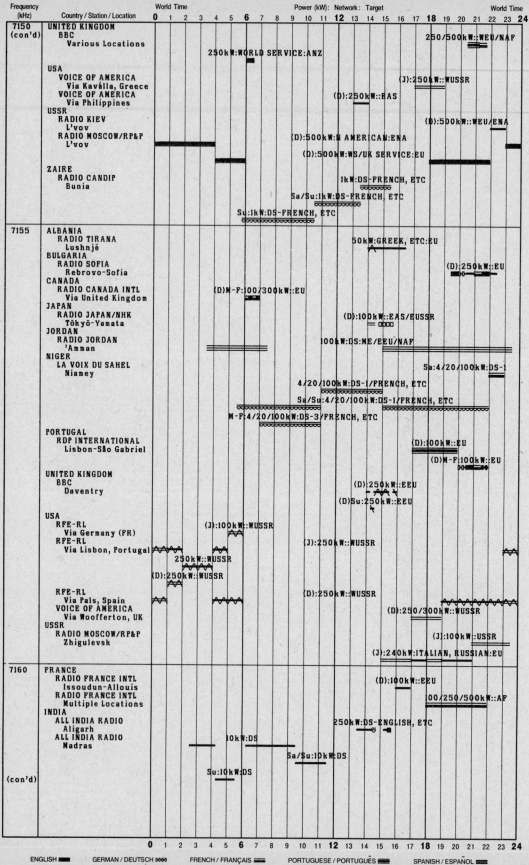

Frequency (kHz)	Country / Station / Location	World Time / Power (kW) : Network : Target
7150 (con'd)	**UNITED KINGDOM** BBC — Various Locations	250/500kW::WEU/NAF 250kW:WORLD SERVICE:ANZ
	USA VOICE OF AMERICA — Via Kaválla, Greece	(J):250kW::WUSSR
	VOICE OF AMERICA — Via Philippines	(D):250kW::EAS
	USSR RADIO KIEV — L'vov	(D):500kW::WEU/ENA
	RADIO MOSCOW/RP&P — L'vov	(D):500kW:N AMERICAN:ENA (D):500kW:WS/UK SERVICE:EU
	ZAIRE RADIO CANDIP — Bunia	1kW:DS-FRENCH, ETC Sa/Su:1kW:DS-FRENCH, ETC Su:1kW:DS-FRENCH, ETC
7155	**ALBANIA** RADIO TIRANA — Lushnjë	50kW:GREEK, ETC:EU
	BULGARIA RADIO SOFIA — Rebrovo-Sofia	(D):250kW::EU
	CANADA RADIO CANADA INTL — Via United Kingdom	(D)M-F:100/300kW::EU
	JAPAN RADIO JAPAN/NHK — Tōkyō-Yamata	(D):100kW::EAS/EUSSR
	JORDAN RADIO JORDAN — 'Amman	100kW:DS:ME/EEU/NAF
	NIGER LA VOIX DU SAHEL — Niamey	Sa:4/20/100kW:DS-1 4/20/100kW:DS-1/FRENCH, ETC Sa/Su:4/20/100kW:DS-1/FRENCH, ETC M-F:4/20/100kW:DS-3/FRENCH, ETC
	PORTUGAL RDP INTERNATIONAL — Lisbon-São Gabriel	(D):100kW::EU (D)M-F:100kW::EU
	UNITED KINGDOM BBC — Daventry	(D):250kW::EEU (D)Su:250kW::EEU
	USA RFE-RL — Via Germany (FR)	(J):100kW::WUSSR
	RFE-RL — Via Lisbon, Portugal	(J):250kW::WUSSR 250kW::WUSSR (D):250kW::WUSSR
	RFE-RL — Via Pals, Spain	(D):250kW::WUSSR
	VOICE OF AMERICA — Via Woofferton, UK	(D):250/300kW::WUSSR
	USSR RADIO MOSCOW/RP&P — Zhigulevsk	(J):100kW::USSR (J):240kW:ITALIAN, RUSSIAN:EU
7160	**FRANCE** RADIO FRANCE INTL — Issoudun-Allouis	(D):100kW::EEU
	RADIO FRANCE INTL — Multiple Locations	100/250/500kW::AF
	INDIA ALL INDIA RADIO — Aligarh	250kW:DS-ENGLISH, ETC
	ALL INDIA RADIO — Madras	10kW:DS Sa/Su:10kW:DS Su:10kW:DS
(con'd)		

Key / Legend:

ENGLISH ▬▬ GERMAN / DEUTSCH ◊◊◊◊ FRENCH / FRANÇAIS ═══ PORTUGUESE / PORTUGUÊS ▬▬ SPANISH / ESPAÑOL ▬▬

ARABIC /ﻉﺏ ≡≡ RUSSIAN / РУССКИИ ═══ CHINESE / ✱✱ ☐☐☐☐ JAPANESE / 日本語 ▬▬▬ MULTILINGUAL ☐☐☐☐ OTHER ▬▬

SUMMER ONLY (J) WINTER ONLY (D) JAMMING ∧∧ or / or \ EARLIEST HEARD ◢ LATEST HEARD ◣ ✦ TENTATIVE

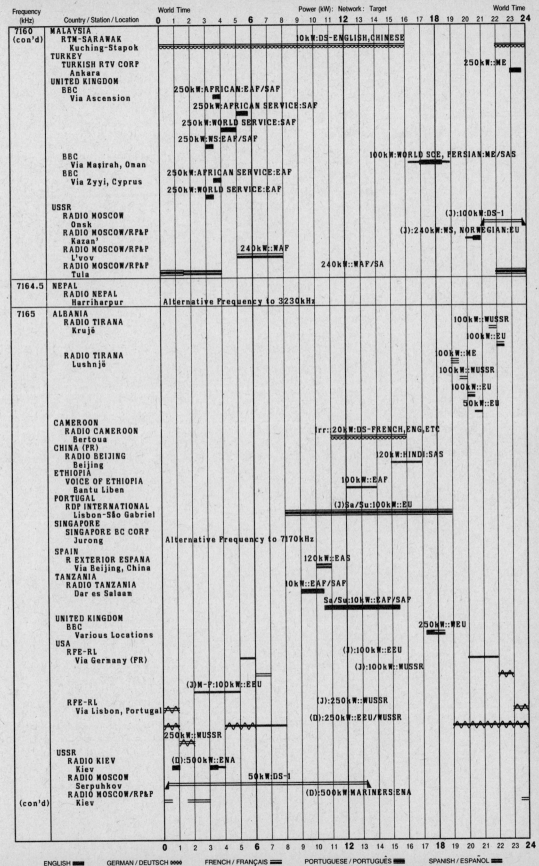

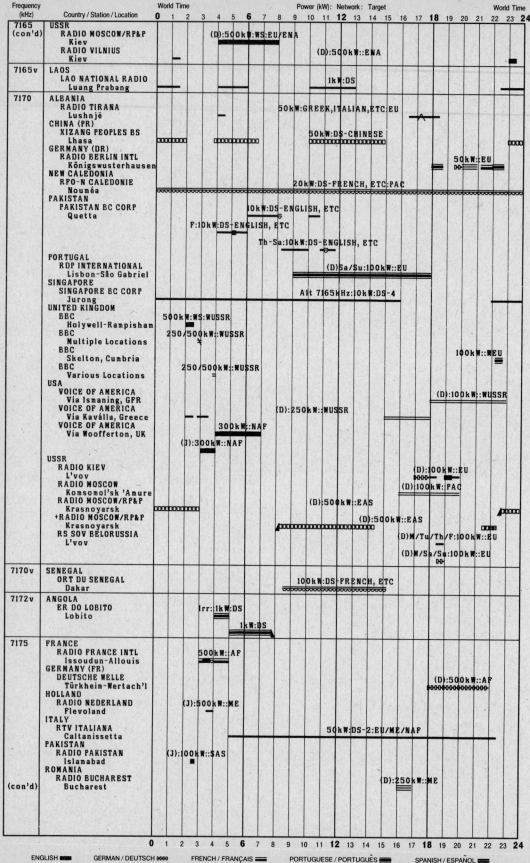

Frequency (kHz)	Country / Station / Location	Schedule
7165 (con'd)	**USSR**	
	RADIO MOSCOW/RP&P Kiev	(D):500kW:WS:EU/ENA
	RADIO VILNIUS Kiev	(D):500kW::ENA
7165v	**LAOS**	
	LAO NATIONAL RADIO Luang Prabang	1kW:DS
7170	**ALBANIA**	
	RADIO TIRANA Lushnjë	50kW:GREEK,ITALIAN,ETC:EU
	CHINA (PR)	
	XIZANG PEOPLES BS Lhasa	50kW:DS-CHINESE
	GERMANY (DR)	
	RADIO BERLIN INTL Königswusterhausen	50kW::EU
	NEW CALEDONIA	
	RFO-N CALEDONIE Nouméa	20kW:DS-FRENCH, ETC:PAC
	PAKISTAN	
	PAKISTAN BC CORP Quetta	10kW:DS-ENGLISH, ETC
		F:10kW:DS-ENGLISH, ETC
		Th-Sa:10kW:DS-ENGLISH, ETC
	PORTUGAL	
	RDP INTERNATIONAL Lisbon-São Gabriel	(D)Sa/Su:100kW::EU
	SINGAPORE	
	SINGAPORE BC CORP Jurong	Alt 7165kHz:10kW:DS-4
	UNITED KINGDOM	
	BBC Holywell-Rampisham	500kW:WS:WUSSR
	BBC Multiple Locations	250/500kW::WUSSR
	BBC Skelton, Cumbria	100kW::WEU
	BBC Various Locations	250/500kW::WUSSR
	USA	
	VOICE OF AMERICA Via Ismaning, GFR	(D):100kW::WUSSR
	VOICE OF AMERICA Via Kaválla, Greece	(D):250kW::WUSSR
	VOICE OF AMERICA Via Woofferton, UK	300kW::NAF
		(J):300kW::NAF
	USSR	
	RADIO KIEV L'vov	(D):100kW::EU
	RADIO MOSCOW Komsomol'sk 'Amure	(D):100kW::PAC
	RADIO MOSCOW/RP&P Krasnoyarsk	(D):500kW::EAS
	+RADIO MOSCOW/RP&P Krasnoyarsk	(D):500kW::EAS
	RS SOV BELORUSSIA L'vov	(D)M/Tu/Th/F:100kW::EU
		(D)W/Sa/Su:100kW::EU
7170v	**SENEGAL**	
	ORT DU SENEGAL Dakar	100kW:DS-FRENCH, ETC
7172v	**ANGOLA**	
	ER DO LOBITO Lobito	Irr:1kW:DS
		1kW:DS
7175	**FRANCE**	
	RADIO FRANCE INTL Issoudun-Allouis	500kW::AF
	GERMANY (FR)	
	DEUTSCHE WELLE Türkheim-Wertach'l	(D):500kW::AF
	HOLLAND	
	RADIO NEDERLAND Flevoland	(J):500kW::ME
	ITALY	
	RTV ITALIANA Caltanissetta	50kW:DS-2:EU/ME/NAF
	PAKISTAN	
	RADIO PAKISTAN Islamabad	(J):100kW::SAS
	ROMANIA	
(con'd)	RADIO BUCHAREST Bucharest	(D):250kW::ME

World Time: 0 1 2 3 4 5 6 7 8 9 10 11 12 13 14 15 16 17 18 19 20 21 22 23 24

Power (kW): Network: Target

ENGLISH ▬   GERMAN / DEUTSCH ∞∞∞   FRENCH / FRANÇAIS ▬   PORTUGUESE / PORTUGUÊS ▬   SPANISH / ESPAÑOL ▬

ARABIC /ﻉ◌◌ ≡   RUSSIAN / РУССКИЙ ▬   CHINESE / ✦✶ ◌◌◌◌   JAPANESE / 日本語 ▬▬   MULTILINGUAL ∞∞∞   OTHER ▬

SUMMER ONLY (J)   WINTER ONLY (D)   JAMMING ∧∧ or / or \   EARLIEST HEARD ◢   LATEST HEARD ◣   + TENTATIVE

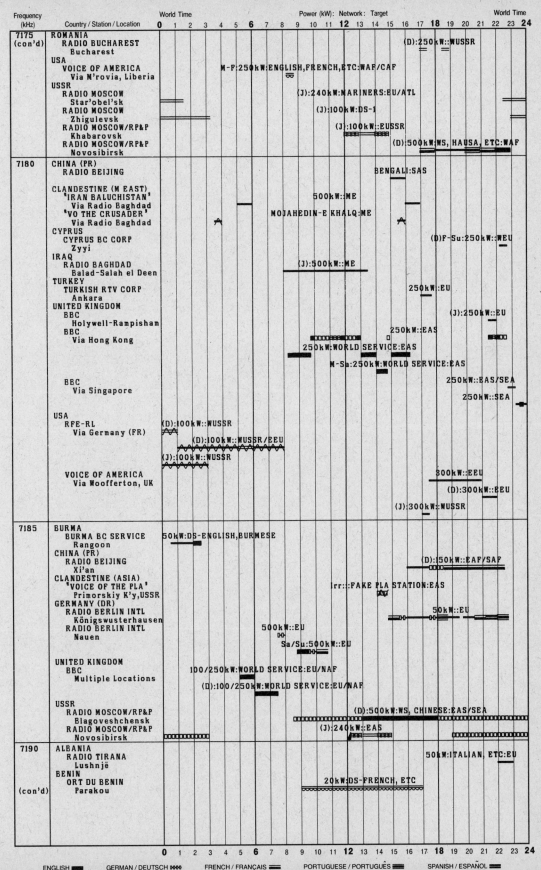

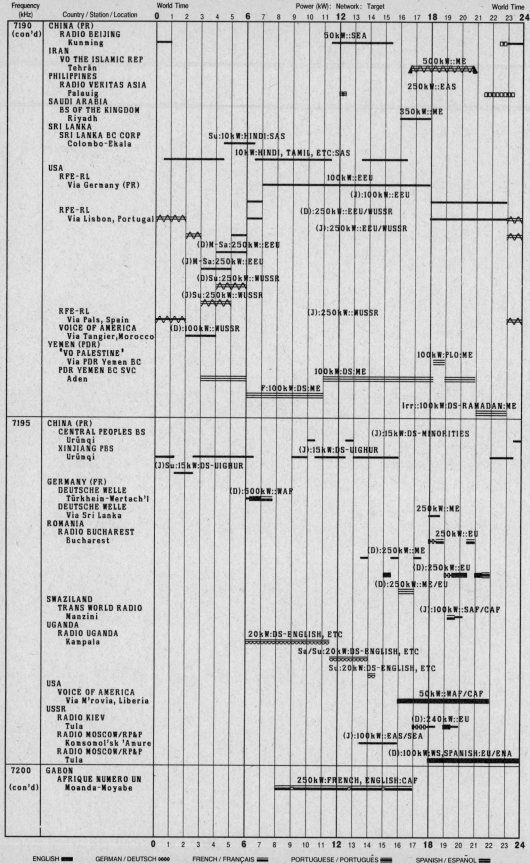

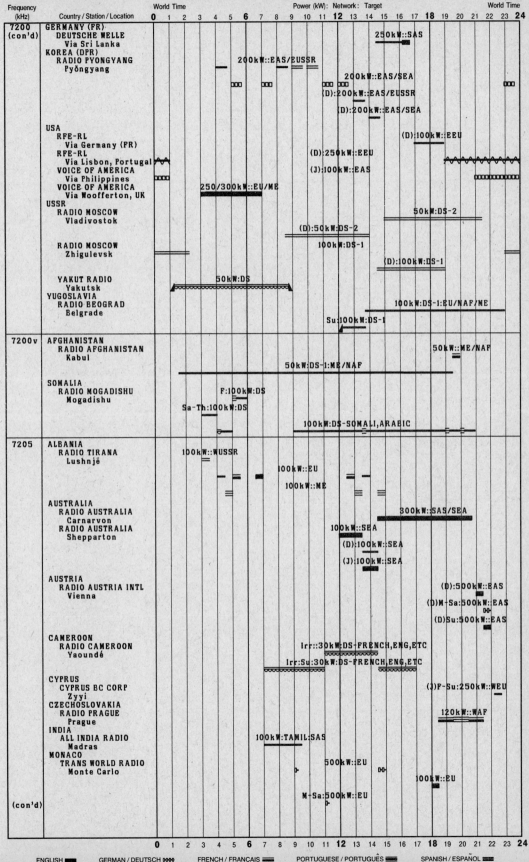

Frequency (kHz)	Country / Station / Location	Power (kW): Network: Target
7200 (con'd)	**GERMANY (FR)** DEUTSCHE WELLE — Via Sri Lanka	250kW::SAS
	KOREA (DPR) RADIO PYONGYANG — Pyŏngyang	200kW::EAS/EUSSR · 200kW::EAS/SEA · (D):200kW::EAS/EUSSR · (D):200kW::EAS/SEA
	USA RFE-RL — Via Germany (FR)	(D):100kW::EEU
	RFE-RL — Via Lisbon, Portugal	(D):250kW::EEU
	VOICE OF AMERICA — Via Philippines	(J):100kW::EAS
	VOICE OF AMERICA — Via Woofferton, UK	250/300kW::EU/ME
	USSR RADIO MOSCOW — Vladivostok	50kW:DS-2 · (D):50kW:DS-2
	RADIO MOSCOW — Zhigulevsk	100kW:DS-1 · (D):100kW:DS-1
	YAKUT RADIO — Yakutsk	50kW:DS
	YUGOSLAVIA RADIO BEOGRAD — Belgrade	100kW:DS-1:EU/NAF/ME · Su:100kW:DS-1
7200v	**AFGHANISTAN** RADIO AFGHANISTAN — Kabul	50kW::ME/NAF · 50kW:DS-1:ME/NAF
	SOMALIA RADIO MOGADISHU — Mogadishu	F:100kW:DS · Sa-Th:100kW:DS · 100kW:DS-SOMALI,ARABIC
7205	**ALBANIA** RADIO TIRANA — Lushnjë	100kW::WUSSR · 100kW::EU · 100kW::ME
	AUSTRALIA RADIO AUSTRALIA — Carnarvon	300kW::SAS/SEA
	RADIO AUSTRALIA — Shepparton	100kW::SEA · (D):100kW::SEA · (J):100kW::SEA
	AUSTRIA RADIO AUSTRIA INTL — Vienna	(D):500kW::EAS · (D)M-Sa:500kW::EAS · (D)Su:500kW::EAS
	CAMEROON RADIO CAMEROON — Yaoundé	Irr::30kW:DS-FRENCH,ENG,ETC · Irr:Su:30kW:DS-FRENCH,ENG,ETC
	CYPRUS CYPRUS BC CORP — Zyyi	(J)F-Su:250kW::WEU
	CZECHOSLOVAKIA RADIO PRAGUE — Prague	120kW::WAF
	INDIA ALL INDIA RADIO — Madras	100kW:TAMIL:SAS
	MONACO TRANS WORLD RADIO — Monte Carlo	500kW::EU · 100kW::EU · M-Sa:500kW::EU
(con'd)		

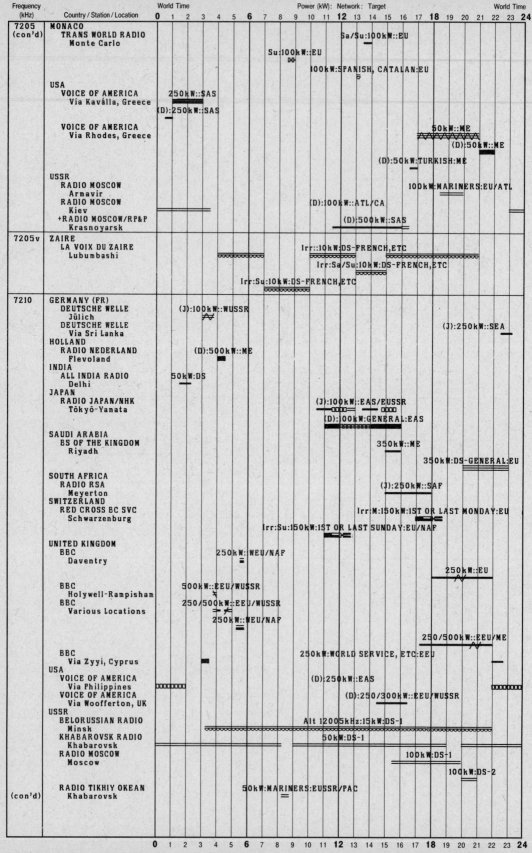

Frequency (kHz)	Country / Station / Location	World Time / Power (kW) : Network : Target

7205 (con'd)

MONACO
TRANS WORLD RADIO
Monte Carlo
- Sa/Su:100kW::EU
- Su:100kW::EU
- 100kW:SPANISH, CATALAN:EU

USA
VOICE OF AMERICA
Via Kaválla, Greece
- 250kW::SAS
- (D):250kW::SAS

VOICE OF AMERICA
Via Rhodes, Greece
- 50kW::ME
- (D):50kW::ME
- (D):50kW:TURKISH:ME

USSR
RADIO MOSCOW
Armavir
- 100kW:MARINERS:EU/ATL

RADIO MOSCOW
Kiev
- (D):100kW::ATL/CA

+RADIO MOSCOW/RP&P
Krasnoyarsk
- (D):500kW::SAS

7205v

ZAIRE
LA VOIX DU ZAIRE
Lubumbashi
- Irr::10kW:DS-FRENCH,ETC
- Irr:Sa/Su:10kW:DS-FRENCH,ETC
- Irr:Su:10kW:DS-FRENCH,ETC

7210

GERMANY (FR)
DEUTSCHE WELLE
Jülich
- (J):100kW::WUSSR

DEUTSCHE WELLE
Via Sri Lanka
- (J):250kW::SEA

HOLLAND
RADIO NEDERLAND
Flevoland
- (D):500kW::ME

INDIA
ALL INDIA RADIO
Delhi
- 50kW:DS

JAPAN
RADIO JAPAN/NHK
Tōkyō-Yamata
- (J):100kW::EAS/EUSSR
- (D):100kW:GENERAL:EAS

SAUDI ARABIA
BS OF THE KINGDOM
Riyadh
- 350kW::ME
- 350kW:DS-GENERAL:EU

SOUTH AFRICA
RADIO RSA
Meyerton
- (J):250kW::SAF

SWITZERLAND
RED CROSS BC SVC
Schwarzenburg
- Irr:M:150kW:1ST OR LAST MONDAY:EU
- Irr:Su:150kW:1ST OR LAST SUNDAY:EU/NAF

UNITED KINGDOM
BBC
Daventry
- 250kW:WEU/NAF
- 250kW::EU

BBC
Holywell-Rampisham
- 500kW::EEU/WUSSR

BBC
Various Locations
- 250/500kW::EEU/WUSSR
- 250kW::WEU/NAF
- 250/500kW::EEU/ME

BBC
Via Zyyi, Cyprus
- 250kW:WORLD SERVICE, ETC:EEU

USA
VOICE OF AMERICA
Via Philippines
- (D):250kW::EAS

VOICE OF AMERICA
Via Woofferton, UK
- (D):250/300kW::EEU/WUSSR

USSR
BELORUSSIAN RADIO
Minsk
- Alt 12005kHz:15kW:DS-1

KHABAROVSK RADIO
Khabarovsk
- 50kW:DS-1

RADIO MOSCOW
Moscow
- 100kW:DS-1
- 100kW:DS-2

(con'd)
RADIO TIKHIY OKEAN
Khabarovsk
- 50kW:MARINERS:EUSSR/PAC

ENGLISH ▬▬ GERMAN / DEUTSCH ◊◊◊◊ FRENCH / FRANÇAIS ▬▬ PORTUGUESE / PORTUGUÊS ▬▬ SPANISH / ESPAÑOL ▬▬

ARABIC / ﻋﺮﺑﻰ ≡ RUSSIAN / РУССКИИ ▬▬ CHINESE / ✦✦ ▭▭▭▭ JAPANESE / 日本語 ▬▬▬ MULTILINGUAL ▭▭▭▭ OTHER ▬▬

SUMMER ONLY (J)   WINTER ONLY (D)   JAMMING ∧∧ or / or \   EARLIEST HEARD ◢   LATEST HEARD ◣   + TENTATIVE

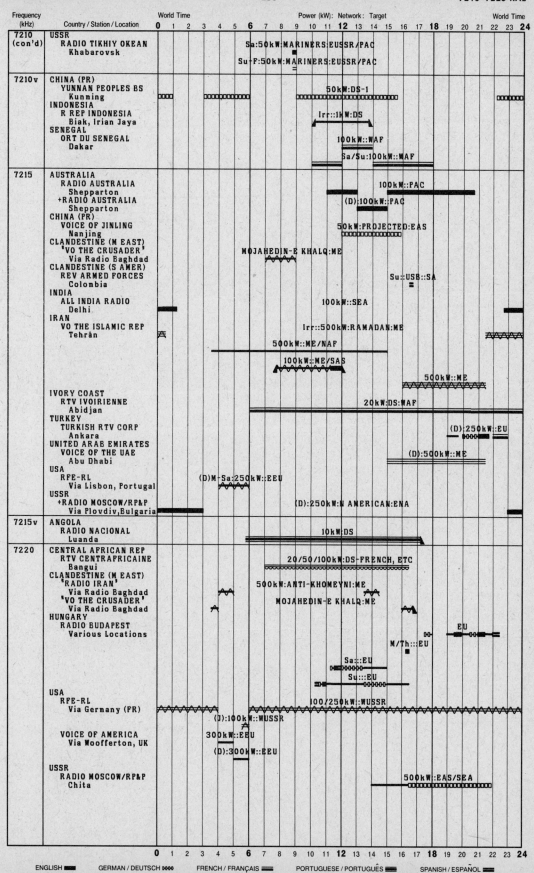

Frequency (kHz)	Country / Station / Location	Power (kW): Network: Target

7210 (con'd)	USSR
	  RADIO TIKHIY OKEAN
	    Khabarovsk
		Sa:50kW:MARINERS:EUSSR/PAC
		Su-F:50kW:MARINERS:EUSSR/PAC

7210v	CHINA (PR)
	  YUNNAN PEOPLES BS
	    Kunming
	INDONESIA
	  R REP INDONESIA
	    Biak, Irian Jaya
	SENEGAL
	  ORT DU SENEGAL
	    Dakar
		50kW:DS-1
		Irr::1kW:DS
		100kW::WAF
		Sa/Su:100kW::WAF

7215	AUSTRALIA
	  RADIO AUSTRALIA
	    Shepparton
	  +RADIO AUSTRALIA
	    Shepparton
	CHINA (PR)
	  VOICE OF JINLING
	    Nanjing
	CLANDESTINE (M EAST)
	  'VO THE CRUSADER'
	    Via Radio Baghdad
	CLANDESTINE (S AMER)
	  REV ARMED FORCES
	    Colombia
	INDIA
	  ALL INDIA RADIO
	    Delhi
	IRAN
	  VO THE ISLAMIC REP
	    Tehrān
	
	IVORY COAST
	  RTV IVOIRIENNE
	    Abidjan
	TURKEY
	  TURKISH RTV CORP
	    Ankara
	UNITED ARAB EMIRATES
	  VOICE OF THE UAE
	    Abu Dhabi
	USA
	  RFE-RL
	    Via Lisbon, Portugal
	USSR
	  +RADIO MOSCOW/RP&P
	    Via Plovdiv,Bulgaria
		100kW::PAC
		(D):100kW:PAC
		50kW:PROJECTED:EAS
		MOJAHEDIN-E KHALQ:ME
		Su::USB::SA
		100kW::SEA
		Irr::500kW:RAMADAN:ME
		500kW::ME/NAF
		100kW::ME/SAS
		500kW::ME
		20kW:DS:WAF
		(D):250kW::EU
		(D):500kW::ME
		(D)M-Sa:250kW::EEU
		(D):250kW:N AMERICAN:ENA

7215v	ANGOLA
	  RADIO NACIONAL
	    Luanda
		10kW:DS

7220	CENTRAL AFRICAN REP
	  RTV CENTRAFRICAINE
	    Bangui
	CLANDESTINE (M EAST)
	  'RADIO IRAN'
	    Via Radio Baghdad
	  'VO THE CRUSADER'
	    Via Radio Baghdad
	HUNGARY
	  RADIO BUDAPEST
	    Various Locations
	
	USA
	  RFE-RL
	    Via Germany (FR)
	
	  VOICE OF AMERICA
	    Via Woofferton, UK
	
	USSR
	  RADIO MOSCOW/RP&P
	    Chita
		20/50/100kW:DS-FRENCH, ETC
		500kW:ANTI-KHOMEYNI:ME
		MOJAHEDIN-E KHALQ:ME
		EU
		M/Th:::EU
		Sa::EU
		Su:::EU
		100/250kW:WUSSR
		(J):100kW::WUSSR
		300kW::EEU
		(D):300kW::EEU
		500kW::EAS/SEA

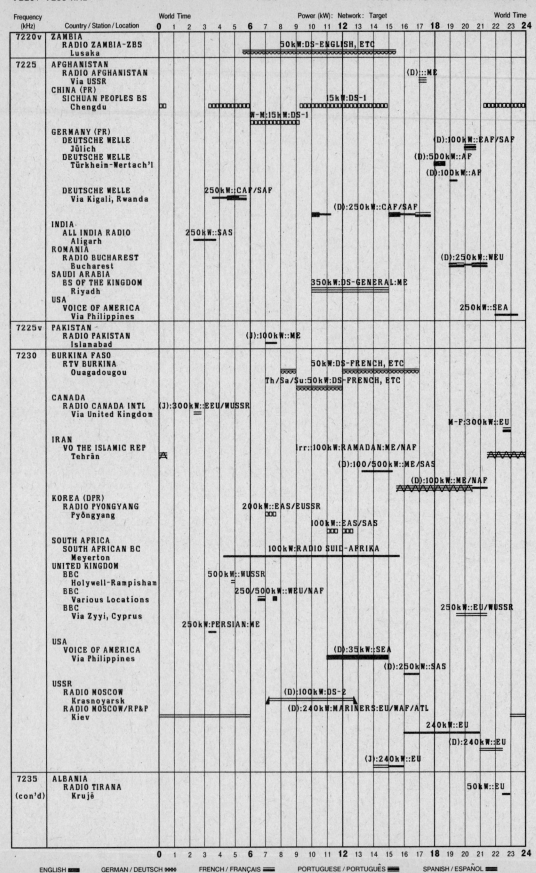

Frequency (kHz)	Country / Station / Location	Details
7220v	**ZAMBIA** RADIO ZAMBIA-ZBS Lusaka	50kW:DS-ENGLISH, ETC
7225	**AFGHANISTAN** RADIO AFGHANISTAN Via USSR	(D):::ME
	CHINA (PR) SICHUAN PEOPLES BS Chengdu	15kW:DS-1 / W-M:15kW:DS-1
	GERMANY (FR) DEUTSCHE WELLE Jülich	(D):100kW::EAF/SAF
	DEUTSCHE WELLE Türkheim-Wertach'l	(D):500kW::AF / (D):100kW::AF
	DEUTSCHE WELLE Via Kigali, Rwanda	250kW::CAF/SAF / (D):250kW::CAF/SAF
	INDIA ALL INDIA RADIO Aligarh	250kW::SAS
	ROMANIA RADIO BUCHAREST Bucharest	(D):250kW::WEU
	SAUDI ARABIA BS OF THE KINGDOM Riyadh	350kW:DS-GENERAL:ME
	USA VOICE OF AMERICA Via Philippines	250kW::SEA
7225v	**PAKISTAN** RADIO PAKISTAN Islamabad	(J):100kW::ME
7230	**BURKINA FASO** RTV BURKINA Ouagadougou	50kW:DS-FRENCH, ETC / Th/Sa/Su:50kW:DS-FRENCH, ETC
	CANADA RADIO CANADA INTL Via United Kingdom	(J):300kW::EEU/WUSSR / M-F:300kW::EU
	IRAN VO THE ISLAMIC REP Tehrān	Irr::100kW:RAMADAN:ME/NAF / (D):100/500kW::ME/SAS / (D):100kW::ME/NAF
	KOREA (DPR) RADIO PYONGYANG Pyŏngyang	200kW::EAS/EUSSR / 100kW::EAS/SAS
	SOUTH AFRICA SOUTH AFRICAN BC Meyerton	100kW:RADIO SUID-AFRIKA
	UNITED KINGDOM BBC Holywell-Rampisham	500kW::WUSSR
	BBC Various Locations	250/500kW::WEU/NAF
	BBC Via Zyyi, Cyprus	250kW::EU/WUSSR / 250kW:PERSIAN:ME
	USA VOICE OF AMERICA Via Philippines	(D):35kW::SEA / (D):250kW::SAS
	USSR RADIO MOSCOW Krasnoyarsk	(D):100kW:DS-2
	RADIO MOSCOW/RP&P Kiev	(D):240kW:MARINERS:EU/WAF/ATL / 240kW::EU / (D):240kW::EU / (J):240kW::EU
7235 (con'd)	**ALBANIA** RADIO TIRANA Krujë	50kW::EU

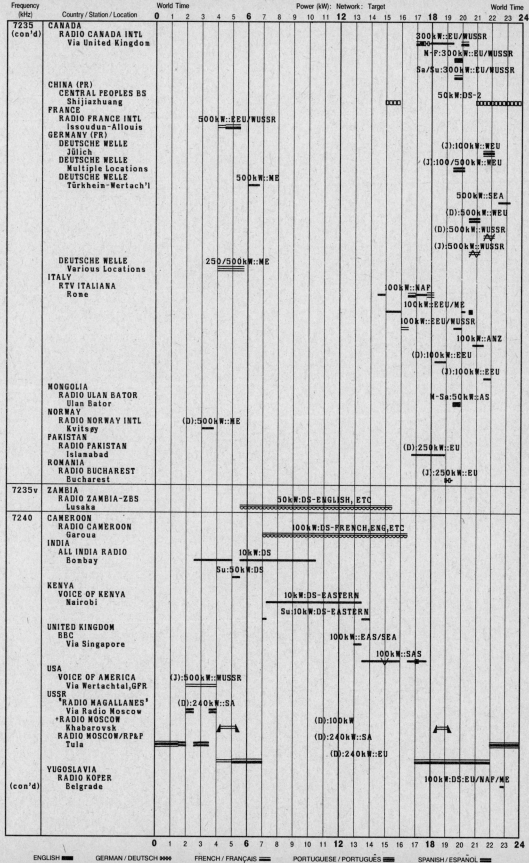

Frequency (kHz)	Country / Station / Location	Schedule (World Time / Power (kW): Network: Target)
7235 (con'd)	**CANADA** RADIO CANADA INTL Via United Kingdom	300kW::EU/WUSSR; M-F:300kW::EU/WUSSR; Sa/Su:300kW::EU/WUSSR
	CHINA (PR) CENTRAL PEOPLES BS Shijiazhuang	50kW:DS-2
	FRANCE RADIO FRANCE INTL Issoudun-Allouis	500kW::EEU/WUSSR
	GERMANY (FR) DEUTSCHE WELLE Jülich	(J):100kW::WEU
	DEUTSCHE WELLE Multiple Locations	(J):100/500kW::WEU
	DEUTSCHE WELLE Türkheim-Wertach'l	500kW::ME; 500kW::SEA; (D):500kW::WEU; (D):500kW::WUSSR; (J):500kW::WUSSR
	DEUTSCHE WELLE Various Locations	250/500kW::ME
	ITALY RTV ITALIANA Rome	100kW::NAF; 100kW::EEU/ME; 100kW::EEU/WUSSR; 100kW::ANZ; (D):100kW::EEU; (J):100kW::EEU
	MONGOLIA RADIO ULAN BATOR Ulan Bator	M-Sa:50kW::AS
	NORWAY RADIO NORWAY INTL Kvitsøy	(D):500kW::ME
	PAKISTAN RADIO PAKISTAN Islamabad	(D):250kW::EU
	ROMANIA RADIO BUCHAREST Bucharest	(J):250kW::EU
7235v	**ZAMBIA** RADIO ZAMBIA-ZBS Lusaka	50kW:DS-ENGLISH, ETC
7240	**CAMEROON** RADIO CAMEROON Garoua	100kW:DS-FRENCH,ENG,ETC
	INDIA ALL INDIA RADIO Bombay	10kW:DS; Su:50kW:DS
	KENYA VOICE OF KENYA Nairobi	10kW:DS-EASTERN; Su:10kW:DS-EASTERN
	UNITED KINGDOM BBC Via Singapore	100kW::EAS/SEA; 100kW::SAS
	USA VOICE OF AMERICA Via Wertachtal,GFR	(J):500kW::WUSSR
	USSR 'RADIO MAGALLANES' Via Radio Moscow	(D):240kW::SA
	+RADIO MOSCOW Khabarovsk	(D):100kW
	RADIO MOSCOW/RP&P Tula	(D):240kW::SA; (D):240kW::EU
(con'd)	**YUGOSLAVIA** RADIO KOPER Belgrade	100kW:DS:EU/NAF/ME

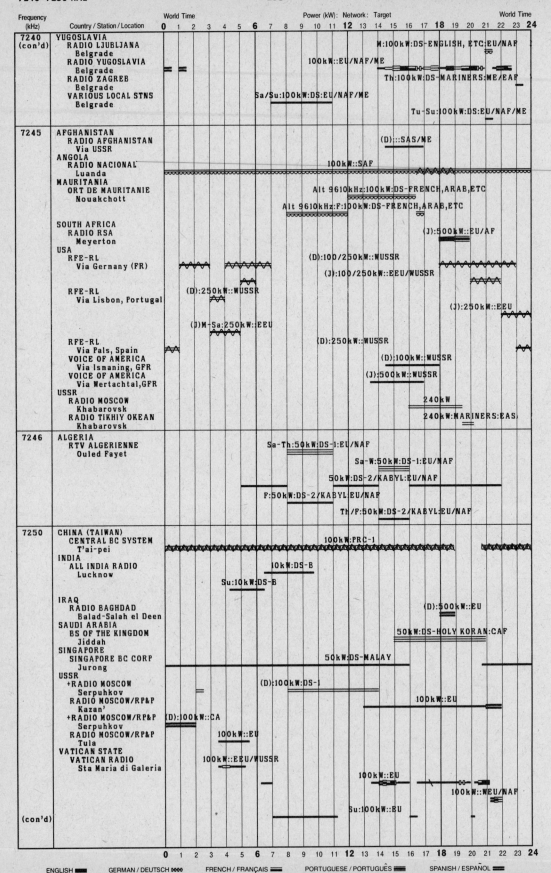

Frequency (kHz)	Country / Station / Location	World Time / Power (kW): Network: Target
7240 (con'd)	**YUGOSLAVIA**	
	RADIO LJUBLJANA Belgrade	M:100kW:DS-ENGLISH, ETC:EU/NAF
	RADIO YUGOSLAVIA Belgrade	100kW::EU/NAF/ME
	RADIO ZAGREB Belgrade	Th:100kW:DS-MARINERS:ME/EAF
	VARIOUS LOCAL STNS Belgrade	Sa/Su:100kW:DS:EU/NAF/ME Tu-Su:100kW:DS:EU/NAF/ME
7245	**AFGHANISTAN**	
	RADIO AFGHANISTAN Via USSR	(D):::SAS/ME
	ANGOLA	
	RADIO NACIONAL Luanda	100kW::SAF
	MAURITANIA	
	ORT DE MAURITANIE Nouakchott	Alt 9610kHz:100kW:DS-FRENCH,ARAB,ETC Alt 9610kHz:F:100kW:DS-FRENCH,ARAB,ETC
	SOUTH AFRICA	
	RADIO RSA Meyerton	(J):500kW::EU/AF
	USA	
	RFE-RL Via Germany (FR)	(D):100/250kW::WUSSR (J):100/250kW::EEU/WUSSR
	RFE-RL Via Lisbon, Portugal	(D):250kW::WUSSR (J):250kW::EEU
	RFE-RL Via Pals, Spain	(J)M-Sa:250kW::EEU (D):250kW::WUSSR
	VOICE OF AMERICA Via Ismaning, GFR	(D):100kW::WUSSR
	VOICE OF AMERICA Via Wertachtal,GFR	(J):500kW::WUSSR
	USSR	
	RADIO MOSCOW Khabarovsk	240kW
	RADIO TIKHIY OKEAN Khabarovsk	240kW:MARINERS:EAS
7246	**ALGERIA**	
	RTV ALGERIENNE Ouled Fayet	Sa-Th:50kW:DS-1:EU/NAF Sa-W:50kW:DS-1:EU/NAF 50kW:DS-2/KABYL:EU/NAF F:50kW:DS-2/KABYL:EU/NAF Th/F:50kW:DS-2/KABYL:EU/NAF
7250	**CHINA (TAIWAN)**	
	CENTRAL BC SYSTEM T'ai-pei	100kW:PRC-1
	INDIA	
	ALL INDIA RADIO Lucknow	10kW:DS-B Su:10kW:DS-B
	IRAQ	
	RADIO BAGHDAD Balad-Salah el Deen	(D):500kW::EU
	SAUDI ARABIA	
	BS OF THE KINGDOM Jiddah	50kW:DS-HOLY KORAN:CAF
	SINGAPORE	
	SINGAPORE BC CORP Jurong	50kW:DS-MALAY
	USSR	
	+RADIO MOSCOW Serpuhkov	(D):100kW:DS-1
	RADIO MOSCOW/RP&P Kazan'	100kW::EU
	+RADIO MOSCOW/RP&P Serpuhkov	(D):100kW::CA
	RADIO MOSCOW/RP&P Tula	100kW::EU
	VATICAN STATE	
	VATICAN RADIO Sta Maria di Galeria	100kW::EEU/WUSSR 100kW::EU 100kW::WEU/NAF Su:100kW::EU
(con'd)		

ENGLISH ▪▪▪ GERMAN / DEUTSCH ◊◊◊◊ FRENCH / FRANÇAIS ≡≡ PORTUGUESE / PORTUGUÊS ≡≡ SPANISH / ESPAÑOL ≡≡

ARABIC / ﻋﺮﺑﻲ ≡ RUSSIAN / PУССКИИ ▬ CHINESE / ♦♣ ▭▭▭▭ JAPANESE / 日本語 ▪▪▪ MULTILINGUAL ◌◌◌◌ OTHER ▬

SUMMER ONLY (J) WINTER ONLY (D) JAMMING ᴧᴧ or / or \ EARLIEST HEARD ◢ LATEST HEARD ◣ ⁺ TENTATIVE

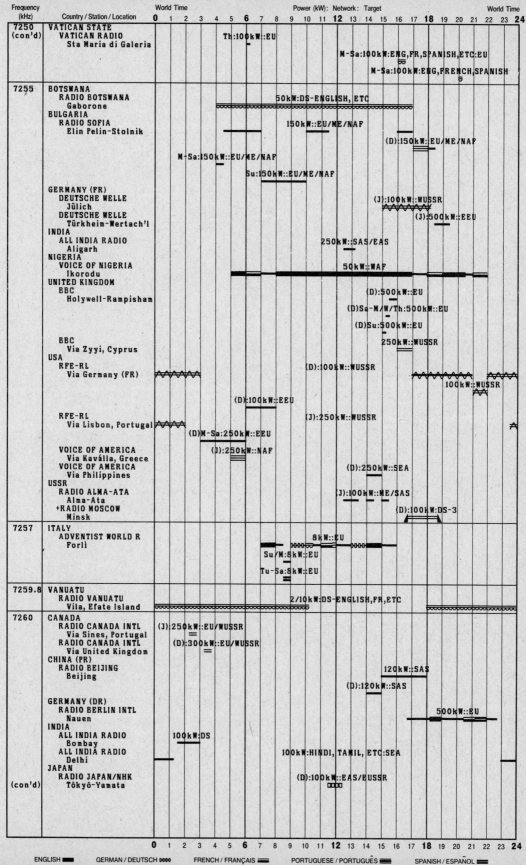

Frequency (kHz) Country / Station / Location	World Time
7250 (con'd) VATICAN STATE VATICAN RADIO Sta Maria di Galeria	Th:100kW::EU / M-Sa:100kW:ENG,FR,SPANISH,ETC:EU / M-Sa:100kW:ENG,FRENCH,SPANISH
7255 BOTSWANA RADIO BOTSWANA Gaborone	50kW:DS-ENGLISH, ETC
BULGARIA RADIO SOFIA Elin Pelin-Stolnik	150kW::EU/ME/NAF / (D):150kW::EU/ME/NAF / M-Sa:150kW::EU/ME/NAF / Su:150kW::EU/ME/NAF
GERMANY (FR) DEUTSCHE WELLE Jülich	(J):100kW::WUSSR
DEUTSCHE WELLE Türkheim-Wertach'l	(J):500kW::EEU
INDIA ALL INDIA RADIO Aligarh	250kW::SAS/EAS
NIGERIA VOICE OF NIGERIA Ikorodu	50kW::WAF
UNITED KINGDOM BBC Holywell-Rampisham	(D):500kW::EU / (D)Sa-M/W/Th:500kW::EU / (D)Su:500kW::EU
BBC Via Zyyi, Cyprus	250kW::WUSSR
USA RFE-RL Via Germany (FR)	(D):100kW::WUSSR / 100kW::WUSSR
RFE-RL Via Lisbon, Portugal	(D):100kW::EEU / (J):250kW::WUSSR / (D)M-Sa:250kW::EEU
VOICE OF AMERICA Via Kaválla, Greece	(J):250kW::NAF
VOICE OF AMERICA Via Philippines	(D):250kW::SEA
USSR RADIO ALMA-ATA Alma-Ata	(J):100kW::ME/SAS
+RADIO MOSCOW Minsk	(D):100kW:DS-3
7257 ITALY ADVENTIST WORLD R Forlì	8kW::EU / Su/M:8kW::EU / Tu-Sa:8kW::EU
7259.8 VANUATU RADIO VANUATU Vila, Efate Island	2/10kW:DS-ENGLISH,FR,ETC
7260 CANADA RADIO CANADA INTL Via Sines, Portugal	(J):250kW::EU/WUSSR
RADIO CANADA INTL Via United Kingdom	(D):300kW::EU/WUSSR
CHINA (PR) RADIO BEIJING Beijing	120kW::SAS / (D):120kW::SAS
GERMANY (DR) RADIO BERLIN INTL Nauen	500kW::EU
INDIA ALL INDIA RADIO Bombay	100kW:DS
ALL INDIA RADIO Delhi	100kW:HINDI, TAMIL, ETC:SEA
JAPAN RADIO JAPAN/NHK **(con'd)** Tōkyō-Yamata	(D):100kW::EAS/EUSSR

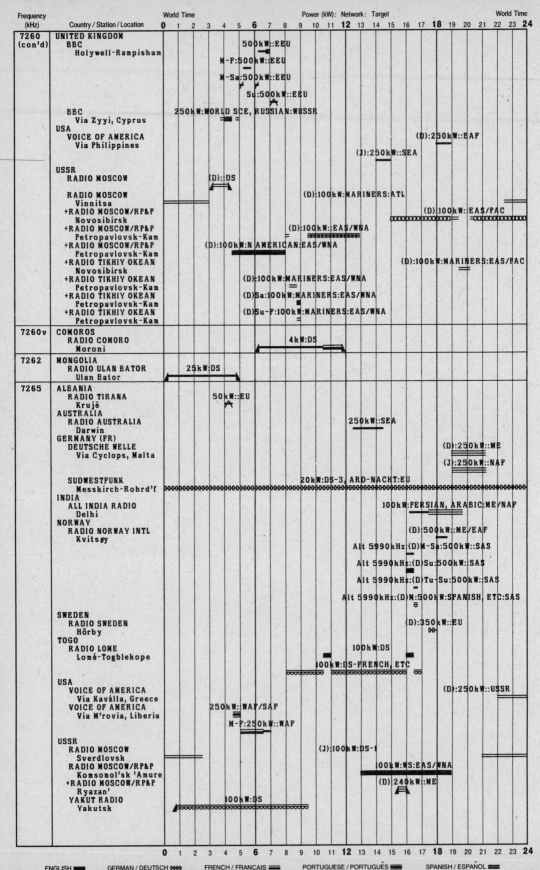

Frequency (kHz)	Country / Station / Location	World Time / Power (kW): Network: Target
7260 (con'd)	**UNITED KINGDOM** BBC Holywell-Rampisham	500kW::EEU M-F:500kW::EEU M-Sa:500kW::EEU Su:500kW::EEU
	BBC Via Zyyi, Cyprus	250kW:WORLD SCE, RUSSIAN:WUSSR
	USA VOICE OF AMERICA Via Philippines	(D):250kW::EAF (J):250kW::SEA
	USSR RADIO MOSCOW	(D)::DS
	RADIO MOSCOW Vinnitsa	(D):100kW:MARINERS:ATL
	+RADIO MOSCOW/RP&P Novosibirsk	(D)100kW:EAS/PAC
	+RADIO MOSCOW/RP&P Petropavlovsk-Kam	(D):100kW::EAS/WNA
	+RADIO MOSCOW/RP&P Petropavlovsk-Kam	(D):100kW:N AMERICAN:EAS/WNA
	+RADIO TIKHIY OKEAN Novosibirsk	(D):100kW:MARINERS:EAS/PAC
	+RADIO TIKHIY OKEAN Petropavlovsk-Kam	(D):100kW:MARINERS:EAS/WNA
	+RADIO TIKHIY OKEAN Petropavlovsk-Kam	(D)Sa:100kW:MARINERS:EAS/WNA
	+RADIO TIKHIY OKEAN Petropavlovsk-Kam	(D)Su-F:100kW:MARINERS:EAS/WNA
7260v	**COMOROS** RADIO COMORO Moroni	4kW:DS
7262	**MONGOLIA** RADIO ULAN BATOR Ulan Bator	25kW:DS
7265	**ALBANIA** RADIO TIRANA Krujë	50kW::EU
	AUSTRALIA RADIO AUSTRALIA Darwin	250kW::SEA
	GERMANY (FR) DEUTSCHE WELLE Via Cyclops, Malta	(D):250kW::ME (J):250kW::NAF
	SUDWESTFUNK Messkirch-Rohrd'f	20kW:DS-3, ARD-NACHT:EU
	INDIA ALL INDIA RADIO Delhi	100kW:PERSIAN, ARABIC:ME/NAF
	NORWAY RADIO NORWAY INTL Kvitsøy	(D):500kW::ME/EAF Alt 5990kHz:(D)M-Sa:500kW::SAS Alt 5990kHz:(D)Su:500kW::SAS Alt 5990kHz:(D)Tu-Su:500kW::SAS Alt 5990kHz:(D)M:500kW:SPANISH, ETC:SAS
	SWEDEN RADIO SWEDEN Hörby	(D):350kW::EU
	TOGO RADIO LOME Lomé-Togblekope	100kW:DS 100kW:DS-FRENCH, ETC
	USA VOICE OF AMERICA Via Kaválla, Greece	(D):250kW::USSR
	VOICE OF AMERICA Via M'rovia, Liberia	250kW::WAF/SAF M-F:250kW::WAF
	USSR RADIO MOSCOW Sverdlovsk	(J):100kW:DS-1
	RADIO MOSCOW/RP&P Komsomol'sk 'Amure	100kW:WS:EAS/WNA
	+RADIO MOSCOW/RP&P Ryazan'	(D):240kW::ME
	YAKUT RADIO Yakutsk	100kW:DS

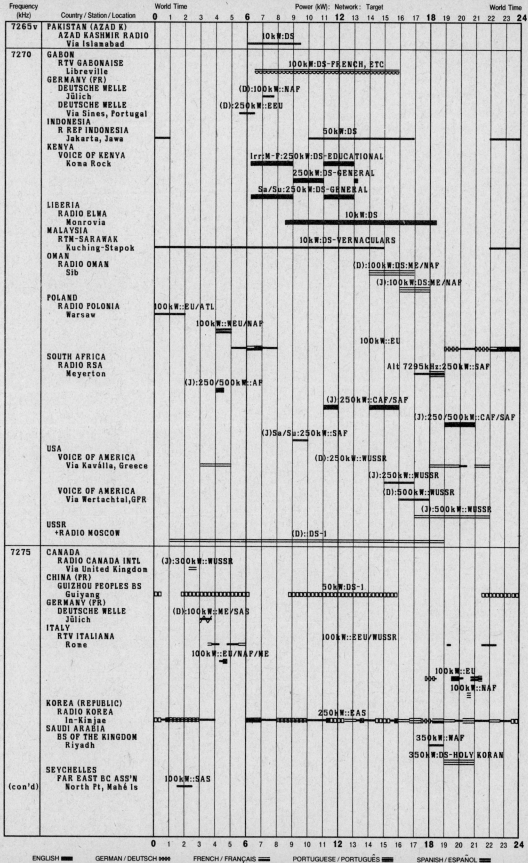

Frequency (kHz)	Country / Station / Location	Schedule
7265v	PAKISTAN (AZAD K) AZAD KASHMIR RADIO Via Islamabad	10kW:DS
7270	GABON RTV GABONAISE Libreville	100kW:DS-FRENCH, ETC
	GERMANY (FR) DEUTSCHE WELLE Jülich	(D):100kW::NAF
	DEUTSCHE WELLE Via Sines, Portugal	(D):250kW::EEU
	INDONESIA R REP INDONESIA Jakarta, Jawa	50kW:DS
	KENYA VOICE OF KENYA Koma Rock	Irr:M-F:250kW:DS-EDUCATIONAL / 250kW:DS-GENERAL / Sa/Su:250kW:DS-GENERAL
	LIBERIA RADIO ELWA Monrovia	10kW:DS
	MALAYSIA RTM-SARAWAK Kuching-Stapok	10kW:DS-VERNACULARS
	OMAN RADIO OMAN Sib	(D):100kW:DS:ME/NAF / (J):100kW:DS:ME/NAF
	POLAND RADIO POLONIA Warsaw	100kW::EU/ATL / 100kW::WEU/NAF / 100kW::EU
	SOUTH AFRICA RADIO RSA Meyerton	Alt 7295kHz:250kW::SAF / (J):250/500kW::AF / (J)250kW::CAF/SAF / (J):250/500kW::CAF/SAF / (J)Sa/Su:250kW::SAF
	USA VOICE OF AMERICA Via Kaválla, Greece	(D):250kW::WUSSR / (J):250kW::WUSSR
	VOICE OF AMERICA Via Wertachtal,GFR	(D):500kW::WUSSR / (J):500kW::WUSSR
	USSR +RADIO MOSCOW	(D)::DS-1
7275	CANADA RADIO CANADA INTL Via United Kingdom	(J):300kW::WUSSR
	CHINA (PR) GUIZHOU PEOPLES BS Guiyang	50kW:DS-1
	GERMANY (FR) DEUTSCHE WELLE Jülich	(D):100kW::ME/SAS
	ITALY RTV ITALIANA Rome	100kW::EEU/WUSSR / 100kW::EU/NAF/ME / 100kW::EU / 100kW::NAF
	KOREA (REPUBLIC) RADIO KOREA In-Kimjae	250kW::EAS
	SAUDI ARABIA BS OF THE KINGDOM Riyadh	350kW::WAF / 350kW:DS-HOLY KORAN
(con'd)	SEYCHELLES FAR EAST BC ASS'N North Pt, Mahé Is	100kW::SAS

World Time: 0 1 2 3 4 5 6 7 8 9 10 11 12 13 14 15 16 17 18 19 20 21 22 23 24
Power (kW): Network: Target

ENGLISH ▬   GERMAN / DEUTSCH ◊◊◊◊   FRENCH / FRANÇAIS ▬   PORTUGUESE / PORTUGUÊS ▬   SPANISH / ESPAÑOL ▬

ARABIC /ﻉﺭ ▬   RUSSIAN / PУCCКИИ ▬   CHINESE / 中文 ◻◻◻◻   JAPANESE / 日本語 ▬   MULTILINGUAL ▭▭▭   OTHER ▬

SUMMER ONLY (J)   WINTER ONLY (D)   JAMMING ∧∧ or / or \   EARLIEST HEARD ◢   LATEST HEARD ◣   + TENTATIVE

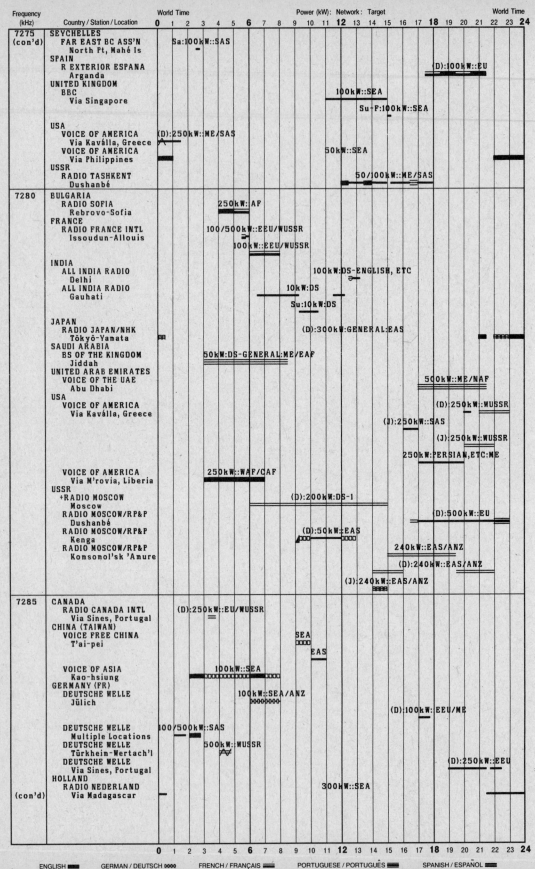

Frequency (kHz)	Country / Station / Location	Schedule
7275 (con'd)	**SEYCHELLES**	
	FAR EAST BC ASS'N — North Pt, Mahé Is	Sa:100kW::SAS
	SPAIN	
	R EXTERIOR ESPANA — Arganda	(D):100kW::EU
	UNITED KINGDOM	
	BBC — Via Singapore	100kW::SEA / Su-F:100kW::SEA
	USA	
	VOICE OF AMERICA — Via Kaválla, Greece	(D):250kW::ME/SAS
	VOICE OF AMERICA — Via Philippines	50kW::SEA
	USSR	
	RADIO TASHKENT — Dushanbé	50/100kW::ME/SAS
7280	**BULGARIA**	
	RADIO SOFIA — Rebrovo-Sofia	250kW:AF
	FRANCE	
	RADIO FRANCE INTL — Issoudun-Allouis	100/500kW::EEU/WUSSR / 100kW::EEU/WUSSR
	INDIA	
	ALL INDIA RADIO — Delhi	100kW:DS-ENGLISH, ETC
	ALL INDIA RADIO — Gauhati	10kW:DS / Su:10kW:DS
	JAPAN	
	RADIO JAPAN/NHK — Tôkyô-Yamata	(D):300kW:GENERAL:EAS
	SAUDI ARABIA	
	BS OF THE KINGDOM — Jiddah	50kW:DS-GENERAL:ME/EAF
	UNITED ARAB EMIRATES	
	VOICE OF THE UAE — Abu Dhabi	500kW::ME/NAF
	USA	
	VOICE OF AMERICA — Via Kaválla, Greece	(D):250kW::WUSSR / (J):250kW::SAS / (J):250kW::WUSSR / 250kW:PERSIAN,ETC:ME
	VOICE OF AMERICA — Via M'rovia, Liberia	250kW::WAF/CAF
	USSR	
	+RADIO MOSCOW — Moscow	(D):200kW:DS-1
	RADIO MOSCOW/RP&P — Dushanbé	(D):500kW::EU
	RADIO MOSCOW/RP&P — Kenga	(D):50kW::EAS
	RADIO MOSCOW/RP&P — Komsomol'sk 'Amure	240kW::EAS/ANZ / (D):240kW::EAS/ANZ / (J):240kW::EAS/ANZ
7285	**CANADA**	
	RADIO CANADA INTL — Via Sines, Portugal	(D):250kW::EU/WUSSR
	CHINA (TAIWAN)	
	VOICE FREE CHINA — T'ai-pei	SEA / EAS
	VOICE OF ASIA — Kao-hsiung	100kW::SEA
	GERMANY (FR)	
	DEUTSCHE WELLE — Jülich	100kW::SEA/ANZ / (D):100kW: EEU/ME
	DEUTSCHE WELLE — Multiple Locations	100/500kW::SAS
	DEUTSCHE WELLE — Türkheim-Wertach'l	500kW::WUSSR
	DEUTSCHE WELLE — Via Sines, Portugal	(D):250kW::EEU
	HOLLAND	
(con'd)	RADIO NEDERLAND — Via Madagascar	300kW::SEA

World Time: 0 1 2 3 4 5 6 7 8 9 10 11 12 13 14 15 16 17 18 19 20 21 22 23 24

Power (kW): Network: Target

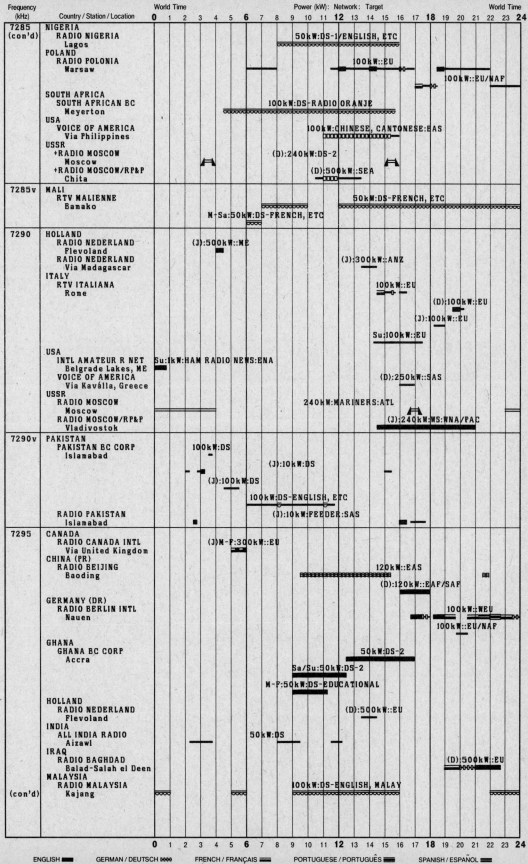

Frequency (kHz)	Country / Station / Location	Power (kW): Network: Target
7285 (con'd)	NIGERIA RADIO NIGERIA Lagos	50kW:DS-1/ENGLISH, ETC
	POLAND RADIO POLONIA Warsaw	100kW::EU / 100kW::EU/NAF
	SOUTH AFRICA SOUTH AFRICAN BC Meyerton	100kW:DS-RADIO ORANJE
	USA VOICE OF AMERICA Via Philippines	100kW:CHINESE, CANTONESE:EAS
	USSR +RADIO MOSCOW Moscow	(D):240kW:DS-2
	+RADIO MOSCOW/RP&P Chita	(D):500kW::SEA
7285v	MALI RTV MALIENNE Bamako	50kW:DS-FRENCH, ETC / M-Sa:50kW:DS-FRENCH, ETC
7290	HOLLAND RADIO NEDERLAND Flevoland	(J):500kW::ME
	RADIO NEDERLAND Via Madagascar	(J):300kW::ANZ
	ITALY RTV ITALIANA Rome	100kW::EU / (D):100kW::EU / (J):100kW::EU / Su:100kW::EU
	USA INTL AMATEUR R NET Belgrade Lakes, ME	Su:1kW:HAM RADIO NEWS:ENA
	VOICE OF AMERICA Via Kaválla, Greece	(D):250kW::SAS
	USSR RADIO MOSCOW Moscow	240kW:MARINERS:ATL
	RADIO MOSCOW/RP&P Vladivostok	(J):240kW:WS:WNA/PAC
7290v	PAKISTAN PAKISTAN BC CORP Islamabad	100kW:DS / (J):10kW:DS / (J):100kW:DS / 100kW:DS-ENGLISH, ETC
	RADIO PAKISTAN Islamabad	(J):10kW:FEEDER:SAS
7295	CANADA RADIO CANADA INTL Via United Kingdom	(J)M-F:300kW::EU
	CHINA (PR) RADIO BEIJING Baoding	120kW::EAS / (D):120kW::EAF/SAF
	GERMANY (DR) RADIO BERLIN INTL Nauen	100kW::WEU / 100kW::EU/NAF
	GHANA GHANA BC CORP Accra	50kW:DS-2 / Sa/Su:50kW:DS-2 / M-F:50kW:DS-EDUCATIONAL
	HOLLAND RADIO NEDERLAND Flevoland	(D):500kW::EU
	INDIA ALL INDIA RADIO Aizawl	50kW:DS
	IRAQ RADIO BAGHDAD Balad-Salah el Deen	(D):500kW::EU
	MALAYSIA RADIO MALAYSIA Kajang	100kW:DS-ENGLISH, MALAY
(con'd)		

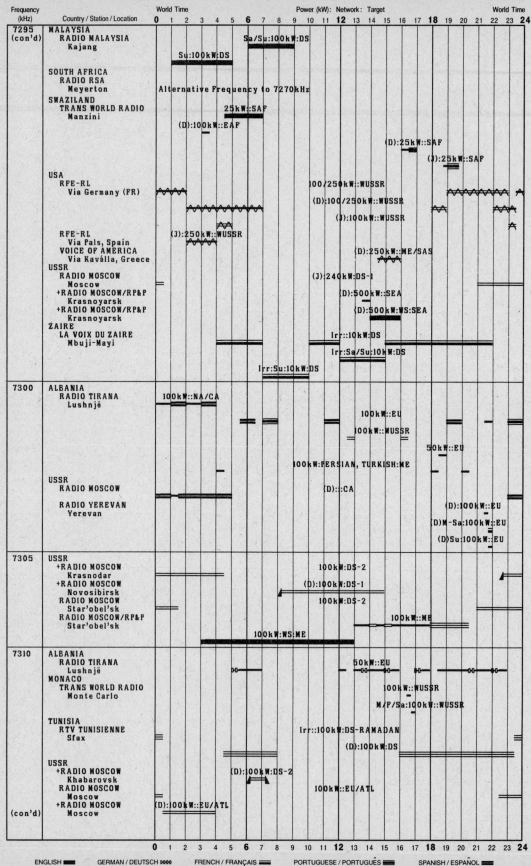

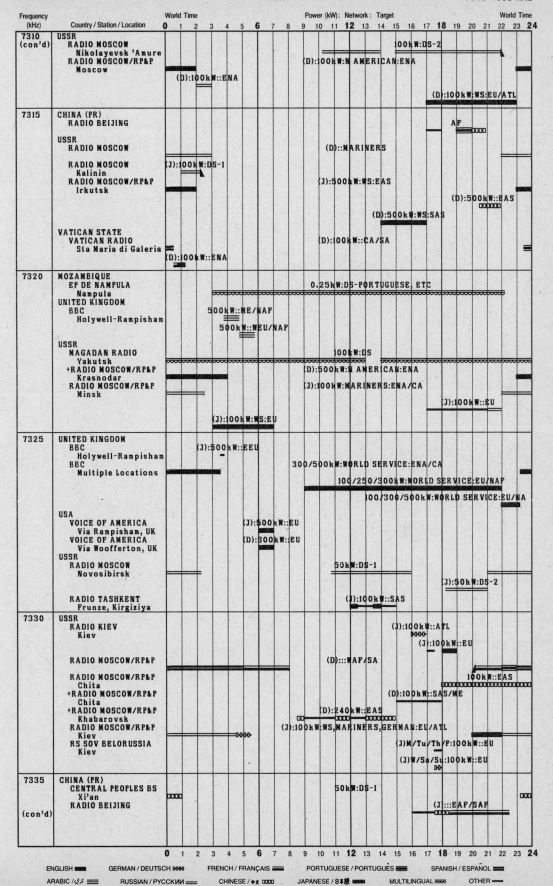

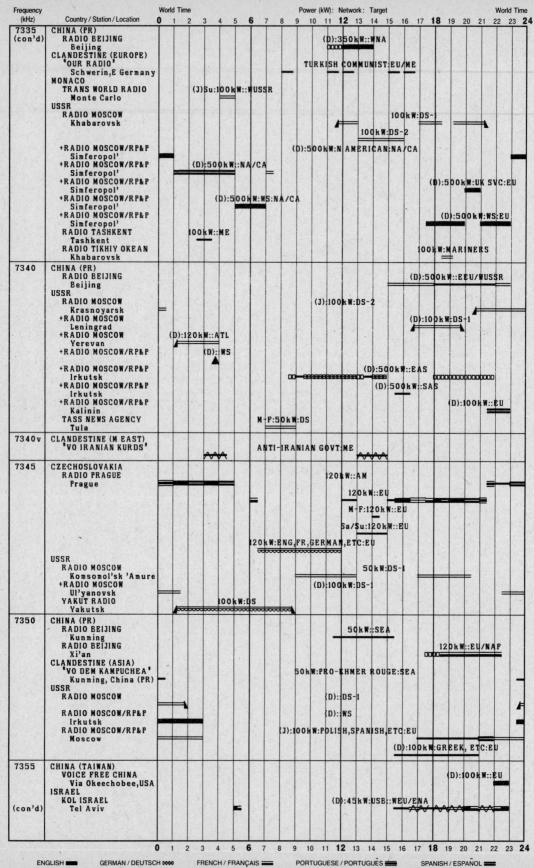

Frequency (kHz) — Country / Station / Location — World Time — Power (kW): Network: Target — World Time

0 1 2 3 4 5 6 7 8 9 10 11 12 13 14 15 16 17 18 19 20 21 22 23 24

7335 (con'd)
CHINA (PR)
RADIO BEIJING — Beijing — (D):350kW::WNA
CLANDESTINE (EUROPE) — "OUR RADIO" — Schwerin, E Germany — TURKISH COMMUNIST:EU/ME
MONACO
TRANS WORLD RADIO — Monte Carlo — (J)Su:100kW::WUSSR
USSR
RADIO MOSCOW — Khabarovsk — 100kW:DS-1 — 100kW:DS-2
+RADIO MOSCOW/RP&P — Simferopol' — (D):500kW:N AMERICAN:NA/CA
+RADIO MOSCOW/RP&P — Simferopol' — (D):500kW::NA/CA
+RADIO MOSCOW/RP&P — Simferopol' — (D):500kW:UK SVC:EU
+RADIO MOSCOW/RP&P — Simferopol' — (D):500kW:WS:NA/CA
+RADIO MOSCOW/RP&P — Simferopol' — (D):500kW:WS:EU
RADIO TASHKENT — Tashkent — 100kW::ME
RADIO TIKHIY OKEAN — Khabarovsk — 100kW:MARINERS

7340
CHINA (PR)
RADIO BEIJING — Beijing — (D):500kW::EEU/WUSSR
USSR
RADIO MOSCOW — Krasnoyarsk — (J):100kW:DS-2
+RADIO MOSCOW — Leningrad — (D):100kW:DS-1
+RADIO MOSCOW — Yerevan — (D):120kW::ATL
+RADIO MOSCOW/RP&P — (D):WS
+RADIO MOSCOW/RP&P — Irkutsk — (D):500kW::EAS
+RADIO MOSCOW/RP&P — Irkutsk — (D):500kW::SAS
+RADIO MOSCOW/RP&P — Kalinin — (D):100kW::EU
TASS NEWS AGENCY — Tula — M-F:50kW:DS

7340v
CLANDESTINE (M EAST)
"VO IRANIAN KURDS" — ANTI-IRANIAN GOVT:ME

7345
CZECHOSLOVAKIA
RADIO PRAGUE — Prague — 120kW::AM — 120kW::EU — M-F:120kW::EU — Sa/Su:120kW::EU — 120kW:ENG,FR,GERMAN,ETC:EU
USSR
RADIO MOSCOW — Komsomol'sk 'Amure — 50kW:DS-1
+RADIO MOSCOW — Ul'yanovsk — (D):100kW:DS-1
YAKUT RADIO — Yakutsk — 100kW:DS

7350
CHINA (PR)
RADIO BEIJING — Kunming — 50kW::SEA
RADIO BEIJING — Xi'an — 120kW::EU/NAF
CLANDESTINE (ASIA)
"VO DEM KAMPUCHEA" — Kunming, China (PR) — 50kW:PRO-KHMER ROUGE:SEA
USSR
RADIO MOSCOW — (D):DS-1
RADIO MOSCOW/RP&P — Irkutsk — (D):WS
RADIO MOSCOW/RP&P — Moscow — (J):100kW:POLISH,SPANISH,ETC:EU — (D):100kW:GREEK, ETC:EU

7355 (con'd)
CHINA (TAIWAN)
VOICE FREE CHINA — Via Okeechobee, USA — (D):100kW::EU
ISRAEL
KOL ISRAEL — Tel Aviv — (D):45kW:USB::WEU/ENA

0 1 2 3 4 5 6 7 8 9 10 11 12 13 14 15 16 17 18 19 20 21 22 23 24

ENGLISH ▬▬   GERMAN / DEUTSCH ০০০০   FRENCH / FRANÇAIS ═══   PORTUGUESE / PORTUGUÊS ▬▬   SPANISH / ESPAÑOL ▬▬

ARABIC / كاكا ═══   RUSSIAN / РУССКИИ ═══   CHINESE / ★★ ০০০০   JAPANESE / 日本語 ▬▬   MULTILINGUAL ০০০০   OTHER ▬▬

SUMMER ONLY (J)   WINTER ONLY (D)   JAMMING ∧∧ or / or \   EARLIEST HEARD ◢   LATEST HEARD ◣   ✦ TENTATIVE

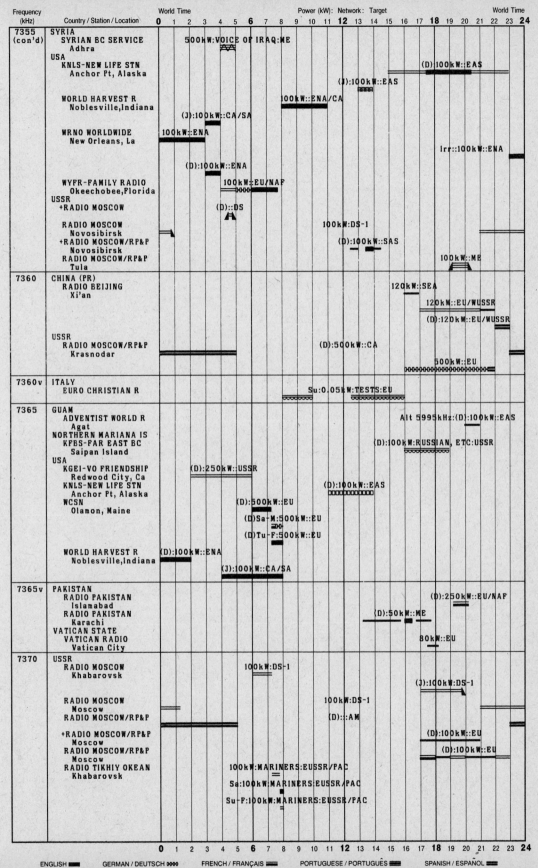

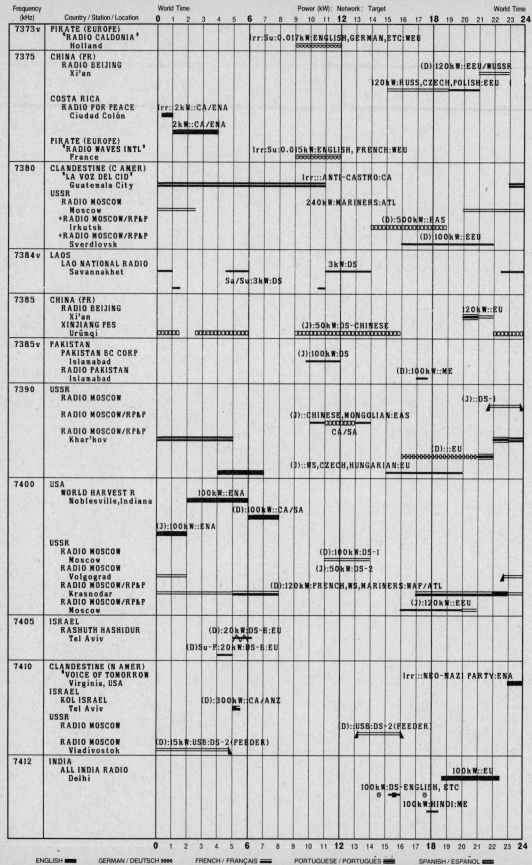

Frequency (kHz)	Country / Station / Location	World Time / Power (kW): Network: Target
7373v	PIRATE (EUROPE) "RADIO CALDONIA" Holland	Irr:Su:0.017kW:ENGLISH,GERMAN,ETC:WEU
7375	CHINA (PR) RADIO BEIJING Xi'an	(D) 120kW::EEU/WUSSR 120kW:RUSS,CZECH,POLISH:EEU
	COSTA RICA RADIO FOR PEACE Ciudad Colón	Irr::2kW::CA/ENA 2kW::CA/ENA
	PIRATE (EUROPE) "RADIO WAVES INTL" France	Irr:Su:0.015kW:ENGLISH, FRENCH:WEU
7380	CLANDESTINE (C AMER) "LA VOZ DEL CID" Guatemala City	Irr:::ANTI-CASTRO:CA
	USSR RADIO MOSCOW Moscow	240kW:MARINERS:ATL
	+RADIO MOSCOW/RP&P Irkutsk	(D):500kW::EAS
	+RADIO MOSCOW/RP&P Sverdlovsk	(D) 100kW::EEU
7384v	LAOS LAO NATIONAL RADIO Savannakhet	3kW:DS Sa/Su:3kW:DS
7385	CHINA (PR) RADIO BEIJING Xi'an	120kW::EU
	XINJIANG PBS Urümqi	(J):50kW:DS-CHINESE
7385v	PAKISTAN PAKISTAN BC CORP Islamabad	(J):100kW:DS
	RADIO PAKISTAN Islamabad	(D):100kW::ME
7390	USSR RADIO MOSCOW	(J)::DS-1
	RADIO MOSCOW/RP&P	(J)::CHINESE,MONGOLIAN:EAS
	RADIO MOSCOW/RP&P Khar'kov	CA/SA (D):::EU (J)::WS,CZECH,HUNGARIAN:EU
7400	USA WORLD HARVEST R Noblesville,Indiana	100kW::ENA (D):100kW::CA/SA (J):100kW::ENA
	USSR RADIO MOSCOW Moscow	(D):100kW:DS-1
	RADIO MOSCOW Volgograd	(J):50kW:DS-2
	RADIO MOSCOW/RP&P Krasnodar	(D):120kW:FRENCH,WS,MARINERS:WAF/ATL
	RADIO MOSCOW/RP&P Moscow	(J):120kW::EEU
7405	ISRAEL RASHUTH HASHIDUR Tel Aviv	(D):20kW:DS-B:EU (D)Su-F:20kW:DS-B:EU
7410	CLANDESTINE (N AMER) "VOICE OF TOMORROW" Virginia, USA	Irr:::NEO-NAZI PARTY:ENA
	ISRAEL KOL ISRAEL Tel Aviv	(D):300kW::CA/ANZ
	USSR RADIO MOSCOW	(D)::USB:DS-2(FEEDER)
	RADIO MOSCOW Vladivostok	(D):15kW:USB:DS-2(FEEDER)
7412	INDIA ALL INDIA RADIO Delhi	100kW::EU 100kW:DS-ENGLISH, ETC 100kW:HINDI:ME

ENGLISH ▰▰▰ GERMAN / DEUTSCH ◊◊◊◊ FRENCH / FRANÇAIS ▬▬ PORTUGUESE / PORTUGUÊS ▰▰ SPANISH / ESPAÑOL ▰▰

ARABIC / ﻉﺏﺭ ▬▬ RUSSIAN / РУССКИИ ▬▬ CHINESE / ★★ ◊◊◊◊ JAPANESE / 日本語 ▰▰▰ MULTILINGUAL ◊◊◊◊ OTHER ▬▬

SUMMER ONLY (J) WINTER ONLY (D) JAMMING ∧∧∧ or / or \ EARLIEST HEARD ◢ LATEST HEARD ◣ ⁺ TENTATIVE

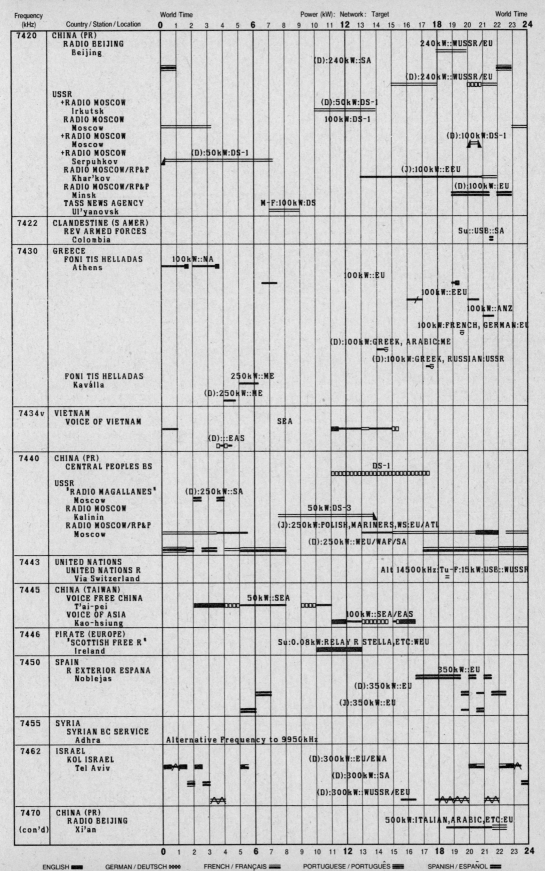

Frequency (kHz)	Country / Station / Location	Schedule (World Time 0–24 · Power (kW): Network: Target)
7420	CHINA (PR) RADIO BEIJING — Beijing	240kW::WUSSR/EU; (D):240kW::SA; (D):240kW::WUSSR/EU
	USSR +RADIO MOSCOW — Irkutsk	(D):50kW:DS-1
	RADIO MOSCOW — Moscow	100kW:DS-1
	+RADIO MOSCOW — Moscow	(D):100kW:DS-1
	+RADIO MOSCOW — Serpuhkov	(D):50kW:DS-1
	RADIO MOSCOW/RP&P — Khar'kov	(J):100kW::EEU
	RADIO MOSCOW/RP&P — Minsk	(D):100kW::EU
	TASS NEWS AGENCY — Ul'yanovsk	M-F:100kW:DS
7422	CLANDESTINE (S AMER) REV ARMED FORCES — Colombia	Su::USB::SA
7430	GREECE FONI TIS HELLADAS — Athens	100kW::NA; 100kW::EU; 100kW::EEU; 100kW::ANZ; 100kW:FRENCH, GERMAN:EU; (D):100kW:GREEK, ARABIC:ME; (D):100kW:GREEK, RUSSIAN:USSR
	FONI TIS HELLADAS — Kaválla	250kW::ME; (D):250kW::ME
7434v	VIETNAM VOICE OF VIETNAM	SEA; (D):::EAS
7440	CHINA (PR) CENTRAL PEOPLES BS	DS-1
	USSR "RADIO MAGALLANES" — Moscow	(D):250kW::SA
	RADIO MOSCOW — Kalinin	50kW:DS-3
	RADIO MOSCOW/RP&P — Moscow	(J):250kW:POLISH,MARINERS,WS:EU/ATL; (D):250kW::WEU/WAF/SA
7443	UNITED NATIONS UNITED NATIONS R — Via Switzerland	Alt 14500kHz:Tu-F:15kW:USB::WUSSR
7445	CHINA (TAIWAN) VOICE FREE CHINA — T'ai-pei	50kW::SEA
	VOICE OF ASIA — Kao-hsiung	100kW::SEA/EAS
7446	PIRATE (EUROPE) "SCOTTISH FREE R" — Ireland	Su:0.08kW:RELAY R STELLA,ETC:WEU
7450	SPAIN R EXTERIOR ESPANA — Noblejas	350kW::EU; (D):350kW::EU; (J):350kW::EU
7455	SYRIA SYRIAN BC SERVICE — Adhra	Alternative Frequency to 9950kHz
7462	ISRAEL KOL ISRAEL — Tel Aviv	(D):300kW::EU/ENA; (D):300kW::SA; (D):300kW::WUSSR/EEU
7470 (con'd)	CHINA (PR) RADIO BEIJING — Xi'an	500kW:ITALIAN,ARABIC,ETC:EU

ENGLISH ▬▬   GERMAN / DEUTSCH ◊◊◊◊   FRENCH / FRANÇAIS ═══   PORTUGUESE / PORTUGUÊS ▬▬   SPANISH / ESPAÑOL ▬▬

ARABIC /ぃﻝ ═══   RUSSIAN / РУССКИИ ═══   CHINESE / ✦✗ ▭▭▭   JAPANESE / 日本語 ▭▭▭   MULTILINGUAL ৯৯৯৯   OTHER ▬▬

SUMMER ONLY (J)   WINTER ONLY (D)   JAMMING ∧∧ or / or \   EARLIEST HEARD ◢   LATEST HEARD ◣   + TENTATIVE

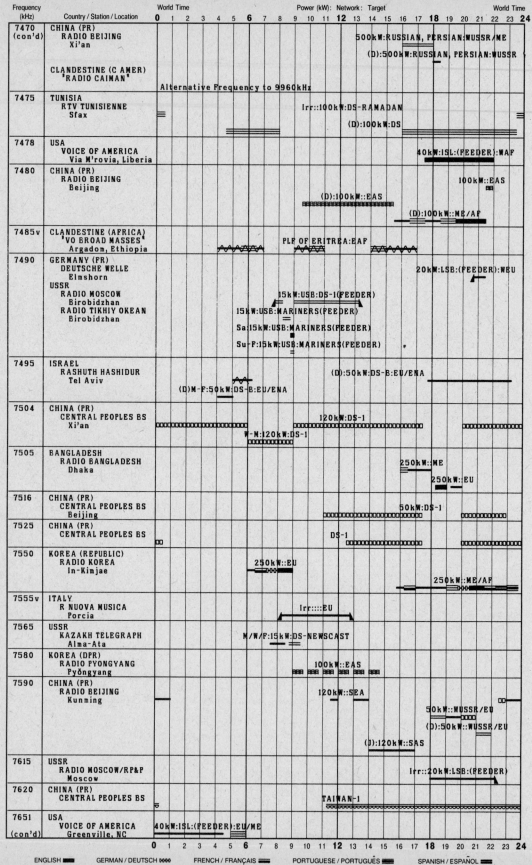

Frequency (kHz)	Country / Station / Location	World Time 0–24 — Power (kW): Network: Target
7470 (con'd)	CHINA (PR) RADIO BEIJING Xi'an	500kW:RUSSIAN, PERSIAN:WUSSR/ME (D):500kW:RUSSIAN, PERSIAN:WUSSR
	CLANDESTINE (C AMER) "RADIO CAIMAN"	Alternative Frequency to 9960kHz
7475	TUNISIA RTV TUNISIENNE Sfax	Irr::100kW:DS-RAMADAN (D):100kW:DS
7478	USA VOICE OF AMERICA Via M'rovia, Liberia	40kW:ISL:(FEEDER):WAF
7480	CHINA (PR) RADIO BEIJING Beijing	100kW::EAS (D):100kW::EAS (D):100kW::ME/AF
7485v	CLANDESTINE (AFRICA) "VO BROAD MASSES" Argadom, Ethiopia	PLF OF ERITREA:EAF
7490	GERMANY (FR) DEUTSCHE WELLE Elmshorn	20kW:LSB:(FEEDER):WEU
	USSR RADIO MOSCOW Birobidzhan	15kW:USB:DS-1(FEEDER)
	RADIO TIKHIY OKEAN Birobidzhan	15kW:USB:MARINERS(FEEDER) Sa:15kW:USB:MARINERS(FEEDER) Su-F:15kW:USB:MARINERS(FEEDER)
7495	ISRAEL RASHUTH HASHIDUR Tel Aviv	(D):50kW:DS-B:EU/ENA (D)M-F:50kW:DS-B:EU/ENA
7504	CHINA (PR) CENTRAL PEOPLES BS Xi'an	120kW:DS-1 W-M:120kW:DS-1
7505	BANGLADESH RADIO BANGLADESH Dhaka	250kW::ME 250kW::EU
7516	CHINA (PR) CENTRAL PEOPLES BS Beijing	50kW:DS-1
7525	CHINA (PR) CENTRAL PEOPLES BS	DS-1
7550	KOREA (REPUBLIC) RADIO KOREA In-Kimjae	250kW::EU 250kW::ME/AF
7555v	ITALY R NUOVA MUSICA Porcia	Irr::::EU
7565	USSR KAZAKH TELEGRAPH Alma-Ata	M/W/F:15kW:DS-NEWSCAST
7580	KOREA (DPR) RADIO PYONGYANG Pyŏngyang	100kW::EAS
7590	CHINA (PR) RADIO BEIJING Kunming	120kW::SEA 50kW::WUSSR/EU (D):50kW::WUSSR/EU (J):120kW::SAS
7615	USSR RADIO MOSCOW/RP&P Moscow	Irr::20kW:LSB:(FEEDER)
7620	CHINA (PR) CENTRAL PEOPLES BS	TAIWAN-1
7651 (con'd)	USA VOICE OF AMERICA Greenville, NC	40kW:ISL:(FEEDER):EU/ME

ENGLISH ▬ GERMAN / DEUTSCH ▭▭▭ FRENCH / FRANÇAIS ═ PORTUGUESE / PORTUGUÊS ▬ SPANISH / ESPAÑOL ▬
ARABIC / عربي ≡ RUSSIAN / РУССКИЙ ═ CHINESE / 中文 ▫▫▫ JAPANESE / 日本語 ▪▪▪ MULTILINGUAL ≈≈ OTHER —
SUMMER ONLY (J) WINTER ONLY (D) JAMMING /\/\ or / or \ EARLIEST HEARD ◢ LATEST HEARD ◣ + TENTATIVE

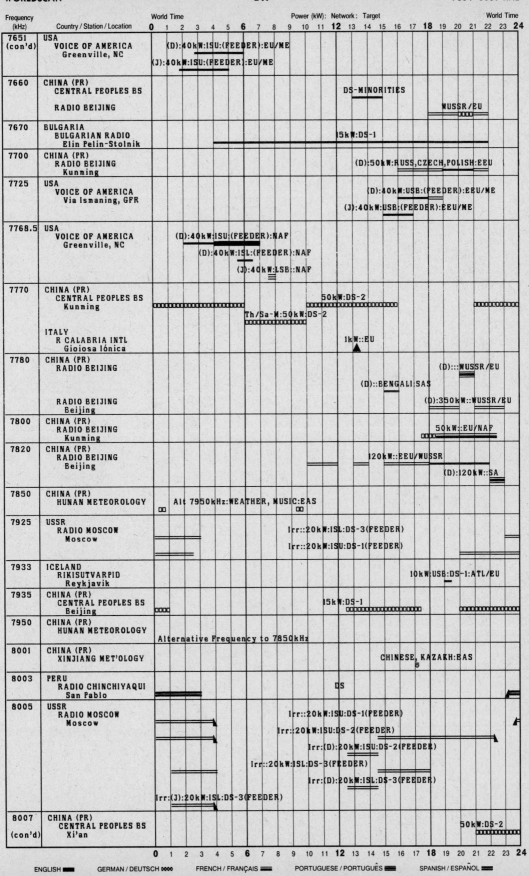

Frequency (kHz)	Country / Station / Location	World Time 0–24 / Power (kW): Network: Target
7651 (con'd)	USA VOICE OF AMERICA Greenville, NC	(D):40kW:ISU:(FEEDER):EU/ME / (J):40kW:ISU:(FEEDER):EU/ME
7660	CHINA (PR) CENTRAL PEOPLES BS / RADIO BEIJING	DS-MINORITIES / WUSSR/EU
7670	BULGARIA BULGARIAN RADIO Elin Pelin-Stolnik	15kW:DS-1
7700	CHINA (PR) RADIO BEIJING Kunming	(D):50kW:RUSS,CZECH,POLISH:EEU
7725	USA VOICE OF AMERICA Via Ismaning, GFR	(D):40kW:USB:(FEEDER):EEU/ME / (J):40kW:USB:(FEEDER):EEU/ME
7768.5	USA VOICE OF AMERICA Greenville, NC	(D):40kW:ISU:(FEEDER):NAF / (D):40kW:ISL:(FEEDER):NAF / (J):40kW:LSB::NAF
7770	CHINA (PR) CENTRAL PEOPLES BS Kunming	50kW:DS-2 / Th/Sa-M:50kW:DS-2
	ITALY R CALABRIA INTL Gioiosa Iónica	1kW::EU
7780	CHINA (PR) RADIO BEIJING / RADIO BEIJING Beijing	(D):::WUSSR/EU / (D)::BENGALI:SAS / (D):350kW::WUSSR/EU
7800	CHINA (PR) RADIO BEIJING Kunming	50kW::EU/NAF
7820	CHINA (PR) RADIO BEIJING Beijing	120kW::EEU/WUSSR / (D):120kW::SA
7850	CHINA (PR) HUNAN METEOROLOGY	Alt 7950kHz:WEATHER, MUSIC:EAS
7925	USSR RADIO MOSCOW Moscow	Irr::20kW:ISL:DS-3(FEEDER) / Irr::20kW:ISU:DS-1(FEEDER)
7933	ICELAND RIKISUTVARPID Reykjavik	10kW:USB:DS-1:ATL/EU
7935	CHINA (PR) CENTRAL PEOPLES BS Beijing	15kW:DS-1
7950	CHINA (PR) HUNAN METEOROLOGY	Alternative Frequency to 7850kHz
8001	CHINA (PR) XINJIANG MET'OLOGY	CHINESE, KAZAKH:EAS
8003	PERU RADIO CHINCHIYAQUI San Pablo	DS
8005	USSR RADIO MOSCOW Moscow	Irr::20kW:ISU:DS-1(FEEDER) / Irr::20kW:ISU:DS-2(FEEDER) / Irr:(D):20kW:ISU:DS-2(FEEDER) / Irr::20kW:ISL:DS-3(FEEDER) / Irr:(D):20kW:ISL:DS-3(FEEDER) / Irr:(J):20kW:ISL:DS-3(FEEDER)
8007 (con'd)	CHINA (PR) CENTRAL PEOPLES BS Xi'an	50kW:DS-2

ENGLISH ▬ GERMAN / DEUTSCH ◊◊◊◊ FRENCH / FRANÇAIS ▬ PORTUGUESE / PORTUGUÊS ▬ SPANISH / ESPAÑOL ▬

ARABIC / ربي ▬ RUSSIAN / РУССКИИ ▬ CHINESE / ✦✗ ◻◻◻◻ JAPANESE / 日本語 ▬ MULTILINGUAL ▭▭▭▭ OTHER ▬

SUMMER ONLY (J) WINTER ONLY (D) JAMMING ∧∧ or / or \ EARLIEST HEARD ◢ LATEST HEARD ◣ ✦ TENTATIVE

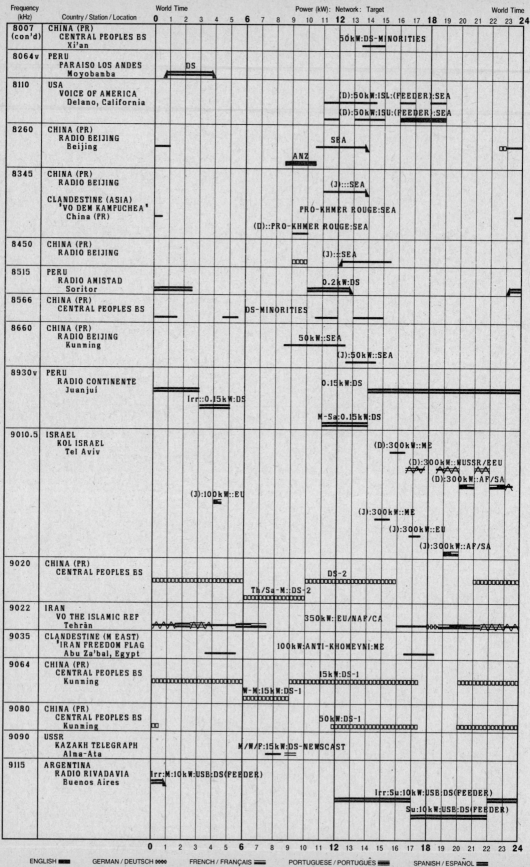

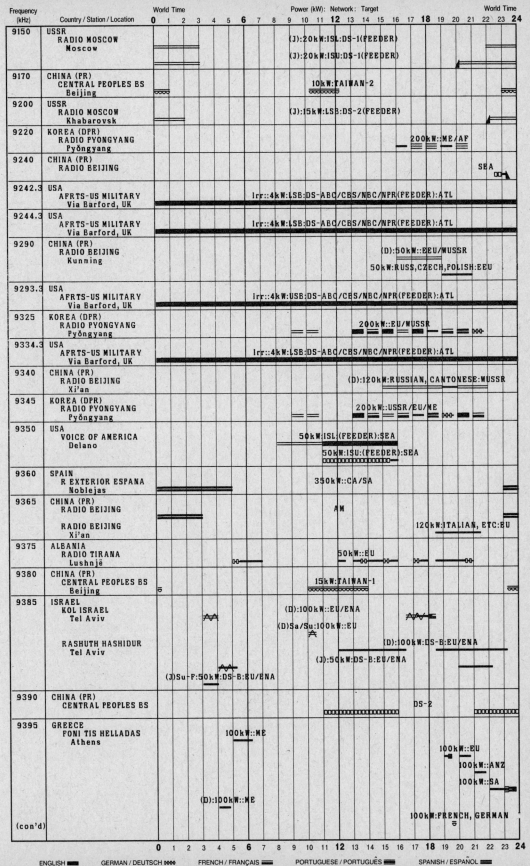

Frequency (kHz)	Country / Station / Location	Power (kW): Network : Target
9150	USSR RADIO MOSCOW Moscow	(J):20kW:ISL:DS-1(FEEDER) (J):20kW:ISU:DS-1(FEEDER)
9170	CHINA (PR) CENTRAL PEOPLES BS Beijing	10kW:TAIWAN-2
9200	USSR RADIO MOSCOW Khabarovsk	(J):15kW:LSB:DS-2(FEEDER)
9220	KOREA (DPR) RADIO PYONGYANG Pyŏngyang	200kW::ME/AF
9240	CHINA (PR) RADIO BEIJING	SEA
9242.3	USA AFRTS-US MILITARY Via Barford, UK	Irr::4kW:LSB:DS-ABC/CBS/NBC/NPR(FEEDER):ATL
9244.3	USA AFRTS-US MILITARY Via Barford, UK	Irr::4kW:LSB:DS-ABC/CBS/NBC/NPR(FEEDER):ATL
9290	CHINA (PR) RADIO BEIJING Kunming	(D):50kW::EEU/WUSSR 50kW:RUSS,CZECH,POLISH:EEU
9293.3	USA AFRTS-US MILITARY Via Barford, UK	Irr::4kW:USB:DS-ABC/CBS/NBC/NPR(FEEDER):ATL
9325	KOREA (DPR) RADIO PYONGYANG Pyŏngyang	200kW::EU/WUSSR
9334.3	USA AFRTS-US MILITARY Via Barford, UK	Irr::4kW:LSB:DS-ABC/CBS/NBC/NPR(FEEDER):ATL
9340	CHINA (PR) RADIO BEIJING Xi'an	(D):120kW:RUSSIAN, CANTONESE:WUSSR
9345	KOREA (DPR) RADIO PYONGYANG Pyŏngyang	200kW::USSR/EU/ME
9350	USA VOICE OF AMERICA Delano	50kW:ISL:(FEEDER):SEA 50kW:ISU:(FEEDER):SEA
9360	SPAIN R EXTERIOR ESPANA Noblejas	350kW::CA/SA
9365	CHINA (PR) RADIO BEIJING	AM
	RADIO BEIJING Xi'an	120kW:ITALIAN, ETC:EU
9375	ALBANIA RADIO TIRANA Lushnjë	50kW::EU
9380	CHINA (PR) CENTRAL PEOPLES BS Beijing	15kW:TAIWAN-1
9385	ISRAEL KOL ISRAEL Tel Aviv	(D):100kW::EU/ENA (D)Sa/Su:100kW::EU
	RASHUTH HASHIDUR Tel Aviv	(D):100kW:DS-B:EU/ENA (J):50kW:DS-B:EU/ENA (J)Su-F:50kW:DS-B:EU/ENA
9390	CHINA (PR) CENTRAL PEOPLES BS	DS-2
9395	GREECE FONI TIS HELLADAS Athens	100kW::ME 100kW::EU 100kW::ANZ 100kW::SA (D):100kW::ME 100kW:FRENCH, GERMAN
(con'd)		

World Time: 0 1 2 3 4 5 6 7 8 9 10 11 12 13 14 15 16 17 18 19 20 21 22 23 24

ENGLISH ▬ GERMAN / DEUTSCH ∞∞ FRENCH / FRANÇAIS ▬ PORTUGUESE / PORTUGUÊS ▬ SPANISH / ESPAÑOL ▬
ARABIC / ≡ RUSSIAN / РУССКИИ ▬ CHINESE / 中文 ▭▭ JAPANESE / 日本語 ▬ MULTILINGUAL ∞∞ OTHER ▬
SUMMER ONLY (J) WINTER ONLY (D) JAMMING /\/\ or / or \ EARLIEST HEARD ◢ LATEST HEARD ◣ + TENTATIVE

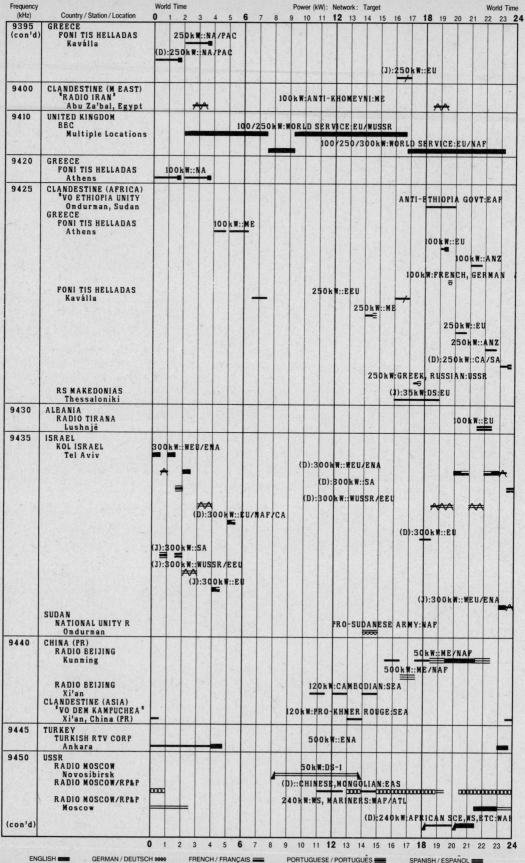

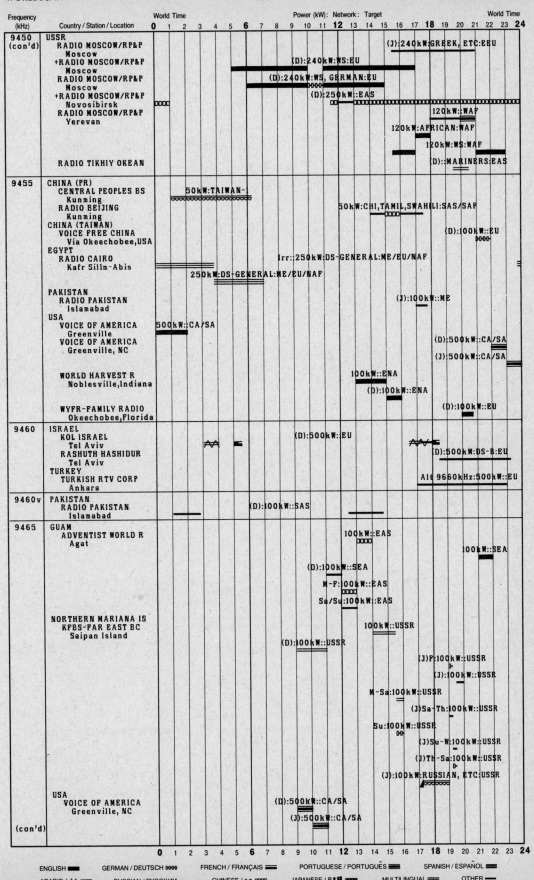

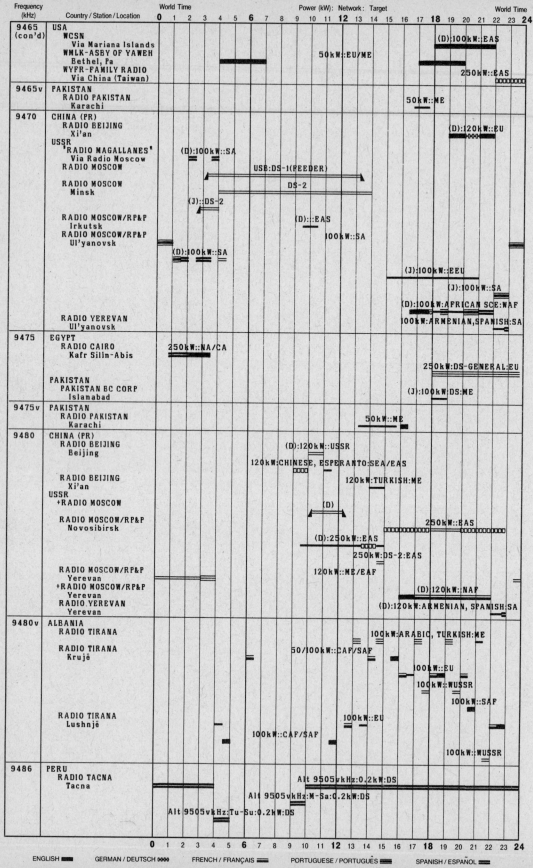

9465 (con'd) — USA

WCSN
Via Mariana Islands — (D):100kW::EAS
WMLK-ASBY OF YAWEH
Bethel, Pa — 50kW::EU/ME
WYFR-FAMILY RADIO
Via China (Taiwan) — 250kW::EAS

9465v — PAKISTAN

RADIO PAKISTAN
Karachi — 50kW::ME

9470 — CHINA (PR)

RADIO BEIJING
Xi'an — (D):120kW::EU
USSR
"RADIO MAGALLANES" — (D):100kW::SA
Via Radio Moscow
RADIO MOSCOW — USB:DS-1(FEEDER)

RADIO MOSCOW — DS-2
Minsk
— (J)::DS-2

RADIO MOSCOW/RP&P — (D)::EAS
Irkutsk
RADIO MOSCOW/RP&P — 100kW::SA
Ul'yanovsk

— (D):100kW::SA

— (J):100kW::EEU

— (J):100kW::SA

— (D):100kW:AFRICAN SCE:WAF

RADIO YEREVAN — 100kW::ARMENIAN,SPANISH:SA
Ul'yanovsk

9475 — EGYPT

RADIO CAIRO — 250kW::NA/CA
Kafr Silim-Abis

— 250kW:DS-GENERAL:EU

PAKISTAN
PAKISTAN BC CORP
Islamabad — (J):100kW:DS:ME

9475v — PAKISTAN

RADIO PAKISTAN
Karachi — 50kW::ME

9480 — CHINA (PR)

RADIO BEIJING
Beijing — (D):120kW::USSR

— 120kW:CHINESE, ESPERANTO:SEA/EAS

RADIO BEIJING
Xi'an — 120kW:TURKISH:ME
USSR
+RADIO MOSCOW

RADIO MOSCOW/RP&P — (D)
Novosibirsk — 250kW::EAS

— (D):250kW::EAS

— 250kW:DS-2:EAS

RADIO MOSCOW/RP&P — 120kW::ME/EAF
Yerevan
+RADIO MOSCOW/RP&P — (D) 120kW::NAF
Yerevan
RADIO YEREVAN — (D):120kW:ARMENIAN, SPANISH:SA
Yerevan

9480v — ALBANIA

RADIO TIRANA — 100kW:ARABIC, TURKISH:ME

RADIO TIRANA — 50/100kW::CAF/SAF
Krujë
— 100kW::EU

— 100kW::WUSSR

— 100kW::SAF

RADIO TIRANA — 100kW::EU
Lushnjë
— 100kW::CAF/SAF

— 100kW::WUSSR

9486 — PERU

RADIO TACNA — Alt 9505vkHz:0.2kW:DS
Tacna

Alt 9505vkHz:M-Sa:0.2kW:DS

Alt 9505vkHz:Tu-Su:0.2kW:DS

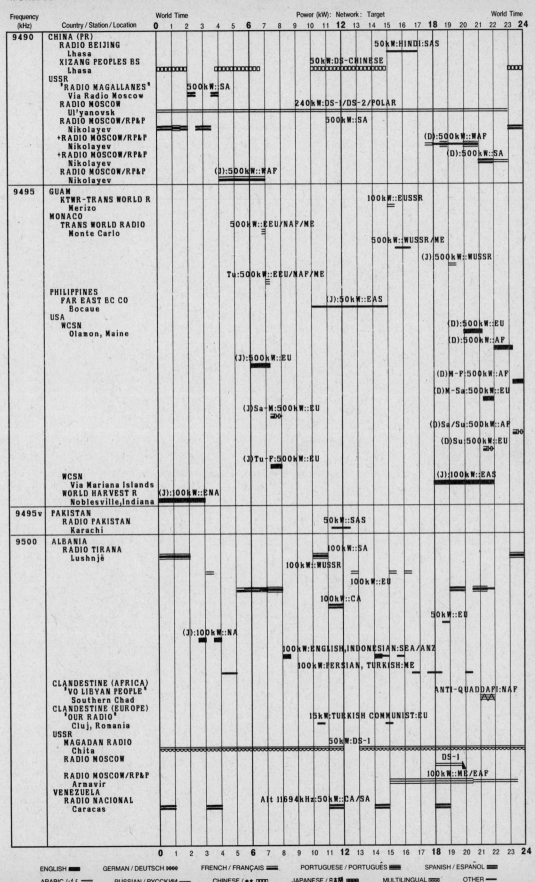

9490 CHINA (PR)
RADIO BEIJING — Lhasa — 50kW:HINDI:SAS
XIZANG PEOPLES BS — Lhasa — 50kW:DS-CHINESE
USSR
'RADIO MAGALLANES' — Via Radio Moscow — 500kW::SA
RADIO MOSCOW — Ul'yanovsk — 240kW:DS-1/DS-2/POLAR
RADIO MOSCOW/RP&P — Nikolayev — 500kW::SA
+RADIO MOSCOW/RP&P — Nikolayev — (D):500kW::WAF
+RADIO MOSCOW/RP&P — Nikolayev — (D):500kW::SA
RADIO MOSCOW/RP&P — Nikolayev — (J):500kW::WAF

9495 GUAM
KTWR-TRANS WORLD R — Merizo — 100kW::EUSSR
MONACO
TRANS WORLD RADIO — Monte Carlo — 500kW::EEU/NAF/ME
500kW::WUSSR/ME
(J):500kW::WUSSR
Tu:500kW::EEU/NAF/ME
PHILIPPINES
FAR EAST BC CO — Bocaue — (J):50kW::EAS
USA
WCSN — Olamon, Maine — (D):500kW::EU
(D):500kW::AF
(J):500kW::EU
(D)M-F:500kW:AF
(D)M-Sa:500kW::EU
(J)Sa-M:500kW::EU
(D)Sa/Su:500kW::AF
(D)Su:500kW::EU
(J)Tu-F:500kW::EU
WCSN — Via Mariana Islands — (J):100kW::EAS
WORLD HARVEST R — Noblesville,Indiana — (J):100kW::ENA

9495v PAKISTAN
RADIO PAKISTAN — Karachi — 50kW::SAS

9500 ALBANIA
RADIO TIRANA — Lushnjë — 100kW::SA
100kW::WUSSR
100kW::EU
100kW::CA
50kW::EU
(J):100kW::NA
100kW:ENGLISH,INDONESIAN:SEA/ANZ
100kW:PERSIAN, TURKISH:ME
CLANDESTINE (AFRICA)
'VO LIBYAN PEOPLE' — Southern Chad — ANTI-QUADDAFI:NAF
CLANDESTINE (EUROPE)
'OUR RADIO' — Cluj, Romania — 15kW:TURKISH COMMUNIST:EU
USSR
MAGADAN RADIO — Chita — 50kW:DS-1
RADIO MOSCOW — DS-1
RADIO MOSCOW/RP&P — Armavir — 100kW::ME/EAF
VENEZUELA
RADIO NACIONAL — Caracas — Alt 11694kHz:50kW::CA/SA

ENGLISH ▰▰▰   GERMAN / DEUTSCH ▨▨▨▨   FRENCH / FRANÇAIS ▬▬   PORTUGUESE / PORTUGUÊS ▰▰▰   SPANISH / ESPAÑOL ▬▬

ARABIC /ﻉﻱﺏ ▦▦   RUSSIAN / РУССКИИ ▬▬   CHINESE / ✶✹ ▨▨▨   JAPANESE / 日本語 ▰▰▰   MULTILINGUAL ▨▨▨   OTHER ▬▬

SUMMER ONLY (J)   WINTER ONLY (D)   JAMMING ∧∧ or / or \   EARLIEST HEARD ◢   LATEST HEARD ◣   ✦ TENTATIVE

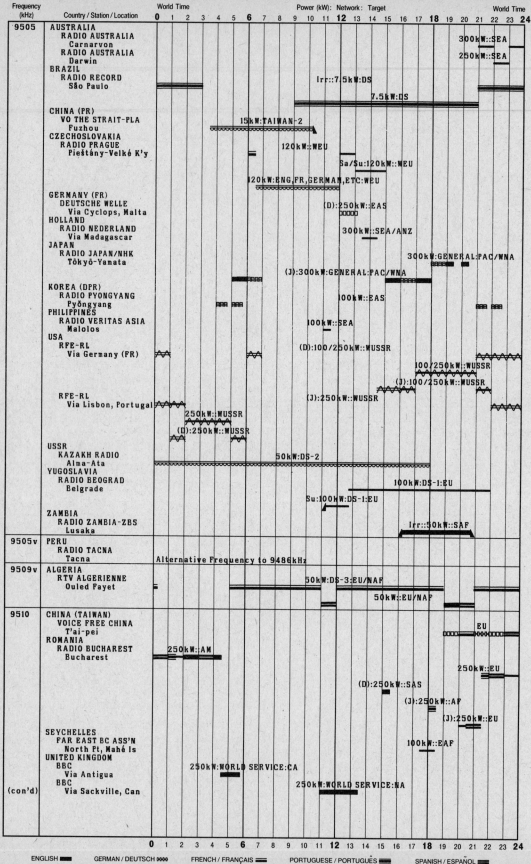

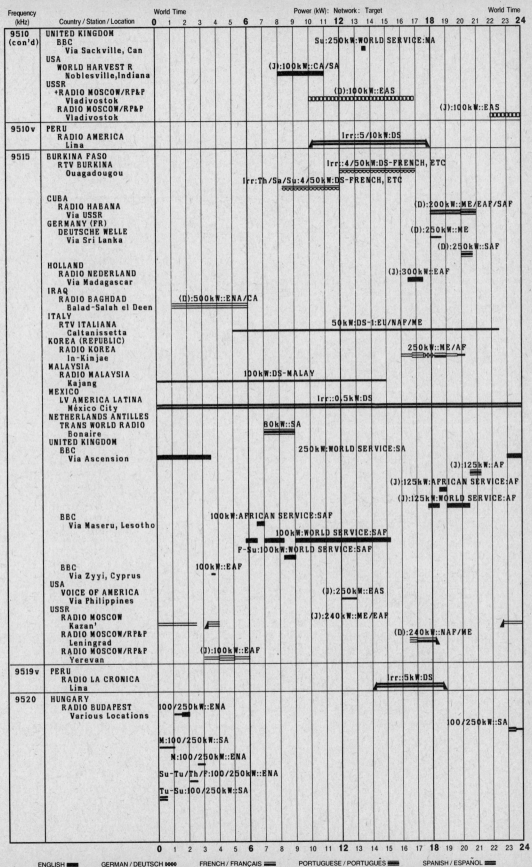

| Frequency (kHz) | Country / Station / Location | | World Time | Power (kW): Network: Target | World Time |

Frequency (kHz)	Country / Station / Location	Schedule
9510 (con'd)	UNITED KINGDOM	
	BBC	Su:250kW:WORLD SERVICE:NA (12-15)
	Via Sackville, Can	
	USA	
	WORLD HARVEST R	(J):100kW::CA/SA (8-11)
	Noblesville, Indiana	
	USSR	
	+RADIO MOSCOW/RP&P	(D):100kW::EAS (11-18)
	Vladivostok	
	RADIO MOSCOW/RP&P	(J):100kW::EAS (22-24)
	Vladivostok	
9510v	PERU	
	RADIO AMERICA	Irr::5/10kW:DS (11-18)
	Lima	
9515	BURKINA FASO	
	RTV BURKINA	Irr::4/50kW:DS-FRENCH, ETC (11-18)
	Ouagadougou	Irr:Th/Sa/Su:4/50kW:DS-FRENCH, ETC (6-11)
	CUBA	
	RADIO HABANA	(D):200kW::ME/EAF/SAF (17-22)
	Via USSR	
	GERMANY (FR)	
	DEUTSCHE WELLE	(D):250kW::ME (16-18)
	Via Sri Lanka	(D):250kW::SAF (17-18)
	HOLLAND	
	RADIO NEDERLAND	(J):300kW::EAF (15-17)
	Via Madagascar	
	IRAQ	
	RADIO BAGHDAD	(D):500kW::ENA/CA (1-7)
	Balad-Salah el Deen	
	ITALY	
	RTV ITALIANA	50kW:DS-1:EU/NAF/ME (6-24)
	Caltanissetta	
	KOREA (REPUBLIC)	
	RADIO KOREA	250kW::ME/AF (16-18)
	In-Kimjae	
	MALAYSIA	
	RADIO MALAYSIA	100kW:DS-MALAY (0-11)
	Kajang	
	MEXICO	
	LV AMERICA LATINA	Irr::0.5kW:DS (0-24)
	México City	
	NETHERLANDS ANTILLES	
	TRANS WORLD RADIO	80kW::SA (7-8)
	Bonaire	
	UNITED KINGDOM	
	BBC	250kW:WORLD SERVICE:SA (0-4)
	Via Ascension	(J):125kW::AF (19-21)
		(J):125kW:AFRICAN SERVICE:AF (18-22)
		(J):125kW:WORLD SERVICE:AF (19-22)
	BBC	100kW:AFRICAN SERVICE:SAF (5-8)
	Via Maseru, Lesotho	100kW:WORLD SERVICE:SAF (8-14)
		F-Su:100kW:WORLD SERVICE:SAF (6-8)
	BBC	100kW::EAF (4-5)
	Via Zyyi, Cyprus	
	USA	
	VOICE OF AMERICA	(J):250kW::EAS (12-14)
	Via Philippines	
	USSR	
	RADIO MOSCOW	(J):240kW::ME/EAF (12-15)
	Kazan'	
	RADIO MOSCOW/RP&P	(D):240kW::NAF/ME (18-20)
	Leningrad	
	RADIO MOSCOW/RP&P	(J):100kW::EAF (4-18)
	Yerevan	
9519v	PERU	
	RADIO LA CRONICA	Irr::5kW:DS (15-18)
	Lima	
9520	HUNGARY	
	RADIO BUDAPEST	100/250kW::ENA (0-2)
	Various Locations	100/250kW::SA (20-23)
		M:100/250kW::SA (0-1)
		M:100/250kW::ENA (1-2)
		Su-Tu/Th/F:100/250kW::ENA (1-2)
		Tu-Su:100/250kW::SA (0-1)

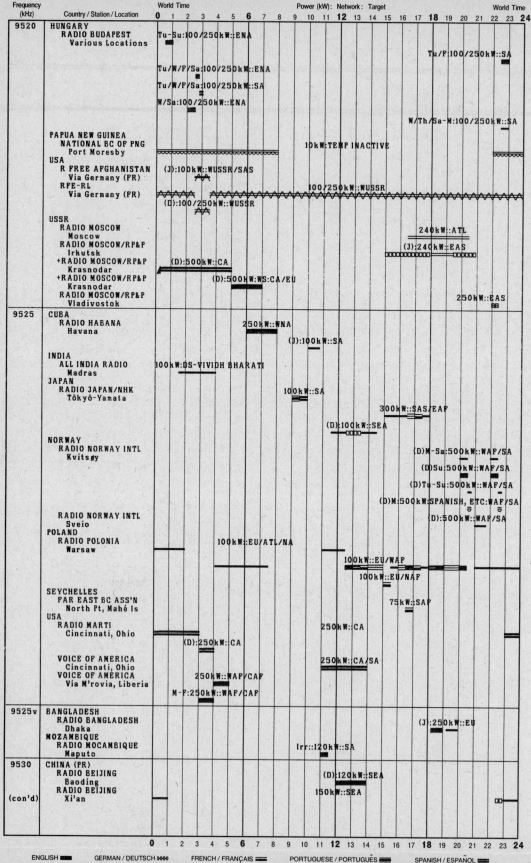

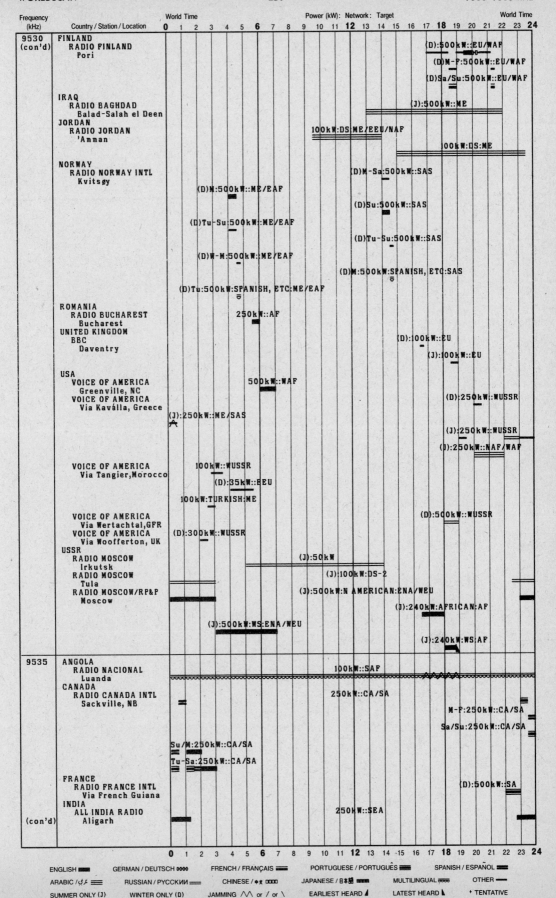

Frequency (kHz)	Country / Station / Location	Schedule
9530 (con'd)	FINLAND RADIO FINLAND Pori	(D):500kW::EU/WAF (D)M-F:500kW::EU/WAF (D)Sa/Su:500kW::EU/WAF
	IRAQ RADIO BAGHDAD Balad-Salah el Deen	(J):500kW::ME
	JORDAN RADIO JORDAN 'Amman	100kW:DS:ME/EEU/NAF 100kW:DS:ME
	NORWAY RADIO NORWAY INTL Kvitsøy	(D)M-Sa:500kW::SAS (D)M:500kW::ME/EAF (D)Su:500kW::SAS (D)Tu-Su:500kW::ME/EAF (D)Tu-Su:500kW::SAS (D)W-M:500kW::ME/EAF (D)M:500kW:SPANISH,ETC:SAS (D)Tu:500kW:SPANISH,ETC:ME/EAF
	ROMANIA RADIO BUCHAREST Bucharest	250kW::AF
	UNITED KINGDOM BBC Daventry	(D):100kW::EU (J):100kW::EU
	USA VOICE OF AMERICA Greenville, NC	500kW::WAF
	VOICE OF AMERICA Via Kaválla, Greece	(J):250kW::ME/SAS (D):250kW::WUSSR (J):250kW::WUSSR (J):250kW::NAF/WAF
	VOICE OF AMERICA Via Tangier, Morocco	100kW::WUSSR (D):35kW::EEU 100kW:TURKISH:ME
	VOICE OF AMERICA Via Wertachtal, GFR	(D):500kW::WUSSR
	VOICE OF AMERICA Via Woofferton, UK	(D):300kW::WUSSR
	USSR RADIO MOSCOW Irkutsk	(J):50kW
	RADIO MOSCOW Tula	(J):100kW:DS-2
	RADIO MOSCOW/RP&P Moscow	(J):500kW:N AMERICAN:ENA/WEU (J):240kW:AFRICAN:AF (J):500kW:WS:ENA/WEU (J):240kW:WS:AF
9535	ANGOLA RADIO NACIONAL Luanda	100kW::SAF
	CANADA RADIO CANADA INTL Sackville, NB	250kW::CA/SA M-F:250kW::CA/SA Sa/Su:250kW::CA/SA Su/M:250kW::CA/SA Tu-Sa:250kW::CA/SA
	FRANCE RADIO FRANCE INTL Via French Guiana	(D):500kW::SA
(con'd)	INDIA ALL INDIA RADIO Aligarh	250kW::SEA

ENGLISH ▰▰▰ GERMAN / DEUTSCH ◊◊◊◊ FRENCH / FRANÇAIS ▭▭▭ PORTUGUESE / PORTUGUÊS ▰▰▰ SPANISH / ESPAÑOL ▰▰▰

ARABIC / جربى ▰▰ RUSSIAN / PУССКИИ ▭▭▭ CHINESE / ✦✗ ◻◻◻◻ JAPANESE / 日本語 ▰▰▰ MULTILINGUAL ▭▭▭ OTHER ▬▬

SUMMER ONLY (J) WINTER ONLY (D) JAMMING ∧∧ or / or \ EARLIEST HEARD ◢ LATEST HEARD ◣ ✦ TENTATIVE

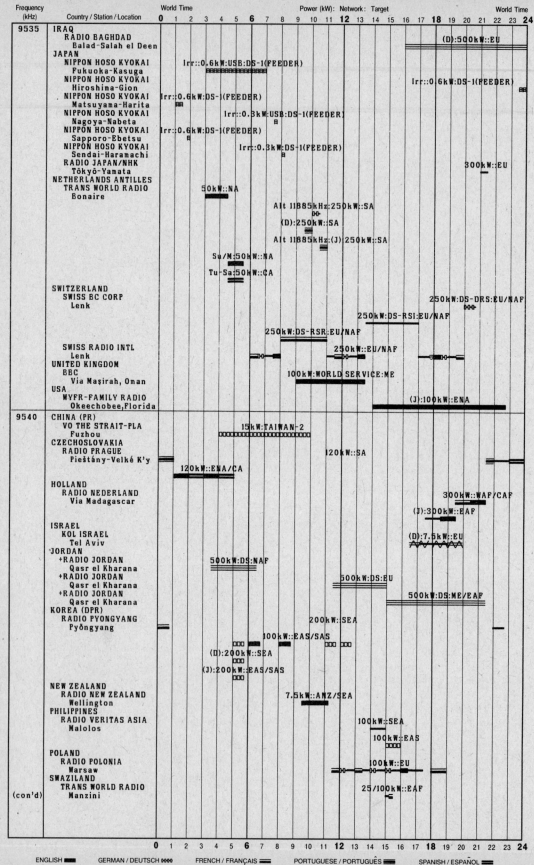

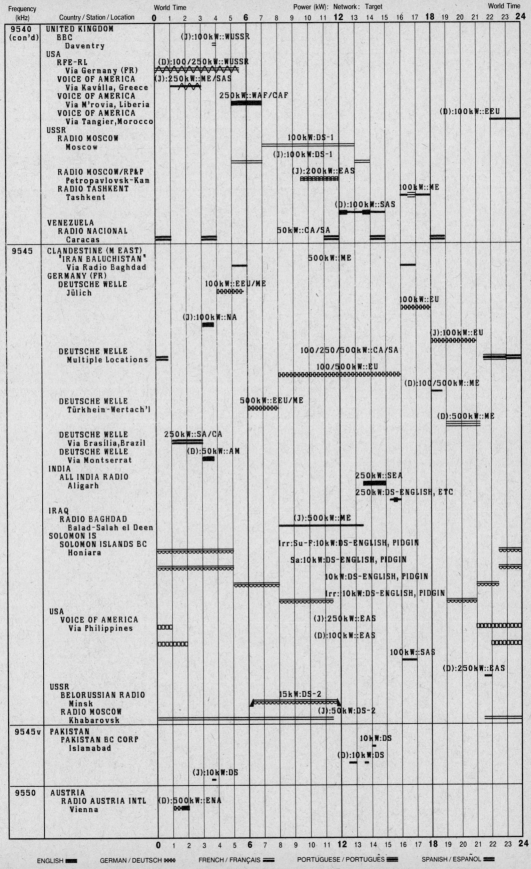

Frequency (kHz)	Country / Station / Location	World Time / Power (kW): Network: Target
9540 (con'd)	**UNITED KINGDOM** BBC, Daventry	(J):100kW::WUSSR
	USA RFE-RL, Via Germany (FR)	(D):100/250kW::WUSSR
	VOICE OF AMERICA, Via Kavälla, Greece	(J):250kW::ME/SAS
	VOICE OF AMERICA, Via M'rovia, Liberia	250kW::WAF/CAF
	VOICE OF AMERICA, Via Tangier, Morocco	(D):100kW::EEU
	USSR RADIO MOSCOW, Moscow	100kW:DS-1 / (J):100kW:DS-1
	RADIO MOSCOW/RP&P, Petropavlovsk-Kam	(J):200kW::EAS
	RADIO TASHKENT, Tashkent	100kW::ME / (D):100kW::SAS
	VENEZUELA RADIO NACIONAL, Caracas	50kW::CA/SA
9545	**CLANDESTINE (M EAST)** "IRAN BALUCHISTAN" Via Radio Baghdad	500kW:ME
	GERMANY (FR) DEUTSCHE WELLE, Jülich	100kW::EEU/ME / 100kW::EU / (J):100kW::EU / (J):100kW::NA
	DEUTSCHE WELLE, Multiple Locations	100/250/500kW::CA/SA / 100/500kW::EU / (D):100/500kW::ME
	DEUTSCHE WELLE, Türkheim-Wertach'l	500kW::EEU/ME / (D):500kW::ME
	DEUTSCHE WELLE, Via Brasília, Brazil	250kW::SA/CA
	DEUTSCHE WELLE, Via Montserrat	(D):50kW::AM
	INDIA ALL INDIA RADIO, Aligarh	250kW::SEA / 250kW:DS-ENGLISH, ETC
	IRAQ RADIO BAGHDAD, Balad-Salah el Deen	(J):500kW::ME
	SOLOMON IS SOLOMON ISLANDS BC, Honiara	Irr:Su-F:10kW:DS-ENGLISH, PIDGIN / Sa:10kW:DS-ENGLISH, PIDGIN / 10kW:DS-ENGLISH, PIDGIN / Irr:10kW:DS-ENGLISH, PIDGIN
	USA VOICE OF AMERICA, Via Philippines	(J):250kW::EAS / (D):100kW::EAS / 100kW::SAS / (D):250kW::EAS
	USSR BELORUSSIAN RADIO, Minsk	15kW:DS-2
	RADIO MOSCOW, Khabarovsk	(J):50kW:DS-2
9545v	**PAKISTAN** PAKISTAN BC CORP, Islamabad	10kW:DS / (D):10kW:DS / (J):10kW:DS
9550	**AUSTRIA** RADIO AUSTRIA INTL, Vienna	(D):500kW::ENA

World Time scale: 0 1 2 3 4 5 6 7 8 9 10 11 12 13 14 15 16 17 18 19 20 21 22 23 24

ENGLISH ▬▬ GERMAN / DEUTSCH ◊◊◊◊ FRENCH / FRANÇAIS ═══ PORTUGUESE / PORTUGUÊS ▬▬ SPANISH / ESPAÑOL ▬▬

ARABIC / ﻉﺭﺏ ═══ RUSSIAN / РУССКИЙ ═══ CHINESE / ✶✶ ◻◻◻◻ JAPANESE / 日本語 ▬▬ MULTILINGUAL ◷◷◷◷ OTHER ▬▬

SUMMER ONLY (J)   WINTER ONLY (D)   JAMMING ∧∧ or / or \   EARLIEST HEARD ◢   LATEST HEARD ◣   + TENTATIVE

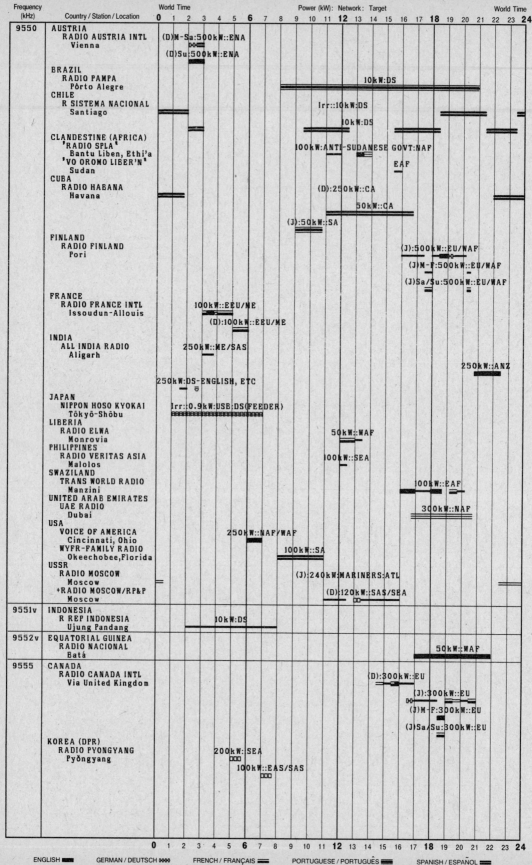

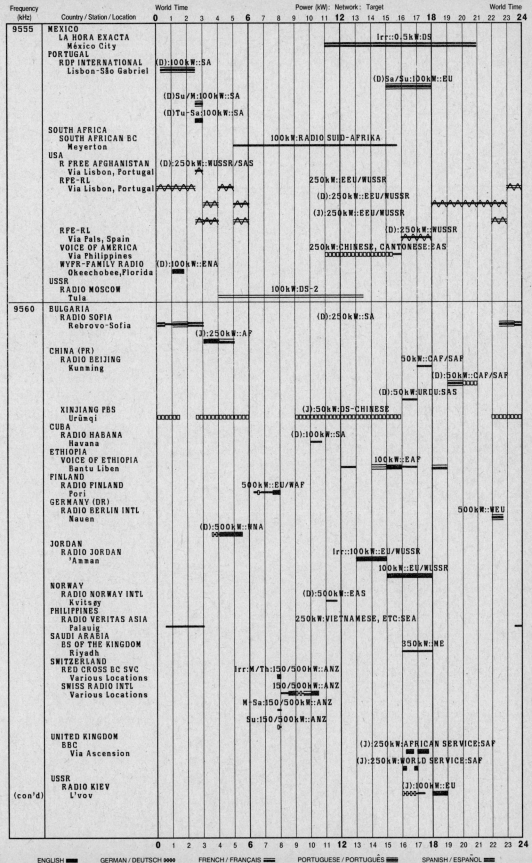

Frequency (kHz)	Country / Station / Location	Schedule
9555	**MEXICO**	
	LA HORA EXACTA	Irr::0.5kW:DS
	México City	
	PORTUGAL	
	RDP INTERNATIONAL	(D):100kW::SA
	Lisbon-São Gabriel	(D)Sa/Su:100kW::EU
		(D)Su/M:100kW::SA
		(D)Tu-Sa:100kW::SA
	SOUTH AFRICA	
	SOUTH AFRICAN BC	100kW:RADIO SUID-AFRIKA
	Meyerton	
	USA	
	R FREE AFGHANISTAN	(D):250kW::WUSSR/SAS
	Via Lisbon, Portugal	
	RFE-RL	250kW::EEU/WUSSR
	Via Lisbon, Portugal	(D):250kW::EEU/WUSSR
		(J):250kW::EEU/WUSSR
	RFE-RL	(D):250kW::WUSSR
	Via Pals, Spain	
	VOICE OF AMERICA	250kW:CHINESE, CANTONESE:EAS
	Via Philippines	
	WYFR-FAMILY RADIO	(D):100kW::ENA
	Okeechobee, Florida	
	USSR	
	RADIO MOSCOW	100kW:DS-2
	Tula	
9560	**BULGARIA**	
	RADIO SOFIA	(D):250kW::SA
	Rebrovo-Sofia	(J):250kW::AF
	CHINA (PR)	
	RADIO BEIJING	50kW::CAF/SAF
	Kunming	(D):50kW::CAF/SAF
		(D):50kW:URDU:SAS
	XINJIANG PBS	(J):50kW:DS-CHINESE
	Urümqi	
	CUBA	
	RADIO HABANA	(D):100kW::SA
	Havana	
	ETHIOPIA	
	VOICE OF ETHIOPIA	100kW::EAF
	Bantu Liben	
	FINLAND	
	RADIO FINLAND	500kW::EU/WAF
	Pori	
	GERMANY (DR)	
	RADIO BERLIN INTL	500kW::WEU
	Nauen	(D):500kW::WNA
	JORDAN	
	RADIO JORDAN	Irr::100kW::EU/WUSSR
	'Amman	100kW::EU/WUSSR
	NORWAY	
	RADIO NORWAY INTL	(D):500kW::EAS
	Kvitsøy	
	PHILIPPINES	
	RADIO VERITAS ASIA	250kW:VIETNAMESE, ETC:SEA
	Palauig	
	SAUDI ARABIA	
	BS OF THE KINGDOM	350kW::ME
	Riyadh	
	SWITZERLAND	
	RED CROSS BC SVC	Irr:M/Th:150/500kW::ANZ
	Various Locations	
	SWISS RADIO INTL	150/500kW::ANZ
	Various Locations	M-Sa:150/500kW::ANZ
		Su:150/500kW::ANZ
	UNITED KINGDOM	
	BBC	(J):250kW:AFRICAN SERVICE:SAF
	Via Ascension	(J):250kW:WORLD SERVICE:SAF
	USSR	
	RADIO KIEV	(J):100kW::EU
(con'd)	L'vov	

Frequency (kHz)   Country / Station / Location   World Time   Power (kW): Network: Target   World Time

0 1 2 3 4 5 6 7 8 9 10 11 12 13 14 15 16 17 18 19 20 21 22 23 24

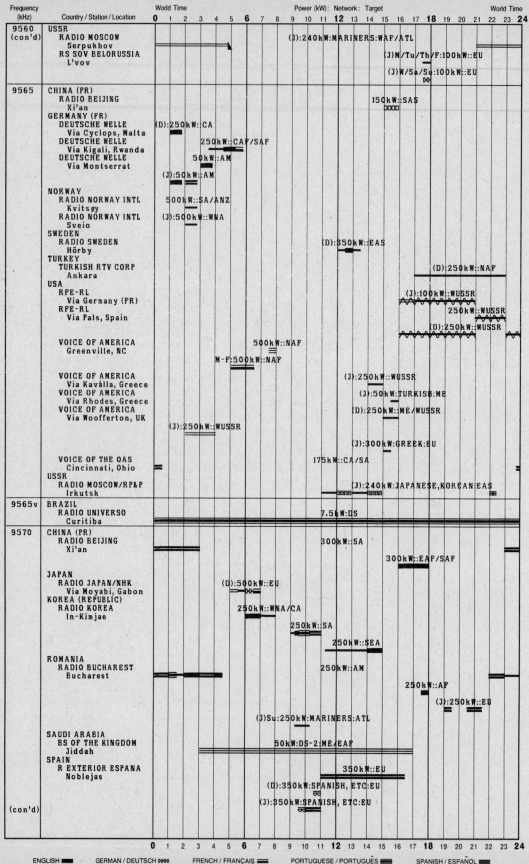

Frequency (kHz)	Country / Station / Location	Schedule (World Time) — Power (kW): Network: Target
9560 (con'd)	**USSR**	
	RADIO MOSCOW — Serpukhov	(J):240kW:MARINERS:WAF/ATL
	RS SOV BELORUSSIA — L'vov	(J)M/Tu/Th/F:100kW::EU
		(J)W/Sa/Su:100kW::EU
9565	**CHINA (PR)**	
	RADIO BEIJING — Xi'an	150kW::SAS
	GERMANY (FR)	
	DEUTSCHE WELLE — Via Cyclops, Malta	(D):250kW::CA
	DEUTSCHE WELLE — Via Kigali, Rwanda	250kW::CAF/SAF
	DEUTSCHE WELLE — Via Montserrat	50kW:AM
		(J):50kW::AM
	NORWAY	
	RADIO NORWAY INTL — Kvitsøy	500kW::SA/ANZ
	RADIO NORWAY INTL — Sveio	(J):500kW::WNA
	SWEDEN	
	RADIO SWEDEN — Hörby	(D):350kW::EAS
	TURKEY	
	TURKISH RTV CORP — Ankara	(D):250kW::NAF
	USA	
	RFE-RL — Via Germany (FR)	(J):100kW::WUSSR
	RFE-RL — Via Pals, Spain	250kW::WUSSR
		(D):250kW::WUSSR
	VOICE OF AMERICA — Greenville, NC	500kW::NAF
		M-F:500kW::NAF
	VOICE OF AMERICA — Via Kaválla, Greece	(J):250kW::WUSSR
	VOICE OF AMERICA — Via Rhodes, Greece	(J):50kW:TURKISH:ME
	VOICE OF AMERICA — Via Woofferton, UK	(D):250kW::ME/WUSSR
		(J):250kW::WUSSR
		(J):300kW:GREEK:EU
	VOICE OF THE OAS — Cincinnati, Ohio	175kW::CA/SA
	USSR	
	RADIO MOSCOW/RP&P — Irkutsk	(J):240kW:JAPANESE,KOREAN:EAS
9565v	**BRAZIL**	
	RADIO UNIVERSO — Curitiba	7.5kW:DS
9570	**CHINA (PR)**	
	RADIO BEIJING — Xi'an	300kW::SA
		300kW::EAF/SAF
	JAPAN	
	RADIO JAPAN/NHK — Via Moyabi, Gabon	(D):500kW::EU
	KOREA (REPUBLIC)	
	RADIO KOREA — In-Kimjae	250kW::WNA/CA
		250kW::SA
		250kW::SEA
	ROMANIA	
	RADIO BUCHAREST — Bucharest	250kW::AM
		250kW::AF
		(J):250kW::EU
		(J)Su:250kW:MARINERS:ATL
	SAUDI ARABIA	
	BS OF THE KINGDOM — Jiddah	50kW:DS-2:ME/EAF
	SPAIN	
	R EXTERIOR ESPANA — Noblejas	350kW::EU
		(D):350kW:SPANISH, ETC:EU
(con'd)		(J):350kW:SPANISH, ETC:EU

Legend:

ENGLISH ▬▬   GERMAN / DEUTSCH ◊◊◊◊   FRENCH / FRANÇAIS ▬▬   PORTUGUESE / PORTUGUÊS ▬▬   SPANISH / ESPAÑOL ▬▬

ARABIC / ﻋﺮﺑﻲ ▭▭   RUSSIAN / РУССКИИ ▬▬   CHINESE / ★★ □□□□   JAPANESE / 日本語 ▬▬   MULTILINGUAL ▭▭▭▭   OTHER ▬▬

SUMMER ONLY (J)   WINTER ONLY (D)   JAMMING ∧∧ or / or \   EARLIEST HEARD ◢   LATEST HEARD ◣   + TENTATIVE

Frequency (kHz) — Country / Station / Location — Power (kW): Network: Target — World Time

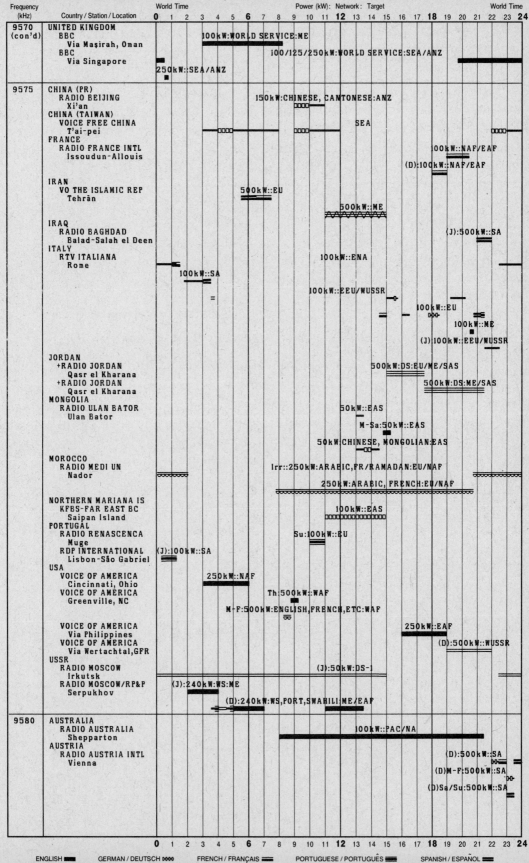

Freq	Country / Station / Location	Schedule
9570 (con'd)	UNITED KINGDOM — BBC — Via Maşirah, Oman	100kW:WORLD SERVICE:ME
	BBC — Via Singapore	100/125/250kW:WORLD SERVICE:SEA/ANZ
		250kW::SEA/ANZ
9575	CHINA (PR) — RADIO BEIJING — Xi'an	150kW:CHINESE, CANTONESE:ANZ
	CHINA (TAIWAN) — VOICE FREE CHINA — T'ai-pei	SEA
	FRANCE — RADIO FRANCE INTL — Issoudun-Allouis	100kW::NAF/EAF / (D)100kW::NAF/EAF
	IRAN — VO THE ISLAMIC REP — Tehrān	500kW::EU / 500kW::ME
	IRAQ — RADIO BAGHDAD — Balad-Salah el Deen	(J):500kW::SA
	ITALY — RTV ITALIANA — Rome	100kW::ENA / 100kW::SA / 100kW::EEU/WUSSR / 100kW::EU / 100kW::ME / (J)100kW::EEU/WUSSR
	JORDAN — +RADIO JORDAN — Qasr el Kharana	500kW:DS:EU/ME/SAS
	+RADIO JORDAN — Qasr el Kharana	500kW:DS:ME/SAS
	MONGOLIA — RADIO ULAN BATOR — Ulan Bator	50kW::EAS / M-Sa:50kW::EAS / 50kW:CHINESE, MONGOLIAN:EAS
	MOROCCO — RADIO MEDI UN — Nador	Irr::250kW:ARABIC,FR/RAMADAN:EU/NAF / 250kW:ARABIC, FRENCH:EU/NAF
	NORTHERN MARIANA IS — KFBS-FAR EAST BC — Saipan Island	100kW::EAS
	PORTUGAL — RADIO RENASCENCA — Muge	Su:100kW::EU
	RDP INTERNATIONAL — Lisbon-São Gabriel	(J):100kW::SA
	USA — VOICE OF AMERICA — Cincinnati, Ohio	250kW::NAF
	VOICE OF AMERICA — Greenville, NC	Th:500kW::WAF / M-F:500kW:ENGLISH,FRENCH,ETC:WAF
	VOICE OF AMERICA — Via Philippines	250kW::EAF
	VOICE OF AMERICA — Via Wertachtal,GFR	(D):500kW::WUSSR
	USSR — RADIO MOSCOW — Irkutsk	(J):50kW:DS-1
	RADIO MOSCOW/RP&P — Serpukhov	(J):240kW:WS:ME / (D):240kW:WS,PORT,SWAHILI:ME/EAF
9580	AUSTRALIA — RADIO AUSTRALIA — Shepparton	100kW::PAC/NA
	AUSTRIA — RADIO AUSTRIA INTL — Vienna	(D):500kW::SA / (D)M-F:500kW::SA / (D)Sa/Su:500kW::SA

ENGLISH ▰▰▰   GERMAN / DEUTSCH ◊◊◊◊   FRENCH / FRANÇAIS ▰▰   PORTUGUESE / PORTUGUÊS ▰▰   SPANISH / ESPAÑOL ▰▰

ARABIC /ﻋﺮﺑﻲ ▰▰   RUSSIAN / РУССКИЙ ▰▰   CHINESE / ◆✕ ◊◊◊◊   JAPANESE / 日本語 ▰▰   MULTILINGUAL ◊◊◊◊   OTHER ▬

SUMMER ONLY (J)   WINTER ONLY (D)   JAMMING ∧∧ or / or \   EARLIEST HEARD ◢   LATEST HEARD ◣   ✦ TENTATIVE

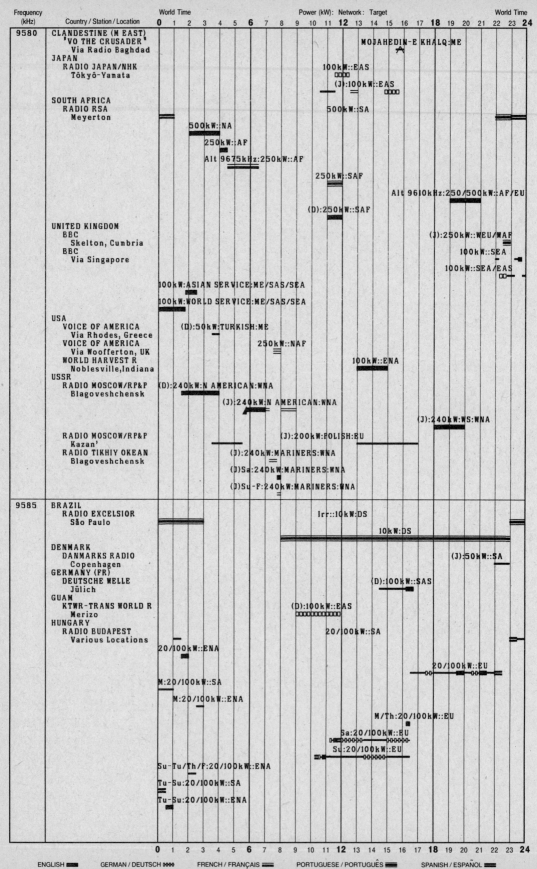

Frequency (kHz)	Country / Station / Location	World Time / Power (kW) : Network : Target
9580	CLANDESTINE (M EAST)	
	'VO THE CRUSADER'	MOJAHEDIN-E KHALQ:ME
	Via Radio Baghdad	
	JAPAN	
	RADIO JAPAN/NHK	100kW::EAS
	Tôkyô-Yamata	(J):100kW::EAS
	SOUTH AFRICA	
	RADIO RSA	500kW::SA
	Meyerton	500kW::NA
		250kW::AF
		Alt 9675kHz:250kW::AF
		250kW::SAF
		Alt 9610kHz:250/500kW::AF/EU
		(D):250kW::SAF
	UNITED KINGDOM	
	BBC	(J):250kW::WEU/WAF
	Skelton, Cumbria	
	BBC	100kW::SEA
	Via Singapore	100kW::SEA/EAS
		100kW:ASIAN SERVICE:ME/SAS/SEA
		100kW:WORLD SERVICE:ME/SAS/SEA
	USA	
	VOICE OF AMERICA	(D):50kW:TURKISH:ME
	Via Rhodes, Greece	
	VOICE OF AMERICA	250kW::NAF
	Via Woofferton, UK	
	WORLD HARVEST R	100kW::ENA
	Noblesville,Indiana	
	USSR	
	RADIO MOSCOW/RP&P	(D):240kW:N AMERICAN:WNA
	Blagoveshchensk	(J):240kW:N AMERICAN:WNA
		(J):240kW:WS:WNA
	RADIO MOSCOW/RP&P	(J):200kW:POLISH:EU
	Kazan'	
	RADIO TIKHIY OKEAN	(J):240kW:MARINERS:WNA
	Blagoveshchensk	(J)Sa:240kW:MARINERS:WNA
		(J)Su-F:240kW:MARINERS:WNA
9585	BRAZIL	
	RADIO EXCELSIOR	Irr::10kW:DS
	São Paulo	10kW:DS
	DENMARK	
	DANMARKS RADIO	(J):50kW::SA
	Copenhagen	
	GERMANY (FR)	
	DEUTSCHE WELLE	(D):100kW::SAS
	Jülich	
	GUAM	
	KTWR-TRANS WORLD R	(D):100kW::EAS
	Merizo	
	HUNGARY	
	RADIO BUDAPEST	20/100kW::SA
	Various Locations	20/100kW::ENA
		20/100kW::EU
		M:20/100kW::SA
		M:20/100kW::ENA
		M/Th:20/100kW::EU
		Sa:20/100kW::EU
		Su:20/100kW::EU
		Su-Tu/Th/F:20/100kW::ENA
		Tu-Su:20/100kW::SA
		Tu-Su:20/100kW::ENA

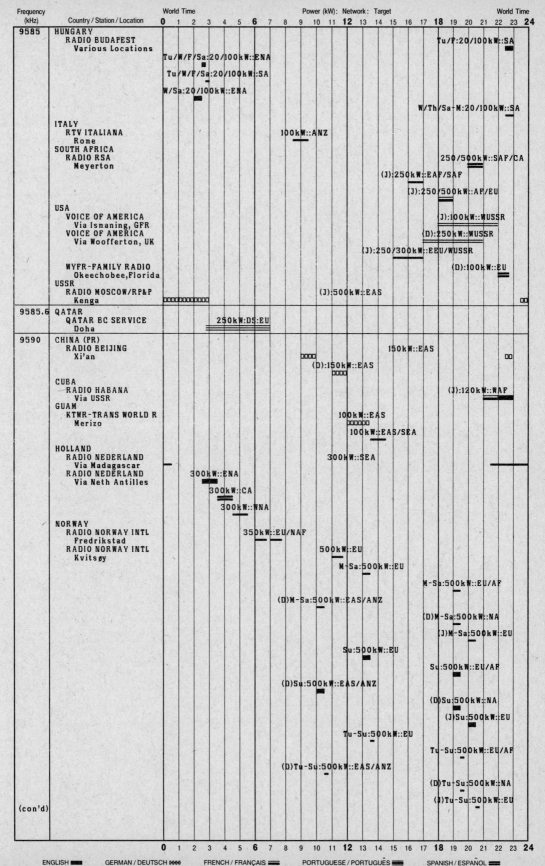

Frequency (kHz)	Country / Station / Location	Transmission details
9585	HUNGARY	
	RADIO BUDAPEST	Tu/F:20/100kW::SA
	Various Locations	Tu/W/F/Sa:20/100kW::ENA
		Tu/W/F/Sa:20/100kW::SA
		W/Sa:20/100kW::ENA
		W/Th/Sa-M:20/100kW::SA
	ITALY	
	RTV ITALIANA	100kW::ANZ
	Rome	
	SOUTH AFRICA	
	RADIO RSA	250/500kW::SAF/CA
	Meyerton	(J):250kW::EAF/SAF
		(J):250/500kW::AF/EU
	USA	
	VOICE OF AMERICA	(J):100kW::WUSSR
	Via Ismaning, GFR	
	VOICE OF AMERICA	(D):250kW::WUSSR
	Via Woofferton, UK	(J):250/300kW::EEU/WUSSR
	WYFR-FAMILY RADIO	(D):100kW::EU
	Okeechobee,Florida	
	USSR	
	RADIO MOSCOW/RP&P	(J):500kW::EAS
	Kenga	
9585.6	QATAR	
	QATAR BC SERVICE	250kW:DS:EU
	Doha	
9590	CHINA (PR)	
	RADIO BEIJING	150kW::EAS
	Xi'an	(D):150kW::EAS
	CUBA	
	RADIO HABANA	(J):120kW::WAF
	Via USSR	
	GUAM	
	KTWR-TRANS WORLD R	100kW::EAS
	Merizo	100kW::EAS/SEA
	HOLLAND	
	RADIO NEDERLAND	300kW::SEA
	Via Madagascar	
	RADIO NEDERLAND	300kW::ENA
	Via Neth Antilles	300kW::CA
		300kW::WNA
	NORWAY	
	RADIO NORWAY INTL	350kW::EU/NAF
	Fredrikstad	
	RADIO NORWAY INTL	500kW::EU
	Kvitsøy	M-Sa:500kW::EU
		M-Sa:500kW::EU/AF
		(D)M-Sa:500kW::EAS/ANZ
		(D)M-Sa:500kW::NA
		(J)M-Sa:500kW::EU
		Su:500kW::EU
		Su:500kW::EU/AF
		(D)Su:500kW::EAS/ANZ
		(D)Su:500kW::NA
		(J)Su:500kW::EU
		Tu-Su:500kW::EU
		Tu-Su:500kW::EU/AF
		(D)Tu-Su:500kW::EAS/ANZ
		(D)Tu-Su:500kW::NA
	(con'd)	(J)Tu-Su:500kW::EU

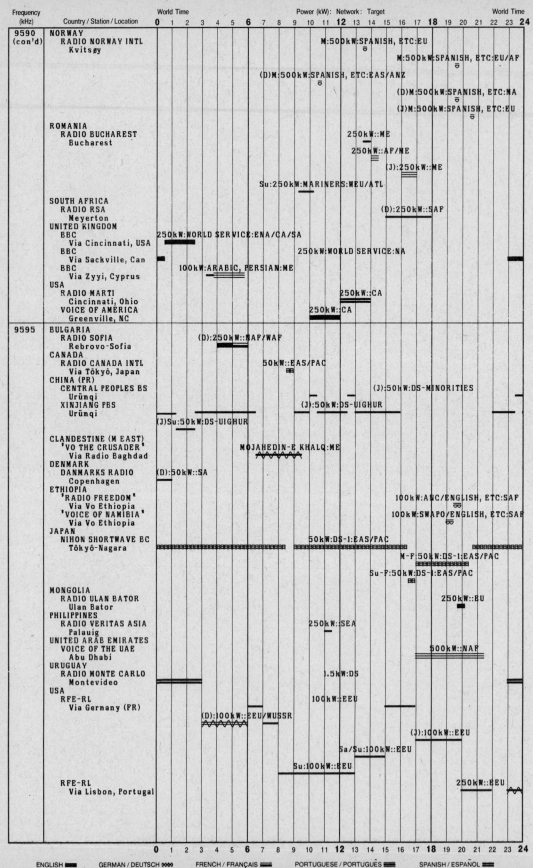

Frequency (kHz)	Country / Station / Location	World Time 0–24 / Power (kW) · Network : Target
9590 (con'd)	**NORWAY**	
	RADIO NORWAY INTL	M:500kW:SPANISH, ETC:EU
	Kvitsøy	M:500kW:SPANISH, ETC:EU/AF
		(D)M:500kW:SPANISH, ETC:EAS/ANZ
		(D)M:500kW:SPANISH, ETC:NA
		(J)M:500kW:SPANISH, ETC:EU
	ROMANIA	
	RADIO BUCHAREST	250kW::ME
	Bucharest	250kW::AF/ME
		(J):250kW::ME
		Su:250kW:MARINERS:WEU/ATL
	SOUTH AFRICA	
	RADIO RSA	(D):250kW::SAF
	Meyerton	
	UNITED KINGDOM	
	BBC	250kW:WORLD SERVICE:ENA/CA/SA
	Via Cincinnati, USA	
	BBC	250kW:WORLD SERVICE:NA
	Via Sackville, Can	
	BBC	100kW:ARABIC, PERSIAN:ME
	Via Zyyi, Cyprus	
	USA	
	RADIO MARTI	250kW::CA
	Cincinnati, Ohio	
	VOICE OF AMERICA	250kW::CA
	Greenville, NC	
9595	**BULGARIA**	
	RADIO SOFIA	(D):250kW::NAF/WAF
	Rebrovo-Sofia	
	CANADA	
	RADIO CANADA INTL	50kW::EAS/PAC
	Via Tōkyō, Japan	
	CHINA (PR)	
	CENTRAL PEOPLES BS	(J):50kW:DS-MINORITIES
	Urümqi	
	XINJIANG PBS	(J):50kW:DS-UIGHUR
	Urümqi	(J)Su:50kW:DS-UIGHUR
	CLANDESTINE (M EAST)	
	"VO THE CRUSADER"	MOJAHEDIN-E KHALQ:ME
	Via Radio Baghdad	
	DENMARK	
	DANMARKS RADIO	(D):50kW::SA
	Copenhagen	
	ETHIOPIA	
	"RADIO FREEDOM"	100kW:ANC/ENGLISH, ETC:SAF
	Via Vo Ethiopia	
	"VOICE OF NAMIBIA"	100kW:SWAPO/ENGLISH, ETC:SAF
	Via Vo Ethiopia	
	JAPAN	
	NIHON SHORTWAVE BC	50kW:DS-1:EAS/PAC
	Tōkyō-Nagara	M-F:50kW:DS-1:EAS/PAC
		Su-F:50kW:DS-1:EAS/PAC
	MONGOLIA	
	RADIO ULAN BATOR	250kW::EU
	Ulan Bator	
	PHILIPPINES	
	RADIO VERITAS ASIA	250kW::SEA
	Palauig	
	UNITED ARAB EMIRATES	
	VOICE OF THE UAE	500kW::NAF
	Abu Dhabi	
	URUGUAY	
	RADIO MONTE CARLO	1.5kW:DS
	Montevideo	
	USA	
	RFE-RL	100kW::EEU
	Via Germany (FR)	(D):100kW::EEU/WUSSR
		(J):100kW::EEU
		Sa/Su:100kW::EEU
		Su:100kW::EEU
	RFE-RL	250kW::EEU
	Via Lisbon, Portugal	

ENGLISH ▪▪▪   **GERMAN / DEUTSCH** ◊◊◊◊   **FRENCH / FRANÇAIS** ══   **PORTUGUESE / PORTUGUÊS** ▬▬   **SPANISH / ESPAÑOL** ▭▭

ARABIC / عربى ═   **RUSSIAN / РУССКИИ** ▬   **CHINESE / 中文** ◻◻◻◻   **JAPANESE / 日本語** ▬▬   **MULTILINGUAL** ▭▭▭▭   **OTHER** ▬

SUMMER ONLY (J)   **WINTER ONLY (D)**   **JAMMING** ∧∧ or / or \   **EARLIEST HEARD** ◢   **LATEST HEARD** ◣   **+ TENTATIVE**

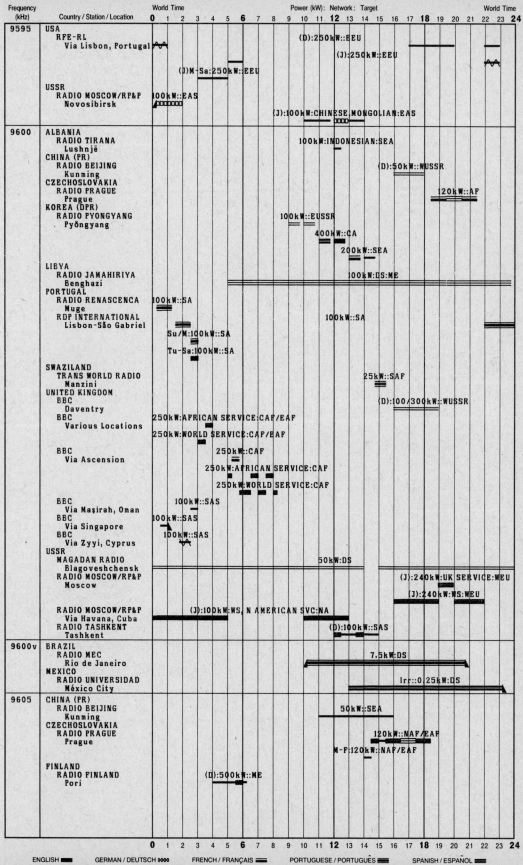

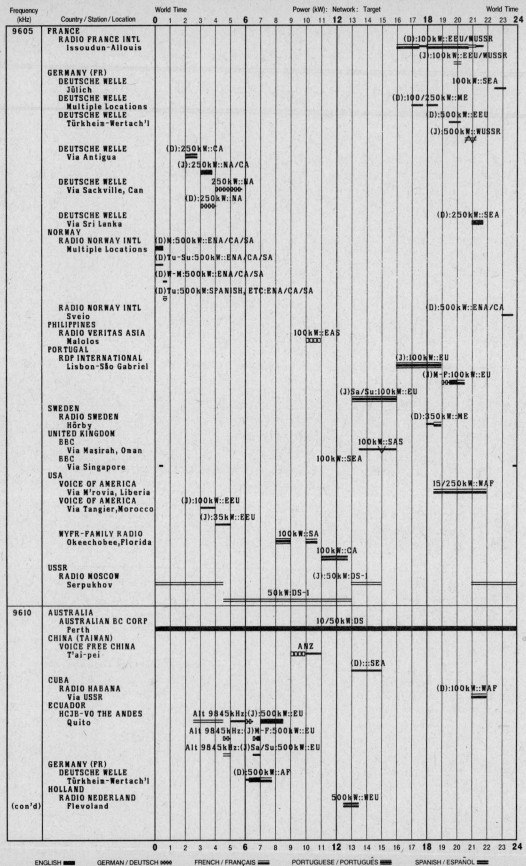

Frequency (kHz)	Country / Station / Location	Schedule
9605	**FRANCE**	
	RADIO FRANCE INTL — Issoudun-Allouis	(D):100kW::EEU/WUSSR; (J):100kW::EEU/WUSSR
	GERMANY (FR)	
	DEUTSCHE WELLE — Jülich	100kW::SEA
	DEUTSCHE WELLE — Multiple Locations	(D):100/250kW::ME
	DEUTSCHE WELLE — Türkheim-Wertach'l	(D):500kW::EEU; (J):500kW::WUSSR
	DEUTSCHE WELLE — Via Antigua	(D):250kW::CA; (J):250kW::NA/CA
	DEUTSCHE WELLE — Via Sackville, Can	250kW::NA; (D):250kW::NA
	DEUTSCHE WELLE — Via Sri Lanka	(D):250kW::SEA
	NORWAY	
	RADIO NORWAY INTL — Multiple Locations	(D)M:500kW::ENA/CA/SA; (D)Tu-Su:500kW::ENA/CA/SA; (D)W-M:500kW::ENA/CA/SA; (D)Tu:500kW:SPANISH, ETC:ENA/CA/SA
	RADIO NORWAY INTL — Sveio	(D):500kW::ENA/CA
	PHILIPPINES	
	RADIO VERITAS ASIA — Malolos	100kW::EAS
	PORTUGAL	
	RDP INTERNATIONAL — Lisbon-São Gabriel	(J):100kW::EU; (J)M-F:100kW::EU; (J)Sa/Su:100kW::EU
	SWEDEN	
	RADIO SWEDEN — Hörby	(D):350kW::ME
	UNITED KINGDOM	
	BBC — Via Maşirah, Oman	100kW::SAS
	BBC — Via Singapore	100kW::SEA
	USA	
	VOICE OF AMERICA — Via M'rovia, Liberia	15/250kW::WAF
	VOICE OF AMERICA — Via Tangier, Morocco	(J):100kW::EEU; (J):35kW::EEU
	WYFR-FAMILY RADIO — Okeechobee, Florida	100kW::SA; 100kW::CA
	USSR	
	RADIO MOSCOW — Serpukhov	(J):50kW:DS-1; 50kW:DS-1
9610	**AUSTRALIA**	
	AUSTRALIAN BC CORP — Perth	10/50kW:DS
	CHINA (TAIWAN)	
	VOICE FREE CHINA — T'ai-pei	ANZ; (D):::SEA
	CUBA	
	RADIO HABANA — Via USSR	(D):100kW::WAF
	ECUADOR	
	HCJB-VO THE ANDES — Quito	Alt 9845kHz:(J):500kW::EU; Alt 9845kHz:(J)M-F:500kW::EU; Alt 9845kHz:(J)Sa/Su:500kW::EU
	GERMANY (FR)	
	DEUTSCHE WELLE — Türkheim-Wertach'l	(D):500kW::AF
	HOLLAND	
(con'd)	RADIO NEDERLAND — Flevoland	500kW::WEU

World Time: 0 1 2 3 4 5 6 7 8 9 10 11 12 13 14 15 16 17 18 19 20 21 22 23 24

Power (kW): Network: Target

ENGLISH ▬▬ GERMAN / DEUTSCH ⋈⋈⋈ FRENCH / FRANÇAIS ═══ PORTUGUESE / PORTUGUÊS ▬▬ SPANISH / ESPAÑOL ▬▬
ARABIC /ﻉﻉ RUSSIAN / РУССКИИ CHINESE / ●¥ ⊡⊡⊡ JAPANESE / 日本語 ▬▬ MULTILINGUAL ⊟⊟⊟ OTHER ▬
SUMMER ONLY (J) WINTER ONLY (D) JAMMING ∧∧ or / or \ EARLIEST HEARD ◢ LATEST HEARD ◣ + TENTATIVE

Frequency (kHz)	Country / Station / Location		

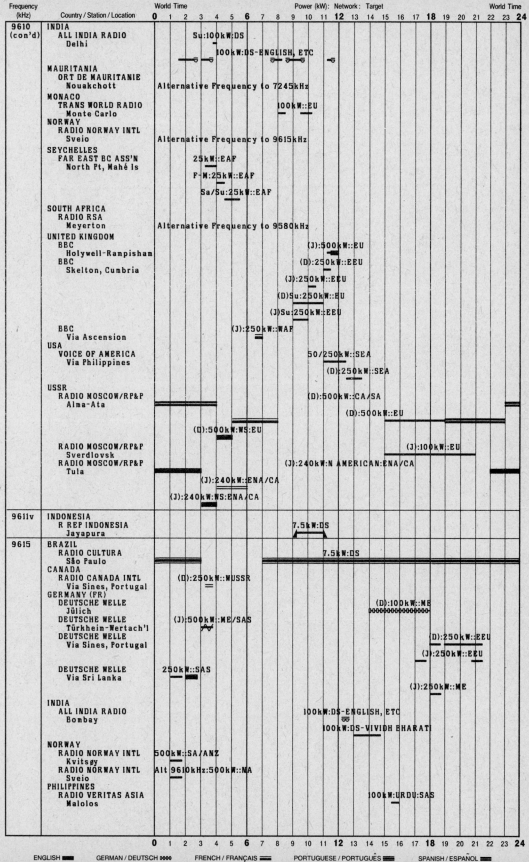

Frequency (kHz)	Country / Station / Location	Schedule
9610 (con'd)	**INDIA**	
	ALL INDIA RADIO, Delhi	Su:100kW:DS
		100kW:DS-ENGLISH, ETC
	MAURITANIA	
	ORT DE MAURITANIE, Nouakchott	Alternative Frequency to 7245kHz
	MONACO	
	TRANS WORLD RADIO, Monte Carlo	100kW::EU
	NORWAY	
	RADIO NORWAY INTL, Sveio	Alternative Frequency to 9615kHz
	SEYCHELLES	
	FAR EAST BC ASS'N, North Pt, Mahé Is	25kW::EAF
		F-M:25kW::EAF
		Sa/Su:25kW::EAF
	SOUTH AFRICA	
	RADIO RSA, Meyerton	Alternative Frequency to 9580kHz
	UNITED KINGDOM	
	BBC, Holywell-Rampisham	(J):500kW::EU
	BBC, Skelton, Cumbria	(D):250kW::EEU
		(J):250kW::EEU
		(D)Su:250kW::EU
		(J)Su:250kW::EEU
	BBC, Via Ascension	(J):250kW::WAF
	USA	
	VOICE OF AMERICA, Via Philippines	50/250kW::SEA
		(D):250kW::SEA
	USSR	
	RADIO MOSCOW/RP&P, Alma-Ata	(D):500kW::CA/SA
		(D):500kW::EU
		(D):500kW:WS:EU
	RADIO MOSCOW/RP&P, Sverdlovsk	(J):100kW::EU
	RADIO MOSCOW/RP&P, Tula	(J):240kW:N AMERICAN:ENA/CA
		(J):240kW::ENA/CA
		(J):240kW:WS:ENA/CA
9611v	**INDONESIA**	
	R REP INDONESIA, Jayapura	7.5kW:DS
9615	**BRAZIL**	
	RADIO CULTURA, São Paulo	7.5kW:DS
	CANADA	
	RADIO CANADA INTL, Via Sines, Portugal	(D):250kW::WUSSR
	GERMANY (FR)	
	DEUTSCHE WELLE, Jülich	(D):100kW::ME
	DEUTSCHE WELLE, Türkheim-Wertach'l	(J):500kW::ME/SAS
	DEUTSCHE WELLE, Via Sines, Portugal	D):250kW::EEU
		(J):250kW::EEU
	DEUTSCHE WELLE, Via Sri Lanka	250kW::SAS
		(J):250kW::ME
	INDIA	
	ALL INDIA RADIO, Bombay	100kW:DS-ENGLISH, ETC
		100kW:DS-VIVIDH BHARATI
	NORWAY	
	RADIO NORWAY INTL, Kvitsøy	500kW:SA/ANZ
	RADIO NORWAY INTL, Sveio	Alt 9610kHz:500kW::NA
	PHILIPPINES	
	RADIO VERITAS ASIA, Malolos	100kW:URDU:SAS

ENGLISH ▬   GERMAN / DEUTSCH ०००   FRENCH / FRANÇAIS ▬   PORTUGUESE / PORTUGUÊS ▬   SPANISH / ESPAÑOL ▬

ARABIC / ﻉﺭﺏ ≡   RUSSIAN / РУССКИЙ ═   CHINESE / 中文 ००००   JAPANESE / 日本語 ▬   MULTILINGUAL ००००   OTHER ▬

SUMMER ONLY (J)   WINTER ONLY (D)   JAMMING /\/\ or / or \   EARLIEST HEARD ◢   LATEST HEARD ◣   ✦ TENTATIVE

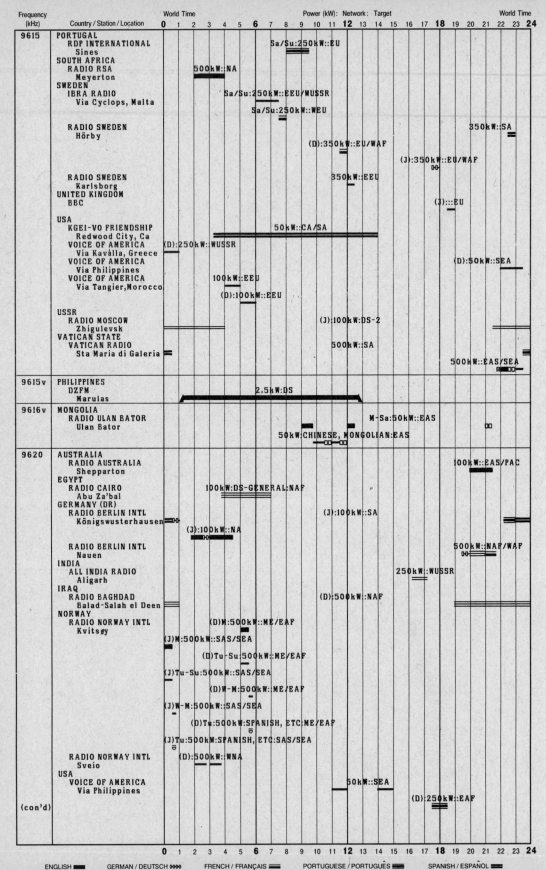

9615

PORTUGAL
  RDP INTERNATIONAL
    Sines — Sa/Su:250kW::EU
SOUTH AFRICA
  RADIO RSA
    Meyerton — 500kW::NA
SWEDEN
  IBRA RADIO
    Via Cyclops, Malta — Sa/Su:250kW::EEU/WUSSR — Sa/Su:250kW::WEU
  RADIO SWEDEN
    Hörby — 350kW::SA / (D):350kW::EU/WAF / (J):350kW::EU/WAF
  RADIO SWEDEN
    Karlsborg — 350kW::EEU
UNITED KINGDOM
  BBC — (J):::EU
USA
  KGEI-VO FRIENDSHIP
    Redwood City, Ca — 50kW::CA/SA
  VOICE OF AMERICA
    Via Kaválla, Greece — (D):250kW::WUSSR
  VOICE OF AMERICA
    Via Philippines — (D):50kW::SEA
  VOICE OF AMERICA
    Via Tangier,Morocco — 100kW::EEU / (D):100kW::EEU
USSR
  RADIO MOSCOW
    Zhigulevsk — (J):100kW::DS-2
VATICAN STATE
  VATICAN RADIO
    Sta Maria di Galeria — 500kW::SA / 500kW::EAS/SEA

9615v

PHILIPPINES
  DZFM
    Marulas — 2.5kW:DS

9616v

MONGOLIA
  RADIO ULAN BATOR
    Ulan Bator — M-Sa:50kW::EAS / 50kW:CHINESE, MONGOLIAN:EAS

9620

AUSTRALIA
  RADIO AUSTRALIA
    Shepparton — 100kW::EAS/PAC
EGYPT
  RADIO CAIRO
    Abu Za'bal — 100kW:DS-GENERAL:NAF
GERMANY (DR)
  RADIO BERLIN INTL
    Königswusterhausen — (J):100kW::SA / (J):100kW::NA
  RADIO BERLIN INTL
    Nauen — 500kW::NAF/WAF
INDIA
  ALL INDIA RADIO
    Aligarh — 250kW::WUSSR
IRAQ
  RADIO BAGHDAD
    Balad-Salah el Deen — (D):500kW::NAF
NORWAY
  RADIO NORWAY INTL
    Kvitsøy — (D)M:500kW::ME/EAF / (J)M:500kW::SAS/SEA / (D)Tu-Su:500kW::ME/EAF / (J)Tu-Su:500kW::SAS/SEA / (D)W-M:500kW::ME/EAF / (J)W-M:500kW::SAS/SEA / (D)Tu:500kW:SPANISH, ETC:ME/EAF / (J)Tu:500kW:SPANISH, ETC:SAS/SEA
  RADIO NORWAY INTL
    Sveio — (D):500kW::WNA
USA
  VOICE OF AMERICA
    Via Philippines — 50kW::SEA / (D):250kW::EAF

(con'd)

ENGLISH ▬ GERMAN / DEUTSCH ◊◊◊◊ FRENCH / FRANÇAIS ▬ PORTUGUESE / PORTUGUÊS ▬ SPANISH / ESPAÑOL ▬
ARABIC / ﻋﺮﺑﻲ ▬ RUSSIAN / РУССКИИ ▬ CHINESE / ✦✦ ◊◊◊◊ JAPANESE / 日本語 ▬ MULTILINGUAL ◊◊◊◊ OTHER ▬
SUMMER ONLY (J)   WINTER ONLY (D)   JAMMING /\/\ or / or \   EARLIEST HEARD ◢   LATEST HEARD ◣   + TENTATIVE

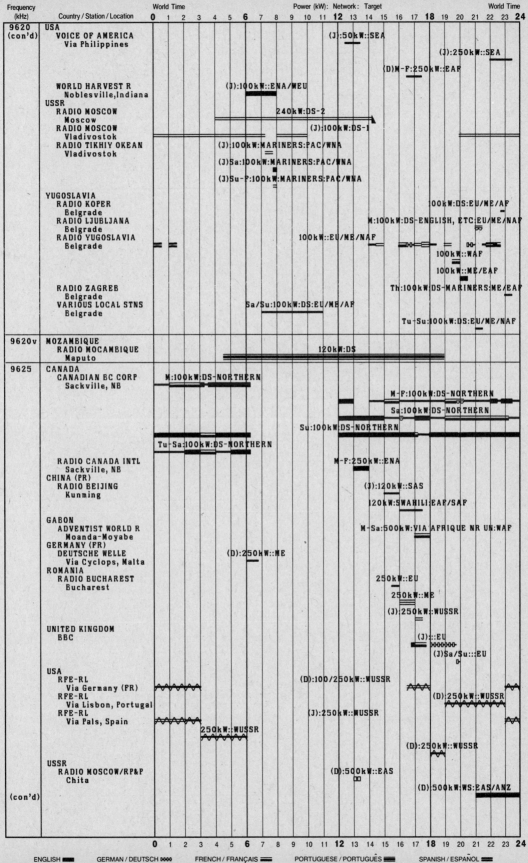

9620 (con'd)

USA
VOICE OF AMERICA
Via Philippines
(J):50kW::SEA
(J):250kW::SEA
(D)M-F:250kW::EAF

WORLD HARVEST R
Noblesville,Indiana
(J):100kW::ENA/WEU

USSR
RADIO MOSCOW
Moscow
240kW:DS-2
RADIO MOSCOW
Vladivostok
(J):100kW:DS-1
RADIO TIKHIY OKEAN
Vladivostok
(J):100kW:MARINERS:PAC/WNA
(J)Sa:100kW:MARINERS:PAC/WNA
(J)Su-F:100kW:MARINERS:PAC/WNA

YUGOSLAVIA
RADIO KOPER
Belgrade
100kW:DS:EU/ME/AF
RADIO LJUBLJANA
Belgrade
M:100kW:DS-ENGLISH, ETC:EU/ME/NAF
RADIO YUGOSLAVIA
Belgrade
100kW::EU/ME/NAF
100kW::WAF
100kW::ME/EAF
RADIO ZAGREB
Belgrade
Th:100kW:DS-MARINERS:ME/EAF
VARIOUS LOCAL STNS
Belgrade
Sa/Su:100kW:DS:EU/ME/AF
Tu-Su:100kW:DS:EU/ME/NAF

9620v

MOZAMBIQUE
RADIO MOCAMBIQUE
Maputo
120kW:DS

9625

CANADA
CANADIAN BC CORP
Sackville, NB
M:100kW:DS-NORTHERN
M-F:100kW:DS-NORTHERN
Sa:100kW:DS-NORTHERN
Su:100kW:DS-NORTHERN
Tu-Sa:100kW:DS-NORTHERN

RADIO CANADA INTL
Sackville, NB
M-F:250kW::ENA

CHINA (PR)
RADIO BEIJING
Kunming
(J):120kW::SAS
120kW:SWAHILI:EAF/SAF

GABON
ADVENTIST WORLD R
Moanda-Moyabe
M-Sa:500kW:VIA AFRIQUE NR UN:WAF

GERMANY (PR)
DEUTSCHE WELLE
Via Cyclops, Malta
(D):250kW::ME

ROMANIA
RADIO BUCHAREST
Bucharest
250kW::EU
250kW::ME
(J):250kW::WUSSR

UNITED KINGDOM
BBC
(J):::EU
(J)Sa/Su:::EU

USA
RFE-RL
Via Germany (FR)
(D):100/250kW::WUSSR
RFE-RL
Via Lisbon, Portugal
(D):250kW::WUSSR
RFE-RL
Via Pals, Spain
(J):250kW::WUSSR
250kW::WUSSR
(D):250kW::WUSSR

USSR
RADIO MOSCOW/RP&P
Chita
(D):500kW::EAS
(D):500kW:WS:EAS/ANZ

(con'd)

ENGLISH ▬▬   GERMAN / DEUTSCH ▨▨▨   FRENCH / FRANÇAIS ▬▬   PORTUGUESE / PORTUGUÊS ▬▬   SPANISH / ESPAÑOL ▬▬

ARABIC / بر ش ▬▬   RUSSIAN / РУССКИИ ▬   CHINESE / 中文 ▨▨▨   JAPANESE / 日本語 ▬▬   MULTILINGUAL ▨▨▨   OTHER ▬

SUMMER ONLY (J)   WINTER ONLY (D)   JAMMING ∧∧ or / or \   EARLIEST HEARD ◢   LATEST HEARD ◣   ⁺ TENTATIVE

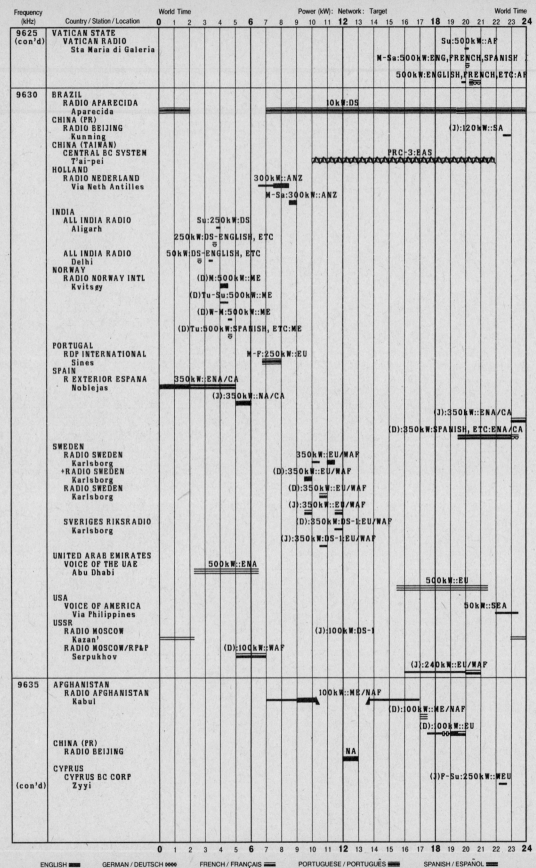

Frequency (kHz)	Country / Station / Location	Schedule
9625 (con'd)	**VATICAN STATE** VATICAN RADIO Sta Maria di Galeria	Su:500kW::AF — M-Sa:500kW:ENG,FRENCH,SPANISH — 500kW:ENGLISH,FRENCH,ETC:AF
9630	**BRAZIL** RADIO APARECIDA Aparecida	10kW:DS
	CHINA (PR) RADIO BEIJING Kunming	(J):120kW::SA
	CHINA (TAIWAN) CENTRAL BC SYSTEM T'ai-pei	PRC-3:EAS
	HOLLAND RADIO NEDERLAND Via Neth Antilles	300kW::ANZ — M-Sa:300kW::ANZ
	INDIA ALL INDIA RADIO Aligarh	Su:250kW:DS — 250kW:DS-ENGLISH, ETC
	ALL INDIA RADIO Delhi	50kW:DS-ENGLISH, ETC
	NORWAY RADIO NORWAY INTL Kvitsøy	(D)M:500kW::ME — (D)Tu-Su:500kW::ME — (D)W-M:500kW::ME — (D)Tu:500kW:SPANISH, ETC:ME
	PORTUGAL RDP INTERNATIONAL Sines	M-F:250kW::EU
	SPAIN R EXTERIOR ESPANA Noblejas	350kW::ENA/CA — (J):350kW::NA/CA — (J):350kW::ENA/CA — (D):350kW:SPANISH, ETC:ENA/CA
	SWEDEN RADIO SWEDEN Karlsborg	350kW::EU/WAF
	+RADIO SWEDEN Karlsborg	(D):350kW::EU/WAF
	RADIO SWEDEN Karlsborg	(D):350kW::EU/WAF — (J):350kW::EU/WAF
	SVERIGES RIKSRADIO Karlsborg	(D):350kW:DS-1:EU/WAF — (J):350kW:DS-1:EU/WAF
	UNITED ARAB EMIRATES VOICE OF THE UAE Abu Dhabi	500kW::ENA — 500kW::EU
	USA VOICE OF AMERICA Via Philippines	50kW::SEA
	USSR RADIO MOSCOW Kazan'	(J):100kW:DS-1
	RADIO MOSCOW/RP&P Serpukhov	(D):100kW::WAF — (J):240kW::EU/WAF
9635	**AFGHANISTAN** RADIO AFGHANISTAN Kabul	100kW::ME/NAF — (D):100kW::ME/NAF — (D):100kW::EU
	CHINA (PR) RADIO BEIJING	NA
(con'd)	**CYPRUS** CYPRUS BC CORP Zyyi	(J)F-Su:250kW::WEU

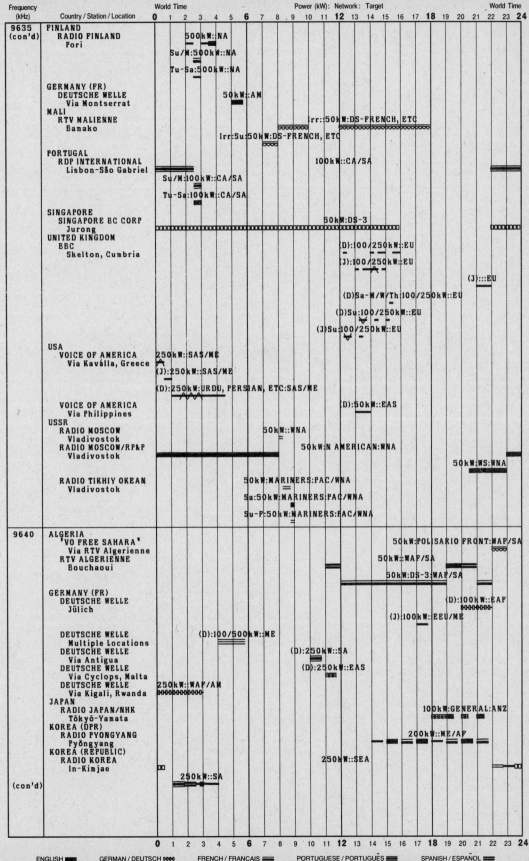

Frequency (kHz)	Country / Station / Location	Power (kW): Network: Target	World Time
9635 (con'd)	FINLAND		
	RADIO FINLAND	500kW::NA	
	Pori	Su/M:500kW::NA	
		Tu-Sa:500kW::NA	
	GERMANY (FR)		
	DEUTSCHE WELLE	50kW::AM	
	Via Montserrat		
	MALI		
	RTV MALIENNE	Irr::50kW:DS-FRENCH, ETC	
	Bamako	Irr:Su:50kW:DS-FRENCH, ETC	
	PORTUGAL		
	RDP INTERNATIONAL	100kW::CA/SA	
	Lisbon-São Gabriel	Su/M:100kW::CA/SA	
		Tu-Sa:100kW::CA/SA	
	SINGAPORE		
	SINGAPORE BC CORP	50kW:DS-3	
	Jurong		
	UNITED KINGDOM		
	BBC	(D):100/250kW::EU	
	Skelton, Cumbria	(J):100/250kW::EU	
		(J):::EU	
		(D)Sa-M/W/Th:100/250kW::EU	
		(D)Su:100/250kW::EU	
		(J)Su:100/250kW::EU	
	USA		
	VOICE OF AMERICA	250kW::SAS/ME	
	Via Kaválla, Greece	(J):250kW::SAS/ME	
		(D):250kW:URDU, PERSIAN, ETC:SAS/ME	
	VOICE OF AMERICA	(D):50kW::EAS	
	Via Philippines		
	USSR		
	RADIO MOSCOW	50kW::WNA	
	Vladivostok		
	RADIO MOSCOW/RP&P	50kW:N AMERICAN:WNA	
	Vladivostok	50kW:WS:WNA	
	RADIO TIKHIY OKEAN	50kW:MARINERS:PAC/WNA	
	Vladivostok	Sa:50kW:MARINERS:PAC/WNA	
		Su-F:50kW:MARINERS:PAC/WNA	
9640	ALGERIA		
	"VO FREE SAHARA"	50kW:POLISARIO FRONT:WAF/SA	
	Via RTV Algerienne		
	RTV ALGERIENNE	50kW::WAF/SA	
	Bouchaoui	50kW:DS-3:WAF/SA	
	GERMANY (FR)		
	DEUTSCHE WELLE	(D):100kW::EAF	
	Jülich	(J):100kW::EEU/ME	
	DEUTSCHE WELLE	(D):100/500kW::ME	
	Multiple Locations		
	DEUTSCHE WELLE	(D):250kW::SA	
	Via Antigua		
	DEUTSCHE WELLE	(D):250kW::EAS	
	Via Cyclops, Malta		
	DEUTSCHE WELLE	250kW::WAF/AM	
	Via Kigali, Rwanda		
	JAPAN		
	RADIO JAPAN/NHK	100kW:GENERAL:ANZ	
	Tōkyō-Yamata		
	KOREA (DPR)		
	RADIO PYONGYANG	200kW:ME/AF	
	Pyŏngyang		
	KOREA (REPUBLIC)		
	RADIO KOREA	250kW::SEA	
	In-Kimjae		
(con'd)		250kW::SA	

ENGLISH ▬ GERMAN / DEUTSCH ∞∞ FRENCH / FRANÇAIS ═══ PORTUGUESE / PORTUGUÊS ▬ SPANISH / ESPAÑOL ▬

ARABIC /ﻉﺭ ≡ RUSSIAN / РУССКИИ ═ CHINESE / 中文 ∞∞ JAPANESE / 日本語 ▬ MULTILINGUAL ∞∞ OTHER ▬

SUMMER ONLY (J) WINTER ONLY (D) JAMMING ∧∧ or / or \ EARLIEST HEARD ◢ LATEST HEARD ◣ + TENTATIVE

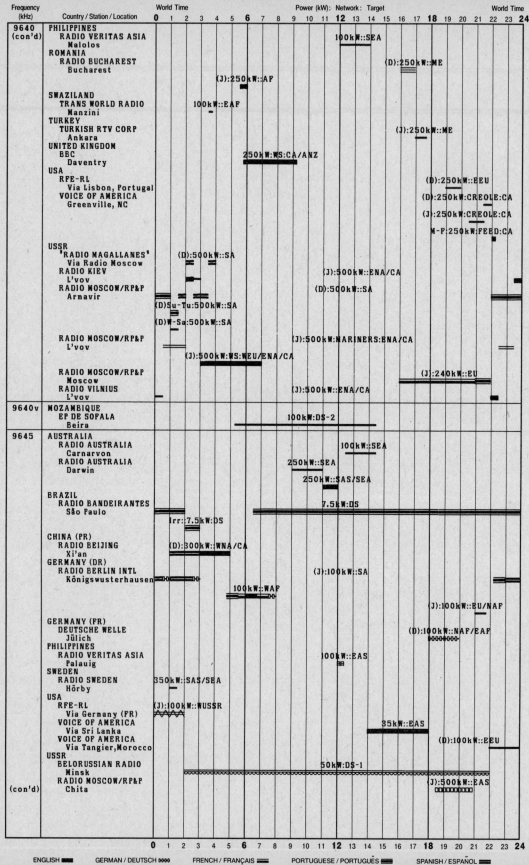

Frequency (kHz)	Country / Station / Location	Schedule (World Time, Power/Network/Target)
9640 (con'd)	**PHILIPPINES** RADIO VERITAS ASIA Malolos	100kW::SEA
	ROMANIA RADIO BUCHAREST Bucharest	(D):250kW::ME / (J):250kW::AF
	SWAZILAND TRANS WORLD RADIO Manzini	100kW::EAF
	TURKEY TURKISH RTV CORP Ankara	(J):250kW::ME
	UNITED KINGDOM BBC Daventry	250kW:WS:CA/ANZ
	USA RFE-RL Via Lisbon, Portugal	(D):250kW::EEU
	VOICE OF AMERICA Greenville, NC	(D):250kW:CREOLE:CA / (J):250kW:CREOLE:CA / M-F:250kW:FEED:CA
	USSR "RADIO MAGALLANES" Via Radio Moscow	(D):500kW::SA
	RADIO KIEV L'vov	(J):500kW::ENA/CA
	RADIO MOSCOW/RP&P Armavir	(D):500kW::SA / (D)Su-Tu:500kW::SA / (D)W-Sa:500kW::SA
	RADIO MOSCOW/RP&P L'vov	(J):500kW:MARINERS:ENA/CA / (J):500kW:WS:WEU/ENA/CA
	RADIO MOSCOW/RP&P Moscow	(J):240kW::EU
	RADIO VILNIUS L'vov	(J):500kW::ENA/CA
9640v	**MOZAMBIQUE** EP DE SOFALA Beira	100kW:DS-2
9645	**AUSTRALIA** RADIO AUSTRALIA Carnarvon	100kW::SEA
	RADIO AUSTRALIA Darwin	250kW::SEA / 250kW::SAS/SEA
	BRAZIL RADIO BANDEIRANTES São Paulo	7.5kW:DS / Irr:7.5kW:DS
	CHINA (PR) RADIO BEIJING Xi'an	(D):300kW::WNA/CA
	GERMANY (DR) RADIO BERLIN INTL Königswusterhausen	(J):100kW::SA / 100kW::WAF
	GERMANY (FR) DEUTSCHE WELLE Jülich	(J):100kW::EU/NAF / (D):100kW::NAF/EAF
	PHILIPPINES RADIO VERITAS ASIA Palauig	100kW::EAS
	SWEDEN RADIO SWEDEN Hörby	350kW:SAS/SEA
	USA RFE-RL Via Germany (FR)	(J):100kW::WUSSR
	VOICE OF AMERICA Via Sri Lanka	35kW::EAS
	VOICE OF AMERICA Via Tangier, Morocco	(D):100kW::EEU
	USSR BELORUSSIAN RADIO Minsk	50kW:DS-1
(con'd)	RADIO MOSCOW/RP&P Chita	(J):500kW::EAS

ENGLISH ▰▰▰   GERMAN / DEUTSCH ◊◊◊◊   FRENCH / FRANÇAIS ▬▬▬   PORTUGUESE / PORTUGUÊS ▰▰▰   SPANISH / ESPAÑOL ▬▬▬

ARABIC / علی ▬▬   RUSSIAN / РУССКИИ ▬▬▬   CHINESE / 中文 ◻◻◻◻   JAPANESE / 日本語 ▰▰▰▰   MULTILINGUAL ▱▱▱▱   OTHER ▬▬▬

SUMMER ONLY (J)   WINTER ONLY (D)   JAMMING ∧∧ or / or \   EARLIEST HEARD ◢   LATEST HEARD ◣   ⁺ TENTATIVE

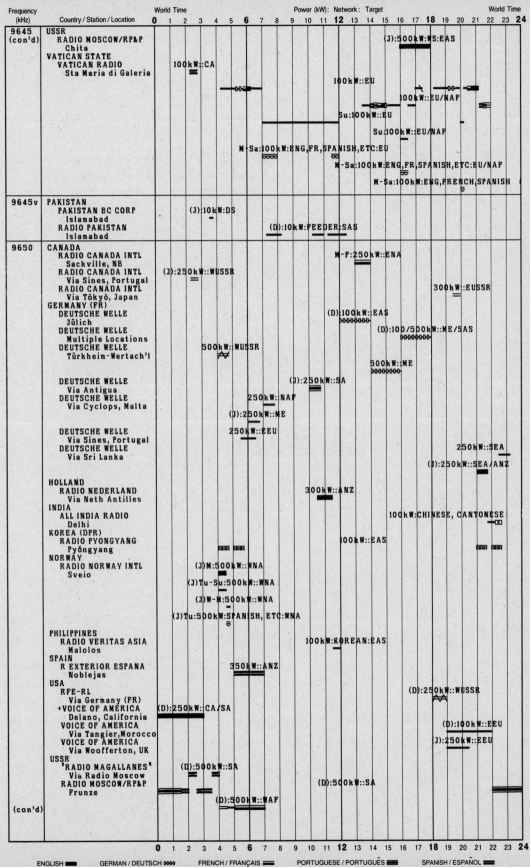

Frequency (kHz)	Country / Station / Location	World Time →	Power (kW): Network: Target
9645 (con'd)	**USSR** RADIO MOSCOW/RP&P Chita		(J):500kW:WS:EAS
	VATICAN STATE VATICAN RADIO Sta Maria di Galeria	100kW::CA	100kW::EU / 100kW::EU/NAF / Su:100kW::EU / Su:100kW::EU/NAF / M-Sa:100kW:ENG,FR,SPANISH,ETC:EU / M-Sa:100kW:ENG,FR,SPANISH,ETC:EU/NAF / M-Sa:100kW:ENG,FRENCH,SPANISH
9645v	**PAKISTAN** PAKISTAN BC CORP Islamabad	(J):10kW:DS	
	RADIO PAKISTAN Islamabad	(D):10kW:FEEDER:SAS	
9650	**CANADA** RADIO CANADA INTL Sackville, NB		M-F:250kW::ENA
	RADIO CANADA INTL Via Sines, Portugal	(J):250kW::WUSSR	
	RADIO CANADA INTL Via Tôkyô, Japan		300kW::EUSSR
	GERMANY (FR) DEUTSCHE WELLE Jülich		(D):100kW::EAS
	DEUTSCHE WELLE Multiple Locations		(D):100/500kW::ME/SAS
	DEUTSCHE WELLE Türkheim-Wertach'l	500kW::WUSSR	500kW::ME
	DEUTSCHE WELLE Via Antigua		(J):250kW::SA
	DEUTSCHE WELLE Via Cyclops, Malta	250kW::NAF / (J):250kW::ME	
	DEUTSCHE WELLE Via Sines, Portugal	250kW::EEU	
	DEUTSCHE WELLE Via Sri Lanka		250kW::SEA / (J):250kW::SEA/ANZ
	HOLLAND RADIO NEDERLAND Via Neth Antilles		300kW::ANZ
	INDIA ALL INDIA RADIO Delhi		100kW:CHINESE, CANTONESE
	KOREA (DPR) RADIO PYONGYANG Pyŏngyang		100kW::EAS
	NORWAY RADIO NORWAY INTL Sveio	(J)M:500kW::WNA / (J)Tu-Su:500kW::WNA / (J)W-M:500kW::WNA / (J)Tu:500kW:SPANISH, ETC:WNA	
	PHILIPPINES RADIO VERITAS ASIA Malolos		100kW:KOREAN:EAS
	SPAIN R EXTERIOR ESPANA Noblejas	350kW::ANZ	
	USA RFE-RL Via Germany (FR)		(D):250kW::WUSSR
	+VOICE OF AMERICA Delano, California	(D):250kW:CA/SA	
	VOICE OF AMERICA Via Tangier, Morocco		(D):100kW::EEU
	VOICE OF AMERICA Via Woofferton, UK		(J):250kW::EEU
	USSR "RADIO MAGALLANES" Via Radio Moscow	(D):500kW::SA	
	RADIO MOSCOW/RP&P Frunze		(D):500kW::SA
(con'd)		(D):500kW::WAF	

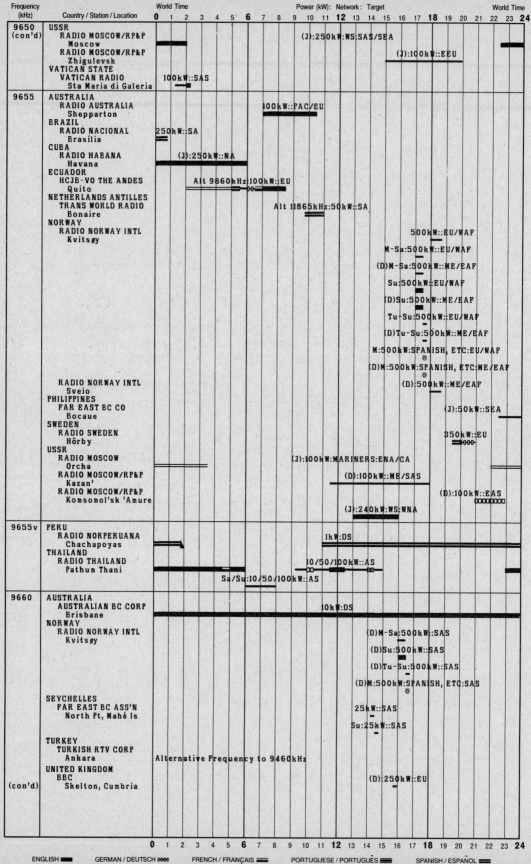

Frequency (kHz)	Country / Station / Location	Notes
9650 (con'd)	USSR — RADIO MOSCOW/RP&P — Moscow	(J):250kW:WS:SAS/SEA
	RADIO MOSCOW/RP&P — Zhigulevsk	(J):100kW::EEU
	VATICAN STATE — VATICAN RADIO — Sta Maria di Galeria	100kW::SAS
9655	AUSTRALIA — RADIO AUSTRALIA — Shepparton	100kW::PAC/EU
	BRAZIL — RADIO NACIONAL — Brasília	250kW::SA
	CUBA — RADIO HABANA — Havana	(J):250kW::NA
	ECUADOR — HCJB-VO THE ANDES — Quito	Alt 9860kHz:100kW::EU
	NETHERLANDS ANTILLES — TRANS WORLD RADIO — Bonaire	Alt 11865kHz:50kW::SA
	NORWAY — RADIO NORWAY INTL — Kvitsøy	500kW::EU/WAF
		M-Sa:500kW::EU/WAF
		(D)M-Sa:500kW::ME/EAF
		Su:500kW::EU/WAF
		(D)Su:500kW::ME/EAF
		Tu-Su:500kW::EU/WAF
		(D)Tu-Su:500kW::ME/EAF
		M:500kW:SPANISH, ETC:EU/WAF
		(D)M:500kW:SPANISH, ETC:ME/EAF
	RADIO NORWAY INTL — Sveio	(D):500kW::ME/EAF
	PHILIPPINES — FAR EAST BC CO — Bocaue	(J):50kW::SEA
	SWEDEN — RADIO SWEDEN — Hörby	350kW::EU
	USSR — RADIO MOSCOW — Orcha	(J):100kW:MARINERS:ENA/CA
	RADIO MOSCOW/RP&P — Kazan'	(D):100kW::ME/SAS
	RADIO MOSCOW/RP&P — Komsomol'sk 'Amure	(D):100kW::EAS
		(J):240kW:WS:WNA
9655v	PERU — RADIO NORPERUANA — Chachapoyas	1kW:DS
	THAILAND — RADIO THAILAND — Pathum Thani	10/50/100kW::AS
		Sa/Su:10/50/100kW::AS
9660	AUSTRALIA — AUSTRALIAN BC CORP — Brisbane	10kW:DS
	NORWAY — RADIO NORWAY INTL — Kvitsøy	(D)M-Sa:500kW::SAS
		(D)Su:500kW::SAS
		(D)Tu-Su:500kW::SAS
		(D)M:500kW:SPANISH, ETC:SAS
	SEYCHELLES — FAR EAST BC ASS'N — North Pt, Mahé Is	25kW::SAS
		Su:25kW::SAS
	TURKEY — TURKISH RTV CORP — Ankara	Alternative Frequency to 9460kHz
	UNITED KINGDOM — BBC — Skelton, Cumbria	(D):250kW::EU
(con'd)		

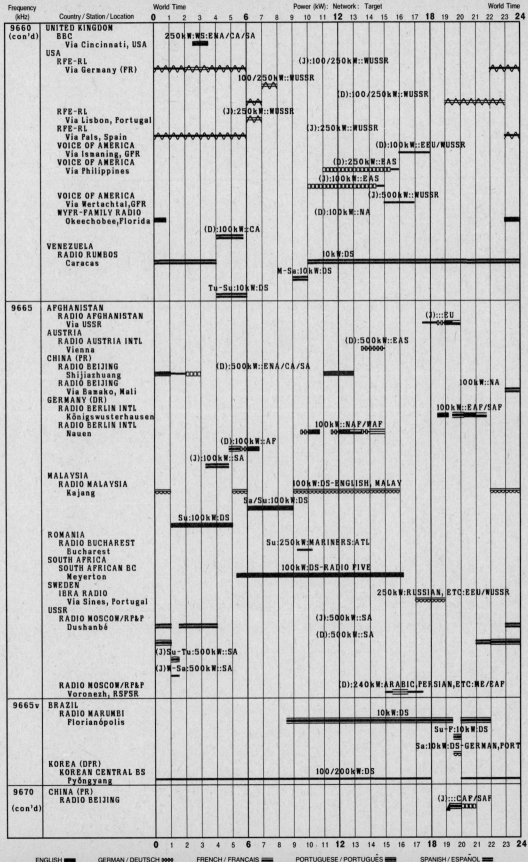

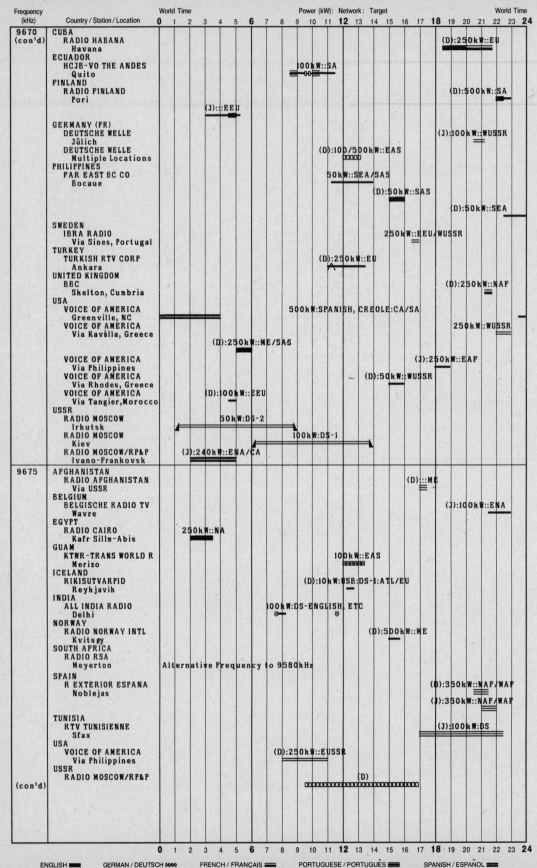

Frequency (kHz)	Country / Station / Location	Details
9670 (con'd)	CUBA	
	RADIO HABANA Havana	(D):250kW::EU
	ECUADOR	
	HCJB–VO THE ANDES Quito	100kW::SA
	FINLAND	
	RADIO FINLAND Pori	(D):500kW::SA
		(J):::EEU
	GERMANY (FR)	
	DEUTSCHE WELLE Jülich	(J):100kW::WUSSR
	DEUTSCHE WELLE Multiple Locations	(D):100/500kW::EAS
	PHILIPPINES	
	FAR EAST BC CO Bocaue	50kW::SEA/SAS
		(D):50kW::SAS
		(D):50kW::SEA
	SWEDEN	
	IBRA RADIO Via Sines, Portugal	250kW::EEU/WUSSR
	TURKEY	
	TURKISH RTV CORP Ankara	(D):250kW::EU
	UNITED KINGDOM	
	BBC Skelton, Cumbria	(D):250kW::NAF
	USA	
	VOICE OF AMERICA Greenville, NC	500kW:SPANISH, CREOLE:CA/SA
	VOICE OF AMERICA Via Kaválla, Greece	250kW::WUSSR
	VOICE OF AMERICA	(D):250kW::ME/SAS
	VOICE OF AMERICA Via Philippines	(J):250kW::EAF
	VOICE OF AMERICA Via Rhodes, Greece	(D):50kW::WUSSR
	VOICE OF AMERICA Via Tangier, Morocco	(D):100kW::EEU
	USSR	
	RADIO MOSCOW Irkutsk	50kW:DS-2
	RADIO MOSCOW Kiev	100kW:DS-1
	RADIO MOSCOW/RP&P Ivano-Frankovsk	(J):240kW::ENA/CA
9675	AFGHANISTAN	
	RADIO AFGHANISTAN Via USSR	(D):::ME
	BELGIUM	
	BELGISCHE RADIO TV Wavre	(J):100kW::ENA
	EGYPT	
	RADIO CAIRO Kafr Silim-Abis	250kW::NA
	GUAM	
	KTWR–TRANS WORLD R Merizo	100kW::EAS
	ICELAND	
	RIKISUTVARPID Reykjavik	(D):10kW:USB:DS-1:ATL/EU
	INDIA	
	ALL INDIA RADIO Delhi	100kW:DS-ENGLISH, ETC
	NORWAY	
	RADIO NORWAY INTL Kvitsøy	(D):500kW::ME
	SOUTH AFRICA	
	RADIO RSA Meyerton	Alternative Frequency to 9580kHz
	SPAIN	
	R EXTERIOR ESPANA Noblejas	(D):350kW::NAF/WAF
		(J):350kW::NAF/WAF
	TUNISIA	
	RTV TUNISIENNE Sfax	(J):100kW:DS
	USA	
	VOICE OF AMERICA Via Philippines	(D):250kW::EUSSR
	USSR	
(con'd)	RADIO MOSCOW/RP&P	(D)

ENGLISH ▬▬ GERMAN / DEUTSCH ∞∞∞ FRENCH / FRANÇAIS ═══ PORTUGUESE / PORTUGUÊS ▬▬ SPANISH / ESPAÑOL ▬▬

ARABIC / ﻋﺮﺑﻲ ≡≡≡ RUSSIAN / РУССКИЙ ≡≡≡ CHINESE / ✸✶ ∞∞∞ JAPANESE / 日本語 ▬▬ MULTILINGUAL ∞∞∞ OTHER ▬▬

SUMMER ONLY (J) WINTER ONLY (D) JAMMING ∧∧ or / or \ EARLIEST HEARD ◢ LATEST HEARD ◣ * TENTATIVE

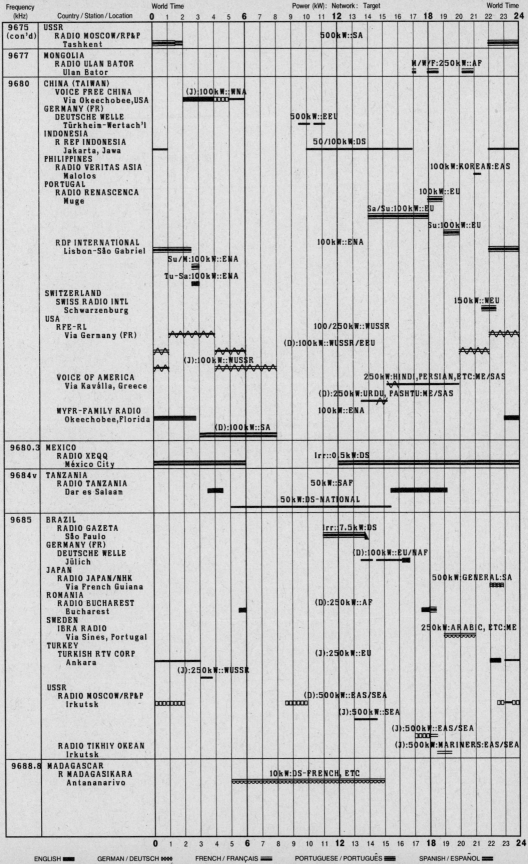

Frequency (kHz)	Country / Station / Location	Power (kW): Network: Target
9675 (con'd)	USSR — RADIO MOSCOW/RP&P — Tashkent	500kW::SA
9677	MONGOLIA — RADIO ULAN BATOR — Ulan Bator	M/W/F:250kW::AF
9680	CHINA (TAIWAN) — VOICE FREE CHINA — Via Okeechobee, USA	(J):100kW::WNA
	GERMANY (FR) — DEUTSCHE WELLE — Türkheim-Wertach'l	500kW::EEU
	INDONESIA — R REP INDONESIA — Jakarta, Jawa	50/100kW:DS
	PHILIPPINES — RADIO VERITAS ASIA — Malolos	100kW:KOREAN:EAS
	PORTUGAL — RADIO RENASCENCA — Muge	100kW::EU / Sa/Su:100kW::EU / Su:100kW::EU
	RDP INTERNATIONAL — Lisbon–São Gabriel	100kW::ENA / Su/M:100kW::ENA / Tu-Sa:100kW::ENA
	SWITZERLAND — SWISS RADIO INTL — Schwarzenburg	150kW::WEU
	USA — RFE-RL — Via Germany (FR)	100/250kW::WUSSR / (D):100kW::WUSSR/EEU / (J):100kW::WUSSR
	VOICE OF AMERICA — Via Kaválla, Greece	250kW:HINDI,PERSIAN,ETC:ME/SAS / (D):250kW:URDU, PASHTU:ME/SAS
	WYFR-FAMILY RADIO — Okeechobee, Florida	100kW::ENA / (D):100kW::SA
9680.3	MEXICO — RADIO XEQQ — México City	Irr::0.5kW:DS
9684v	TANZANIA — RADIO TANZANIA — Dar es Salaam	50kW::SAF / 50kW:DS-NATIONAL
9685	BRAZIL — RADIO GAZETA — São Paulo	Irr:7.5kW:DS
	GERMANY (FR) — DEUTSCHE WELLE — Jülich	(D):100kW::EU/NAF
	JAPAN — RADIO JAPAN/NHK — Via French Guiana	500kW:GENERAL:SA
	ROMANIA — RADIO BUCHAREST — Bucharest	(D):250kW::AF
	SWEDEN — IBRA RADIO — Via Sines, Portugal	250kW:ARABIC, ETC:ME
	TURKEY — TURKISH RTV CORP — Ankara	(J):250kW::EU / (J):250kW::WUSSR
	USSR — RADIO MOSCOW/RP&P — Irkutsk	(D):500kW::EAS/SEA / (J):500kW::SEA / (J):500kW::EAS/SEA
	RADIO TIKHIY OKEAN — Irkutsk	(J):500kW:MARINERS:EAS/SEA
9688.8	MADAGASCAR — R MADAGASIKARA — Antananarivo	10kW:DS-FRENCH, ETC

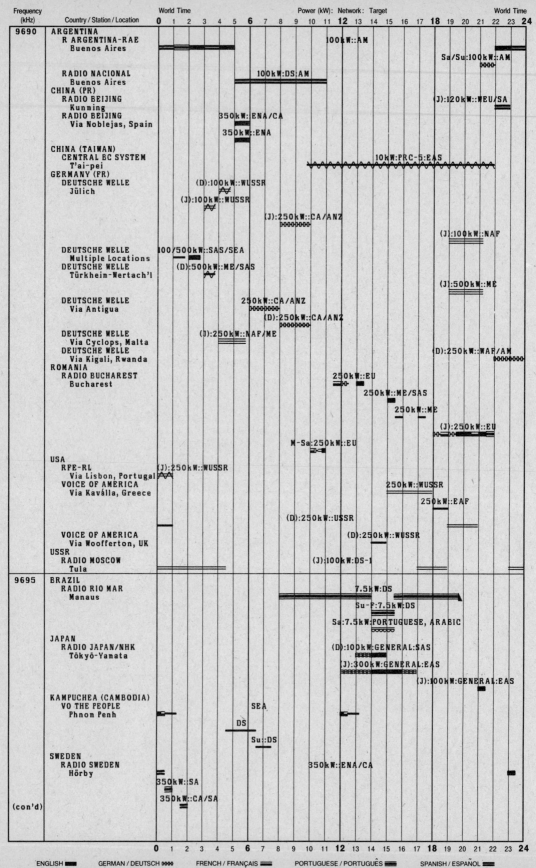

9690 ARGENTINA
R ARGENTINA-RAE
Buenos Aires — 100kW::AM — Sa/Su:100kW::AM

RADIO NACIONAL
Buenos Aires — 100kW:DS:AM
CHINA (PR)
RADIO BEIJING
Kunming — (J):120kW::WEU/SA
RADIO BEIJING
Via Noblejas, Spain — 350kW::ENA/CA — 350kW::ENA

CHINA (TAIWAN)
CENTRAL BC SYSTEM
T'ai-pei — 10kW:PRC-5:EAS
GERMANY (FR)
DEUTSCHE WELLE
Jülich — (D):100kW::WUSSR — (J):100kW::WUSSR — (J):250kW::CA/ANZ — (J):100kW::NAF

DEUTSCHE WELLE
Multiple Locations — 100/500kW::SAS/SEA
DEUTSCHE WELLE
Türkheim-Wertach'l — (D):500kW::ME/SAS — (J):500kW::ME

DEUTSCHE WELLE
Via Antigua — 250kW::CA/ANZ — (D):250kW::CA/ANZ

DEUTSCHE WELLE
Via Cyclops, Malta — (J):250kW::NAF/ME
DEUTSCHE WELLE
Via Kigali, Rwanda — (D):250kW::WAF/AM
ROMANIA
RADIO BUCHAREST
Bucharest — 250kW::EU — 250kW::ME/SAS — 250kW::ME — (J):250kW::EU — M-Sa:250kW::EU

USA
RFE-RL
Via Lisbon, Portugal — (J):250kW::WUSSR
VOICE OF AMERICA
Via Kaválla, Greece — 250kW::WUSSR — 250kW::EAF — (D):250kW::USSR

VOICE OF AMERICA
Via Woofferton, UK — (D):250kW::WUSSR
USSR
RADIO MOSCOW
Tula — (J):100kW:DS-1

9695 BRAZIL
RADIO RIO MAR
Manaus — 7.5kW:DS — Su-?:7.5kW:DS — Sa:7.5kW:PORTUGUESE, ARABIC

JAPAN
RADIO JAPAN/NHK
Tōkyō-Yamata — (D):100kW:GENERAL:SAS — (J):300kW:GENERAL:EAS — (J):100kW:GENERAL:EAS

KAMPUCHEA (CAMBODIA)
VO THE PEOPLE
Phnom Penh — SEA — DS — Su::DS

SWEDEN
RADIO SWEDEN
Hörby — 350kW::ENA/CA — 350kW::SA — 350kW::CA/SA

(con'd)

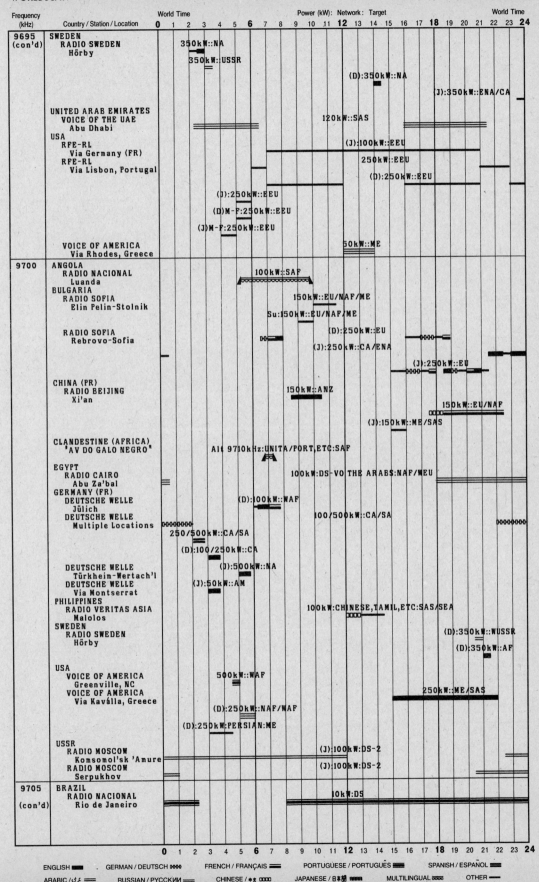

Frequency (kHz)	Country / Station / Location	World Time / Power (kW) : Network : Target
9695 (con'd)	SWEDEN	
	RADIO SWEDEN	350kW::NA
	Hörby	350kW::USSR
		(D):350kW::NA
		(J):350kW::ENA/CA
	UNITED ARAB EMIRATES	
	VOICE OF THE UAE	120kW::SAS
	Abu Dhabi	
	USA	
	RFE-RL	(J):100kW::EEU
	Via Germany (FR)	
	RFE-RL	250kW::EEU
	Via Lisbon, Portugal	(D):250kW::EEU
		(J):250kW::EEU
		(D)M-F:250kW::EEU
		(J)M-F:250kW::EEU
	VOICE OF AMERICA	50kW::ME
	Via Rhodes, Greece	
9700	ANGOLA	
	RADIO NACIONAL	100kW::SAF
	Luanda	
	BULGARIA	
	RADIO SOFIA	150kW::EU/NAF/ME
	Elin Pelin-Stolnik	Su:150kW::EU/NAF/ME
	RADIO SOFIA	(D):250kW::EU
	Rebrovo-Sofia	(J):250kW::CA/ENA
		(J):250kW::EU
	CHINA (PR)	
	RADIO BEIJING	150kW::ANZ
	Xi'an	150kW::EU/NAF
		(J):150kW::ME/SAS
	CLANDESTINE (AFRICA)	
	"AV DO GALO NEGRO"	Alt 9710kHz:UNITA/PORT,ETC:SAF
	EGYPT	
	RADIO CAIRO	100kW:DS-VO THE ARABS:NAF/WEU
	Abu Za'bal	
	GERMANY (FR)	
	DEUTSCHE WELLE	(D):100kW::WAF
	Jülich	
	DEUTSCHE WELLE	100/500kW::CA/SA
	Multiple Locations	250/500kW::CA/SA
		(D):100/250kW::CA
	DEUTSCHE WELLE	(J):500kW::NA
	Türkheim-Wertach'l	
	DEUTSCHE WELLE	(J):50kW::AM
	Via Montserrat	
	PHILIPPINES	
	RADIO VERITAS ASIA	100kW:CHINESE,TAMIL,ETC:SAS/SEA
	Malolos	
	SWEDEN	
	RADIO SWEDEN	(D):350kW::WUSSR
	Hörby	(D):350kW::AF
	USA	
	VOICE OF AMERICA	500kW::WAF
	Greenville, NC	
	VOICE OF AMERICA	250kW::ME/SAS
	Via Kaválla, Greece	(D):250kW::NAF/WAF
		(D):250kW:PERSIAN:ME
	USSR	
	RADIO MOSCOW	(J):100kW:DS-2
	Komsomol'sk 'Amure	
	RADIO MOSCOW	(J):100kW:DS-2
	Serpukhov	
9705 (con'd)	BRAZIL	
	RADIO NACIONAL	10kW:DS
	Rio de Janeiro	

ENGLISH ▬ · GERMAN / DEUTSCH ∞∞∞ FRENCH / FRANÇAIS ═ PORTUGUESE / PORTUGUÊS ▬ SPANISH / ESPAÑOL ▬
ARABIC / ﻉﺮﺑ ═ RUSSIAN / РУССКИИ ═ CHINESE / ★★ ∞∞∞ JAPANESE / 日本語 ▬ MULTILINGUAL ∞∞∞ OTHER ▬
SUMMER ONLY (J) WINTER ONLY (D) JAMMING ∧∧ or / or \ EARLIEST HEARD ◢ LATEST HEARD ◣ ✦ TENTATIVE

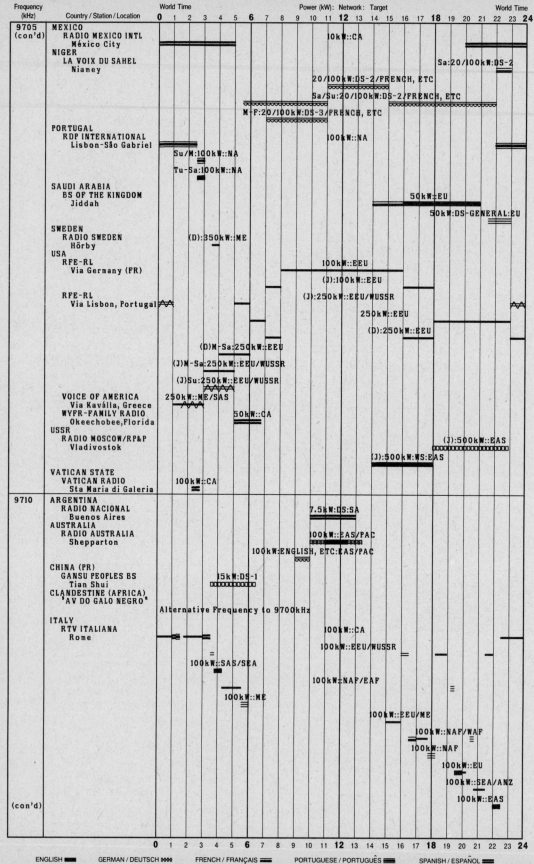

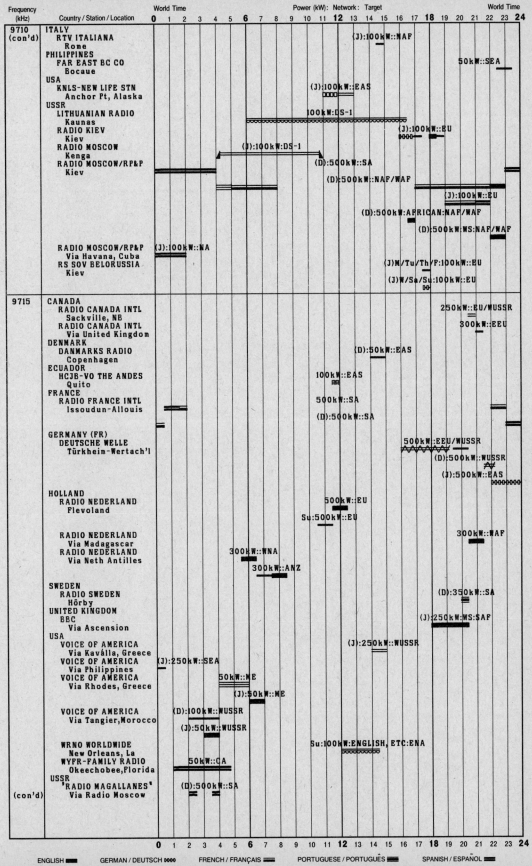

9710 (con'd)

ITALY
 RTV ITALIANA
  Rome — (J):100kW::NAF

PHILIPPINES
 FAR EAST BC CO
  Bocaue — 50kW::SEA

USA
 KNLS-NEW LIFE STN
  Anchor Pt, Alaska — (J):100kW::EAS

USSR
 LITHUANIAN RADIO
  Kaunas — 100kW:DS-1
 RADIO KIEV
  Kiev — (J):100kW::EU
 RADIO MOSCOW
  Kenga — (J):100kW:DS-1
 RADIO MOSCOW/RP&P
  Kiev — (D):500kW::SA
  (D):500kW::NAF/WAF
  (J):100kW::EU
  (D):500kW:AFRICAN:NAF/WAF
  (D):500kW:WS:NAF/WAF

 RADIO MOSCOW/RP&P
  Via Havana, Cuba — (J):100kW::NA
 RS SOV BELORUSSIA
  Kiev — (J)M/Tu/Th/F:100kW::EU
  (J)W/Sa/Su:100kW::EU

9715

CANADA
 RADIO CANADA INTL
  Sackville, NB — 250kW::EU/WUSSR
 RADIO CANADA INTL
  Via United Kingdom — 300kW::EEU

DENMARK
 DANMARKS RADIO
  Copenhagen — (D):50kW::EAS

ECUADOR
 HCJB-VO THE ANDES
  Quito — 100kW::EAS

FRANCE
 RADIO FRANCE INTL
  Issoudun-Allouis — 500kW::SA
  (D):500kW::SA

GERMANY (FR)
 DEUTSCHE WELLE
  Türkheim-Wertach'l — 500kW:EEU/WUSSR
  (D):500kW::WUSSR
  (J):500kW::EAS

HOLLAND
 RADIO NEDERLAND
  Flevoland — 500kW::EU
  Su:500kW::EU

 RADIO NEDERLAND
  Via Madagascar — 300kW::NAF
 RADIO NEDERLAND
  Via Neth Antilles — 300kW::WNA
  300kW::ANZ

SWEDEN
 RADIO SWEDEN
  Hörby — (D):350kW::SA
UNITED KINGDOM
 BBC
  Via Ascension — (J):250kW:WS:SAF
USA
 VOICE OF AMERICA
  Via Kaválla, Greece — (J):250kW::WUSSR
 VOICE OF AMERICA
  Via Philippines — (J):250kW::SEA
 VOICE OF AMERICA
  Via Rhodes, Greece — 50kW::ME
  (J):50kW::ME

 VOICE OF AMERICA
  Via Tangier, Morocco — (D):100kW::WUSSR
  (J):50kW::WUSSR

 WRNO WORLDWIDE
  New Orleans, La — Su:100kW:ENGLISH, ETC:ENA
 WYFR-FAMILY RADIO
  Okeechobee, Florida — 50kW::CA
USSR
 'RADIO MAGALLANES'
  (con'd) Via Radio Moscow — (D):500kW::SA

ENGLISH ▬▬ GERMAN / DEUTSCH ००००० FRENCH / FRANÇAIS ▰▰▰ PORTUGUESE / PORTUGUÊS ▰▰▰ SPANISH / ESPAÑOL ▰▰▰

ARABIC / ﺍﻟﻌﺮﺑﻴﺔ ≡≡ RUSSIAN / РУССКИИ ══ CHINESE / ✱✱ ०००० JAPANESE / 日本語 ▬▬ MULTILINGUAL ०००० OTHER ▬▬

SUMMER ONLY (J) WINTER ONLY (D) JAMMING /∧\ or / or \ EARLIEST HEARD ◢ LATEST HEARD ◣ ♦ TENTATIVE

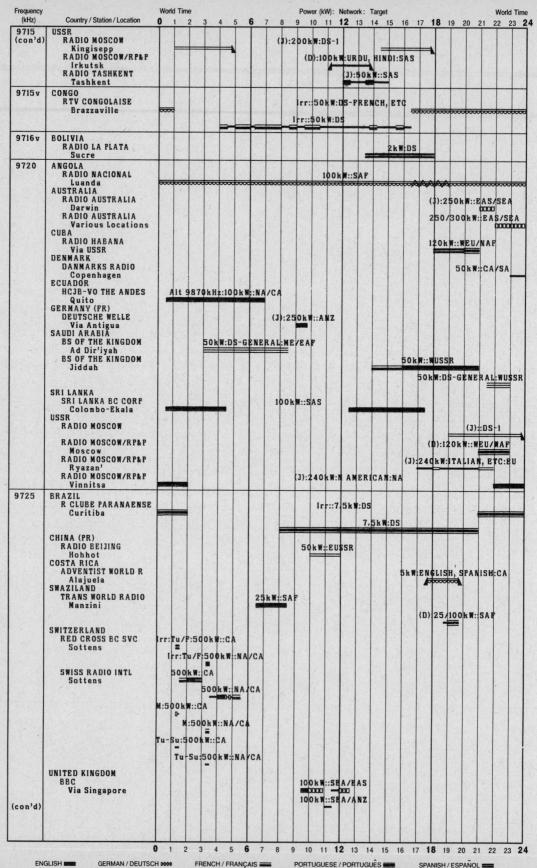

Frequency (kHz)	Country / Station / Location	Notes
9715 (con'd)	USSR / RADIO MOSCOW / Kingisepp	(J):200kW:DS-1
	RADIO MOSCOW/RP&P / Irkutsk	(D):100kW:URDU, HINDI:SAS
	RADIO TASHKENT / Tashkent	(J):50kW::SAS
9715v	CONGO / RTV CONGOLAISE / Brazzaville	Irr::50kW:DS-FRENCH, ETC; Irr::50kW:DS
9716v	BOLIVIA / RADIO LA PLATA / Sucre	2kW:DS
9720	ANGOLA / RADIO NACIONAL / Luanda	100kW::SAF
	AUSTRALIA / RADIO AUSTRALIA / Darwin	(J):250kW::EAS/SEA
	RADIO AUSTRALIA / Various Locations	250/300kW::EAS/SEA
	CUBA / RADIO HABANA / Via USSR	120kW::WEU/NAF
	DENMARK / DANMARKS RADIO / Copenhagen	50kW::CA/SA
	ECUADOR / HCJB-VO THE ANDES / Quito	Alt 9870kHz:100kW::NA/CA
	GERMANY (FR) / DEUTSCHE WELLE / Via Antigua	(J):250kW::ANZ
	SAUDI ARABIA / BS OF THE KINGDOM / Ad Dir'iyah	50kW:DS-GENERAL:ME/EAF
	BS OF THE KINGDOM / Jiddah	50kW::WUSSR; 50kW:DS-GENERAL:WUSSR
	SRI LANKA / SRI LANKA BC CORP / Colombo-Ekala	100kW::SAS
	USSR / RADIO MOSCOW	(J)::DS-1
	RADIO MOSCOW/RP&P / Moscow	(D):120kW::WEU/NAF
	RADIO MOSCOW/RP&P / Ryazan'	(J):240kW:ITALIAN, ETC:EU
	RADIO MOSCOW/RP&P / Vinnitsa	(J):240kW:N AMERICAN:NA
9725	BRAZIL / R CLUBE PARANAENSE / Curitiba	Irr::7.5kW:DS; 7.5kW:DS
	CHINA (PR) / RADIO BEIJING / Hohhot	50kW::EUSSR
	COSTA RICA / ADVENTIST WORLD R / Alajuela	5kW:ENGLISH, SPANISH:CA
	SWAZILAND / TRANS WORLD RADIO / Manzini	25kW:SAF; (D) 25/100kW::SAF
	SWITZERLAND / RED CROSS BC SVC / Sottens	Irr:Tu/F:500kW::CA; Irr:Tu/F:500kW::NA/CA
	SWISS RADIO INTL / Sottens	500kW::CA; 500kW::NA/CA; M:500kW::CA; M:500kW::NA/CA; Tu-Su:500kW::CA; Tu-Su:500kW::NA/CA
	UNITED KINGDOM / BBC / Via Singapore	100kW::SEA/EAS; 100kW::SEA/ANZ
(con'd)		

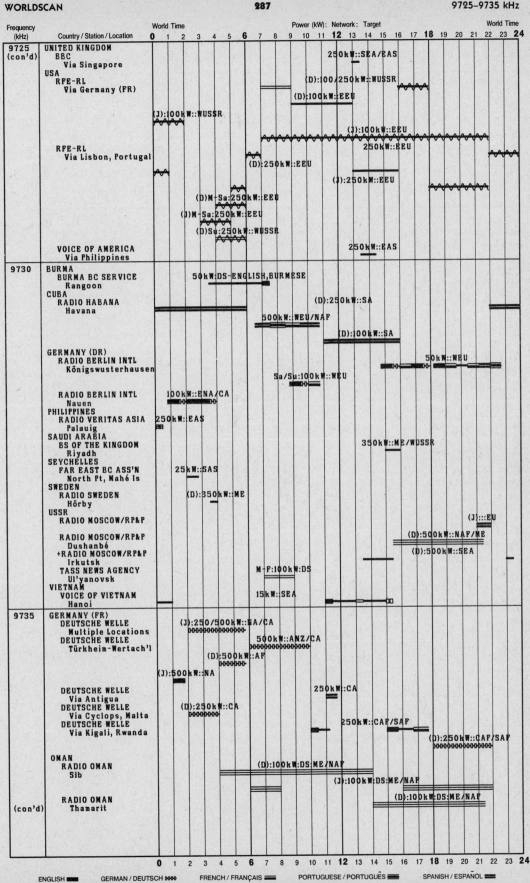

Frequency (kHz)	Country / Station / Location
9725 (con'd)	**UNITED KINGDOM**
	BBC
	Via Singapore — 250kW::SEA/EAS
	USA
	RFE-RL
	Via Germany (FR) — (D):100/250kW::WUSSR
	(D):100kW::EEU
	(J):100kW::WUSSR
	RFE-RL
	Via Lisbon, Portugal
	(J):100kW::EEU
	250kW::EEU
	(D):250kW::EEU
	(J):250kW::EEU
	(D)M-Sa:250kW::EEU
	(J)M-Sa:250kW::EEU
	(D)Su:250kW::WUSSR
	VOICE OF AMERICA
	Via Philippines — 250kW::EAS
9730	**BURMA**
	BURMA BC SERVICE
	Rangoon — 50kW:DS-ENGLISH,BURMESE
	CUBA
	RADIO HABANA
	Havana — (D):250kW::SA
	500kW::WEU/NAF
	(D):100kW::SA
	GERMANY (DR)
	RADIO BERLIN INTL
	Königswusterhausen — 50kW::WEU
	Sa/Su:100kW::WEU
	RADIO BERLIN INTL
	Nauen — 100kW::ENA/CA
	PHILIPPINES
	RADIO VERITAS ASIA
	Palauig — 250kW::EAS
	SAUDI ARABIA
	BS OF THE KINGDOM
	Riyadh — 350kW::ME/WUSSR
	SEYCHELLES
	FAR EAST BC ASS'N
	North Pt, Mahé Is — 25kW::SAS
	SWEDEN
	RADIO SWEDEN
	Hörby — (D):350kW::ME
	USSR
	RADIO MOSCOW/RP&P — (J):::EU
	RADIO MOSCOW/RP&P
	Dushanbé — (D):500kW::NAF/ME
	+RADIO MOSCOW/RP&P
	Irkutsk — (D):500kW::SEA
	TASS NEWS AGENCY
	Ul'yanovsk — M-F:100kW:DS
	VIETNAM
	VOICE OF VIETNAM
	Hanoi — 15kW::SEA
9735	**GERMANY (FR)**
	DEUTSCHE WELLE
	Multiple Locations — (J):250/500kW::NA/CA
	DEUTSCHE WELLE
	Türkheim-Wertach'l — 500kW::ANZ/CA
	(D):500kW::AF
	(J):500kW::NA
	DEUTSCHE WELLE
	Via Antigua — 250kW::CA
	DEUTSCHE WELLE
	Via Cyclops, Malta — (D):250kW::CA
	DEUTSCHE WELLE
	Via Kigali, Rwanda — 250kW::CAF/SAF
	(D):250kW::CAF/SAF
	OMAN
	RADIO OMAN
	Sib — (D):100kW:DS:ME/NAF
	(J):100kW:DS:ME/NAF
(con'd)	RADIO OMAN
	Thamarit — (D):100kW:DS:ME/NAF

World Time: 0 1 2 3 4 5 6 7 8 9 10 11 12 13 14 15 16 17 18 19 20 21 22 23 24

Power (kW): Network: Target

ENGLISH ▬ GERMAN / DEUTSCH ◊◊◊◊ FRENCH / FRANÇAIS ═══ PORTUGUESE / PORTUGUÊS ▬ SPANISH / ESPAÑOL ═══

ARABIC /ﺍﺏﺝﺩ ═ RUSSIAN / РУССКИЙ ─── CHINESE / ✦✖ ◊◊◊◊ JAPANESE / 日本語 ▬▬ MULTILINGUAL ◌◌◌◌ OTHER ▬

SUMMER ONLY (J)   WINTER ONLY (D)   JAMMING ∧∧ or / or \   EARLIEST HEARD ◢   LATEST HEARD ◣   + TENTATIVE

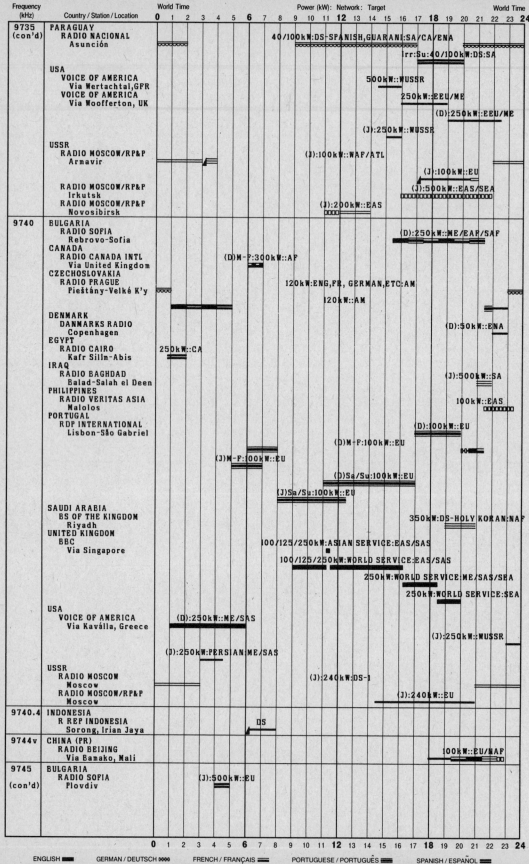

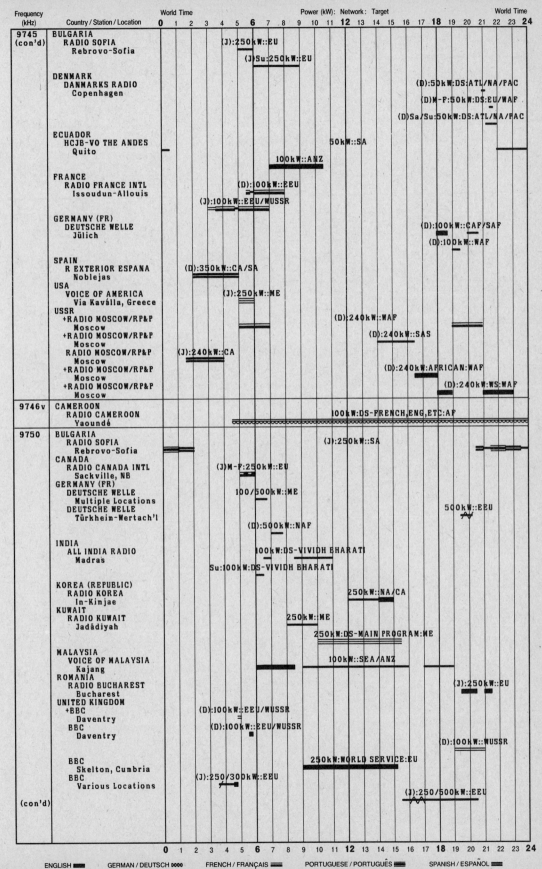

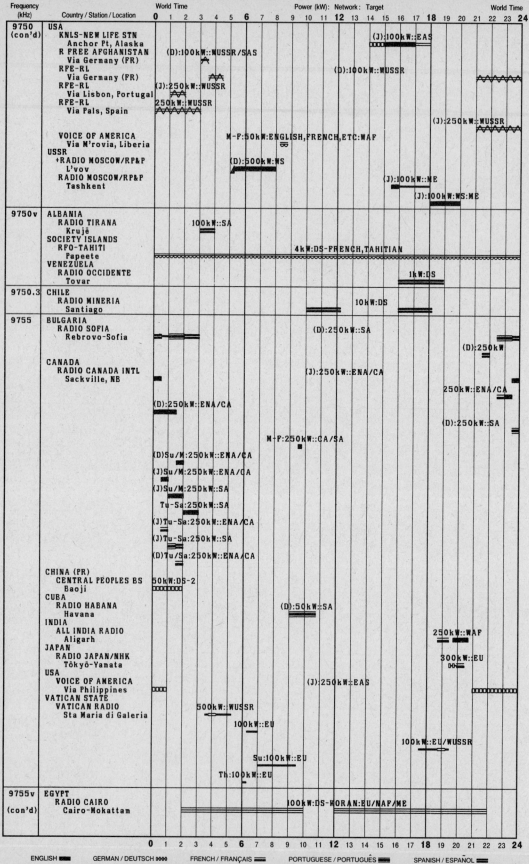

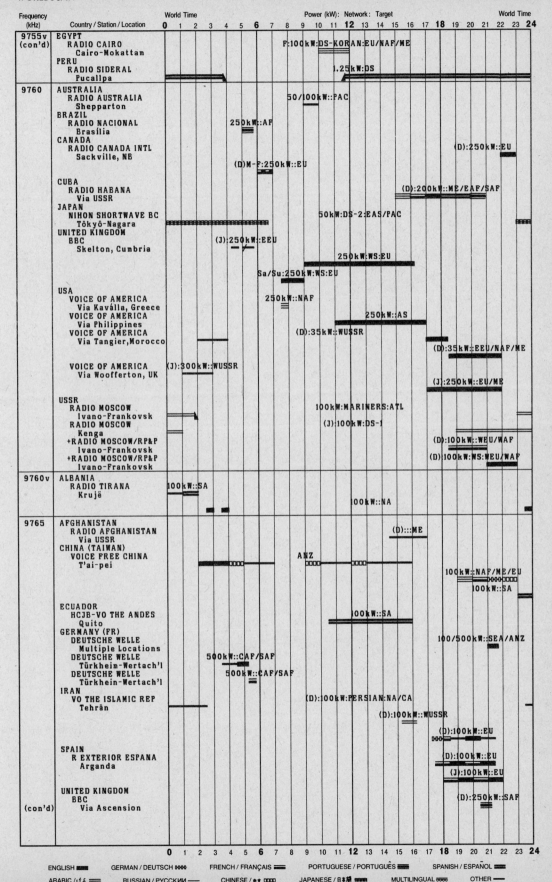

Frequency (kHz)	Country / Station / Location		Power (kW): Network: Target

9755v (con'd) — EGYPT / RADIO CAIRO / Cairo-Mokattam — F:100kW:DS-KORAN:EU/NAF/ME

PERU / RADIO SIDERAL / Pucallpa — 1.25kW:DS

9760 — AUSTRALIA / RADIO AUSTRALIA / Shepparton — 50/100kW::PAC

BRAZIL / RADIO NACIONAL / Brasília — 250kW::AF

CANADA / RADIO CANADA INTL / Sackville, NB — (D):250kW::EU ; (D)M-F:250kW::EU

CUBA / RADIO HABANA / Via USSR — (D):200kW::ME/EAF/SAF

JAPAN / NIHON SHORTWAVE BC / Tōkyō-Nagara — 50kW:DS-2:EAS/PAC

UNITED KINGDOM / BBC / Skelton, Cumbria — (J):250kW::EEU ; 250kW:WS:EU ; Sa/Su:250kW:WS:EU

USA / VOICE OF AMERICA / Via Kaválla, Greece — 250kW::NAF

VOICE OF AMERICA / Via Philippines — 250kW::AS

VOICE OF AMERICA / Via Tangier, Morocco — (D):35kW::WUSSR ; (D):35kW::EEU/NAF/ME

VOICE OF AMERICA / Via Woofferton, UK — (J):300kW::WUSSR ; (J):250kW::EU/ME

USSR / RADIO MOSCOW / Ivano-Frankovsk — 100kW:MARINERS:ATL

RADIO MOSCOW / Kenga — (J):100kW:DS-1

+RADIO MOSCOW/RP&P / Ivano-Frankovsk — (D):100kW::WEU/WAF

+RADIO MOSCOW/RP&P / Ivano-Frankovsk — (D):100kW:WS:WEU/WAF

9760v — ALBANIA / RADIO TIRANA / Krujë — 100kW::SA ; 100kW::NA

9765 — AFGHANISTAN / RADIO AFGHANISTAN / Via USSR — (D):::ME

CHINA (TAIWAN) / VOICE FREE CHINA / T'ai-pei — ANZ ; 100kW::NAF/ME/EU ; 100kW::SA

ECUADOR / HCJB-VO THE ANDES / Quito — 100kW::SA

GERMANY (FR) / DEUTSCHE WELLE / Multiple Locations — 100/500kW::SEA/ANZ

DEUTSCHE WELLE / Türkhein-Wertach'l — 500kW::CAF/SAF

DEUTSCHE WELLE / Türkhein-Wertach'l — 500kW::CAF/SAF

IRAN / VO THE ISLAMIC REP / Tehrān — (D):100kW:PERSIAN:NA/CA ; (D):100kW::WUSSR

SPAIN / R EXTERIOR ESPANA / Arganda — (D):100kW::EU ; (D):100kW::EU ; (J):100kW::EU

UNITED KINGDOM / BBC / Via Ascension — (D):250kW::SAF

(con'd)

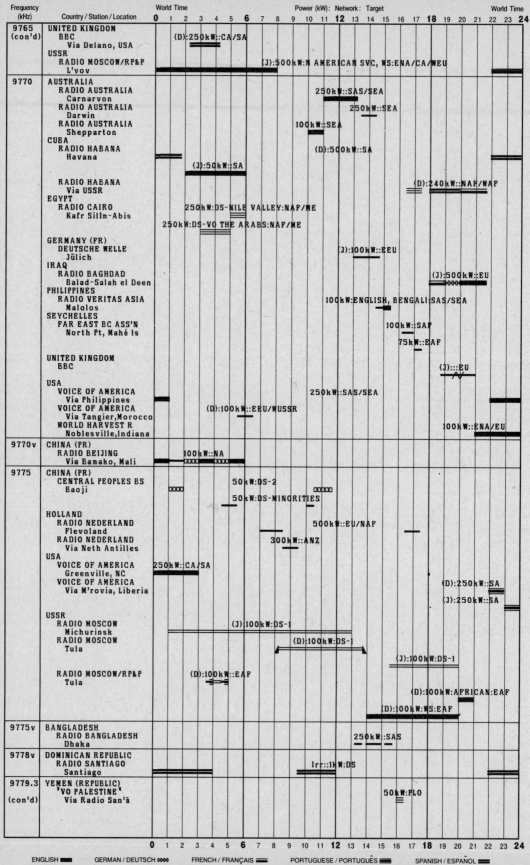

Frequency (kHz)	Country / Station / Location	
9765 (con'd)	UNITED KINGDOM BBC Via Delano, USA	(D):250kW::CA/SA
	USSR RADIO MOSCOW/RP&P L'vov	(J):500kW:N AMERICAN SVC, WS:ENA/CA/WEU
9770	AUSTRALIA RADIO AUSTRALIA Carnarvon	250kW::SAS/SEA
	RADIO AUSTRALIA Darwin	250kW::SEA
	RADIO AUSTRALIA Shepparton	100kW::SEA
	CUBA RADIO HABANA Havana	(D):500kW::SA / (J):50kW::SA
	RADIO HABANA Via USSR	(D):240kW::NAF/WAF
	EGYPT RADIO CAIRO Kafr Silim-Abis	250kW:DS-NILE VALLEY:NAF/ME / 250kW:DS-VO THE ARABS:NAF/ME
	GERMANY (FR) DEUTSCHE WELLE Jülich	(J):100kW::EEU
	IRAQ RADIO BAGHDAD Balad-Salah el Deen	(J):500kW::EU
	PHILIPPINES RADIO VERITAS ASIA Malolos	100kW:ENGLISH, BENGALI:SAS/SEA
	SEYCHELLES FAR EAST BC ASS'N North Pt, Mahé Is	100kW::SAF / 75kW::EAF
	UNITED KINGDOM BBC	(J):::EU
	USA VOICE OF AMERICA Via Philippines	250kW::SAS/SEA
	VOICE OF AMERICA Via Tangier,Morocco	(D):100kW::EEU/WUSSR
	WORLD HARVEST R Noblesville,Indiana	100kW::ENA/EU
9770v	CHINA (PR) RADIO BEIJING Via Bamako, Mali	100kW::NA
9775	CHINA (PR) CENTRAL PEOPLES BS Baoji	50kW:DS-2 / 50kW:DS-MINORITIES
	HOLLAND RADIO NEDERLAND Flevoland	500kW::EU/NAF
	RADIO NEDERLAND Via Neth Antilles	300kW::ANZ
	USA VOICE OF AMERICA Greenville, NC	250kW::CA/SA
	VOICE OF AMERICA Via M'rovia, Liberia	(D):250kW::SA / (J):250kW::SA
	USSR RADIO MOSCOW Michurinsk	(J)100kW:DS-1
	RADIO MOSCOW Tula	(D):100kW:DS-1
		(J):100kW:DS-1
	RADIO MOSCOW/RP&P Tula	(D):100kW::EAF
		(D):100kW:AFRICAN:EAF
		(D):100kW:WS:EAF
9775v	BANGLADESH RADIO BANGLADESH Dhaka	250kW::SAS
9778v	DOMINICAN REPUBLIC RADIO SANTIAGO Santiago	Irr::1kW:DS
9779.3 (con'd)	YEMEN (REPUBLIC) 'VO PALESTINE' Via Radio San'ā	50kW:FLO

ENGLISH ▰▰▰   GERMAN / DEUTSCH ◊◊◊◊   FRENCH / FRANÇAIS ▭▭▭   PORTUGUESE / PORTUGUÊS ▭▭▭   SPANISH / ESPAÑOL ▭▭▭

ARABIC / المعة ▰▰▰   RUSSIAN / РУССКИЙ ▭▭▭   CHINESE / 中文 ◊◊◊◊   JAPANESE / 日本語 ▰▰▰   MULTILINGUAL ◊◊◊◊   OTHER ▬▬

SUMMER ONLY (J)   WINTER ONLY (D)   JAMMING ∧∧ or / or \   EARLIEST HEARD ◢   LATEST HEARD ◣   ⁺ TENTATIVE

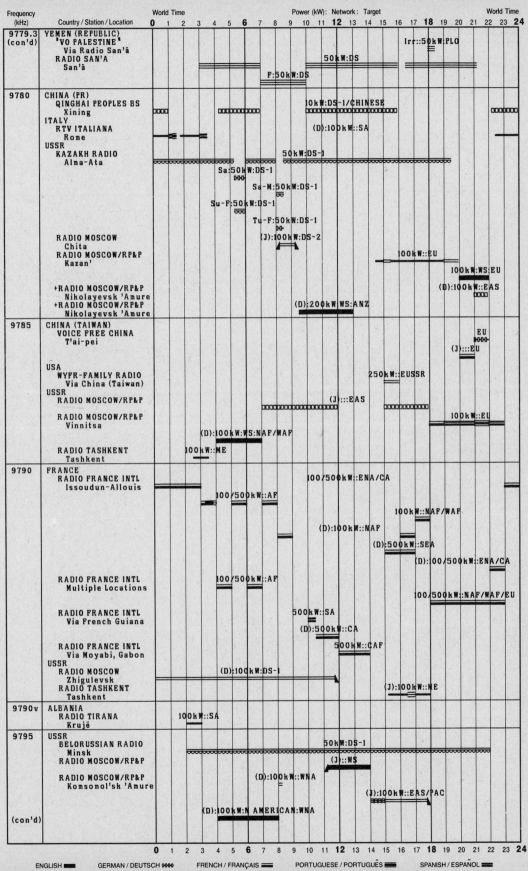

Frequency (kHz)	Country / Station / Location		

9779.3 (con'd) — YEMEN (REPUBLIC), 'VO PALESTINE' Via Radio San'ā — Irr::50kW:PLO

RADIO SAN'A, San'ā — 50kW:DS — F:50kW:DS

9780 — CHINA (PR), QINGHAI PEOPLES BS, Xining — 10kW:DS-1/CHINESE

ITALY, RTV ITALIANA, Rome — (D):100kW::SA

USSR, KAZAKH RADIO, Alma-Ata — 50kW:DS-1 — Sa:50kW:DS-1 — Sa-M:50kW:DS-1 — Su-F:50kW:DS-1 — Tu-F:50kW:DS-1

RADIO MOSCOW, Chita — (J):100kW:DS-2

RADIO MOSCOW/RP&P, Kazan' — 100kW::EU — 100kW:WS:EU — (D):100kW::EAS

+RADIO MOSCOW/RP&P, Nikolayevsk 'Amure

+RADIO MOSCOW/RP&P, Nikolayevsk 'Amure — (D):200kW:WS:ANZ

9785 — CHINA (TAIWAN), VOICE FREE CHINA, T'ai-pei — EU — (J):::EU

USA, WYFR-FAMILY RADIO Via China (Taiwan) — 250kW::EUSSR

USSR, RADIO MOSCOW/RP&P — (J):::EAS

RADIO MOSCOW/RP&P, Vinnitsa — 100kW::EU — (D):100kW:WS:NAF/WAF

RADIO TASHKENT, Tashkent — 100kW::ME

9790 — FRANCE, RADIO FRANCE INTL, Issoudun-Allouis — 100/500kW::ENA/CA — 100/500kW::AF — 100kW::NAF/WAF — (D):100kW::NAF — (D):500kW::SEA — (D):100/500kW::ENA/CA

RADIO FRANCE INTL, Multiple Locations — 100/500kW::AF — 100/500kW::NAF/WAF/EU

RADIO FRANCE INTL Via French Guiana — 500kW::SA — (D):500kW::CA

RADIO FRANCE INTL Via Moyabi, Gabon — 500kW::CAF

USSR, RADIO MOSCOW, Zhigulevsk — (D):100kW:DS-1

RADIO TASHKENT, Tashkent — (J):100kW::ME

9790v — ALBANIA, RADIO TIRANA, Krujë — 100kW::SA

9795 — USSR, BELORUSSIAN RADIO, Minsk — 50kW:DS-1

RADIO MOSCOW/RP&P — (J)::WS

RADIO MOSCOW/RP&P, Komsomol'sk 'Amure — (D):100kW::WNA — (J):100kW::EAS/PAC

(con'd) — (D):100kW:N AMERICAN:WNA

ENGLISH ▬▬   GERMAN / DEUTSCH ◊◊◊◊   FRENCH / FRANÇAIS ▬▬   PORTUGUESE / PORTUGUÊS ▬▬   SPANISH / ESPAÑOL ▬▬

ARABIC / ﻋﺮﺑﻲ ▬▬   RUSSIAN / РУССКИИ ▬▬   CHINESE / 中文 ◊◊◊◊   JAPANESE / 日本語 ▬▬   MULTILINGUAL ◊◊◊◊   OTHER ▬▬

SUMMER ONLY (J)   WINTER ONLY (D)   JAMMING ∧∧ or / or \   EARLIEST HEARD ◢   LATEST HEARD ◣   + TENTATIVE

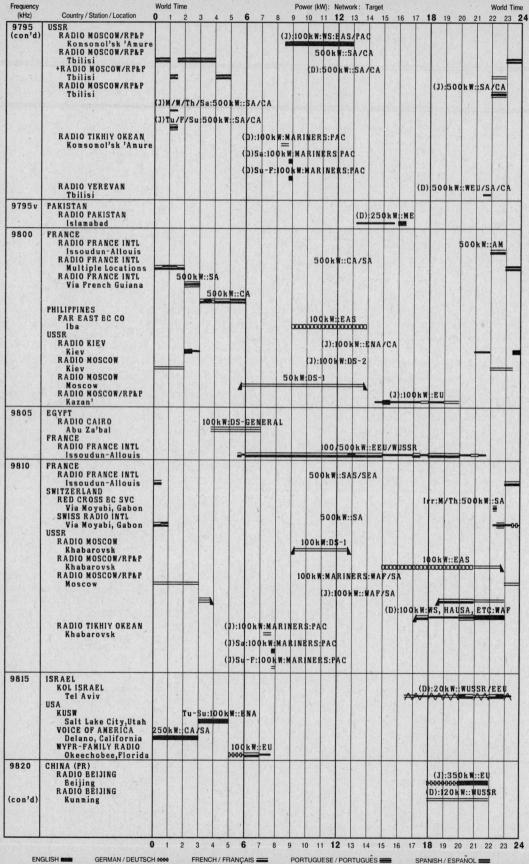

Frequency (kHz)	Country / Station / Location	Schedule (World Time 0–24, Power (kW): Network: Target)
9795 (con'd)	USSR	
	RADIO MOSCOW/RP&P Komsomol'sk 'Amure	(J):100kW:WS:EAS/PAC
	RADIO MOSCOW/RP&P Tbilisi	500kW::SA/CA
	+RADIO MOSCOW/RP&P Tbilisi	(D):500kW::SA/CA
	RADIO MOSCOW/RP&P Tbilisi	(J):500kW::SA/CA
		(J)M/W/Th/Sa:500kW::SA/CA
		(J)Tu/F/Su:500kW::SA/CA
	RADIO TIKHIY OKEAN Komsomol'sk 'Amure	(D):100kW:MARINERS:PAC
		(D)Sa:100kW:MARINERS:PAC
		(D)Su-F:100kW:MARINERS:PAC
	RADIO YEREVAN Tbilisi	(D):500kW::WEU/SA/CA
9795v	PAKISTAN	
	RADIO PAKISTAN Islamabad	(D):250kW::ME
9800	FRANCE	
	RADIO FRANCE INTL Issoudun-Allouis	500kW::AM
	RADIO FRANCE INTL Multiple Locations	500kW::CA/SA
	RADIO FRANCE INTL Via French Guiana	500kW::SA
		500kW::CA
	PHILIPPINES	
	FAR EAST BC CO Iba	100kW::EAS
	USSR	
	RADIO KIEV Kiev	(J):100kW::ENA/CA
	RADIO MOSCOW Kiev	(J):100kW:DS-2
	RADIO MOSCOW Moscow	50kW:DS-1
	RADIO MOSCOW/RP&P Kazan'	(J):100kW::EU
9805	EGYPT	
	RADIO CAIRO Abu Za'bal	100kW:DS-GENERAL
	FRANCE	
	RADIO FRANCE INTL Issoudun-Allouis	100/500kW::EEU/WUSSR
9810	FRANCE	
	RADIO FRANCE INTL Issoudun-Allouis	500kW::SAS/SEA
	SWITZERLAND	
	RED CROSS BC SVC Via Moyabi, Gabon	Irr:M/Th:500kW::SA
	SWISS RADIO INTL Via Moyabi, Gabon	500kW::SA
	USSR	
	RADIO MOSCOW Khabarovsk	100kW:DS-1
	RADIO MOSCOW/RP&P Khabarovsk	100kW::EAS
	RADIO MOSCOW/RP&P Moscow	100kW:MARINERS:WAF/SA
		(J):100kW::WAF/SA
		(D):100kW:WS, HAUSA, ETC:WAF
	RADIO TIKHIY OKEAN Khabarovsk	(J):100kW:MARINERS:PAC
		(J)Sa:100kW:MARINERS:PAC
		(J)Su-F:100kW:MARINERS:PAC
9815	ISRAEL	
	KOL ISRAEL Tel Aviv	(D):20kW::WUSSR/EEU
	USA	
	KUSW Salt Lake City,Utah	Tu-Su:100kW::ENA
	VOICE OF AMERICA Delano, California	250kW:CA/SA
	WYFR-FAMILY RADIO Okeechobee,Florida	100kW::EU
9820	CHINA (PR)	
	RADIO BEIJING Beijing	(J):350kW::EU
(con'd)	RADIO BEIJING Kunming	(D):120kW::WUSSR

World Time: 0 1 2 3 4 5 6 7 8 9 10 11 12 13 14 15 16 17 18 19 20 21 22 23 24

ENGLISH ▬▬   GERMAN / DEUTSCH ◊◊◊◊   FRENCH / FRANÇAIS ▬▬   PORTUGUESE / PORTUGUÊS ▬▬   SPANISH / ESPAÑOL ▬▬

ARABIC / العربية ▬▬   RUSSIAN / РУССКИИ ▬▬   CHINESE / ★★ ◊◊◊◊   JAPANESE / 日本語 ▬▬   MULTILINGUAL ◊◊◊◊   OTHER ▬▬

SUMMER ONLY (J)   WINTER ONLY (D)   JAMMING ∧∧ or / or \   EARLIEST HEARD ◢   LATEST HEARD ◣   + TENTATIVE

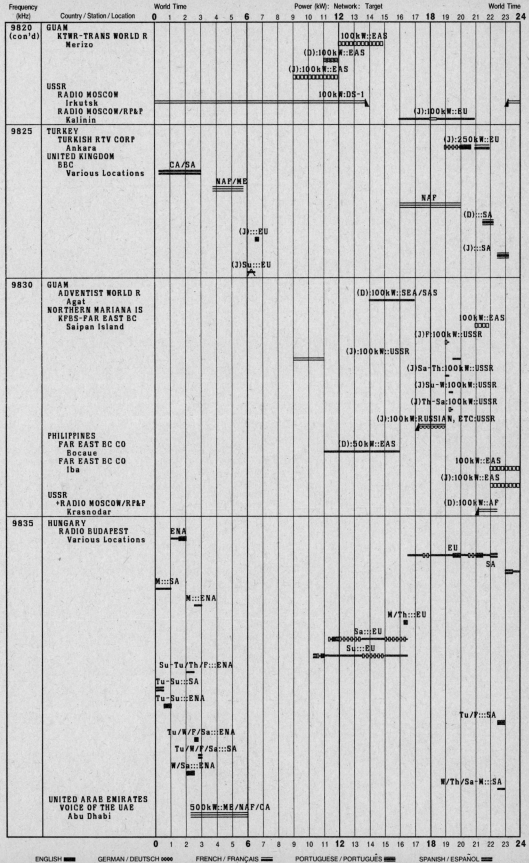

9820 (con'd) — GUAM — KTWR-TRANS WORLD R — Merizo — 100kW::EAS, (D):100kW::EAS, (J):100kW::EAS
USSR — RADIO MOSCOW — Irkutsk — 100kW:DS-1
RADIO MOSCOW/RP&P — Kalinin — (J):100kW::EU

9825 — TURKEY — TURKISH RTV CORP — Ankara — (J):250kW::EU
UNITED KINGDOM — BBC — Various Locations — CA/SA, NAF/ME, NAF, (D):::SA, (J):::EU, (J)Su:::EU, (J):::SA

9830 — GUAM — ADVENTIST WORLD R — Agat — (D):100kW::SEA/SAS
NORTHERN MARIANA IS — KFBS-FAR EAST BC — Saipan Island — 100kW::EAS, (J)F:100kW::USSR, (J):100kW::USSR, (J)Sa-Th:100kW::USSR, (J)Su-W:100kW::USSR, (J)Th-Sa:100kW::USSR, (J):100kW:RUSSIAN, ETC:USSR
PHILIPPINES — FAR EAST BC CO — Bocaue — (D):50kW::EAS
FAR EAST BC CO — Iba — 100kW::EAS, (J):100kW::EAS
USSR — +RADIO MOSCOW/RP&P — Krasnodar — (D):100kW::AF

9835 — HUNGARY — RADIO BUDAPEST — Various Locations — ENA, EU, SA, M:::SA, M:::ENA, M/Th:::EU, Sa:::EU, Su:::EU, Su-Tu/Th/F:::ENA, Tu-Su:::SA, Tu-Su:::ENA, Tu/F:::SA, Tu/W/F/Sa:::ENA, Tu/W/F/Sa:::SA, W/Sa:::ENA, W/Th/Sa-M:::SA
UNITED ARAB EMIRATES — VOICE OF THE UAE — Abu Dhabi — 500kW::ME/NAF/CA

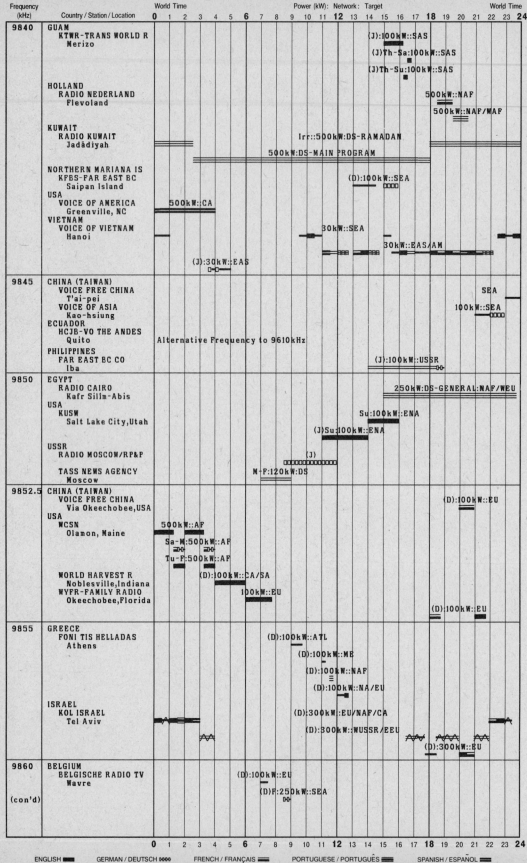

Frequency (kHz)	Country / Station / Location	Power (kW): Network: Target / World Time schedule
9840	**GUAM** KTWR-TRANS WORLD R — Merizo	(J):100kW::SAS / (J)Th-Sa:100kW::SAS / (J)Th-Su:100kW::SAS
	HOLLAND RADIO NEDERLAND — Flevoland	500kW::NAF / 500kW::NAF/WAF
	KUWAIT RADIO KUWAIT — Jadâdiyah	Irr::500kW:DS-RAMADAN / 500kW:DS-MAIN PROGRAM
	NORTHERN MARIANA IS KFBS-FAR EAST BC — Saipan Island	(D):100kW::SEA
	USA VOICE OF AMERICA — Greenville, NC	500kW::CA
	VIETNAM VOICE OF VIETNAM — Hanoi	30kW::SEA / 30kW::EAS/AM / (J):30kW::EAS
9845	**CHINA (TAIWAN)** VOICE FREE CHINA — T'ai-pei	SEA
	VOICE OF ASIA — Kao-hsiung	100kW::SEA
	ECUADOR HCJB-VO THE ANDES — Quito	Alternative Frequency to 9610kHz
	PHILIPPINES FAR EAST BC CO — Iba	(J):100kW::USSR
9850	**EGYPT** RADIO CAIRO — Kafr Silim-Abis	250kW:DS-GENERAL:NAF/WEU
	USA KUSW — Salt Lake City, Utah	Su:100kW::ENA / (J)Su:100kW::ENA
	USSR RADIO MOSCOW/RP&P	(J)
	TASS NEWS AGENCY — Moscow	M-F:120kW:DS
9852.5	**CHINA (TAIWAN)** VOICE FREE CHINA — Via Okeechobee, USA	(D):100kW::EU
	USA WCSN — Olamon, Maine	500kW::AF / Sa-M:500kW::AF / Tu-F:500kW::AF
	WORLD HARVEST R — Noblesville, Indiana	(D):100kW::CA/SA
	WYFR-FAMILY RADIO — Okeechobee, Florida	100kW::EU / (D):100kW::EU
9855	**GREECE** FONI TIS HELLADAS — Athens	(D):100kW::ATL / (D):100kW::ME / (D):100kW::NAF / (D):100kW::NA/EU
	ISRAEL KOL ISRAEL — Tel Aviv	(D):300kW::EU/NAF/CA / (D):300kW::WUSSR/EEU / (D):300kW::EU
9860 (con'd)	**BELGIUM** BELGISCHE RADIO TV — Wavre	(D):100kW::EU / (D)F:250kW::SEA

ENGLISH ▅▅▅   GERMAN / DEUTSCH ◊◊◊◊   FRENCH / FRANÇAIS ═══   PORTUGUESE / PORTUGUÊS ▬▬▬   SPANISH / ESPAÑOL ▬▬▬

ARABIC / ﻋﺮﺑﻰ ═══   RUSSIAN / РУССКИИ ═══   CHINESE / 中文 □□□□   JAPANESE / 日本語 ▬▬▬   MULTILINGUAL ▭▭▭   OTHER ▬▬

SUMMER ONLY (J)   WINTER ONLY (D)   JAMMING ∧∧∧ or / or \   EARLIEST HEARD ◢   LATEST HEARD ◣   ✦ TENTATIVE

Frequency (kHz)	Country / Station / Location	World Time 0 ... Power (kW): Network: Target ... 24

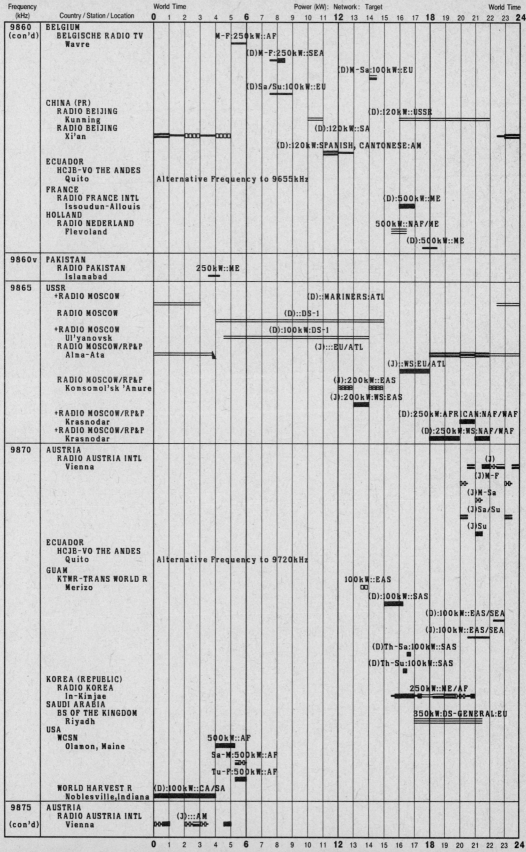

9860 (con'd) BELGIUM
  BELGISCHE RADIO TV
    Wavre
      M-F:250kW::AF
      (D)M-F:250kW::SEA
      (D)M-Sa:100kW::EU
      (D)Sa/Su:100kW::EU

CHINA (PR)
  RADIO BEIJING
    Kunming
      (D)::120kW::USSR
  RADIO BEIJING
    Xi'an
      (D)::120kW::SA
      (D):120kW:SPANISH, CANTONESE:AM

ECUADOR
  HCJB-VO THE ANDES
    Quito
      Alternative Frequency to 9655kHz
FRANCE
  RADIO FRANCE INTL
    Issoudun-Allouis
      (D)::500kW::ME
HOLLAND
  RADIO NEDERLAND
    Flevoland
      500kW::NAF/ME
      (D):500kW::ME

9860v PAKISTAN
  RADIO PAKISTAN
    Islamabad
      250kW::ME

9865 USSR
  +RADIO MOSCOW
      (D)::MARINERS:ATL
  RADIO MOSCOW
      (D)::DS-1
  +RADIO MOSCOW
    Ul'yanovsk
      (D):100kW:DS-1
  RADIO MOSCOW/RP&P
    Alma-Ata
      (J):::EU/ATL
      (J)::WS:EU/ATL
  RADIO MOSCOW/RP&P
    Komsomol'sk 'Amure
      (J):200kW::EAS
      (J):200kW:WS:EAS
  +RADIO MOSCOW/RP&P
    Krasnodar
      (D):250kW:AFRICAN:NAF/WAF
  +RADIO MOSCOW/RP&P
    Krasnodar
      (D):250kW:WS:NAF/WAF

9870 AUSTRIA
  RADIO AUSTRIA INTL
    Vienna
      (J)
      (J)M-F
      (J)M-Sa
      (J)Sa/Su
      (J)Su

ECUADOR
  HCJB-VO THE ANDES
    Quito
      Alternative Frequency to 9720kHz
GUAM
  KTWR-TRANS WORLD R
    Merizo
      100kW::EAS
      (D):100kW::SAS
      (D):100kW::EAS/SEA
      (J):100kW::EAS/SEA
      (D)Th-Sa:100kW::SAS
      (D)Th-Su:100kW::SAS
KOREA (REPUBLIC)
  RADIO KOREA
    In-Kimjae
      250kW::ME/AF
SAUDI ARABIA
  BS OF THE KINGDOM
    Riyadh
      350kW:DS-GENERAL:EU
USA
  WCSN
    Olamon, Maine
      500kW::AF
      Sa-M:500kW::AF
      Tu-F:500kW::AF
WORLD HARVEST R
  Noblesville, Indiana
      (D):100kW::CA/SA

9875 (con'd) AUSTRIA
  RADIO AUSTRIA INTL
    Vienna
      (J):::AM

ENGLISH ▬   GERMAN / DEUTSCH ◊◊◊◊   FRENCH / FRANÇAIS ═══   PORTUGUESE / PORTUGUÊS ▬▬   SPANISH / ESPAÑOL ▬▬

ARABIC / عربى ▤   RUSSIAN / РУССКИЙ ▬   CHINESE / ◆ x ◊◊◊◊   JAPANESE / 日本語 ▬▬   MULTILINGUAL ▦▦   OTHER ▬

SUMMER ONLY (J)   WINTER ONLY (D)   JAMMING /\/\ or / or \   EARLIEST HEARD ◢   LATEST HEARD ◣   * TENTATIVE

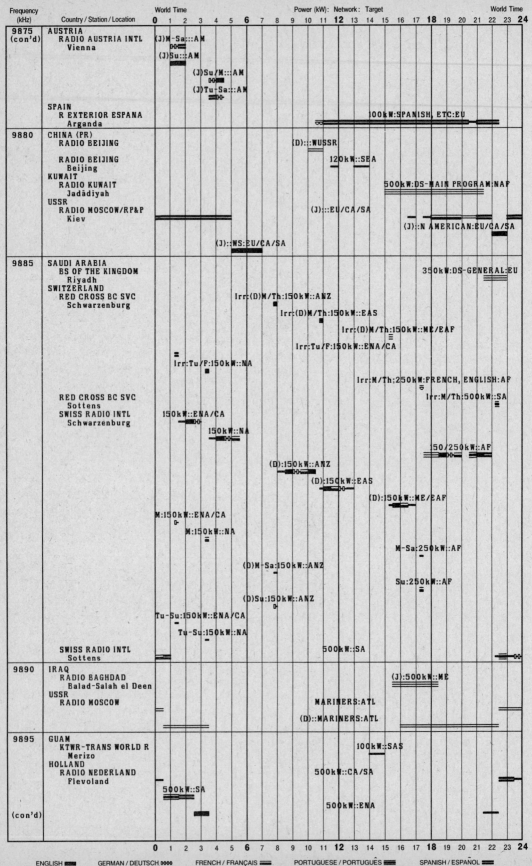

Frequency (kHz)	Country / Station / Location	
9875 (con'd)	AUSTRIA	
	RADIO AUSTRIA INTL Vienna	(J)M-Sa:::AM / (J)Su:::AM / (J)Su/M:::AM / (J)Tu-Sa:::AM
	SPAIN	
	R EXTERIOR ESPANA Arganda	100kW:SPANISH, ETC:EU
9880	CHINA (PR)	
	RADIO BEIJING	(D):::WUSSR
	RADIO BEIJING Beijing	120kW::SEA
	KUWAIT	
	RADIO KUWAIT Jadādiyah	500kW:DS-MAIN PROGRAM:NAF
	USSR	
	RADIO MOSCOW/RP&P Kiev	(J):::EU/CA/SA / (J)::N AMERICAN:EU/CA/SA / (J)::WS:EU/CA/SA
9885	SAUDI ARABIA	
	BS OF THE KINGDOM Riyadh	350kW:DS-GENERAL:EU
	SWITZERLAND	
	RED CROSS BC SVC Schwarzenburg	Irr:(D)M/Th:150kW::ANZ / Irr:(D)M/Th:150kW::EAS / Irr:(D)M/Th:150kW::ME/EAF / Irr:Tu/F:150kW::ENA/CA / Irr:Tu/F:150kW::NA
	RED CROSS BC SVC Sottens	Irr:M/Th:250kW:FRENCH, ENGLISH:AF / Irr:M/Th:500kW::SA
	SWISS RADIO INTL Schwarzenburg	150kW::ENA/CA / 150kW::NA / 50/250kW::AF / (D):150kW::ANZ / (D):150kW::EAS / (D):150kW::ME/EAF / M:150kW::ENA/CA / M:150kW::NA / M-Sa:250kW::AF / (D)M-Sa:150kW::ANZ / Su:250kW::AF / (D)Su:150kW::ANZ / Tu-Su:150kW::ENA/CA / Tu-Su:150kW::NA
	SWISS RADIO INTL Sottens	500kW::SA
9890	IRAQ	
	RADIO BAGHDAD Balad-Salah el Deen	(J):500kW::ME
	USSR	
	RADIO MOSCOW	MARINERS:ATL / (D)::MARINERS:ATL
9895	GUAM	
	KTWR-TRANS WORLD R Merizo	100kW::SAS
	HOLLAND	
	RADIO NEDERLAND Flevoland	500kW::CA/SA / 500kW::SA / 500kW::ENA
(con'd)		

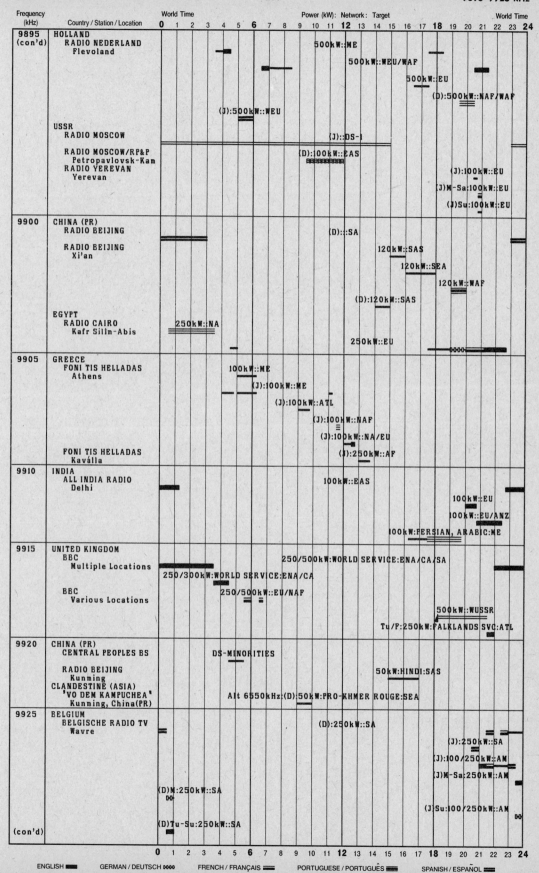

ENGLISH ▬▬   GERMAN / DEUTSCH 0000   FRENCH / FRANÇAIS ══   PORTUGUESE / PORTUGUÊS ▬▬   SPANISH / ESPAÑOL ══

ARABIC / ‫ربی‬ ══   RUSSIAN / РУССКИИ ══   CHINESE / 中文 0000   JAPANESE / 日本語 ▬▬   MULTILINGUAL ▭▭   OTHER ▬

SUMMER ONLY (J)   WINTER ONLY (D)   JAMMING /\/\ or / or \   EARLIEST HEARD ◢   LATEST HEARD ◣   + TENTATIVE

Frequency (kHz)	Country / Station / Location	World Time — Power (kW): Network: Target

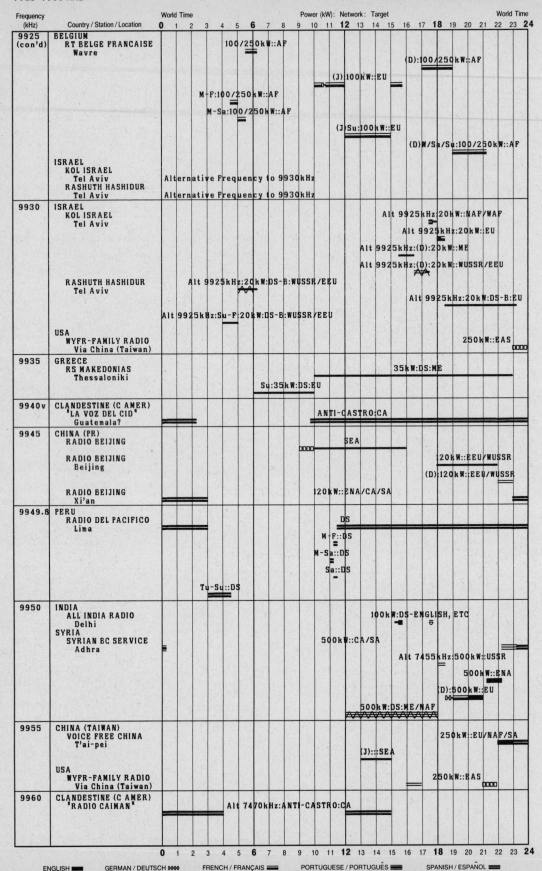

9925 (con'd) — **BELGIUM** — RT BELGE FRANCAISE, Wavre
- 100/250kW::AF
- (D):100/250kW::AF
- (J):100kW::EU
- M-F:100/250kW::AF
- M-Sa:100/250kW::AF
- (J):Su:100kW::EU
- (D)W/Sa/Su:100/250kW::AF

ISRAEL — KOL ISRAEL, Tel Aviv — Alternative Frequency to 9930kHz
RASHUTH HASHIDUR, Tel Aviv — Alternative Frequency to 9930kHz

9930 — **ISRAEL** — KOL ISRAEL, Tel Aviv
- Alt 9925kHz:20kW::NAF/WAF
- Alt 9925kHz:20kW::EU
- Alt 9925kHz:(D):20kW::ME
- Alt 9925kHz:(D):20kW::WUSSR/EEU

RASHUTH HASHIDUR, Tel Aviv
- Alt 9925kHz:20kW:DS-B:WUSSR/EEU
- Alt 9925kHz:20kW:DS-B:EU
- Alt 9925kHz:Su-F:20kW:DS-B:WUSSR/EEU

USA — WYFR-FAMILY RADIO, Via China (Taiwan) — 250kW::EAS

9935 — **GREECE** — RS MAKEDONIAS, Thessaloniki
- 35kW:DS:ME
- Su:35kW:DS:EU

9940v — **CLANDESTINE (C AMER)** — "LA VOZ DEL CID", Guatemala? — ANTI-CASTRO:CA

9945 — **CHINA (PR)** — RADIO BEIJING — SEA
RADIO BEIJING, Beijing
- 120kW::EEU/WUSSR
- (D):120kW::EEU/WUSSR
RADIO BEIJING, Xi'an — 120kW::ENA/CA/SA

9949.8 — **PERU** — RADIO DEL PACIFICO, Lima
- DS
- M-F::DS
- M-Sa::DS
- Sa::DS
- Tu-Su::DS

9950 — **INDIA** — ALL INDIA RADIO, Delhi — 100kW:DS-ENGLISH, ETC
SYRIA — SYRIAN BC SERVICE, Adhra
- 500kW::CA/SA
- Alt 7455kHz:500kW::USSR
- 500kW::ENA
- (D):500kW::EU
- 500kW:DS:ME/NAF

9955 — **CHINA (TAIWAN)** — VOICE FREE CHINA, T'ai-pei
- 250kW::EU/NAF/SA
- (J):::SEA
USA — WYFR-FAMILY RADIO, Via China (Taiwan) — 250kW::EAS

9960 — **CLANDESTINE (C AMER)** — "RADIO CAIMAN" — Alt 7470kHz:ANTI-CASTRO:CA

ENGLISH ▬▬ GERMAN / DEUTSCH ◊◊◊◊ FRENCH / FRANÇAIS ▭▭ PORTUGUESE / PORTUGUÊS ▬▬ SPANISH / ESPAÑOL ▬▬
ARABIC / ﻉﺏ ▬ RUSSIAN / РУССКИИ ▭ CHINESE / 中文 ◊◊◊◊ JAPANESE / 日本語 ▬ MULTILINGUAL ◊◊◊◊ OTHER ▬
SUMMER ONLY (J) WINTER ONLY (D) JAMMING ∧∧ or / or \ EARLIEST HEARD ◢ LATEST HEARD ◣ + TENTATIVE

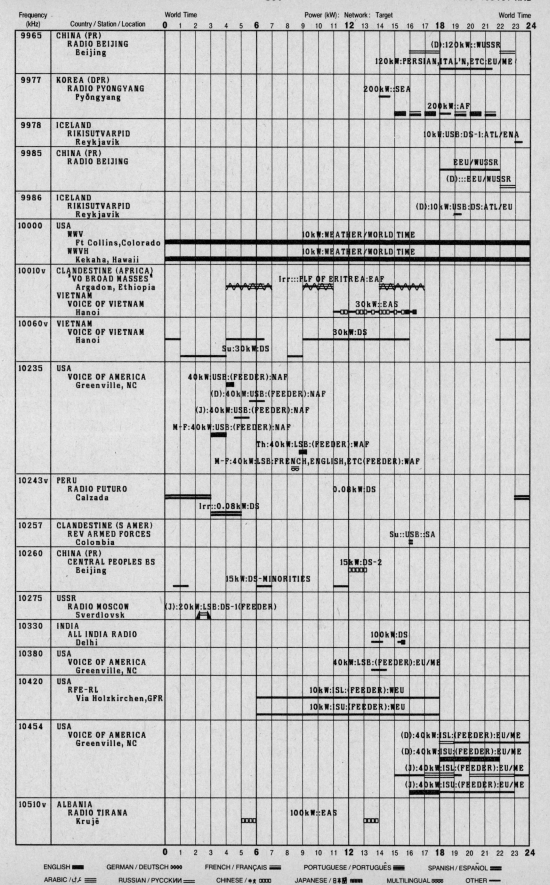

Frequency (kHz)	Country / Station / Location	World Time / Power (kW): Network: Target
9965	CHINA (PR) RADIO BEIJING Beijing	(D):120kW::WUSSR 120kW:PERSIAN,ITAL'N,ETC:EU/ME
9977	KOREA (DPR) RADIO PYONGYANG Pyŏngyang	200kW::SEA 200kW::AF
9978	ICELAND RIKISUTVARPID Reykjavik	10kW:USB:DS-1:ATL/ENA
9985	CHINA (PR) RADIO BEIJING	EEU/WUSSR (D):::EEU/WUSSR
9986	ICELAND RIKISUTVARPID Reykjavik	(D):10kW:USB:DS:ATL/EU
10000	USA WWV Ft Collins,Colorado WWVH Kekaha, Hawaii	10kW:WEATHER/WORLD TIME 10kW:WEATHER/WORLD TIME
10010v	CLANDESTINE (AFRICA) VO BROAD MASSES Argadom, Ethiopia VIETNAM VOICE OF VIETNAM Hanoi	Irr:::FLF OF ERITREA:EAF 30kW::EAS
10060v	VIETNAM VOICE OF VIETNAM Hanoi	30kW:DS Su:30kW:DS
10235	USA VOICE OF AMERICA Greenville, NC	40kW:USB:(FEEDER):NAF (D):40kW:USB:(FEEDER):NAF (J):40kW:USB:(FEEDER):NAF M-F:40kW:USB:(FEEDER):NAF Th:40kW:LSB:(FEEDER):WAF M-F:40kW:LSB:FRENCH,ENGLISH,ETC(FEEDER):WAF
10243v	PERU RADIO FUTURO Calzada	0.08kW:DS Irr::0.08kW:DS
10257	CLANDESTINE (S AMER) REV ARMED FORCES Colombia	Su::USB::SA
10260	CHINA (PR) CENTRAL PEOPLES BS Beijing	15kW:DS-2 15kW:DS-MINORITIES
10275	USSR RADIO MOSCOW Sverdlovsk	(J):20kW:LSB:DS-1(FEEDER)
10330	INDIA ALL INDIA RADIO Delhi	100kW:DS
10380	USA VOICE OF AMERICA Greenville, NC	40kW:LSB:(FEEDER):EU/ME
10420	USA RFE-RL Via Holzkirchen,GFR	10kW:ISL:(FEEDER):WEU 10kW:ISU:(FEEDER):WEU
10454	USA VOICE OF AMERICA Greenville, NC	(D):40kW:ISL:(FEEDER):EU/ME (D):40kW:ISU:(FEEDER):EU/ME (J):40kW:ISL:(FEEDER):EU/ME (J):40kW:ISU:(FEEDER):EU/ME
10510v	ALBANIA RADIO TIRANA Krujë	100kW::EAS

World Time: 0 1 2 3 4 5 6 7 8 9 10 11 12 13 14 15 16 17 18 19 20 21 22 23 24

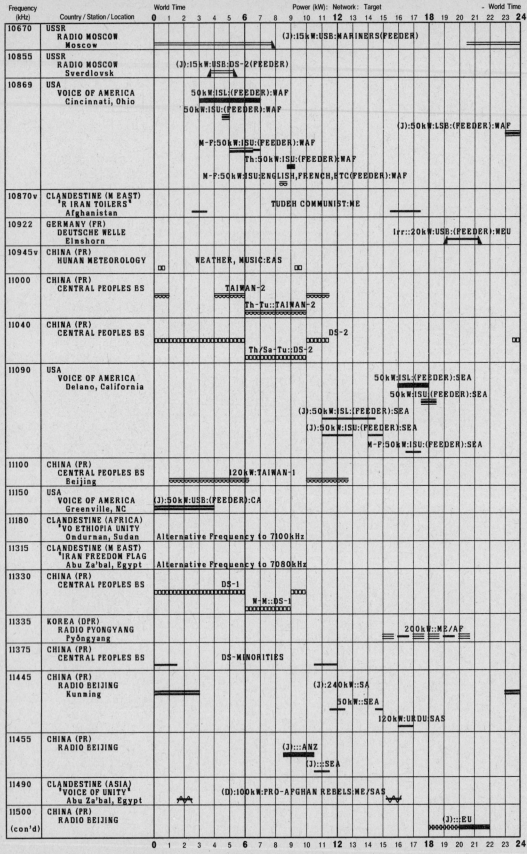

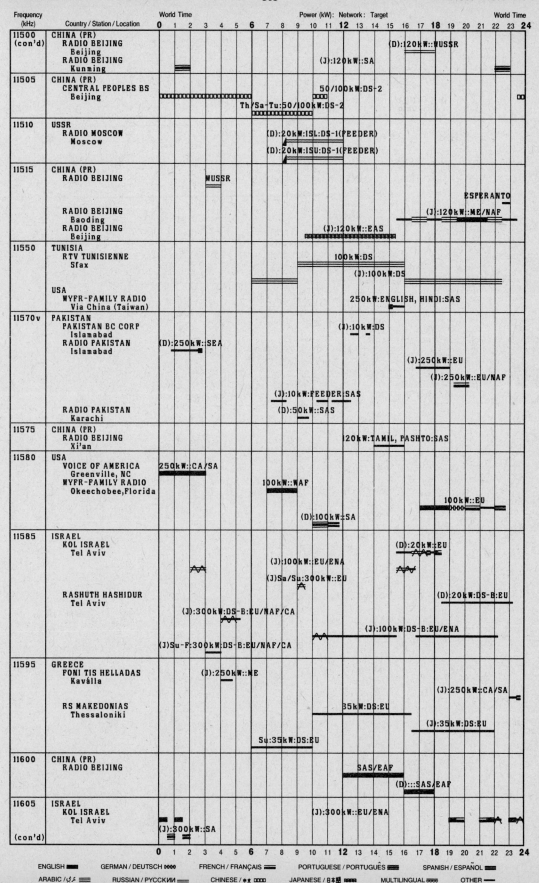

11500 (con'd) CHINA (PR)
RADIO BEIJING — Beijing — (D):120kW::WUSSR
RADIO BEIJING — Kunming — (J):120kW::SA

11505 CHINA (PR)
CENTRAL PEOPLES BS — Beijing — 50/100kW:DS-2
Th/Sa-Tu:50/100kW:DS-2

11510 USSR
RADIO MOSCOW — Moscow — (D):20kW:ISL:DS-1(FEEDER)
(D):20kW:ISU:DS-1(FEEDER)

11515 CHINA (PR)
RADIO BEIJING — WUSSR
ESPERANTO
RADIO BEIJING — Baoding — (J):120kW::ME/NAF
RADIO BEIJING — Beijing — (J):120kW::EAS

11550 TUNISIA
RTV TUNISIENNE — Sfax — 100kW:DS
(J):100kW:DS
USA
WYFR-FAMILY RADIO — Via China (Taiwan) — 250kW:ENGLISH, HINDI:SAS

11570v PAKISTAN
PAKISTAN BC CORP — Islamabad — (J):10kW:DS
RADIO PAKISTAN — Islamabad — (D):250kW::SEA
(J):250kW::EU
(J):250kW::EU/NAF
(J):10kW:FEEDER:SAS
RADIO PAKISTAN — Karachi — (D):50kW::SAS

11575 CHINA (PR)
RADIO BEIJING — Xi'an — 120kW:TAMIL, PASHTO:SAS

11580 USA
VOICE OF AMERICA — Greenville, NC — 250kW::CA/SA
WYFR-FAMILY RADIO — Okeechobee, Florida — 100kW::NAF
100kW::EU
(D):100kW::SA

11585 ISRAEL
KOL ISRAEL — Tel Aviv — (D):20kW::EU
(J):100kW::EU/ENA
(J)Sa/Su:300kW::EU
RASHUTH HASHIDUR — Tel Aviv — (D):20kW:DS-B:EU
(J):300kW:DS-B:EU/NAF/CA
(J):100kW:DS-B:EU/ENA
(J)Su-F:300kW:DS-B:EU/NAF/CA

11595 GREECE
FONI TIS HELLADAS — Kaválla — (J):250kW::ME
(J):250kW::CA/SA
RS MAKEDONIAS — Thessaloniki — 35kW:DS:EU
(J):35kW:DS:EU
Su:35kW:DS:EU

11600 CHINA (PR)
RADIO BEIJING — SAS/EAF
(D):::SAS/EAF

11605 (con'd) ISRAEL
KOL ISRAEL — Tel Aviv — (J):300kW::EU/ENA
(J):300kW::SA

Frequency (kHz)	Country / Station / Location	Power (kW): Network: Target

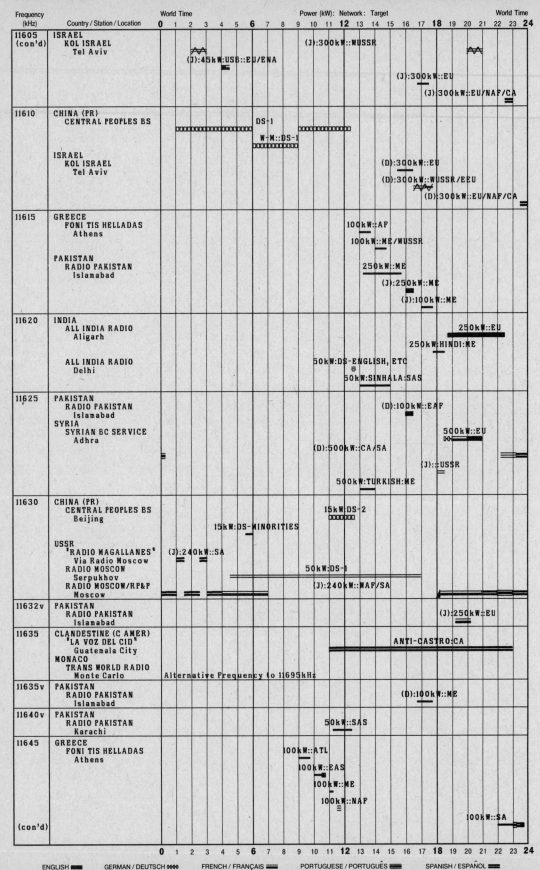

Chart content (World Time 0–24):

11605 (con'd) — ISRAEL, KOL ISRAEL, Tel Aviv
- (J):300kW::WUSSR
- (J):45kW:USB::EU/ENA
- (J):300kW::EU
- (J):300kW::EU/NAF/CA

11610 — CHINA (PR), CENTRAL PEOPLES BS
- DS-1
- W-M::DS-1

ISRAEL, KOL ISRAEL, Tel Aviv
- (D):300kW::EU
- (D):300kW::WUSSR/EEU
- (D):300kW::EU/NAF/CA

11615 — GREECE, FONI TIS HELLADAS, Athens
- 100kW::AF
- 100kW::ME/WUSSR

PAKISTAN, RADIO PAKISTAN, Islamabad
- 250kW::ME
- (J):250kW::ME
- (J):100kW::ME

11620 — INDIA, ALL INDIA RADIO, Aligarh
- 250kW::EU
- 250kW:HINDI:ME

ALL INDIA RADIO, Delhi
- 50kW:DS-ENGLISH, ETC
- 50kW:SINHALA:SAS

11625 — PAKISTAN, RADIO PAKISTAN, Islamabad
- (D):100kW::EAF

SYRIA, SYRIAN BC SERVICE, Adhra
- 500kW::EU
- (D):500kW::CA/SA
- (J)::USSR
- 500kW:TURKISH:ME

11630 — CHINA (PR), CENTRAL PEOPLES BS, Beijing
- 15kW:DS-2
- 15kW:DS-MINORITIES

USSR, "RADIO MAGALLANES" Via Radio Moscow
- (J):240kW::SA

RADIO MOSCOW, Serpukhov
- 50kW:DS-1

RADIO MOSCOW/RP&P, Moscow
- (J):240kW::WAF/SA

11632v — PAKISTAN, RADIO PAKISTAN, Islamabad
- (J):250kW::EU

11635 — CLANDESTINE (C AMER), "LA VOZ DEL CID", Guatemala City
- ANTI-CASTRO:CA

MONACO, TRANS WORLD RADIO, Monte Carlo
- Alternative Frequency to 11695kHz

11635v — PAKISTAN, RADIO PAKISTAN, Islamabad
- (D):100kW::ME

11640v — PAKISTAN, RADIO PAKISTAN, Karachi
- 50kW::SAS

11645 — GREECE, FONI TIS HELLADAS, Athens
- 100kW::ATL
- 100kW::EAS
- 100kW::ME
- 100kW::NAF
- 100kW::SA

(con'd)

Legend:
ENGLISH ▪▪▪   GERMAN / DEUTSCH ००००   FRENCH / FRANÇAIS ▬▬   PORTUGUESE / PORTUGUÊS ▬▬   SPANISH / ESPAÑOL ▬▬
ARABIC / عربى ▬▬   RUSSIAN / РУССКИИ ▬▬   CHINESE / 中文 ००००   JAPANESE / 日本語 ▬▬   MULTILINGUAL ००००   OTHER ▬
SUMMER ONLY (J)   WINTER ONLY (D)   JAMMING /\/\ or / or \   EARLIEST HEARD ◢   LATEST HEARD ◣   + TENTATIVE

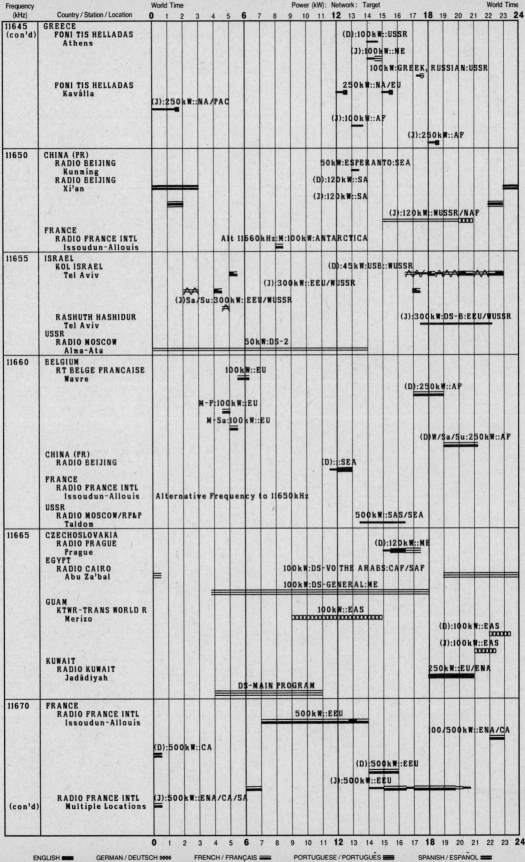

Frequency (kHz)	Country / Station / Location	Schedule (World Time / Power (kW): Network: Target)
11645 (con'd)	**GREECE** FONI TIS HELLADAS Athens	(D):100kW::USSR (J):100kW::ME 100kW:GREEK, RUSSIAN:USSR
	FONI TIS HELLADAS Kaválla	250kW::NA/EU (J):250kW::NA/PAC (J):100kW::AF (J):250kW::AF
11650	**CHINA (PR)** RADIO BEIJING Kunming RADIO BEIJING Xi'an	50kW:ESPERANTO:SEA (D):120kW::SA (J):120kW::SA (J):120kW::WUSSR/NAF
	FRANCE RADIO FRANCE INTL Issoudun-Allouis	Alt 11660kHz:M:100kW:ANTARCTICA
11655	**ISRAEL** KOL ISRAEL Tel Aviv	(D):45kW:USB::WUSSR (J):300kW::EEU/WUSSR (J)Sa/Su:300kW::EEU/WUSSR
	RASHUTH HASHIDUR Tel Aviv	(J):300kW:DS-B:EEU/WUSSR
	USSR RADIO MOSCOW Alma-Ata	50kW:DS-2
11660	**BELGIUM** RT BELGE FRANCAISE Wavre	100kW::EU (D):250kW::AF M-F:100kW::EU M-Sa:100kW::EU (D)W/Sa/Su:250kW::AF
	CHINA (PR) RADIO BEIJING	(D):::SEA
	FRANCE RADIO FRANCE INTL Issoudun-Allouis	Alternative Frequency to 11650kHz
	USSR RADIO MOSCOW/RP&P Taldom	500kW::SAS/SEA
11665	**CZECHOSLOVAKIA** RADIO PRAGUE Prague	(D):120kW::ME
	EGYPT RADIO CAIRO Abu Za'bal	100kW:DS-VO THE ARABS:CAF/SAF 100kW:DS-GENERAL:ME
	GUAM KTWR-TRANS WORLD R Merizo	100kW::EAS (D):100kW::EAS (J):100kW::EAS
	KUWAIT RADIO KUWAIT Jadâdiyah	250kW::EU/ENA DS-MAIN PROGRAM
11670	**FRANCE** RADIO FRANCE INTL Issoudun-Allouis	500kW::EEU 00/500kW::ENA/CA (D):500kW:CA (D):500kW::EEU (J):500kW::EEU
(con'd)	RADIO FRANCE INTL Multiple Locations	(J):500kW::ENA/CA/SA

World Time: 0 1 2 3 4 5 6 7 8 9 10 11 12 13 14 15 16 17 18 19 20 21 22 23 24

ENGLISH ▬   GERMAN / DEUTSCH ∞∞∞   FRENCH / FRANÇAIS ═══   PORTUGUESE / PORTUGUÊS ≡≡≡   SPANISH / ESPAÑOL ═══

ARABIC / عربي ▬   RUSSIAN / РУССКИЙ ═══   CHINESE / 中文 ▭▭▭   JAPANESE / 日本語 ▬▬▬   MULTILINGUAL ▭▭▭   OTHER ▬

SUMMER ONLY (J)   WINTER ONLY (D)   JAMMING ∧∧∧ or / or \   EARLIEST HEARD ◢   LATEST HEARD ◣   + TENTATIVE

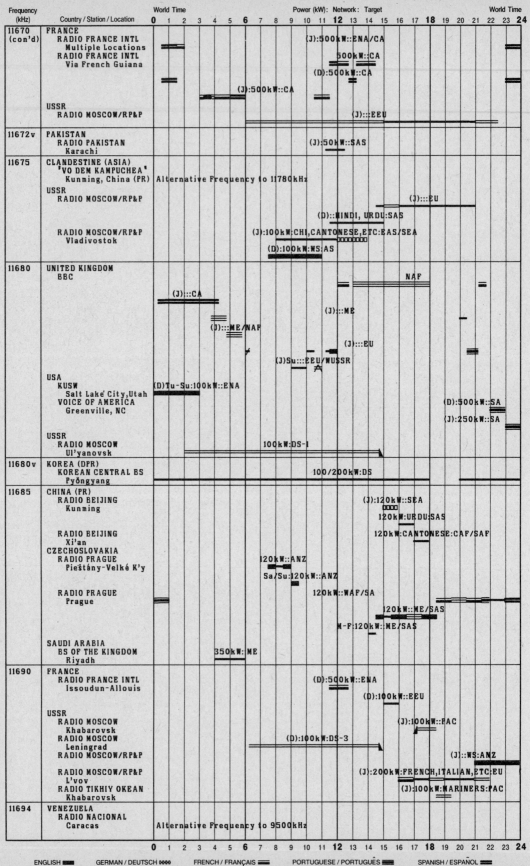

Frequency (kHz)	Country / Station / Location	World Time 0–24 schedule · Power (kW) : Network : Target
11670 (con'd)	FRANCE — RADIO FRANCE INTL, Multiple Locations	(J):500kW::ENA/CA
	RADIO FRANCE INTL, Via French Guiana	500kW::CA · (D):500kW::CA · (J):500kW::CA
	USSR — RADIO MOSCOW/RP&P	(J):::EEU
11672v	PAKISTAN — RADIO PAKISTAN, Karachi	(J):50kW::SAS
11675	CLANDESTINE (ASIA) "VO DEM KAMPUCHEA", Kunming, China (PR)	Alternative Frequency to 11780kHz
	USSR — RADIO MOSCOW/RP&P	(J):::EU · (D)::HINDI, URDU:SAS
	RADIO MOSCOW/RP&P, Vladivostok	(J):100kW:CHI,CANTONESE,ETC:EAS/SEA · (D):100kW:WS:AS
11680	UNITED KINGDOM — BBC	(J):::CA · (J):::ME · (J):::ME/NAF · (J):::EU · (J)Su:::EEU/WUSSR · NAF
	USA — KUSW, Salt Lake City,Utah	(D)Tu-Su:100kW::ENA
	VOICE OF AMERICA, Greenville, NC	(D):500kW::SA · (J):250kW::SA
	USSR — RADIO MOSCOW, Ul'yanovsk	100kW:DS-1
11680v	KOREA (DPR) — KOREAN CENTRAL BS, Pyŏngyang	100/200kW:DS
11685	CHINA (PR) — RADIO BEIJING, Kunming	(J):120kW::SEA · 120kW:URDU:SAS
	RADIO BEIJING, Xi'an	120kW:CANTONESE:CAF/SAF
	CZECHOSLOVAKIA — RADIO PRAGUE, Piešťany-Velké K'y	120kW::ANZ · Sa/Su:120kW::ANZ
	RADIO PRAGUE, Prague	120kW::WAF/SA · 120kW::ME/SAS · M-F:120kW::ME/SAS
	SAUDI ARABIA — BS OF THE KINGDOM, Riyadh	350kW:ME
11690	FRANCE — RADIO FRANCE INTL, Issoudun-Allouis	(D):500kW::ENA · (D):100kW::EEU
	USSR — RADIO MOSCOW, Khabarovsk	(J):100kW::PAC
	RADIO MOSCOW, Leningrad	(D):100kW:DS-3
	RADIO MOSCOW/RP&P	(J)::WS:ANZ
	RADIO MOSCOW/RP&P, L'vov	(J):200kW:FRENCH,ITALIAN,ETC:EU
	RADIO TIKHIY OKEAN, Khabarovsk	(J):100kW:MARINERS:PAC
11694	VENEZUELA — RADIO NACIONAL, Caracas	Alternative Frequency to 9500kHz

ENGLISH ▬▬ GERMAN / DEUTSCH ∞∞ FRENCH / FRANÇAIS ▬▬ PORTUGUESE / PORTUGUÊS ▬▬ SPANISH / ESPAÑOL ▬▬

ARABIC / ﻋﺮﺑﻲ ▬▬ RUSSIAN / РУССКИЙ ▬▬ CHINESE / 中文 ∞∞ JAPANESE / 日本語 ▬▬ MULTILINGUAL ∞∞ OTHER ▬▬

SUMMER ONLY (J) WINTER ONLY (D) JAMMING ∧∧ or / or \ EARLIEST HEARD ◢ LATEST HEARD ◣ † TENTATIVE

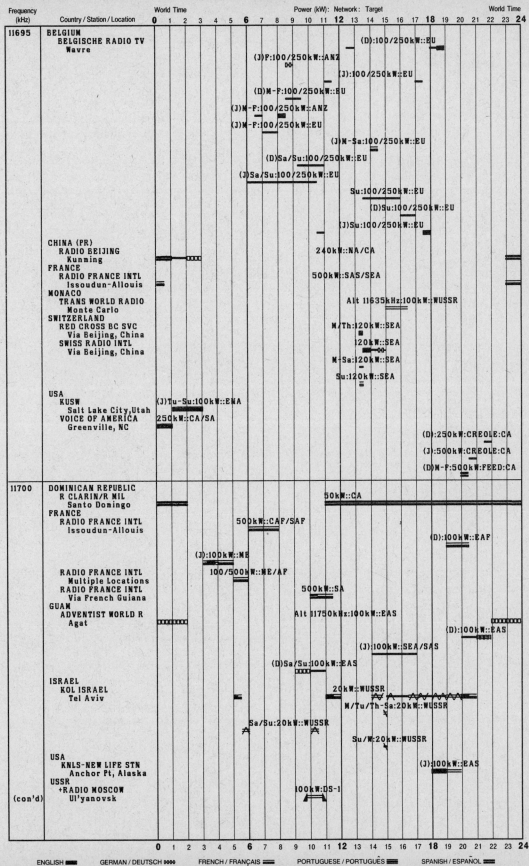

Frequency (kHz)   Country / Station / Location   World Time   Power (kW): Network: Target   World Time

11695

BELGIUM
BELGISCHE RADIO TV
Wavre
- (D):100/250kW::EU
- (J)F:100/250kW::ANZ
- (J):100/250kW::EU
- (D)M-F:100/250kW::EU
- (J)M-F:100/250kW::ANZ
- (J)M-F:100/250kW::EU
- (J)M-Sa:100/250kW::EU
- (D)Sa/Su:100/250kW::EU
- (J)Sa/Su:100/250kW::EU
- Su:100/250kW::EU
- (D)Su:100/250kW::EU
- (J)Su:100/250kW::EU

CHINA (PR)
RADIO BEIJING
Kunming
- 240kW::NA/CA

FRANCE
RADIO FRANCE INTL
Issoudun-Allouis
- 500kW::SAS/SEA

MONACO
TRANS WORLD RADIO
Monte Carlo
- Alt 11635kHz:100kW::WUSSR

SWITZERLAND
RED CROSS BC SVC
Via Beijing, China
- M/Th:120kW::SEA

SWISS RADIO INTL
Via Beijing, China
- 120kW::SEA
- M-Sa:120kW::SEA
- Su:120kW::SEA

USA
KUSW
Salt Lake City, Utah
- (J)Tu-Su:100kW::ENA

VOICE OF AMERICA
Greenville, NC
- 250kW::CA/SA
- (D):250kW:CREOLE:CA
- (J):500kW:CREOLE:CA
- (D)M-F:500kW:FEED:CA

11700

DOMINICAN REPUBLIC
R CLARIN/R MIL
Santo Domingo
- 50kW::CA

FRANCE
RADIO FRANCE INTL
Issoudun-Allouis
- 500kW::CAF/SAF
- (D):100kW::EAF
- (J):100kW::ME

RADIO FRANCE INTL
Multiple Locations
- 100/500kW::ME/AF

RADIO FRANCE INTL
Via French Guiana
- 500kW::SA

GUAM
ADVENTIST WORLD R
Agat
- Alt 11750kHz:100kW::EAS
- (D):100kW::EAS
- (J):100kW::SEA/SAS
- (D)Sa/Su:100kW::EAS

ISRAEL
KOL ISRAEL
Tel Aviv
- 20kW::WUSSR
- M/Tu/Th-Sa:20kW::WUSSR
- Sa/Su:20kW::WUSSR
- Su/W:20kW::WUSSR

USA
KNLS-NEW LIFE STN
Anchor Pt, Alaska
- (J):100kW::EAS

USSR
+RADIO MOSCOW
Ul'yanovsk
- 100kW:DS-1

(con'd)

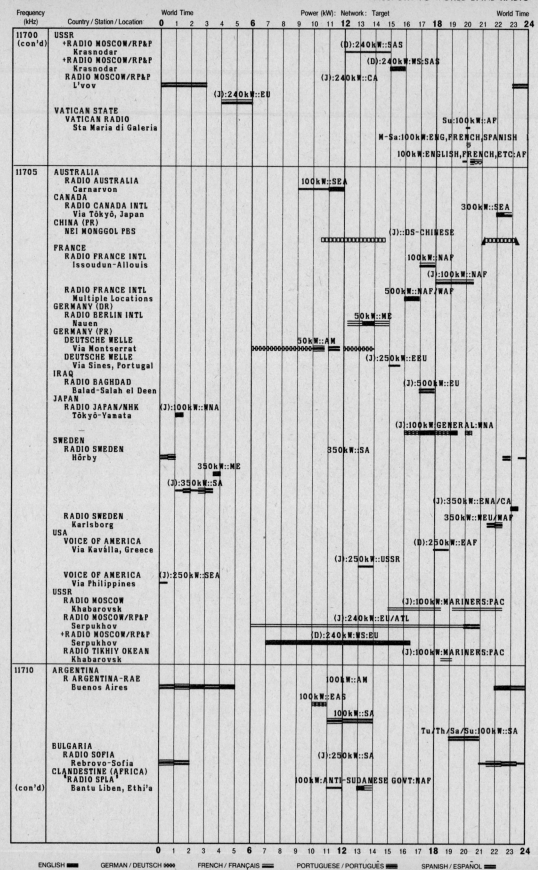

Frequency (kHz)	Country / Station / Location	World Time 0–6	Power (kW): Network: Target 6–18	World Time 18–24

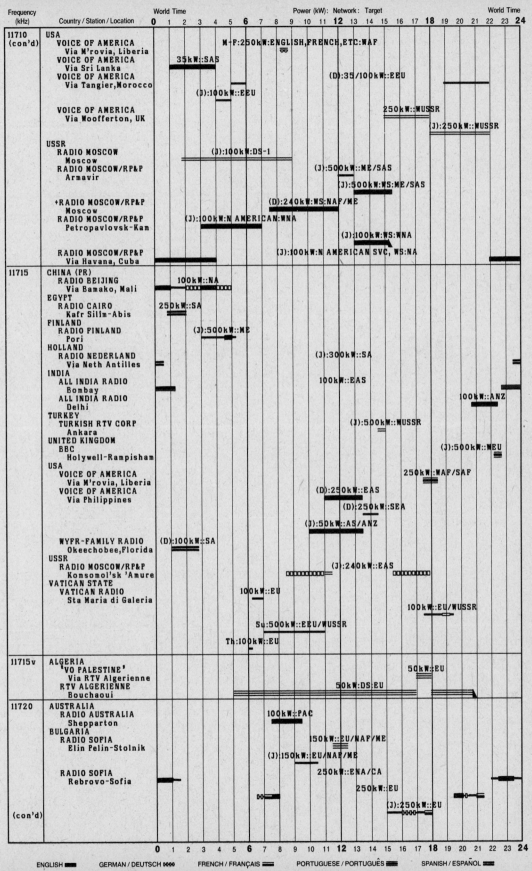

Frequency (kHz)	Country / Station / Location	Power (kW): Network: Target
11710 (con'd)	USA	
	VOICE OF AMERICA Via M'rovia, Liberia	M-F:250kW:ENGLISH,FRENCH,ETC:WAF
	VOICE OF AMERICA Via Sri Lanka	35kW::SAS
	VOICE OF AMERICA Via Tangier,Morocco	(D):35/100kW::EEU
		(J):100kW::EEU
	VOICE OF AMERICA Via Woofferton, UK	250kW::WUSSR
		(J):250kW::WUSSR
	USSR	
	RADIO MOSCOW Moscow	(J):100kW:DS-1
	RADIO MOSCOW/RP&P Armavir	(J):500kW:ME/SAS
		(J):500kW:WS:ME/SAS
	+RADIO MOSCOW/RP&P Moscow	(D):240kW:WS:NAF/ME
	RADIO MOSCOW/RP&P Petropavlovsk-Kam	(J):100kW:N AMERICAN:WNA
		(J):100kW:WS:WNA
	RADIO MOSCOW/RP&P Via Havana, Cuba	(J):100kW:N AMERICAN SVC, WS:NA
11715	CHINA (PR)	
	RADIO BEIJING Via Bamako, Mali	100kW::NA
	EGYPT	
	RADIO CAIRO Kafr Silim-Abis	250kW::SA
	FINLAND	
	RADIO FINLAND Pori	(J):500kW::ME
	HOLLAND	
	RADIO NEDERLAND Via Neth Antilles	(J):300kW::SA
	INDIA	
	ALL INDIA RADIO Bombay	100kW::EAS
	ALL INDIA RADIO Delhi	100kW::ANZ
	TURKEY	
	TURKISH RTV CORP Ankara	(J):500kW::WUSSR
	UNITED KINGDOM	
	BBC Holywell-Rampisham	(J):500kW::WEU
	USA	
	VOICE OF AMERICA Via M'rovia, Liberia	250kW::WAF/SAF
	VOICE OF AMERICA Via Philippines	(D):250kW::EAS
		(D):250kW::SEA
		(J):50kW::AS/ANZ
	WYFR-FAMILY RADIO Okeechobee,Florida	(D):100kW::SA
	USSR	
	RADIO MOSCOW/RP&P Komsomol'sk 'Amure	(J):240kW::EAS
	VATICAN STATE	
	VATICAN RADIO Sta Maria di Galeria	100kW::EU
		100kW::EU/WUSSR
		Su:500kW::EEU/WUSSR
		Th:100kW::EU
11715v	ALGERIA	
	'VO PALESTINE' Via RTV Algerienne	50kW::EU
	RTV ALGERIENNE Bouchaoui	50kW:DS:EU
11720	AUSTRALIA	
	RADIO AUSTRALIA Shepparton	100kW::PAC
	BULGARIA	
	RADIO SOFIA Elin Pelin-Stolnik	150kW::EU/NAF/ME
		(J):150kW::EU/NAF/ME
	RADIO SOFIA Rebrovo-Sofia	250kW::ENA/CA
		250kW::EU
		(J):250kW::EU
(con'd)		

ENGLISH ■■■ GERMAN / DEUTSCH ᴐᴐᴐᴐ FRENCH / FRANÇAIS ▬▬ PORTUGUESE / PORTUGUÊS ▬▬ SPANISH / ESPAÑOL ▬▬

ARABIC /ئ/ RUSSIAN / РУССКИИ ▬▬ CHINESE / 中文 ᴐᴐᴐᴐ JAPANESE / 日本語 ▬▬ MULTILINGUAL ᴐᴐᴐᴐ OTHER ▬

SUMMER ONLY (J) WINTER ONLY (D) JAMMING ∧∧ or / or \ EARLIEST HEARD ◢ LATEST HEARD ◣ + TENTATIVE

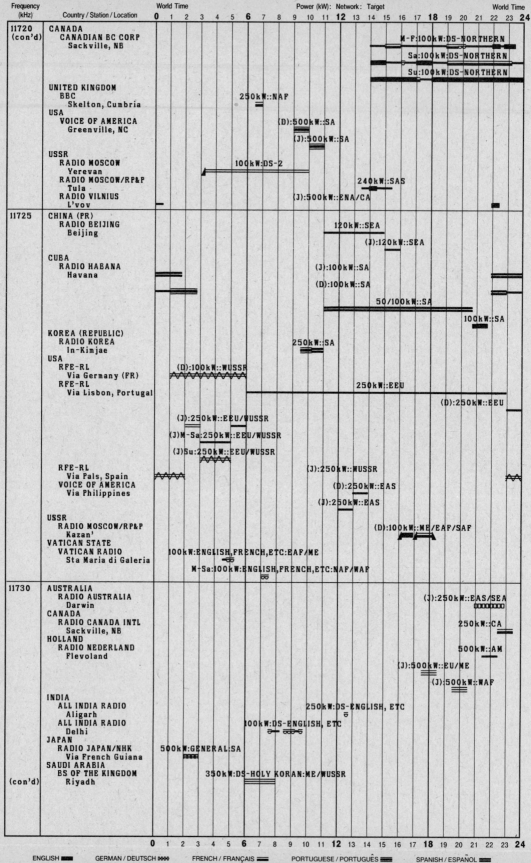

Frequency (kHz)	Country / Station / Location	World Time ... Power (kW) : Network : Target

11720 (con'd)

CANADA
CANADIAN BC CORP
Sackville, NB
M-F:100kW:DS-NORTHERN
Sa:100kW:DS-NORTHERN
Su:100kW:DS-NORTHERN

UNITED KINGDOM
BBC
Skelton, Cumbria
250kW::NAF

USA
VOICE OF AMERICA
Greenville, NC
(D):500kW::SA
(J):500kW::SA

USSR
RADIO MOSCOW
Yerevan
100kW:DS-2
RADIO MOSCOW/RP&P
Tula
240kW::SAS
RADIO VILNIUS
L'vov
(J):500kW::ENA/CA

11725

CHINA (PR)
RADIO BEIJING
Beijing
120kW::SEA
(J):120kW::SEA

CUBA
RADIO HABANA
Havana
(J):100kW::SA
(D):100kW::SA
50/100kW::SA
100kW::SA

KOREA (REPUBLIC)
RADIO KOREA
In-Kimjae
250kW::SA

USA
RFE-RL
Via Germany (FR)
(D):100kW::WUSSR
RFE-RL
Via Lisbon, Portugal
250kW::EEU
(D):250kW::EEU
(J):250kW::EEU/WUSSR
(J)M-Sa:250kW::EEU/WUSSR
(J)Su:250kW::EEU/WUSSR
RFE-RL
Via Pals, Spain
(J):250kW::WUSSR
VOICE OF AMERICA
Via Philippines
(D):250kW::EAS
(J):250kW::EAS

USSR
RADIO MOSCOW/RP&P
Kazan'
(D):100kW::ME/EAF/SAF
VATICAN STATE
VATICAN RADIO
Sta Maria di Galeria
100kW:ENGLISH,FRENCH,ETC:EAF/ME
M-Sa:100kW:ENGLISH,FRENCH,ETC:NAF/WAF

11730

AUSTRALIA
RADIO AUSTRALIA
Darwin
(J):250kW::EAS/SEA
CANADA
RADIO CANADA INTL
Sackville, NB
250kW::CA
HOLLAND
RADIO NEDERLAND
Flevoland
500kW::AM
(J):500kW::EU/ME
(J):500kW::WAF

INDIA
ALL INDIA RADIO
Aligarh
250kW:DS-ENGLISH, ETC
ALL INDIA RADIO
Delhi
100kW:DS-ENGLISH, ETC
JAPAN
RADIO JAPAN/NHK
Via French Guiana
500kW:GENERAL:SA
SAUDI ARABIA
BS OF THE KINGDOM
Riyadh
350kW:DS-HOLY KORAN:ME/WUSSR

(con'd)

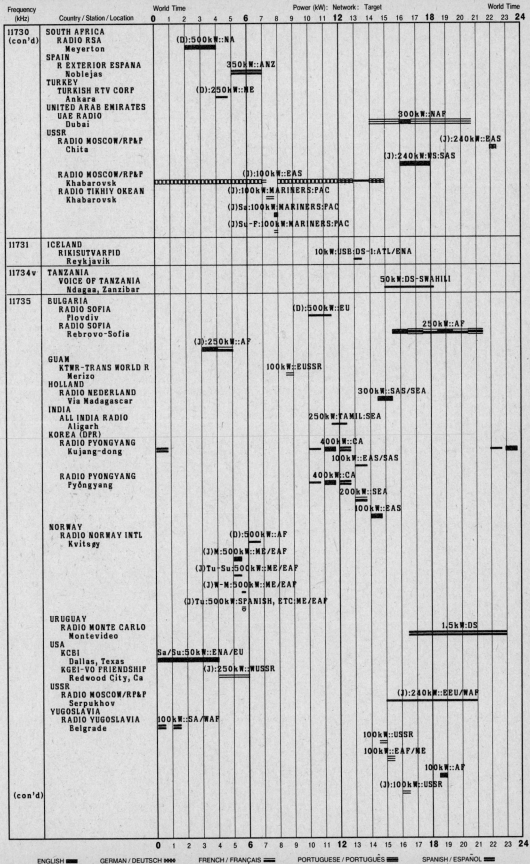

Frequency (kHz)	Country / Station / Location	Power (kW) : Network : Target
11730 (con'd)	SOUTH AFRICA	
	RADIO RSA	(D):500kW::NA
	Meyerton	
	SPAIN	
	R EXTERIOR ESPANA	350kW::ANZ
	Noblejas	
	TURKEY	
	TURKISH RTV CORP	(D):250kW::ME
	Ankara	
	UNITED ARAB EMIRATES	
	UAE RADIO	300kW::NAF
	Dubai	
	USSR	
	RADIO MOSCOW/RP&P	(J):240kW::EAS
	Chita	(J):240kW:WS:SAS
	RADIO MOSCOW/RP&P	(D):100kW::EAS
	Khabarovsk	
	RADIO TIKHIY OKEAN	(J):100kW:MARINERS:PAC
	Khabarovsk	(J)Sa:100kW:MARINERS:PAC
		(J)Su-F:100kW:MARINERS:PAC
11731	ICELAND	
	RIKISUTVARPID	10kW:USB:DS-1:ATL/ENA
	Reykjavik	
11734v	TANZANIA	
	VOICE OF TANZANIA	50kW:DS-SWAHILI
	Ndagaa, Zanzibar	
11735	BULGARIA	
	RADIO SOFIA	(D):500kW::EU
	Plovdiv	
	RADIO SOFIA	250kW::AF
	Rebrovo-Sofia	(J):250kW::AF
	GUAM	
	KTWR-TRANS WORLD R	100kW::EUSSR
	Merizo	
	HOLLAND	
	RADIO NEDERLAND	300kW::SAS/SEA
	Via Madagascar	
	INDIA	
	ALL INDIA RADIO	250kW:TAMIL:SEA
	Aligarh	
	KOREA (DPR)	
	RADIO PYONGYANG	400kW::CA
	Kujang-dong	100kW::EAS/SAS
	RADIO PYONGYANG	400kW::CA
	Pyŏngyang	200kW::SEA
		100kW::EAS
	NORWAY	
	RADIO NORWAY INTL	(D):500kW::AF
	Kvitsøy	(J)M:500kW::ME/EAF
		(J)Tu-Su:500kW::ME/EAF
		(J)W-M:500kW::ME/EAF
		(J)Tu:500kW:SPANISH, ETC:ME/EAF
	URUGUAY	
	RADIO MONTE CARLO	1.5kW:DS
	Montevideo	
	USA	
	KCBI	Sa/Su:50kW::ENA/EU
	Dallas, Texas	
	KGEI-VO FRIENDSHIP	(J):250kW:WUSSR
	Redwood City, Ca	
	USSR	
	RADIO MOSCOW/RP&P	(J):240kW::EEU/WAF
	Serpukhov	
	YUGOSLAVIA	
	RADIO YUGOSLAVIA	100kW::SA/WAF
	Belgrade	100kW::USSR
		100kW::EAF/ME
		100kW::AF
		(J):100kW::USSR
(con'd)		

ENGLISH ▬   GERMAN / DEUTSCH ᴅᴅᴅᴅ   FRENCH / FRANÇAIS ▭▭   PORTUGUESE / PORTUGUÊS ▭▬   SPANISH / ESPAÑOL ▭▭

ARABIC / العربية ▭   RUSSIAN / РУССКИИ ▭   CHINESE / ★★ ᴅᴅᴅᴅ   JAPANESE / 日本語 ▭   MULTILINGUAL ᴅᴅᴅᴅ   OTHER ▬

SUMMER ONLY (J)   WINTER ONLY (D)   JAMMING ∧∧ or / or \   EARLIEST HEARD ◢   LATEST HEARD ◣   + TENTATIVE

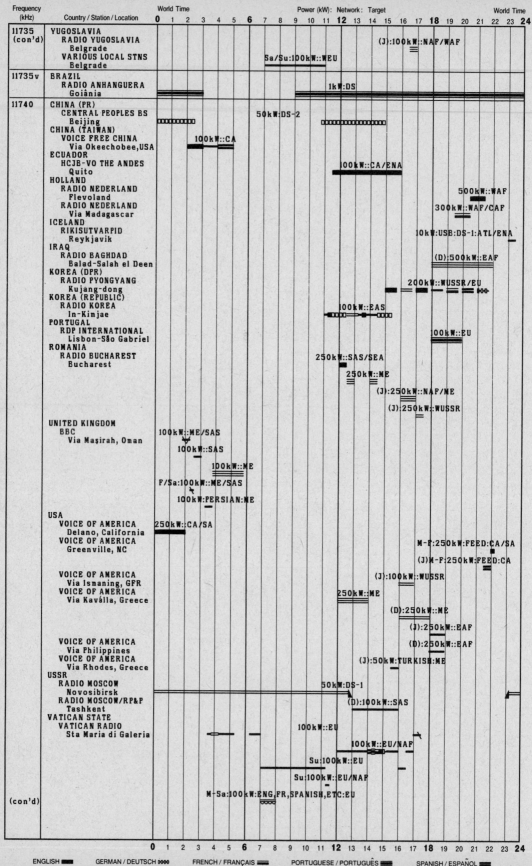

Frequency (kHz)	Country / Station / Location		Power (kW) : Network : Target

11735 (con'd) YUGOSLAVIA
   RADIO YUGOSLAVIA Belgrade — (J):100kW::NAF/WAF
   VARIOUS LOCAL STNS Belgrade — Sa/Su:100kW::WEU

11735v BRAZIL
   RADIO ANHANGUERA Goiânia — 1kW:DS

11740 CHINA (PR)
   CENTRAL PEOPLES BS Beijing — 50kW:DS-2
CHINA (TAIWAN)
   VOICE FREE CHINA Via Okeechobee,USA — 100kW::CA
ECUADOR
   HCJB-VO THE ANDES Quito — 100kW::CA/ENA
HOLLAND
   RADIO NEDERLAND Flevoland — 500kW::WAF
   RADIO NEDERLAND Via Madagascar — 300kW::WAF/CAF
ICELAND
   RIKISUTVARPID Reykjavik — 10kW:USB:DS-1:ATL/ENA
IRAQ
   RADIO BAGHDAD Balad-Salah el Deen — (D):500kW::EAF
KOREA (DPR)
   RADIO PYONGYANG Kujang-dong — 200kW::WUSSR/EU
KOREA (REPUBLIC)
   RADIO KOREA In-Kimjae — 100kW::EAS
PORTUGAL
   RDP INTERNATIONAL Lisbon-São Gabriel — 100kW::EU
ROMANIA
   RADIO BUCHAREST Bucharest — 250kW::SAS/SEA
   — 250kW::ME
   — (J):250kW::NAF/ME
   — (J):250kW::WUSSR

UNITED KINGDOM
   BBC Via Maṣirah, Oman — 100kW::ME/SAS
   — 100kW::SAS
   — 100kW::ME
   — F/Sa:100kW::ME/SAS
   — 100kW:PERSIAN:ME

USA
   VOICE OF AMERICA Delano, California — 250kW::CA/SA
   VOICE OF AMERICA Greenville, NC — M-F:250kW:FEED:CA/SA
   — (J)M-F:250kW:FEED:CA
   VOICE OF AMERICA Via Ismaning, GFR — (J):100kW::WUSSR
   VOICE OF AMERICA Via Kaválla, Greece — 250kW::ME
   — (D):250kW::ME
   — (J):250kW::EAF
   VOICE OF AMERICA Via Philippines — (D):250kW::EAF
   VOICE OF AMERICA Via Rhodes, Greece — (J):50kW:TURKISH:ME
USSR
   RADIO MOSCOW Novosibirsk — 50kW:DS-1
   RADIO MOSCOW/RP&P Tashkent — (D):100kW::SAS
VATICAN STATE
   VATICAN RADIO Sta Maria di Galeria — 100kW::EU
   — 100kW::EU/NAF
   — Su:100kW::EU
   — Su:100kW::EU/NAF
   — M-Sa:100kW:ENG,FR,SPANISH,ETC:EU

(con'd)

Frequency (kHz)	Country / Station / Location	Power (kW) : Network : Target

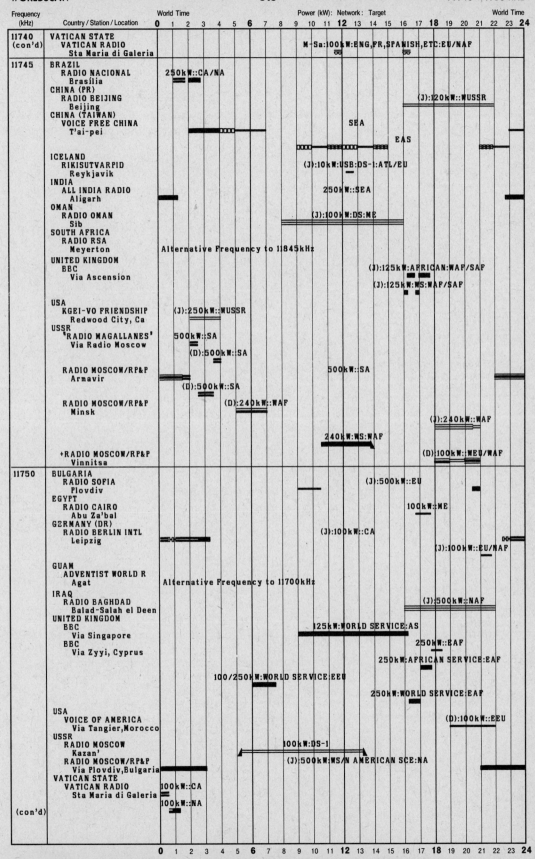

11740 (con'd)
VATICAN STATE
  VATICAN RADIO
    Sta Maria di Galeria — M-Sa:100kW:ENG,FR,SPANISH,ETC:EU/NAF

11745
BRAZIL
  RADIO NACIONAL
    Brasília — 250kW::CA/NA
CHINA (PR)
  RADIO BEIJING
    Beijing — (J):120kW::WUSSR
CHINA (TAIWAN)
  VOICE FREE CHINA
    T'ai-pei — SEA / EAS
ICELAND
  RIKISUTVARPID
    Reykjavik — (J):10kW:USB:DS-1:ATL/EU
INDIA
  ALL INDIA RADIO
    Aligarh — 250kW::SEA
OMAN
  RADIO OMAN
    Sib — (J):100kW:DS:ME
SOUTH AFRICA
  RADIO RSA
    Meyerton — Alternative Frequency to 11845kHz
UNITED KINGDOM
  BBC
    Via Ascension — (J):125kW:AFRICAN:WAF/SAF / (J):125kW:WS:WAF/SAF
USA
  KGEI-VO FRIENDSHIP
    Redwood City, Ca — (J):250kW::WUSSR
USSR
  'RADIO MAGALLANES'
    Via Radio Moscow — 500kW::SA / (D):500kW::SA
  RADIO MOSCOW/RP&P
    Armavir — 500kW::SA / (D):500kW::SA
  RADIO MOSCOW/RP&P
    Minsk — (D):240kW::WAF / (J):240kW::WAF
  +RADIO MOSCOW/RP&P
    Vinnitsa — 240kW:WS:WAF / (D):100kW::WEU/WAF

11750
BULGARIA
  RADIO SOFIA
    Plovdiv — (J):500kW::EU
EGYPT
  RADIO CAIRO
    Abu Za'bal — 100kW::ME
GERMANY (DR)
  RADIO BERLIN INTL
    Leipzig — (J):100kW::CA / (J):100kW::EU/NAF
GUAM
  ADVENTIST WORLD R
    Agat — Alternative Frequency to 11700kHz
IRAQ
  RADIO BAGHDAD
    Balad-Salah el Deen — (J):500kW::NAF
UNITED KINGDOM
  BBC
    Via Singapore — 125kW:WORLD SERVICE:AS
  BBC
    Via Zyyi, Cyprus — 250kW::EAF / 250kW:AFRICAN SERVICE:EAF / 100/250kW:WORLD SERVICE:EEU / 250kW:WORLD SERVICE:EAF
USA
  VOICE OF AMERICA
    Via Tangier,Morocco — (D):100kW::EEU
USSR
  RADIO MOSCOW
    Kazan' — 100kW:DS-1
  RADIO MOSCOW/RP&P
    Via Plovdiv,Bulgaria — (J):500kW:WS/N AMERICAN SCE:NA
VATICAN STATE
  VATICAN RADIO
    Sta Maria di Galeria — 100kW::CA / 100kW::NA

(con'd)

ENGLISH ■■■   GERMAN / DEUTSCH ◊◊◊◊   FRENCH / FRANÇAIS ══   PORTUGUESE / PORTUGUÊS ≡≡≡   SPANISH / ESPAÑOL ══

ARABIC / بى ≡≡   RUSSIAN / РУССКИЙ ══   CHINESE / **※ ◻◻◻◻   JAPANESE / 日本語 ■■■   MULTILINGUAL ◓◓◓◓   OTHER ━━

SUMMER ONLY (J)   WINTER ONLY (D)   JAMMING ∧∧ or / or \   EARLIEST HEARD ◢   LATEST HEARD ◣   + TENTATIVE

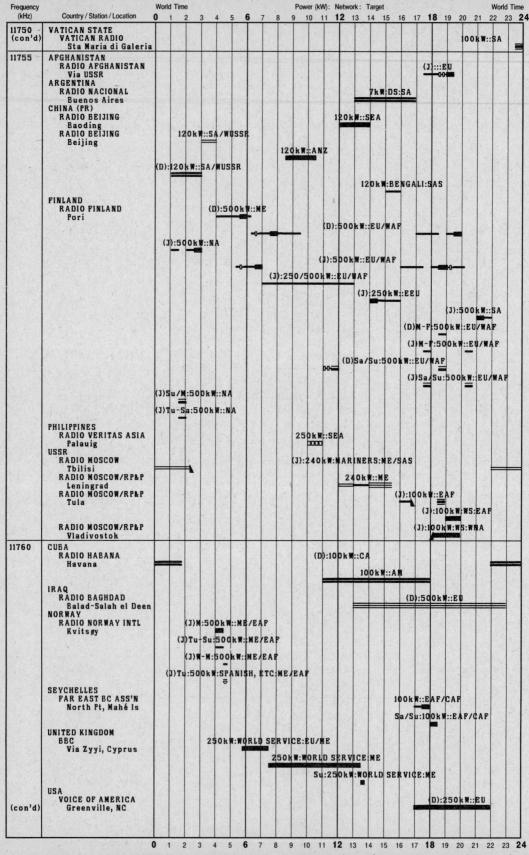

Frequency (kHz)	Country / Station / Location	World Time / Power (kW) : Network : Target
11750 (con'd)	**VATICAN STATE** **VATICAN RADIO** Sta Maria di Galeria	100kW::SA
11755	**AFGHANISTAN** **RADIO AFGHANISTAN** Via USSR	(J):::EU
	ARGENTINA **RADIO NACIONAL** Buenos Aires	7kW:DS:SA
	CHINA (PR) **RADIO BEIJING** Baoding	120kW::SEA
	RADIO BEIJING Beijing	120kW::SA/WUSSR 120kW::ANZ (D):120kW::SA/WUSSR 120kW:BENGALI:SAS
	FINLAND **RADIO FINLAND** Pori	(D):500kW::ME (D):500kW::EU/WAF (J):500kW::NA (J):500kW::EU/WAF (J):250/500kW::EU/WAF (J):250kW::EEU (J):500kW::SA (D)M-F:500kW::EU/WAF (J)M-F:500kW::EU/WAF (D)Sa/Su:500kW::EU/WAF (J)Sa/Su:500kW::EU/WAF (J)Su/M:500kW::NA (J)Tu-Sa:500kW::NA
	PHILIPPINES **RADIO VERITAS ASIA** Palauig	250kW::SEA
	USSR **RADIO MOSCOW** Tbilisi	(J):240kW:MARINERS:ME/SAS
	RADIO MOSCOW/RP&P Leningrad	240kW::ME
	RADIO MOSCOW/RP&P Tula	(J):100kW::EAF (J):100kW:WS:EAF
	RADIO MOSCOW/RP&P Vladivostok	(J):100kW:WS:WNA
11760	**CUBA** **RADIO HABANA** Havana	(D):100kW::CA 100kW::AM
	IRAQ **RADIO BAGHDAD** Balad-Salah el Deen	(D):500kW::EU
	NORWAY **RADIO NORWAY INTL** Kvitsøy	(J)M:500kW::ME/EAF (J)Tu-Su:500kW::ME/EAF (J)W-M:500kW::ME/EAF (J)Tu:500kW:SPANISH, ETC:ME/EAF
	SEYCHELLES **FAR EAST BC ASS'N** North Pt, Mahé Is	100kW::EAF/CAF Sa/Su:100kW::EAF/CAF
	UNITED KINGDOM **BBC** Via Zyyi, Cyprus	250kW:WORLD SERVICE:EU/ME 250kW:WORLD SERVICE:ME Su:250kW:WORLD SERVICE:ME
(con'd)	**USA** **VOICE OF AMERICA** Greenville, NC	(D):250kW::EU

ENGLISH ▰▰▰   GERMAN / DEUTSCH ◊◊◊◊   FRENCH / FRANÇAIS ▰▰▰   PORTUGUESE / PORTUGUÊS ▰▰▰   SPANISH / ESPAÑOL ▰▰▰

ARABIC / ﻉﺏﻉ ▰▰▰   RUSSIAN / РУССКИИ ▰▰▰   CHINESE / ✶✶ ◻◻◻◻   JAPANESE / 日本語 ▰▰▰   MULTILINGUAL ▭▭▭▭   OTHER ▬▬

SUMMER ONLY (J)   WINTER ONLY (D)   JAMMING ∧∧ or / or \   EARLIEST HEARD ◢   LATEST HEARD ◣   † TENTATIVE

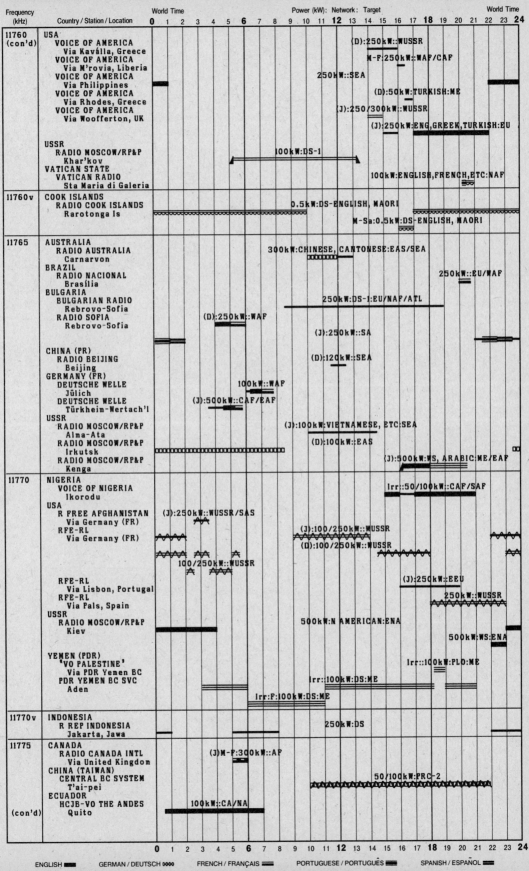

Frequency (kHz)	Country / Station / Location	Power (kW): Network: Target
11760 (con'd)	USA — VOICE OF AMERICA Via Kaválla, Greece	(D):250kW::WUSSR
	VOICE OF AMERICA Via M'rovia, Liberia	M-F:250kW::WAF/CAF
	VOICE OF AMERICA Via Philippines	250kW::SEA
	VOICE OF AMERICA Via Rhodes, Greece	(D):50kW:TURKISH:ME
	VOICE OF AMERICA Via Woofferton, UK	(J):250/300kW::WUSSR / (J):250kW:ENG,GREEK,TURKISH:EU
	USSR — RADIO MOSCOW/RP&P Khar'kov	100kW:DS-1
	VATICAN STATE — VATICAN RADIO Sta Maria di Galeria	100kW:ENGLISH,FRENCH,ETC:NAF
11760v	COOK ISLANDS — RADIO COOK ISLANDS Rarotonga Is	0.5kW:DS-ENGLISH, MAORI / M-Sa:0.5kW:DS-ENGLISH, MAORI
11765	AUSTRALIA — RADIO AUSTRALIA Carnarvon	300kW:CHINESE, CANTONESE:EAS/SEA
	BRAZIL — RADIO NACIONAL Brasília	250kW::EU/WAF
	BULGARIA — BULGARIAN RADIO Rebrovo-Sofia	250kW:DS-1:EU/NAF/ATL
	RADIO SOFIA Rebrovo-Sofia	(D):250kW::WAF / (J):250kW::SA
	CHINA (PR) — RADIO BEIJING Beijing	(D):120kW::SEA
	GERMANY (FR) — DEUTSCHE WELLE Jülich	100kW::WAF
	DEUTSCHE WELLE Türkheim-Wertach'l	(J):500kW::CAF/EAF
	USSR — RADIO MOSCOW/RP&P Alma-Ata	(J):100kW:VIETNAMESE, ETC:SEA
	RADIO MOSCOW/RP&P Irkutsk	(D):100kW::EAS
	RADIO MOSCOW/RP&P Kenga	(J):500kW:WS, ARABIC:ME/EAP
11770	NIGERIA — VOICE OF NIGERIA Ikorodu	Irr::50/100kW::CAF/SAF
	USA — R FREE AFGHANISTAN Via Germany (FR)	(J):250kW::WUSSR/SAS
	RFE-RL Via Germany (FR)	(J):100/250kW::WUSSR / (D):100/250kW::WUSSR / 100/250kW::WUSSR
	RFE-RL Via Lisbon, Portugal	(J):250kW::EEU
	RFE-RL Via Pals, Spain	250kW::WUSSR
	USSR — RADIO MOSCOW/RP&P Kiev	500kW:N AMERICAN:ENA / 500kW:WS:ENA
	YEMEN (PDR) — 'VO PALESTINE' Via PDR Yemen BC	Irr::100kW:PLO:ME
	PDR YEMEN BC SVC Aden	Irr::100kW:DS:ME / Irr:F:100kW:DS:ME
11770v	INDONESIA — R REP INDONESIA Jakarta, Jawa	250kW:DS
11775	CANADA — RADIO CANADA INTL Via United Kingdom	(J)M-F:300kW::AF
	CHINA (TAIWAN) — CENTRAL BC SYSTEM T'ai-pei	50/100kW:PRC-2
(con'd)	ECUADOR — HCJB-VO THE ANDES Quito	100kW::CA/NA

ENGLISH ▬▬ GERMAN / DEUTSCH ∞∞∞ FRENCH / FRANÇAIS ▭▭ PORTUGUESE / PORTUGUÊS ▬▬ SPANISH / ESPAÑOL ▬▬

ARABIC /ﻉﻑ ≡ RUSSIAN / РУССКИИ ▭ CHINESE / ✦✦ ▭▭ JAPANESE / 日本語 ▬▬ MULTILINGUAL ∞∞∞ OTHER ▬

SUMMER ONLY (J) WINTER ONLY (D) JAMMING ∧∧ or / or \ EARLIEST HEARD ◢ LATEST HEARD ◣ ✦ TENTATIVE

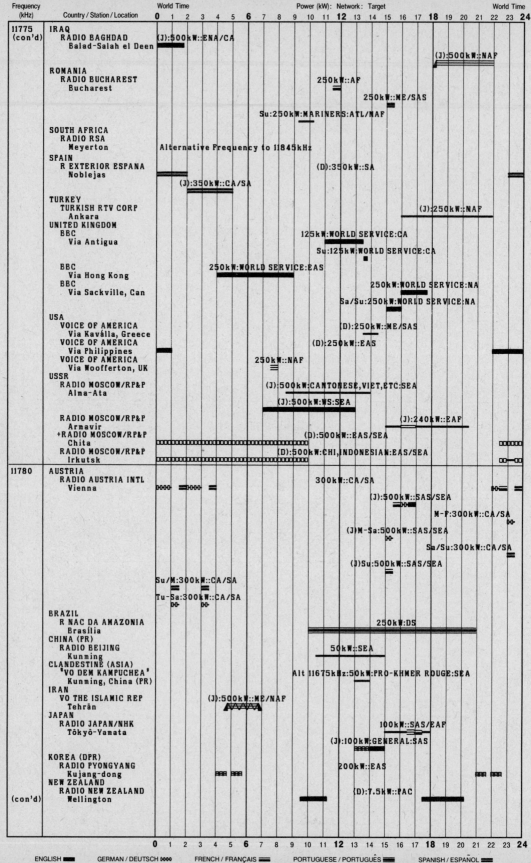

Frequency (kHz)	Country / Station / Location		World Time 0 1 2 3 4 5 6 7 8 9 10 11 12 13 14 15 16 17 18 19 20 21 22 23 24	Power (kW) : Network : Target

11775 (con'd)

IRAQ
RADIO BAGHDAD
Balad-Salah el Deen — (J):500kW::ENA/CA ; (J):500kW::NAF

ROMANIA
RADIO BUCHAREST
Bucharest — 250kW::AF ; 250kW::ME/SAS ; Su:250kW:MARINERS:ATL/NAF

SOUTH AFRICA
RADIO RSA
Meyerton — Alternative Frequency to 11845kHz

SPAIN
R EXTERIOR ESPANA
Noblejas — (D):350kW::SA ; (J):350kW::CA/SA

TURKEY
TURKISH RTV CORP
Ankara — (J):250kW::NAF

UNITED KINGDOM
BBC
Via Antigua — 125kW:WORLD SERVICE:CA ; Su:125kW:WORLD SERVICE:CA

BBC
Via Hong Kong — 250kW:WORLD SERVICE:EAS

BBC
Via Sackville, Can — 250kW:WORLD SERVICE:NA ; Sa/Su:250kW:WORLD SERVICE:NA

USA
VOICE OF AMERICA
Via Kaválla, Greece — (D):250kW::ME/SAS

VOICE OF AMERICA
Via Philippines — (D):250kW::EAS

VOICE OF AMERICA
Via Woofferton, UK — 250kW::NAF

USSR
RADIO MOSCOW/RP&P
Alma-Ata — (J):500kW:CANTONESE,VIET,ETC:SEA ; (J):500kW:WS:SEA

RADIO MOSCOW/RP&P
Armavir — (J):240kW::EAF

+RADIO MOSCOW/RP&P
Chita — (D):500kW::EAS/SEA

RADIO MOSCOW/RP&P
Irkutsk — (D):500kW:CHI,INDONESIAN:EAS/SEA

11780

AUSTRIA
RADIO AUSTRIA INTL
Vienna — 300kW::CA/SA ; (J):500kW::SAS/SEA ; M-F:300kW::CA/SA ; (J)M-Sa:500kW::SAS/SEA ; Sa/Su:300kW::CA/SA ; (J)Su:500kW::SAS/SEA ; Su/M:300kW::CA/SA ; Tu-Sa:300kW::CA/SA

BRAZIL
R NAC DA AMAZONIA
Brasília — 250kW:DS

CHINA (PR)
RADIO BEIJING
Kunming — 50kW::SEA

CLANDESTINE (ASIA)
'VO DEM KAMPUCHEA'
Kunming, China (PR) — Alt 11675kHz:50kW:PRO-KHMER ROUGE:SEA

IRAN
VO THE ISLAMIC REP
Tehrān — (J):500kW::ME/NAF

JAPAN
RADIO JAPAN/NHK
Tōkyō-Yamata — 100kW::SAS/EAF ; (J):100kW:GENERAL:SAS

KOREA (DPR)
RADIO PYONGYANG
Kujang-dong — 200kW::EAS

NEW ZEALAND
RADIO NEW ZEALAND
(con'd) Wellington — (D):7.5kW::PAC

World Time	0 1 2 3 4 5 6 7 8 9 10 11 12 13 14 15 16 17 18 19 20 21 22 23 24

ENGLISH ▬▬ GERMAN / DEUTSCH ◊◊◊◊ FRENCH / FRANÇAIS ▬▬ PORTUGUESE / PORTUGUÊS ▬▬ SPANISH / ESPAÑOL ▬▬

ARABIC / عربي ▬ RUSSIAN / РУССКИИ ▬ CHINESE / 中文 ▭▭▭▭ JAPANESE / 日本語 ▬▬ MULTILINGUAL ▬▬ OTHER ▬▬

SUMMER ONLY (J)   WINTER ONLY (D)   JAMMING ∧∧ or / or \   EARLIEST HEARD ◢   LATEST HEARD ◣   + TENTATIVE

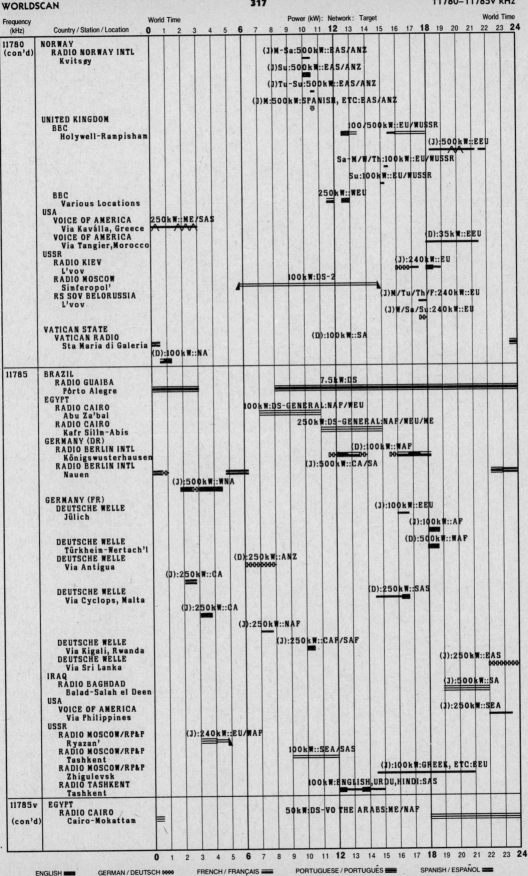

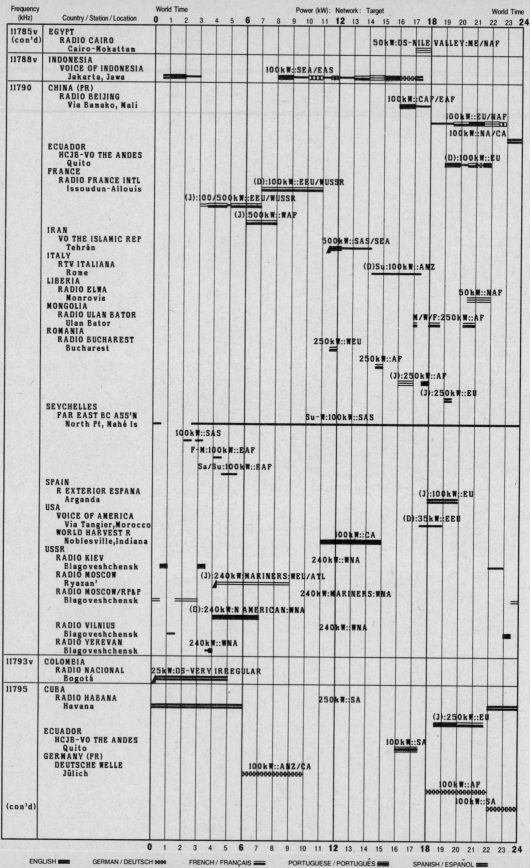

Frequency (kHz)	Country / Station / Location	World Time / Power (kW) : Network : Target
11785v (con'd)	EGYPT RADIO CAIRO Cairo-Mokattam	50kW:DS-NILE VALLEY:ME/NAF
11788v	INDONESIA VOICE OF INDONESIA Jakarta, Jawa	100kW::SEA/EAS
11790	CHINA (PR) RADIO BEIJING Via Bamako, Mali	100kW::CAF/EAF 100kW::EU/NAF 100kW::NA/CA
	ECUADOR HCJB-VO THE ANDES Quito	(D):100kW::EU
	FRANCE RADIO FRANCE INTL Issoudun-Allouis	(D):100kW::EEU/WUSSR (J):100/500kW::EEU/WUSSR (J):500kW::WAF
	IRAN VO THE ISLAMIC REP Tehrān	500kW::SAS/SEA
	ITALY RTV ITALIANA Rome	(D)Su:100kW::ANZ
	LIBERIA RADIO ELWA Monrovia	50kW::NAF
	MONGOLIA RADIO ULAN BATOR Ulan Bator	M/W/F:250kW::AF
	ROMANIA RADIO BUCHAREST Bucharest	250kW::WEU 250kW::AF (J):250kW::AF (J):250kW::EU
	SEYCHELLES FAR EAST BC ASS'N North Pt, Mahé Is	Su-W:100kW::SAS 100kW::SAS F-M:100kW::EAF Sa/Su:100kW::EAF
	SPAIN R EXTERIOR ESPANA Arganda	(J):100kW::EU
	USA VOICE OF AMERICA Via Tangier,Morocco	(D):35kW::EEU
	WORLD HARVEST R Noblesville,Indiana	100kW::CA
	USSR RADIO KIEV Blagoveshchensk	240kW::WNA
	RADIO MOSCOW Ryazan'	(J):240kW:MARINERS:WEU/ATL
	RADIO MOSCOW/RP&P Blagoveshchensk	240kW:MARINERS:WNA (D):240kW:N AMERICAN:WNA
	RADIO VILNIUS Blagoveshchensk	240kW::WNA
	RADIO YEREVAN Blagoveshchensk	240kW::WNA
11793v	COLOMBIA RADIO NACIONAL Bogotá	25kW:DS-VERY IRREGULAR
11795	CUBA RADIO HABANA Havana	250kW::SA (J):250kW::EU
	ECUADOR HCJB-VO THE ANDES Quito	100kW::SA
	GERMANY (FR) DEUTSCHE WELLE Jülich	100kW::ANZ/CA
(con'd)		100kW::AF 100kW::SA

ENGLISH ▬▬   GERMAN / DEUTSCH ०००   FRENCH / FRANÇAIS ═══   PORTUGUESE / PORTUGUÊS ▬▬   SPANISH / ESPAÑOL ▬▬

ARABIC /للغة ═══   RUSSIAN / РУССКИИ ═══   CHINESE / 中文 ००००   JAPANESE / 日本語 ▬▬   MULTILINGUAL ००००   OTHER ▬▬

SUMMER ONLY (J)   WINTER ONLY (D)   JAMMING ∧∧ or / or \   EARLIEST HEARD ◢   LATEST HEARD ◣   ✦ TENTATIVE

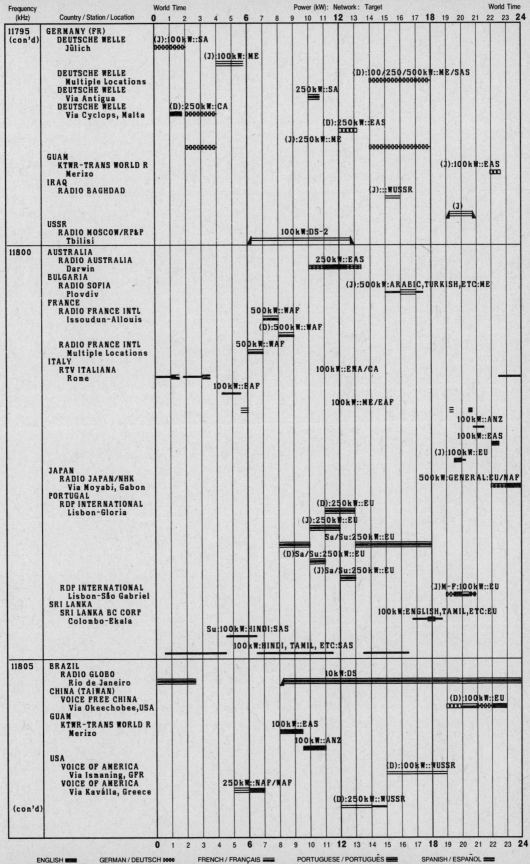

Frequency (kHz)	Country / Station / Location	Schedule

11795 (con'd)

GERMANY (FR)
- DEUTSCHE WELLE — Jülich — (J):100kW::SA / (J):100kW::ME
- DEUTSCHE WELLE — Multiple Locations — (D):100/250/500kW::ME/SAS
- DEUTSCHE WELLE — Via Antigua — 250kW::SA
- DEUTSCHE WELLE — Via Cyclops, Malta — (D):250kW::CA / (D):250kW::EAS / (J):250kW::ME

GUAM
- KTWR-TRANS WORLD R — Merizo — (J):100kW::EAS

IRAQ
- RADIO BAGHDAD — (J):::WUSSR / (J)

USSR
- RADIO MOSCOW/RP&P — Tbilisi — 100kW:DS-2

11800

AUSTRALIA
- RADIO AUSTRALIA — Darwin — 250kW::EAS

BULGARIA
- RADIO SOFIA — Plovdiv — (J):500kW:ARABIC,TURKISH,ETC:ME

FRANCE
- RADIO FRANCE INTL — Issoudun-Allouis — 500kW::WAF / (D):500kW::WAF
- RADIO FRANCE INTL — Multiple Locations — 500kW::WAF

ITALY
- RTV ITALIANA — Rome — 100kW::ENA/CA / 100kW::EAF / 100kW::ME/EAF / 100kW::ANZ / 100kW::EAS / (J):100kW::EU

JAPAN
- RADIO JAPAN/NHK — Via Moyabi, Gabon — 500kW:GENERAL:EU/NAF

PORTUGAL
- RDP INTERNATIONAL — Lisbon-Gloria — (D):250kW::EU / (J):250kW::EU / Sa/Su:250kW::EU / (D)Sa/Su:250kW::EU / (J)Sa/Su:250kW::EU
- RDP INTERNATIONAL — Lisbon-São Gabriel — (J)M-F:100kW::EU

SRI LANKA
- SRI LANKA BC CORP — Colombo-Ekala — 100kW:ENGLISH,TAMIL,ETC:EU / Su:100kW:HINDI:SAS / 100kW:HINDI, TAMIL, ETC:SAS

11805

BRAZIL
- RADIO GLOBO — Rio de Janeiro — 10kW:DS

CHINA (TAIWAN)
- VOICE FREE CHINA — Via Okeechobee,USA — (D):100kW::EU

GUAM
- KTWR-TRANS WORLD R — Merizo — 100kW::EAS / 100kW::ANZ

USA
- VOICE OF AMERICA — Via Ismaning, GFR — (D):100kW::WUSSR
- VOICE OF AMERICA — Via Kaválla, Greece — 250kW::NAF/WAF / (D):250kW::WUSSR

(con'd)

Legend:
ENGLISH ▬ GERMAN / DEUTSCH ◊◊◊◊ FRENCH / FRANÇAIS ▬ PORTUGUESE / PORTUGUÊS ▬ SPANISH / ESPAÑOL ▬
ARABIC /ﻉﻑ ▬ RUSSIAN / РУССКИИ ▬ CHINESE /✦✷ ▭▭ JAPANESE / 日本語 ▬ MULTILINGUAL ▭▭ OTHER ▬
SUMMER ONLY (J) WINTER ONLY (D) JAMMING ∧∧ or / or \ EARLIEST HEARD ◢ LATEST HEARD ◣ † TENTATIVE

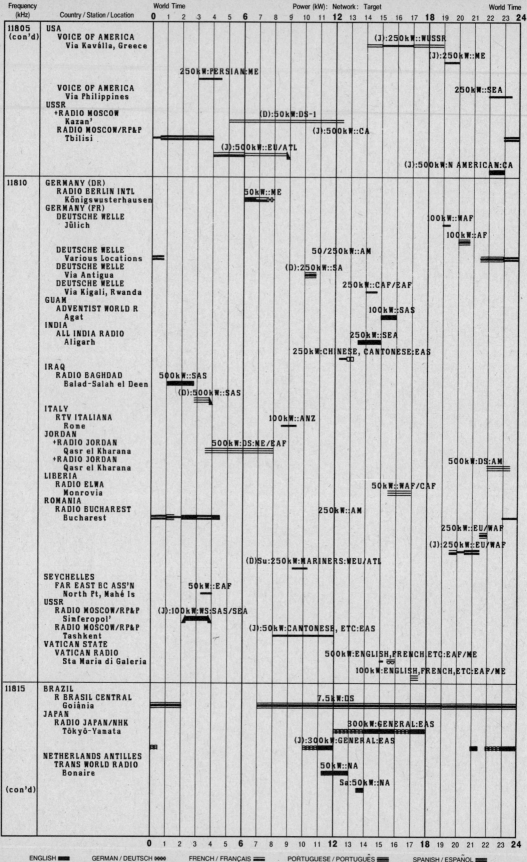

Frequency (kHz) / Country / Station / Location

Frequency (kHz)	Country / Station / Location	Details
11805 (con'd)	USA	
	VOICE OF AMERICA, Via Kaválla, Greece	(J):250kW::WUSSR; (J):250kW::ME; 250kW:PERSIAN:ME
	VOICE OF AMERICA, Via Philippines	250kW::SEA
	USSR +RADIO MOSCOW, Kazan'	(D):50kW:DS-1
	RADIO MOSCOW/RP&P, Tbilisi	(J):500kW::CA; (J):500kW::EU/ATL; (J):500kW::N AMERICAN:CA
11810	GERMANY (DR)	
	RADIO BERLIN INTL, Königswusterhausen	50kW::ME
	GERMANY (FR) DEUTSCHE WELLE, Jülich	100kW::WAF; 100kW::AF
	DEUTSCHE WELLE, Various Locations	50/250kW::AM
	DEUTSCHE WELLE, Via Antigua	(D):250kW::SA
	DEUTSCHE WELLE, Via Kigali, Rwanda	250kW::CAF/EAF
	GUAM ADVENTIST WORLD R, Agat	100kW::SAS
	INDIA ALL INDIA RADIO, Aligarh	250kW::SEA; 250kW:CHINESE, CANTONESE:EAS
	IRAQ RADIO BAGHDAD, Balad-Salah el Deen	500kW::SAS; (D):500kW::SAS
	ITALY RTV ITALIANA, Rome	100kW::ANZ
	JORDAN +RADIO JORDAN, Qasr el Kharana	500kW:DS:NE/EAF
	+RADIO JORDAN, Qasr el Kharana	500kW:DS:AM
	LIBERIA RADIO ELWA, Monrovia	50kW::WAF/CAF
	ROMANIA RADIO BUCHAREST, Bucharest	250kW::AM; 250kW::EU/WAF; (J):250kW::EU/WAF; (D)Su:250kW:MARINERS:WEU/ATL
	SEYCHELLES FAR EAST BC ASS'N, North Pt, Mahé Is	50kW::EAF
	USSR RADIO MOSCOW/RP&P, Simferopol'	(J):100kW:WS:SAS/SEA
	RADIO MOSCOW/RP&P, Tashkent	(J):50kW:CANTONESE, ETC:EAS
	VATICAN STATE VATICAN RADIO, Sta Maria di Galeria	500kW:ENGLISH,FRENCH,ETC:EAF/ME; 100kW:ENGLISH,FRENCH,ETC:EAF/ME
11815	BRAZIL	
	R BRASIL CENTRAL, Goiânia	7.5kW:DS
	JAPAN RADIO JAPAN/NHK, Tōkyō-Yamata	300kW:GENERAL:EAS; (J):300kW:GENERAL:EAS
	NETHERLANDS ANTILLES TRANS WORLD RADIO, Bonaire	50kW::NA; Sa:50kW::NA
(con'd)		

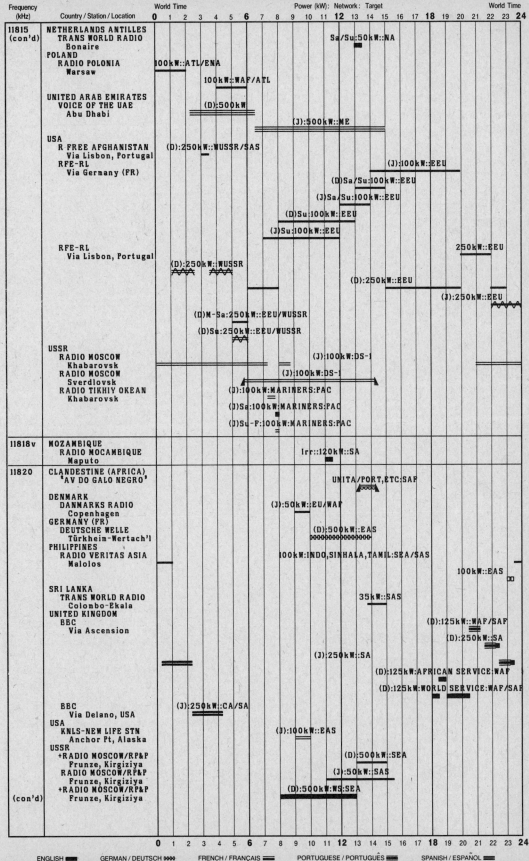

Frequency (kHz)	Country / Station / Location	Transmission details
11815 (con'd)	**NETHERLANDS ANTILLES** TRANS WORLD RADIO Bonaire	Sa/Su:50kW::NA
	POLAND RADIO POLONIA Warsaw	100kW::ATL/ENA ; 100kW::WAF/ATL
	UNITED ARAB EMIRATES VOICE OF THE UAE Abu Dhabi	(D):500kW ; (J):500kW::ME
	USA R FREE AFGHANISTAN Via Lisbon, Portugal	(D):250kW::WUSSR/SAS
	RFE-RL Via Germany (FR)	(J):100kW::EEU ; (D)Sa/Su:100kW::EEU ; (J)Sa/Su:100kW::EEU ; (D)Su:100kW::EEU ; (J)Su:100kW::EEU
	RFE-RL Via Lisbon, Portugal	250kW::EEU ; (D):250kW::WUSSR ; (D):250kW::EEU ; (J):250kW::EEU ; (D)M-Sa:250kW::EEU/WUSSR ; (D)Su:250kW::EEU/WUSSR
	USSR RADIO MOSCOW Khabarovsk	(J):100kW::DS-1
	RADIO MOSCOW Sverdlovsk	(J):100kW::DS-1
	RADIO TIKHIY OKEAN Khabarovsk	(J):100kW::MARINERS:PAC ; (J)Sa:100kW::MARINERS:PAC ; (J)Su-F:100kW::MARINERS:PAC
11818 v	**MOZAMBIQUE** RADIO MOCAMBIQUE Maputo	Irr::120kW::SA
11820	**CLANDESTINE (AFRICA)** "AV DO GALO NEGRO"	UNITA/PORT,ETC:SAF
	DENMARK DANMARKS RADIO Copenhagen	(J):50kW::EU/WAF
	GERMANY (FR) DEUTSCHE WELLE Türkheim-Wertach'l	(D):500kW::EAS
	PHILIPPINES RADIO VERITAS ASIA Malolos	100kW:INDO,SINHALA,TAMIL:SEA/SAS ; 100kW::EAS
	SRI LANKA TRANS WORLD RADIO Colombo-Ekala	35kW::SAS
	UNITED KINGDOM BBC Via Ascension	(D):125kW::WAF/SAF ; (D):250kW::SA ; (J):250kW::SA ; (D):125kW:AFRICAN SERVICE:WAF ; (D):125kW:WORLD SERVICE:WAF/SAF
	BBC Via Delano, USA	(J):250kW::CA/SA
	USA KNLS-NEW LIFE STN Anchor Pt, Alaska	(J):100kW::EAS
	USSR +RADIO MOSCOW/RP&P Frunze, Kirgiziya	(D):500kW::SEA
	RADIO MOSCOW/RP&P Frunze, Kirgiziya	(J):50kW::SAS
(con'd)	+RADIO MOSCOW/RP&P Frunze, Kirgiziya	(D):500kW:WS:SEA

ENGLISH ▬▬   GERMAN / DEUTSCH ◊◊◊◊   FRENCH / FRANÇAIS ▭▭▭   PORTUGUESE / PORTUGUÊS ▦▦▦   SPANISH / ESPAÑOL ▬▬

ARABIC / العربية ▤▤   RUSSIAN / РУССКИИ ▬▬   CHINESE / 中文 ◻◻◻◻   JAPANESE / 日本語 ▰▰▰   MULTILINGUAL ▧▧▧   OTHER ▬

SUMMER ONLY (J)   WINTER ONLY (D)   JAMMING ∧∧ or / or \   EARLIEST HEARD ◢   LATEST HEARD ◣   + TENTATIVE

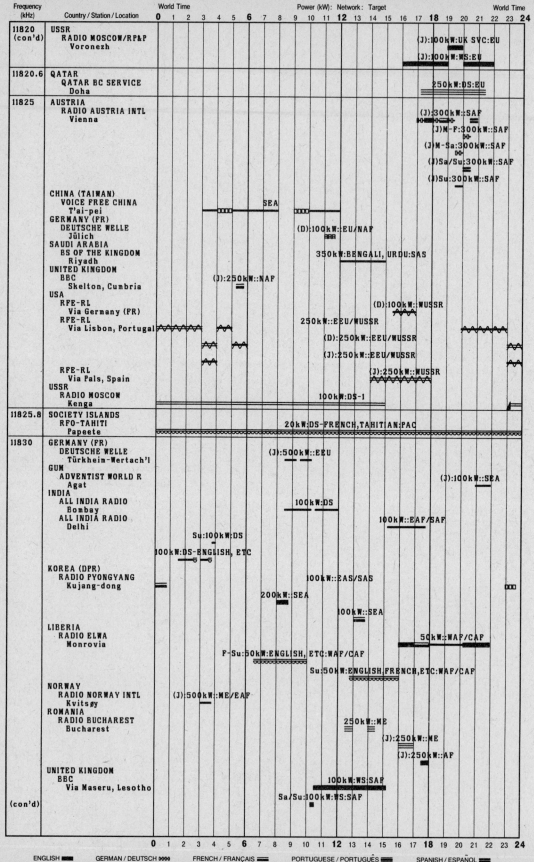

Frequency (kHz)	Country / Station / Location	Schedule (World Time 0–24)
11820 (con'd)	**USSR** RADIO MOSCOW/RP&P — Voronezh	(J):100kW:UK SVC:EU (18–20) · (J):100kW:WS:EU (18–22)
11820.6	**QATAR** QATAR BC SERVICE — Doha	250kW:DS:EU (16–22)
11825	**AUSTRIA** RADIO AUSTRIA INTL — Vienna	(J):300kW::SAF · (J)M-F:300kW::SAF · (J)M-Sa:300kW::SAF · (J)Sa/Su:300kW::SAF · (J)Su:300kW::SAF
	CHINA (TAIWAN) VOICE FREE CHINA — T'ai-pei	SEA (3–9)
	GERMANY (FR) DEUTSCHE WELLE — Jülich	(D):100kW::EU/NAF (11)
	SAUDI ARABIA BS OF THE KINGDOM — Riyadh	350kW:BENGALI, URDU:SAS (12–15)
	UNITED KINGDOM BBC — Skelton, Cumbria	(J):250kW::NAF (4)
	USA RFE-RL — Via Germany (FR)	(D):100kW:WUSSR (16–17)
	RFE-RL — Via Lisbon, Portugal	250kW::EEU/WUSSR · (D):250kW::EEU/WUSSR · (J):250kW::EEU/WUSSR
	RFE-RL — Via Pals, Spain	(J):250kW::WUSSR (14–17)
	USSR RADIO MOSCOW — Kenga	100kW:DS-1
11825.8	**SOCIETY ISLANDS** RFO-TAHITI — Papeete	20kW:DS-FRENCH,TAHITIAN:PAC
11830	**GERMANY (FR)** DEUTSCHE WELLE — Türkheim-Wertach'l	(J):500kW::EEU (7–8)
	GUM ADVENTIST WORLD R — Agat	(J):100kW::SEA (20–22)
	INDIA ALL INDIA RADIO — Bombay	100kW:DS (8–10)
	ALL INDIA RADIO — Delhi	100kW::EAF/SAF (15–16)
		Su:100kW:DS · 100kW:DS-ENGLISH, ETC
	KOREA (DPR) RADIO PYONGYANG — Kujang-dong	100kW::EAS/SAS · 200kW::SEA · 100kW::SEA
	LIBERIA RADIO ELWA — Monrovia	50kW::WAF/CAF · F-Su:50kW:ENGLISH, ETC:WAF/CAF · Su:50kW:ENGLISH,FRENCH,ETC:WAF/CAF
	NORWAY RADIO NORWAY INTL — Kvitsøy	(J):500kW:ME/EAF (3–4)
	ROMANIA RADIO BUCHAREST — Bucharest	250kW::ME · (J):250kW::ME · (J):250kW::AF
	UNITED KINGDOM BBC — Via Maseru, Lesotho	100kW:WS:SAF · Sa/Su:100kW:WS:SAF
(con'd)		

ENGLISH ▬▬   GERMAN / DEUTSCH ◊◊◊◊   FRENCH / FRANÇAIS ═══   PORTUGUESE / PORTUGUÊS ▬▬   SPANISH / ESPAÑOL ▬▬

ARABIC /ﻉﺏﻍ ═══   RUSSIAN / РУССКИИ ═══   CHINESE / ✳✗ ◊◊◊◊   JAPANESE / 日本語 ▬▬   MULTILINGUAL ▭▭▭   OTHER ▬▬

SUMMER ONLY (J)   WINTER ONLY (D)   JAMMING ∧∧ or / or \   EARLIEST HEARD ◢   LATEST HEARD ◣   + TENTATIVE

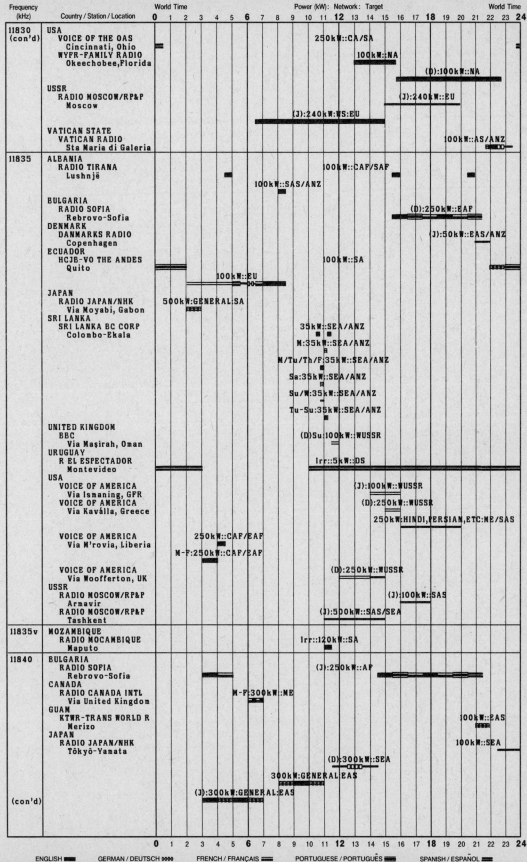

Frequency (kHz)	Country / Station / Location	World Time / Power (kW): Network: Target

11830 (con'd)

USA
- VOICE OF THE OAS — Cincinnati, Ohio — 250kW::CA/SA
- WYFR-FAMILY RADIO — Okeechobee, Florida — 100kW::NA / (D):100kW::NA

USSR
- RADIO MOSCOW/RP&P — Moscow — (J):240kW::EU / (J):240kW:WS:EU

VATICAN STATE
- VATICAN RADIO — Sta Maria di Galeria — 100kW::AS/ANZ

11835

ALBANIA
- RADIO TIRANA — Lushnjë — 100kW::CAF/SAF / 100kW::SAS/ANZ

BULGARIA
- RADIO SOFIA — Rebrovo-Sofia — (D):250kW::EAF

DENMARK
- DANMARKS RADIO — Copenhagen — (J):50kW::EAS/ANZ

ECUADOR
- HCJB-VO THE ANDES — Quito — 100kW::SA / 100kW::EU

JAPAN
- RADIO JAPAN/NHK — Via Moyabi, Gabon — 500kW:GENERAL:SA

SRI LANKA
- SRI LANKA BC CORP — Colombo-Ekala — 35kW::SEA/ANZ
  - M:35kW::SEA/ANZ
  - M/Tu/Th/F:35kW::SEA/ANZ
  - Sa:35kW::SEA/ANZ
  - Su/W:35kW::SEA/ANZ
  - Tu-Su:35kW::SEA/ANZ

UNITED KINGDOM
- BBC — Via Maşirah, Oman — (D)Su:100kW::WUSSR

URUGUAY
- R EL ESPECTADOR — Montevideo — Irr::5kW::DS

USA
- VOICE OF AMERICA — Via Ismaning, GFR — (J):100kW::WUSSR
- VOICE OF AMERICA — Via Kaválla, Greece — (D):250kW::WUSSR / 250kW:HINDI,PERSIAN,ETC:ME/SAS
- VOICE OF AMERICA — Via M'rovia, Liberia — 250kW::CAF/EAF / M-F:250kW::CAF/EAF
- VOICE OF AMERICA — Via Woofferton, UK — (D):250kW::WUSSR

USSR
- RADIO MOSCOW/RP&P — Armavir — (J):100kW::SAS
- RADIO MOSCOW/RP&P — Tashkent — (J):500kW::SAS/SEA

11835v

MOZAMBIQUE
- RADIO MOCAMBIQUE — Maputo — Irr::120kW::SA

11840

BULGARIA
- RADIO SOFIA — Rebrovo-Sofia — (J):250kW::AF

CANADA
- RADIO CANADA INTL — Via United Kingdom — M-F:300kW::ME

GUAM
- KTWR-TRANS WORLD R — Merizo — 100kW::EAS

JAPAN
- RADIO JAPAN/NHK — Tōkyō-Yamata — 100kW::SEA / (D):300kW::SEA / 300kW:GENERAL:EAS / (J):300kW:GENERAL:EAS

(con'd)

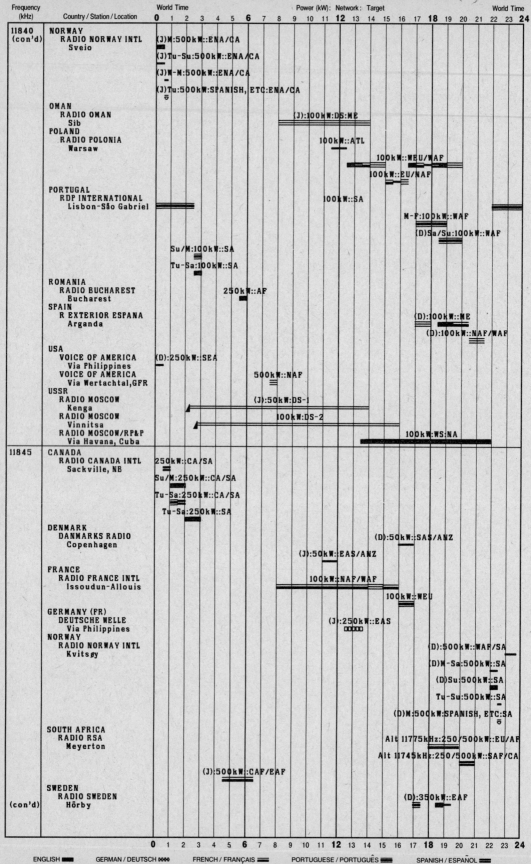

11840 (con'd)

NORWAY
RADIO NORWAY INTL
Sveio
- (J)M:500kW::ENA/CA
- (J)Tu-Su:500kW::ENA/CA
- (J)W-M:500kW:ENA/CA
- (J)Tu:500kW:SPANISH, ETC:ENA/CA

OMAN
RADIO OMAN
Sib
- (J):100kW:DS:ME

POLAND
RADIO POLONIA
Warsaw
- 100kW::ATL
- 100kW::WEU/WAF
- 100kW::EU/NAF

PORTUGAL
RDP INTERNATIONAL
Lisbon-São Gabriel
- 100kW::SA
- M-F:100kW::WAF
- (D)Sa/Su:100kW::WAF
- Su/M:100kW::SA
- Tu-Sa:100kW::SA

ROMANIA
RADIO BUCHAREST
Bucharest
- 250kW::AF

SPAIN
R EXTERIOR ESPANA
Arganda
- (D):100kW::ME
- (D):100kW::NAF/WAF

USA
VOICE OF AMERICA
Via Philippines
- (D):250kW::SEA

VOICE OF AMERICA
Via Wertachtal,GFR
- 500kW::NAF

USSR
RADIO MOSCOW
Kenga
- (J):50kW:DS-1

RADIO MOSCOW
Vinnitsa
- 100kW:DS-2

RADIO MOSCOW/RP&P
Via Havana, Cuba
- 100kW:WS:NA

11845

CANADA
RADIO CANADA INTL
Sackville, NB
- 250kW::CA/SA
- Su/M:250kW::CA/SA
- Tu-Sa:250kW::CA/SA
- Tu-Sa:250kW::SA

DENMARK
DANMARKS RADIO
Copenhagen
- (D):50kW::SAS/ANZ
- (J):50kW::EAS/ANZ

FRANCE
RADIO FRANCE INTL
Issoudun-Allouis
- 100kW::NAF/WAF
- 100kW::WEU

GERMANY (FR)
DEUTSCHE WELLE
Via Philippines
- (J):250kW::EAS

NORWAY
RADIO NORWAY INTL
Kvitsøy
- (D):500kW::WAF/SA
- (D)M-Sa:500kW::SA
- (D)Su:500kW::SA
- Tu-Su:500kW::SA
- (D)M:500kW:SPANISH, ETC:SA

SOUTH AFRICA
RADIO RSA
Meyerton
- Alt 11775kHz:250/500kW::EU/AF
- Alt 11745kHz:250/500kW::SAF/CA
- (J):500kW::CAF/EAF

SWEDEN
RADIO SWEDEN
Hörby **(con'd)**
- (D):350kW::EAF

ENGLISH ▬▬ GERMAN / DEUTSCH ◊◊◊◊ FRENCH / FRANÇAIS ═══ PORTUGUESE / PORTUGUÊS ▬▬ SPANISH / ESPAÑOL ═══
ARABIC / ﻋﺮﺑﻲ ≡≡ RUSSIAN / РУССКИИ ═══ CHINESE / ◆χ □□□□ JAPANESE / 日本語 ▬▬ MULTILINGUAL ◌◌◌◌ OTHER ▬▬
SUMMER ONLY (J) WINTER ONLY (D) JAMMING ∧∧ or / or \ EARLIEST HEARD ◢ LATEST HEARD ◣ ✦ TENTATIVE

Frequency (kHz)	Country / Station / Location		World Time → 0 ... 12 ... 24 (Power (kW): Network: Target)

11845 (con'd) SWEDEN
- RADIO SWEDEN, Hörby — (J):350kW::AF
- SVERIGES RIKSRADIO, Hörby — (D):350kW:DS-1/DS-3:AF

USA
- VOICE OF AMERICA, Via Kaválla, Greece — (D):250kW::ME/SAS

USSR
- RADIO MOSCOW/RP&P, Kazan' — (J):100kW:URDU, HINDI, ETC:SAS/SEA
- 100kW:WS:SAS/SEA

11850 CANADA
- RADIO CANADA INTL, Sackville, NB — M-F:250kW::CA/SA

FINLAND
- RADIO FINLAND, Pori — (D):500kW::ME/SAS/EAF

GERMANY (FR)
- DEUTSCHE WELLE, Türkheim-Wertach'l — (D):500kW::EEU
- DEUTSCHE WELLE, Via Sri Lanka — (J):250kW::ME

GUAM
- KTWR-TRANS WORLD R, Merizo — 100kW::SEA
- (D):100kW::EAS

INDIA
- ALL INDIA RADIO, Delhi — 100kW:DS-ENGLISH, ETC

JAPAN
- RADIO JAPAN/NHK, Tōkyō-Yamata — (J):100kW:GENERAL:ANZ

NORWAY
- RADIO NORWAY INTL, Kvitsøy — (D):500kW::SA
- RADIO NORWAY INTL, Sveio — (D)M-Sa:500kW::WNA
- (D)Su:500kW::WNA
- (D)Tu-Su:500kW::WNA
- (D)M:500kW::SPANISH, ETC:WNA

PHILIPPINES
- FAR EAST BC CO, Bocaue — 50kW::ANZ/EAS
- 50kW::SEA/SAS
- (J):50kW::SAS

UNITED KINGDOM
- BBC, Via Singapore — 250kW::SAS/SEA
- 250kW::SAS/ME

USA
- VOICE OF AMERICA, Via M'rovia, Liberia — 250kW::WAF/SAF
- M-F:250kW::WAF/SAF
- M-F:250kW::WAF/CAF
- VOICE OF AMERICA, Via Tangier, Morocco — (D):100kW::EEU/WUSSR

USSR
- RADIO MOSCOW, Konevo — (D):240kW::EU
- RADIO MOSCOW/RP&P, Ryazan' — 200kW:AFRICAN:ME/EAF
- 200kW:WS:ME/EAF
- RADIO MOSCOW/RP&P, Via Plovdiv, Bulgaria — (J):500kW::CA

11852v VENEZUELA
- RADIO NACIONAL, Caracas — Alternative Frequency to 11862vkHz

11855 ALBANIA
- RADIO TIRANA, Lushnjë — 100kW::CAF/SAF
- 100kW::SAS/ANZ

AUSTRALIA
- RADIO AUSTRALIA, Carnarvon — 100kW::SEA

BRAZIL
- RADIO APARECIDA, Aparecida — 7.5kW:DS

(con'd)

ENGLISH ▬▬　GERMAN / DEUTSCH ▨▨▨　FRENCH / FRANÇAIS ═══　PORTUGUESE / PORTUGUÊS ▤▤▤　SPANISH / ESPAÑOL ▬═

ARABIC / عربى ═══　RUSSIAN / РУССКИИ ═══　CHINESE / ✦✦ ▨▨▨　JAPANESE / 日本語 ▬▬　MULTILINGUAL ▨▨▨　OTHER ▬▬

SUMMER ONLY (J)　WINTER ONLY (D)　JAMMING ∧∧ or / or \　EARLIEST HEARD ◢　LATEST HEARD ◣　✦ TENTATIVE

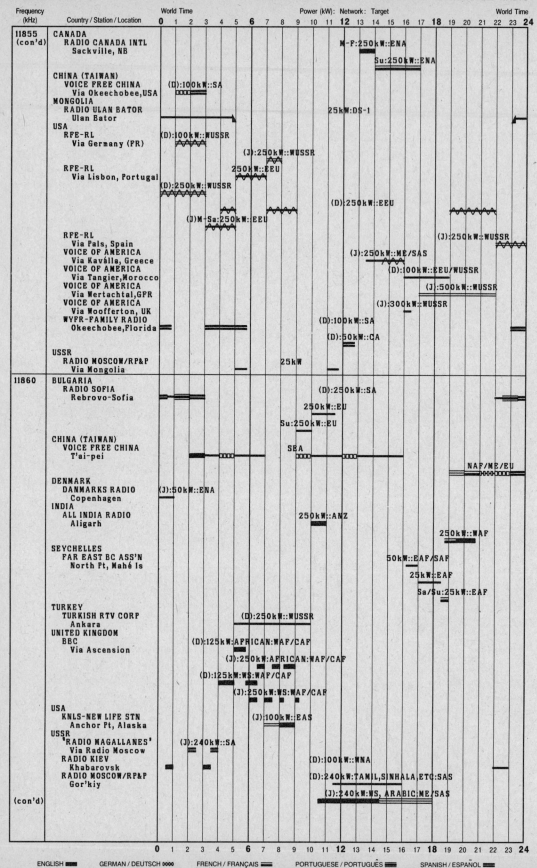

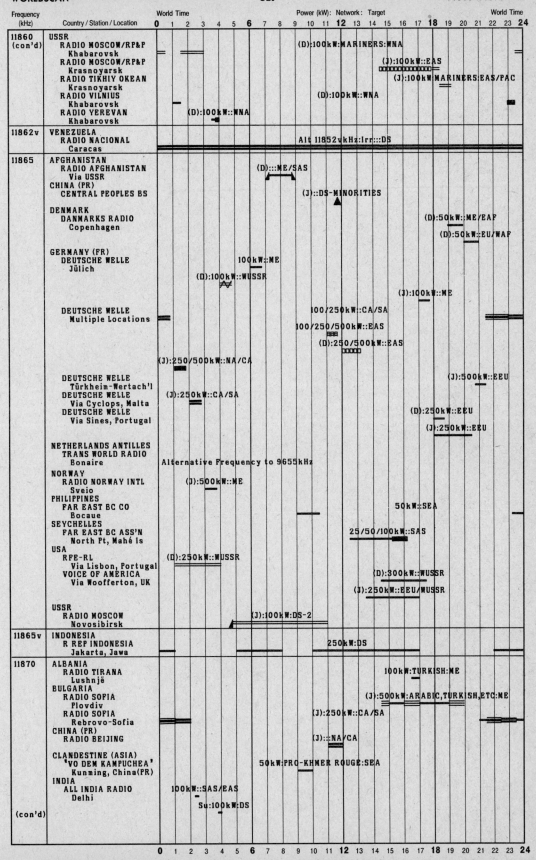

Frequency (kHz)	Country / Station / Location	Power (kW): Network: Target
11860 (con'd)	USSR RADIO MOSCOW/RP&P Khabarovsk	(D):100kW:MARINERS:WNA
	RADIO MOSCOW/RP&P Krasnoyarsk	(J):100kW::EAS
	RADIO TIKHIY OKEAN Krasnoyarsk	(J):100kW MARINERS:EAS/PAC
	RADIO VILNIUS Khabarovsk	(D):100kW::WNA
	RADIO YEREVAN Khabarovsk	(D):100kW::WNA
11862v	VENEZUELA RADIO NACIONAL Caracas	Alt 11852vkHz:Irr:::DS
11865	AFGHANISTAN RADIO AFGHANISTAN Via USSR	(D):::ME/SAS
	CHINA (PR) CENTRAL PEOPLES BS	(J)::DS-MINORITIES
	DENMARK DANMARKS RADIO Copenhagen	(D):50kW::ME/EAF (D):50kW::EU/WAF
	GERMANY (FR) DEUTSCHE WELLE Jülich	100kW::ME (D):100kW::WUSSR (J):100kW::ME
	DEUTSCHE WELLE Multiple Locations	100/250kW::CA/SA 100/250/500kW::EAS (D):250/500kW::EAS
	DEUTSCHE WELLE Türkheim-Wertach'l	(J):250/500kW::NA/CA (J):500kW::EEU
	DEUTSCHE WELLE Via Cyclops, Malta	(J):250kW::CA/SA
	DEUTSCHE WELLE Via Sines, Portugal	(D):250kW::EEU (J):250kW::EEU
	NETHERLANDS ANTILLES TRANS WORLD RADIO Bonaire	Alternative Frequency to 9655kHz
	NORWAY RADIO NORWAY INTL Sveio	(J):500kW::ME
	PHILIPPINES FAR EAST BC CO Bocaue	50kW::SEA
	SEYCHELLES FAR EAST BC ASS'N North Pt, Mahé Is	25/50/100kW::SAS
	USA RFE-RL Via Lisbon, Portugal	(D):250kW::WUSSR
	VOICE OF AMERICA Via Woofferton, UK	(D):300kW::WUSSR (J):250kW::EEU/WUSSR
	USSR RADIO MOSCOW Novosibirsk	(J):100kW:DS-2
11865v	INDONESIA R REP INDONESIA Jakarta, Jawa	250kW:DS
11870	ALBANIA RADIO TIRANA Lushnjë	100kW:TURKISH:ME
	BULGARIA RADIO SOFIA Plovdiv	(J):500kW:ARABIC,TURKISH,ETC:ME
	RADIO SOFIA Rebrovo-Sofia	(J):250kW::CA/SA
	CHINA (PR) RADIO BEIJING	(J)::NA/CA
	CLANDESTINE (ASIA) 'VO DEM KAMPUCHEA' Kunming, China(PR)	50kW:PRO-KHMER ROUGE:SEA
	INDIA ALL INDIA RADIO Delhi	100kW::SAS/EAS Su:100kW:DS
(con'd)		

ENGLISH ▬▬ GERMAN / DEUTSCH ⬡⬡⬡⬡ FRENCH / FRANÇAIS ═══ PORTUGUESE / PORTUGUÊS ▬▬ SPANISH / ESPAÑOL ═══

ARABIC / ﻋﺮﺑﻲ ═▬ RUSSIAN / РУССКИЙ ═══ CHINESE / 中文 ⬡⬡⬡⬡ JAPANESE / 日本語 ▬▬▬ MULTILINGUAL ⬡⬡⬡⬡ OTHER ▬▬

SUMMER ONLY (J)   WINTER ONLY (D)   JAMMING ∧∧ or / or \   EARLIEST HEARD ◢   LATEST HEARD ◣   ⁺ TENTATIVE

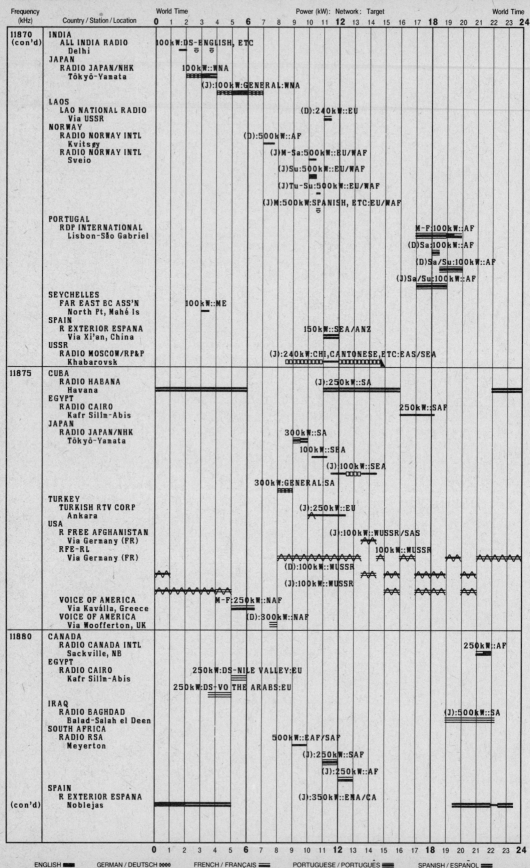

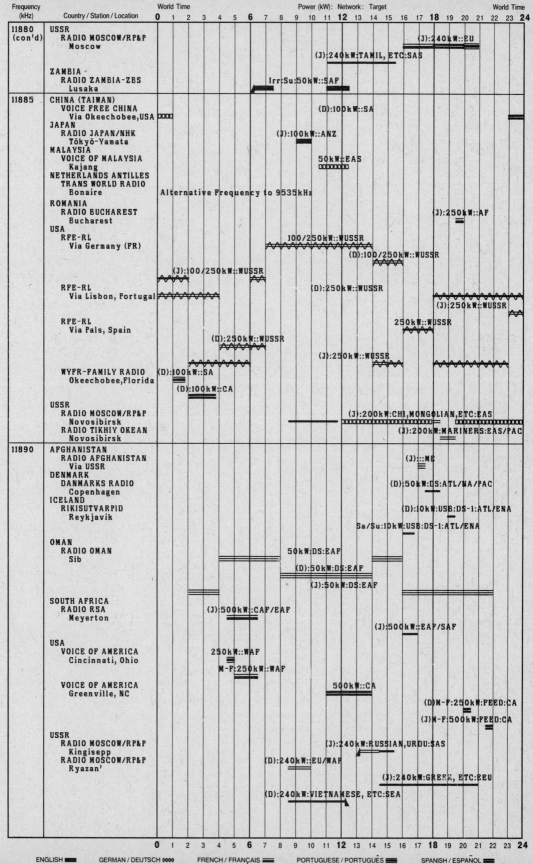

Frequency (kHz)   Country / Station / Location   World Time   Power (kW): Network: Target   World Time

0 1 2 3 4 5 6 7 8 9 10 11 12 13 14 15 16 17 18 19 20 21 22 23 24

11880 (con'd)

USSR
RADIO MOSCOW/RP&P
Moscow
- (J):240kW::EU
- (J):240kW:TAMIL,ETC:SAS

ZAMBIA
RADIO ZAMBIA-ZBS
Lusaka
- Irr:Su:50kW::SAF

11885

CHINA (TAIWAN)
VOICE FREE CHINA
Via Okeechobee,USA
- (D):100kW::SA

JAPAN
RADIO JAPAN/NHK
Tōkyō-Yamata
- (J):100kW::ANZ

MALAYSIA
VOICE OF MALAYSIA
Kajang
- 50kW::EAS

NETHERLANDS ANTILLES
TRANS WORLD RADIO
Bonaire
- Alternative Frequency to 9535kHz

ROMANIA
RADIO BUCHAREST
Bucharest
- (J):250kW::AF

USA
RFE-RL
Via Germany (FR)
- 100/250kW::WUSSR
- (D):100/250kW::WUSSR

RFE-RL
Via Lisbon, Portugal
- (J):100/250kW::WUSSR
- (D):250kW::WUSSR
- (J):250kW::WUSSR

RFE-RL
Via Pals, Spain
- 250kW::WUSSR
- (D):250kW::WUSSR
- (J):250kW::WUSSR

WYFR-FAMILY RADIO
Okeechobee,Florida
- (D):100kW::SA
- (D):100kW::CA

USSR
RADIO MOSCOW/RP&P
Novosibirsk
- (J):200kW:CHI,MONGOLIAN,ETC:EAS

RADIO TIKHIY OKEAN
Novosibirsk
- (J):200kW:MARINERS:EAS/PAC

11890

AFGHANISTAN
RADIO AFGHANISTAN
Via USSR
- (J):::ME

DENMARK
DANMARKS RADIO
Copenhagen
- (D):50kW:DS:ATL/NA/PAC

ICELAND
RIKISUTVARPID
Reykjavik
- (D):10kW:USB:DS-1:ATL/ENA
- Sa/Su:10kW:USB:DS-1:ATL/ENA

OMAN
RADIO OMAN
Sib
- 50kW:DS:EAF
- (D):50kW:DS:EAF
- (J):50kW:DS:EAF

SOUTH AFRICA
RADIO RSA
Meyerton
- (J):500kW::CAF/EAF
- (J):500kW::EAF/SAF

USA
VOICE OF AMERICA
Cincinnati, Ohio
- 250kW::WAF
- M-F:250kW::WAF

VOICE OF AMERICA
Greenville, NC
- 500kW::CA
- (D)M-F:250kW:FEED:CA
- (J)M-F:500kW:FEED:CA

USSR
RADIO MOSCOW/RP&P
Kingisepp
- (J):240kW:RUSSIAN,URDU:SAS

RADIO MOSCOW/RP&P
Ryazan'
- (D):240kW::EU/WAF
- (J):240kW:GREEK,ETC:EEU
- (D):240kW:VIETNAMESE,ETC:SEA

0 1 2 3 4 5 6 7 8 9 10 11 12 13 14 15 16 17 18 19 20 21 22 23 24

ENGLISH ▬▬ GERMAN / DEUTSCH ◊◊◊◊ FRENCH / FRANÇAIS ═══ PORTUGUESE / PORTUGUÊS ▬▬ SPANISH / ESPAÑOL ▬▬

ARABIC /‏عربي‎ ═══ RUSSIAN / РУССКИИ ═══ CHINESE / 中文 ◊◊◊◊ JAPANESE / 日本語 ▬▬ MULTILINGUAL ◊◊◊◊ OTHER ▬▬

SUMMER ONLY (J) WINTER ONLY (D) JAMMING /\/\ or / or \ EARLIEST HEARD ◢ LATEST HEARD ◣ ✝ TENTATIVE

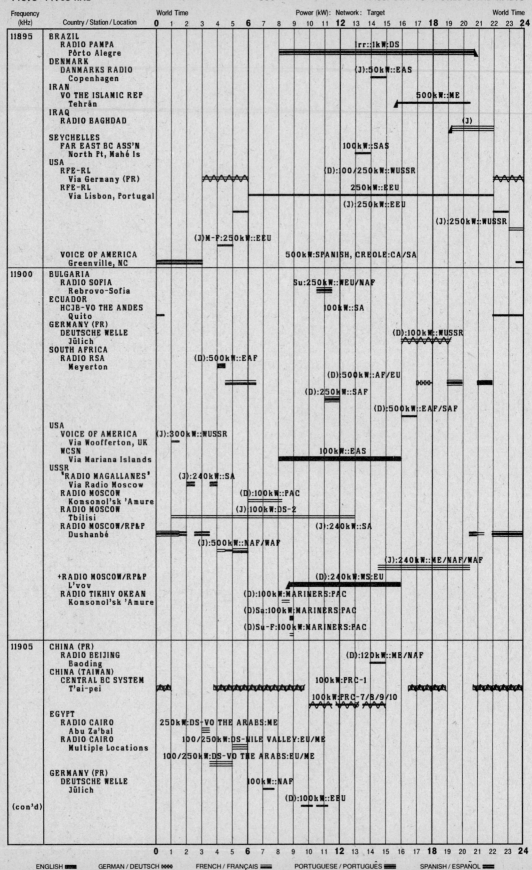

Frequency (kHz)	Country / Station / Location	World Time	Power (kW): Network: Target	World Time

11895

BRAZIL
RADIO PAMPA
Pôrto Alegre — Irr::1kW:DS

DENMARK
DANMARKS RADIO
Copenhagen — (J):50kW::EAS

IRAN
VO THE ISLAMIC REP
Tehrän — 500kW::ME

IRAQ
RADIO BAGHDAD — (J)

SEYCHELLES
FAR EAST BC ASS'N
North Pt, Mahé Is — 100kW::SAS

USA
RFE-RL
Via Germany (FR) — (D):00/250kW::WUSSR
RFE-RL
Via Lisbon, Portugal — 250kW::EEU
— (J):250kW::EEU
— (J):250kW::WUSSR
— (J)M-F:250kW::EEU

VOICE OF AMERICA
Greenville, NC — 500kW:SPANISH, CREOLE:CA/SA

11900

BULGARIA
RADIO SOFIA
Rebrovo-Sofia — Su:250kW::WEU/NAF

ECUADOR
HCJB-VO THE ANDES
Quito — 100kW::SA

GERMANY (FR)
DEUTSCHE WELLE
Jülich — (D):100kW::WUSSR

SOUTH AFRICA
RADIO RSA
Meyerton — (D):500kW::EAF
— (D):500kW::AF/EU
— (D):250kW::SAF
— (D):500kW::EAF/SAF

USA
VOICE OF AMERICA
Via Woofferton, UK — (J):300kW::WUSSR
WCSN
Via Mariana Islands — 100kW::EAS

USSR
'RADIO MAGALLANES'
Via Radio Moscow — (J):240kW::SA
RADIO MOSCOW
Komsomol'sk 'Amure — (D):100kW::PAC
RADIO MOSCOW
Tbilisi — (J)100kW::DS-2
RADIO MOSCOW/RP&P
Dushanbé — (J):240kW::SA
— (J):500kW::NAF/WAF
— (J):240kW::ME/NAF/WAF

+RADIO MOSCOW/RP&P
L'vov — (D):240kW:WS:EU
RADIO TIKHIY OKEAN
Komsomol'sk 'Amure — (D):100kW:MARINERS:PAC
— (D)Sa:100kW:MARINERS:PAC
— (D)Su-F:100kW:MARINERS:PAC

11905

CHINA (PR)
RADIO BEIJING
Baoding — (D):120kW::ME/NAF

CHINA (TAIWAN)
CENTRAL BC SYSTEM
T'ai-pei — 100kW:PRC-1
— 100kW:PRC-7/8/9/10

EGYPT
RADIO CAIRO
Abu Za'bal — 250kW:DS-VO THE ARABS:ME
RADIO CAIRO
Multiple Locations — 100/250kW:DS-NILE VALLEY:EU/ME
— 100/250kW:DS-VO THE ARABS:EU/ME

GERMANY (FR)
DEUTSCHE WELLE
Jülich — 100kW::NAF
— (D):100kW::EEU

(con'd)

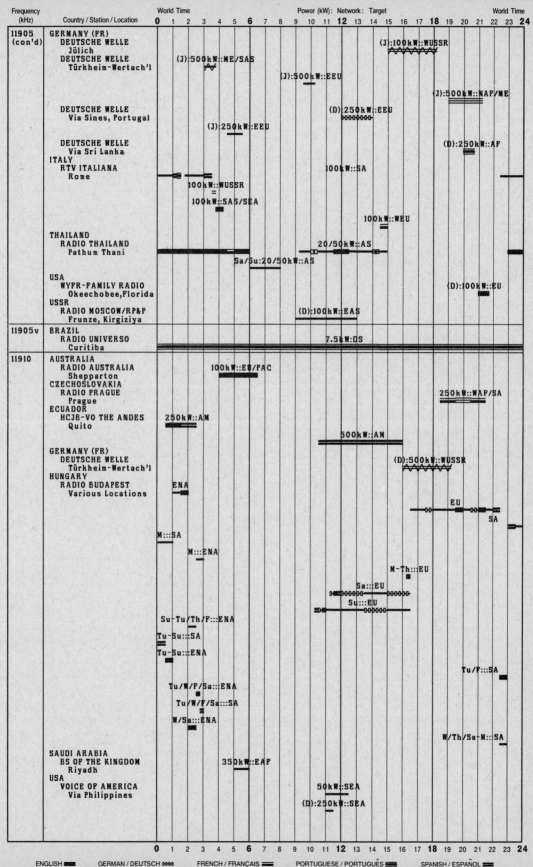

Frequency (kHz)	Country / Station / Location	Details
11905 (con'd)	**GERMANY (FR)** DEUTSCHE WELLE Jülich	(J):100kW::WUSSR
	DEUTSCHE WELLE Türkheim-Wertach'l	(J):500kW::ME/SAS
		(J):500kW::EEU
		(J):500kW::NAF/ME
	DEUTSCHE WELLE Via Sines, Portugal	(D):250kW::EEU
		(J):250kW::EEU
	DEUTSCHE WELLE Via Sri Lanka	(D):250kW::AF
	ITALY RTV ITALIANA Rome	100kW::SA
		100kW::WUSSR
		100kW::SAS/SEA
		100kW::WEU
	THAILAND RADIO THAILAND Pathum Thani	20/50kW::AS
		Sa/Su:20/50kW::AS
	USA WYFR–FAMILY RADIO Okeechobee, Florida	(D):100kW::EU
	USSR RADIO MOSCOW/RP&P Frunze, Kirgiziya	(D):100kW::EAS
11905v	**BRAZIL** RADIO UNIVERSO Curitiba	7.5kW::DS
11910	**AUSTRALIA** RADIO AUSTRALIA Shepparton	100kW::EU/PAC
	CZECHOSLOVAKIA RADIO PRAGUE Prague	250kW::WAF/SA
	ECUADOR HCJB–VO THE ANDES Quito	250kW::AM
		500kW::AM
	GERMANY (FR) DEUTSCHE WELLE Türkheim-Wertach'l	(D):500kW::WUSSR
	HUNGARY RADIO BUDAPEST Various Locations	ENA
		EU
		SA
		M:::SA
		M:::ENA
		M-Th:::EU
		Sa:::EU
		Su:::EU
		Su-Tu/Th/F:::ENA
		Tu-Su:::SA
		Tu-Su:::ENA
		Tu/F:::SA
		Tu/W/F/Sa:::ENA
		Tu/W/F/Sa:::SA
		W/Sa:::ENA
		W/Th/Sa-M:::SA
	SAUDI ARABIA BS OF THE KINGDOM Riyadh	350kW::EAF
	USA VOICE OF AMERICA Via Philippines	50kW::SEA
		(D):250kW::SEA

ENGLISH ▪▪▪   GERMAN / DEUTSCH ◊◊◊◊   FRENCH / FRANÇAIS ═══   PORTUGUESE / PORTUGUÊS ▰▰▰   SPANISH / ESPAÑOL ▰▰▰

ARABIC /ﻉﺏﺃ ≡≡   RUSSIAN / РУССКИИ ═══   CHINESE / ★☆ ◊◊◊◊   JAPANESE / 日本語 ▰▰▰   MULTILINGUAL ◊◊◊◊   OTHER ▬▬

SUMMER ONLY (J)   WINTER ONLY (D)   JAMMING /\/\ or / or \   EARLIEST HEARD ◢   LATEST HEARD ◣   + TENTATIVE

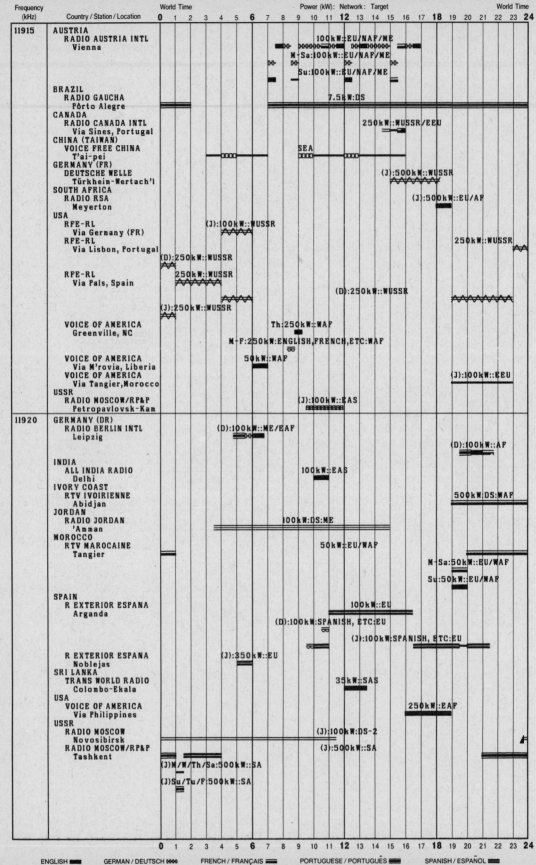

Frequency (kHz)	Country / Station / Location	World Time 0–24 / Power (kW): Network: Target
11915	**AUSTRIA** RADIO AUSTRIA INTL — Vienna	100kW::EU/NAF/ME; M-Sa:100kW::EU/NAF/ME; Su:100kW::EU/NAF/ME
	BRAZIL RADIO GAUCHA — Pôrto Alegre	7.5kW:DS
	CANADA RADIO CANADA INTL — Via Sines, Portugal	250kW::WUSSR/EEU
	CHINA (TAIWAN) VOICE FREE CHINA — T'ai-pei	SEA
	GERMANY (FR) DEUTSCHE WELLE — Türkheim-Wertach'l	(J):500kW::WUSSR
	SOUTH AFRICA RADIO RSA — Meyerton	(J):500kW::EU/AF
	USA RFE-RL — Via Germany (FR)	(J):100kW::WUSSR
	RFE-RL — Via Lisbon, Portugal	250kW::WUSSR
	RFE-RL — Via Pals, Spain	(D):250kW::WUSSR; 250kW::WUSSR; (D):250kW::WUSSR; (J):250kW::WUSSR
	VOICE OF AMERICA — Greenville, NC	Th:250kW::WAF; M-F:250kW:ENGLISH,FRENCH,ETC:WAF
	VOICE OF AMERICA — Via M'rovia, Liberia	50kW::WAF
	VOICE OF AMERICA — Via Tangier, Morocco	(J):100kW::EEU
	USSR RADIO MOSCOW/RP&P — Petropavlovsk-Kam	(J):100kW::EAS
11920	**GERMANY (DR)** RADIO BERLIN INTL — Leipzig	(D):100kW::ME/EAF; (D):100kW::AF
	INDIA ALL INDIA RADIO — Delhi	100kW::EAS
	IVORY COAST RTV IVOIRIENNE — Abidjan	500kW:DS:WAF
	JORDAN RADIO JORDAN — 'Amman	100kW:DS:ME
	MOROCCO RTV MAROCAINE — Tangier	50kW::EU/WAF; M-Sa:50kW::EU/WAF; Su:50kW::EU/WAF
	SPAIN R EXTERIOR ESPANA — Arganda	100kW::EU; (D):100kW:SPANISH,ETC:EU; (J):100kW:SPANISH,ETC:EU
	R EXTERIOR ESPANA — Noblejas	(J):350kW::EU
	SRI LANKA TRANS WORLD RADIO — Colombo-Ekala	35kW::SAS
	USA VOICE OF AMERICA — Via Philippines	250kW:EAF
	USSR RADIO MOSCOW — Novosibirsk	(J):100kW:DS-2
	RADIO MOSCOW/RP&P — Tashkent	(J):500kW::SA; (J)M/W/Th/Sa:500kW::SA; (J)Su/Tu/F:500kW::SA

ENGLISH ▪▪▪   GERMAN / DEUTSCH ◊◊◊◊   FRENCH / FRANÇAIS ▬▬   PORTUGUESE / PORTUGUÊS ▬▬   SPANISH / ESPAÑOL ▬▬

ARABIC / ﻉﺮﺑ ▬▬   RUSSIAN / РУССКИЙ ══   CHINESE / ⋆✗ ◊◊◊◊   JAPANESE / 日本語 ▬▬   MULTILINGUAL ▒▒▒▒   OTHER ▬▬

SUMMER ONLY (J)   WINTER ONLY (D)   JAMMING /\/\ or / or \   EARLIEST HEARD ◢   LATEST HEARD ◣   † TENTATIVE

Frequency (kHz)	Country / Station / Location	World Time — Power (kW) : Network : Target

11925

BRAZIL
RADIO BANDEIRANTES
São Paulo
— 10kW:DS
Irr::10kW:DS

CHINA (PR)
CENTRAL PEOPLES BS
Beijing
— 50kW:TAIWAN-1

ECUADOR
HCJB-VO THE ANDES
Quito
— 100kW::ANZ/PAC

PHILIPPINES
RADIO VERITAS ASIA
Malolos
— 100kW::SEA

SWEDEN
SVERIGES RIKSRADIO
Varberg
— (D):100kW:USB:DS-1:WAF/SA

UNITED KINGDOM
BBC
Skelton, Cumbria
— (J):250kW::EEU

USA
RFE-RL
Via Germany (FR)
— (D):100kW::WUSSR

RFE-RL
Via Lisbon, Portugal
— (D):250kW::EEU

VOICE OF AMERICA
Via Kaválla, Greece
— (D):250kW::ME/SAS
— (J):250kW::ME/SAS

VOICE OF AMERICA
Via Philippines
— 250kW::EAS

VOICE OF AMERICA
Via Wertachtal, GFR
— (J):500kW::ME

VOICE OF AMERICA
Via Woofferton, UK
— (D):300kW:GREEK:EU

USSR
+RADIO MOSCOW/RP&P
Krasnoyarsk
— (D):500kW::EAS/SEA

11930

CUBA
RADIO HABANA
Havana
— (J):50kW::CA

EGYPT
RADIO CAIRO
Kafr Silim-Abis
— 250kW::ME

FRANCE
RADIO FRANCE INTL
Issoudun-Allouis
— (D):500kW::AF
— (J):100/500kW::AF

HOLLAND
RADIO NEDERLAND
Flevoland
— 500kW::WAF
— 500kW::WEU

IRAN
VO THE ISLAMIC REP
Tehrãn
— (J):100kW::EU

USA
KNLS-NEW LIFE STN
Anchor Pt, Alaska
— (J):100kW::EAS

RADIO MARTI
Greenville, NC
— 500kW::CA

VOICE OF AMERICA
Via Philippines
— 250kW::EUSSR
— 250kW::SEA
— (J):50kW::SEA

USSR
RADIO MOSCOW
Armavir
— (D):100kW:DS-1

RADIO MOSCOW/RP&P
Ashkhabad
— (J):100kW::CA/SA
— (J):500kW::EU

11935

ALBANIA
RADIO TIRANA
Lushnjë
— 100kW:INDONESIAN:SEA

BRAZIL
R CLUBE PARANAENSE
Curitiba
— Irr:7.5kW:DS

CANADA
RADIO CANADA INTL
Via United Kingdom
— (D):300kW::EU/WUSSR
— (J):300kW::EU/WUSSR

GERMANY (FR)
DEUTSCHE WELLE
Via Sines, Portugal
— (J):250kW::EEU

(con'd)

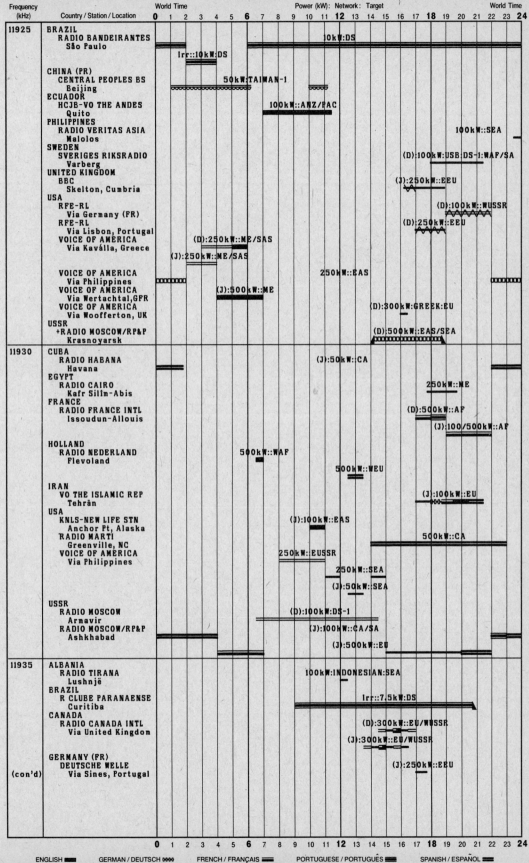

ENGLISH ■■■ GERMAN / DEUTSCH ◊◊◊◊ FRENCH / FRANÇAIS ═══ PORTUGUESE / PORTUGUÊS ▬▬▬ SPANISH / ESPAÑOL ▬▬▬
ARABIC /ﻉﺏ ▬ RUSSIAN / РУССКИИ ▬ CHINESE / 中文 ◊◊◊◊ JAPANESE / 日本語 ■■■ MULTILINGUAL ▭▭▭ OTHER ▬▬
SUMMER ONLY (J) WINTER ONLY (D) JAMMING ∧∧ or / or \ EARLIEST HEARD ◢ LATEST HEARD ◣ + TENTATIVE

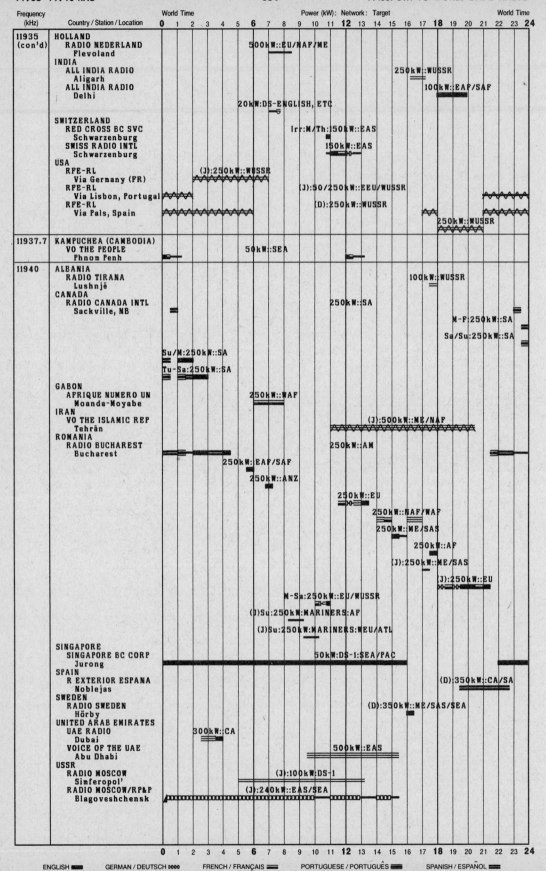

Frequency (kHz)	Country / Station / Location		World Time — Power (kW): Network: Target
11935 (con'd)	HOLLAND		
	RADIO NEDERLAND, Flevoland		500kW::EU/NAF/ME
	INDIA		
	ALL INDIA RADIO, Aligarh		250kW::WUSSR
	ALL INDIA RADIO, Delhi		100kW::EAF/SAF
			20kW:DS-ENGLISH, ETC
	SWITZERLAND		
	RED CROSS BC SVC, Schwarzenburg		Irr:M/Th:150kW::EAS
	SWISS RADIO INTL, Schwarzenburg		150kW::EAS
	USA		
	RFE-RL, Via Germany (FR)		(J):250kW::WUSSR
	RFE-RL, Via Lisbon, Portugal		(J):50/250kW::EEU/WUSSR
	RFE-RL, Via Pals, Spain		(D):250kW::WUSSR / 250kW::WUSSR
11937.7	KAMPUCHEA (CAMBODIA)		
	VO THE PEOPLE, Phnom Penh		50kW::SEA
11940	ALBANIA		
	RADIO TIRANA, Lushnjë		100kW::WUSSR
	CANADA		
	RADIO CANADA INTL, Sackville, NB		250kW::SA
			M-F:250kW::SA
			Sa/Su:250kW::SA
			Su/M:250kW::SA
			Tu-Sa:250kW::SA
	GABON		
	AFRIQUE NUMERO UN, Moanda-Moyabe		250kW::WAF
	IRAN		
	VO THE ISLAMIC REP, Tehrän		(J):500kW::ME/NAF
	ROMANIA		
	RADIO BUCHAREST, Bucharest		250kW::AM
			250kW:EAF/SAF
			250kW::ANZ
			250kW::EU
			250kW::NAF/WAF
			250kW::ME/SAS
			250kW::AF
			(J):250kW::ME/SAS
			(J):250kW::EU
			M-Sa:250kW::EU/WUSSR
			(J)Su:250kW::MARINERS:AF
			(J)Su:250kW::MARINERS:WEU/ATL
	SINGAPORE		
	SINGAPORE BC CORP, Jurong		50kW:DS-1:SEA/PAC
	SPAIN		
	R EXTERIOR ESPANA, Noblejas		(D):350kW::CA/SA
	SWEDEN		
	RADIO SWEDEN, Hörby		(D):350kW::ME/SAS/SEA
	UNITED ARAB EMIRATES		
	UAE RADIO, Dubai		300kW::CA
	VOICE OF THE UAE, Abu Dhabi		500kW::EAS
	USSR		
	RADIO MOSCOW, Simferopol'		(J):100kW:DS-1
	RADIO MOSCOW/RP&P, Blagoveshchensk		(J):240kW::EAS/SEA

World Time scale: 0 1 2 3 4 5 6 7 8 9 10 11 12 13 14 15 16 17 18 19 20 21 22 23 24

ENGLISH ▰▰ GERMAN / DEUTSCH ◊◊◊◊ FRENCH / FRANÇAIS ═══ PORTUGUESE / PORTUGUÊS ▰▰▰ SPANISH / ESPAÑOL ═══

ARABIC / عربي ═══ RUSSIAN / РУССКИЙ ═══ CHINESE / 中文 ◊◊◊◊ JAPANESE / 日本語 ▰▰▰ MULTILINGUAL ◊◊◊◊ OTHER ───

SUMMER ONLY (J) WINTER ONLY (D) JAMMING ∧∧ or / or \ EARLIEST HEARD ◢ LATEST HEARD ◣ + TENTATIVE

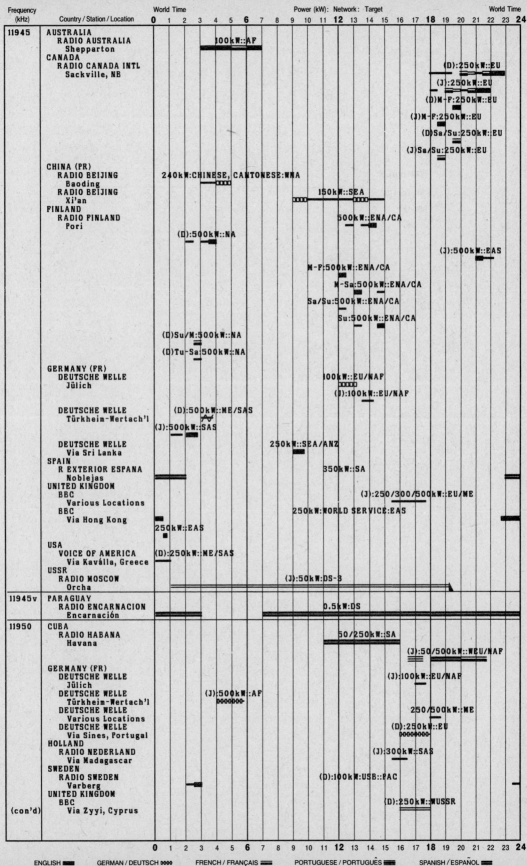

Frequency (kHz)	Country / Station / Location	Power (kW) : Network : Target
11945	AUSTRALIA	
	RADIO AUSTRALIA Shepparton	100kW::AF
	CANADA	
	RADIO CANADA INTL Sackville, NB	(D):250kW::EU / (J):250kW::EU / (D)M-F:250kW::EU / (J)M-F:250kW::EU / (D)Sa/Su:250kW::EU / (J)Sa/Su:250kW::EU
	CHINA (PR)	
	RADIO BEIJING Baoding	240kW:CHINESE, CANTONESE:WNA
	RADIO BEIJING Xi'an	150kW::SEA
	FINLAND	
	RADIO FINLAND Pori	500kW::ENA/CA / (D):500kW::NA / (J):500kW::EAS / M-F:500kW::ENA/CA / M-Sa:500kW::ENA/CA / Sa/Su:500kW::ENA/CA / Su:500kW::ENA/CA / (D)Su/M:500kW::NA / (D)Tu-Sa:500kW::NA
	GERMANY (FR)	
	DEUTSCHE WELLE Jülich	100kW::EU/NAF / (J):100kW::EU/NAF
	DEUTSCHE WELLE Türkheim-Wertach'l	(D):500kW::ME/SAS / (J):500kW::SAS
	DEUTSCHE WELLE Via Sri Lanka	250kW::SEA/ANZ
	SPAIN	
	R EXTERIOR ESPANA Noblejas	350kW::SA
	UNITED KINGDOM	
	BBC Various Locations	(J):250/300/500kW::EU/ME
	BBC Via Hong Kong	250kW:WORLD SERVICE:EAS / 250kW::EAS
	USA	
	VOICE OF AMERICA Via Kaválla, Greece	(D):250kW::ME/SAS
	USSR	
	RADIO MOSCOW Orcha	(J):50kW:DS-3
11945v	PARAGUAY	
	RADIO ENCARNACION Encarnación	0.5kW:DS
11950	CUBA	
	RADIO HABANA Havana	50/250kW::SA / (J):50/500kW::WEU/NAF
	GERMANY (FR)	
	DEUTSCHE WELLE Jülich	(J):100kW::EU/NAF
	DEUTSCHE WELLE Türkheim-Wertach'l	(J):500kW::AF
	DEUTSCHE WELLE Various Locations	250/500kW::ME
	DEUTSCHE WELLE Via Sines, Portugal	(D):250kW::EU
	HOLLAND	
	RADIO NEDERLAND Via Madagascar	(J):300kW::SAS
	SWEDEN	
	RADIO SWEDEN Varberg	(D):100kW:USB::PAC
	UNITED KINGDOM	
	BBC	(D):250kW::WUSSR
(con'd)	Via Zyyi, Cyprus	

ENGLISH ▬▬ GERMAN / DEUTSCH ▭▭▭▭ FRENCH / FRANÇAIS ▬▬ PORTUGUESE / PORTUGUÊS ▬▬ SPANISH / ESPAÑOL ▬▬

ARABIC / عربى ▬▬ RUSSIAN / РУССКИИ ▬▬ CHINESE / 中文 ▭▭▭▭ JAPANESE / 日本語 ▬▬ MULTILINGUAL ▭▭▭▭ OTHER ▬▬

SUMMER ONLY (J)   WINTER ONLY (D)   JAMMING ∧∧ or / or \   EARLIEST HEARD ◢   LATEST HEARD ◣   * TENTATIVE

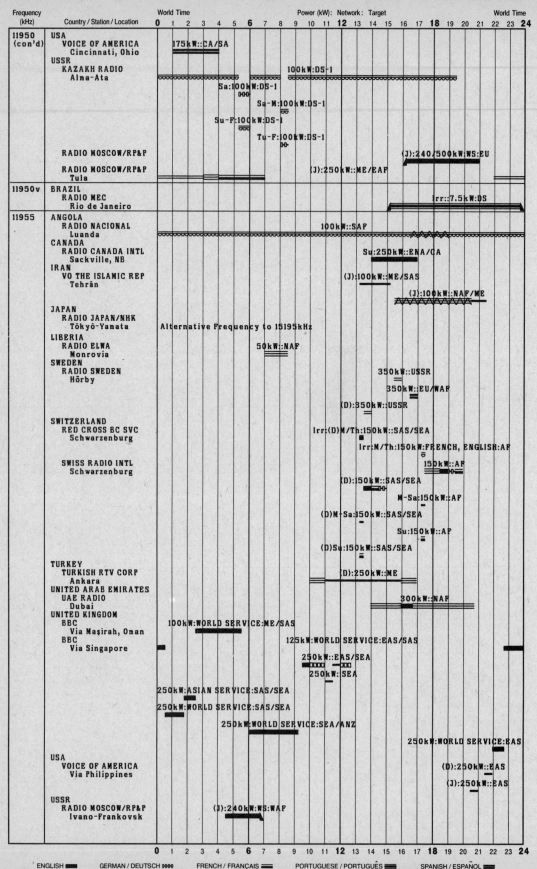

Frequency (kHz)	Country / Station / Location		World Time / Power (kW): Network: Target
11950 (con'd)	USA	VOICE OF AMERICA Cincinnati, Ohio	175kW::CA/SA
	USSR	KAZAKH RADIO Alma-Ata	100kW:DS-1
			Sa:100kW:DS-1
			Sa-M:100kW:DS-1
			Su-F:100kW:DS-1
			Tu-F:100kW:DS-1
		RADIO MOSCOW/RP&P	(J):240/500kW:WS:EU
		RADIO MOSCOW/RP&P Tula	(J):250kW::ME/EAF
11950v	BRAZIL	RADIO MEC Rio de Janeiro	Irr::7.5kW:DS
11955	ANGOLA	RADIO NACIONAL Luanda	100kW::SAF
	CANADA	RADIO CANADA INTL Sackville, NB	Su:250kW::ENA/CA
	IRAN	VO THE ISLAMIC REP Tehrān	(J):100kW::ME/SAS
			(J):100kW::NAF/ME
	JAPAN	RADIO JAPAN/NHK Tōkyō-Yamata	Alternative Frequency to 15195kHz
	LIBERIA	RADIO ELWA Monrovia	50kW::NAF
	SWEDEN	RADIO SWEDEN Hörby	350kW::USSR
			350kW::EU/WAF
			(D):350kW::USSR
	SWITZERLAND	RED CROSS BC SVC Schwarzenburg	Irr:(D)M/Th:150kW::SAS/SEA
			Irr:M/Th:150kW:FRENCH, ENGLISH:AF
		SWISS RADIO INTL Schwarzenburg	150kW::AF
			(D):150kW::SAS/SEA
			M-Sa:150kW::AF
			(D)M-Sa:150kW::SAS/SEA
			Su:150kW::AF
			(D)Su:150kW::SAS/SEA
	TURKEY	TURKISH RTV CORP Ankara	(D):250kW::ME
	UNITED ARAB EMIRATES	UAE RADIO Dubai	300kW::NAF
	UNITED KINGDOM	BBC Via Maşirah, Oman	100kW:WORLD SERVICE:ME/SAS
		BBC Via Singapore	125kW:WORLD SERVICE:EAS/SAS
			250kW::EAS/SEA
			250kW::SEA
			250kW:ASIAN SERVICE:SAS/SEA
			250kW:WORLD SERVICE:SAS/SEA
			250kW:WORLD SERVICE:SEA/ANZ
			250kW:WORLD SERVICE:EAS
	USA	VOICE OF AMERICA Via Philippines	(D):250kW::EAS
			(J):250kW::EAS
	USSR	RADIO MOSCOW/RP&P Ivano-Frankovsk	(J):240kW:WS:WAF

World Time 0 1 2 3 4 5 6 7 8 9 10 11 12 13 14 15 16 17 18 19 20 21 22 23 24

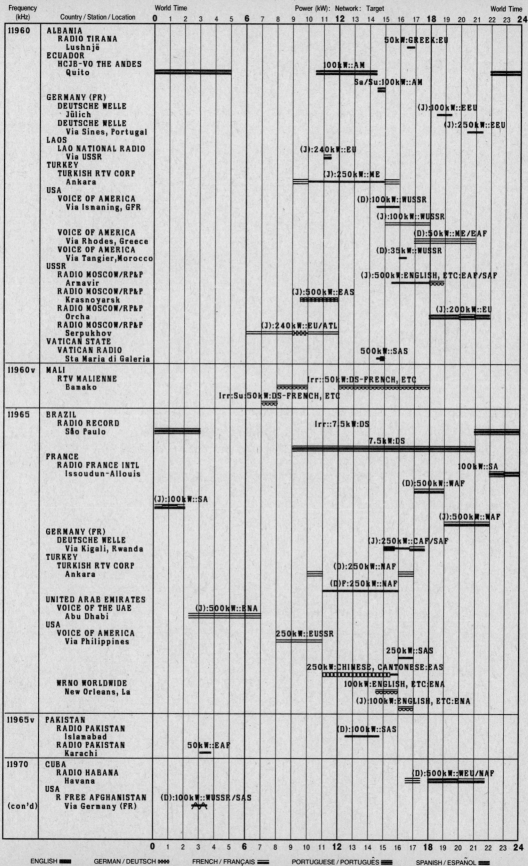

Frequency (kHz) | Country / Station / Location

World Time   Power (kW): Network: Target   **World Time**
0 1 2 3 4 5 6 7 8 9 10 11 12 13 14 15 16 17 18 19 20 21 22 23 24

11960

ALBANIA
RADIO TIRANA
Lushnjë — 50kW:GREEK:EU

ECUADOR
HCJB–VO THE ANDES
Quito — 100kW::AM
Sa/Su:100kW::AM

GERMANY (FR)
DEUTSCHE WELLE
Jülich — (J):100kW::EEU
DEUTSCHE WELLE
Via Sines, Portugal — (J):250kW::EEU

LAOS
LAO NATIONAL RADIO
Via USSR — (J):240kW::EU

TURKEY
TURKISH RTV CORP
Ankara — (J):250kW::ME

USA
VOICE OF AMERICA
Via Ismaning, GFR — (D):100kW:WUSSR
(J):100kW:WUSSR

VOICE OF AMERICA
Via Rhodes, Greece — (D):50kW::ME/EAF

VOICE OF AMERICA
Via Tangier,Morocco — (D):35kW::WUSSR

USSR
RADIO MOSCOW/RP&P
Armavir — (J):500kW:ENGLISH, ETC:EAF/SAF
RADIO MOSCOW/RP&P
Krasnoyarsk — (J):500kW::EAS
RADIO MOSCOW/RP&P
Orcha — (J):200kW::EU
RADIO MOSCOW/RP&P
Serpukhov — (J):240kW::EU/ATL

VATICAN STATE
VATICAN RADIO
Sta Maria di Galeria — 500kW::SAS

11960v

MALI
RTV MALIENNE
Bamako — Irr::50kW:DS-FRENCH, ETC
Irr:Su:50kW:DS-FRENCH, ETC

11965

BRAZIL
RADIO RECORD
São Paulo — Irr::7.5kW:DS
7.5kW:DS

FRANCE
RADIO FRANCE INTL
Issoudun-Allouis — 100kW::SA
(D):500kW::WAF
(J):500kW::WAF
(J):100kW::SA

GERMANY (FR)
DEUTSCHE WELLE
Via Kigali, Rwanda — (J):250kW::CAF/SAF

TURKEY
TURKISH RTV CORP
Ankara — (D):250kW::NAF
(D)F:250kW::NAF

UNITED ARAB EMIRATES
VOICE OF THE UAE
Abu Dhabi — (J):500kW::ENA

USA
VOICE OF AMERICA
Via Philippines — 250kW:EUSSR
250kW::SAS
250kW:CHINESE, CANTONESE:EAS

WRNO WORLDWIDE
New Orleans, La — 100kW:ENGLISH, ETC:ENA
(J):100kW:ENGLISH, ETC:ENA

11965v

PAKISTAN
RADIO PAKISTAN
Islamabad — (D):100kW::SAS
RADIO PAKISTAN
Karachi — 50kW::EAF

11970

CUBA
RADIO HABANA
Havana — (D):500kW::WEU/NAF

USA
R FREE AFGHANISTAN
Via Germany (FR) — (D):100kW::WUSSR/SAS

(con'd)

0 1 2 3 4 5 6 7 8 9 10 11 12 13 14 15 16 17 18 19 20 21 22 23 24

ENGLISH ▰▰▰   GERMAN / DEUTSCH ০০০০   FRENCH / FRANÇAIS ═══   PORTUGUESE / PORTUGUÊS ▰▰▰   SPANISH / ESPAÑOL ▰▰▰

ARABIC / عربى ═══   RUSSIAN / РУССКИИ ═══   CHINESE / ☀☀ ০০০০   JAPANESE / 日本語 ▰▰▰   MULTILINGUAL ০০০   OTHER ━━

SUMMER ONLY (J)   WINTER ONLY (D)   JAMMING ∧∧ or / or \   EARLIEST HEARD ◢   LATEST HEARD ◣   + TENTATIVE

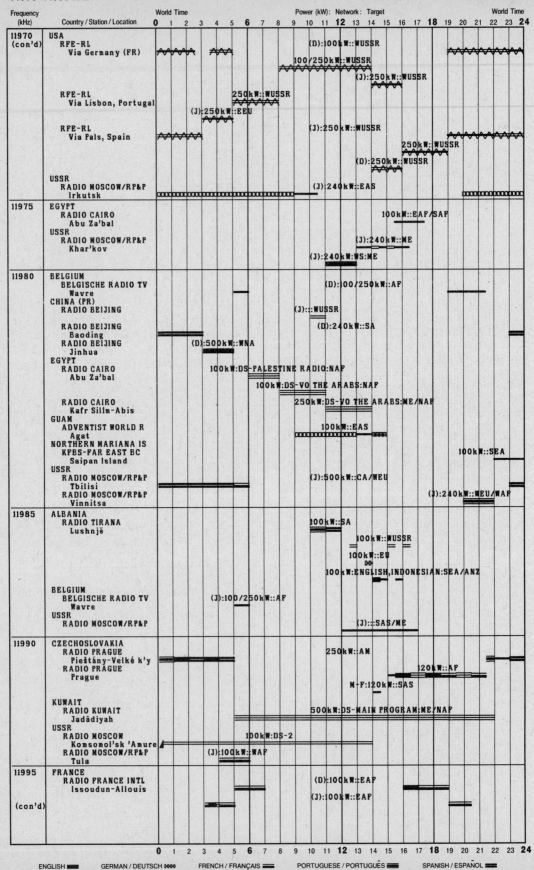

Frequency (kHz)	Country / Station / Location		Power (kW): Network: Target	World Time

11970 (con'd) USA
RFE-RL Via Germany (FR) — (D):100kW::WUSSR / 100/250kW::WUSSR / (J):250kW::WUSSR
RFE-RL Via Lisbon, Portugal — 250kW::WUSSR / (J):250kW::EEU
RFE-RL Via Pals, Spain — 250kW::WUSSR / (D):250kW::WUSSR / (J):250kW::WUSSR
USSR RADIO MOSCOW/RP&P Irkutsk — (J):240kW::EAS

11975 EGYPT
RADIO CAIRO Abu Za'bal — 100kW::EAF/SAF
USSR RADIO MOSCOW/RP&P Khar'kov — (J):240kW::ME
(J):240kW:WS:ME

11980 BELGIUM
BELGISCHE RADIO TV Wavre — (D):100/250kW::AF
CHINA (PR) RADIO BEIJING — (J):::WUSSR
RADIO BEIJING Baoding — (D):240kW::SA
RADIO BEIJING Jinhua — (D):500kW::WNA
EGYPT RADIO CAIRO Abu Za'bal — 100kW:DS-PALESTINE RADIO:NAF / 100kW:DS-VO THE ARABS:NAF
RADIO CAIRO Kafr Sillm-Abis — 250kW:DS-VO THE ARABS:ME/NAF
GUAM ADVENTIST WORLD R Agat — 100kW::EAS
NORTHERN MARIANA IS KFBS-FAR EAST BC Saipan Island — 100kW::SEA
USSR RADIO MOSCOW/RP&P Tbilisi — (J):500kW::CA/WEU
RADIO MOSCOW/RP&P Vinnitsa — (J):240kW::WEU/WAF

11985 ALBANIA
RADIO TIRANA Lushnjë — 100kW::SA / 100kW::WUSSR / 100kW::EU / 100kW:ENGLISH,INDONESIAN:SEA/ANZ
BELGIUM BELGISCHE RADIO TV Wavre — (J):100/250kW::AF
USSR RADIO MOSCOW/RP&P — (J):::SAS/ME

11990 CZECHOSLOVAKIA
RADIO PRAGUE Piešťany-Velké k'y — 250kW::AM
RADIO PRAGUE Prague — 120kW::AF / M-F:120kW::SAS
KUWAIT RADIO KUWAIT Jadādiyah — 500kW:DS-MAIN PROGRAM:ME/NAF
USSR RADIO MOSCOW Komsomol'sk 'Amure — 100kW:DS-2
RADIO MOSCOW/RP&P Tula — (J):100kW::WAF

11995 FRANCE
RADIO FRANCE INTL Issoudun-Allouis — (D):100kW::EAF / (J):100kW::EAF

(con'd)

Legend: 0 1 2 3 4 5 6 7 8 9 10 11 12 13 14 15 16 17 18 19 20 21 22 23 24

ENGLISH ▬▬   GERMAN / DEUTSCH ◊◊◊◊   FRENCH / FRANÇAIS ▭▭   PORTUGUESE / PORTUGUÊS ▬▬   SPANISH / ESPAÑOL ▬▬
ARABIC / العربية ▬▬   RUSSIAN / РУССКИИ ▬▬   CHINESE / 中文 ▭▭▭   JAPANESE / 日本語 ▬▬   MULTILINGUAL ▭▭▭▭   OTHER ▬
SUMMER ONLY (J)   WINTER ONLY (D)   JAMMING /\/\ or / or \   EARLIEST HEARD ◢   LATEST HEARD ◣   ✦ TENTATIVE

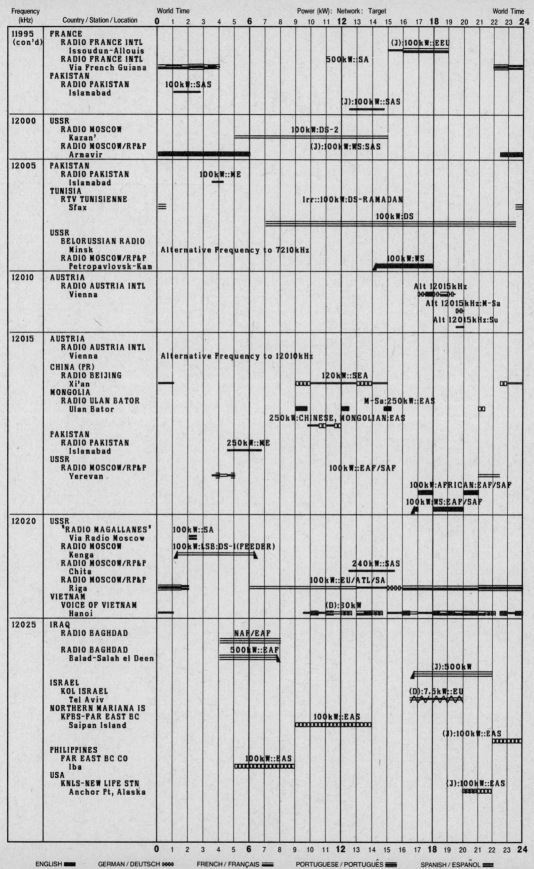

Frequency (kHz)	Country / Station / Location	Schedule (World Time / Power (kW): Network: Target)
11995 (con'd)	FRANCE	
	RADIO FRANCE INTL Issoudun-Allouis	(J):100kW::EEU
	RADIO FRANCE INTL Via French Guiana	500kW::SA
	PAKISTAN	
	RADIO PAKISTAN Islamabad	100kW::SAS / (J):100kW::SAS
12000	USSR	
	RADIO MOSCOW Kazan'	100kW:DS-2
	RADIO MOSCOW/RP&P Armavir	(J):100kW:WS:SAS
12005	PAKISTAN	
	RADIO PAKISTAN Islamabad	100kW::ME
	TUNISIA	
	RTV TUNISIENNE Sfax	Irr::100kW:DS-RAMADAN / 100kW:DS
	USSR	
	BELORUSSIAN RADIO Minsk	Alternative Frequency to 7210kHz
	RADIO MOSCOW/RP&P Petropavlovsk-Kam	100kW:WS
12010	AUSTRIA	
	RADIO AUSTRIA INTL Vienna	Alt 12015kHz / Alt 12015kHz:M-Sa / Alt 12015kHz:Su
12015	AUSTRIA	
	RADIO AUSTRIA INTL Vienna	Alternative Frequency to 12010kHz
	CHINA (PR)	
	RADIO BEIJING Xi'an	120kW::SEA
	MONGOLIA	
	RADIO ULAN BATOR Ulan Bator	M-Sa:250kW::EAS / 250kW:CHINESE, MONGOLIAN:EAS
	PAKISTAN	
	RADIO PAKISTAN Islamabad	250kW::ME
	USSR	
	RADIO MOSCOW/RP&P Yerevan	100kW::EAF/SAF / 100kW:AFRICAN:EAF/SAF / 100kW:WS:EAF/SAF
12020	USSR	
	'RADIO MAGALLANES' Via Radio Moscow	100kW::SA
	RADIO MOSCOW Kenga	100kW:LSB:DS-I(FEEDER)
	RADIO MOSCOW/RP&P Chita	240kW::SAS
	RADIO MOSCOW/RP&P Riga	100kW::EU/ATL/SA
	VIETNAM	
	VOICE OF VIETNAM Hanoi	(D):30kW
12025	IRAQ	
	RADIO BAGHDAD	NAF/EAF
	RADIO BAGHDAD Balad-Salah el Deen	500kW::EAF / (J):500kW
	ISRAEL	
	KOL ISRAEL Tel Aviv	(D):7.5kW::EU
	NORTHERN MARIANA IS	
	KFBS-FAR EAST BC Saipan Island	100kW::EAS / (J):100kW::EAS
	PHILIPPINES	
	FAR EAST BC CO Iba	100kW::EAS
	USA	
	KNLS-NEW LIFE STN Anchor Pt, Alaska	(J):100kW::EAS

ENGLISH ▄▄▄   GERMAN / DEUTSCH ०००○   FRENCH / FRANÇAIS ▬▬▬   PORTUGUESE / PORTUGUÊS ▬▬▬   SPANISH / ESPAÑOL ▬▬▬

ARABIC / ﻉﺭﺑﻲ ▬▬▬   RUSSIAN / РУССКИИ ▬▬▬   CHINESE / ✦☆ ▭▭▭   JAPANESE / 日本語 ▬▬▬   MULTILINGUAL ▭▭▭   OTHER ▬▬▬

SUMMER ONLY (J)   WINTER ONLY (D)   JAMMING ∧∧ or / or \   EARLIEST HEARD ◢   LATEST HEARD ◣   ◦ TENTATIVE

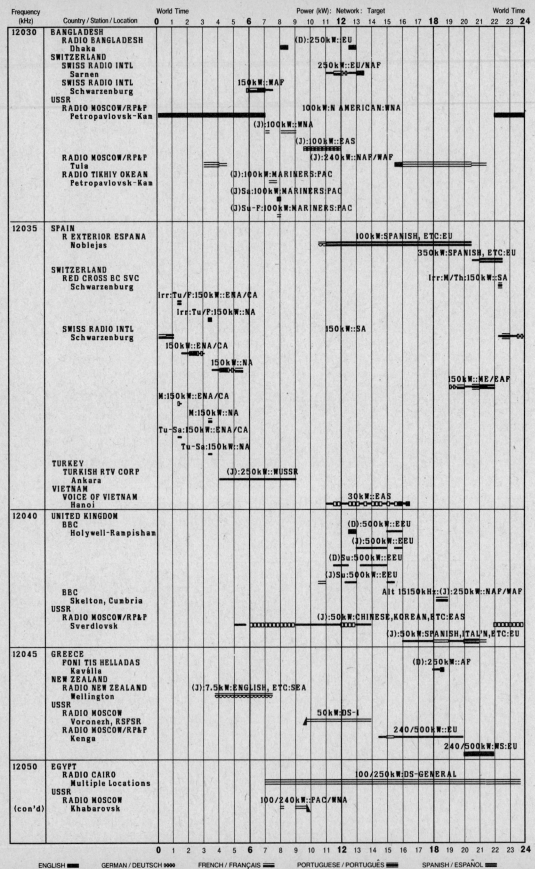

Frequency
(kHz) Country / Station / Location
World Time
0 1 2 3 4 5 6 7 8 9 10 11 12 13 14 15 16 17 18 19 20 21 22 23 24
Power (kW): Network: Target
World Time

12030
BANGLADESH
  RADIO BANGLADESH
    Dhaka — (D):250kW::EU
SWITZERLAND
  SWISS RADIO INTL
    Sarnen — 250kW::EU/NAF
  SWISS RADIO INTL
    Schwarzenburg — 150kW::WAF
USSR
  RADIO MOSCOW/RP&P
    Petropavlovsk-Kam — 100kW:N AMERICAN:WNA
    (J):100kW::WNA
    (J):100kW::EAS
  RADIO MOSCOW/RP&P
    Tula — (J):240kW::NAF/WAF
  RADIO TIKHIY OKEAN
    Petropavlovsk-Kam — (J):100kW:MARINERS:PAC
    (J)Sa:100kW:MARINERS:PAC
    (J)Su-F:100kW:MARINERS:PAC

12035
SPAIN
  R EXTERIOR ESPANA
    Noblejas — 100kW:SPANISH, ETC:EU
    350kW:SPANISH, ETC:EU
SWITZERLAND
  RED CROSS BC SVC
    Schwarzenburg — Irr:M/Th:150kW::SA
    Irr:Tu/F:150kW::ENA/CA
    Irr:Tu/F:150kW::NA
  SWISS RADIO INTL
    Schwarzenburg — 150kW::SA
    150kW::ENA/CA
    150kW::NA
    150kW::ME/EAF
    M:150kW::ENA/CA
    M:150kW::NA
    Tu-Sa:150kW::ENA/CA
    Tu-Sa:150kW::NA
TURKEY
  TURKISH RTV CORP
    Ankara — (J):250kW::WUSSR
VIETNAM
  VOICE OF VIETNAM
    Hanoi — 30kW::EAS

12040
UNITED KINGDOM
  BBC
    Holywell-Rampisham — (D):500kW::EEU
    (J):500kW::EEU
    (D)Su:500kW::EEU
    (J)Su:500kW::EEU
  BBC
    Skelton, Cumbria — Alt 15150kHz:(J):250kW::NAF/WAF
USSR
  RADIO MOSCOW/RP&P
    Sverdlovsk — (J):50kW:CHINESE,KOREAN,ETC:EAS
    (J):50kW:SPANISH,ITAL'N,ETC:EU

12045
GREECE
  FONI TIS HELLADAS
    Kaválla — (D):250kW::AF
NEW ZEALAND
  RADIO NEW ZEALAND
    Wellington — (J):7.5kW:ENGLISH, ETC:SEA
USSR
  RADIO MOSCOW
    Voronezh, RSFSR — 50kW:DS-1
  RADIO MOSCOW/RP&P
    Kenga — 240/500kW::EU
    240/500kW:WS:EU

12050
EGYPT
  RADIO CAIRO
    Multiple Locations — 100/250kW:DS-GENERAL
USSR
  RADIO MOSCOW
(con'd)   Khabarovsk — 100/240kW::PAC/WNA

ENGLISH ▬▬   GERMAN / DEUTSCH ∞∞∞   FRENCH / FRANÇAIS ═══   PORTUGUESE / PORTUGUÊS ▬▬   SPANISH / ESPAÑOL ▬▬

ARABIC / عربي ═══   RUSSIAN / РУССКИЙ ═══   CHINESE / 中文 ▭▭▭▭   JAPANESE / 日本語 ▬▬   MULTILINGUAL ∞∞∞   OTHER ▬▬

SUMMER ONLY (J)   WINTER ONLY (D)   JAMMING /\/\ or / or \   EARLIEST HEARD ◢   LATEST HEARD ◣   + TENTATIVE

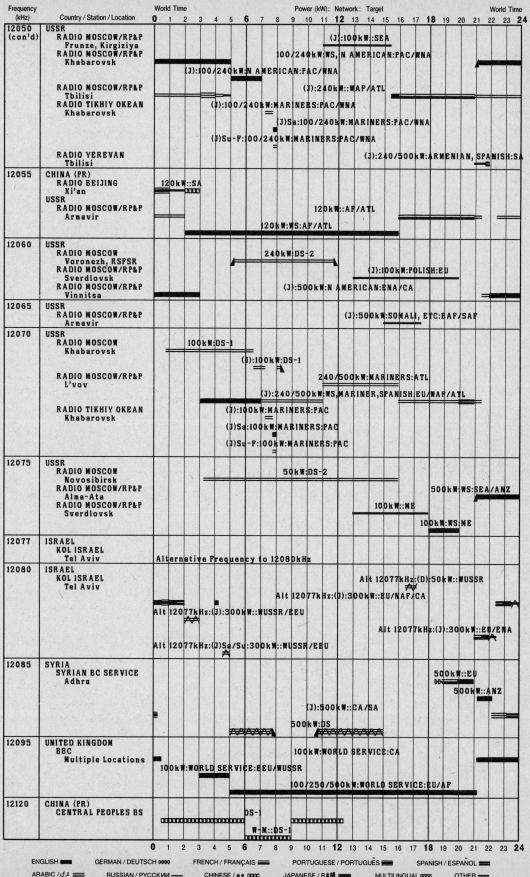

Frequency (kHz)	Country / Station / Location	Details
12050 (con'd)	USSR	
	RADIO MOSCOW/RP&P Frunze, Kirgiziya	(J):100kW::SEA
	RADIO MOSCOW/RP&P Khabarovsk	100/240kW:WS, N AMERICAN:PAC/WNA / (J):100/240kW:N AMERICAN:PAC/WNA
	RADIO MOSCOW/RP&P Tbilisi	(J):240kW::WAF/ATL
	RADIO TIKHIY OKEAN Khabarovsk	(J):100/240kW:MARINERS:PAC/WNA / (J)Sa:100/240kW:MARINERS:PAC/WNA / (J)Su-F:100/240kW:MARINERS:PAC/WNA
	RADIO YEREVAN Tbilisi	(J):240/500kW:ARMENIAN, SPANISH:SA
12055	CHINA (PR)	
	RADIO BEIJING Xi'an	120kW::SA
	USSR	
	RADIO MOSCOW/RP&P Armavir	120kW::AF/ATL / 120kW:WS:AF/ATL
12060	USSR	
	RADIO MOSCOW Voronezh, RSFSR	240kW:DS-2
	RADIO MOSCOW/RP&P Sverdlovsk	(J):100kW:POLISH:EU
	RADIO MOSCOW/RP&P Vinnitsa	(J):500kW:N AMERICAN:ENA/CA
12065	USSR	
	RADIO MOSCOW/RP&P Armavir	(J):500kW:SOMALI, ETC:EAF/SAF
12070	USSR	
	RADIO MOSCOW Khabarovsk	100kW:DS-1 / (J):100kW:DS-1
	RADIO MOSCOW/RP&P L'vov	240/500kW:MARINERS:ATL / (J):240/500kW:WS,MARINER,SPANISH:EU/WAF/ATL
	RADIO TIKHIY OKEAN Khabarovsk	(J):100kW:MARINERS:PAC / (J)Sa:100kW:MARINERS:PAC / (J)Su-F:100kW:MARINERS:PAC
12075	USSR	
	RADIO MOSCOW Novosibirsk	50kW:DS-2
	RADIO MOSCOW/RP&P Alma-Ata	500kW:WS:SEA/ANZ
	RADIO MOSCOW/RP&P Sverdlovsk	100kW::ME / 100kW:WS:ME
12077	ISRAEL	
	KOL ISRAEL Tel Aviv	Alternative Frequency to 12080kHz
12080	ISRAEL	
	KOL ISRAEL Tel Aviv	Alt 12077kHz:(D):50kW::WUSSR / Alt 12077kHz:(J):300kW::EU/NAF/CA / Alt 12077kHz:(J):300kW::WUSSR/EEU / Alt 12077kHz:(J):300kW::EU/ENA / Alt 12077kHz:(J)Sa/Su:300kW::WUSSR/EEU
12085	SYRIA	
	SYRIAN BC SERVICE Adhra	500kW::EU / 500kW::ANZ / (J):500kW::CA/SA / 500kW:DS
12095	UNITED KINGDOM	
	BBC Multiple Locations	100kW:WORLD SERVICE:CA / 100kW:WORLD SERVICE:EEU/WUSSR / 100/250/500kW:WORLD SERVICE:EU/AF
12120	CHINA (PR)	
	CENTRAL PEOPLES BS	DS-1 / W-M::DS-1

ENGLISH ▬ GERMAN / DEUTSCH ◊◊◊◊ FRENCH / FRANÇAIS ▬ PORTUGUESE / PORTUGUÊS ▬ SPANISH / ESPAÑOL ▬

ARABIC /ﻋﺮﺑﻲ ▬ RUSSIAN / РУССКИЙ ▬ CHINESE /◆✦ ▭▭▭▭ JAPANESE / 日本語 ▬▬ MULTILINGUAL ▭▭▭▭ OTHER ▬

SUMMER ONLY (J) WINTER ONLY (D) JAMMING /\/\ or / or \ EARLIEST HEARD ◢ LATEST HEARD ◣ + TENTATIVE

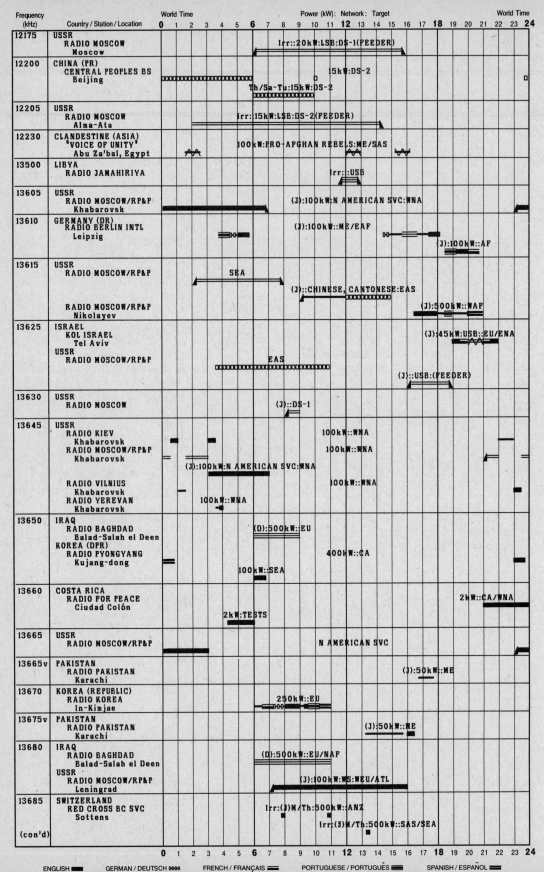

Frequency (kHz)	Country / Station / Location	Description
12175	USSR RADIO MOSCOW Moscow	Irr::20kW:LSB:DS-1(FEEDER)
12200	CHINA (PR) CENTRAL PEOPLES BS Beijing	15kW:DS-2 / Th/Sa-Tu:15kW:DS-2
12205	USSR RADIO MOSCOW Alma-Ata	Irr:15kW:LSB:DS-2(FEEDER)
12230	CLANDESTINE (ASIA) 'VOICE OF UNITY' Abu Za'bal, Egypt	100kW:PRO-AFGHAN REBELS:ME/SAS
13500	LIBYA RADIO JAMAHIRIYA	Irr::USB
13605	USSR RADIO MOSCOW/RP&P Khabarovsk	(J):100kW:N AMERICAN SVC:WNA
13610	GERMANY (DR) RADIO BERLIN INTL Leipzig	(J):100kW::ME/EAF / (J):100kW::AF
13615	USSR RADIO MOSCOW/RP&P	SEA / (J)::CHINESE, CANTONESE:EAS
	RADIO MOSCOW/RP&P Nikolayev	(J):500kW::WAF
13625	ISRAEL KOL ISRAEL Tel Aviv	(J):45kW:USB::EU/ENA
	USSR RADIO MOSCOW/RP&P	EAS / (J)::USB:(FEEDER)
13630	USSR RADIO MOSCOW	(J)::DS-1
13645	USSR RADIO KIEV Khabarovsk	100kW::WNA
	RADIO MOSCOW/RP&P Khabarovsk	100kW::WNA / (J):100kW:N AMERICAN SVC:WNA
	RADIO VILNIUS Khabarovsk	100kW::WNA
	RADIO YEREVAN Khabarovsk	100kW::WNA
13650	IRAQ RADIO BAGHDAD Balad-Salah el Deen	(D):500kW::EU
	KOREA (DPR) RADIO PYONGYANG Kujang-dong	400kW::CA / 100kW::SEA
13660	COSTA RICA RADIO FOR PEACE Ciudad Colón	2kW::CA/WNA / 2kW:TESTS
13665	USSR RADIO MOSCOW/RP&P	N AMERICAN SVC
13665v	PAKISTAN RADIO PAKISTAN Karachi	(J):50kW::ME
13670	KOREA (REPUBLIC) RADIO KOREA In-Kimjae	250kW::EU
13675v	PAKISTAN RADIO PAKISTAN Karachi	(J):50kW::ME
13680	IRAQ RADIO BAGHDAD Balad-Salah el Deen	(D):500kW::EU/NAF
	USSR RADIO MOSCOW/RP&P Leningrad	(J):100kW:WS:WEU/ATL
13685 (con'd)	SWITZERLAND RED CROSS BC SVC Sottens	Irr:(J)M/Th:500kW::ANZ / Irr:(J)M/Th:500kW::SAS/SEA

ENGLISH ▬▬   GERMAN / DEUTSCH ◊◊◊◊   FRENCH / FRANÇAIS ▬▬   PORTUGUESE / PORTUGUÊS ▬▬   SPANISH / ESPAÑOL ▬▬

ARABIC / العربية ▬▬   RUSSIAN / РУССКИИ ▬▬   CHINESE / 中文 ◊◊◊◊   JAPANESE / 日本語 ▬▬   MULTILINGUAL ▬▬   OTHER ▬▬

SUMMER ONLY (J)   WINTER ONLY (D)   JAMMING /\/\ or / or \   EARLIEST HEARD ◢   LATEST HEARD ◣   ♦ TENTATIVE

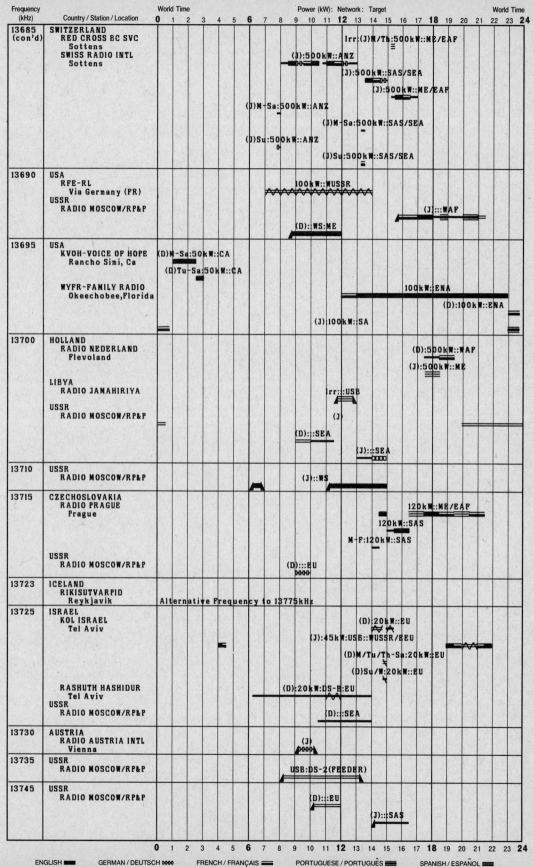

Frequency (kHz)	Country / Station / Location
13685 (con'd)	**SWITZERLAND** **RED CROSS BC SVC** Sottens — Irr:(J)M/Th:500kW::ME/EAF **SWISS RADIO INTL** Sottens — (J):500kW::ANZ; (J):500kW::SAS/SEA; (J):500kW::ME/EAF; (J)M-Sa:500kW::ANZ; (J)M-Sa:500kW::SAS/SEA; (J)Su:500kW::ANZ; (J)Su:500kW::SAS/SEA
13690	**USA** **RFE-RL** Via Germany (FR) — 100kW::WUSSR **USSR** **RADIO MOSCOW/RP&P** — (J):::WAF; (D)::WS:ME
13695	**USA** **KVOH-VOICE OF HOPE** Rancho Simi, Ca — (D)M-Sa:50kW::CA; (D)Tu-Sa:50kW::CA **WYFR-FAMILY RADIO** Okeechobee,Florida — 100kW::ENA; (D):100kW::ENA; (J):100kW::SA
13700	**HOLLAND** **RADIO NEDERLAND** Flevoland — (D):500kW::WAF; (J):500kW::ME **LIBYA** **RADIO JAMAHIRIYA** — Irr::USB **USSR** **RADIO MOSCOW/RP&P** — (J); (D):::SEA; (J):::SEA
13710	**USSR** **RADIO MOSCOW/RP&P** — (J)::WS
13715	**CZECHOSLOVAKIA** **RADIO PRAGUE** Prague — 120kW::ME/EAF; 120kW::SAS; M-F:120kW::SAS **USSR** **RADIO MOSCOW/RP&P** — (D):::EU
13723	**ICELAND** **RIKISUTVARPID** Reykjavik — Alternative Frequency to 13775kHz
13725	**ISRAEL** **KOL ISRAEL** Tel Aviv — (D):20kW::EU; (J):45kW:USB::WUSSR/EEU; (D)M/Tu/Th-Sa:20kW::EU; (D)Su/W:20kW::EU **RASHUTH HASHIDUR** Tel Aviv — (D):20kW:DS-B:EU **USSR** **RADIO MOSCOW/RP&P** — (D):::SEA
13730	**AUSTRIA** **RADIO AUSTRIA INTL** Vienna — (J)
13735	**USSR** **RADIO MOSCOW/RP&P** — USB:DS-2(FEEDER)
13745	**USSR** **RADIO MOSCOW/RP&P** — (D):::EU; (J):::SAS

World Time: 0 1 2 3 4 5 6 7 8 9 10 11 12 13 14 15 16 17 18 19 20 21 22 23 24

ENGLISH ▬▬   GERMAN / DEUTSCH ▭▭▭   FRENCH / FRANÇAIS ▬▬   PORTUGUESE / PORTUGUÊS ▬▬   SPANISH / ESPAÑOL ▬▬

ARABIC / ﻉﺮﺑ ▬▬   RUSSIAN / РУССКИЙ ▬▬   CHINESE / 中文 ▭▭▭   JAPANESE / 日本語 ▬▬   MULTILINGUAL ▭▭▭   OTHER ▬▬

SUMMER ONLY (J)   WINTER ONLY (D)   JAMMING /\/\ or / or \   EARLIEST HEARD ◢   LATEST HEARD ◣   + TENTATIVE

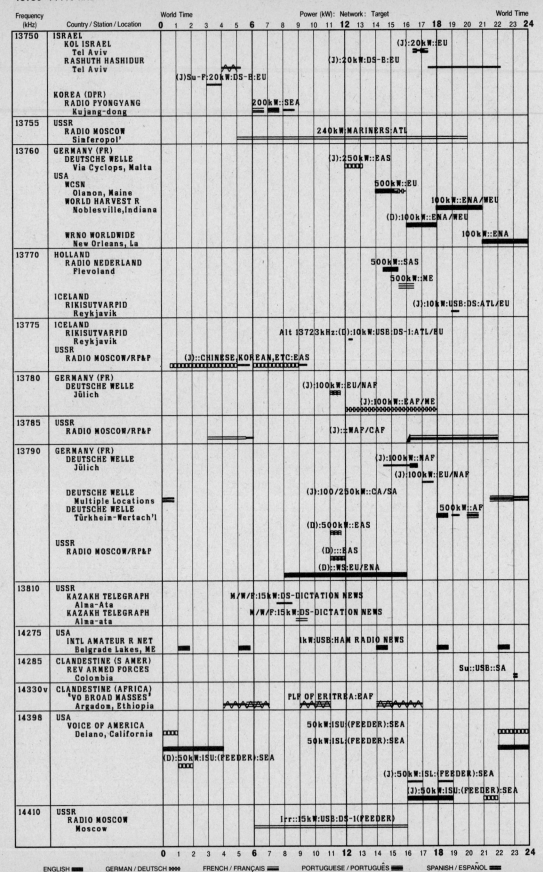

ENGLISH ▬▬ GERMAN / DEUTSCH ◊◊◊◊ FRENCH / FRANÇAIS ▭▭ PORTUGUESE / PORTUGUÊS ▤▤ SPANISH / ESPAÑOL ▬▬

ARABIC /ﻉﺏ ▬ RUSSIAN / РУССКИИ ▬ CHINESE / ◆◇ ▫▫▫ JAPANESE / 日本語 ▬ MULTILINGUAL ▨▨ OTHER ▬

SUMMER ONLY (J) WINTER ONLY (D) JAMMING ∧∧ or / or \ EARLIEST HEARD ◢ LATEST HEARD ◣ + TENTATIVE

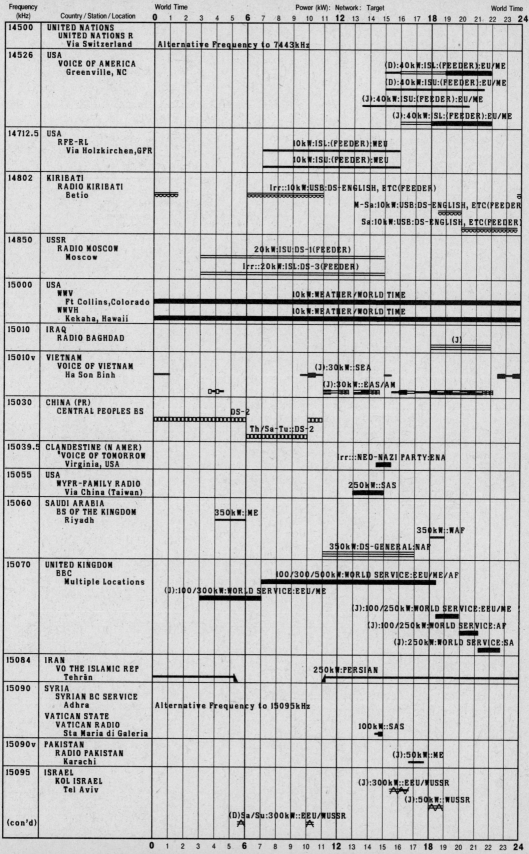

Frequency (kHz)	Country / Station / Location	Broadcast details
14500	UNITED NATIONS — UNITED NATIONS R — Via Switzerland	Alternative Frequency to 7443kHz
14526	USA — VOICE OF AMERICA — Greenville, NC	(D):40kW:ISL:(FEEDER):EU/ME; (D):40kW:ISU:(FEEDER):EU/ME; (J):40kW:ISU:(FEEDER):EU/ME; (J):40kW:ISL:(FEEDER):EU/ME
14712.5	USA — RFE-RL — Via Holzkirchen,GFR	10kW:ISL:(FEEDER):WEU; 10kW:ISU:(FEEDER):WEU
14802	KIRIBATI — RADIO KIRIBATI — Betio	Irr::10kW:USB:DS-ENGLISH, ETC(FEEDER); M-Sa:10kW:USB:DS-ENGLISH, ETC(FEEDER); Sa:10kW:USB:DS-ENGLISH, ETC(FEEDER)
14850	USSR — RADIO MOSCOW — Moscow	20kW:ISU:DS-1(FEEDER); Irr::20kW:ISL:DS-3(FEEDER)
15000	USA — WWV — Ft Collins,Colorado — WWVH — Kekaha, Hawaii	10kW:WEATHER/WORLD TIME; 10kW:WEATHER/WORLD TIME
15010	IRAQ — RADIO BAGHDAD	(J)
15010v	VIETNAM — VOICE OF VIETNAM — Ha Son Binh	(J):30kW::SEA; (J):30kW::EAS/AM
15030	CHINA (PR) — CENTRAL PEOPLES BS	DS-2; Th/Sa-Tu::DS-2
15039.5	CLANDESTINE (N AMER) — VOICE OF TOMORROW — Virginia, USA	Irr:::NEO-NAZI PARTY:ENA
15055	USA — WYFR-FAMILY RADIO — Via China (Taiwan)	250kW::SAS
15060	SAUDI ARABIA — BS OF THE KINGDOM — Riyadh	350kW:ME; 350kW::WAF; 350kW:DS-GENERAL:NAF
15070	UNITED KINGDOM — BBC — Multiple Locations	100/300/500kW:WORLD SERVICE:EEU/ME/AF; (J):100/300kW:WORLD SERVICE:EEU/ME; (J):100/250kW:WORLD SERVICE:EEU/ME; (J):100/250kW:WORLD SERVICE:AF; (J):250kW:WORLD SERVICE:SA
15084	IRAN — VO THE ISLAMIC REP — Tehrān	250kW:PERSIAN
15090	SYRIA — SYRIAN BC SERVICE — Adhra	Alternative Frequency to 15095kHz
	VATICAN STATE — VATICAN RADIO — Sta Maria di Galeria	100kW::SAS
15090v	PAKISTAN — RADIO PAKISTAN — Karachi	(J):50kW::ME
15095 (con'd)	ISRAEL — KOL ISRAEL — Tel Aviv	(J):300kW::EEU/WUSSR; (J):50kW::WUSSR; (D)Sa/Su:300kW::EEU/WUSSR

ENGLISH ▬▬ GERMAN / DEUTSCH ∞∞∞ FRENCH / FRANÇAIS ══ PORTUGUESE / PORTUGUÊS ▬▬ SPANISH / ESPAÑOL ▬▬

ARABIC / عربى ══ RUSSIAN / РУССКИИ CHINESE / 中文 □□□□ JAPANESE / 日本語 ▬▬ MULTILINGUAL ∞∞∞ OTHER ▬

SUMMER ONLY (J)   WINTER ONLY (D)   JAMMING /\/\ or / or \   EARLIEST HEARD ◢   LATEST HEARD ◣   + TENTATIVE

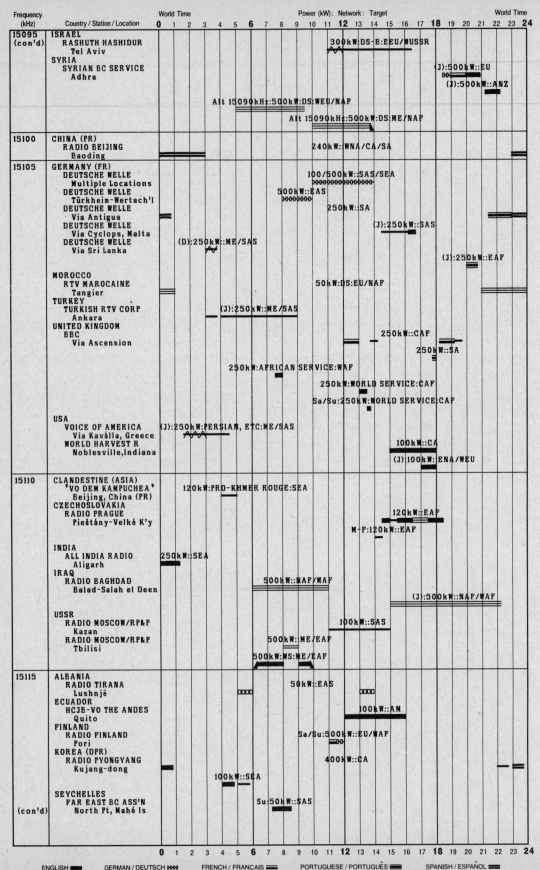

Frequency (kHz)	Country / Station / Location	World Time
15095 (con'd)	ISRAEL	
	RASHUTH HASHIDUR Tel Aviv	300kW:DS-B:EEU/WUSSR
	SYRIA	
	SYRIAN BC SERVICE Adhra	(J):500kW::EU (J):500kW::ANZ
		Alt 15090kHz:500kW:DS:WEU/NAF
		Alt 15090kHz:500kW:DS:ME/NAF
15100	CHINA (PR)	
	RADIO BEIJING Baoding	240kW::WNA/CA/SA
15105	GERMANY (FR)	
	DEUTSCHE WELLE Multiple Locations	100/500kW::SAS/SEA
	DEUTSCHE WELLE Türkheim-Wertach'l	500kW::EAS
	DEUTSCHE WELLE Via Antigua	250kW::SA
	DEUTSCHE WELLE Via Cyclops, Malta	(J):250kW::SAS
	DEUTSCHE WELLE Via Sri Lanka	(D):250kW::ME/SAS (J):250kW::EAF
	MOROCCO	
	RTV MAROCAINE Tangier	50kW:DS:EU/NAF
	TURKEY	
	TURKISH RTV CORP Ankara	(J):250kW::ME/SAS
	UNITED KINGDOM	
	BBC Via Ascension	250kW::CAF 250kW::SA
		250kW:AFRICAN SERVICE:WAF
		250kW:WORLD SERVICE:CAF
		Sa/Su:250kW:WORLD SERVICE:CAF
	USA	
	VOICE OF AMERICA Via Kaválla, Greece	(J):250kW:PERSIAN, ETC:ME/SAS
	WORLD HARVEST R Noblesville,Indiana	100kW::CA (J):100kW::ENA/WEU
15110	CLANDESTINE (ASIA)	
	"VO DEM KAMPUCHEA" Beijing, China (PR)	120kW:PRO-KHMER ROUGE:SEA
	CZECHOSLOVAKIA	
	RADIO PRAGUE Piešťany-Velké K'y	120kW::EAF M-F:120kW::EAF
	INDIA	
	ALL INDIA RADIO Aligarh	250kW::SEA
	IRAQ	
	RADIO BAGHDAD Balad-Salah el Deen	500kW::NAF/WAF (J):500kW::NAF/WAF
	USSR	
	RADIO MOSCOW/RP&P Kazan	100kW::SAS
	RADIO MOSCOW/RP&P Tbilisi	500kW::ME/EAF 500kW:WS:ME/EAF
15115	ALBANIA	
	RADIO TIRANA Lushnjë	50kW::EAS
	ECUADOR	
	HCJB-VO THE ANDES Quito	100kW::AM
	FINLAND	
	RADIO FINLAND Pori	Sa/Su:500kW::EU/WAF
	KOREA (DPR)	
	RADIO PYONGYANG Kujang-dong	400kW::CA
		100kW::SEA
	SEYCHELLES	
(con'd)	FAR EAST BC ASS'N North Pt, Mahé Is	Su:50kW::SAS

ENGLISH ▬▬   GERMAN / DEUTSCH ∞∞∞   FRENCH / FRANÇAIS ▭▭   PORTUGUESE / PORTUGUÊS ▬▬   SPANISH / ESPAÑOL ▬▬

ARABIC / ▬▬   RUSSIAN / РУССКИИ ▭▭   CHINESE / 中文 ∞∞∞   JAPANESE / 日本語 ▬▬   MULTILINGUAL ∞∞∞   OTHER ▬▬

SUMMER ONLY (J)   WINTER ONLY (D)   JAMMING /\/\ or / or \   EARLIEST HEARD ◢   LATEST HEARD ◣   ✦ TENTATIVE

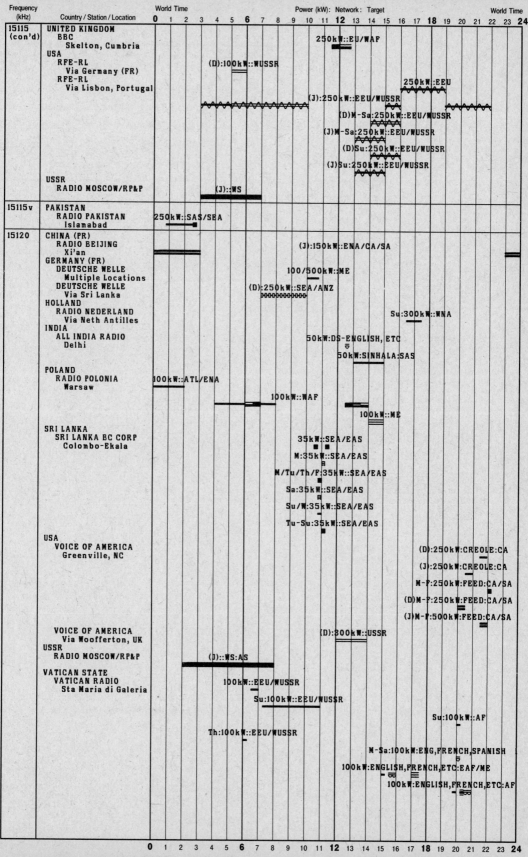

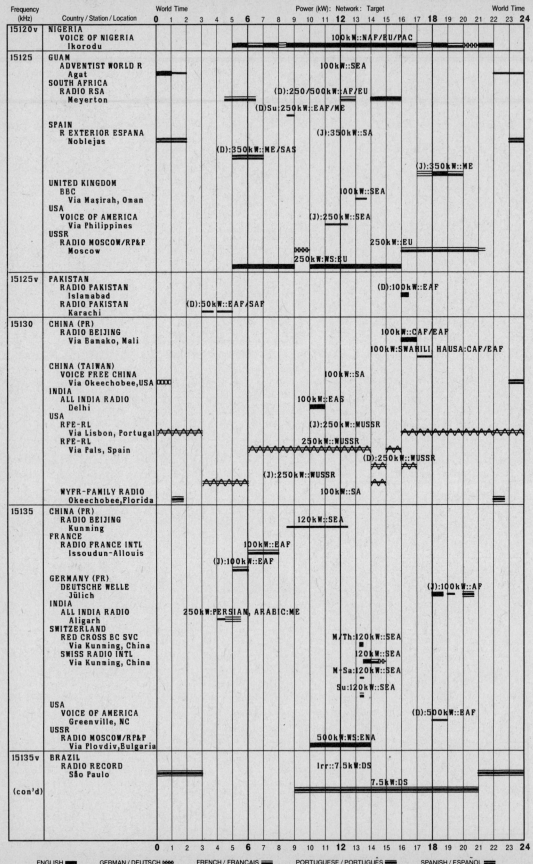

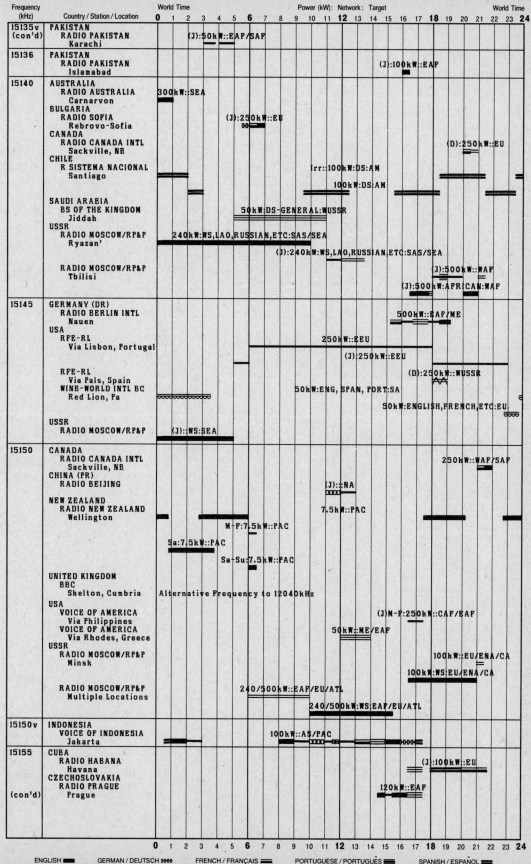

Frequency (kHz)	Country / Station / Location		World Time / Power (kW) : Network : Target
15135v (con'd)	PAKISTAN — RADIO PAKISTAN — Karachi		(J):50kW::EAF/SAF
15136	PAKISTAN — RADIO PAKISTAN — Islamabad		(J):100kW::EAF
15140	AUSTRALIA — RADIO AUSTRALIA — Carnarvon		300kW::SEA
	BULGARIA — RADIO SOFIA — Rebrovo-Sofia		(J):250kW::EU
	CANADA — RADIO CANADA INTL — Sackville, NB		(D):250kW::EU
	CHILE — R SISTEMA NACIONAL — Santiago		Irr::100kW:DS:AM / 100kW:DS:AM
	SAUDI ARABIA — BS OF THE KINGDOM — Jiddah		50kW:DS-GENERAL:WUSSR
	USSR — RADIO MOSCOW/RP&P — Ryazan'		240kW:WS,LAO,RUSSIAN,ETC:SAS/SEA / (J):240kW:WS,LAO,RUSSIAN,ETC:SAS/SEA
	RADIO MOSCOW/RP&P — Tbilisi		(J):500kW::WAF / (J):500kW:AFRICAN:WAF
15145	GERMANY (DR) — RADIO BERLIN INTL — Nauen		500kW::EAF/ME
	USA — RFE-RL — Via Lisbon, Portugal		250kW::EEU / (J):250kW::EEU
	RFE-RL — Via Pals, Spain		(D):250kW::WUSSR
	WINB-WORLD INTL BC — Red Lion, Pa		50kW:ENG, SPAN, PORT:SA / 50kW:ENGLISH,FRENCH,ETC:EU
	USSR — RADIO MOSCOW/RP&P		(J)::WS:SEA
15150	CANADA — RADIO CANADA INTL — Sackville, NB		250kW::WAF/SAF
	CHINA (PR) — RADIO BEIJING		(J)::NA
	NEW ZEALAND — RADIO NEW ZEALAND — Wellington		7.5kW::PAC / M-F:7.5kW::PAC / Sa:7.5kW::PAC / Sa-Su:7.5kW::PAC
	UNITED KINGDOM — BBC — Skelton, Cumbria		Alternative Frequency to 12040kHz
	USA — VOICE OF AMERICA — Via Philippines		(J)M-F:250kW::CAF/EAF
	VOICE OF AMERICA — Via Rhodes, Greece		50kW::ME/EAF
	USSR — RADIO MOSCOW/RP&P — Minsk		100kW::EU/ENA/CA / 100kW:WS:EU/ENA/CA
	RADIO MOSCOW/RP&P — Multiple Locations		240/500kW::EAF/EU/ATL / 240/500kW:WS:EAF/EU/ATL
15150v	INDONESIA — VOICE OF INDONESIA — Jakarta		100kW::AS/PAC
15155	CUBA — RADIO HABANA — Havana		(J)::100kW::EU
(con'd)	CZECHOSLOVAKIA — RADIO PRAGUE — Prague		120kW::EAF

World Time: 0 1 2 3 4 5 6 7 8 9 10 11 12 13 14 15 16 17 18 19 20 21 22 23 24

ENGLISH ▬▬ GERMAN / DEUTSCH ◊◊◊◊ FRENCH / FRANÇAIS ═══ PORTUGUESE / PORTUGUÊS ▬▬ SPANISH / ESPAÑOL ▬▬

ARABIC / ﻉﺭﺏ ═══ RUSSIAN / РУССКИЙ ▬▬ CHINESE / 中文 ◻◻◻◻ JAPANESE / 日本語 ▬▬ MULTILINGUAL ◊◊◊◊ OTHER ▬▬

SUMMER ONLY (J) WINTER ONLY (D) JAMMING ∧∧ or / or \ EARLIEST HEARD ◢ LATEST HEARD ◣ + TENTATIVE

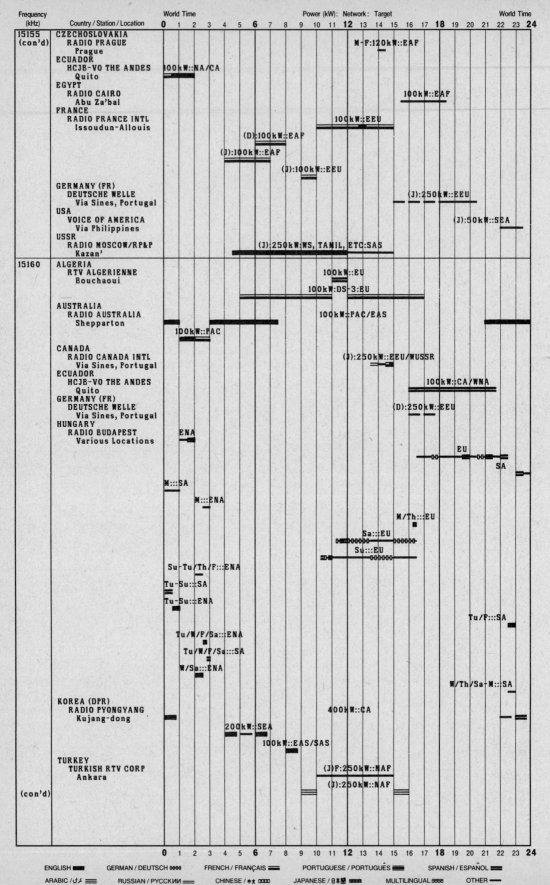

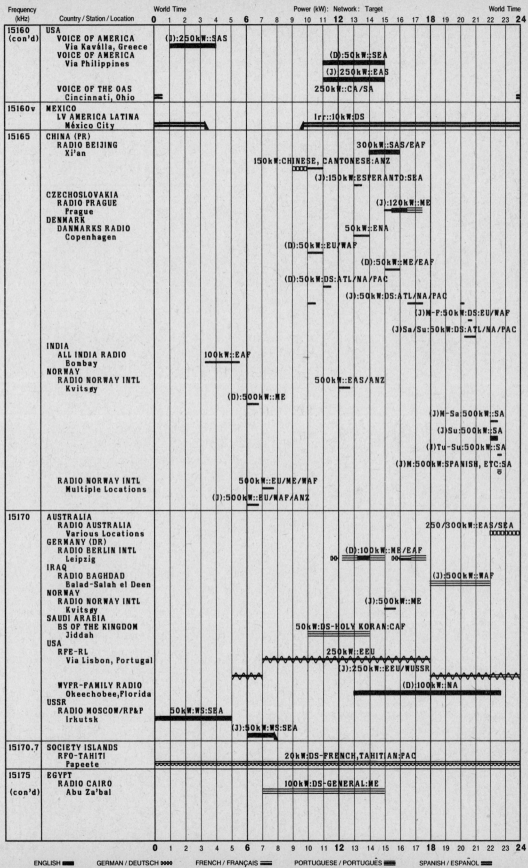

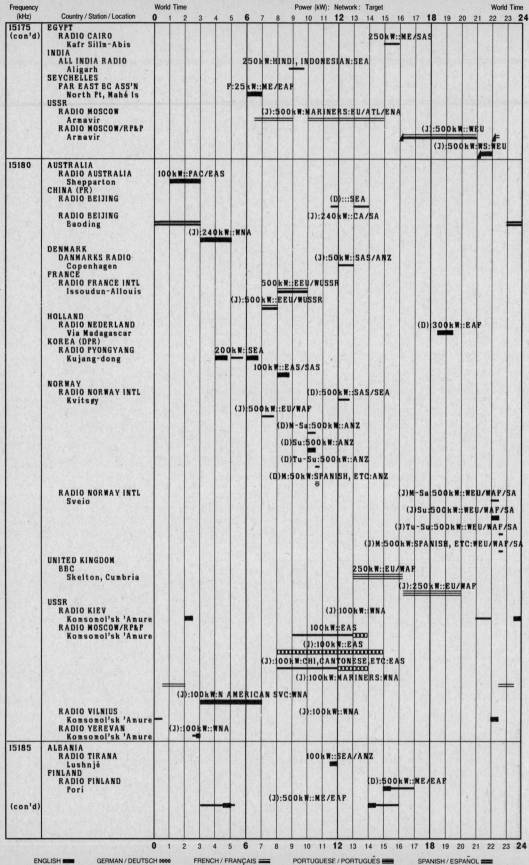

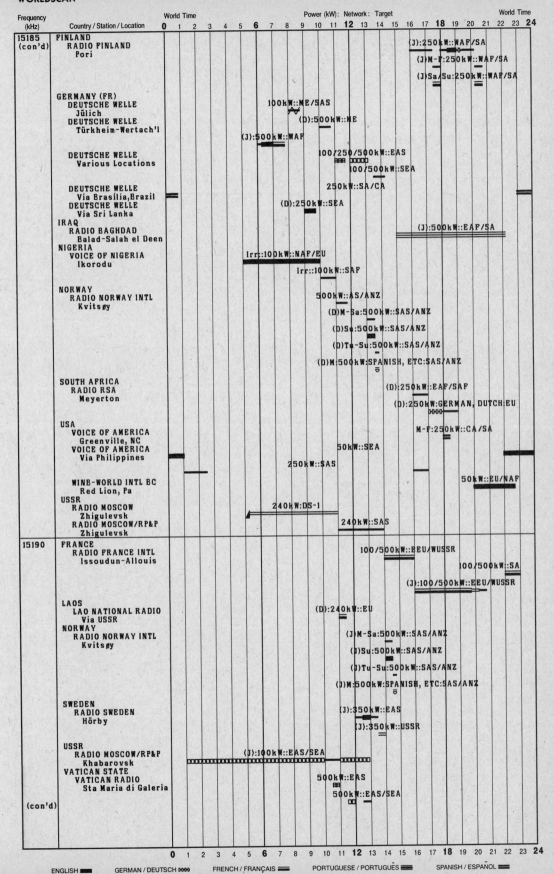

Frequency
(kHz)   Country / Station / Location

15185 (con'd)

FINLAND
 RADIO FINLAND
  Pori — (J):250kW::WAF/SA; (J)M–F:250kW::WAF/SA; (J)Sa/Su:250kW::WAF/SA

GERMANY (FR)
 DEUTSCHE WELLE
  Jülich — 100kW::ME/SAS
 DEUTSCHE WELLE
  Türkheim-Wertach'l — (D):500kW::ME; (J):500kW::WAF
 DEUTSCHE WELLE
  Various Locations — 100/250/500kW::EAS; 100/500kW::SEA
 DEUTSCHE WELLE
  Via Brasília, Brazil — 250kW::SA/CA
 DEUTSCHE WELLE
  Via Sri Lanka — (D):250kW::SEA
IRAQ
 RADIO BAGHDAD
  Balad-Salah el Deen — (J):500kW::EAF/SA
NIGERIA
 VOICE OF NIGERIA
  Ikorodu — Irr::100kW::NAF/EU; Irr::100kW::SAF

NORWAY
 RADIO NORWAY INTL
  Kvitsøy — 500kW::AS/ANZ; (D)M–Sa:500kW::SAS/ANZ; (D)Su:500kW::SAS/ANZ; (D)Tu–Su:500kW::SAS/ANZ; (D)M:500kW:SPANISH, ETC:SAS/ANZ

SOUTH AFRICA
 RADIO RSA
  Meyerton — (D):250kW::EAF/SAF; (D):250kW::GERMAN, DUTCH:EU

USA
 VOICE OF AMERICA
  Greenville, NC — M–F:250kW::CA/SA
 VOICE OF AMERICA
  Via Philippines — 50kW::SEA; 250kW::SAS; 50kW::EU/NAF
 WINB–WORLD INTL BC
  Red Lion, Pa
USSR
 RADIO MOSCOW
  Zhigulevsk — 240kW:DS-1
 RADIO MOSCOW/RP&P
  Zhigulevsk — 240kW::SAS

15190

FRANCE
 RADIO FRANCE INTL
  Issoudun-Allouis — 100/500kW::EEU/WUSSR; 100/500kW::SA; (J):100/500kW::EEU/WUSSR

LAOS
 LAO NATIONAL RADIO
  Via USSR — (D):240kW::EU
NORWAY
 RADIO NORWAY INTL
  Kvitsøy — (J)M–Sa:500kW::SAS/ANZ; (J)Su:500kW::SAS/ANZ; (J)Tu–Su:500kW::SAS/ANZ; (J)M:500kW:SPANISH, ETC:SAS/ANZ

SWEDEN
 RADIO SWEDEN
  Hörby — (J):350kW::EAS; (J):350kW::USSR

USSR
 RADIO MOSCOW/RP&P
  Khabarovsk — (J):100kW::EAS/SEA
VATICAN STATE
 VATICAN RADIO
  Sta Maria di Galeria — 500kW::EAS; 500kW::EAS/SEA

(con'd)

ENGLISH ▬▬   GERMAN / DEUTSCH ◊◊◊◊   FRENCH / FRANÇAIS ▬▬   PORTUGUESE / PORTUGUÊS ▬▬   SPANISH / ESPAÑOL ▬▬

ARABIC / بی عر ▬▬   RUSSIAN / РУССКИИ ▬▬   CHINESE / ✱✱ ◊◊◊◊   JAPANESE / 日本語 ▬▬   MULTILINGUAL ◊◊◊◊   OTHER ▬▬

SUMMER ONLY (J)   WINTER ONLY (D)   JAMMING ∧∧ or / or \   EARLIEST HEARD ◢   LATEST HEARD ◣   + TENTATIVE

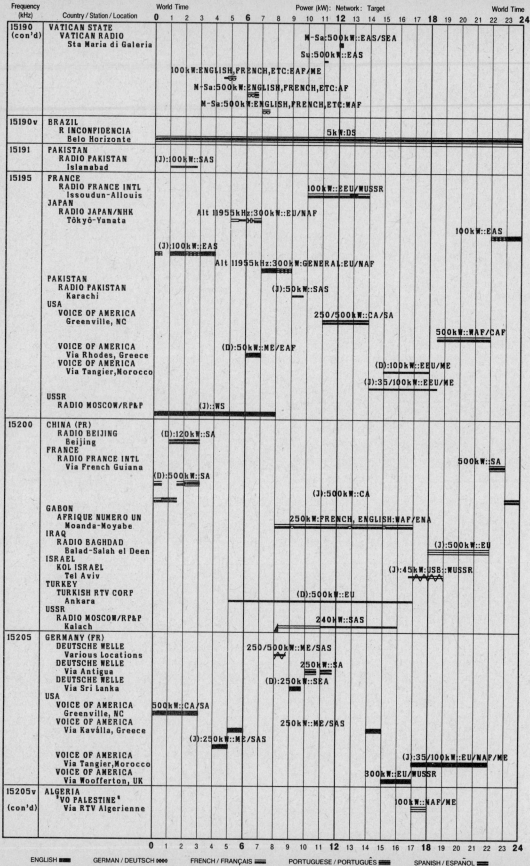

Frequency (kHz)	Country / Station / Location	World Time	Power (kW) : Network : Target
15190 (con'd)	VATICAN STATE — VATICAN RADIO, Sta Maria di Galeria		M-Sa:500kW::EAS/SEA; Su:500kW::EAS; 100kW:ENGLISH,FRENCH,ETC:EAF/ME; M-Sa:500kW:ENGLISH,FRENCH,ETC:AF; M-Sa:500kW:ENGLISH,FRENCH,ETC:WAF
15190v	BRAZIL — R INCONFIDENCIA, Belo Horizonte		5kW:DS
15191	PAKISTAN — RADIO PAKISTAN, Islamabad		(J):100kW::SAS
15195	FRANCE — RADIO FRANCE INTL, Issoudun-Allouis		100kW::EEU/WUSSR
	JAPAN — RADIO JAPAN/NHK, Tōkyō-Yamata		Alt 11955kHz:300kW::EU/NAF; 100kW::EAS; (J):100kW::EAS; Alt 11955kHz:300kW:GENERAL:EU/NAF
	PAKISTAN — RADIO PAKISTAN, Karachi		(J):50kW::SAS
	USA — VOICE OF AMERICA, Greenville, NC		250/500kW::CA/SA; 500kW::WAF/CAF
	VOICE OF AMERICA, Via Rhodes, Greece		(D):50kW::ME/EAF
	VOICE OF AMERICA, Via Tangier, Morocco		(D):100kW::EEU/ME; (J):35/100kW::EEU/ME
	USSR — RADIO MOSCOW/RP&P		(J)::WS
15200	CHINA (PR) — RADIO BEIJING, Beijing		(D):120kW::SA
	FRANCE — RADIO FRANCE INTL, Via French Guiana		(D):500kW::SA; 500kW::SA; (J):500kW::CA
	GABON — AFRIQUE NUMERO UN, Moanda-Moyabe		250kW:FRENCH, ENGLISH:WAF/ENA
	IRAQ — RADIO BAGHDAD, Balad-Salah el Deen		(J):500kW::EU
	ISRAEL — KOL ISRAEL, Tel Aviv		(J):45kW:USB::WUSSR
	TURKEY — TURKISH RTV CORP, Ankara		(D):500kW::EU
	USSR — RADIO MOSCOW/RP&P, Kalach		240kW::SAS
15205	GERMANY (FR) — DEUTSCHE WELLE, Various Locations		250/500kW::ME/SAS
	DEUTSCHE WELLE, Via Antigua		250kW::SA
	DEUTSCHE WELLE, Via Sri Lanka		(D):250kW::SEA
	USA — VOICE OF AMERICA, Greenville, NC		500kW::CA/SA
	VOICE OF AMERICA, Via Kaválla, Greece		250kW::ME/SAS; (J):250kW::ME/SAS
	VOICE OF AMERICA, Via Tangier, Morocco		(J):35/100kW::EU/NAF/ME
	VOICE OF AMERICA, Via Woofferton, UK		300kW::EU/WUSSR
15205v (con'd)	ALGERIA — "VO PALESTINE", Via RTV Algerienne		100kW::NAF/ME

World Time: 0 1 2 3 4 5 6 7 8 9 10 11 12 13 14 15 16 17 18 19 20 21 22 23 24

ENGLISH ▬▬ GERMAN / DEUTSCH ◊◊◊◊ FRENCH / FRANÇAIS ▬▬ PORTUGUESE / PORTUGUÊS ▬▬ SPANISH / ESPAÑOL ▬▬
ARABIC / عربي ▬▬ RUSSIAN / РУССКИИ ▬▬ CHINESE / 中文 ◊◊◊◊ JAPANESE / 日本語 ▬▬ MULTILINGUAL ◊◊◊◊ OTHER ▬▬
SUMMER ONLY (J) WINTER ONLY (D) JAMMING ∧∧ or / or \ EARLIEST HEARD ◢ LATEST HEARD ◣ + TENTATIVE

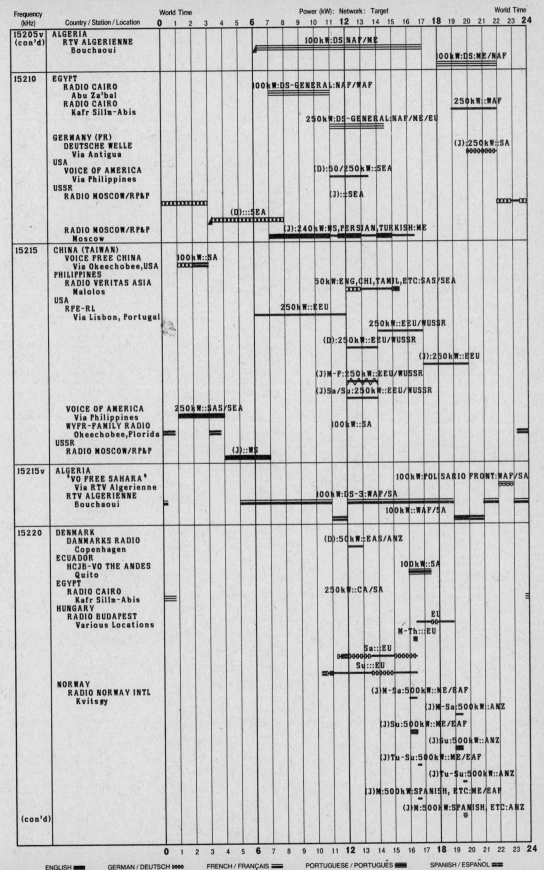

Frequency (kHz) — Country / Station / Location — World Time / Power (kW): Network: Target

15205v (con'd) — ALGERIA, RTV ALGERIENNE, Bouchaoui
- 100kW:DS:NAF/ME
- 100kW:DS:ME/NAF

15210 — EGYPT
- RADIO CAIRO, Abu Za'bal — 100kW:DS-GENERAL:NAF/WAF
- RADIO CAIRO, Kafr Sillm-Abis — 250kW::WAF
- 250kW:DS-GENERAL:NAF/ME/EU
- GERMANY (FR), DEUTSCHE WELLE, Via Antigua — (J):250kW::SA
- USA, VOICE OF AMERICA, Via Philippines — (D):50/250kW::SEA
- USSR, RADIO MOSCOW/RP&P — (J)::SEA
- (D):::SEA
- RADIO MOSCOW/RP&P, Moscow — (J):240kW:WS,PERSIAN,TURKISH:ME

15215 — CHINA (TAIWAN)
- VOICE FREE CHINA, Via Okeechobee, USA — 100kW::SA
- PHILIPPINES, RADIO VERITAS ASIA, Malolos — 50kW:ENG,CHI,TAMIL,ETC:SAS/SEA
- USA, RFE-RL, Via Lisbon, Portugal — 250kW::EEU
- 250kW::EEU/WUSSR
- (D):250kW::EEU/WUSSR
- (J):250kW::EEU
- (J)M-F:250kW::EEU/WUSSR
- (J)Sa/Su:250kW::EEU/WUSSR
- VOICE OF AMERICA, Via Philippines — 250kW::SAS/SEA
- WYFR-FAMILY RADIO, Okeechobee, Florida — 100kW::SA
- USSR, RADIO MOSCOW/RP&P — (J)::WS

15215v — ALGERIA
- 'VO FREE SAHARA', Via RTV Algerienne — 100kW:POLISARIO FRONT:WAF/SA
- RTV ALGERIENNE, Bouchaoui — 100kW:DS-3:WAF/SA
- 100kW::WAF/SA

15220 — DENMARK
- DANMARKS RADIO, Copenhagen — (D):50kW::EAS/ANZ
- ECUADOR, HCJB-VO THE ANDES, Quito — 100kW::SA
- EGYPT, RADIO CAIRO, Kafr Sillm-Abis — 250kW::CA/SA
- HUNGARY, RADIO BUDAPEST, Various Locations — EU
- M-Th:::EU
- Sa:::EU
- Su:::EU
- NORWAY, RADIO NORWAY INTL, Kvitsøy — (J)M-Sa:500kW::ME/EAF
- (J)M-Sa:500kW::ANZ
- (J)Su:500kW::ME/EAF
- (J)Su:500kW::ANZ
- (J)Tu-Su:500kW::ME/EAF
- (J)Tu-Su:500kW::ANZ
- (J)M:500kW:SPANISH, ETC:ME/EAF
- (J)M:500kW:SPANISH, ETC:ANZ

(con'd)

ENGLISH ▬   GERMAN / DEUTSCH ∞∞   FRENCH / FRANÇAIS ▬   PORTUGUESE / PORTUGUÊS ▬   SPANISH / ESPAÑOL ▬

ARABIC / عربي ▬   RUSSIAN / РУССКИЙ ▬   CHINESE / 中文 ∞∞   JAPANESE / 日本語 ▬   MULTILINGUAL ∞∞   OTHER ▬

SUMMER ONLY (J)   WINTER ONLY (D)   JAMMING ∧∧ or / or \   EARLIEST HEARD ◢   LATEST HEARD ◣   + TENTATIVE

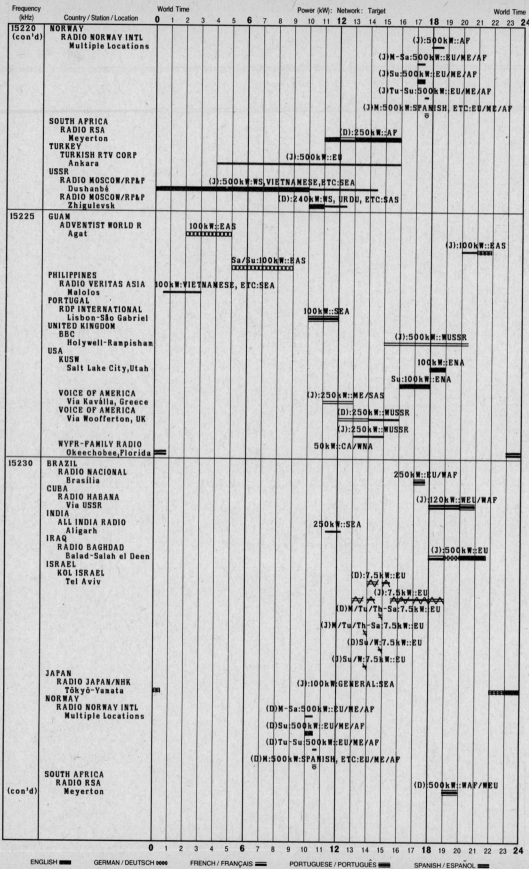

Frequency (kHz)	Country / Station / Location	World Time 0–24 / Power (kW): Network: Target
15220 (con'd)	**NORWAY** RADIO NORWAY INTL Multiple Locations	(J):500kW::AF
		(J)M-Sa:500kW::EU/ME/AF
		(J)Su:500kW:EU/ME/AF
		(J)Tu-Su:500kW:EU/ME/AF
		(J)M:500kW:SPANISH, ETC:EU/ME/AF
	SOUTH AFRICA RADIO RSA Meyerton	(D):250kW::AF
	TURKEY TURKISH RTV CORP Ankara	(J):500kW::EU
	USSR RADIO MOSCOW/RP&P Dushanbé	(J):500kW:WS,VIETNAMESE,ETC:SEA
	RADIO MOSCOW/RP&P Zhigulevsk	(D):240kW:WS, URDU, ETC:SAS
15225	**GUAM** ADVENTIST WORLD R Agat	100kW:EAS
		(J):100kW::EAS
		Sa/Su:100kW::EAS
	PHILIPPINES RADIO VERITAS ASIA Malolos	100kW:VIETNANESE, ETC:SEA
	PORTUGAL RDP INTERNATIONAL Lisbon-São Gabriel	100kW::SEA
	UNITED KINGDOM BBC Holywell-Rampisham	(J):500kW::WUSSR
	USA KUSW Salt Lake City,Utah	100kW::ENA
		Su:100kW::ENA
	VOICE OF AMERICA Via Kaválla, Greece	(J):250kW::ME/SAS
	VOICE OF AMERICA Via Woofferton, UK	(D):250kW::WUSSR
		(J):250kW::WUSSR
	WYFR-FAMILY RADIO Okeechobee,Florida	50kW::CA/WNA
15230	**BRAZIL** RADIO NACIONAL Brasília	250kW::EU/WAF
	CUBA RADIO HABANA Via USSR	(J):120kW::WEU/WAF
	INDIA ALL INDIA RADIO Aligarh	250kW::SEA
	IRAQ RADIO BAGHDAD Balad-Salah el Deen	(J):500kW::EU
	ISRAEL KOL ISRAEL Tel Aviv	(D):7.5kW::EU
		(J):7.5kW::EU
		(D)M/Tu/Th-Sa:7.5kW::EU
		(J)M/Tu/Th-Sa:7.5kW::EU
		(D)Su/W:7.5kW::EU
		(J)Su/W:7.5kW::EU
	JAPAN RADIO JAPAN/NHK Tōkyō-Yamata	(J):100kW:GENERAL:SEA
	NORWAY RADIO NORWAY INTL Multiple Locations	(D)M-Sa:500kW::EU/ME/AF
		(D)Su:500kW:EU/ME/AF
		(D)Tu-Su:500kW:EU/ME/AF
		(D)M:500kW:SPANISH, ETC:EU/ME/AF
(con'd)	**SOUTH AFRICA** RADIO RSA Meyerton	(D):500kW::WAF/WEU

ENGLISH ▬   GERMAN / DEUTSCH ∞∞   FRENCH / FRANÇAIS ▬   PORTUGUESE / PORTUGUÊS ▬   SPANISH / ESPAÑOL ▬

ARABIC / ﻉﺮﺑ ▬   RUSSIAN / РУССКИИ ▬   CHINESE / ✦✧ ∞∞   JAPANESE / 日本語 ▬   MULTILINGUAL ∞∞   OTHER ▬

SUMMER ONLY (J)   WINTER ONLY (D)   JAMMING ∧∧ or / or \   EARLIEST HEARD ◢   LATEST HEARD ◣   † TENTATIVE

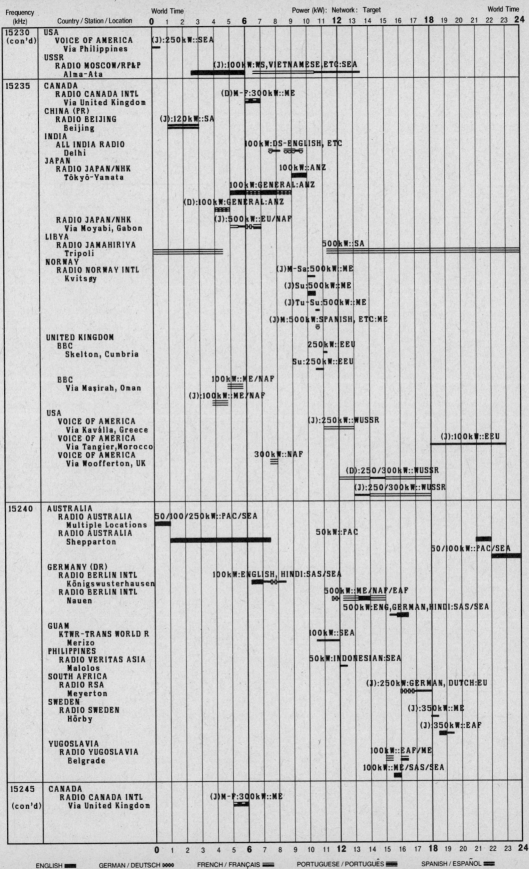

15230 (con'd)

USA
  VOICE OF AMERICA
    Via Philippines — (J):250kW::SEA

USSR
  RADIO MOSCOW/RP&P
    Alma-Ata — (J):100kW:WS,VIETNAMESE,ETC:SEA

15235

CANADA
  RADIO CANADA INTL
    Via United Kingdom — (D)M-F:300kW::ME

CHINA (PR)
  RADIO BEIJING
    Beijing — (J):120kW::SA

INDIA
  ALL INDIA RADIO
    Delhi — 100kW:DS-ENGLISH, ETC

JAPAN
  RADIO JAPAN/NHK
    Tōkyō-Yamata — 100kW::ANZ
      100kW:GENERAL:ANZ
      (D):100kW:GENERAL:ANZ

  RADIO JAPAN/NHK
    Via Moyabi, Gabon — (J):500kW::EU/NAF

LIBYA
  RADIO JAMAHIRIYA
    Tripoli — 500kW::SA

NORWAY
  RADIO NORWAY INTL
    Kvitsøy — (J)M-Sa:500kW::ME
      (J)Su:500kW::ME
      (J)Tu-Su:500kW::ME
      (J)M:500kW:SPANISH, ETC:ME

UNITED KINGDOM
  BBC
    Skelton, Cumbria — 250kW::EEU
      Su:250kW::EEU

  BBC
    Via Maşirah, Oman — 100kW::ME/NAF
      (J):100kW::ME/NAF

USA
  VOICE OF AMERICA
    Via Kaválla, Greece — (J):250kW::WUSSR
  VOICE OF AMERICA
    Via Tangier, Morocco — (J):100kW::EEU
  VOICE OF AMERICA
    Via Woofferton, UK — 300kW::NAF
      (D):250/300kW::WUSSR
      (J):250/300kW::WUSSR

15240

AUSTRALIA
  RADIO AUSTRALIA
    Multiple Locations — 50/100/250kW::PAC/SEA
  RADIO AUSTRALIA
    Shepparton — 50kW::PAC
      50/100kW::PAC/SEA

GERMANY (DR)
  RADIO BERLIN INTL
    Königswusterhausen — 100kW:ENGLISH, HINDI:SAS/SEA
  RADIO BERLIN INTL
    Nauen — 500kW::ME/NAF/EAF
      500kW:ENG,GERMAN,HINDI:SAS/SEA

GUAM
  KTWR-TRANS WORLD R
    Merizo — 100kW::SEA

PHILIPPINES
  RADIO VERITAS ASIA
    Malolos — 50kW:INDONESIAN:SEA

SOUTH AFRICA
  RADIO RSA
    Meyerton — (J):250kW:GERMAN, DUTCH:EU

SWEDEN
  RADIO SWEDEN
    Hörby — (J):350kW::ME
      (J):350kW::EAF

YUGOSLAVIA
  RADIO YUGOSLAVIA
    Belgrade — 100kW::EAF/ME
      100kW::ME/SAS/SEA

15245 (con'd)

CANADA
  RADIO CANADA INTL
    Via United Kingdom — (J)M-F:300kW::ME

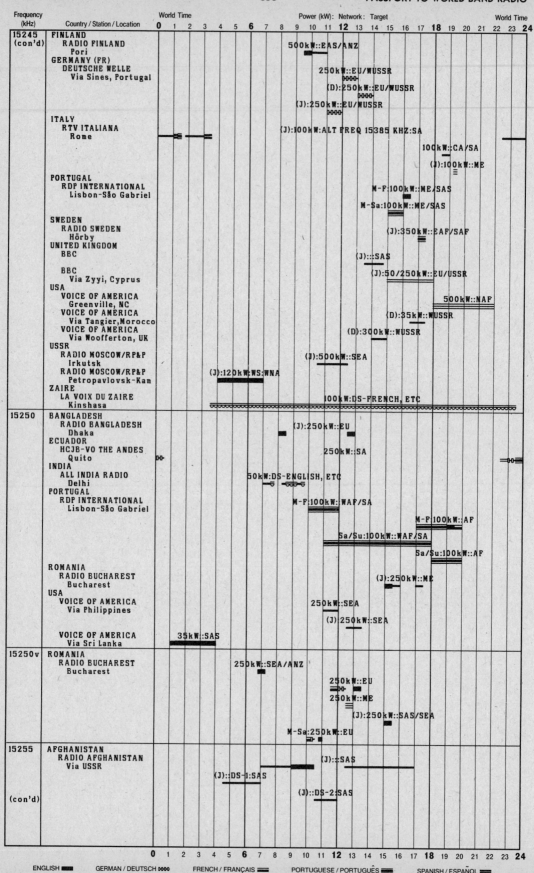

Frequency (kHz)	Country / Station / Location	Power (kW) : Network : Target (World Time 0–24)

15245 (con'd)	FINLAND
	  RADIO FINLAND
	    Pori
		500kW::EAS/ANZ

	GERMANY (FR)
	  DEUTSCHE WELLE
	    Via Sines, Portugal
		250kW::EU/WUSSR
		(D):250kW::EU/WUSSR
		(J):250kW::EU/WUSSR

	ITALY
	  RTV ITALIANA
	    Rome
		(J):100kW:ALT FREQ 15385 KHZ:SA
		100kW::CA/SA
		(J):100kW::ME

	PORTUGAL
	  RDP INTERNATIONAL
	    Lisbon-São Gabriel
		M-F:100kW::ME/SAS
		M-Sa:100kW::ME/SAS

	SWEDEN
	  RADIO SWEDEN
	    Hörby
		(J):350kW::EAF/SAF

	UNITED KINGDOM BBC	(J):::SAS
	BBC Via Zyyi, Cyprus	(J):50/250kW::EU/USSR

	USA
	  VOICE OF AMERICA
	    Greenville, NC
		500kW::NAF

	VOICE OF AMERICA Via Tangier,Morocco	(D):35kW::WUSSR
	VOICE OF AMERICA Via Woofferton, UK	(D):300kW::WUSSR

	USSR
	  RADIO MOSCOW/RP&P
	    Irkutsk
		(J):500kW::SEA

	RADIO MOSCOW/RP&P Petropavlovsk-Kam	(J):120kW:WS:WNA

	ZAIRE
	  LA VOIX DU ZAIRE
	    Kinshasa
		100kW:DS-FRENCH, ETC

15250	BANGLADESH
	  RADIO BANGLADESH
	    Dhaka
		(J):250kW::EU

	ECUADOR
	  HCJB-VO THE ANDES
	    Quito
		250kW::SA

	INDIA
	  ALL INDIA RADIO
	    Delhi
		50kW:DS-ENGLISH, ETC

	PORTUGAL
	  RDP INTERNATIONAL
	    Lisbon-São Gabriel
		M-F:100kW::WAF/SA
		M-F:100kW::AF
		Sa/Su:100kW::WAF/SA
		Sa/Su:100kW::AF

	ROMANIA
	  RADIO BUCHAREST
	    Bucharest
		(J):250kW::ME

	USA
	  VOICE OF AMERICA
	    Via Philippines
		250kW::SEA
		(J):250kW::SEA

	VOICE OF AMERICA Via Sri Lanka	35kW::SAS

15250v	ROMANIA
	  RADIO BUCHAREST
	    Bucharest
		250kW::SEA/ANZ
		250kW::EU
		250kW::ME
		(J):250kW::SAS/SEA
		M-Sa:250kW::EU

15255	AFGHANISTAN
	  RADIO AFGHANISTAN
	    Via USSR
		(J):::SAS
		(J)::DS-1:SAS
		(J)::DS-2:SAS

(con'd)		

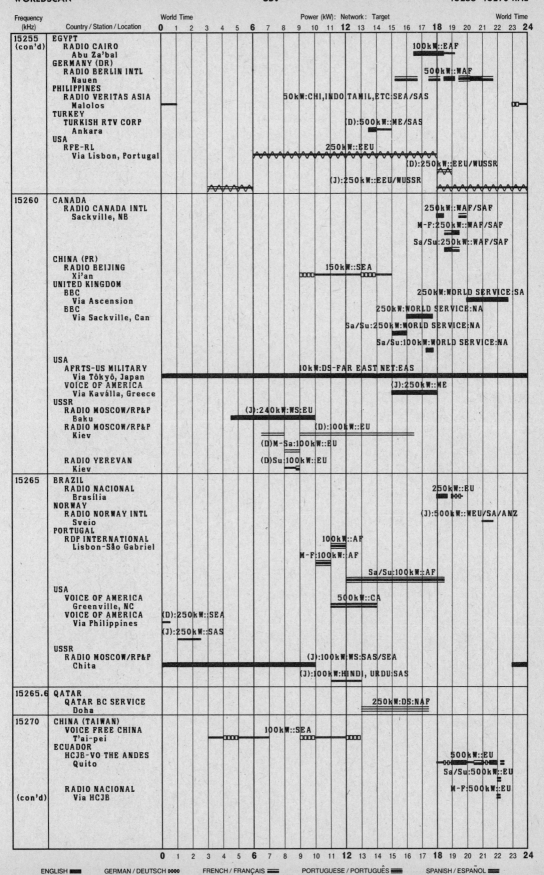

Frequency (kHz)	Country / Station / Location	Power (kW): Network : Target
15255 (con'd)	EGYPT	
	RADIO CAIRO Abu Za'bal	100kW::EAF
	GERMANY (DR)	
	RADIO BERLIN INTL Nauen	500kW::WAF
	PHILIPPINES	
	RADIO VERITAS ASIA Malolos	50kW:CHI,INDO,TAMIL,ETC:SEA/SAS
	TURKEY	
	TURKISH RTV CORP Ankara	(D):500kW::ME/SAS
	USA	
	RFE-RL Via Lisbon, Portugal	250kW::EEU (D):250kW::EEU/WUSSR (J):250kW::EEU/WUSSR
15260	CANADA	
	RADIO CANADA INTL Sackville, NB	250kW::WAF/SAF M-F:250kW::WAF/SAF Sa/Su:250kW::WAF/SAF
	CHINA (PR)	
	RADIO BEIJING Xi'an	150kW::SEA
	UNITED KINGDOM	
	BBC Via Ascension	250kW:WORLD SERVICE:SA
	BBC Via Sackville, Can	250kW:WORLD SERVICE:NA Sa/Su:250kW:WORLD SERVICE:NA Sa/Su:100kW:WORLD SERVICE:NA
	USA	
	AFRTS-US MILITARY Via Tōkyō, Japan	10kW:DS-FAR EAST NET:EAS
	VOICE OF AMERICA Via Kaválla, Greece	(J):250kW::ME
	USSR	
	RADIO MOSCOW/RP&P Baku	(J):240kW:WS:EU
	RADIO MOSCOW/RP&P Kiev	(D):100kW::EU (D)M-Sa:100kW::EU
	RADIO YEREVAN Kiev	(D)Su:100kW::EU
15265	BRAZIL	
	RADIO NACIONAL Brasília	250kW::EU
	NORWAY	
	RADIO NORWAY INTL Sveio	(J):500kW::WEU/SA/ANZ
	PORTUGAL	
	RDP INTERNATIONAL Lisbon-São Gabriel	100kW::AF M-F:100kW::AF Sa/Su:100kW::AF
	USA	
	VOICE OF AMERICA Greenville, NC	500kW::CA
	VOICE OF AMERICA Via Philippines	(D):250kW::SEA (J):250kW::SAS
	USSR	
	RADIO MOSCOW/RP&P Chita	(J):100kW:WS:SAS/SEA (J):100kW:HINDI, URDU:SAS
15265.6	QATAR	
	QATAR BC SERVICE Doha	250kW:DS:NAF
15270	CHINA (TAIWAN)	
	VOICE FREE CHINA T'ai-pei	100kW::SEA
	ECUADOR	
	HCJB-VO THE ANDES Quito	500kW::EU Sa/Su:500kW::EU
(con'd)	RADIO NACIONAL Via HCJB	M-F:500kW::EU

ENGLISH ▬ GERMAN / DEUTSCH ০০০০ FRENCH / FRANÇAIS ═ PORTUGUESE / PORTUGUÊS ▬ SPANISH / ESPAÑOL ▬

ARABIC /العبية ▬ RUSSIAN / РУССКИИ ═ CHINESE / ✳✖ ০০০০ JAPANESE / 日本語 ▬ MULTILINGUAL ▥ OTHER ▬

SUMMER ONLY (J) WINTER ONLY (D) JAMMING ∧∧ or / or \ EARLIEST HEARD ◢ LATEST HEARD ◣ ✝ TENTATIVE

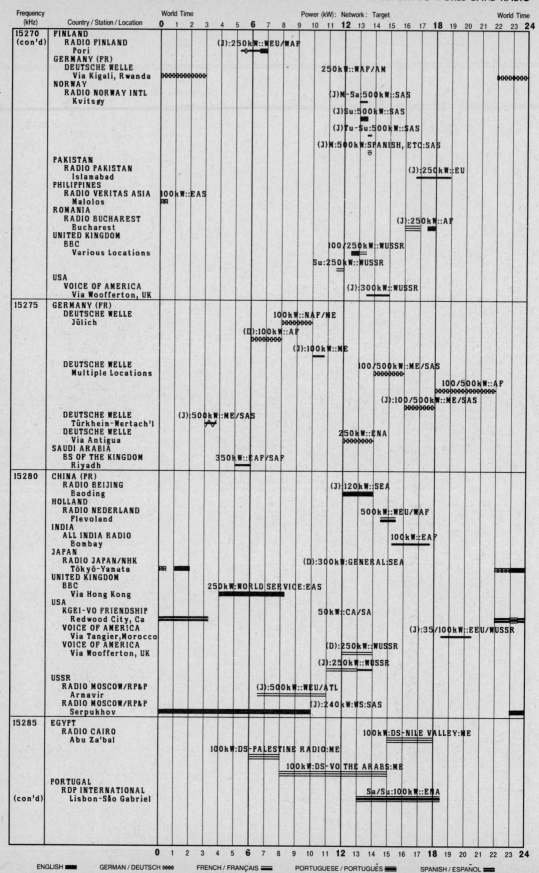

Frequency (kHz)	Country / Station / Location	World Time 0–24 / Power (kW) / Network / Target
15270 (con'd)	**FINLAND**	
	RADIO FINLAND Pori	(J):250kW::WEU/WAF
	GERMANY (FR)	
	DEUTSCHE WELLE Via Kigali, Rwanda	250kW::WAF/AM
	NORWAY	
	RADIO NORWAY INTL Kvitsøy	(J)M-Sa:500kW::SAS; (J)Su:500kW::SAS; (J)Tu-Su:500kW::SAS; (J)M:500kW:SPANISH, ETC:SAS
	PAKISTAN	
	RADIO PAKISTAN Islamabad	(J):250kW::EU
	PHILIPPINES	
	RADIO VERITAS ASIA Malolos	100kW::EAS
	ROMANIA	
	RADIO BUCHAREST Bucharest	(J):250kW::AF
	UNITED KINGDOM	
	BBC Various Locations	100/250kW::WUSSR; Su:250kW::WUSSR
	USA	
	VOICE OF AMERICA Via Woofferton, UK	(J):300kW::WUSSR
15275	**GERMANY (FR)**	
	DEUTSCHE WELLE Jülich	100kW::NAF/ME; (D):100kW::AF; (J):100kW::ME
	DEUTSCHE WELLE Multiple Locations	100/500kW::ME/SAS; 100/500kW::AF; (J):100/500kW::ME/SAS
	DEUTSCHE WELLE Türkheim-Wertach'l	(J):500kW::ME/SAS
	DEUTSCHE WELLE Via Antigua	250kW::ENA
	SAUDI ARABIA	
	BS OF THE KINGDOM Riyadh	350kW::EAF/SAF
15280	**CHINA (PR)**	
	RADIO BEIJING Baoding	(J):120kW::SEA
	HOLLAND	
	RADIO NEDERLAND Flevoland	500kW::WEU/WAF
	INDIA	
	ALL INDIA RADIO Bombay	100kW::EAF
	JAPAN	
	RADIO JAPAN/NHK Tōkyō-Yamata	(D):300kW:GENERAL:SEA
	UNITED KINGDOM	
	BBC Via Hong Kong	250kW:WORLD SERVICE:EAS
	USA	
	KGEI-VO FRIENDSHIP Redwood City, Ca	50kW::CA/SA
	VOICE OF AMERICA Via Tangier, Morocco	(J):35/100kW::EEU/WUSSR
	VOICE OF AMERICA Via Woofferton, UK	(D):250kW::WUSSR; (J):250kW::WUSSR
	USSR	
	RADIO MOSCOW/RP&P Armavir	(J):500kW::WEU/ATL
	RADIO MOSCOW/RP&P Serpukhov	(J):240kW:WS:SAS
15285	**EGYPT**	
	RADIO CAIRO Abu Za'bal	100kW:DS-NILE VALLEY:ME; 100kW:DS-PALESTINE RADIO:ME; 100kW:DS-VO THE ARABS:ME
(con'd)	**PORTUGAL**	
	RDP INTERNATIONAL Lisbon-São Gabriel	Sa/Su:100kW::ENA

ENGLISH ▬▬   GERMAN / DEUTSCH ◊◊◊◊   FRENCH / FRANÇAIS ═══   PORTUGUESE / PORTUGUÊS ▬▬   SPANISH / ESPAÑOL ▬▬

ARABIC / عربي ═══   RUSSIAN / РУССКИИ ═══   CHINESE / ▲✗ ◊◊◊◊   JAPANESE / 日本語 ▬▬▬   MULTILINGUAL ◙◙◙◙   OTHER ▬▬

SUMMER ONLY (J)   WINTER ONLY (D)   JAMMING /\/\ or / or \   EARLIEST HEARD ◢   LATEST HEARD ◣   + TENTATIVE

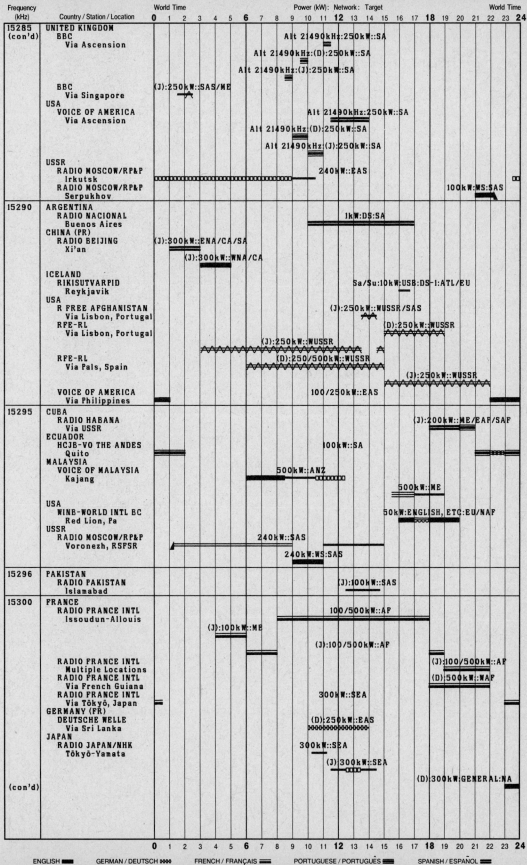

Frequency (kHz)	Country / Station / Location	Power (kW): Network: Target
15285 (con'd)	UNITED KINGDOM BBC Via Ascension	Alt 21490kHz:250kW::SA
		Alt 21490kHz:(D):250kW::SA
		Alt 21490kHz:(J):250kW::SA
	BBC Via Singapore	(J):250kW::SAS/ME
	USA VOICE OF AMERICA Via Ascension	Alt 21490kHz:250kW::SA
		Alt 21490kHz:(D):250kW::SA
		Alt 21490kHz:(J):250kW::SA
	USSR RADIO MOSCOW/RP&P Irkutsk	240kW::EAS
	RADIO MOSCOW/RP&P Serpukhov	100kW::WS:SAS
15290	ARGENTINA RADIO NACIONAL Buenos Aires	1kW:DS:SA
	CHINA (PR) RADIO BEIJING Xi'an	(J):300kW::ENA/CA/SA
		(J):300kW::WNA/CA
	ICELAND RIKISUTVARPID Reykjavik	Sa/Su:10kW:USB:DS-1:ATL/EU
	USA R FREE AFGHANISTAN Via Lisbon, Portugal	(J):250kW::WUSSR/SAS
	RFE-RL Via Lisbon, Portugal	(D):250kW::WUSSR
		(J):250kW::WUSSR
	RFE-RL Via Pals, Spain	(D):250/500kW::WUSSR
		(J):250kW::WUSSR
	VOICE OF AMERICA Via Philippines	100/250kW::EAS
15295	CUBA RADIO HABANA Via USSR	(J):200kW::ME/EAF/SAF
	ECUADOR HCJB-VO THE ANDES Quito	100kW::SA
	MALAYSIA VOICE OF MALAYSIA Kajang	500kW::ANZ
		500kW::ME
	USA WINB-WORLD INTL BC Red Lion, Pa	50kW:ENGLISH, ETC:EU/NAF
	USSR RADIO MOSCOW/RP&P Voronezh, RSFSR	240kW::SAS
		240kW:WS:SAS
15296	PAKISTAN RADIO PAKISTAN Islamabad	(J):100kW::SAS
15300	FRANCE RADIO FRANCE INTL Issoudun-Allouis	100/500kW::AF
		(J):100kW::ME
		(J):100/500kW::AF
	RADIO FRANCE INTL Multiple Locations	(J):100/500kW::AF
	RADIO FRANCE INTL Via French Guiana	(D):500kW::WAF
	RADIO FRANCE INTL Via Tōkyō, Japan	300kW::SEA
	GERMANY (FR) DEUTSCHE WELLE Via Sri Lanka	(D):250kW::EAS
	JAPAN RADIO JAPAN/NHK Tōkyō-Yamata	300kW::SEA
		(J):300kW::SEA
(con'd)		(D):300kW:GENERAL:NA

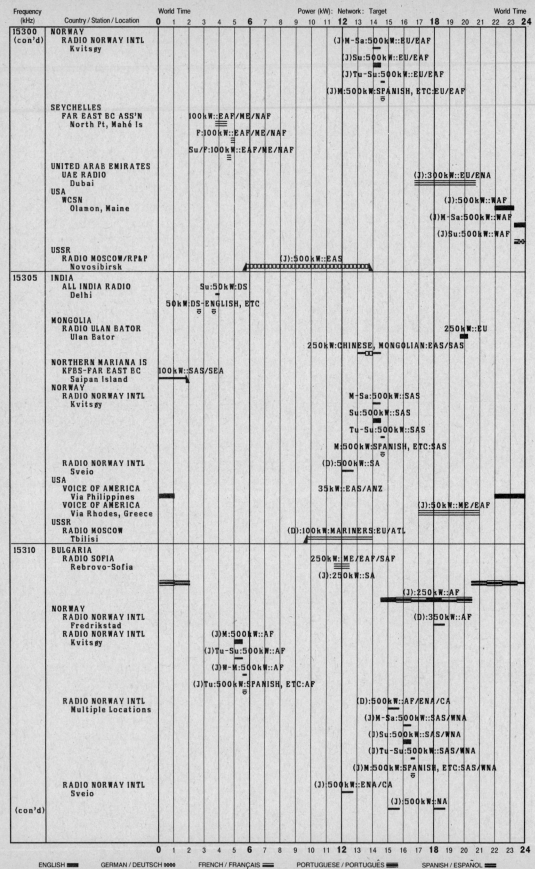

Frequency (kHz)	Country / Station / Location	Schedule
15300 (con'd)	**NORWAY** RADIO NORWAY INTL — Kvitsøy	(J)M-Sa:500kW::EU/EAF
		(J)Su:500kW::EU/EAF
		(J)Tu-Su:500kW::EU/EAF
		(J)M:500kW:SPANISH, ETC:EU/EAF
	SEYCHELLES FAR EAST BC ASS'N — North Pt, Mahé Is	100kW::EAF/ME/NAF
		F:100kW::EAF/ME/NAF
		Su/F:100kW::EAF/ME/NAF
	UNITED ARAB EMIRATES UAE RADIO — Dubai	(J):300kW::EU/ENA
	USA WCSN — Olamon, Maine	(J):500kW::WAF
		(J)M-Sa:500kW::WAF
		(J)Su:500kW::WAF
	USSR RADIO MOSCOW/RP&P — Novosibirsk	(J):500kW::EAS
15305	**INDIA** ALL INDIA RADIO — Delhi	Su:50kW:DS
		50kW:DS-ENGLISH, ETC
	MONGOLIA RADIO ULAN BATOR — Ulan Bator	250kW::EU
		250kW:CHINESE, MONGOLIAN:EAS/SAS
	NORTHERN MARIANA IS KFBS-FAR EAST BC — Saipan Island	100kW::SAS/SEA
	NORWAY RADIO NORWAY INTL — Kvitsøy	M-Sa:500kW::SAS
		Su:500kW::SAS
		Tu-Su:500kW::SAS
		M:500kW:SPANISH, ETC:SAS
	RADIO NORWAY INTL — Sveio	(D):500kW::SA
	USA VOICE OF AMERICA — Via Philippines	35kW::EAS/ANZ
	VOICE OF AMERICA — Via Rhodes, Greece	(J):50kW::ME/EAF
	USSR RADIO MOSCOW — Tbilisi	(D):100kW:MARINERS:EU/ATL
15310	**BULGARIA** RADIO SOFIA — Rebrovo-Sofia	250kW:ME/EAF/SAF
		(J):250kW::SA
		(J):250kW::AF
	NORWAY RADIO NORWAY INTL — Fredrikstad	(D):350kW::AF
	RADIO NORWAY INTL — Kvitsøy	(J)M:500kW::AF
		(J)Tu-Su:500kW::AF
		(J)W-M:500kW::AF
		(J)Tu:500kW:SPANISH, ETC:AF
	RADIO NORWAY INTL — Multiple Locations	(D):500kW::AF/ENA/CA
		(J)M-Sa:500kW::SAS/WNA
		(J)Su:500kW::SAS/WNA
		(J)Tu-Su:500kW::SAS/WNA
		(J)M:500kW:SPANISH, ETC:SAS/WNA
	RADIO NORWAY INTL — Sveio	(J):500kW::ENA/CA
		(J):500kW::NA
(con'd)		

Frequency (kHz)   Country / Station / Location   World Time   Power (kW): Network: Target   World Time

0 1 2 3 4 5 6 7 8 9 10 11 12 13 14 15 16 17 18 19 20 21 22 23 24

ENGLISH ▬▬▬   GERMAN / DEUTSCH ΟΟΟΟ   FRENCH / FRANÇAIS ▬▬   PORTUGUESE / PORTUGUÊS ▬▬   SPANISH / ESPAÑOL ▬▬

ARABIC / ﻋﺮﺑﻰ ≡≡≡   RUSSIAN / РУССКИЙ ═══   CHINESE / 中文 ΟΟΟΟ   JAPANESE / 日本語 ▬▬▬   MULTILINGUAL ▬▬▬   OTHER ▬▬

SUMMER ONLY (J)   WINTER ONLY (D)   JAMMING ∿∿ or / or \   EARLIEST HEARD ◢   LATEST HEARD ◣   † TENTATIVE

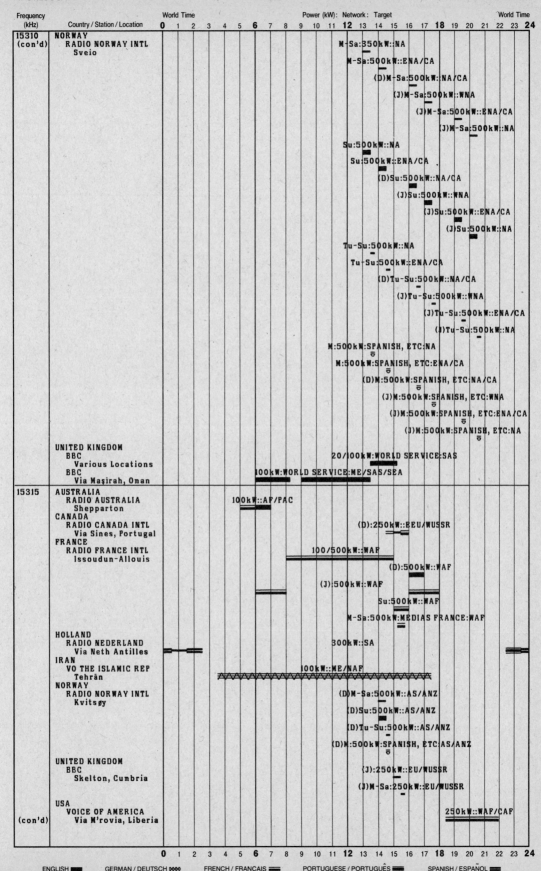

Frequency (kHz)	Country / Station / Location	Power (kW): Network: Target
15310 (con'd)	**NORWAY**	
	RADIO NORWAY INTL	M-Sa:350kW::NA
	Sveio	M-Sa:500kW::ENA/CA
		(D)M-Sa:500kW::NA/CA
		(J)M-Sa:500kW::WNA
		(J)M-Sa:500kW::ENA/CA
		(J)M-Sa:500kW::NA
		Su:500kW::NA
		Su:500kW::ENA/CA
		(D)Su:500kW::NA/CA
		(J)Su:500kW::WNA
		(J)Su:500kW::ENA/CA
		(J)Su:500kW::NA
		Tu-Su:500kW::NA
		Tu-Su:500kW::ENA/CA
		(D)Tu-Su:500kW::NA/CA
		(J)Tu-Su:500kW::WNA
		(J)Tu-Su:500kW::ENA/CA
		(J)Tu-Su:500kW::NA
		M:500kW:SPANISH, ETC:NA
		M:500kW:SPANISH, ETC:ENA/CA
		(D)M:500kW:SPANISH, ETC:NA/CA
		(J)M:500kW:SPANISH, ETC:WNA
		(J)M:500kW:SPANISH, ETC:ENA/CA
		(J)M:500kW:SPANISH, ETC:NA
	UNITED KINGDOM	
	BBC	20/100kW:WORLD SERVICE:SAS
	Various Locations	
	BBC	100kW:WORLD SERVICE:ME/SAS/SEA
	Via Maşirah, Oman	
15315	**AUSTRALIA**	
	RADIO AUSTRALIA	100kW::AF/PAC
	Shepparton	
	CANADA	
	RADIO CANADA INTL	(D):250kW::EEU/WUSSR
	Via Sines, Portugal	
	FRANCE	
	RADIO FRANCE INTL	100/500kW::WAF
	Issoudun-Allouis	(D):500kW::WAF
		(J):500kW::WAF
		Su:500kW::WAF
		M-Sa:500kW:MEDIAS FRANCE:WAF
	HOLLAND	
	RADIO NEDERLAND	300kW::SA
	Via Neth Antilles	
	IRAN	
	VO THE ISLAMIC REP	100kW::ME/NAF
	Tehrān	
	NORWAY	
	RADIO NORWAY INTL	(D)M-Sa:500kW::AS/ANZ
	Kvitsøy	(D)Su:500kW::AS/ANZ
		(D)Tu-Su:500kW::AS/ANZ
		(D)M:500kW:SPANISH, ETC:AS/ANZ
	UNITED KINGDOM	
	BBC	(J):250kW::EU/WUSSR
	Skelton, Cumbria	(J)M-Sa:250kW::EU/WUSSR
	USA	
(con'd)	VOICE OF AMERICA	250kW::WAF/CAF
	Via M'rovia, Liberia	

ENGLISH ▬▬   GERMAN / DEUTSCH ◊◊◊◊   FRENCH / FRANÇAIS ▭▭   PORTUGUESE / PORTUGUÊS ▤▤   SPANISH / ESPAÑOL ▬▬

ARABIC / عربی ▤▤   RUSSIAN / РУССКИИ ▭▭   CHINESE / 中文 ◊◊◊◊   JAPANESE / 日本語 ▨▨▨   MULTILINGUAL ◊◊◊◊   OTHER ▬▬

SUMMER ONLY (J)   WINTER ONLY (D)   JAMMING ∧∧ or / or \   EARLIEST HEARD ◢   LATEST HEARD ◣   + TENTATIVE

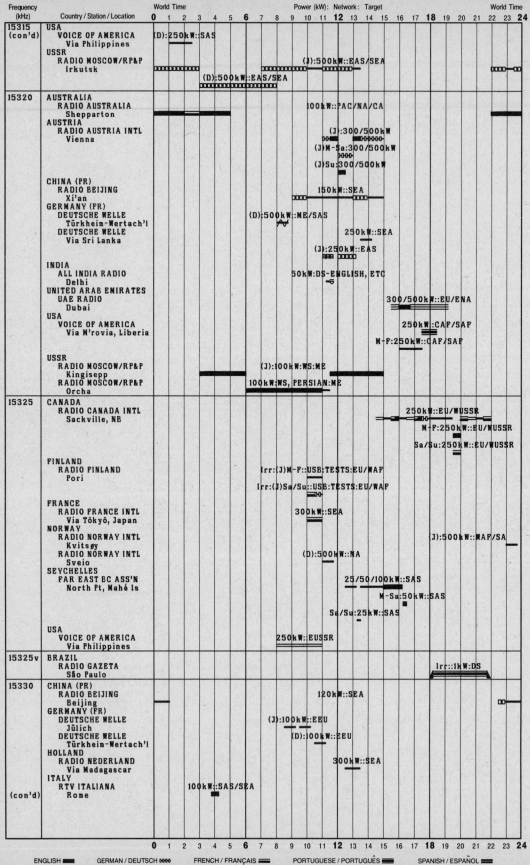

ENGLISH ▬▬   GERMAN / DEUTSCH ◕◕◕◕   FRENCH / FRANÇAIS ▬▬   PORTUGUESE / PORTUGUÊS ▬▬   SPANISH / ESPAÑOL ▬▬

ARABIC / ى‌ف‌ر ▬▬   RUSSIAN / РУССКИИ ▬▬   CHINESE / 中文 ◕◕◕◕   JAPANESE / 日本語 ▬▬   MULTILINGUAL ◕◕◕◕   OTHER ▬▬

SUMMER ONLY (J)   WINTER ONLY (D)   JAMMING ∧∧∧ or / or \   EARLIEST HEARD ◢   LATEST HEARD ◣   + TENTATIVE

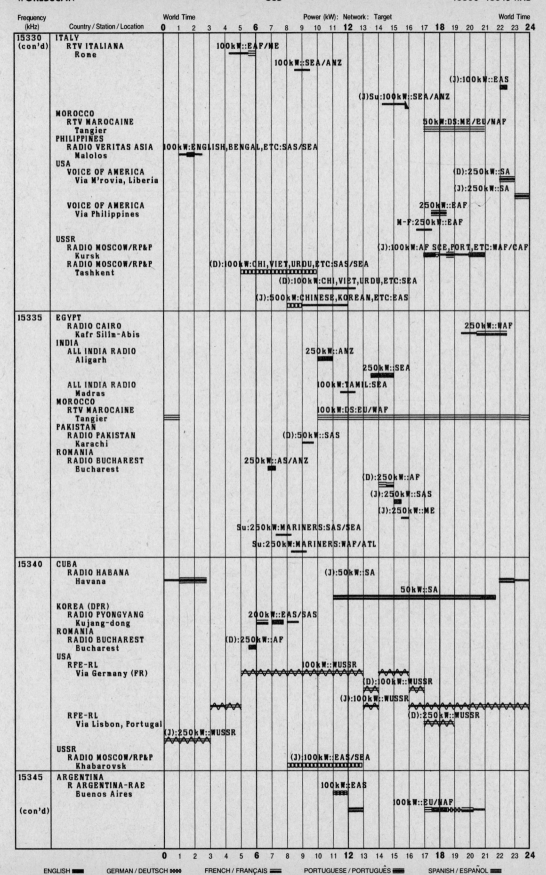

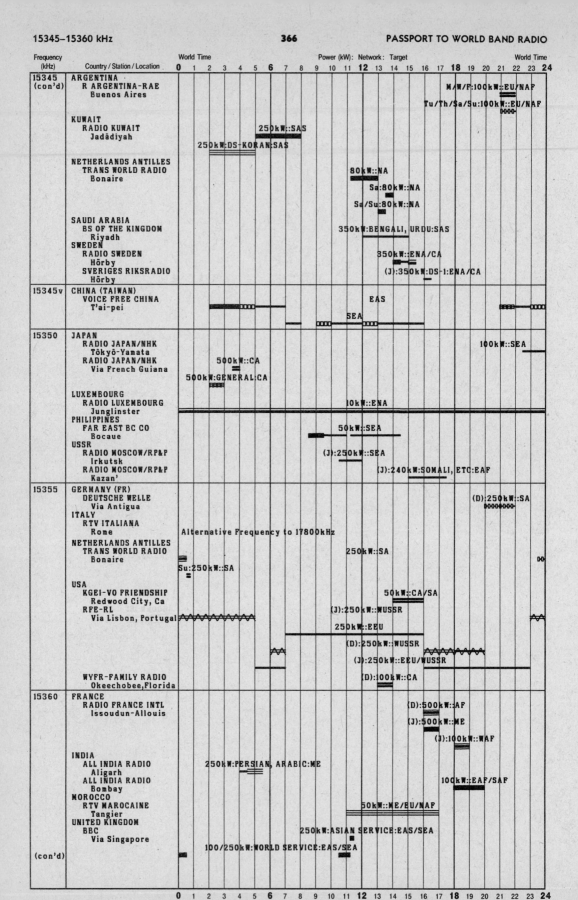

15345 (con'd)

ARGENTINA
R ARGENTINA-RAE
Buenos Aires
— M/W/F:100kW::EU/NAF
— Tu/Th/Sa/Su:100kW::EU/NAF

KUWAIT
RADIO KUWAIT
Jadādiyah
— 250kW::SAS
— 250kW:DS-KORAN:SAS

NETHERLANDS ANTILLES
TRANS WORLD RADIO
Bonaire
— 80kW::NA
— Sa:80kW::NA
— Sa/Su:80kW::NA

SAUDI ARABIA
BS OF THE KINGDOM
Riyadh
— 350kW:BENGALI, URDU:SAS

SWEDEN
RADIO SWEDEN
Hörby
— 350kW::ENA/CA
SVERIGES RIKSRADIO
Hörby
— (J):350kW:DS-1:ENA/CA

15345v

CHINA (TAIWAN)
VOICE FREE CHINA
T'ai-pei
— EAS
— SEA

15350

JAPAN
RADIO JAPAN/NHK
Tōkyō-Yamata
— 100kW::SEA
RADIO JAPAN/NHK
Via French Guiana
— 500kW::CA
— 500kW:GENERAL:CA

LUXEMBOURG
RADIO LUXEMBOURG
Junglinster
— 10kW::ENA

PHILIPPINES
FAR EAST BC CO
Bocaue
— 50kW::SEA

USSR
RADIO MOSCOW/RP&P
Irkutsk
— (J):250kW::SEA
RADIO MOSCOW/RP&P
Kazan'
— (J):240kW:SOMALI, ETC:EAF

15355

GERMANY (FR)
DEUTSCHE WELLE
Via Antigua
— (D):250kW::SA

ITALY
RTV ITALIANA
Rome
— Alternative Frequency to 17800kHz

NETHERLANDS ANTILLES
TRANS WORLD RADIO
Bonaire
— 250kW::SA
— Su:250kW::SA

USA
KGEI-VO FRIENDSHIP
Redwood City, Ca
— 50kW::CA/SA
RFE-RL
Via Lisbon, Portugal
— (J):250kW::WUSSR
— 250kW::EEU
— (D):250kW::WUSSR
— (J):250kW::EEU/WUSSR

WYFR-FAMILY RADIO
Okeechobee,Florida
— (D):100kW::CA

15360

FRANCE
RADIO FRANCE INTL
Issoudun-Allouis
— (D):500kW::AF
— (J):500kW::ME
— (J):100kW::WAF

INDIA
ALL INDIA RADIO
Aligarh
— 250kW:PERSIAN, ARABIC:ME
ALL INDIA RADIO
Bombay
— 100kW::EAF/SAF

MOROCCO
RTV MAROCAINE
Tangier
— 50kW::ME/EU/NAF

UNITED KINGDOM
BBC
Via Singapore
— 250kW:ASIAN SERVICE:EAS/SEA
— 100/250kW:WORLD SERVICE:EAS/SEA

(con'd)

ENGLISH ▮▮▮   GERMAN / DEUTSCH ◇◇◇◇   FRENCH / FRANÇAIS ═══   PORTUGUESE / PORTUGUÊS ▬▬▬   SPANISH / ESPAÑOL ▬▬▬

ARABIC / ﻉﺏﺭ ═══   RUSSIAN / РУССКИЙ ═══   CHINESE / 中文 ◇◇◇◇   JAPANESE / 日本語 ▬▬▬   MULTILINGUAL ◇◇◇◇   OTHER ▬▬▬

SUMMER ONLY (J)   WINTER ONLY (D)   JAMMING ∧∧ or / or \   EARLIEST HEARD ◢   LATEST HEARD ◣   + TENTATIVE

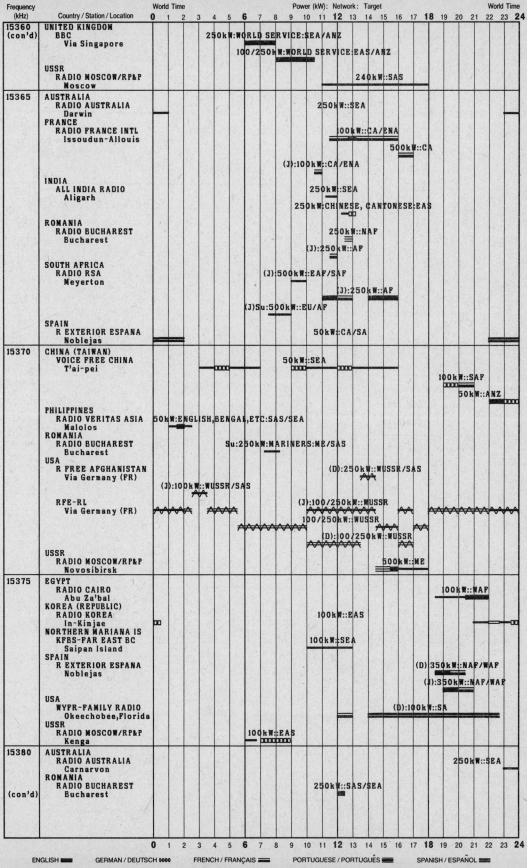

Frequency (kHz)	Country / Station / Location	World Time
15360 (con'd)	**UNITED KINGDOM** BBC Via Singapore	250kW:WORLD SERVICE:SEA/ANZ 100/250kW:WORLD SERVICE:EAS/ANZ
	USSR RADIO MOSCOW/RP&P Moscow	240kW::SAS
15365	**AUSTRALIA** RADIO AUSTRALIA Darwin	250kW::SEA
	FRANCE RADIO FRANCE INTL Issoudun-Allouis	100kW::CA/ENA 500kW::CA (J):100kW::CA/ENA
	INDIA ALL INDIA RADIO Aligarh	250kW::SEA 250kW:CHINESE, CANTONESE:EAS
	ROMANIA RADIO BUCHAREST Bucharest	250kW::NAF (J):250kW::AF
	SOUTH AFRICA RADIO RSA Meyerton	(J):500kW::EAF/SAF (J):250kW::AF (J)Su:500kW::EU/AF
	SPAIN R EXTERIOR ESPANA Noblejas	50kW::CA/SA
15370	**CHINA (TAIWAN)** VOICE FREE CHINA T'ai-pei	50kW::SEA 100kW::SAF 50kW::ANZ
	PHILIPPINES RADIO VERITAS ASIA Malolos	50kW:ENGLISH,BENGAL,ETC:SAS/SEA
	ROMANIA RADIO BUCHAREST Bucharest	Su:250kW:MARINERS:ME/SAS
	USA R FREE AFGHANISTAN Via Germany (FR)	(D):250kW::WUSSR/SAS (J):100kW::WUSSR/SAS
	RFE-RL Via Germany (FR)	(J):100/250kW::WUSSR 100/250kW::WUSSR (D):100/250kW::WUSSR
	USSR RADIO MOSCOW/RP&P Novosibirsk	500kW::ME
15375	**EGYPT** RADIO CAIRO Abu Za'bal	100kW::WAF
	KOREA (REPUBLIC) RADIO KOREA In-Kimjae	100kW::EAS
	NORTHERN MARIANA IS KFBS-FAR EAST BC Saipan Island	100kW::SEA
	SPAIN R EXTERIOR ESPANA Noblejas	(D):350kW::NAF/WAF (J):350kW::NAF/WAF
	USA WYFR-FAMILY RADIO Okeechobee,Florida	(D):100kW::SA
	USSR RADIO MOSCOW/RP&P Kenga	100kW::EAS
15380 (con'd)	**AUSTRALIA** RADIO AUSTRALIA Carnarvon	250kW::SEA
	ROMANIA RADIO BUCHAREST Bucharest	250kW::SAS/SEA

World Time: 0 1 2 3 4 5 6 7 8 9 10 11 12 13 14 15 16 17 18 19 20 21 22 23 24

ENGLISH ▮▮▮   GERMAN / DEUTSCH ᴅᴏᴏᴏ   FRENCH / FRANÇAIS ▬▬   PORTUGUESE / PORTUGUÊS ▬▬   SPANISH / ESPAÑOL ▬▬

ARABIC / ﻋﺮﺑﻰ ≣   RUSSIAN / РУССКИИ ▬   CHINESE / ✳✳ ᴅᴏᴏᴏ   JAPANESE / 日本語 ▬▬   MULTILINGUAL ᴏᴏᴏᴏ   OTHER ▬

SUMMER ONLY (J)   WINTER ONLY (D)   JAMMING /\/\ or / or \   EARLIEST HEARD ◢   LATEST HEARD ◣   ✦ TENTATIVE

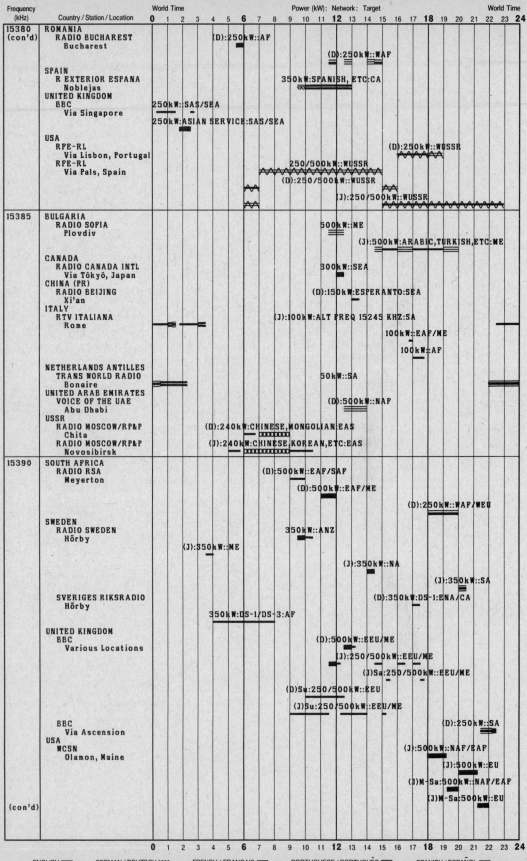

Frequency (kHz)	Country / Station / Location	World Time / Power (kW): Network: Target
15380 (con'd)	**ROMANIA** RADIO BUCHAREST Bucharest	(D):250kW::AF (D):250kW::WAF
	SPAIN R EXTERIOR ESPANA Noblejas	350kW:SPANISH, ETC:CA
	UNITED KINGDOM BBC Via Singapore	250kW::SAS/SEA 250kW:ASIAN SERVICE:SAS/SEA
	USA RFE-RL Via Lisbon, Portugal	(D):250kW::WUSSR
	RFE-RL Via Pals, Spain	250/500kW::WUSSR (D):250/500kW::WUSSR (J):250/500kW::WUSSR
15385	**BULGARIA** RADIO SOFIA Plovdiv	500kW::ME (J):500kW:ARABIC,TURKISH,ETC:ME
	CANADA RADIO CANADA INTL Via Tōkyō, Japan	300kW::SEA
	CHINA (PR) RADIO BEIJING Xi'an	(D):150kW:ESPERANTO:SEA
	ITALY RTV ITALIANA Rome	(J):100kW:ALT FREQ 15245 KHZ:SA 100kW::EAF/ME 100kW::AF
	NETHERLANDS ANTILLES TRANS WORLD RADIO Bonaire	50kW::SA
	UNITED ARAB EMIRATES VOICE OF THE UAE Abu Dhabi	(D):500kW::NAF
	USSR RADIO MOSCOW/RP&P Chita	(D):240kW:CHINESE,MONGOLIAN:EAS
	RADIO MOSCOW/RP&P Novosibirsk	(J):240kW:CHINESE,KOREAN,ETC:EAS
15390	**SOUTH AFRICA** RADIO RSA Meyerton	(D):500kW::EAF/SAF (D):500kW::EAF/ME (D):250kW::WAF/WEU
	SWEDEN RADIO SWEDEN Hörby	350kW::ANZ (J):350kW::ME (J):350kW::NA (J):350kW::SA
	SVERIGES RIKSRADIO Hörby	(D):350kW:DS-1:ENA/CA 350kW:DS-1/DS-3:AF
	UNITED KINGDOM BBC Various Locations	(D):500kW::EEU/ME (J):250/500kW::EEU/ME (J)Sa:250/500kW::EEU/ME (D)Su:250/500kW::EEU (J)Su:250/500kW::EEU/ME
	BBC Via Ascension	(D):250kW::SA
	USA WCSN Olamon, Maine	(J):500kW::NAF/EAF (J):500kW::EU (J)M-Sa:500kW::NAF/EAF (J)M-Sa:500kW::EU
(con'd)		

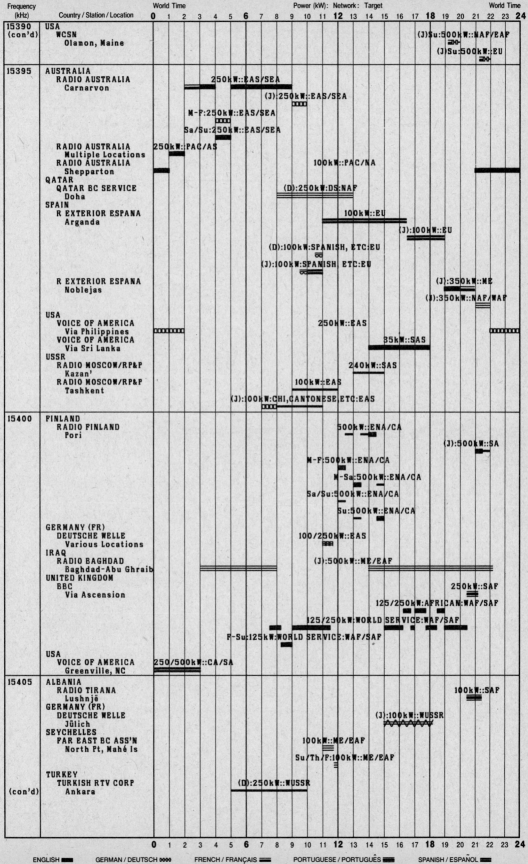

Frequency (kHz)	Country / Station / Location	Power (kW) : Network : Target
15390 (con'd)	USA WCSN Olamon, Maine	(J):Su:500kW::NAF/EAF (J):Su:500kW::EU
15395	AUSTRALIA RADIO AUSTRALIA Carnarvon	250kW::EAS/SEA (J):250kW::EAS/SEA M-F:250kW::EAS/SEA Sa/Su:250kW::EAS/SEA
	RADIO AUSTRALIA Multiple Locations	250kW::PAC/AS
	RADIO AUSTRALIA Shepparton	100kW::PAC/NA
	QATAR QATAR BC SERVICE Doha	(D):250kW:DS:NAF
	SPAIN R EXTERIOR ESPANA Arganda	100kW::EU (J):100kW::EU (D):100kW:SPANISH, ETC:EU (J):100kW:SPANISH, ETC:EU
	R EXTERIOR ESPANA Noblejas	(J):350kW::ME (J):350kW::NAF/WAF
	USA VOICE OF AMERICA Via Philippines	250kW::EAS
	VOICE OF AMERICA Via Sri Lanka	35kW::SAS
	USSR RADIO MOSCOW/RP&P Kazan'	240kW::SAS
	RADIO MOSCOW/RP&P Tashkent	100kW::EAS (J):100kW:CHI,CANTONESE,ETC:EAS
15400	FINLAND RADIO FINLAND Pori	500kW::ENA/CA (J):500kW::SA M-F:500kW::ENA/CA M-Sa:500kW::ENA/CA Sa/Su:500kW::ENA/CA Su:500kW::ENA/CA
	GERMANY (FR) DEUTSCHE WELLE Various Locations	100/250kW::EAS
	IRAQ RADIO BAGHDAD Baghdad-Abu Ghraib	(J):500kW::ME/EAF
	UNITED KINGDOM BBC Via Ascension	250kW::SAF 125/250kW:AFRICAN:WAF/SAF 125/250kW:WORLD SERVICE:WAF/SAF F-Su:125kW:WORLD SERVICE:WAF/SAF
	USA VOICE OF AMERICA Greenville, NC	250/500kW::CA/SA
15405	ALBANIA RADIO TIRANA Lushnjë	100kW::SAF
	GERMANY (FR) DEUTSCHE WELLE Jülich	(J):100kW::WUSSR
	SEYCHELLES FAR EAST BC ASS'N North Pt, Mahé Is	100kW::ME/EAF Su/Th/F:100kW::ME/EAF
(con'd)	TURKEY TURKISH RTV CORP Ankara	(D):250kW::WUSSR

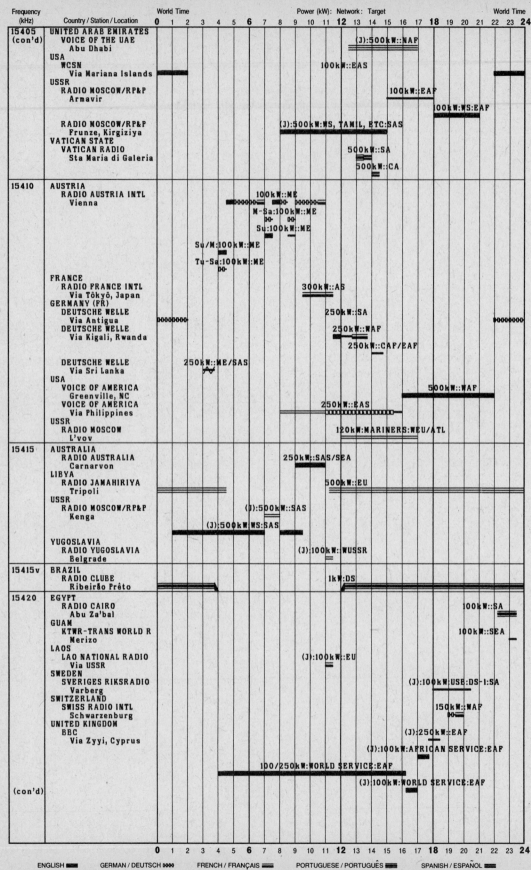

Frequency (kHz)	Country / Station / Location	World Time	Power (kW): Network: Target
15405 (con'd)	UNITED ARAB EMIRATES VOICE OF THE UAE Abu Dhabi		(J):500kW::NAF
	USA WCSN Via Mariana Islands	0–2	100kW::EAS
	USSR RADIO MOSCOW/RP&P Armavir		100kW::EAF
			100kW:WS:EAF
	RADIO MOSCOW/RP&P Frunze, Kirgiziya		(J):500kW:WS, TAMIL, ETC:SAS
	VATICAN STATE VATICAN RADIO Sta Maria di Galeria		500kW::SA
			500kW::CA
15410	AUSTRIA RADIO AUSTRIA INTL Vienna		100kW::ME
			M-Sa:100kW::ME
			Su:100kW::ME
			Su/M:100kW::ME
			Tu-Sa:100kW::ME
	FRANCE RADIO FRANCE INTL Via Tōkyō, Japan		300kW::AS
	GERMANY (FR) DEUTSCHE WELLE Via Antigua		250kW::SA
	DEUTSCHE WELLE Via Kigali, Rwanda		250kW::WAF
			250kW::CAF/EAF
	DEUTSCHE WELLE Via Sri Lanka		250kW::ME/SAS
	USA VOICE OF AMERICA Greenville, NC		500kW::WAF
	VOICE OF AMERICA Via Philippines		250kW::EAS
	USSR RADIO MOSCOW L'vov		120kW:MARINERS:WEU/ATL
15415	AUSTRALIA RADIO AUSTRALIA Carnarvon		250kW::SAS/SEA
	LIBYA RADIO JAMAHIRIYA Tripoli		500kW::EU
	USSR RADIO MOSCOW/RP&P Kenga		(J):500kW::SAS
			(J):500kW:WS:SAS
	YUGOSLAVIA RADIO YUGOSLAVIA Belgrade		(J):100kW:W:USSR
15415v	BRAZIL RADIO CLUBE Ribeirão Prêto		1kW:DS
15420	EGYPT RADIO CAIRO Abu Za'bal		100kW::SA
	GUAM KTWR-TRANS WORLD R Merizo		100kW::SEA
	LAOS LAO NATIONAL RADIO Via USSR		(J):100kW::EU
	SWEDEN SVERIGES RIKSRADIO Varberg		(J):100kW:USE:DS-1:SA
	SWITZERLAND SWISS RADIO INTL Schwarzenburg		150kW::WAF
	UNITED KINGDOM BBC Via Zyyi, Cyprus		(J):250kW::EAF
			(J):100kW:AFRICAN SERVICE:EAF
			100/250kW:WORLD SERVICE:EAF
(con'd)			(J):100kW:WORLD SERVICE:EAF

ENGLISH ▬ GERMAN / DEUTSCH ००० FRENCH / FRANÇAIS ▬ PORTUGUESE / PORTUGUÊS ▬ SPANISH / ESPAÑOL ▬
ARABIC / ▬ RUSSIAN / РУССКИИ ▬ CHINESE / 中文 ०००० JAPANESE / 日本語 ▬ MULTILINGUAL ०००० OTHER ▬
SUMMER ONLY (J) WINTER ONLY (D) JAMMING /\/\ or / or \ EARLIEST HEARD ◀ LATEST HEARD ▶ + TENTATIVE

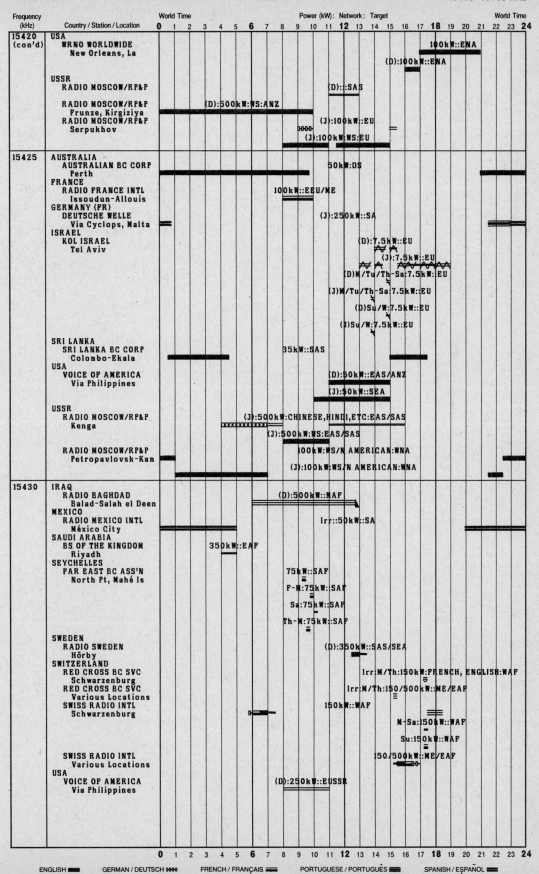

Frequency (kHz)	Country / Station / Location	World Time — Power (kW): Network: Target

15420 (con'd)

USA
　WRNO WORLDWIDE
　　New Orleans, La — 100kW::ENA (17-21); (D):100kW::ENA (16-18)

USSR
　RADIO MOSCOW/RP&P — (D):::SAS (11-12)
　RADIO MOSCOW/RP&P
　　Frunze, Kirgiziya — (D):500kW:WS:ANZ (0-9)
　RADIO MOSCOW/RP&P
　　Serpukhov — (J):100kW::EU; (J):100kW:WS:EU (8-18)

15425

AUSTRALIA
　AUSTRALIAN BC CORP
　　Perth — 50kW:DS
FRANCE
　RADIO FRANCE INTL
　　Issoudun-Allouis — 100kW::EEU/ME (8-12)
GERMANY (FR)
　DEUTSCHE WELLE
　　Via Cyclops, Malta — (J):250kW::SA (11-14)
ISRAEL
　KOL ISRAEL
　　Tel Aviv — (D):7.5kW::EU; (J):7.5kW::EU; (D)M/Tu/Th-Sa:7.5kW::EU; (J)M/Tu/Th-Sa:7.5kW::EU; (D)Su/W:7.5kW::EU; (J)Su/W:7.5kW::EU

SRI LANKA
　SRI LANKA BC CORP
　　Colombo-Ekala — 35kW::SAS
USA
　VOICE OF AMERICA
　　Via Philippines — (D):50kW::EAS/ANZ; (J):50kW::SEA

USSR
　RADIO MOSCOW/RP&P
　　Kenga — (J):500kW:CHINESE,HINDI,ETC:EAS/SAS; (J):500kW:WS:EAS/SAS

　RADIO MOSCOW/RP&P
　　Petropavlovsk-Kam — 100kW:WS/N AMERICAN:WNA; (J):100kW:WS/N AMERICAN:WNA

15430

IRAQ
　RADIO BAGHDAD
　　Balad-Salah el Deen — (D):500kW::NAF
MEXICO
　RADIO MEXICO INTL
　　México City — Irr::50kW::SA
SAUDI ARABIA
　BS OF THE KINGDOM
　　Riyadh — 350kW::EAF
SEYCHELLES
　FAR EAST BC ASS'N
　　North Pt, Mahé Is — 75kW::SAF; F-M:75kW::SAF; Sa:75kW::SAF; Th-M:75kW::SAF

SWEDEN
　RADIO SWEDEN
　　Hörby — (D):350kW::SAS/SEA
SWITZERLAND
　RED CROSS BC SVC
　　Schwarzenburg — Irr:M/Th:150kW:FRENCH, ENGLISH:WAF
　RED CROSS BC SVC
　　Various Locations — Irr:M/Th:150/500kW::ME/EAF
　SWISS RADIO INTL
　　Schwarzenburg — 150kW::WAF; M-Sa:150kW::WAF; Su:150kW::WAF

　SWISS RADIO INTL
　　Various Locations — 150/500kW::ME/EAF
USA
　VOICE OF AMERICA
　　Via Philippines — (D):250kW::EUSSR

ENGLISH ▄▄▄　GERMAN / DEUTSCH ◊◊◊◊　FRENCH / FRANÇAIS ═══　PORTUGUESE / PORTUGUÊS ▬▬▬　SPANISH / ESPAÑOL ▬▬▬

ARABIC /ﻉﺭﻉ ≡≡≡　RUSSIAN / РУССКИИ ═══　CHINESE /✦✕ ▭▭▭▭　JAPANESE / 日本語 ▬▬▬　MULTILINGUAL ◊◊◊◊　OTHER ▬▬▬

SUMMER ONLY (J)　WINTER ONLY (D)　JAMMING ∧∧ or / or \　EARLIEST HEARD ◢　LATEST HEARD ◣　✝ TENTATIVE

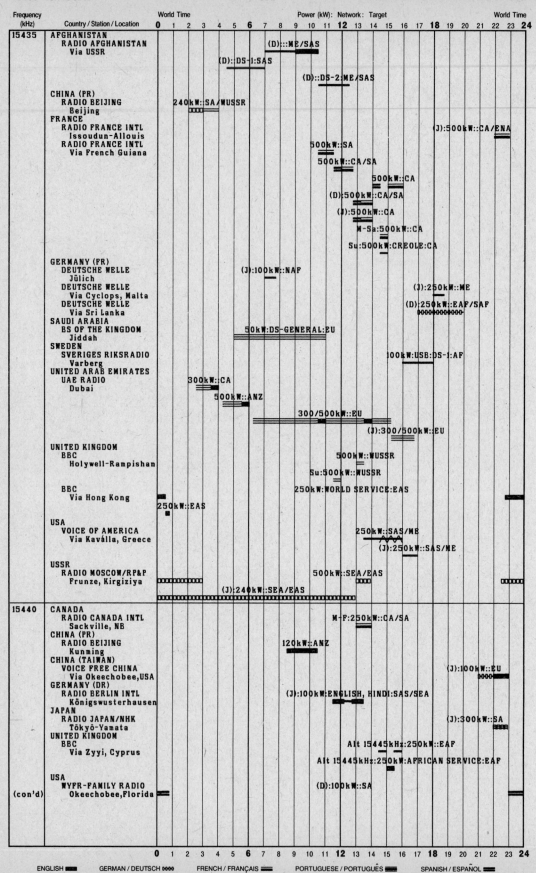

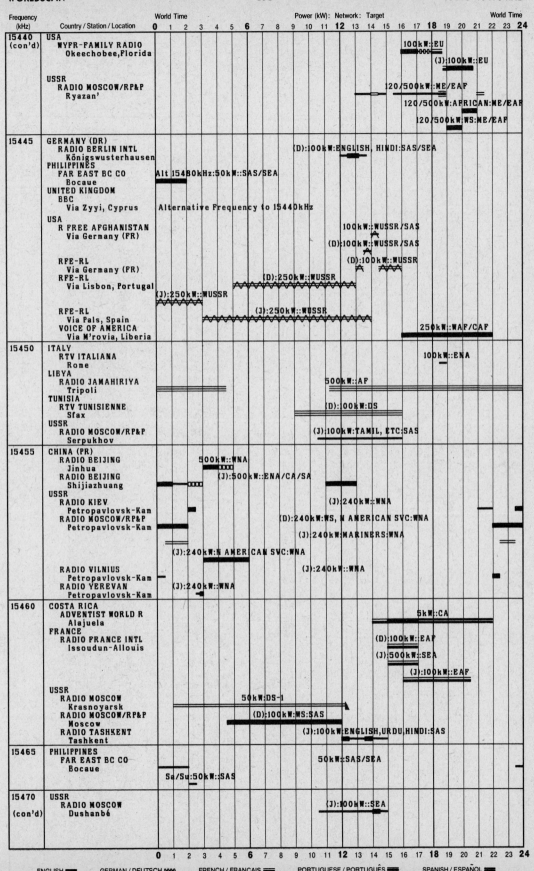

Frequency (kHz)	Country / Station / Location	Power (kW): Network : Target
15440 (con'd)	USA WYFR–FAMILY RADIO Okeechobee, Florida	100kW::EU / (J):100kW::EU
	USSR RADIO MOSCOW/RP&P Ryazan'	120/500kW::ME/EAF / 120/500kW:AFRICAN:ME/EAF / 120/500kW:WS–ME/EAF
15445	GERMANY (DR) RADIO BERLIN INTL Königswusterhausen	(D):100kW:ENGLISH, HINDI:SAS/SEA
	PHILIPPINES FAR EAST BC CO Bocaue	Alt 15480kHz:50kW::SAS/SEA
	UNITED KINGDOM BBC Via Zyyi, Cyprus	Alternative Frequency to 15440kHz
	USA R FREE AFGHANISTAN Via Germany (FR)	100kW::WUSSR/SAS / (D):100kW::WUSSR/SAS
	RFE–RL Via Germany (FR)	(D):100kW::WUSSR
	RFE–RL Via Lisbon, Portugal	(D):250kW::WUSSR / (J):250kW::WUSSR
	RFE–RL Via Pals, Spain	(J):250kW::WUSSR
	VOICE OF AMERICA Via M'rovia, Liberia	250kW::WAF/CAF
15450	ITALY RTV ITALIANA Rome	100kW::ENA
	LIBYA RADIO JAMAHIRIYA Tripoli	500kW::AF
	TUNISIA RTV TUNISIENNE Sfax	(D):100kW:DS
	USSR RADIO MOSCOW/RP&P Serpukhov	(J):100kW:TAMIL, ETC:SAS
15455	CHINA (PR) RADIO BEIJING Jinhua	500kW::WNA
	RADIO BEIJING Shijiazhuang	(J):500kW::ENA/CA/SA
	USSR RADIO KIEV Petropavlovsk-Kam	(J):240kW::WNA
	RADIO MOSCOW/RP&P Petropavlovsk-Kam	(D):240kW:WS, N AMERICAN SVC:WNA / (J):240kW:MARINERS:WNA / (J):240kW:N AMERICAN SVC:WNA
	RADIO VILNIUS Petropavlovsk-Kam	(J):240kW::WNA
	RADIO YEREVAN Petropavlovsk-Kam	(J):240kW::WNA
15460	COSTA RICA ADVENTIST WORLD R Alajuela	5kW::CA
	FRANCE RADIO FRANCE INTL Issoudun-Allouis	(D):100kW::EAF / (J):500kW::SEA / (J):100kW::EAF
	USSR RADIO MOSCOW Krasnoyarsk	50kW:DS-1
	RADIO MOSCOW/RP&P Moscow	(D):100kW:WS:SAS
	RADIO TASHKENT Tashkent	(J):100kW:ENGLISH, URDU, HINDI:SAS
15465	PHILIPPINES FAR EAST BC CO Bocaue	50kW::SAS/SEA / Sa/Su:50kW::SAS
15470 (con'd)	USSR RADIO MOSCOW Dushanbé	(J):100kW::SEA

ENGLISH ▬▬ GERMAN / DEUTSCH ∞∞∞ FRENCH / FRANÇAIS ▭▭ PORTUGUESE / PORTUGUÊS ▬▬ SPANISH / ESPAÑOL ▬▬

ARABIC / ﻋﺮﺑﻲ ▬▬ RUSSIAN / РУССКИЙ ▬▬ CHINESE / ♠☆ ∞∞∞ JAPANESE / 日本語 ▬▬ MULTILINGUAL ∞∞∞ OTHER ▬▬

SUMMER ONLY (J) WINTER ONLY (D) JAMMING ∧∧ or / or \ EARLIEST HEARD ◢ LATEST HEARD ◣ ♦ TENTATIVE

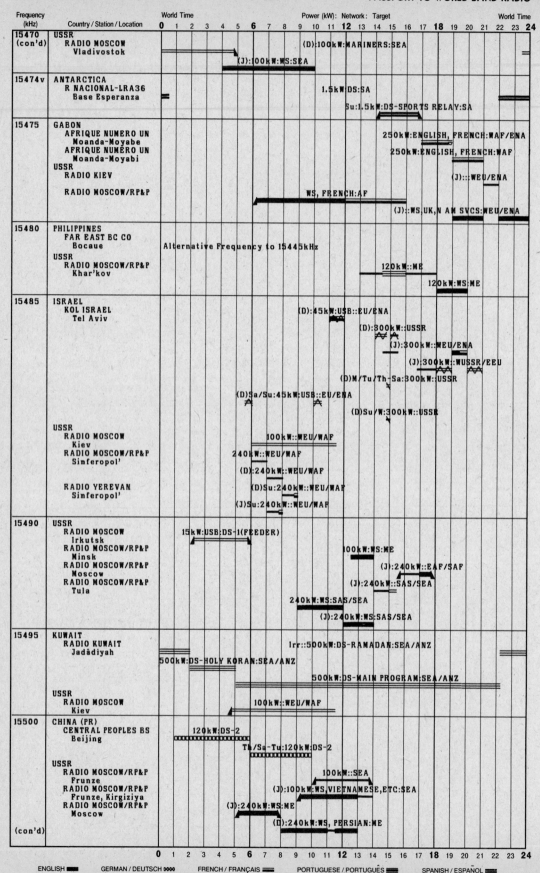

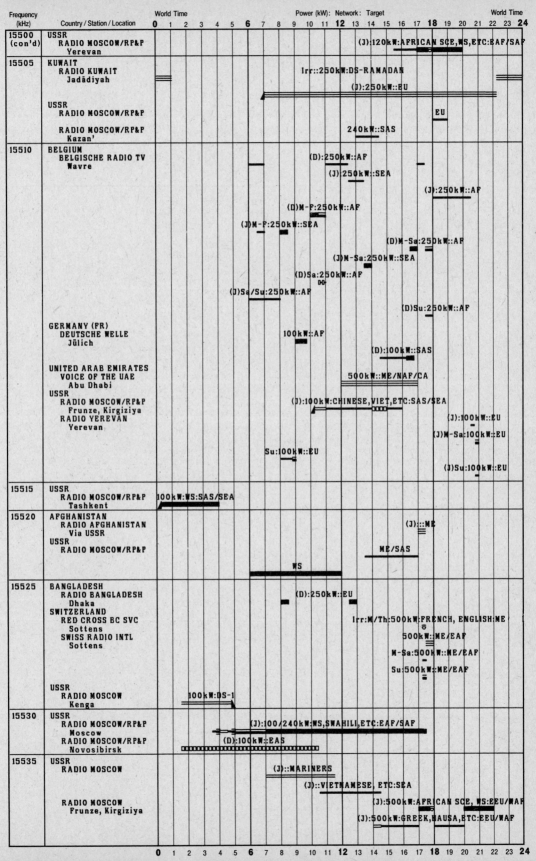

Frequency (kHz)	Country / Station / Location	Schedule (World Time / Power (kW) : Network : Target)
15500 (con'd)	**USSR** RADIO MOSCOW/RP&P Yerevan	(J):120kW:AFRICAN SCE,WS,ETC:EAF/SAF
15505	**KUWAIT** RADIO KUWAIT Jadādiyah	Irr::250kW:DS-RAMADAN / (J):250kW::EU
	USSR RADIO MOSCOW/RP&P	EU
	RADIO MOSCOW/RP&P Kazan'	240kW::SAS
15510	**BELGIUM** BELGISCHE RADIO TV Wavre	(D):250kW::AF / (J):250kW::SEA / (J):250kW::AF / (D)M-F:250kW::AF / (J)M-F:250kW::SEA / (D)M-Sa:250kW::AF / (J)M-Sa:250kW::SEA / (D)Sa:250kW::AF / (J)Sa/Su:250kW::AF / (D)Su:250kW::AF
	GERMANY (FR) DEUTSCHE WELLE Jülich	100kW::AF / (D)::100kW::SAS
	UNITED ARAB EMIRATES VOICE OF THE UAE Abu Dhabi	500kW::ME/NAF/CA
	USSR RADIO MOSCOW/RP&P Frunze, Kirgiziya	(J):100kW:CHINESE,VIET,ETC:SAS/SEA
	RADIO YEREVAN Yerevan	(J):100kW::EU / (J)M-Sa:100kW::EU / Su:100kW::EU / (J)Su:100kW::EU
15515	**USSR** RADIO MOSCOW/RP&P Tashkent	100kW:WS:SAS/SEA
15520	**AFGHANISTAN** RADIO AFGHANISTAN Via USSR	(J):::ME
	USSR RADIO MOSCOW/RP&P	ME/SAS / WS
15525	**BANGLADESH** RADIO BANGLADESH Dhaka	(D):250kW::EU
	SWITZERLAND RED CROSS BC SVC Sottens	Irr:M/Th:500kW:FRENCH, ENGLISH:ME
	SWISS RADIO INTL Sottens	500kW::ME/EAF / M-Sa:500kW::ME/EAF / Su:500kW::ME/EAF
	USSR RADIO MOSCOW Kenga	100kW:DS-1
15530	**USSR** RADIO MOSCOW/RP&P Moscow	(J):100/240kW:WS,SWAHILI,ETC:EAF/SAF
	RADIO MOSCOW/RP&P Novosibirsk	(D):100kW::EAS
15535	**USSR** RADIO MOSCOW	(J)::MARINERS / (J)::VIETNAMESE, ETC:SEA
	RADIO MOSCOW Frunze, Kirgiziya	(J):500kW:AFRICAN SCE, WS:EEU/WAF / (J):500kW:GREEK,HAUSA,ETC:EEU/WAF

ENGLISH ■■■   GERMAN / DEUTSCH ∞∞∞   FRENCH / FRANÇAIS ≡≡≡   PORTUGUESE / PORTUGUÊS ▬▬▬   SPANISH / ESPAÑOL ▬▬▬

ARABIC / العربية ≡≡≡   RUSSIAN / РУССКИИ ═══   CHINESE / 中文 ▫▫▫▫   JAPANESE / 日本語 ▬▬▬   MULTILINGUAL ∞∞∞   OTHER ▬▬

SUMMER ONLY (J)   WINTER ONLY (D)   JAMMING ∧∧ or / or \   EARLIEST HEARD ◢   LATEST HEARD ◣   + TENTATIVE

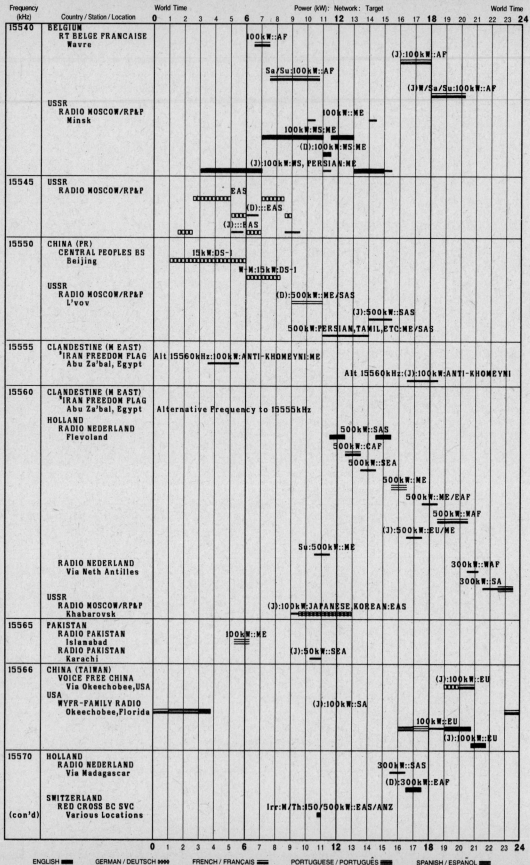

Frequency (kHz)	Country / Station / Location	World Time ... Power (kW): Network: Target ... World Time
15540	BELGIUM RT BELGE FRANCAISE Wavre	100kW::AF / (J):100kW::AF / Sa/Su:100kW::AF / (J)W/Sa/Su:100kW::AF
	USSR RADIO MOSCOW/RP&P Minsk	100kW::ME / 100kW:WS:ME / (D):100kW:WS:ME / (J):100kW:WS, PERSIAN:ME
15545	USSR RADIO MOSCOW/RP&P	EAS / (D):::EAS / (J):::EAS
15550	CHINA (PR) CENTRAL PEOPLES BS Beijing	15kW:DS-1 / W+M:15kW:DS-1
	USSR RADIO MOSCOW/RP&P L'vov	(D):500kW::ME/SAS / (J):500kW::SAS / 500kW:PERSIAN,TAMIL,ETC:ME/SAS
15555	CLANDESTINE (M EAST) 'IRAN FREEDOM FLAG Abu Za'bal, Egypt	Alt 15560kHz:100kW:ANTI-KHOMEYNI:ME / Alt 15560kHz:(J):100kW:ANTI-KHOMEYNI
15560	CLANDESTINE (M EAST) 'IRAN FREEDOM FLAG Abu Za'bal, Egypt	Alternative Frequency to 15555kHz
	HOLLAND RADIO NEDERLAND Flevoland	500kW::SAS / 500kW::CAF / 500kW::SEA / 500kW::ME / 500kW::ME/EAF / 500kW::WAF / (J):500kW::EU/ME / Su:500kW::ME
	RADIO NEDERLAND Via Neth Antilles	300kW::WAF / 300kW::SA
	USSR RADIO MOSCOW/RP&P Khabarovsk	(J):100kW:JAPANESE,KOREAN:EAS
15565	PAKISTAN RADIO PAKISTAN Islamabad	100kW::ME
	RADIO PAKISTAN Karachi	(J):50kW::SEA
15566	CHINA (TAIWAN) VOICE FREE CHINA Via Okeechobee,USA	(J):100kW::EU
	USA WYFR-FAMILY RADIO Okeechobee,Florida	(J):100kW::SA / 100kW::EU / (J):100kW::EU
15570 (con'd)	HOLLAND RADIO NEDERLAND Via Madagascar	300kW::SAS / (D):300kW::EAF
	SWITZERLAND RED CROSS BC SVC Various Locations	Irr:M/Th:150/500kW::EAS/ANZ

ENGLISH ▬ GERMAN / DEUTSCH ∞∞ FRENCH / FRANÇAIS ═ PORTUGUESE / PORTUGUÊS ▦ SPANISH / ESPAÑOL ▬

ARABIC / ﻉﺮﺑ ≡ RUSSIAN / РУССКИИ CHINESE / ★☆ ⬚⬚⬚ JAPANESE / 日本語 MULTILINGUAL ⬚⬚⬚ OTHER ▬

SUMMER ONLY (J) WINTER ONLY (D) JAMMING ∧∧ or / or \ EARLIEST HEARD ◢ LATEST HEARD ◣ + TENTATIVE

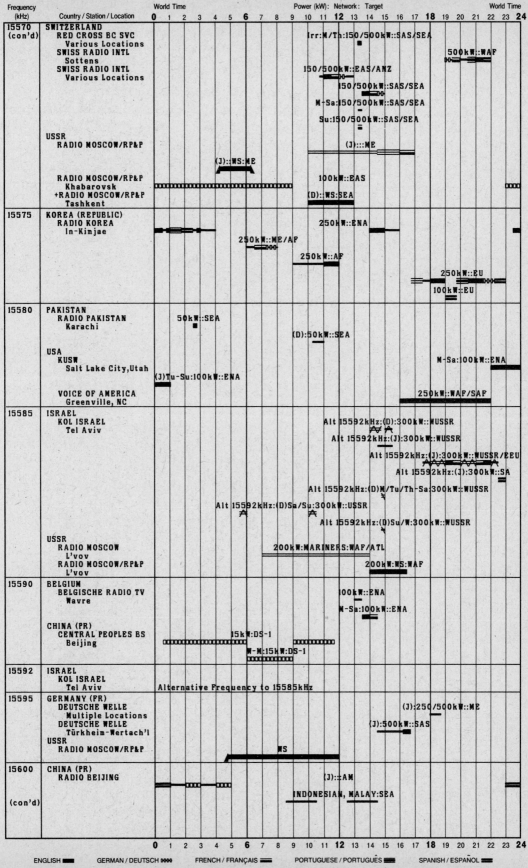

Frequency (kHz)	Country / Station / Location	Details
15570 (con'd)	SWITZERLAND	
	RED CROSS BC SVC — Various Locations	Irr:M/Th:150/500kW::SAS/SEA
	SWISS RADIO INTL — Sottens	500kW::WAF
	SWISS RADIO INTL — Various Locations	150/500kW::EAS/ANZ; 150/500kW::SAS/SEA; M-Sa:150/500kW::SAS/SEA; Su:150/500kW::SAS/SEA
	USSR	
	RADIO MOSCOW/RP&P	(J):::ME; (J)::WS:ME
	RADIO MOSCOW/RP&P — Khabarovsk	100kW::EAS
	+RADIO MOSCOW/RP&P — Tashkent	(D)::WS:SEA
15575	KOREA (REPUBLIC)	
	RADIO KOREA — In-Kimjae	250kW::ENA; 250kW::ME/AF; 250kW::AF; 250kW::EU; 100kW::EU
15580	PAKISTAN	
	RADIO PAKISTAN — Karachi	50kW::SEA; (D):50kW::SEA
	USA	
	KUSW — Salt Lake City, Utah	M-Sa:100kW::ENA; (J)Tu-Su:100kW::ENA
	VOICE OF AMERICA — Greenville, NC	250kW::WAF/SAF
15585	ISRAEL	
	KOL ISRAEL — Tel Aviv	Alt 15592kHz:(D):300kW::WUSSR; Alt 15592kHz:(J):300kW::WUSSR; Alt 15592kHz:(J):300kW::WUSSR/EEU; Alt 15592kHz:(J):300kW::SA; Alt 15592kHz:(D)M/Tu/Th-Sa:300kW::WUSSR; Alt 15592kHz:(D)Sa/Su:300kW::USSR; Alt 15592kHz:(D)Su/W:300kW::WUSSR
	USSR	
	RADIO MOSCOW — L'vov	200kW:MARINERS:WAF/ATL
	RADIO MOSCOW/RP&P — L'vov	200kW:WS:WAF
15590	BELGIUM	
	BELGISCHE RADIO TV — Wavre	100kW::ENA; M-Sa:100kW::ENA
	CHINA (PR)	
	CENTRAL PEOPLES BS — Beijing	15kW:DS-1; W-M:15kW:DS-1
15592	ISRAEL	
	KOL ISRAEL — Tel Aviv	Alternative Frequency to 15585kHz
15595	GERMANY (PR)	
	DEUTSCHE WELLE — Multiple Locations	(J):250/500kW::ME
	DEUTSCHE WELLE — Türkheim-Wertach'l	(J):500kW::SAS
	USSR	
	RADIO MOSCOW/RP&P	WS
15600 (con'd)	CHINA (PR)	
	RADIO BEIJING	(J):::AM; INDONESIAN, MALAY:SEA

ENGLISH ▆   GERMAN / DEUTSCH ∞∞∞   FRENCH / FRANÇAIS ▬   PORTUGUESE / PORTUGUÊS ▭   SPANISH / ESPAÑOL ▬

ARABIC / ﻋﺮﺑﻲ ▬   RUSSIAN / РУССКИИ ▬   CHINESE / 中文 ▭▭   JAPANESE / 日本語 ▬   MULTILINGUAL ▭▭▭   OTHER ▬

SUMMER ONLY (J)   WINTER ONLY (D)   JAMMING ∧∧∧ or / or \   EARLIEST HEARD ◢   LATEST HEARD ◣   + TENTATIVE

Frequency (kHz)	Country / Station / Location	World Time / Power (kW): Network: Target

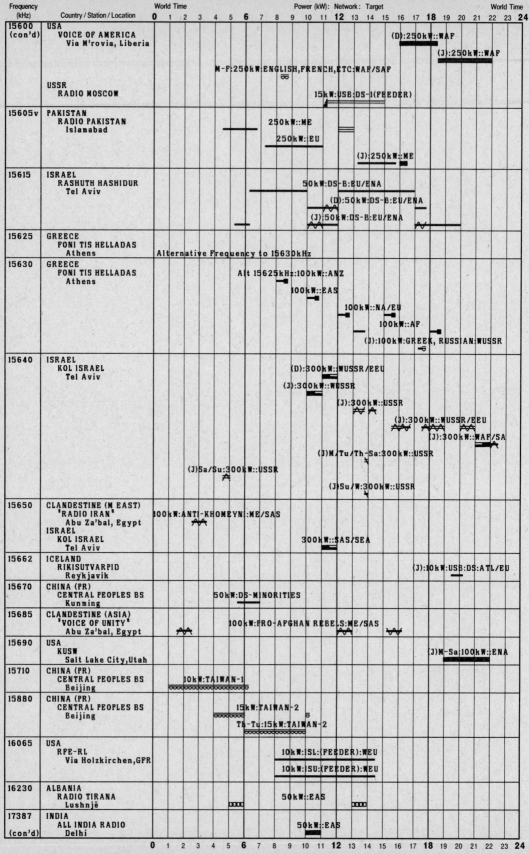

15600 (con'd) — USA — VOICE OF AMERICA, Via M'rovia, Liberia
- (D):250kW::WAF
- (J):250kW::WAF
- M-F:250kW:ENGLISH,FRENCH,ETC:WAF/SAF

USSR — RADIO MOSCOW
- 15kW:USB:DS-1(FEEDER)

15605v — PAKISTAN — RADIO PAKISTAN, Islamabad
- 250kW::ME
- 250kW::EU
- (J):250kW::ME

15615 — ISRAEL — RASHUTH HASHIDUR, Tel Aviv
- 50kW:DS-B:EU/ENA
- (D):50kW:DS-B:EU/ENA
- (J):50kW:DS-B:EU/ENA

15625 — GREECE — FONI TIS HELLADAS, Athens
- Alternative Frequency to 15630kHz

15630 — GREECE — FONI TIS HELLADAS, Athens
- Alt 15625kHz:100kW::ANZ
- 100kW::EAS
- 100kW::NA/EU
- 100kW::AF
- (J):100kW:GREEK, RUSSIAN:WUSSR

15640 — ISRAEL — KOL ISRAEL, Tel Aviv
- (D):300kW::WUSSR/EEU
- (J):300kW::WUSSR
- (J):300kW::USSR
- (J):300kW::WUSSR/EEU
- (J):300kW::WAF/SA
- (J)M/Tu/Th-Sa:300kW::USSR
- (J)Sa/Su:300kW::USSR
- (J)Su/W:300kW::USSR

15650 — CLANDESTINE (M EAST) — "RADIO IRAN", Abu Za'bal, Egypt
- 100kW:ANTI-KHOMEYNI:ME/SAS

ISRAEL — KOL ISRAEL, Tel Aviv
- 300kW:SAS/SEA

15662 — ICELAND — RIKISUTVARPID, Reykjavik
- (J):10kW:USB:DS:ATL/EU

15670 — CHINA (PR) — CENTRAL PEOPLES BS, Kunming
- 50kW:DS-MINORITIES

15685 — CLANDESTINE (ASIA) — "VOICE OF UNITY", Abu Za'bal, Egypt
- 100kW:PRO-AFGHAN REBELS:ME/SAS

15690 — USA — KUSW, Salt Lake City, Utah
- (J)M-Sa:100kW::ENA

15710 — CHINA (PR) — CENTRAL PEOPLES BS, Beijing
- 10kW:TAIWAN-1

15880 — CHINA (PR) — CENTRAL PEOPLES BS, Beijing
- 15kW:TAIWAN-2
- Th-Tu:15kW:TAIWAN-2

16065 — USA — RFE-RL, Via Holzkirchen, GFR
- 10kW:ISL:(FEEDER):WEU
- 10kW:ISU:(FEEDER):WEU

16230 — ALBANIA — RADIO TIRANA, Lushnjë
- 50kW::EAS

17387 (con'd) — INDIA — ALL INDIA RADIO, Delhi
- 50kW::EAS

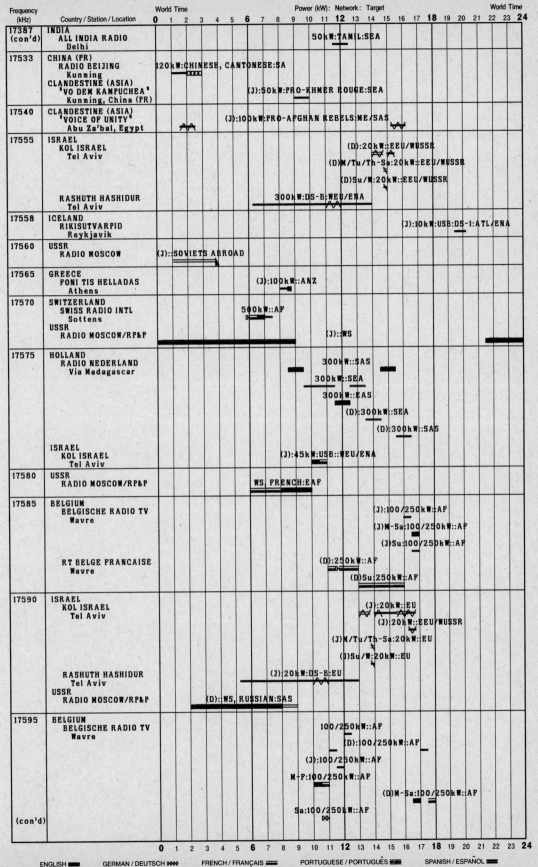

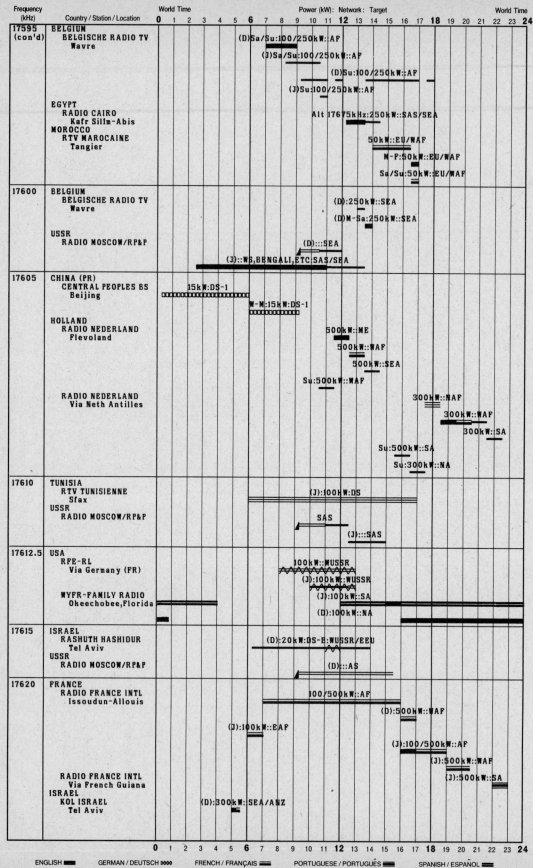

Frequency (kHz)	Country / Station / Location	Schedule
17595 (con'd)	BELGIUM BELGISCHE RADIO TV Wavre	(D)Sa/Su:100/250kW:AF (J)Sa/Su:100/250kW::AF (D)Su:100/250kW::AF (J)Su:100/250kW::AF
	EGYPT RADIO CAIRO Kafr Sillm-Abis	Alt 17675kHz:250kW::SAS/SEA
	MOROCCO RTV MAROCAINE Tangier	50kW::EU/WAF M-F:50kW::EU/WAF Sa/Su:50kW::EU/WAF
17600	BELGIUM BELGISCHE RADIO TV Wavre	(D):250kW::SEA (D)M-Sa:250kW::SEA
	USSR RADIO MOSCOW/RP&P	(D):::SEA (J)::WS,BENGALI,ETC.SAS/SEA
17605	CHINA (PR) CENTRAL PEOPLES BS Beijing	15kW:DS-1 W-M:15kW:DS-1
	HOLLAND RADIO NEDERLAND Flevoland	500kW::ME 500kW::WAF 500kW::SEA Su:500kW::WAF
	RADIO NEDERLAND Via Neth Antilles	300kW::NAF 300kW::WAF 300kW::SA Su:500kW::SA Su:300kW::NA
17610	TUNISIA RTV TUNISIENNE Sfax	(J):100kW:DS
	USSR RADIO MOSCOW/RP&P	SAS (J):::SAS
17612.5	USA RFE-RL Via Germany (FR)	100kW::WUSSR (J):100kW::WUSSR
	WYFR-FAMILY RADIO Okeechobee,Florida	(J):100kW::SA (D):100kW::NA
17615	ISRAEL RASHUTH HASHIDUR Tel Aviv	(D):20kW:DS-E:WUSSR/EEU
	USSR RADIO MOSCOW/RP&P	(D):::AS
17620	FRANCE RADIO FRANCE INTL Issoudun-Allouis	100/500kW::AF (D):500kW::WAF (J):100kW::EAP (J):100/500kW::AF (J):500kW::WAF (J):500kW::SA
	RADIO FRANCE INTL Via French Guiana	
	ISRAEL KOL ISRAEL Tel Aviv	(D):300kW::SEA/ANZ

        0 1 2 3 4 5 6 7 8 9 10 11 12 13 14 15 16 17 18 19 20 21 22 23 24

ENGLISH ▃▃▃   GERMAN / DEUTSCH ◊◊◊◊   FRENCH / FRANÇAIS ▬▬   PORTUGUESE / PORTUGUÊS ▬▬   SPANISH / ESPAÑOL ▬▬

ARABIC / ﺍﻟﻌﺮﺑﻴﺔ ▬▬   RUSSIAN / РУССКИИ ▬▬   CHINESE / ✶✶ ◻◻◻◻   JAPANESE / 日本語 ▬▬   MULTILINGUAL ▭▭▭   OTHER ▬▬

SUMMER ONLY (J)   WINTER ONLY (D)   JAMMING ⋀⋀ or / or \   EARLIEST HEARD ◢   LATEST HEARD ◣   ⁺ TENTATIVE

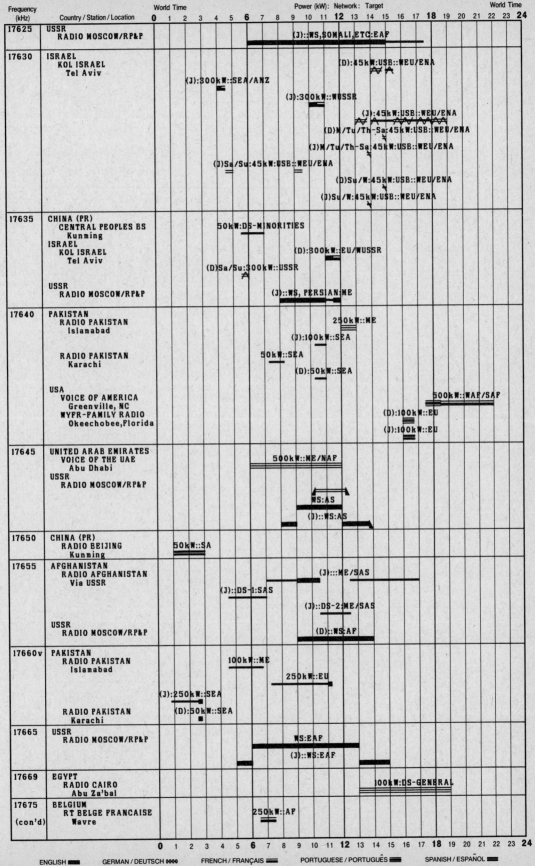

17625 USSR
RADIO MOSCOW/RP&P — (J)::WS,SOMALI,ETC:EAF

17630 ISRAEL
KOL ISRAEL
Tel Aviv — (D):45kW:USB::WEU/ENA
(J):300kW::SEA/ANZ
(J):300kW::WUSSR
(J):45kW:USB::WEU/ENA
(D)M/Tu/Th-Sa:45kW:USB::WEU/ENA
(J)M/Tu/Th-Sa:45kW:USB::WEU/ENA
(J)Sa/Su:45kW:USB::WEU/ENA
(D)Su/W:45kW:USB::WEU/ENA
(J)Su/W:45kW:USB::WEU/ENA

17635 CHINA (PR)
CENTRAL PEOPLES BS
Kunming — 50kW:DS-MINORITIES
ISRAEL
KOL ISRAEL
Tel Aviv — (D):300kW::EU/WUSSR
(D)Sa/Su:300kW::USSR
USSR
RADIO MOSCOW/RP&P — (J)::WS, PERSIAN:ME

17640 PAKISTAN
RADIO PAKISTAN
Islamabad — 250kW::ME
(J):100kW::SEA
RADIO PAKISTAN
Karachi — 50kW::SEA
(D):50kW::SEA
USA
VOICE OF AMERICA
Greenville, NC — 500kW::WAF/SAF
WYFR-FAMILY RADIO
Okeechobee,Florida — (D):100kW::EU
(J):100kW::EU

17645 UNITED ARAB EMIRATES
VOICE OF THE UAE
Abu Dhabi — 500kW::ME/NAF
USSR
RADIO MOSCOW/RP&P — WS:AS
(D)::WS:AS

17650 CHINA (PR)
RADIO BEIJING
Kunming — 50kW::SA

17655 AFGHANISTAN
RADIO AFGHANISTAN
Via USSR — (J):::ME/SAS
(J)::DS-1:SAS
(J)::DS-2:ME/SAS
USSR
RADIO MOSCOW/RP&P — (D)::WS:AF

17660v PAKISTAN
RADIO PAKISTAN
Islamabad — 100kW::ME
250kW::EU
(J):250kW::SEA
RADIO PAKISTAN
Karachi — (D):50kW::SEA

17665 USSR
RADIO MOSCOW/RP&P — WS:EAF
(J)::WS:EAF

17669 EGYPT
RADIO CAIRO
Abu Za'bal — 100kW:DS-GENERAL

17675 BELGIUM
RT BELGE FRANCAISE
(con'd) Wavre — 250kW::AF

ENGLISH ▬▬ GERMAN / DEUTSCH ००० FRENCH / FRANÇAIS ═══ PORTUGUESE / PORTUGUÊS ═══ SPANISH / ESPAÑOL ▬▬

ARABIC /ﻉﺏﺭ ═══ RUSSIAN / РУССКИЙ ▬▬ CHINESE / 中文 ०००० JAPANESE / 日本語 ▬▬ MULTILINGUAL ०००० OTHER ▬▬

SUMMER ONLY (J)   WINTER ONLY (D)   JAMMING ∧∧ or / or \   EARLIEST HEARD ◢   LATEST HEARD ◣   + TENTATIVE

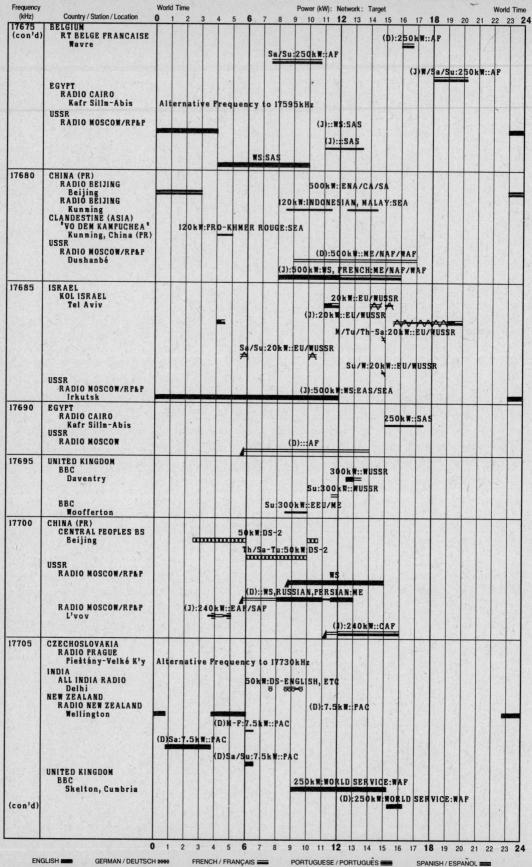

The table charts for frequencies 17675 to 17705 kHz, showing World Time (0–24), Frequency (kHz), Country / Station / Location, and Power (kW): Network : Target.

17675 (con'd)

- **BELGIUM** — RT BELGE FRANCAISE, Wavre
  - (D):250kW::AF
  - Sa/Su:250kW::AF
  - (J)W/Sa/Su:250kW::AF
- **EGYPT** — RADIO CAIRO, Kafr Sillm-Abis — Alternative Frequency to 17595kHz
- **USSR** — RADIO MOSCOW/RP&P
  - (J)::WS:SAS
  - (J)::SAS
  - WS:SAS

17680

- **CHINA (PR)** — RADIO BEIJING, Beijing — 500kW:ENA/CA/SA
- **RADIO BEIJING**, Kunming — 120kW:INDONESIAN, MALAY:SEA
- **CLANDESTINE (ASIA)** — 'VO DEM KAMPUCHEA', Kunming, China (PR) — 120kW:PRO-KHMER ROUGE:SEA
- **USSR** — RADIO MOSCOW/RP&P, Dushanbé
  - (D):500kW::ME/NAF/WAF
  - (J):500kW:WS, FRENCH:ME/NAF/WAF

17685

- **ISRAEL** — KOL ISRAEL, Tel Aviv
  - 20kW::EU/WUSSR
  - (J):20kW::EU/WUSSR
  - M/Tu/Th-Sa:20kW::EU/WUSSR
  - Sa/Su:20kW::EU/WUSSR
  - Su/W:20kW::EU/WUSSR
- **USSR** — RADIO MOSCOW/RP&P, Irkutsk — (J):500kW:WS:EAS/SEA

17690

- **EGYPT** — RADIO CAIRO, Kafr Sillm-Abis — 250kW::SAS
- **USSR** — RADIO MOSCOW — (D)::AF

17695

- **UNITED KINGDOM** — BBC, Daventry
  - 300kW::WUSSR
  - Su:300kW::WUSSR
- **BBC**, Woofferton — Su:300kW::EEU/ME

17700

- **CHINA (PR)** — CENTRAL PEOPLES BS, Beijing
  - 50kW:DS-2
  - Th/Sa-Tu:50kW:DS-2
- **USSR** — RADIO MOSCOW/RP&P
  - WS
  - (D)::WS,RUSSIAN,PERSIAN:ME
- **RADIO MOSCOW/RP&P**, L'vov
  - (J):240kW::EAF/SAF
  - (J):240kW::CAF

17705

- **CZECHOSLOVAKIA** — RADIO PRAGUE, Piešťany-Velké K'y — Alternative Frequency to 17730kHz
- **INDIA** — ALL INDIA RADIO, Delhi — 50kW:DS-ENGLISH, ETC
- **NEW ZEALAND** — RADIO NEW ZEALAND, Wellington
  - (D):7.5kW::PAC
  - (D)M-F:7.5kW::PAC
  - (D)Sa:7.5kW::PAC
  - (D)Sa/Su:7.5kW::PAC
- **UNITED KINGDOM** — BBC, Skelton, Cumbria
  - 250kW:WORLD SERVICE:WAF
  - (D):250kW:WORLD SERVICE:WAF

(con'd)

ENGLISH ▪▪▪   GERMAN / DEUTSCH ▨▨▨   FRENCH / FRANÇAIS ▭▭▭   PORTUGUESE / PORTUGUÊS ▤▤▤   SPANISH / ESPAÑOL ▬▬

ARABIC / ﻋﺮﺑﻲ ▭▭   RUSSIAN / РУССКИИ ▭▭   CHINESE / 中文 ▭▭▭   JAPANESE / 日本語 ▬▬   MULTILINGUAL ▨▨   OTHER ▬▬

SUMMER ONLY (J)   WINTER ONLY (D)   JAMMING ∧∧∧ or / or \   EARLIEST HEARD ◢   LATEST HEARD ◣   ✦ TENTATIVE

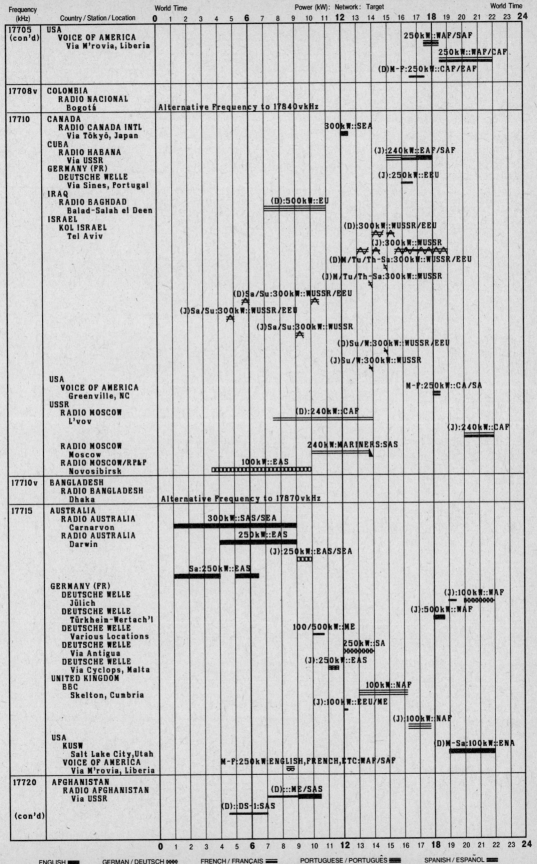

Frequency (kHz)	Country / Station / Location		Power (kW): Network: Target
17705 (con'd)	USA — VOICE OF AMERICA, Via M'rovia, Liberia		250kW::WAF/SAF / 250kW::WAF/CAF / (D)M–F:250kW::CAF/EAF
17708v	COLOMBIA — RADIO NACIONAL, Bogotá		Alternative Frequency to 17840vkHz
17710	CANADA — RADIO CANADA INTL, Via Tōkyō, Japan		300kW::SEA
	CUBA — RADIO HABANA, Via USSR		(J):240kW::EAF/SAF
	GERMANY (FR) — DEUTSCHE WELLE, Via Sines, Portugal		(J):250kW::EEU
	IRAQ — RADIO BAGHDAD, Balad-Salah el Deen		(D):500kW::EU
	ISRAEL — KOL ISRAEL, Tel Aviv		(D):300kW::WUSSR/EEU / (J):300kW::WUSSR / (D)M/Tu/Th-Sa:300kW::WUSSR/EEU / (J)M/Tu/Th-Sa:300kW::WUSSR / (D)Sa/Su:300kW::WUSSR/EEU / (J)Sa/Su:300kW::WUSSR/EEU / (J)Sa/Su:300kW::WUSSR / (D)Su/W:300kW::WUSSR/EEU / (J)Su/W:300kW::WUSSR
	USA — VOICE OF AMERICA, Greenville, NC		M–F:250kW::CA/SA
	USSR — RADIO MOSCOW, L'vov		(D):240kW::CAF / (J):240kW::CAF
	RADIO MOSCOW, Moscow		240kW:MARINERS:SAS
	RADIO MOSCOW/RP&P, Novosibirsk		100kW::EAS
17710v	BANGLADESH — RADIO BANGLADESH, Dhaka		Alternative Frequency to 17870vkHz
17715	AUSTRALIA — RADIO AUSTRALIA, Carnarvon		300kW::SAS/SEA
	RADIO AUSTRALIA, Darwin		250kW::EAS / (J):250kW::EAS/SEA / Sa:250kW::EAS
	GERMANY (FR) — DEUTSCHE WELLE, Jülich		(J):100kW::WAF
	DEUTSCHE WELLE, Türkheim-Wertach'l		(J):500kW::WAF
	DEUTSCHE WELLE, Various Locations		100/500kW::ME
	DEUTSCHE WELLE, Via Antigua		250kW::SA
	DEUTSCHE WELLE, Via Cyclops, Malta		(J):250kW::EAS
	UNITED KINGDOM — BBC, Skelton, Cumbria		100kW::NAF / (J):100kW::EEU/ME / (J):100kW::NAF
	USA — KUSW, Salt Lake City, Utah		(D)M–Sa:100kW::ENA
	VOICE OF AMERICA, Via M'rovia, Liberia		M–F:250kW:ENGLISH,FRENCH,ETC:WAF/SAF
17720 (con'd)	AFGHANISTAN — RADIO AFGHANISTAN, Via USSR		(D):::ME/SAS / (D)::DS-1:SAS

ENGLISH ▬ GERMAN / DEUTSCH ∞∞∞ FRENCH / FRANÇAIS ▬ PORTUGUESE / PORTUGUÊS ▬ SPANISH / ESPAÑOL ▬

ARABIC / عربى ▬ RUSSIAN / РУССКИЙ ▬ CHINESE / 中文 ▭▭ JAPANESE / 日本語 ▬ MULTILINGUAL ∞∞∞ OTHER ▬

SUMMER ONLY (J)   WINTER ONLY (D)   JAMMING ∧∧ or / or \   EARLIEST HEARD ◢   LATEST HEARD ◣   + TENTATIVE

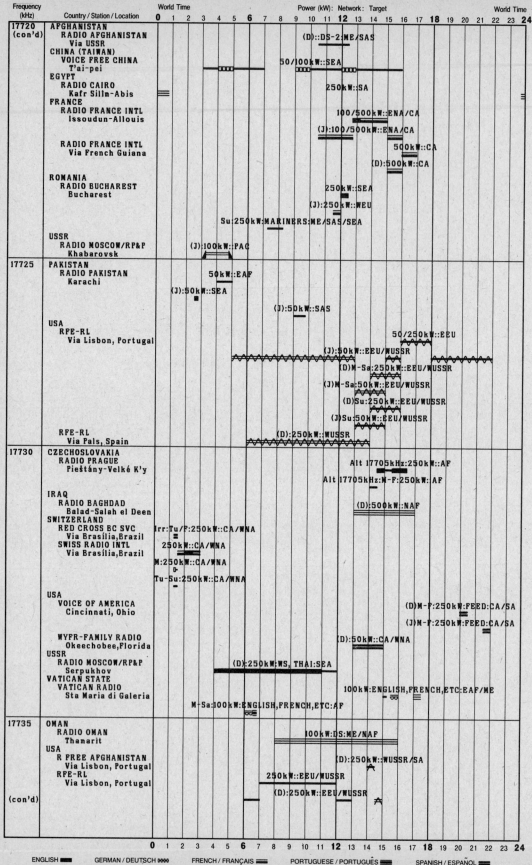

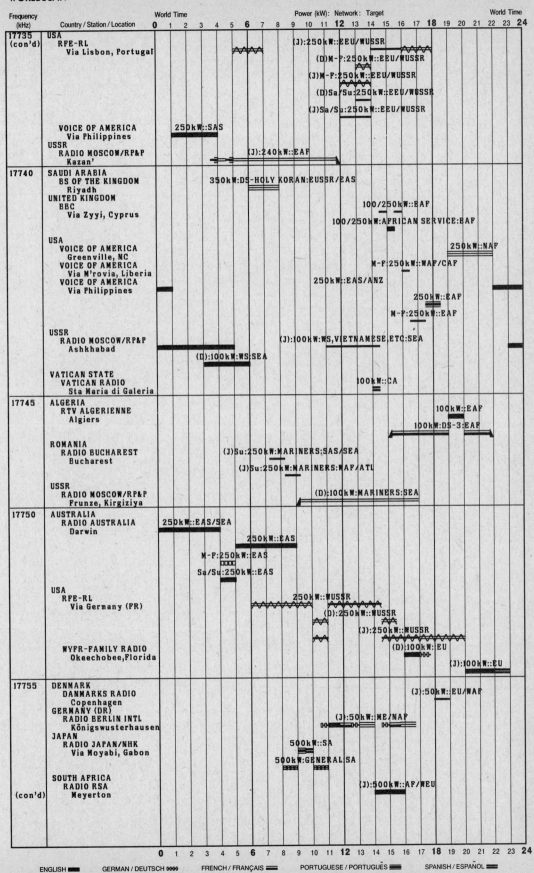

Frequency (kHz)	Country / Station / Location	World Time	Power (kW): Network: Target	World Time

17735 (con'd) — USA
- RFE-RL Via Lisbon, Portugal — (J):250kW::EEU/WUSSR; (D)M-F:250kW::EEU/WUSSR; (J)M-F:250kW:EEU/WUSSR; (D)Sa/Su:250kW::EEU/WUSSR; (J)Sa/Su:250kW::EEU/WUSSR
- VOICE OF AMERICA Via Philippines — 250kW::SAS
- USSR RADIO MOSCOW/RP&P Kazan' — (J):240kW::EAF

17740 — SAUDI ARABIA
- BS OF THE KINGDOM Riyadh — 350kW:DS-HOLY KORAN:EUSSR/EAS
- UNITED KINGDOM BBC Via Zyyi, Cyprus — 100/250kW::EAF; 100/250kW:AFRICAN SERVICE:EAF
- USA VOICE OF AMERICA Greenville, NC — 250kW::NAF
- VOICE OF AMERICA Via M'rovia, Liberia — M-F:250kW::WAF/CAF
- VOICE OF AMERICA Via Philippines — 250kW::EAS/ANZ; 250kW::EAF; M-F:250kW::EAF
- USSR RADIO MOSCOW/RP&P Ashkhabad — (J):100kW:WS,VIETNAMESE,ETC:SEA; (D):100kW:WS:SEA
- VATICAN STATE VATICAN RADIO Sta Maria di Galeria — 100kW::CA

17745 — ALGERIA
- RTV ALGERIENNE Algiers — 100kW::EAF; 100kW:DS-3:EAF
- ROMANIA RADIO BUCHAREST Bucharest — (J)Su:250kW:MARINERS:SAS/SEA; (J)Su:250kW:MARINERS:WAF/ATL
- USSR RADIO MOSCOW/RP&P Frunze, Kirgiziya — (D):100kW:MARINERS:SEA

17750 — AUSTRALIA
- RADIO AUSTRALIA Darwin — 250kW::EAS/SEA; 250kW::EAS; M-F:250kW::EAS; Sa/Su:250kW::EAS
- USA RFE-RL Via Germany (FR) — 250kW::WUSSR; (D):250kW::WUSSR; (J):250kW::WUSSR
- WYFR-FAMILY RADIO Okeechobee,Florida — (D):100kW::EU; (J):100kW::EU

17755 — DENMARK
- DANMARKS RADIO Copenhagen — (J):50kW::EU/WAF
- GERMANY (DR) RADIO BERLIN INTL Königswusterhausen — (J):50kW::ME/NAF
- JAPAN RADIO JAPAN/NHK Via Moyabi, Gabon — 500kW::SA; 500kW:GENERAL:SA
- SOUTH AFRICA RADIO RSA Meyerton **(con'd)** — (J):500kW::AF/WEU

ENGLISH ■■■   GERMAN / DEUTSCH ▨▨▨   FRENCH / FRANÇAIS ▬▬▬   PORTUGUESE / PORTUGUÊS ▬▬▬   SPANISH / ESPAÑOL ▬▬▬

ARABIC / عربي ≡≡   RUSSIAN / РУССКИИ ▬▬   CHINESE / 中文 ▢▢▢▢   JAPANESE / 日本語 ▨▨▨   MULTILINGUAL ▨▨▨▨   OTHER ▬▬

SUMMER ONLY (J)   WINTER ONLY (D)   JAMMING ∧∧ or / or \   EARLIEST HEARD ◢   LATEST HEARD ◣   + TENTATIVE

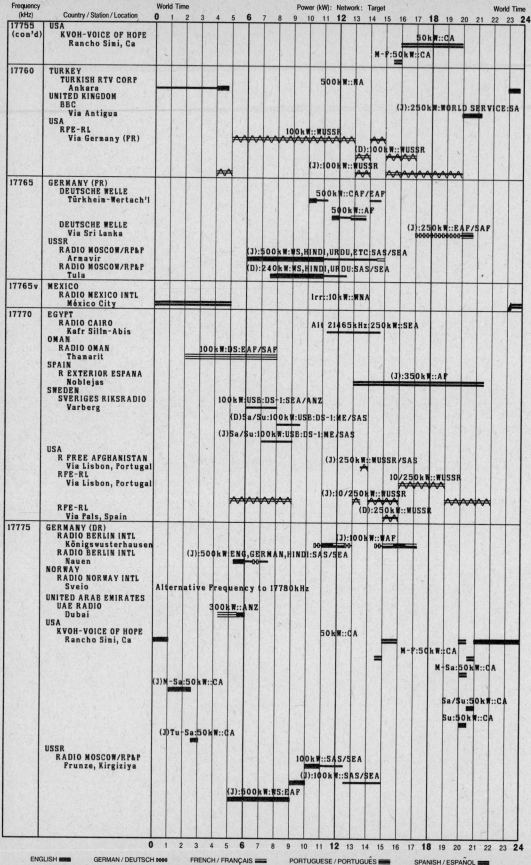

Frequency (kHz)	Country / Station / Location	Schedule (World Time 0–24), Power (kW) : Network : Target
17755 (con'd)	USA — KVOH-VOICE OF HOPE, Rancho Simi, Ca	50kW::CA; M-F:50kW::CA
17760	TURKEY — TURKISH RTV CORP, Ankara	500kW::NA
	UNITED KINGDOM — BBC, Via Antigua	(J):250kW:WORLD SERVICE:SA
	USA — RFE-RL, Via Germany (FR)	100kW::WUSSR; (D):100kW::WUSSR; (J):100kW::WUSSR
17765	GERMANY (FR) — DEUTSCHE WELLE, Türkheim-Wertach'l	500kW::CAF/EAF; 500kW::AF
	DEUTSCHE WELLE, Via Sri Lanka	(J):250kW::EAF/SAF
	USSR — RADIO MOSCOW/RP&P, Armavir	(J):500kW:WS,HINDI,URDU,ETC:SAS/SEA
	RADIO MOSCOW/RP&P, Tula	(D):240kW:WS,HINDI,URDU:SAS/SEA
17765v	MEXICO — RADIO MEXICO INTL, México City	Irr::10kW::WNA
17770	EGYPT — RADIO CAIRO, Kafr Sillm-Abis	Alt 21465kHz:250kW::SEA
	OMAN — RADIO OMAN, Thamarit	100kW:DS:EAF/SAF
	SPAIN — R EXTERIOR ESPANA, Noblejas	(J):350kW::AF
	SWEDEN — SVERIGES RIKSRADIO, Varberg	100kW:USB:DS-1:SEA/ANZ; (D)Sa/Su:100kW:USB:DS-1:ME/SAS; (J)Sa/Su:100kW:USB:DS-1:ME/SAS
	USA — R FREE AFGHANISTAN, Via Lisbon, Portugal	(J):250kW::WUSSR/SAS
	RFE-RL, Via Lisbon, Portugal	10/250kW::WUSSR; (J):10/250kW::WUSSR
	RFE-RL, Via Pals, Spain	(D):250kW::WUSSR
17775	GERMANY (DR) — RADIO BERLIN INTL, Königswusterhausen	(J):100kW::WAF
	RADIO BERLIN INTL, Nauen	(J):500kW:ENG,GERMAN,HINDI:SAS/SEA
	NORWAY — RADIO NORWAY INTL, Sveio	Alternative Frequency to 17780kHz
	UNITED ARAB EMIRATES — UAE RADIO, Dubai	300kW::ANZ
	USA — KVOH-VOICE OF HOPE, Rancho Simi, Ca	50kW::CA; M-F:50kW::CA; M-Sa:50kW::CA; Sa/Su:50kW::CA; Su:50kW::CA; (J)M-Sa:50kW::CA; (J)Tu-Sa:50kW::CA
	USSR — RADIO MOSCOW/RP&P, Frunze, Kirgiziya	100kW::SAS/SEA; (J):100kW::SAS/SEA; (J):500kW:WS:EAF

ENGLISH ▬▬ GERMAN / DEUTSCH ◊◊◊◊ FRENCH / FRANÇAIS ▬▬ PORTUGUESE / PORTUGUÊS ▬▬ SPANISH / ESPAÑOL ▬▬

ARABIC /ﻉﺭﺏ ≡ RUSSIAN / РУССКИИ ▬ CHINESE / 中文 ◻◻◻◻ JAPANESE / 日本語 ▬▬ MULTILINGUAL ▭▭▭ OTHER ▬

SUMMER ONLY (J) WINTER ONLY (D) JAMMING ∧∧ or / or \ EARLIEST HEARD ◢ LATEST HEARD ◣ + TENTATIVE

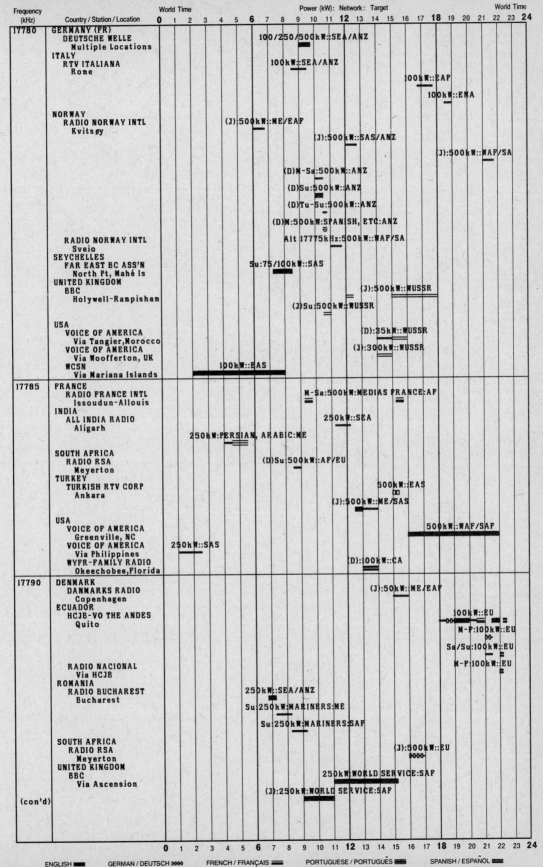

Frequency (kHz)	Country / Station / Location	World Time 0–24 (Power (kW): Network: Target)
17780	**GERMANY (FR)**	
	DEUTSCHE WELLE	
	Multiple Locations	100/250/500kW::SEA/ANZ
	ITALY	
	RTV ITALIANA	100kW::SEA/ANZ
	Rome	100kW::EAF
		100kW::ENA
	NORWAY	
	RADIO NORWAY INTL	(J):500kW::ME/EAF
	Kvitsøy	(J):500kW::SAS/ANZ
		(J):500kW::WAF/SA
		(D)M-Sa:500kW::ANZ
		(D)Su:500kW::ANZ
		(D)Tu-Su:500kW::ANZ
		(D)M:500kW:SPANISH,ETC:ANZ
	RADIO NORWAY INTL	Alt 17775kHz:500kW::WAF/SA
	Sveio	
	SEYCHELLES	
	FAR EAST BC ASS'N	Su:75/100kW::SAS
	North Pt, Mahé Is	
	UNITED KINGDOM	
	BBC	(J):500kW::WUSSR
	Holywell-Rampisham	(J)Su:500kW::WUSSR
	USA	
	VOICE OF AMERICA	(D):35kW::WUSSR
	Via Tangier,Morocco	
	VOICE OF AMERICA	(J):300kW::WUSSR
	Via Woofferton, UK	
	WCSN	100kW::EAS
	Via Mariana Islands	
17785	**FRANCE**	
	RADIO FRANCE INTL	M-Sa:500kW:MEDIAS FRANCE:AF
	Issoudun-Allouis	
	INDIA	
	ALL INDIA RADIO	250kW::SEA
	Aligarh	250kW:PERSIAN, ARABIC:ME
	SOUTH AFRICA	
	RADIO RSA	(D)Su:500kW::AF/EU
	Meyerton	
	TURKEY	
	TURKISH RTV CORP	500kW::EAS
	Ankara	(J):500kW::ME/SAS
	USA	
	VOICE OF AMERICA	500kW::WAF/SAF
	Greenville, NC	
	VOICE OF AMERICA	250kW::SAS
	Via Philippines	
	WYFR-FAMILY RADIO	(D):100kW::CA
	Okeechobee,Florida	
17790	**DENMARK**	
	DANMARKS RADIO	(J):50kW:ME/EAF
	Copenhagen	
	ECUADOR	
	HCJB-VO THE ANDES	100kW::EU
	Quito	M-F:100kW::EU
		Sa/Su:100kW::EU
		M-F:100kW::EU
	RADIO NACIONAL	
	Via HCJB	
	ROMANIA	
	RADIO BUCHAREST	250kW::SEA/ANZ
	Bucharest	Su:250kW:MARINERS:ME
		Su:250kW:MARINERS:SAF
	SOUTH AFRICA	
	RADIO RSA	(J):500kW::EU
	Meyerton	
	UNITED KINGDOM	
	BBC	250kW:WORLD SERVICE:SAF
	Via Ascension	(J):250kW:WORLD SERVICE:SAF
(con'd)		

World Time: 0 1 2 3 4 5 6 7 8 9 10 11 12 13 14 15 16 17 18 19 20 21 22 23 24

ENGLISH ▬▬   GERMAN / DEUTSCH ◊◊◊◊   FRENCH / FRANÇAIS ▭▭▭   PORTUGUESE / PORTUGUÊS ▦▦▦   SPANISH / ESPAÑOL ▦▦▦

ARABIC / عربى ▭▭   RUSSIAN / РУССКИИ ▭▭▭   CHINESE / 中文 ◊◊◊◊   JAPANESE / 日本語 ▦▦▦   MULTILINGUAL ◊◊◊◊   OTHER ▬▬

SUMMER ONLY (J)   WINTER ONLY (D)   JAMMING ∧∧ or / or \   EARLIEST HEARD ◢   LATEST HEARD ◣   + TENTATIVE

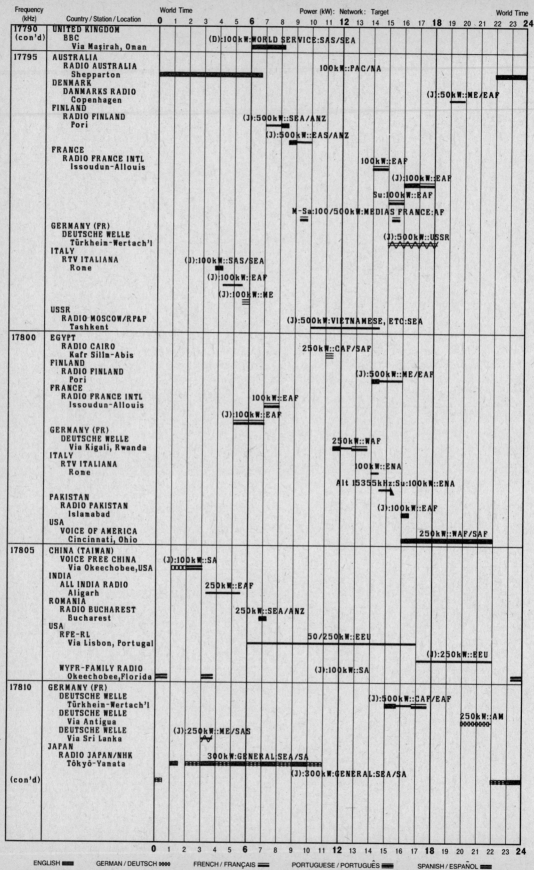

Frequency (kHz)	Country / Station / Location	World Time / Power (kW) / Network / Target
17790 (con'd)	UNITED KINGDOM BBC Via Maşirah, Oman	(D):100kW:WORLD SERVICE:SAS/SEA
17795	AUSTRALIA RADIO AUSTRALIA Shepparton	100kW::PAC/NA
	DENMARK DANMARKS RADIO Copenhagen	(J):50kW::ME/EAF
	FINLAND RADIO FINLAND Pori	(J):500kW::SEA/ANZ (J):500kW:EAS/ANZ
	FRANCE RADIO FRANCE INTL Issoudun-Allouis	100kW::EAF (J):100kW::EAF Su:100kW::EAF M-Sa:100/500kW:MEDIAS FRANCE:AF
	GERMANY (FR) DEUTSCHE WELLE Türkheim-Wertach'l	(J):500kW::USSR
	ITALY RTV ITALIANA Rome	(J):100kW::SAS/SEA (J):100kW:EAF (J):100kW::ME
	USSR RADIO MOSCOW/RP&P Tashkent	(J):500kW:VIETNAMESE, ETC:SEA
17800	EGYPT RADIO CAIRO Kafr Sillm-Abis	250kW::CAF/SAF
	FINLAND RADIO FINLAND Pori	(J):500kW::ME/EAF
	FRANCE RADIO FRANCE INTL Issoudun-Allouis	100kW::EAF (J):100kW::EAF
	GERMANY (FR) DEUTSCHE WELLE Via Kigali, Rwanda	250kW::WAF
	ITALY RTV ITALIANA Rome	100kW::ENA Alt 15355kHz:Su:100kW::ENA
	PAKISTAN RADIO PAKISTAN Islamabad	(J):100kW::EAF
	USA VOICE OF AMERICA Cincinnati, Ohio	250kW::WAF/SAF
17805	CHINA (TAIWAN) VOICE FREE CHINA Via Okeechobee, USA	(J):100kW::SA
	INDIA ALL INDIA RADIO Aligarh	250kW::EAF
	ROMANIA RADIO BUCHAREST Bucharest	250kW::SEA/ANZ
	USA RFE-RL Via Lisbon, Portugal	50/250kW::EEU (J):250kW::EEU
	WYFR-FAMILY RADIO Okeechobee, Florida	(J):100kW::SA
17810	GERMANY (FR) DEUTSCHE WELLE Türkheim-Wertach'l	(J):500kW::CAF/EAF
	DEUTSCHE WELLE Via Antigua	250kW::AM
	DEUTSCHE WELLE Via Sri Lanka	(J):250kW::ME/SAS
	JAPAN RADIO JAPAN/NHK Tōkyō-Yamata	300kW:GENERAL:SEA/SA
(con'd)		(J):300kW:GENERAL:SEA/SA

0 1 2 3 4 5 6 7 8 9 10 11 12 13 14 15 16 17 18 19 20 21 22 23 24

ENGLISH ▰▰▰   GERMAN / DEUTSCH ◊◊◊◊   FRENCH / FRANÇAIS ▰▰▰   PORTUGUESE / PORTUGUÊS ▰▰▰   SPANISH / ESPAÑOL ▰▰▰

ARABIC / عربي ▰▰▰   RUSSIAN / РУССКИИ ▰▰▰   CHINESE / 中文 ▭▭▭▭   JAPANESE / 日本語 ▰▰▰▰   MULTILINGUAL ▭▭▭▭   OTHER ▬▬▬

SUMMER ONLY (J)   WINTER ONLY (D)   JAMMING ∧∧ or / or \   EARLIEST HEARD ◢   LATEST HEARD ◣   * TENTATIVE

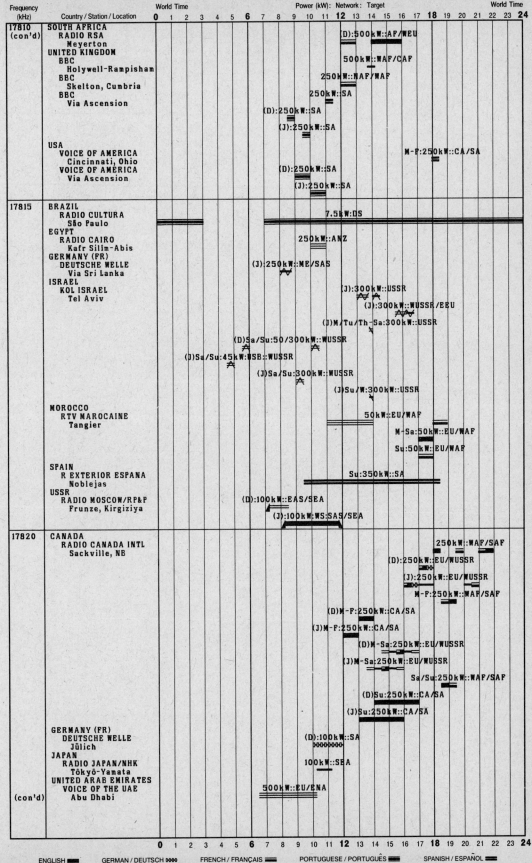

Frequency (kHz)	Country / Station / Location	Schedule
17810 (con'd)	**SOUTH AFRICA**	
	RADIO RSA	(D):500kW::AF/WEU
	Meyerton	
	UNITED KINGDOM	
	BBC	500kW::WAF/CAF
	Holywell-Rampisham	
	BBC	250kW::NAF/WAF
	Skelton, Cumbria	
	BBC	250kW::SA
	Via Ascension	(D):250kW::SA
		(J):250kW::SA
	USA	
	VOICE OF AMERICA	M-F:250kW::CA/SA
	Cincinnati, Ohio	
	VOICE OF AMERICA	(D):250kW::SA
	Via Ascension	(J):250kW::SA
17815	**BRAZIL**	
	RADIO CULTURA	7.5kW:DS
	São Paulo	
	EGYPT	
	RADIO CAIRO	250kW::ANZ
	Kafr Silim-Abis	
	GERMANY (FR)	
	DEUTSCHE WELLE	(J):250kW::ME/SAS
	Via Sri Lanka	
	ISRAEL	
	KOL ISRAEL	(J):300kW::USSR
	Tel Aviv	(J):300kW::WUSSR/EEU
		(J)M/Tu/Th-Sa:300kW::USSR
		(D)Sa/Su:50/300kW::WUSSR
		(J)Sa/Su:45kW:USB:WUSSR
		(J)Sa/Su:300kW::WUSSR
		(J)Su/W:300kW::USSR
	MOROCCO	
	RTV MAROCAINE	50kW::EU/WAF
	Tangier	M-Sa:50kW::EU/WAF
		Su:50kW::EU/WAF
	SPAIN	
	R EXTERIOR ESPANA	Su:350kW::SA
	Noblejas	
	USSR	
	RADIO MOSCOW/RP&P	(D):100kW::EAS/SEA
	Frunze, Kirgiziya	(J):100kW:WS:SAS/SEA
17820	**CANADA**	
	RADIO CANADA INTL	250kW::WAF/SAF
	Sackville, NB	(D):250kW::EU/WUSSR
		(J):250kW::EU/WUSSR
		M-F:250kW::WAF/SAF
		(D)M-F:250kW::CA/SA
		(J)M-F:250kW::CA/SA
		(D)M-Sa:250kW::EU/WUSSR
		(J)M-Sa:250kW::EU/WUSSR
		Sa/Su:250kW::WAF/SAF
		(D)Su:250kW::CA/SA
		(J)Su:250kW::CA/SA
	GERMANY (FR)	
	DEUTSCHE WELLE	(D):100kW::SA
	Jülich	
	JAPAN	
	RADIO JAPAN/NHK	100kW::SEA
	Tōkyō-Yamata	
	UNITED ARAB EMIRATES	
	VOICE OF THE UAE	500kW::EU/ENA
(con'd)	Abu Dhabi	

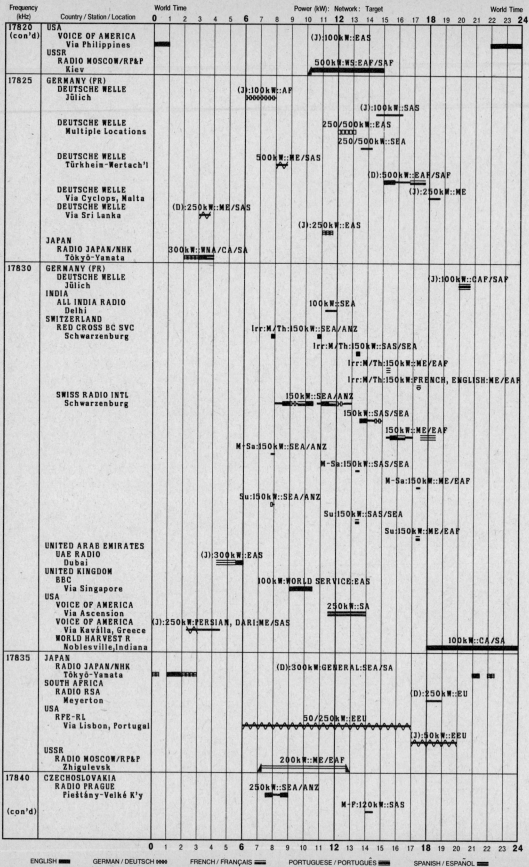

Frequency (kHz)	Country / Station / Location	World Time 0 ... 12 ... 24

17820 (con'd)

USA
VOICE OF AMERICA
Via Philippines — (J):100kW::EAS

USSR
RADIO MOSCOW/RP&P
Kiev — 500kW:WS:EAF/SAF

17825

GERMANY (FR)
DEUTSCHE WELLE
Jülich — (J):100kW::AF

DEUTSCHE WELLE — (J):100kW::SAS
Multiple Locations — 250/500kW::EAS
— 250/500kW::SEA

DEUTSCHE WELLE
Türkheim-Wertach'l — 500kW::ME/SAS
— (D):500kW::EAF/SAF

DEUTSCHE WELLE
Via Cyclops, Malta — (J):250kW::ME
DEUTSCHE WELLE
Via Sri Lanka — (D):250kW::ME/SAS
— (J):250kW::EAS

JAPAN
RADIO JAPAN/NHK
Tōkyō-Yamata — 300kW::WNA/CA/SA

17830

GERMANY (FR)
DEUTSCHE WELLE
Jülich — (J):100kW::CAF/SAF
INDIA
ALL INDIA RADIO
Delhi — 100kW::SEA
SWITZERLAND
RED CROSS BC SVC
Schwarzenburg — Irr:M/Th:150kW::SEA/ANZ
— Irr:M/Th:150kW::SAS/SEA
— Irr:M/Th:150kW::ME/EAF
— Irr:M/Th:150kW:FRENCH, ENGLISH:ME/EAF

SWISS RADIO INTL
Schwarzenburg — 150kW::SEA/ANZ
— 150kW::SAS/SEA
— 150kW::ME/EAF
— M-Sa:150kW::SEA/ANZ
— M-Sa:150kW::SAS/SEA
— M-Sa:150kW::ME/EAF
— Su:150kW::SEA/ANZ
— Su:150kW::SAS/SEA
— Su:150kW::ME/EAF

UNITED ARAB EMIRATES
UAE RADIO
Dubai — (J):300kW::EAS
UNITED KINGDOM
BBC
Via Singapore — 100kW:WORLD SERVICE:EAS
USA
VOICE OF AMERICA
Via Ascension — 250kW::SA
VOICE OF AMERICA
Via Kaválla, Greece — (J):250kW:PERSIAN, DARI:ME/SAS
WORLD HARVEST R
Noblesville,Indiana — 100kW::CA/SA

17835

JAPAN
RADIO JAPAN/NHK
Tōkyō-Yamata — (D):300kW:GENERAL:SEA/SA
SOUTH AFRICA
RADIO RSA
Meyerton — (D):250kW::EU
USA
RFE-RL
Via Lisbon, Portugal — 50/250kW::EEU
— (J):50kW::EEU

USSR
RADIO MOSCOW/RP&P
Zhigulevsk — 200kW::ME/EAF

17840 (con'd)

CZECHOSLOVAKIA
RADIO PRAGUE
Pieštány-Velké K'y — 250kW::SEA/ANZ
— M-F:120kW::SAS

World Time 0 1 2 3 4 5 6 7 8 9 10 11 12 13 14 15 16 17 18 19 20 21 22 23 24

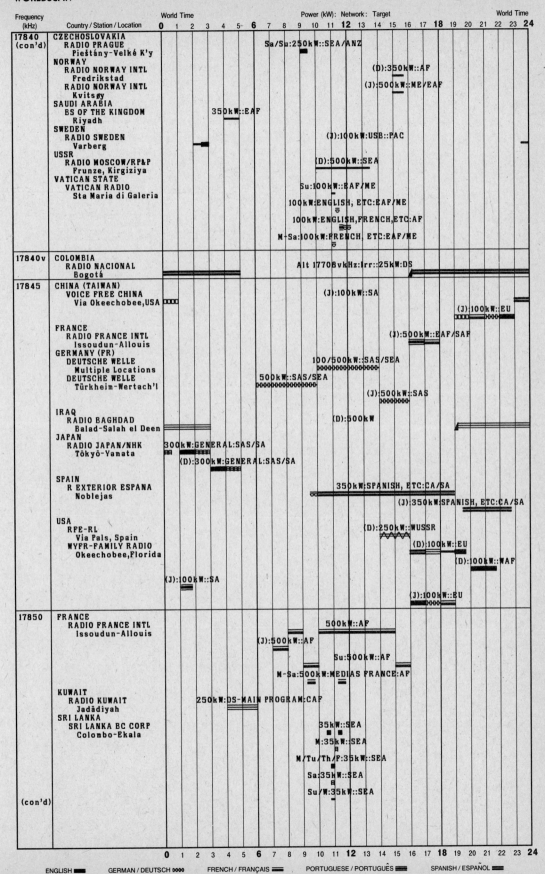

Frequency (kHz)	Country / Station / Location		Power (kW): Network : Target

17840 (con'd)

CZECHOSLOVAKIA
  RADIO PRAGUE
    Piešťany-Velké K'y — Sa/Su:250kW::SEA/ANZ
NORWAY
  RADIO NORWAY INTL
    Fredrikstad — (D):350kW::AF
  RADIO NORWAY INTL
    Kvitsøy — (J):500kW::ME/EAF
SAUDI ARABIA
  BS OF THE KINGDOM
    Riyadh — 350kW::EAF
SWEDEN
  RADIO SWEDEN
    Varberg — (J):100kW:USB::PAC
USSR
  RADIO MOSCOW/RP&P
    Frunze, Kirgiziya — (D):500kW::SEA
VATICAN STATE
  VATICAN RADIO
    Sta Maria di Galeria — Su:100kW::EAF/ME
    100kW:ENGLISH, ETC:EAF/ME
    100kW:ENGLISH,FRENCH,ETC:AF
    M-Sa:100kW:FRENCH, ETC:EAF/ME

17840v

COLOMBIA
  RADIO NACIONAL
    Bogotá — Alt 17770BvkHz:Irr::25kW:DS

17845

CHINA (TAIWAN)
  VOICE FREE CHINA
    Via Okeechobee,USA — (J):100kW::SA
    (J):100kW::EU
FRANCE
  RADIO FRANCE INTL
    Issoudun-Allouis — (J):500kW::EAF/SAF
GERMANY (FR)
  DEUTSCHE WELLE
    Multiple Locations — 100/500kW::SAS/SEA
  DEUTSCHE WELLE
    Türkheim-Wertach'l — 500kW::SAS/SEA
    (J):500kW::SAS
IRAQ
  RADIO BAGHDAD
    Balad-Salah el Deen — (D):500kW
JAPAN
  RADIO JAPAN/NHK
    Tōkyō-Yamata — 300kW:GENERAL:SAS/SA
    (D):300kW:GENERAL:SAS/SA
SPAIN
  R EXTERIOR ESPANA
    Noblejas — 350kW:SPANISH, ETC:CA/SA
    (J):350kW:SPANISH, ETC:CA/SA
USA
  RPE-RL
    Via Pals, Spain — (D):250kW::WUSSR
  WYFR-FAMILY RADIO
    Okeechobee,Florida — (D):100kW::EU
    (D):100kW::WAF
    (J):100kW::SA
    (J):100kW::EU

17850

FRANCE
  RADIO FRANCE INTL
    Issoudun-Allouis — 500kW::AF
    (J):500kW::AF
    Su:500kW::AF
    M-Sa:500kW:MEDIAS FRANCE:AF
KUWAIT
  RADIO KUWAIT
    Jadādiyah — 250kW:DS-MAIN PROGRAM:CAF
SRI LANKA
  SRI LANKA BC CORP
    Colombo-Ekala — 35kW::SEA
    M:35kW::SEA
    M/Tu/Th/F:35kW::SEA
    Sa:35kW::SEA
    Su/W:35kW::SEA

(con'd)

World Time: 0 1 2 3 4 5 6 7 8 9 10 11 12 13 14 15 16 17 18 19 20 21 22 23 24

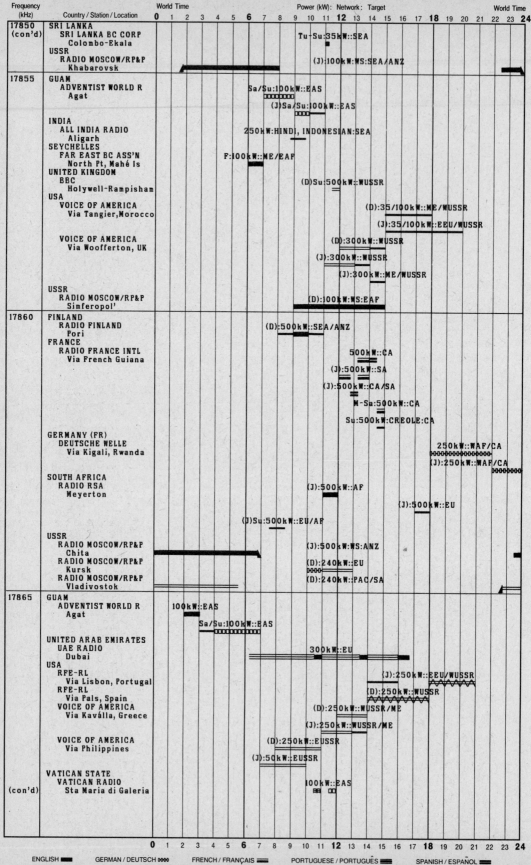

Frequency (kHz)	Country / Station / Location		World Time	Power (kW): Network: Target	World Time

17850 (con'd)

SRI LANKA
  SRI LANKA BC CORP
    Colombo-Ekala — Tu–Su:35kW::SEA
USSR
  RADIO MOSCOW/RP&P
    Khabarovsk — (J):100kW:WS:SEA/ANZ

17855

GUAM
  ADVENTIST WORLD R
    Agat — Sa/Su:100kW::EAS / (J)Sa/Su:100kW::EAS

INDIA
  ALL INDIA RADIO
    Aligarh — 250kW:HINDI, INDONESIAN:SEA
SEYCHELLES
  FAR EAST BC ASS'N
    North Pt, Mahé Is — F:100kW::ME/EAF
UNITED KINGDOM
  BBC
    Holywell-Rampisham — (D)Su:500kW::WUSSR
USA
  VOICE OF AMERICA
    Via Tangier, Morocco — (D):35/100kW::ME/WUSSR / (J):35/100kW::EEU/WUSSR

  VOICE OF AMERICA
    Via Woofferton, UK — (D):300kW::WUSSR / (J):300kW::WUSSR / (J):300kW::ME/WUSSR

USSR
  RADIO MOSCOW/RP&P
    Simferopol' — (D):100kW:WS:EAF

17860

FINLAND
  RADIO FINLAND
    Pori — (D):500kW::SEA/ANZ
FRANCE
  RADIO FRANCE INTL
    Via French Guiana — 500kW::CA / (J):500kW::SA / (J):500kW::CA/SA / M-Sa:500kW::CA / Su:500kW:CREOLE:CA

GERMANY (FR)
  DEUTSCHE WELLE
    Via Kigali, Rwanda — 250kW::WAF/CA / (J):250kW::WAF/CA

SOUTH AFRICA
  RADIO RSA
    Meyerton — (J):500kW::AF / (J):500kW::EU / (J)Su:500kW::EU/AF

USSR
  RADIO MOSCOW/RP&P
    Chita — (J):500kW:WS:ANZ
  RADIO MOSCOW/RP&P
    Kursk — (D):240kW::EU
  RADIO MOSCOW/RP&P
    Vladivostok — (D):240kW::PAC/SA

17865

GUAM
  ADVENTIST WORLD R
    Agat — 100kW::EAS / Sa/Su:100kW::EAS

UNITED ARAB EMIRATES
  UAE RADIO
    Dubai — 300kW::EU
USA
  RFE-RL
    Via Lisbon, Portugal — (J):250kW::EEU/WUSSR
  RFE-RL
    Via Pals, Spain — (D):250kW::WUSSR
  VOICE OF AMERICA
    Via Kaválla, Greece — (D):250kW::WUSSR/ME / (J):250kW::WUSSR/ME

  VOICE OF AMERICA
    Via Philippines — (D):250kW::EUSSR / (J):50kW::EUSSR

VATICAN STATE
  VATICAN RADIO
(con'd)   Sta Maria di Galeria — 100kW::EAS

World Time scale: 0 1 2 3 4 5 6 7 8 9 10 11 12 13 14 15 16 17 18 19 20 21 22 23 24

ENGLISH ▬▬   GERMAN / DEUTSCH ◊◊◊◊   FRENCH / FRANÇAIS ▬▬   PORTUGUESE / PORTUGUÊS ▬▬   SPANISH / ESPAÑOL ▬▬

ARABIC / ﻉﺏﻉ ≡   RUSSIAN / РУССКИЙ ▬   CHINESE / 中文 ◊◊◊◊   JAPANESE / 日本語 ▬▬   MULTILINGUAL ◊◊◊◊   OTHER ▬

SUMMER ONLY (J)   WINTER ONLY (D)   JAMMING /\/\ or / or \   EARLIEST HEARD ◢   LATEST HEARD ◣   + TENTATIVE

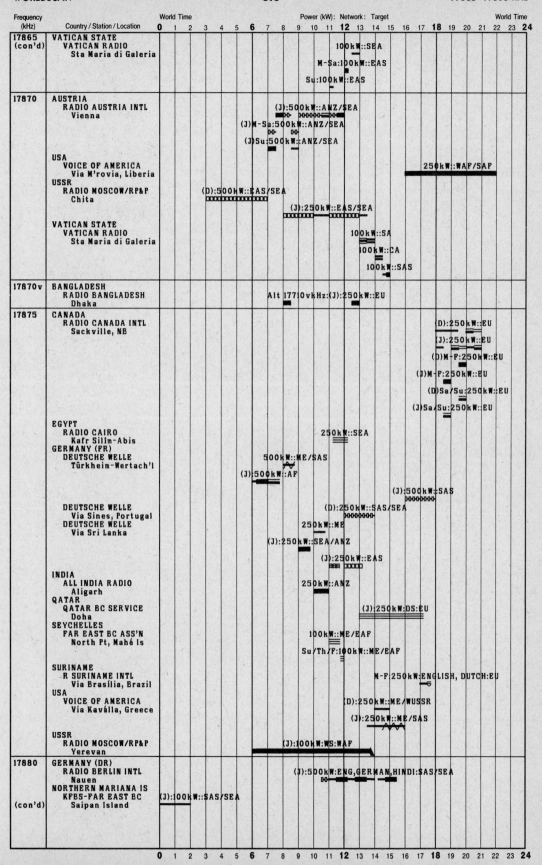

ENGLISH ▬▬   GERMAN / DEUTSCH ◊◊◊◊   FRENCH / FRANÇAIS ═══   PORTUGUESE / PORTUGUÊS ▬▬   SPANISH / ESPAÑOL ▬▬

ARABIC / ﻉﺭ ≡≡≡   RUSSIAN / РУССКИИ ═══   CHINESE / ✷✷ ◻◻◻◻   JAPANESE / 日本語 ▦▦   MULTILINGUAL ▩▩▩▩   OTHER ▬▬

SUMMER ONLY (J)   WINTER ONLY (D)   JAMMING /\/\ or / or \   EARLIEST HEARD ◢   LATEST HEARD ◣   + TENTATIVE

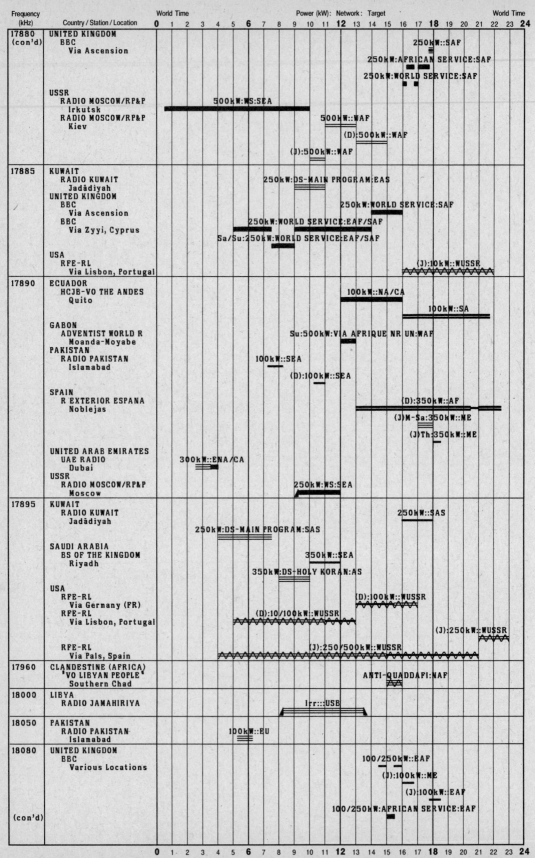

Frequency (kHz)	Country / Station / Location	Broadcast schedule
17880 (con'd)	**UNITED KINGDOM** BBC / Via Ascension	250kW::SAF ; 250kW:AFRICAN SERVICE:SAF ; 250kW:WORLD SERVICE:SAF
	USSR RADIO MOSCOW/RP&P Irkutsk	500kW:WS:SEA
	RADIO MOSCOW/RP&P Kiev	500kW::WAF ; (D):500kW::WAF ; (J):500kW::WAF
17885	**KUWAIT** RADIO KUWAIT Jadādiyah	250kW:DS-MAIN PROGRAM:EAS
	UNITED KINGDOM BBC / Via Ascension	250kW:WORLD SERVICE:SAF
	BBC / Via Zyyi, Cyprus	250kW:WORLD SERVICE:EAF/SAF ; Sa/Su:250kW:WORLD SERVICE:EAF/SAF
	USA RFE-RL / Via Lisbon, Portugal	(J):10kW::WUSSR
17890	**ECUADOR** HCJB-VO THE ANDES Quito	100kW::NA/CA ; 100kW::SA
	GABON ADVENTIST WORLD R Moanda-Moyabe	Su:500kW:VIA AFRIQUE NR UN:WAF
	PAKISTAN RADIO PAKISTAN Islamabad	100kW::SEA ; (D):100kW::SEA
	SPAIN R EXTERIOR ESPANA Noblejas	(D):350kW::AF ; (J)M-Sa:350kW::ME ; (J)Th:350kW::ME
	UNITED ARAB EMIRATES UAE RADIO Dubai	300kW::ENA/CA
	USSR RADIO MOSCOW/RP&P Moscow	250kW:WS:SEA
17895	**KUWAIT** RADIO KUWAIT Jadādiyah	250kW::SAS ; 250kW:DS-MAIN PROGRAM:SAS
	SAUDI ARABIA BS OF THE KINGDOM Riyadh	350kW::SEA ; 350kW:DS-HOLY KORAN:AS
	USA RFE-RL / Via Germany (FR)	(D):100kW::WUSSR
	RFE-RL / Via Lisbon, Portugal	(D):10/100kW::WUSSR ; (J):250kW::WUSSR
	RFE-RL / Via Pals, Spain	(J):250/500kW::WUSSR
17960	**CLANDESTINE (AFRICA)** "VO LIBYAN PEOPLE" Southern Chad	ANTI-QUADDAFI:NAF
18000	**LIBYA** RADIO JAMAHIRIYA	Irr:::USB
18050	**PAKISTAN** RADIO PAKISTAN Islamabad	100kW::EU
18080	**UNITED KINGDOM** BBC / Various Locations	100/250kW::EAF ; (J):100kW::ME ; (J):100kW::EAF
(con'd)		100/250kW:AFRICAN SERVICE:EAF

ENGLISH ▬▬   GERMAN / DEUTSCH ∞∞∞   FRENCH / FRANÇAIS ══   PORTUGUESE / PORTUGUÊS ▬▬   SPANISH / ESPAÑOL ▬▬

ARABIC / عربي ≡≡≡   RUSSIAN / РУССКИЙ ══   CHINESE / 中文 □□□□   JAPANESE / 日本語 ▬▬   MULTILINGUAL ▤▤▤   OTHER ▬

SUMMER ONLY (J)   WINTER ONLY (D)   JAMMING ∧∧∧ or / or \   EARLIEST HEARD ◢   LATEST HEARD ◣   + TENTATIVE

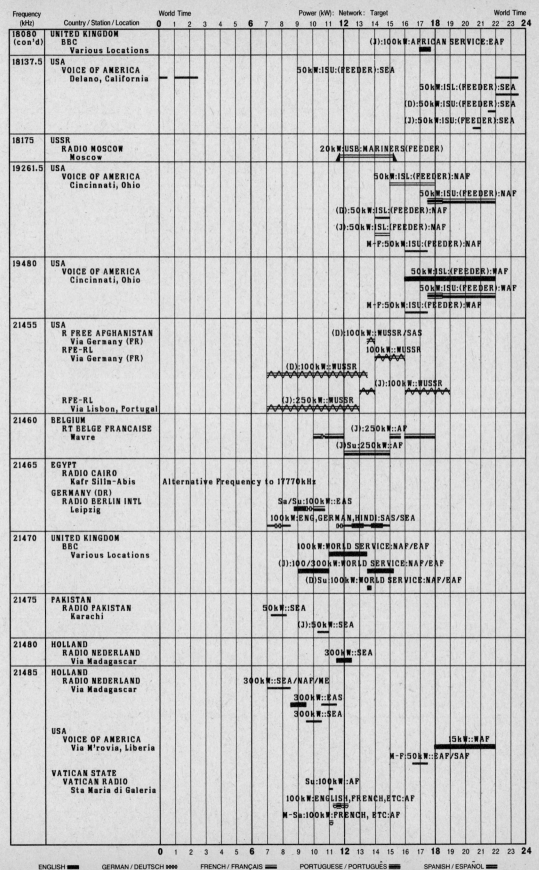

Frequency (kHz)	Country / Station / Location	World Time / Power (kW): Network: Target
18080 (con'd)	UNITED KINGDOM BBC Various Locations	(J):100kW:AFRICAN SERVICE:EAF
18137.5	USA VOICE OF AMERICA Delano, California	50kW:ISU:(FEEDER):SEA / 50kW:ISL:(FEEDER):SEA / (D):50kW:ISU:(FEEDER):SEA / (J):50kW:ISU:(FEEDER):SEA
18175	USSR RADIO MOSCOW Moscow	20kW:USB:MARINERS(FEEDER)
19261.5	USA VOICE OF AMERICA Cincinnati, Ohio	50kW:ISL:(FEEDER):NAF / 50kW:ISU:(FEEDER):NAF / (D):50kW:ISL:(FEEDER):NAF / (J):50kW:ISL:(FEEDER):NAF / M-F:50kW:ISU:(FEEDER):NAF
19480	USA VOICE OF AMERICA Cincinnati, Ohio	50kW:ISL:(FEEDER):WAF / 50kW:ISU:(FEEDER):WAF / M-F:50kW:ISU:(FEEDER):WAF
21455	USA R FREE AFGHANISTAN Via Germany (FR) RFE-RL Via Germany (FR) RFE-RL Via Lisbon, Portugal	(D):100kW::WUSSR/SAS / 100kW::WUSSR / (D):100kW::WUSSR / (J):100kW::WUSSR / (J):250kW::WUSSR
21460	BELGIUM RT BELGE FRANCAISE Wavre	(J):250kW::AF / (J)Su:250kW::AF
21465	EGYPT RADIO CAIRO Kafr Silim-Abis GERMANY (DR) RADIO BERLIN INTL Leipzig	Alternative Frequency to 17770kHz / Sa/Su:100kW::EAS / 100kW:ENG,GERMAN,HINDI:SAS/SEA
21470	UNITED KINGDOM BBC Various Locations	100kW:WORLD SERVICE:NAF/EAF / (J):100/300kW:WORLD SERVICE:NAF/EAF / (D)Su:100kW:WORLD SERVICE:NAF/EAF
21475	PAKISTAN RADIO PAKISTAN Karachi	50kW::SEA / (J):50kW::SEA
21480	HOLLAND RADIO NEDERLAND Via Madagascar	300kW::SEA
21485	HOLLAND RADIO NEDERLAND Via Madagascar USA VOICE OF AMERICA Via M'rovia, Liberia VATICAN STATE VATICAN RADIO Sta Maria di Galeria	300kW::SEA/NAF/ME / 300kW::EAS / 300kW::SEA / 15kW::WAF / M-F:50kW::EAF/SAF / Su:100kW::AF / 100kW:ENGLISH,FRENCH,ETC:AF / M-Sa:100kW:FRENCH, ETC:AF

ENGLISH ▬▬ GERMAN / DEUTSCH ∞∞ FRENCH / FRANÇAIS ═══ PORTUGUESE / PORTUGUÊS ▬▬ SPANISH / ESPAÑOL ═══

ARABIC / عربي ≡≡≡ RUSSIAN / РУССКИЙ ═══ CHINESE / 中文 ∞∞∞ JAPANESE / 日本語 ▬▬ MULTILINGUAL ∞∞∞ OTHER ▬▬

SUMMER ONLY (J)   WINTER ONLY (D)   JAMMING /\/\ or / or \   EARLIEST HEARD ◢   LATEST HEARD ◣   † TENTATIVE

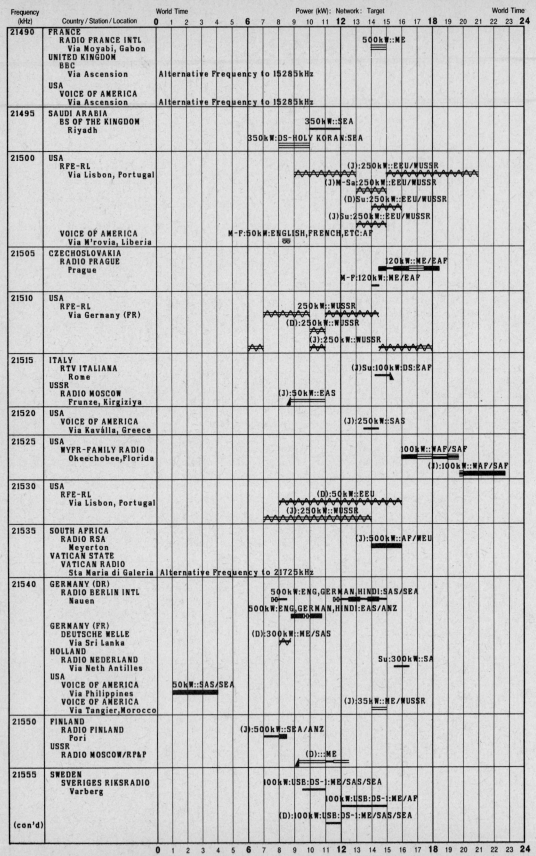

Frequency (kHz) Country / Station / Location	World Time	Power (kW): Network: Target	World Time

21490 FRANCE
   RADIO FRANCE INTL
      Via Moyabi, Gabon — 500kW::ME
   UNITED KINGDOM
   BBC
      Via Ascension — Alternative Frequency to 15285kHz
   USA
   VOICE OF AMERICA
      Via Ascension — Alternative Frequency to 15285kHz

21495 SAUDI ARABIA
   BS OF THE KINGDOM
      Riyadh — 350kW::SEA
      350kW:DS-HOLY KORAN:SEA

21500 USA
   RFE-RL
      Via Lisbon, Portugal — (J):250kW::EEU/WUSSR
         (J)M-Sa:250kW::EEU/WUSSR
         (D)Su:250kW::EEU/WUSSR
         (J)Su:250kW::EEU/WUSSR
   VOICE OF AMERICA
      Via M'rovia, Liberia — M-F:50kW:ENGLISH,FRENCH,ETC:AF

21505 CZECHOSLOVAKIA
   RADIO PRAGUE
      Prague — 120kW::ME/EAF
         M-F:120kW::ME/EAF

21510 USA
   RFE-RL
      Via Germany (FR) — 250kW::WUSSR
         (D):250kW::WUSSR
         (J):250kW::WUSSR

21515 ITALY
   RTV ITALIANA
      Rome — (J)Su:100kW:DS:EAF
   USSR
   RADIO MOSCOW
      Frunze, Kirgiziya — (J):50kW::EAS

21520 USA
   VOICE OF AMERICA
      Via Kaválla, Greece — (J):250kW::SAS

21525 USA
   WYFR-FAMILY RADIO
      Okeechobee,Florida — 100kW::WAF/SAF
         (J):100kW::WAF/SAF

21530 USA
   RFE-RL
      Via Lisbon, Portugal — (D):50kW::EEU
         (J):250kW::WUSSR

21535 SOUTH AFRICA
   RADIO RSA
      Meyerton — (J):500kW::AF/WEU
   VATICAN STATE
   VATICAN RADIO
      Sta Maria di Galeria — Alternative Frequency to 21725kHz

21540 GERMANY (DR)
   RADIO BERLIN INTL
      Nauen — 500kW:ENG,GERMAN,HINDI:SAS/SEA
         500kW:ENG,GERMAN,HINDI:EAS/ANZ
   GERMANY (FR)
   DEUTSCHE WELLE
      Via Sri Lanka — (D):300kW::ME/SAS
   HOLLAND
   RADIO NEDERLAND
      Via Neth Antilles — Su:300kW::SA
   USA
   VOICE OF AMERICA
      Via Philippines — 50kW::SAS/SEA
   VOICE OF AMERICA
      Via Tangier,Morocco — (J):35kW::ME/WUSSR

21550 FINLAND
   RADIO FINLAND
      Pori — (J):500kW::SEA/ANZ
   USSR
   RADIO MOSCOW/RP&P — (D):::ME

21555 SWEDEN
   SVERIGES RIKSRADIO
      Varberg — 100kW:USB:DS-1:ME/SAS/SEA
         100kW:USB:DS-1:ME/AF
         (D):100kW:USB:DS-1:ME/SAS/SEA

(con'd)

ENGLISH ▬▬   GERMAN / DEUTSCH ◦◦◦◦   FRENCH / FRANÇAIS ▬▬   PORTUGUESE / PORTUGUÊS ▬▬   SPANISH / ESPAÑOL ▬▬
ARABIC / عربي   RUSSIAN / РУССКИЙ ▬▬   CHINESE / 中文 ◦◦◦◦   JAPANESE / 日本語 ▬▬   MULTILINGUAL ▬▬   OTHER ▬▬
SUMMER ONLY (J)   WINTER ONLY (D)   JAMMING ∧∧ or / or \   EARLIEST HEARD ◢   LATEST HEARD ◣   * TENTATIVE

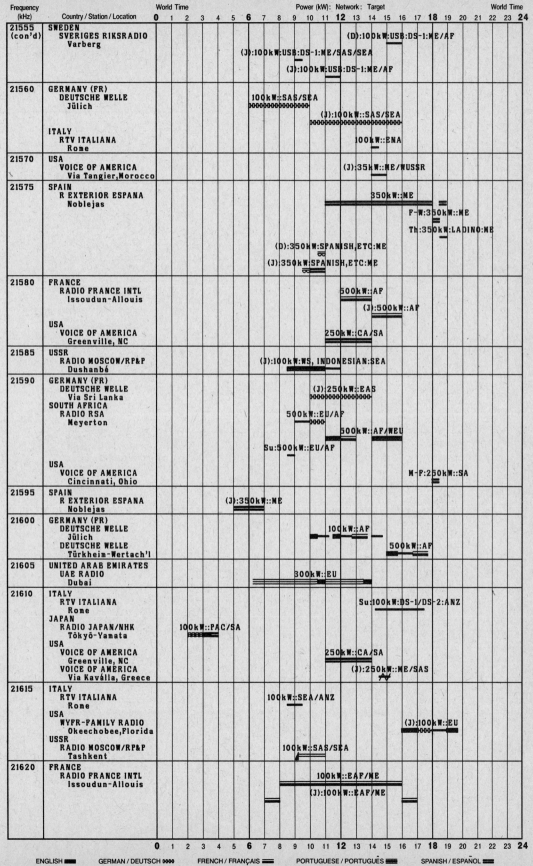

Frequency (kHz)	Country / Station / Location	Power (kW): Network: Target
21555 (con'd)	SWEDEN SVERIGES RIKSRADIO Varberg	(D):100kW:USB:DS-1:ME/AF — (J):100kW:USB:DS-1:ME/SAS/SEA — (J):100kW:USB:DS-1:ME/AF
21560	GERMANY (FR) DEUTSCHE WELLE Jülich	100kW::SAS/SEA — (J):100kW::SAS/SEA
	ITALY RTV ITALIANA Rome	100kW::ENA
21570	USA VOICE OF AMERICA Via Tangier, Morocco	(J):35kW::ME/WUSSR
21575	SPAIN R EXTERIOR ESPANA Noblejas	350kW::ME — F-W:350kW::ME — Th:350kW:LADINO:ME — (D):350kW:SPANISH,ETC:ME — (J):350kW:SPANISH,ETC:ME
21580	FRANCE RADIO FRANCE INTL Issoudun-Allouis	500kW::AF — (J):500kW::AF
	USA VOICE OF AMERICA Greenville, NC	250kW::CA/SA
21585	USSR RADIO MOSCOW/RP&P Dushanbé	(J):100kW:WS, INDONESIAN:SEA
21590	GERMANY (FR) DEUTSCHE WELLE Via Sri Lanka	(J):250kW::EAS
	SOUTH AFRICA RADIO RSA Meyerton	500kW::EU/AF — 500kW::AF/WEU — Su:500kW::EU/AF
	USA VOICE OF AMERICA Cincinnati, Ohio	M-F:250kW::SA
21595	SPAIN R EXTERIOR ESPANA Noblejas	(J):350kW::ME
21600	GERMANY (FR) DEUTSCHE WELLE Jülich	100kW::AF
	DEUTSCHE WELLE Türkheim-Wertach'l	500kW::AF
21605	UNITED ARAB EMIRATES UAE RADIO Dubai	300kW::EU
21610	ITALY RTV ITALIANA Rome	Su:100kW:DS-1/DS-2:ANZ
	JAPAN RADIO JAPAN/NHK Tōkyō-Yamata	100kW::PAC/SA
	USA VOICE OF AMERICA Greenville, NC	250kW::CA/SA
	VOICE OF AMERICA Via Kaválla, Greece	(J):250kW::ME/SAS
21615	ITALY RTV ITALIANA Rome	100kW::SEA/ANZ
	USA WYFR-FAMILY RADIO Okeechobee, Florida	(J):100kW::EU
	USSR RADIO MOSCOW/RP&P Tashkent	100kW::SAS/SEA
21620	FRANCE RADIO FRANCE INTL Issoudun-Allouis	100kW::EAF/ME — (J):100kW::EAF/ME

ENGLISH ▰▰▰   GERMAN / DEUTSCH ◊◊◊◊   FRENCH / FRANÇAIS ▬▬   PORTUGUESE / PORTUGUÊS ▬▬   SPANISH / ESPAÑOL ▬▬

ARABIC /ﻉﺏﺭ ▬▬   RUSSIAN / РУССКИИ ▬▬   CHINESE / 中文 ◊◊◊◊   JAPANESE / 日本語 ▰▰▰   MULTILINGUAL ▭▭▭   OTHER ▬▬

SUMMER ONLY (J)   WINTER ONLY (D)   JAMMING ∧∧ or / or \   EARLIEST HEARD ◢   LATEST HEARD ◣   ⁺ TENTATIVE

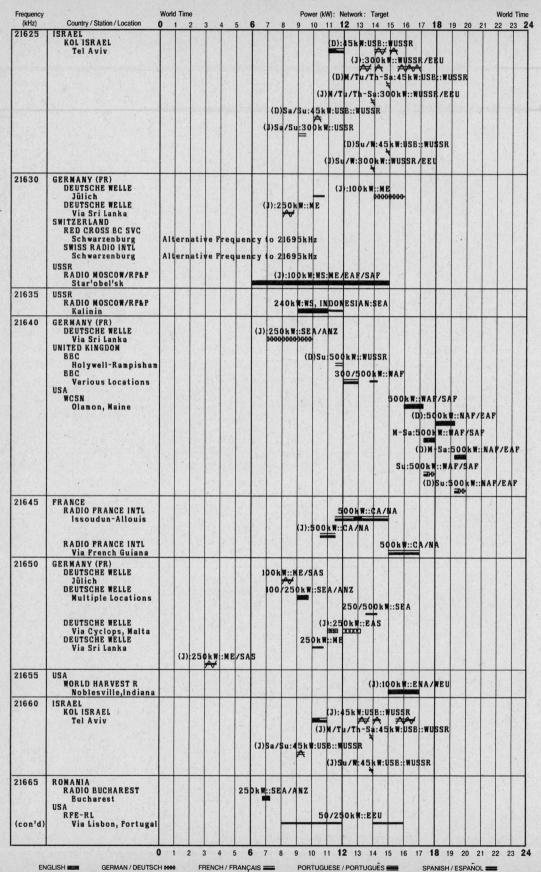

Frequency (kHz)	Country / Station / Location	World Time 0-24 schedule
21625	**ISRAEL** KOL ISRAEL Tel Aviv	(D):45kW:USB::WUSSR / (J):300kW::WUSSR/EEU / (D)M/Tu/Th-Sa:45kW:USB::WUSSR / (J)M/Tu/Th-Sa:300kW::WUSSR/EEU / (D)Sa/Su:45kW:USB::WUSSR / (J)Sa/Su:300kW::USSR / (D)Su/W:45kW:USB::WUSSR / (J)Su/W:300kW::WUSSR/EEU
21630	**GERMANY (FR)** DEUTSCHE WELLE Jülich	(J):100kW::ME
	DEUTSCHE WELLE Via Sri Lanka	(J):250kW::ME
	SWITZERLAND RED CROSS BC SVC Schwarzenburg	Alternative Frequency to 21695kHz
	SWISS RADIO INTL Schwarzenburg	Alternative Frequency to 21695kHz
	USSR RADIO MOSCOW/RP&P Star'obel'sk	(J):100kW:WS:ME/EAF/SAF
21635	**USSR** RADIO MOSCOW/RP&P Kalinin	240kW:WS, INDONESIAN:SEA
21640	**GERMANY (FR)** DEUTSCHE WELLE Via Sri Lanka	(J):250kW::SEA/ANZ
	UNITED KINGDOM BBC Holywell-Rampisham	(D)Su:500kW::WUSSR
	BBC Various Locations	300/500kW::WAF
	USA WCSN Olamon, Maine	500kW::WAF/SAF / (D):500kW::NAF/EAF / M-Sa:500kW::WAF/SAF / (D)M-Sa:500kW::NAF/EAF / Su:500kW::WAF/SAF / (D)Su:500kW::NAF/EAF
21645	**FRANCE** RADIO FRANCE INTL Issoudun-Allouis	500kW::CA/NA / (J):500kW::CA/NA
	RADIO FRANCE INTL Via French Guiana	500kW::CA/NA
21650	**GERMANY (FR)** DEUTSCHE WELLE Jülich	100kW::ME/SAS
	DEUTSCHE WELLE Multiple Locations	100/250kW::SEA/ANZ / 250/500kW::SEA
	DEUTSCHE WELLE Via Cyclops, Malta	(J):250kW::EAS
	DEUTSCHE WELLE Via Sri Lanka	250kW::ME
		(J):250kW::ME/SAS
21655	**USA** WORLD HARVEST R Noblesville,Indiana	(J):100kW::ENA/WEU
21660	**ISRAEL** KOL ISRAEL Tel Aviv	(J):45kW:USB::WUSSR / (J)M/Tu/Th-Sa:45kW:USB::WUSSR / (J)Sa/Su:45kW:USB::WUSSR / (J)Su/W:45kW:USB::WUSSR
21665 (con'd)	**ROMANIA** RADIO BUCHAREST Bucharest	250kW::SEA/ANZ
	USA RFE-RL Via Lisbon, Portugal	50/250kW::EEU

ENGLISH ▄▄▄   GERMAN / DEUTSCH ∞∞   FRENCH / FRANÇAIS ▬▬   PORTUGUESE / PORTUGUÊS ▬▬   SPANISH / ESPAÑOL ▬▬

ARABIC /ﻉﺏﺭ ▬   RUSSIAN / РУССКИИ ▬   CHINESE / 中文 □□□   JAPANESE / 日本語 ▩   MULTILINGUAL ▭▭   OTHER ▬

SUMMER ONLY (J)   WINTER ONLY (D)   JAMMING ∧∧ or / or \   EARLIEST HEARD ◢   LATEST HEARD ◣   + TENTATIVE

Frequency (kHz)	Country / Station / Location	World Time 0 1 2 3 4 5 6 7 8 9 10 11 12 13 14 15 16 17 18 19 20 21 22 23 24	Power (kW): Network: Target

21665 (con'd) — USA — RFE-RL, Via Lisbon, Portugal
- (D):50kW::EEU
- (J):250kW::WUSSR
- (J):250kW::EEU
- (J)M-Sa:250kW::EEU/WUSSR
- (J)Su:250kW::EEU/WUSSR

21675 — ISRAEL — KOL ISRAEL, Tel Aviv
- (J)Sa/Su:300kW::EU/WUSSR
RASHUTH HASHIDUR, Tel Aviv
- (J):300kW:DS-E:EU/WUSSR

21680 — GERMANY (FR) — DEUTSCHE WELLE, Jülich
- 100kW::ME/SAS
DEUTSCHE WELLE, Türkheim-Wertach'l
- 500kW::SEA/ANZ
DEUTSCHE WELLE, Via Cyclops, Malta
- (J):250kW::SAS
DEUTSCHE WELLE, Via Sines, Portugal
- (J):250kW::EU/ME/SAS
HOLLAND — RADIO NEDERLAND, Via Neth Antilles
- 300kW::WAF/CAF

21685 — HOLLAND — RADIO NEDERLAND, Via Neth Antilles
- 300kW::WAF/CAF

21690 — ITALY — RTV ITALIANA, Rome
- 100kW::EAF
- 100kW::AF
- Su:50kW:DS:AF/SA
SWEDEN — RADIO SWEDEN, Hörby
- 350kW::ME
- (D):350kW::ME
- (J):350kW::ME
- (J):350kW::SAS
SVERIGES RIKSRADIO, Hörby
- (J):350kW:DS-1:ME/EAF

21695 — JAPAN — RADIO JAPAN/NHK, Via Moyabi, Gabon
- 500kW:GENERAL:EU/NAF
SWITZERLAND — RED CROSS BC SVC, Schwarzenburg
- Irr:M/Th:150kW::ANZ
- Irr:M/Th:150kW::SAS/SEA
- Alt 21630kHz:Irr:M/Th:150kW::ME
SWISS RADIO INTL, Schwarzenburg
- 150kW::ANZ
- 150kW::SAS/SEA
- Alt 21630kHz:150kW::ME
- M-Sa:150kW::ANZ
- M-Sa:150kW::SAS/SEA
- Su:150kW::ANZ
- Su:150kW::SAS/SEA

21700 — JAPAN — RADIO JAPAN/NHK, Via Moyabi, Gabon
- 500kW:GENERAL:EU
NORWAY — RADIO NORWAY INTL, Fredrikstad
- (J):120/350kW::AF
- (J)M-Sa:120/350kW::AF
- (J)Su:120/350kW::AF
- (J)Tu-Su:120/350kW::AF
- (J)M:120/350kW:SPANISH, ETC:AF
PORTUGAL — RDP INTERNATIONAL, Lisbon-São Gabriel
- M-F:100kW::AF
UNITED ARAB EMIRATES — UAE RADIO, Dubai **(con'd)**
- 300kW::ANZ

World Time 0 1 2 3 4 5 6 7 8 9 10 11 12 13 14 15 16 17 18 19 20 21 22 23 24

ENGLISH ▭▭▭   GERMAN / DEUTSCH ◊◊◊◊   FRENCH / FRANÇAIS ▬▬▬   PORTUGUESE / PORTUGUÊS ▭▭▭   SPANISH / ESPAÑOL ▬▬▬

ARABIC / العربية ≡≡≡   RUSSIAN / РУССКИЙ ▬▬▬   CHINESE / 中文 □□□□   JAPANESE / 日本語 ▬▬▬   MULTILINGUAL ▭▭▭   OTHER ▬▬▬

SUMMER ONLY (J)   WINTER ONLY (D)   JAMMING /\/\ or / or \   EARLIEST HEARD ◢   LATEST HEARD ◣   † TENTATIVE

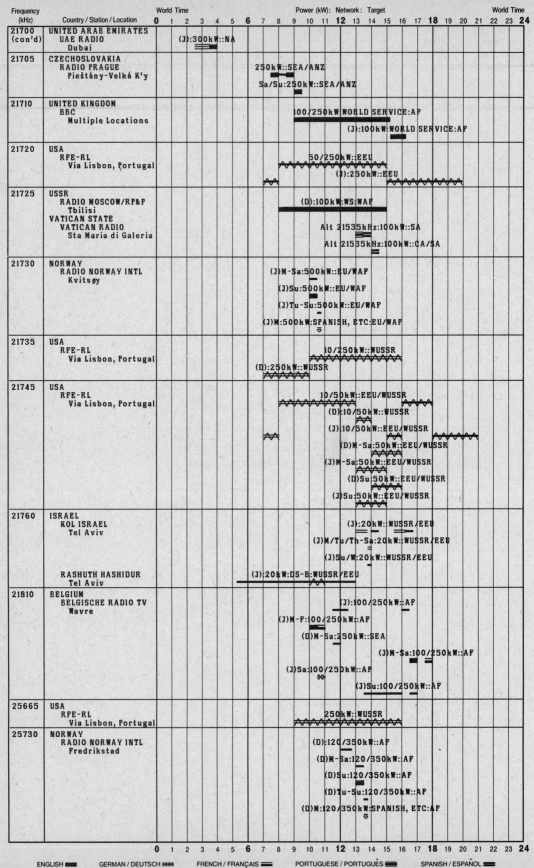

Frequency (kHz)	Country / Station / Location	World Time / Power (kW): Network: Target
21700 (con'd)	**UNITED ARAB EMIRATES** UAE RADIO / Dubai	(J):300kW::NA
21705	**CZECHOSLOVAKIA** RADIO PRAGUE / Pieštány-Velké K'y	250kW::SEA/ANZ Sa/Su:250kW::SEA/ANZ
21710	**UNITED KINGDOM** BBC / Multiple Locations	100/250kW:WORLD SERVICE:AF (J):100kW:WORLD SERVICE:AF
21720	**USA** RFE-RL / Via Lisbon, Portugal	50/250kW::EEU (J):250kW::EEU
21725	**USSR** RADIO MOSCOW/RP&P / Tbilisi **VATICAN STATE** VATICAN RADIO / Sta Maria di Galeria	(D):100kW:WS:WAF Alt 21535kHz:100kW::SA Alt 21535kHz:100kW::CA/SA
21730	**NORWAY** RADIO NORWAY INTL / Kvitsøy	(J)M-Sa:500kW::EU/WAF (J)Su:500kW::EU/WAF (J)Tu-Su:500kW::EU/WAF (J)M:500kW:SPANISH, ETC:EU/WAF
21735	**USA** RFE-RL / Via Lisbon, Portugal	10/250kW::WUSSR (D):250kW::WUSSR
21745	**USA** RFE-RL / Via Lisbon, Portugal	10/50kW::EEU/WUSSR (D):10/50kW::WUSSR (J):10/50kW::EEU/WUSSR (D)M-Sa:50kW::EEU/WUSSR (J)M-Sa:50kW::EEU/WUSSR (D)Su:50kW::EEU/WUSSR (J)Su:50kW::EEU/WUSSR
21760	**ISRAEL** KOL ISRAEL / Tel Aviv RASHUTH HASHIDUR / Tel Aviv	(J):20kW::WUSSR/EEU (J)M/Tu/Th-Sa:20kW::WUSSR/EEU (J)Su/W:20kW::WUSSR/EEU (J):20kW:DS-B:WUSSR/EEU
21810	**BELGIUM** BELGISCHE RADIO TV / Wavre	(J):100/250kW::AF (J)M-F:100/250kW::AF (D)M-Sa:250kW::SEA (J)M-Sa:100/250kW::AF (J)Sa:100/250kW::AF (J)Su:100/250kW::AF
25665	**USA** RFE-RL / Via Lisbon, Portugal	250kW::WUSSR
25730	**NORWAY** RADIO NORWAY INTL / Fredrikstad	(D):120/350kW::AF (D)M-Sa:120/350kW::AF (D)Su:120/350kW::AF (D)Tu-Su:120/350kW::AF (D)M:120/350kW:SPANISH, ETC:AF

World Time: 0 1 2 3 4 5 6 7 8 9 10 11 12 13 14 15 16 17 18 19 20 21 22 23 24

Glossaries and Guides

Terms and Abbreviations Used in World Band Radio

A wide variety of terms and abbreviations is used in world band radio. Some are specialized and need explanation; a few are foreign words that need translation; and yet others are simply adaptations of common usage. Here, then, is *Passport's* guide to what's what in world band terminology and abbreviations—including what each one means. For a thorough writeup on what determines how well a world band radio performs, please see the *RDI White Paper*, "How to Interpret Receiver Specifications and Lab Tests."

Adjacent-Channel Rejection. *See* Selectivity.

AGC. *See* Automatic Gain Control.

Alt. Alternative frequency or channel. Frequency or channel that may be used irregularly or unexpectedly in place of the regularly scheduled frequency or channel.

Amateur Radio. *See* Hams.

AM Band. The local radio band, which currently runs from 520 to 1,611 kHz (530–1700 kHz in North America as of mid-1990), within the Medium Frequency (MF) range. In many countries it is called the mediumwave (MW) band.

Artificial Intelligence. The ability of a computer to operate similarly to the human brain.

Audio Quality, Audio Fidelity. *See* High Fidelity.

Automatic Gain Control. Smoothes out the fluctuations in signal strength brought about by fading, a common occurrence with world band signals.

AV. A Voz—Portuguese for Voice of.

Bandwidth. One of the variables that determines selectivity (*see*), bandwidth is the amount of radio signal a set will let pass through. With world band channel spacing at 5 kHz, the best single bandwidths are usually in the vicinity of 3–6 kHz. Better radios offer two or more selectable bandwidths: one of 5–7 kHz or so for when a station is "in the clear," and one or more others between 2–4 kHz for when a station is hemmed in by other stations next to it.

BC, BS. Broadcasting, Broadcasting Company, Broadcasting Corporation, Broadcasting Station, Broadcasting Service.

Broadcast. A radio or TV transmission meant for the general public. *Compare* Utility Stations.

Cd. Ciudad—Spanish for City.

Channel. An everyday term to indicate where a station is supposed to be located on the dial. World band channels are exactly 5 kHz apart. Stations operating outside this norm are "off channel" (for these, *Passport* provides resolution to better than one kHz to aid in station identification). Measured in units of 5 kHz; that is, world band channels, unlike some other radio/TV channels, aren't assigned sequentially, like street numbers, in an $n + 1$ fashion.

Cl. Club, Clube.

Cu, Cult. Cultura, Cultural, Culture.

(D). Frequency operates at this time winters only. Not heard summers.

Digital Channel Display, Digital Frequency Display, Digital Tuning Display. *See* Synthesizer.

DS. Domestic Service—Broadcasting intended for audiences in the broadcaster's home country. *Compare* ES.

DXers. From an old telegraph term "to DX"; that is, to communicate over a great distance. Thus, "DXers" are those who specialize in finding distant or exotic stations.

Dynamic Range. The ability of a set to handle weak signals in the presence of strong competing signals within the same world band segment (*see* World Band Spectrum). Sets with inferior dynamic range sometimes "overload," causing a mishmash of false signals mixed together up and down—and even beyond—the band segment being received.

Earliest Heard (or **Latest Heard**). See the key at the bottom of each "Blue Page." If the *Passport* monitoring team cannot establish the definite sign-on (or sign-off) time of a station, the earliest (or latest) time the station could be traced is indicated, instead, by a triangular "flag." This means that the station almost certainly operates beyond the time shown by that "flag." It also means that, unless you live relatively close to the station, you're unlikely to be able to hear it beyond that "flagged" time.

Ed, Educ. Educational, Educação, Educadora.

Em. Emissora, Emisora, Emissor, Emetteur—In effect, station in various languages.

EP. Emissor Provincial—Portuguese for Provincial Station.

ER. Emissor Regional—Portuguese for Regional Station.

Ergonomics. How handy and comfortable a set is to operate, especially hour after hour.

ES. External Service—Broadcasting intended for foreign audiences. *Compare* DS.

F. Friday.

Feeder. A "utility" station that transmits programs from the broadcaster's home country to a relay site abroad. Although these stations are not intended to be received by the general public, many world band radios can handle these quasi-broadcasts anyway. Feeders operate in lower sideband (LSB), upper sideband (USB) or independent sideband (termed ISL if heard on the lower side, ISU if heard on the upper side) modes. *See* Single Sideband.

FM Band. The local radio band, usually from 88–108 MHz, within the Very High Frequency (VHF) range. Exceptions: In Japan, the FM band is from 76–90 MHz, and in parts of Eastern Europe and the Soviet Union it runs from 66–73 MHz.

FR. Federal Republic.

Frequency. The standard term to indicate where a station is located on the dial—regardless whether it's "on-channel" or "off-channel" (*see* channel). Measured in kilohertz (kHz) or Megahertz (MHz).

GMT. Greenwich Mean Time—*See* UTC.

Hams. Government-licensed amateur radio hobbyists that communicate with each other by radio for pleasure within special "amateur bands."

High Fidelity, Enhanced Fidelity. World band reception is ordinarily of only fair audio quality, or fidelity,

---

Photo page 401: Steep roofed houses in snowy Shirakawa Village, Japan. Photo by NHK

with some stations sounding even worse. Advanced radios with good audio performance and certain high-tech circuits already can improve on this, and radios of the 21st century are expected to provide genuine high fidelity; i.e., smooth wideband audio and freedom from distortion.

Independent Sideband. *See* Single Sideband.

Interference. Sounds from other stations that are disturbing the station you're trying to hear.

Ionosphere. *See* Propagation.

Irr. Irregular operation or hours of operation; i.e., schedule tends to be unpredictable.

(J). Frequency operates at this time summers only. Not heard winters.

Jamming. Deliberate interference to a transmission with the intent of making reception impossible.

kHz. Kilohertz, the most common unit for measuring where a station is on the dial. Formerly known as "kilocycles/second." 1,000 kilohertz equals one Megahertz.

kW. Kilowatt(s), the most common unit of measurement for transmitter power (*see*).

Loc. Local.

Location. The physical location of the station's transmitter, which may be different from the studio location. Transmitter location is useful as a guide to reception quality. For example, if you're in Eastern North America and wish to listen to Radio Moscow, a transmitter located in the Western USSR will almost certainly provide better reception than one located in Siberia, and one located in Cuba will probably be better yet.

LV. La Voix, La Voz—French and Spanish for The Voice.

M. Monday.

Mediumwave Band. *See* AM Band.

Meters. The unit of measurement used for individual world band segments of the shortwave spectrum. The frequency range covered by a given meters designation—also known as "wavelength"—can be gleaned from the following formula: frequency (kHz) = 299,792/meters. Thus, 49 meters comes out to a frequency of 6118 kHz—well within the range of frequencies included in that segment (*see* World Band Spectrum). Inversely, meters can be derived from the following: meters = 299,792/frequency (kHz).

MHz. Megahertz, a common unit to measure where a station is on the dial. Formerly known as "Megacycles/second." One Megahertz equals 1,000 kilohertz.

Multilingual. See graphics keys at the bottom of each "Blue Page." "Multilingual" is used for programs that are partly in one of the world's primary languages (*Arabic, Chinese, English, French, German, Japanese, Portuguese, Russian, Spanish*) and partly in one or more other languages. Thus, a transmission in *English* and Urdu would be designated as "Multilingual" rather than English, whereas a transmission in Tamil and Urdu—neither of which is a primary language—would be designated simply as "Other."

N. New, Nueva, Nuevo, Nouvelle, Nacional, National.

Nac. Nacional.

Narrow-Band Facsimile Video. A technique in which pictures can be transmitted without taking up a great deal of radio spectrum space.

Nat, Natl. National, Nationale.

Other. Programs are in a language *other* than one of the world's primary languages (*see* Multilingual).

Overloading. *See* Dynamic Range.

PBS. People's Broadcasting Station.

Power. Transmitter power *before* amplification by the antenna, expressed in kilowatts (kW). The present range of world band powers is 0.01 to 600 kW.

PR. People's Republic.

Programmable Channel Memory. Allows you to push one button, as on a car radio, to select a station.

Propagation. World band signals travel, like a basketball, up and down from the station to your radio. The "floor" below is the earth's surface, whereas the "player's hand" on high is the *ionosphere*, a gaseous layer that envelops the earth. While the earth's surface remains pretty much the same from day-to-day, the ionosphere—nature's own satellite—varies in how it propagates radio signals, depending on how much sunlight hits the "bounce points."

This is why some world band segments do well mainly by day, whereas others are best by night. During winter there's less sunlight, so the "night bands" become unusually active, while the "day bands" become correspondingly less useful (*see* World Band Spectrum). Day-to-day changes in the sun's weather also cause shortterm changes in world band radio reception; thisexplains why some days you hear rare signals. Additionally, the 11-year sunspot cycle has a long-term effect on propagation. It's now peaking, so the high bands should be even better than usual through about 1993.

PS. Provincial Station, Pangsong.

Pto. Puerto, Pôrto.

QSL. A card or letter from a station verifying that a listener indeed heard that particular station.

R. Radio, Radiodiffusion, Radiodifusora, Radiodifusão, Radiofonikos, Radiostansiya, Radyo, Radyosu, and so forth.

Receiver. Synonym for a radio. In practice, "receiver" is often used to designate a set—usually a tabletop model—with superior ability to ferret out weak, hard-to-hear signals.

Reg. Regional.

Relay. A retransmission facility—shown in **bold** in "Worldwide Broadcasts"—located outside the broadcaster's country. Relay signals, being closer to the target audience, usually provide superior reception. *See* Feeder.

Rep. Republic, République, República.

RN. *See* R and N.

RS. Radio Station, Radiostantsiya, Radiofonikos Stathmos.

RT, RTV. Radiodiffusion Télévision, Radio Télévision, and so forth.

S. San, Santa, Santo, São, Saint.

Sa. Saturday.

Selectivity. The ability of a set to ignore strong signals next to the one being heard. *See* Bandwidth.

Sensitivity. The ability of a set to receive weak signals.

Shortwave Spectrum. The shortwave spectrum—also known as the High Frequency (HF) spectrum—is, strictly speaking, that portion of the radio spectrum from 3–30 MHz (3,000–30,000 kHz). However, common usage places it between 2–30 MHz (2,000–30,000 kHz). It includes not only world band stations, but also "utility" stations and "hams." *See* World Band

Spectrum, Utility Stations and Hams.

Single Sideband, Independent Sideband. Spectrum-conserving modes of transmission commonly used by "utility" stations and "hams." Very few broadcasters—world band or other—use these modes, but this is expected to change early in the 21st century. Many world band radios are already capable of receiving single sideband transmissions, and some can even receive independent sideband transmissions. *See* Feeder.

St, Sta, Sto. Saint.

Su. Sunday.

Synchronous Detector. World band radios are increasingly coming equipped with this hightech circuit that improves adjacent-channel rejection (*see*).

Synthesizer. Simple radios use ordinary needle-and-dial tuning that makes it difficult to find a desired channel, or to tell what you are hearing, except by ear. Advanced models utilize a digital frequency *synthesizer* to tune in signals without your having to "hunt and peck." Among other things, synthesizers allow for pushbutton tuning and display the exact frequency digitally—two plusses that make tuning in the world much easier.

Target. Where a transmission is beamed if it is intended to be heard outside the country.

          AF — Africa
          AM — Americas
          ANZ — Australia & New Zealand
          AS — Asia
          ATL — Atlantic Ocean & Islands
          CA — Central America, Caribbean & Mexico
          CAF — Central Africa
          EAF — East Africa
          EAS — East Asia
          EEU — Eastern Europe
          ENA — Eastern North America
          EU — Europe
     EUSSR — Eastern USSR
          ME — Middle East
          NA — North America
          NAF — North Africa
          PAC — Pacific Ocean & Islands
          SA — South America
          SAF — Southern Africa
          SAS — South Asia
          SEA — Southeast Asia
          USSR — Soviet Union
          WAF — West Africa
          WEU — Western Europe
          WNA — Western North America
     WUSSR — Western USSR

(+) Tent. Tentative listing. This indicates there is some degree of uncertainty concerning one or more details of the station, such as its exact name or location.

Th. Thursday.

Tu. Tuesday.

Universal Time. *See* UTC.

UTC. Coordinated Universal Time, also known as World Time, Greenwich Mean Time and Zulu. With 161 countries on world band radio, if each announced its own local time you would need a calculator to figure it all out. To get around this, a single international time—UTC—is used. The difference between UTC and local time is determined simply by listening to UTC time checks given on the hour by world band

broadcasters. A 24-hour clock is used, so "1800 UTC" means 6:00 PM UTC. If you're in North America, Eastern Time is five hours behind UTC winters and four hours behind UTC summers, so 1800 UTC would be 1:00 PM EST or 2:00 PM EDT. The easiest solution is to use a 24-hour clock set to UTC. Many radios already have these built in, and UTC clocks are also available as accessories.

"Utility" Stations. Most signals within the shortwave spectrum are not world band stations. Rather, they are professional "utility" stations—radio telephones, ships at sea, aircraft and the like—that transmit point-to-point and are not intended to be heard by the general public. *Compare* Broadcast, Hams and Feeders.

v. Variable frequency; i.e., one that is unstable or drifting because of a transmitter malfunction.

Vo. Voice of.

W. Wednesday.

Wavelength. *See* Meters.

World Band Radio. Similar to regular AM band and FM band radio, except that world band broadcasts can be heard for enormous distances and thus often carry programs created especially for audiences abroad. Hundreds of millions of people on every continent now listen to world band radio.

World Band Spectrum. The collected segments of the shortwave spectrum set aside by the International Telecommunication Union (ITU) for broadcasting. The ITU also allows some world band broadcasting to take place outside these segments. The official world band segments—along with, when appropriate, the "real world" segments [in brackets]—follow, with general guides as to when reception may be best. Remember, these are only *general* guides—actual reception will vary according to your location, the station's location, the time of year, and other factors (*see* Propagation).

Weak Reception Winter Nights

*120 Meters:
 2300–2498 kHz (Tropical Domestic Stations)
*90 Meters:
 3200–3400 kHz (Tropical Domestic Stations)

Fair Reception Winter Nights

*75 Meters:
 3900–3950 kHz (Asia & Pacific only)
 3950–4000 kHz (except Americas)
*60 Meters:
 4750–5060 kHz [4000–5730 kHz] (Tropical Domestic Stations)

Strong Nighttime Reception

49 Meters:
 5950–6200 kHz [5850–6600 kHz]
*41 Meters:
 7100–7300 kHz [6800–7600 kHz]

Strong Night and Day Reception

31 Meters:
9500–9900 kHz [9000–9100 & 9300–10100 kHz]
25 Meters:
11650–12050 kHz [11500–12100 kHz]

Strong Daytime Reception

21 Meters:
13600–13800 kHz
19 Meters:
15100–15600 kHz [15000–15700 kHz]
16 Meters:
17550–17900 kHz
13 Meters:
21450–21850 kHz

Fair Daytime Reception

11 Meters:
25670–26100 kHz**
World Time. *See* UTC.
WS. World Service.

---

*Shared with other radio services, such as "utility" stations and "hams."
**Provides interference-free reception briefly many days.

Termes et abréviations

Il existe, dans le domaine de la radiodiffusion par bandes internationales, une multiplicité de termes techniques et d'abréviations: acceptions spécialisées à définir, locutions étrangères à traduire, expressions usuelles à préciser. Pour rendre accessible ce vocabulaire international nous avons dressé la liste des termes couramment employés.

Alt. Fréquence alternative. Fréquence qui s'emploie de façon irrégulière ou exceptionnellement à la place d'une fréquence régulière.
AV. A Voz—portugais: Voix de.
BC, BS. Radiodiffusion, Société de Radiodiffusion, station de radiodiffusion, service de radiodiffusion.

Cd. Ciudad—espagnol: ville.
Cl. Club, clube.
Cu, Cult. Cultura, Cultural, Culture.
(D). Fréquence en opération à l'heure indiquée seulement en hiver.
DS. Service interne—radiodiffusion à l'intention de l'auditoire national, *v.* ES.
Earliest Heard (or **Latest Heard**). Début d'Ecoute (ou Fin d'Ecoute). V. en bas de la page bleue. Dans le cas où notre équipe de contrôle ne réussissait pas à établir, de façon définitive, le début ou la fin d'une émission, l'heure de la première réception captée est indiquée au moyen d'un triangle. Il faut en déduire que la station émet probablement en dehors de

GUIDE DE WORLDSCAN

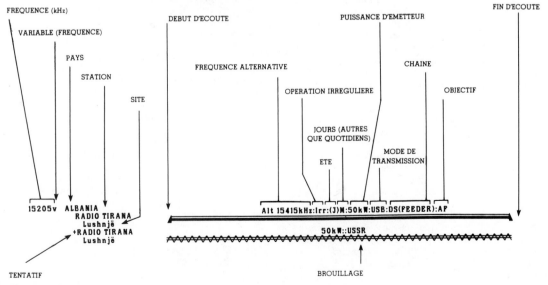

l'heure indiquée au triangle et, qu'à moins d'habiter à proximité de la station d'émission, on ne peut la capter en dehors de l'heure indiquée au triangle.

Ed, Educ. Educational, Educação, Educadora—éducatif.

Em. Emissora, Emisora, Emissor, Emetteur—équivalence dans plusieurs langues de "station."

EP. Emissor Provincial—portugais: Station provinciale.

ER. Emissor Regional—portugais: Station régionale.

ES. Service externe—radiodiffusion à l'intention d'auditoires étrangers, v. DS.

F. Vendredi.

Feeder. Station réservée à l'intention de certains usagers diffusant des programmes du pays d'origine vers un site de relais situé à l'étranger. Bien que ces émissions ne s'adressent pas à des auditoires généraux, il est cependant possible de les capter au moyen de postes récepteurs à gammes mondiales. Les lignes d'alimentation opèrent en différents modes: bandes latérales inférieures LSB), bandes latérales supérieures (USB), bandeslatérales indépendantes (désignées ISL dans le cas des bandes inférieures, ISU dans le cas des bandes supérieures.)

FR. République Fédérale.

Frequency. Fréquence: terme normalement employé pour indiquer la position exacte au cadran d'une station, et qui se mesure en kilohertz (kHz.) or Mégahertz (MHz.).

Irr. Heures d'écoute irrégulières, c'est-à-dire que l'horaire tend à changer d'une façon imprévisible.

Jamming. Brouillage intentionnel occasionné afin de perturber la réception d'une station.

kHz. Kilohertz: l'unité de mesure la plus employée pour indiquer au cadran la situation exacte d'une station. Autrefois se calculait en "kilocycles/seconde." 1 000 kilohertz égale un Mégahertz.

kW. Kilowatt(s): l'unité normalement employée pour mesurer la puissance d'émetteur.

Loc. Local.

Location. Le lieu où est situé l'émetteur d'une station et qui n'est pas nécéssairement celui des studios de programmation. Il existe entre le site de l'émetteur et la qualité de réception une corrélation certaine. Par exemple, si l'on est en Europe et que l'on veut écouter Radio Moscou, la réception assurée par un émetteur situé à l'ouest de l'URSS sera sans doute meilleure que celle en provenance de la Sibérie, et celle en provenance de la Bulgarie sera encore mieux.

LV. La Voix, La Voz (Espagnol).

M. Lundi.

Meters. L'unité de mesure utilisée pour désigner des segments de bandes du spectre ondes courtes. La gamme des fréquences désignée par un certain nombre de mètres donnés—ou longueur d'onde—se déduit d'après la formule suivante: fréquence (kHz.) = 299 792/mètres. Par conséquent, 49 mètres répond à une fréquence de 6 118 kHz.—étant bien dans la gamme des fréquences comprises dans ce segment. (V. World Band Spectrum). A l'opposé, on peut calculer la fréquence en mètres d'après la formule suivante: mètres = 299 792/fréquence (kHz.).

Multilingual. V. les symboles en bas de chaque "page bleue." "Multilinguistique" désigne les programmes diffusés en partie dans une des langues universelles (*arabe, chinois, anglais, français, allemand, japonais, portugais, russe, espagnol*), et, en partie, dans une ou plusieurs autres langues. Une émission,

par exemple, en *anglais* et en ourdou serait désignée comme "Multilingual" plutôt que "English," tandis qu'une émission en tamoul et en ourdou—dont ni l'une ni l'autre ne sont des langues universelles—serait tout simplement désignée comme "Other."

N. New, Nueva, Nuevo, Nouveau, Nouvelle, Nacional, National.

Nac. Nacional.

Nat., Natl. National, Nationale.

Other. Programmes diffusés dans une langue *autre* qu'une des langues universelles (v. Multilingual).

PBS People's Broadcasting Station: Station de Radiodiffusion Populaire.

Power. Puissance d'émetteur *avant* l'amplification par antenne, exprimée en kilowatts (kW.). Le spectre actuel des gammes mondiales se situe entre 0,01 et 600 kW.

PR. People's Republic: République Populaire.

PS. Station Provinciale, Pangsong.

Pto. Puerto, Pôrto.

R. Radio, Radiodiffusion, Radiodifusora, Radio-difusão, Radiofonikos, Radiostansiya, Radyo, Radyosu, et cetera.

Reg. Régional.

Relay. Installation de radiodiffusion—indiquée en **caractères gras** dans "Worldwide Broadcasts"—située à l'étranger. Les signaux de relais, étant plus proches des auditeurs ciblés, assurent généralement une meilleure réception. V. Feeder.

Rep. Republic, République, Republica.

RN. V. R. et N.

RS. Station de Radio, Radiostantsiya, Radiofonikos Stathmos.

RT, RTV. Radiodiffusion Télévision, Radio Televisión, et cetera.

S. Saint, San, Santo, Santa, São.

Sa. Samedi.

Shortwave Spectrum. Spectre Ondes Courtes. Le spectre ondes courtes ou spectre à hautes fréquences (HF) correspond à la partie du spectre située entre 3 et 30 MHz. (3 000–30 000 kHz.). Les fréquences normalement employées, cependant, se situent entre 2 et 30 MHz. (2 000– 30 000 kHz.). Cette gamme comporte non seulement les bandes ondes courtes captées à traverle monde mais aussi les stations réservées à certains usagers dans les domaines de la radiotéléphonie, des services maritimes, de la radio amateur, et cetera.

St., Sta., Sto. Saint.

Su. Dimanche.

Target. Région-cible. Pays vers lequel une émission est diffusée à l'intention d'un auditoire étranger.

    AF — Afrique
    AM — Amériques
    ANZ — Australie et Nouvelle Zélande
    AS — Asie
    ATL — Atlantique: Océan et Iles
    CA — Amérique Centrale, les Caraïbes et le Mexique
    CAF — Afrique Centrale
    EAF — Afrique de l'Est
    EAS — Asie de l'Est
    EEU — Europe de l'Est
    ENA — L'Est de l'Amérique du Nord
    EU — Europe

EUSSR — Partie Est de l'URSS
ME — Moyen Orient
NA — Amérique du Nord
NAF — Afrique du Nord
PAC — Pacifique: Océan et Iles
SA — Amérique du Sud
SAF — Afrique du Sud
SAS — Asie du Sud
SEA — Asie du Sud-est
USSR — URSS
WAF — Afrique de l'Ouest
WEU — Europe de l'Ouest
WNA — Ouest de l'Amérique du Nord
WUSSR — Ouest de l'URSS

(+) **Tent.** Donnée approximative. Cette notation indique un degré d'incertitude concernant, par exemple, le site précis ou le nom exact de la station.

Th. Jeudi.

Tu. Mardi.

Universal Time. *V.* UTC.

UTC. Heure Universelle Coordonnée. Si chacun des 161 pays à diffuser sur bandes mondiales annonçait l'heure locale, l'auditeur aurait à faire, sans cesse, des calculs compliqués. Pour résoudre ce problème, on a recours à l'emploi d'une heure universelle coordonnée. Afin de déterminer la différence entre l'heure universellecoordonnée et l'heure locale, il suffit simplement d'écouter les annonces de vérification régulièrement programmées au début de chaque heure par les Chaînes Internationales deRadiodiffusion. On utilise l'horloge de 24 heures. Ainsi par "1800 UTC" il faut comprendre 6:00 du soir UTC. Pour l'auditeur de Paris l'heure locale, l'hiver, avance d'une heure sur celle d'UTC, tandis que, l'été, l'heure locale avance de deux heures sur celle d'UTC. Ainsi, 1800 UTC serait l'équivalence, en hiver, de 7:00 du soir, heure locale, et de 8:00 du soir, heure locale, en été. Pour effectuer cetter conversion il est possible de se servir d'horloges munies d'un cadran 24-heures réglé sur l'UTC. Il existe de nombreux récepteurs prémunis de ces cadrans qui peuvent également s'acheter comme accessoires.

v. Fréquence variable; c'est-à-dire peu stable ou fluctuante à cause du fonctionnement défectueux d'un émetteur.

Vo. Voix de.

W. Mercredi.

World Band Radio. Semblable à la radiodiffusion sur ondes moyennes (AM) et en modulation de fréquence (FM), sauf que la radiodiffusion à gammes mondiales peut être captée à longue distance et diffuse donc des programmes destinés à des auditoires étrangers. Des millions d'auditeurs dans tous les continents écoutent à présent des émissions à gammes mondiales.

World Band Spectrum. L'ensemble des bandes du spectre ondes courtes attribuées à la radiodiffusion universelle par l'Union Internationale de Télécommunication (ITU). L'ITU autorise également la diffusion de certaines émissions en dehors des bandes prévues. La liste des bandes universelles conférées—et, s'il y a lieu, des bandes réservées à des usagers spécialisés [entre parenthèses]—s'accompagne de recommandations quant aux meilleures heures d'écoute. Il ne faut pas oublier qu'il s'agit

simplement d'indications générales et que la qualité de réception varie suivant le lieu de réception, la situation géographique de la station, la saison de l'année, et d'autres facteurs encore.

Réception de nuit médiocre en hiver

*120 Mètres:
2300–2498 kHz. (Stations Tropicales Internes)

*90 Mètres:
3200–3400 kHz. (Stations Tropicales Internes)

Réception de nuit satisfaisante en hiver

*75 Mètres:
3900–3950 kHz. (Asie et Pacifique exclusivement)

*60 Mètres:
4750–5060 kHz. [4000–5730 kHz.] (Stations Tropicales Internes)

Réception de nuit excellente

49 Mètres:
5950–6200 kHz. [5850–6600 kHz.]

*41 Mètres:
9500–9900 kHz. [6800–7600 kHz.]

31 Mètres:
9500–9900 kHz. [9000–9100 & 9300–10100 kHz.]

25 Mètres:
11760–12050 kHz. [11500–12100 kHz.]

Réception de jour excellente

21 Mètres:
13600–13800 kHz.

19 Mètres:
15100–15600 kHz. [15000–15700 kHz.]

16 Mètres:
17550–17900 kHz.

13 Mètres:
21450–21850 kHz.

Réception de jour satisfaisante

11 Mètres:
25670–26100 kHz.**

World Time. *V.* UTC.

WS. World Service: service mondial.

---

*Bandes réparties entre plusieurs services: stations réservées aux usagers spécialisés et aux amateurs.
**Permet une réception sans interférence pendant de courtes périodes. Les meilleures conditions d'écoute se produiront d'ici vers 1993.

Terminos y abreviaturas

Se utiliza una amplia gama de términos y abreviaturas en este libro. Algunos son especializados y necesitan un explicación; otros son de procedencia extranjera y requieren una traducción; y algunos son adaptaciones de uso común. Lo que sigue es una guía de las abreviaturas y terminología utilizadas, incluyendo las explicaciones correspondientes.

Alt. Frecuencia alternativa; una frecuencia cuyo uso sea imprevisto o irregular y en lugar de la frecuencia asignada.

AV. A Voz.

BC, BS. Broadcasting, Broadcasting Company, Broadcasting Corporation; Broadcasting Station, Broadcasting Service.

Cd. Ciudad.

Cl. Club, Clube.

Cu, Cult. Cultura, Cultural, Culture.

(D). Indica que los detalles refieren solamente al período 'D' que corresponde al invierno en el hemisferio del norte y al verano en los países del sur.

DS. Domestic Service (Servicio Doméstico).

Earliest Heard (or **Latest Heard**). Vease la clave al pie de cada 'Hoja Azul'. Si el equipo de monitores del *Passport* no puede establecer definitivamente el comienzo (o fin) de una transmisión, se entra en cambio la hora más temprana (o tarde) en que pudo rastrearse la estación, indicándola con una banderita triangular.

Ed, Educ. Educational, Educação, Educadora.

Em. Emisora, Emissor, Emissora, Emetteur.

EP. Emissor Provinical.

ER. Emissor Regional.

ES. External Service (Servicio al Exterior).

F. Friday (Viernes).

Feeder. Una transmisión de servicio fijo (punto a punto) usualmente en modo de banda lateral única o independiente, dirigida a la estación de redifusión desde el país de origen de la transmisión. Aunque no destinadas para la recepcióngeneral, las transmisiones de eslabón de onda corta a veces proporcionan la mejor o única oportunidad para la recepción de una emisora determinada a una hora dada. Por esta razón se incluyen en el *Passport* datos sobre este tipo de transmisión, aunque el uso no sea regular. Los modos de transmisión para los eslabones de onda corta son:
LSB—Banda lateral inferior (señal banda lateral única)
ISL—Banda lateral inferior (de una señal banda lateral independiente)
USB—Banda lateral superior (señal banda lateral única)
ISU—Banda lateral superior (de una señal banda lateral independiente)

FR. Federal Republic (República Federal).

Frequency. Frecuencia. La medida más ampliamente aceptada para indicar la ubicación de una estación dentro de la gama radial. La frecuencia se expresa en kilohertz (kHz) o Megahertz (MHz).

Irr. Operación irregular; horas de recepción irregulares.

(J.) Indica que los detalles refieren solamente al período 'J' que corresponde al verano en el hemisferio del norte y al invierno en los países del sur.

Jamming. Interferencia intencional a una transmisión con el propósito de hacer imposible la recepción de la misma.

kHz. Kilohertz. Anteriormente conocido como 'kilociclo(s) por segundo'. *Vease* 'Frequency'.

kW. Kilovatio(s) (*vease* 'Power').

COMO UTILIZAR EL WORLDSCAN

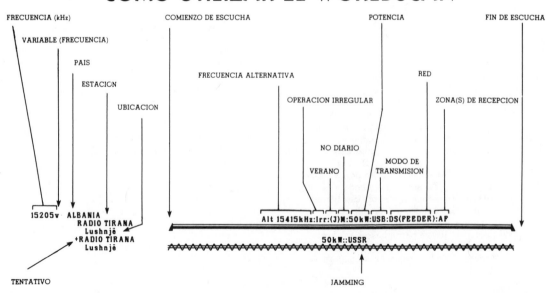

Loc. Local.

Location La ubicación física del complejo transmisor/antena. Esta ubicación pudiera no corresponder a la de los estudios donde se preparan los programas.

LV. La Voix, La Voz.

M. Monday (Lunes).

Meters. Metros. La unidad para definir segmentos determinados de la gama de onda corta. La gama de frecuencias cubierta por una designación en metros (también conocida como 'longitud de onda') puede calcularse de la siguiente fórmula: frecuencia (kHz) = 299.792/metros. Así 49 metros corresponde a la frecuencia de 6118 kHz—bien dentro de la gama de frecuencias incluidas en ese segmento (*vease* 'World Band Spectrum'). Inversamente, metros pueden derivarse de la fórmula: metros = 299.792/frecuencia.

MHz. Megahertz. Anteriormente conocido como 'Megaciclo(s) por segundo'. Un Megahertz equivale a 1.000 kilohertz.

Multilingual. Vease la clave al pie de cada 'Hoja Azul'. 'Multilingual' es utilizado cuando hay programas parcialmente en uno de los idiomas principales del mundo (*alemán, árabe, chino, español, francés, inglés, japonés, portugués o ruso*) y parcialmente en otro(s) idioma(s). Así una transmisión en español y quechua sería designada como 'Multilingual', mientras que una emisión en quechua y aymara sería designada como 'Other' = (Otro).

N. New, Nouvelle, Nova, Novo, Nueva, Nuevo; Nacional, National, Nationale.

Nac. Nacional.

Nat, Natl. National, Nationale.

Network. La red o el servicio de una emisión. Transmisiones de servicios domésticos son indicadas por 'DS'.

Other. Otro. Cualquier idioma fuera de los principales idiomas del mundo (*vease* 'Multilingual').

PBS. People's Broadcasting Station (Estación de Radiodifusión del Pueblo).

Power. La potencia de salida de RF (radiofrecuencia)—eso es, antes de la amplificación—expresado en kilovatios. La gama actual de potencias de emisoras de onda corta es 0.01–600kW.

PR. People's Republic (República Popular).

PS. Provincial Station, Pangsong.

Pto. Puerto, Pôrto.

R. Radio, Radiodiffusion, Radiodifusora, Radiodifusão, Radioemisora, Radiofonikos, Radiostantsiya, Radyo, Radyosu, etc.

Reg. Regional.

Relay Instalaciones transmisoras extraterritoriales que retransmiten programas recibidos por satélite, eslabón de onda corta, o en forma de grabación.

Rep. Republic, República, République.

RN. *Vease* 'R' y 'N'.

RS. Radio Station, Radiostantsiya, Radiofonikos Stathmos.

RT, RTV. Radiodiffusion Télévision, Radio Televisión, etc.

n, Santa, Santo, São.

Sa. Saturday (Sábado).

Shortwave Spectrum. Gama de onda corta. Estrictamente hablando, la gama de onda corta (o alta frecuencia) es esa porción de la gama radial que se encuentra entre 3 y 30 MHz (3.000–30.000 kHz). Sin embargo, de ordinario se ubica la gama de onda corta entre 2 y 30 MHz aproximadamente, e incluye no solo

estaciones de radiodifusión sino también radioaficionados y servicios utilitarios tal como radiotelefonía y radioteletipo.

St. Saint.

Sta, Sto. Santa; Santo.

Su. Sunday (Domingo).

Target. Adonde se dirige un transmisión, con tal que está destinada fuera del país de origen.

  AF—África
  AM—Américas
  ANZ—Australia & Nueva Zelandia
  AS—Asia
  ATL—Océano Atlántico
  CA—América Central, Caribe & México
  CAF—África Central
  EAF—África Oriental
  EAS—Asia Oriental
  EEU—Europa Oriental
  ENA—América del Norte (Este)
  EU—Europa
EUSSR—URSS Oriental
  ME—Oriente Medio
  NA—América del Norte
  NAF—África del Norte
  PAC—Pacífico
  SA—América del Sur
  SAF—África Meridional
  SAS—Sud Asia
  SEA—Asia (Sudeste)
  USSR—URSS (Unión Soviética)
  WAF—África Occidental
  WEU—Europa Occidental
  WNA—América del Norte (Oeste)
 WUSSR—URSS Occidental

(+) Tent. Tentativo (-a); eso es, la exactitud de algunos detalles (p.ej. el nombre exacto de la estación) está incierta.

Th. Thursday (Jueves).

Tu. Tuesday (Martes).

Universal Time. *Vease* 'UTC'.

UTC. Hora Universal Coordinada. Con unos 160 países transmitiendo sus programas en onda corta, es necesario utilizar una hora única para evitar confusión entre las emisoras y sus oyentes. Esta referencia internacional de 24 horas para la radiodifusión se llama UTC. La diferencia entre UTC y la hora local puede determinarse escuchando los avisos rutinarios de la hora UTC transmitidos por emisoras internacionales. Si uno está en Madrid, la hora local de invierno es UTC + 1, y de verano, UTC + 2. Así 1800 UTC sería las siete de la noche en invierno, y ocho de la noche en verano.

v. Frecuencia variable, eso es, una que es inestable.

Vo. Voice of (Voz de).

W. Wednesday (Miércoles).

Wavelength. Longitud de onda (*vease* 'Meters').

World Band Radio. Similar a onda media y frecuencia modulada, con la excepción de que las emisiones pueden ser captadas sobre enormes distancias. Por eso las transmisiones contienen a menudo programas creados especialmente para audiencias en el exterior. Hoy en día cientos de millones de gente en todos los continentes escuchan estas emisiones.

World Band Spectrum. Todos los segmentos de la gama de onda corta autorizados por la Unión Internacional de Telecomunicaciones (UIT) para la radiodifusión.

La UIT también permite el uso de algunas frecuencias fuera de estos segmentos. Los segmentos oficialmente autorizados—junto con los segmentos actualmente utilizados [entre paréntesis rectangular]—siguen, con algunas sugerencias generales para indicar cuando la recepción podría ser óptima. Conviene recordar que estas sugerencias son generales ya que la recepción variará de acuerdo a la ubicación de la emisora, la estación del año, y otros factores.

Recepción débil, noches de invierno

*120 Metros:
2300–2498 kHz (Emisoras domésticas tropicales)

*90 Metros:
3200–3400 kHz (Emisoras domésticas tropicales)

*75 Metros:
3900–3950 kHz (Asia & Pacífico solamente)
3950–4000 kHz (excepto las Américas)

*60 Metros:
4750–5060 kHz [4000–5730 kHz] (Emisoras domésticas tropicales)

Buena recepción nocturna

49 Metros:
5950–6200 kHz [5800–6600 kHz]

*41 Metros:
7100–7300 kHz [6800–7600 kHz]

Buena recepción, día y noche

31 Metros:
9500–9900 kHz [9000–9100 & 9300–10100 kHz]

25 Metros:
11650–12050 kHz [11500–12100 kHz]

Buena recepción diurna

21 Metros:
13600–13800 kHz

19 Metros:
13600–13800 kHz

19 Metros:
15100–15600 kHz [15000–15700 kHz]

16 Metros:
17550–17900 kHz

13 Metros:
21450–21850 kHz

Recepción diurna regular

11 Metros:
25670–26100 kHz**

---

*Compartido con otros servicios radiofónicos, tal como estaciones utilitarias y radioaficionados.
**Proporciona breves períodos de recepción sin interferencia durante muchos días, con los mejores resultados desde ahora hasta 1993 aproximadamente.

WORLDSCAN: GEBRAUCHSANWEISUNG

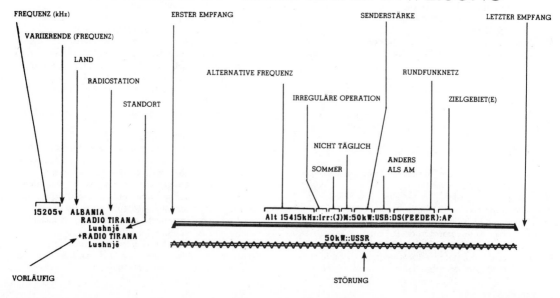

Begriffe und Abkuerzungen die im Weltbandradio vorkommen

Im Weltbandradio wird eine große Anzahl technischer, ausländischer und aus der Allgemeinsprache übernommene Begriffe verwendet. Der folgende Glossar dient als Orientierungshilfe für den *Passport* Benützer.

Alt. Alternative frequency: Alternative Frequenz die abwechselnd an Stelle der regelmäßigen Frequenz verwendet werden kann.

AV. A Voz: Portugiesisch für Stimme von.

BC. Broadcasting, Broadcasting Company, Broadcasting Corporation: Rundfunksendung, Rundfunkgesellschaft.

BS. Broadcasting Station, Broadcasting Service: Rundfunksender, Rundfunkdienst.

Cd. Ciudad: Spanisch für Stadt.

Cl. Club, Clube: Klub.

Cu. Cult., Cultura, Culture, Cultural: Kultur, kulturell.

(D). Frequenz kann zur Zeit nur im Winter empfangen werden. Empfang im Sommer nicht möglich.

DS. Domestic Service: Rundfunkdienst fürs Inland. *Vergleiche* ES.

Earliest Heard (or Latest Heard). Hineinschwinden (oder Herausschwinden). Siehe Schlüssel am unteren Rande der „Blue Pages." Falls das *Passport*-Rundfunkerfasserteam den Anfang oder das Ende einer Sendung nicht genau bestimmen kann, wird die früheste (oder späteste) mögliche Empfangszeit durch ein schwarzes Dreieck (,) angegeben. Das heißt, die Rundfundsendug kann nur mit aller Wahrscheinlichkeit über die mit dem schwarzen Dreieck angegebene Zeit hinaus empfangen werden, wenn man in unmittelbarer Nähe des Rundfunksenders wohnt.

Ed., Educ. Educational, Educação, Educadora: Bildungsprogramm.

Em. Emissora, Emisora, Emissor, Emetteur: Begriff für Sender in verschiedenen Sprachen.

EP. Emissor Provincial: Portugiesisch für Landkreis-Sender.

ER. Emissor Regional: Portugiesisch für Regional-Sender.

ES. External Service: Rundfunkdienst fürs Ausland. *Siehe* DS.

F. Friday: Freitag.

Feeder. Versorger: Eine „Versorgungsstation" die Programme vom Rundfunkdienst im Inland an eine Relaisstelle im Ausland sendet. Obwohl der Empfang dieser Stationen für die öffentlichkeit nicht beabsichtigt ist, können viele der Weltbandradios diese Neo-Rundfunksendungen auf jeden Fall empfangen. „Feeder" Sendearten sind:
1. Unteres Seitenband (LSB—Lower Sideband)
2. Oberes Seitenband (USB—Upper Sideband)
3. Unabhängiges Seitenband (Independent Sideband)
   a. Unteres (ISL—lower)
   b. Oberes (ISU—upper)

FR. Federal Republic: Bundesrepublik.

Frequency. Frequenz: Das Standardmaß um die Lage einer Sendung im Radiospektrum anzugeben. Wird in Kilohertz (kHz) oder Megahertz (MHz) ausgedrückt.

Irr. Irregular Operation or Hours of Operation: Unregelmäßige Sendung, das heißt Sendeprogramm ist nicht vorhersagbar.

(J). Frequenz kann zur Zeit nur im Sommer empfangen werden. Empfang im Winter nicht möglich.

Jamming. Störung durch andere Sender: Der Empfang einer Sendung wird mit Absicht gestört.

kHz. Kilohertz: Allgemeine Maßeinheit um die Lage einer Sendung im Radiospektrum anzugeben. Früher bekannt als „Kilocycles/second." 1000 kHz = 1 MHz.

kW. Kilowatt(s): Allgemeine Maßeinheit der Senderleistung.

Loc. Local: örtlich.

Location. Standort des Radiosenders, der mit dem Standort des Studios nicht übereinstimmen muß. Der Standort des Radiosenders ist für die Empfangsqualität wichtig. Z.B. ist der Empfang Radio Moskaus in Europa bei einem Senderstandort im Westen der Sowjetunion wahrscheinlicher als bei einem Senderstandort in Sibirien. Ein Standort in Bulgarien wäre günstiger.

LV. La Voix, La Voz: Französisch und Spanisch für Die Stimme.

M. Monday: Montag.

Meters. Maßeinheit für einzelne Weltbandabschnitte des Kurzwellenspektrums. Der Frequenzbereich gemessen in Meter, auch als Wellenlänge bekannt, kann mit folgender Formel errechnet werden: Frequenz (kHz) = 299,792/Meter. D.h. 49 m = Frequenz von 6118 kHz liegt mit Sicherheit im Kurzwellenbereich (*siehe* Weltbandspektrum). Umgekehrt, können Meter errechnet werden: Meter = 299,792/Frequenz (kHz).

MHz. Megahertz: Allgemeine Maßeinheit um die Lage einer Sendung im Radiospektrum anzugeben. Früher bekannt als „Megacycles/second." 1 MHz = 1000 kHz.

Multilingual. Mehrsprachig. Siehe graphischer Schlüssel am unteren Rand der „Blue Pages." „Muitilingual"— Programme werden zu einem Teil in einer der Weltsprachen (*Arabisch, Chinesisch, Englisch, Französisch, Deutsch, Japanisch, Portugiesisch, Russisch, Spanisch*) und zum anderen Teil in einer oder mehreren anderen Sprachen ausgestrahlt. D.h. eine Sendung in Englisch und Urdu wird als „Multilingual" bezeichnet (anstatt nur „Englisch"), während eine Sendung in Tamil und Urdu nur als „Other" („Andere") bezeichnet wird, da keine der beiden eine Weltsprache ist.

N. New, Nueva, Nuevo, Novelle: Neu.

Nac. Nacional: National.

Nat. Natl., National, Nationale: National.

Other. Andere. Programme in anderen Sprachen als Weltsprachen. (*Siehe* Multilingual).

PBS. People's Broadcasting Station: Volksrundfunkstation.

Power. Kraft. Senderleistung vor der Amplifikation durch die Antenne, ausgedrückt in Kilowatt (kW). Der Empfangsbereich des Weltbandradios liegt z.Zt. zwischen 0.01 und 600 kW.

PR. People's Republic: Volksrepublik.

PS. Provincial Station, Pangsong: Landkreis-Sender.

Pto. Puerto, Pôrto: Hafen.

R. Radio, Radiodiffusion, Radiodifusora, Radiodifusão, Radiofonikos, Radiostansiya, Radyo, Radyosu, usw.: Radio

Reg. Regional: Regional.

Relay. Relais. Eine zusätzliche Sendestation (fettgedruckt im „Worldwide Broadcasts") im Ausland. Relaissignale in der Nähe des Empfängers ermöglichen einen besseren Empfang. (*Siehe* Feeder.)

Rep. Republic, République, Republica: Republik.

RN. *Siehe* R. und N.

RS. Radio Station, Radiostansiya, Radiofonikos Stathmos: Radiostation.

RT, RTV. Radiodiffusion Télévision, Radio Television, etc.: Radio und Fernsehen.

S. San, Santa, Santo, São, Saint: Sankt (St.).

Sa. Saturday: Samstag.

Shortwave Spectrum. Kurzwellenspektrum. Das Kurzwellenspektrum, auch als Hochfrequenzspektrum (HF) bekannt, liegt genau gesagt zwischen 3 und 30 MHz (3,000–30,000 kHz) im Radiospektrum. Die allgemeine Empfangsmöglichkeit liegt jedoch zwischen 2 und 30 MHz (2,000–30,000 kHz). Enthalten sind nicht nur die Weltbandstationen, sondern auch die Versorgerstationen („Feeder")–Radiotelephone, Schiffe auf See, usw.–und Radioamateure.

St., Sta., Sto. Saint: Sankt (St.).

Su. Sunday: Sonntag.

Target. Zielgebiet einer Sendung, wenn sie außerhalb des Landes gehört werden soll. „Targets" sind:

AF – Africa: Afrika

AM – Americas: Die amerikanischen Kontinente

ANZ – Australia & New Zealand: Australien & Neuseeland

AS – Asia: Asien

ATL – Atlantic Ocean & Islands: Atlantischer Ozean & Inseln

CA – Central America, Caribbean, & Mexico: Mittelamerika, Karibik, & Mexiko

CAF – Central Africa: Zentralafrika

EAF – East Africa: Ostafrika

EAS – East Asia: Ostasien

EEU – Eastern Europe: Osteuropa

ENA – Eastern North America: Ostnordamerika

EU – Europe: Europa

EUSSR – Eastern USSR: UdSSR (Ost)

ME – Middle East: Nahost

NA – North America: Nordamerika

NAF – North Africa: Nordafrika

PAC – Pacific Ocean & Islands: Pazifischer Ozean & Inseln

SA – South America: Südamerika

SAF – Southern Africa: Südliches Afrika

SAS – South Asia: Südasien

SEA – Southeast Asia: Südostasien

USSR – Soviet Union: Sowjetunion

WAF – West Africa: Westafrika

WEU – Western Europe: Westeuropa

WNA – Western North America: Westnordamerika

WUSSR – Western USSR: UdSSR (West)

(+) Tent. Tentative listing: Probeverzeichnis. Hinweis auf unbestimmte Einzelheiten einer Station, wie z.B. Name und Standort.

Th. Thursday: Donnerstag.

Tu. Tuesday: Dienstag.

Universal Time. Universalzeit. *Siehe* UTC.

UTC. Coordinated Universal Time: Koordinierte Universalzeit. 161 Länder der Welt beteiligen sich am Weltbandradio. Wenn jedes Land seine Ortszeit angeben würde, so müßte der Empfänger einen Rechner benützen um seine Zeit zu kalkulieren. Um das zu vermeiden wird eine internationale Zeit–UTC–verwendet. Stündliche UTC-Zeitansagen im Weltbandrundfunk geben die Differenz zwischen UTC und der jeweiligen Ortszeit an. Eine 24-Stunden-Uhr wird verwendet, d.h. „1800" UTC = 6:00 PM UTC. Die deutsche Winter-/Sommerzeit is 1 bzw. 2 Stunden später als UTC-Zeit. (D.h. 1800 UTC = 7:00 PM Winterzeit und 8:00 PM Sommerzeit). Am einfachsten ist es eine 24-Stunden-Uhr auf UTC-Zeit einzustellen. Bei vielen Radios ist diese schon eingebaut und außerdem sind UTC-Uhren als Zusatz erhältlich.

v. Variable frequency: Variierende Frequenz. D.h. eine Frequenz die wegen Funktionsstörung des Senders unstabil oder schwankend ist.

Vo. Voice of: Stimme von.

W. Wednesday: Mittwoch.

Wavelength. Wellenlänge. *Siehe* Meters.

World Band Radio. Weltbandradio. Ähnlich dem normalen Mittelwellenband (AM, FM) mit der Ausnahme, daß es möglich ist Programme über große Entfernungen ins Ausland zu senden. Weltbandradio kann nun von Hunderten von Millionen Menschen auf jedem Kontinent empfangen werden.

World Band Spectrum. Weltbandspektrum. Es besteht aus den gesamten Abschnitten des Kurzwellenspektrums, bestimmt von der „International Telecommunication Union" (ITU). Die ITU erlaubt auch einige Weltbandradiosendungen außerhalb des Kurzwellenspektrums. Es folgt eine Liste der offiziellen und [effektiven] Weltband-Abschnitte des Kurzwellenspektrums, in der die günstigste Empfangzeit angegeben wird. Bemerke daß diese Liste nur zur Orientierung dient–der effektive Empfang kann sich je nach Standort des Empfängers oder Senders, Jahreszeit und anderen Faktoren ändern.

Schwacher Empfang im Winter bei Nacht

*120 Meters:
2300–2498 kHz (Tropische Inlandstationen)

*90 Meters:
3200–3400 kHz (Tropische Inlandstationen)

Mittelmäßiger Empfang im Winter bei Nacht

*75 Meters:
3900–3950 kHz (nur Asien und Pazifik)
3950–4000 kHz (außer Americas)

*60 Meters:
4750–5060 kHz [4000–5730 kHz] (Tropische Inlandstationen)

Guter Empfang bei Nacht

49 Meters:
5950–6200 kHz [5850–6600 kHz]

*41 Meters:
7100–7300 kHz [6800–7600 kHz]

Guter Empfang bei Nacht und Tag

31 Meters:
9500–9900 kHz [9000–9100 & 9300–10100 kHz]

25 Meters:
11650–12050 kHz [11500–12100 kHz]

Guter Empfang bei Tage

21 Meters:
13600–13800 kHz

19 Meters:
15100–15600 kHz [15000–15700 kHz]

16 Meters:
17550–17900 kHz

13 Meters:
21450–21850 kHz

Mittelmäßiger Empfang bei Tage

11 Meters:
**25670–26100 kHz

World Time. Weltzeit. *Siehe* UTC.
WS. World Service: Weltdienst.

---

*„Feeder"-Stationen und „Hams"-Stationen (Radio-amateure) teilen sich den Rundfunkdienst.
**Von jetzt an bis 1993 gibt es für kurze Zeit (außer im Sommer) den bestmöglichen störungsfreien Empfang.*

Summary of Broadcasting Activity

Nearly 160 of the world's countries, from the giant USSR to tiny Bhutan—and various extralegal stations—air world band broadcasts within the shortwave spectrum. This spectrum is divided into two major parts: that containing *Tropical* world band segments, found within the ranges 2.2-3.9 and 4.0-5.73 MHz; and that containing *International* world band segments, found within the ranges 3.9-4.0 and 5.73-26.1 MHz.

Although the Tropical segments consist almost entirely of broadcasts intended for domestic audiences, the nature of world band radio is such that even these stations can be heard continents away when conditions are right. The International segments, on the other hand, are composed largely of powerful stations targeted to audiences abroad. These are routinely heard well over great distances.

Jamming is deliberate interference directed against a broadcaster by those trying to keep certain programs from being heard. Jamming takes place within both Tropical and International segments, but is much more common within the International portion. Jammed hours given here are listed alongside the "victim" country—not the country actually doing the jamming.

Countries listed are those responsible for the material being broadcast. So the BBC, for example, is listed under "United Kingdom," regardless of whether it is being aired from transmitters within the UK or from relay sites abroad. For specific sites, please refer to the "Blue Pages."

As listings in *Passport to World Band Radio* are normally based on signals actually monitored at various locations worldwide, there can be slight year-to-year variations resulting from such reception variables as interference levels and propagation conditions.

Tropical Broadcasting—Hours per Week

	Country	Total Hours	Hours Jammed		Country	Total Hours	Hours Jammed		Country	Total Hours	Hours Jammed
1	BRAZIL	10286	None	34	GHANA	186	None	62	GUINEA	108	None
2	PERU	6607	None	35	BENIN	185	None	63	SOLOMON IS	106	None
3	CHINA (PR)	5542	None	36	BOTSWANA	182	None	64	MADAGASCAR	104	None
4	USSR	5346	None	37	PAKISTAN	175	None	65	DJIBOUTI (JIBUTI)	104	None
5	INDONESIA	4497	None	38	CLANDESTINE (M EAST)	173	89	66	KAMPUCHEA (CAMBODIA)	102	None
6	BOLIVIA	2511	None	39	NEW CALEDONIA	168	None	67	PAKISTAN—AZAD K	95	None
7	ECUADOR	2495	None	40	COLOMBIA	168	None	68	CHINA—TAIWAN	89	89
8	COLOMBIA	1609	None	41	LIBERIA	166	None	69	MALAWI	83	None
9	USA	1507	None	42	UGANDA	160	None	70	SENEGAL	81	None
10	PAPUA NEW GUINEA	1332	None	43	(M EAST)	173	89	71	ZIMBABWE	73	None
11	VENEZUELA	1196	None	39	NEW CALEDONIA	168	None	72	CENTRAL AFRICAN REP	72	None
12	INDIA	1035	None	40	COLOMBIA	168	None	73	BURUNDI	70	None
13	KOREA (DPR)	902	None	41	LIBERIA	166	None	74	BURKINA FASO	66	None
14	MALAYSIA	834	None	42	UGANDA	160	None	75	MAURITANIA	58	None
15	ANGOLA	745	None	43	SWAZILAND	157	None	76	EQUATORIAL GUINEA	55	None
16	MONGOLIA	667	None	44	TOGO	155	None	77	CLANDESTINE (AFRICA)	55	22
17	AUSTRALIA	594	None	45	LAOS	155	None	78	AUSTRIA	54	None
18	GUATEMALA	553	None	46	SURINAME	139	None	79	MALI	54	None
19	CLANDESTINE (ASIA)	538	397	47	LESOTHO	138	None	80	BANGLADESH	50	None
20	MOZAMBIQUE	396	None	48	NIGER	134	None	81	MEXICO	49	None
21	NIGERIA	354	None	49	BELIZE	133	None	82	ARGENTINA	44	None
22	NAMIBIA	344	None	50	ZAMBIA	126	None	83	BURMA	36	None
23	SRI LANKA	334	None	51	IVORY COAST	126	None	84	COMOROS	35	None
24	AFGHANISTAN	308	None	52	SUDAN	126	None	85	CLANDESTINE (C. AMER)	24	24
25	CAMEROON	294	None	53	ALBANIA	126	None	86	DOMINICAN REPUBLIC	21	None
26	KENYA	286	None	54	THAILAND	125	None	87	TRISTAN DA CUNHA	15	None
27	HONDURAS	271	None	55	HAITI	126	None	88	IRAN	14	None
28	VIETNAM	261	None	56	COSTA RICA	125	None	89	FRANCE	14	None
29	SINGAPORE	252	None	57	GABON	122	None	90	ICELAND	4	None
30	TANZANIA	246	None	58	CHAD	117	None				
31	NEPAL	198	None	59	ZAIRE	115	None		Total Tropical Jamming		621
32	SOUTH AFRICA	194	None	60	YEMEN (PDR)	113	None		Total Tropical Broadcasting		58,484
33	FRENCH GUIANA	187	None	61	RWANDA	108	None				

International Broadcasting—Hours per Week

	Country	Total Hours	Hours Jammed		Country	Total Hours	Hours Jammed		Country	Total Hours	Hours Jammed
1	USSR	28892	None	21	ECUADOR	1434	None	41	COLOMBIA	900	None
2	USA	17853	5283	22	SWITZERLAND	1421	None	42	KUWAIT	870	None
3	CHINA (PR)	10870	None	23	ITALY	1405	None	43	PAKISTAN	844	None
4	BRAZIL	5558	None	24	HOLLAND	1331	None	44	VIETNAM	834	None
5	UNITED KINGDOM	4985	25	25	ALBANIA	1233	27	45	HUNGARY	804	None
6	GERMANY (FR)	4399	261	26	ALGERIA	1184	None	46	SINGAPORE	798	None
7	PERU	3706	None	27	BOLIVIA	1174	None	47	PHILIPPINES	746	None
8	CHINA—TAIWAN	2588	1040	28	NIGERIA	1127	None	48	IRAQ	745	None
9	FRANCE	2489	None	29	BULGARIA	1127	None	49	ARGENTINA	718	None
10	CANADA	2135	None	30	CZECHOSLOVAKIA	1121	None	50	AFGHANISTAN	708	None
11	KOREA (DPR)	2074	None	31	SPAIN	1101	None	51	AUSTRIA	682	None
12	AUSTRALIA	1993	None	32	UNITED ARAB EMIRATES	1078	None	52	SOCIETY ISLANDS	672	None
13	INDIA	1913	None	33	IRAN	1043	375	53	TURKEY	667	2
14	GERMANY (DR)	1837	None	34	SOUTH AFRICA	1035	None	54	CLANDESTINE (MIDDLE EAST)	637	462
15	MALAYSIA	1727	None	35	VATICAN STATE	1018	5	55	SWEDEN	622	None
16	INDONESIA	1661	None	36	POLAND	1002	None	56	LIBYA	622	None
17	JAPAN	1626	None	37	ANGOLA	963	88	57	PORTUGAL	561	None
18	ISRAEL	1599	589	38	SAUDI ARABIA	962	None	58	CHILE	514	None
19	EGYPT	1500	None	39	CUBA	952	None	59	GREECE	507	2
20	KOREA (REP)	1444	None	40	ROMANIA	947	None				

	Country	Total Hours	Hours Jammed
60	MOZAMBIQUE	506	None
61	FINLAND	5021	None
62	YUGOSLAVIA	494	None
63	JORDAN	474	None
64	CLANDESTINE (C. AMERICA)	455	47
65	GUAM	445	None
66	OMAN	399	None
67	ZAMBIA	398	None
68	SRI LANKA	397	None
69	MOROCCO	395	None
70	CLANDESTINE (ASIA)	380	76
71	LAOS	366	None
72	TUNISIA	357	None
73	THAILAND	337	None
74	PARAGUAY	336	None
75	CLANDESTINE (AFRICA)	335	134
76	LEBANON	330	None
77	LUXEMBOURG	327	None
78	VENEZUELA	326	None
79	CAMEROON	325	None
80	SEYCHELLES	318	None
81	BELGIUM	317	None
82	LIBERIA	313	None
83	MONGOLIA	306	None
84	URUGUAY	303	None
85	KENYA	295	None
86	SYRIA	274	105
87	COSTA RICA	269	None
88	GABON	264	None
89	IVORY COAST	252	None
90	ZIMBABWE	249	None
91	MALI	237	None

	Country	Total Hours	Hours Jammed
92	TANZANIA	234	None
93	PAPUA NEW GUINEA	229	None
94	VANUATU	226	None
95	YEMEN (REPUBLIC)	226	None
96	NIGER	225	None
97	SOMALIA	214	None
98	BANGLADESH	207	None
99	NORWAY	205	None
100	NORTHERN MARIANA IS	205	None
101	BOTSWANA	203	None
102	YEMEN (PDR)	198	None
103	ETHIOPIA	196	None
104	SENEGAL	189	None
105	GUATEMALA	178	None
106	SWAZILAND	171	None
107	NEW CALEDONIA	168	None
108	FALKLAND ISLANDS	168	None
109	NICARAGUA	168	None
110	ZAIRE	165	None
111	MADAGASCAR	154	None
112	EQUATORIAL GUINEA	154	None
113	MEXICO	154	None
114	NETHERLANDS ANTILLES	152	None
115	ANTARCTICA	149	88
116	NEW ZEALAND	147	None
117	KAMPUCHEA (CAMBODIA)	138	None
118	SIERRA LEONE	130	None
119	COOK ISLANDS	125	None
120	BURMA	121	None
121	GREENLAND	120	None
122	HONDURAS	119	None
123	MALAWI	118	None
124	QATAR	114	None

	Country	Total Hours	Hours Jammed
125	RWANDA	108	None
126	GUINEA	108	None
127	MARSHALL ISLANDS	108	None
128	CYPRUS	106	None
129	DOMINICAN REPUBLIC	105	None
130	MONACO	105	None
131	TOGO	100	None
132	GHANA	93	None
133	UGANDA	88	None
134	FRENCH GUIANA	77	None
135	DENMARK	77	None
136	CENTRAL AFRICAN REP	66	None
137	BENIN	56	None
138	BURKINA FASO	51	None
139	BURUNDI	50	None
140	(UNIDENTIFIED)	50	None
141	SOLOMON IS	48	None
142	CLANDESTINE (EUROPE)	48	None
143	COMOROS	46	None
144	CHAD	45	None
145	ICELAND	45	None
146	MAURITANIA	36	None
147	BHUTAN	25	None
148	PAKISTAN-AZAD KASHMIR	24	None
149	MALTA	21	None
150	PIRATE (EUROPE)	19	None
151	KIRIBATI	16	None
152	SUDAN	14	None
153	SURINAME	3	None

Total International Jamming	8,521
Total International Broadcasting	55,647

Directory of Advertisers

Advanced Electronic Applications • 30
Alpha Delta Communications • 20
American Radio Relay League • 32, 413
Antenna Supermarket • 12
Atlantic Ham Radio • 40
Barry Electronics Corp. • 60
Com-Rad Industries • 62
Com-West Radio Systems, Ltd. • 54
Datong Electronics, Ltd. • 52
Dubberley's on Davie • 59
Electronic Equipment Bank • 14, 18, 21, 24, 28
Electronics Center • 58
G & G Electronics • 50
Gilfer Shortwave • 26
Glenwood Trading Company • 80
Grove Enterprises, Inc. • 6, 22
Grundig AG • 4–5
Hobbytronique • 29
ICOM America, Inc. • 10
Interbooks • 72
Japan Radio Company, Ltd. • 36
Kenwood USA Corporation • 416, Inside Back Cover
Klingenfuss Publications • 34
Librarie Postale PIF • 92
MFJ Enterprises, Ltd. • 42–43
Phase Track Ltd. • 64
Philips Consumer Electronics • Inside Front Cover
Popular Communications • 27

Radio KUSW • 44
Radio Canada International • 126
Radio West • 130
RDI White Papers • 70
Sangean America, Inc. • 15
Sherwood Engineering, Inc. • 75
Stoner Communications, Inc. • 8
The Ant Farm • 66
The Radio Works • 68
Universal Shortwave Radio • 16, 38, 48
Voice of Free China • 7
World Calendar • 56
World Press Review • 74
Yaesu USA • 39

Advertising representative:
Mary Kroszner
IBS, Ltd.
Box 300
Penn's Park, PA 18943 USA
215/794–8252

Made in USA

KENWOOD

...pacesetter in Amateur Radio

Scan the World

R-2000
All-mode receiver

Superior engineering, quality, and performance describe Kenwood's multi-mode communications receiver.

The R-2000 receiver has the most often- needed features for the serious or casual shortwave broadcast listener. Listen in on overseas news, music, and commentary. "Listen up" on the VHF public service and Amateur radio frequencies, as well as aircraft and business band communications with the R-2000 and VC-10 option. The R-2000 has a muting circuit so you can monitor your Amateur radio station's signal quality.

- Covers 150 kHz –30 MHz in 30 bands.
- All mode: USB, LSB, CW, AM, FM.
- Digital VFO's. 50-Hz, 500-Hz or 5-kHz steps. F. LOCK switch.

- Ten memories store frequency, band, and mode data. Each memory may be tuned as a VFO.
- Lithium batt. memory back-up.
- Memory scan.
- Programmable band scan.
- Fluorescent tube digital display of frequency (100 Hz resolution) or time.
- Dual 24-hour quartz clocks, with timer.
- Three built-in IF filters with NARROW/WIDE selector switch. (CW filter optional.)
- Squelch circuit, all mode, built-in.
- Noise blanker built-in.
- Large front mounted speaker.
- RF step attenuator. (0-10-20-30 dB.)
- AGC switch. (Slow-Fast.)
- "S" meter, with SINPO scale.
- High and low impedance antenna terminals.
- 100/120/220/240 VAC operation.
- RECORD output jack.
- Timer REMOTE output (not for AC power).
- Muting terminals.

Optional accessories:

- VC-10 VHF converter for R-2000 covers 118-174 MHz
- YG-455C 500 Hz CW filter for R-2000
- HS-4 Headphones
- HS-5 Deluxe headphones
- HS-6 Lightweight headphones
- HS-7 Micro headphones
- DCK-1 DC cable kit for 13.8 VDC operation

Additional information on Kenwood all-band receivers is available from authorized dealers

KENWOOD

KENWOOD U.S.A. CORPORATION
2201 E. Dominguez St., Long Beach, CA 9081C
P.O. Box 22745, Long Beach, CA 90801-5745

Service manuals are available for all receivers and most accessories.
Specifications and prices subject to change without notice or obligation.